D. W. Robertson, Jr.
(1914-1992)

Uncollected Essays

With a Foreword by Paul A. Olson

Zea Books
Lincoln, Nebraska 2017

Collection copyright © 1945–1991 estate of D. W. Robertson, Jr.
Foreword copyright © 2017 Paul A. Olson.

ISBN: 978-1-60962-113-1

doi: 10.13014/K23776W6

Composed in Sitka types by Paul Royster.

Zea Books are published by the University of Nebraska–Lincoln Libraries

Electronic (pdf) edition available online at
http://digitalcommons.unl.edu/zeabook/

Print edition available from
http://www.lulu.com/spotlight/unlib

UNL does not discriminate based upon any protected status.
Please go to unl.edu/nondiscrimination.

Contents

Foreword, by Paul A. Olson vii

Buzones, an Alternative Etymology 1
  Studies in Philology 42:4 (October 1945), pp. 741-744.

The *Manuel des Péchés* and an English Episcopal Decree 5
  Modern Language Notes 60:7 (November 1945), pp. 439-477.

Correspondence – The Manuel des Péchés 15
  Modern Language Notes 61:2 (February 1946), p. 144.

A Note on the Classical Origin of 'Circumstances' in
  the Medieval Confessional 16
  Studies in Philology 43:1 (January 1946), pp. 6-14.

A Study of Certain Aspects of the Cultural Tradition
  of 'Handlyng Synne' 26
  University of North Carolina Record (1946), pp. 146-147.

The Cultural Tradition of *Handlyng Synne* 27
  Speculum 22:2 (April 1947), pp. 162-185.

Marie de France, *Lais*, Prologue, 13-16 64
  Modern Language Notes 64:5 (May 1949), pp. 336-338.

Cumhthach Labhras an Lonsa 67
  Modern Language Notes 67:2 (February 1952): 123-125.

Chaucerian Tragedy 70
  ELH: A Journal of English Literary History 19:1 (March 1952), pp. 1-37.

St. Foy among the Thorns 107
  Modern Language Notes 67:5 (May 1952), pp. 295-299.

Amors de terra lonhdana 112
  Studies in Philology 49:4 (October 1952): 566-582.

The Subject of the *De Amore* of Andreas Capellanus . . 130
  Modern Philology 50:3 (February 1953), pp. 145-161.

iii

Why the Devil Wears Green 159
    Modern Language Notes 69:7 (November 1954), pp. 470-472.

A Further Note on *Conjointure* 162
    Modern Language Notes 70:6 (June 1955), pp. 415-416.

The Book of the Duchess 164
    Companion to Chaucer Studies, ed. Beryl Rowland (New York:
    Oxford University Press, 1968), pp. 332-340.
    [Updated bibliography, Revised Edition, 1979, pp. 409-413].

Chaucer Criticism 175
    Medievalia et Humanistica 8 (1977), pp. 252-255.

"And for my land thus hastow mordred me?" Land
Tenure, the Cloth Industry, and the Wife of Bath . . 181
    Chaucer Review 14:4 (Spring 1980), pp. 403-20.

Chaucer and the "Commune Profit": The Manor . . 203
    Mediaevalia 6 (1980), pp. 239-259.

The Intellectual, Artistic and Historical Context . . 224
    Approaches to Teaching Chaucer's Canterbury Tales,
    ed. Joseph Gibaldi (New York: Modern Language Association
    of America, 1980), pp. 129-135.

Religion and Stylistic History 232
    Theolinguistics Brussels, ed. J. P. van Noppen (Brussels:
    Vrije Universiteit Brussel, 1981), pp. 215-229.

Simple Signs from Everyday Life in Chaucer . . . 247
    Signs and Symbols in Chaucer's Poetry, ed. John P. Hermann
    and John J. Burke Jr. (Tuscaloosa, AL: University of Alabama
    Press, 1981), pp. 12-26 & 208-215.

Chaucer and Christian Tradition 274
    Chaucer and Scriptural Tradition, ed. David Lyle Jeffrey
    (Ottawa: University of Ottawa Press, 1984), pp. 3-32.

The Wife of Bath and Midas 317
    Studies in the Age of Chaucer 6 (1984), pp. 1-20.

The Probable Date and Purpose of Chaucer's *Troilus* . 337
    Medievalia et Humanistica 13 (1985), pp. 143-171.

Who Were "The People"?. 374
   The Popular Literature of Medieval England, ed. Thomas
   J. Heffernan (Knoxville, TN: University of Tennessee Press,
   1985), pp. 3-29.

Chaucer and the Economic and Social Consequences
of the Plague 405
   Social Unrest in the Late Middle Ages. Papers of Fifteenth Annual
   Conference of the Center for Medieval and Early Renaissance Studies,
   ed. Francis X. Newman (Binghamton, NY: SUNY Binghamton Press,
   1986), pp. 49-74.

The Probable Date and Purpose of Chaucer's
Knight's Tale 433
   Studies in Philology 84:4 (Autumn 1987): 418-439.

The Physician's Comic Tale 457
   Chaucer Review 23:2 (Fall 1988), pp. 129-139.

Wisdom and "The Manciple's Tale": A Chaucerian
Comic Interlude 470
   Essays in Honor of Edward B. King. Ed. Robert G. Benson &
   Eric W. Naylor (Sewanee, TN: The University of the South, 1991),
   pp. 223-237.

Foreword

by Paul A. Olson

I

During the late summer of 1992, I received a call from Darryl Gless, a professor of Renaissance literature at the University of North Carolina and my former student, asking me if it would be all right if he and other people looking after the literary remains of D. W. Robertson would send me a package of published and unpublished articles that Robertson had left behind upon his death in July of that year. Gless had been a friend of Dr. and Mrs. Robertson in Chapel Hill, visiting with them frequently while trying a bit to look after their well-being in old age.

Professor Gless said that he and other former students of Professor Robertson wanted me to see what could be done about collecting and publishing Robbie's literary remains. Though I was slightly intimidated, I consented to take on the project. I offered to receive the items and promised to try to distribute the materials. At the time, I had good contacts with the University of Nebraska Press, which had published a number of Robertsonian pieces, and with a number of other places that had published analyses much in the vein of Robertson's. I also had a telephone call from Robbie's son, expressing his interest in my making public the items in the package through computerized publication if book avenues were not available.

When I received the aforesaid items, I added to them a large package of letters that I had received from Robbie across the years—from 1957 to just before his death.

Unfortunately, in the 1990s there was little interest in publishing Robertsonian material, largely because his research and interpretive methods, always controversial, had become increasingly unpopular with the rise of deconstructionism and New Historicism. Indeed,

Robbie told me, late in his life, that he had refused to have *A Preface to Chaucer* translated into Japanese because he thought that his way of doing things no longer had any serious following. Though the *New York Times* obituary said that he was "widely regarded as this [the twentieth] century's most influential Chaucer scholar," the halls of academe echoed with the idea that his methods were losing all of the battles with the French fancies. Eventually, after talking to a few people about methods of publication and failing to find one, I deposited the trove in the University of Nebraska–Lincoln Libraries' Special Collections so scholars could at least access them at another time. In later years, I felt guilty that I had not succeeded in fulfilling the trust that Gless and members of the Robertson family placed in me. I hoped that digitized access to the work could be prepared but was not clear about how.

Recently, Kathleen Johnson, a humanities librarian at the University of Nebraska–Lincoln, called my attention to Paul Royster of the DigitalCommons@University of Nebraska–Lincoln, who also had been a student of Robertson. She indicated that he might well be interested in seeing to it that the materials would be made widely available. I had a few meetings with Dr. Royster, exploring what could be done, and he set about the task of editing first the uncollected published essays of Professor Robertson, those in this book. Later, he plans a publication of the written but unpublished materials that Robbie had in process when he died, unfinished materials containing wonderful insights and hypotheses that will give another generation of Chaucer scholars and late medieval students something to fight with. I am grateful to Dr. Royster for taking on the task I could not do.

II

Though many critics and scholars have recently written of Professor Robertson and his overall contributions to medieval studies, it may be useful at this juncture for me to say a little about my personal experience with him, about the evolution of his methods as illustrated in the essays in this book, and about what scholarship might carry away from these materials. There is, of course, no substitute for reading

Robertson's major books and the pieces in *Essays in Mediaeval Culture* (1980), collected at the time of his retirement by Thomas P. Roche with Robbie's help. However, the pieces in this book add to the record and give us a more comprehensive picture of the evolution of Robertson's methods between the 1940s and the 1990s.

I first met D. W. Robertson in 1954 when I came to Princeton after having spent a year on a Fulbright, studying the construction of artificial languages in the late 17th and early 18th centuries, languages that anticipated in their assumptions the early work of Ludwig Wittgenstein and the Vienna Circle. I soon learned that Princeton was not a place to further such explorations, and I was looking for a direction. I met Dr. Robertson in a Medieval Romance class that included John Benton, Alan Gaylord, and other able students. He had come to Princeton in 1946, and I was told that he had been held over from getting tenure in 1953 at the end of seven years, the normal period for granting it, so Princeton could further review his record to see if it wished to keep him. Robertson was, in short, already a controversial figure, though naïve as I was about academia and attracted as I was to his course, I could not understand why.

Robertson was also already an extraordinary teacher—in the Romance class trying out hypotheses about the romances right and left, tracing iconological motifs from the Latin church fathers to the 14th-century from memory, and treating of romances in Old Gaelic, Provençal, Old and Middle French, and Middle English, while citing sources in a variety of other languages. As he taught, he would smoke stinky cigars, crouch down with his chin near the edge of the seminar table, and page through the romances as he formulated theories about them, raising his eyebrows from time to time while he laughed a *basso profundo* laugh. He was great fun.

Though I thought that Robertson might be let go when the next tenure review came up, I didn't care. I wanted him to guide my studies. In the Romance course, I encountered his revisionist hypotheses about so-called "courtly love," and, using his approach, wrote my first scholarly paper—on the *Roman de Flamenca*. Although he initially rejected my historical hypotheses, he put aside whatever reservations he might have had about my argument and eventually guided me toward its publication, a typical gesture. Though often awkward in guiding discussion, he was a fine teacher because he was willing to throw out hypotheses that might be wrong but that were provocative, because he was always willing to have his approach shaped by his students when they had something to say, and because he cared intensely about his students' welfare. After my initial taste of Robertsonianism, I took his courses in Chaucer and in the Medieval Drama and Lyric, and wrote my dissertation under him. (For a fairly good account of what Robertson emphasized intellectually in his graduate Chaucer class late in his career when court, town, and estate history had become important to him, read his essay [pp. 224–31] in this volume; his teaching in my time emphasized biblical and classical iconology much more than does this 1980 account.) During the next nearly forty years of Robbie's life, he and I exchanged letters every few weeks, sharing ideas about Chaucer, Shakespeare, and the other bards, gossiping about our personal lives and occasional medical complaints, his letters typed impeccably, mine written in an almost illegible hand.

All of this is to illustrate that when Robbie took a student on, he took him or her on for life. Some of my most vivid memories of Robbie have nothing to do with medieval studies but with his reading the Chicken Little story to my son Lars when he was tiny, his telling me during his summer of teaching students at the University of Nebraska (1961) that "the University of Nebraska has no reason to exist save to serve the people of Nebraska," his quoting paragraphs from the Anna Livia Plurabelle section of *Finnegan's Wake* to illustrate Joyce's Chaucerian sense of what storytelling is about ("Well, you know or don't you kennet or haven't I told you every telling has a taling and that's the he and the she of it"), his restrained sorrow in the Princeton Chapel at the sudden, untimely death of his son at a very early age—the son to whom he dedicated *A Preface to Chaucer*, his meditations on the great sins and strengths of the South, and his offering of a wonderful dinner of oysters at Lahiere's Restaurant in Princeton where we both drank a bit too much wine and lurched in his car to a nearby airport. For Robbie, the business of teaching literature, that of lifetime friendship, and that of culture-creation were of a piece. In reading his essays, it is important to keep in mind the larger project of which they are a part.

III

To assist the reader in understanding the larger project, I wish to look at the evolution of Robbie's methodology from the 1940s to the 1990s, as this evolution is quite clearly represented in this book.

Robertson began as a medievalist trained at the University of North Carolina—he always had enormous respect for state universities—in the traditional methods of study of the history of language and the study of sources, methods that had evolved in Germany and were dominant in American vernacular literary study through the 1930s and for many scholars into the 1940s and 1950s. The UNC teachers whom he mentioned to me as having had a considerable influence on him were B. L. Ullman, the editor of Coluccio Salutati's *De laboribus Herculis*; George R. Coffman, the polymath scholar of medieval vernacular and Latin literature; and Urban T. Holmes, the distinguished scholar of Old French and Middle French literature. All three were well schooled in traditional philological methods but extended that work toward exploring the implications of philology for literary interpretation. The history of language tradition appears in the essays on the Latin meaning of *buzones* (pp. 1-4 in this book) and the Old Gaelic meaning of certain phrases in "Cumhthach Labhras an Lonsa" (pp. 67-69), but Robertson always retained an interest in the semantic reconstruction of the precise meanings of the amatory, civic, theological, and legal terms in the medieval works he studied, an interest illustrated in many essays in this work. One of his first lectures in the Chaucer course stressed the great contributions of 19th and early 20th century philological analyses to the development of our understanding of earlier literatures.

The study of sources and literary genetics also appears in Robertson's early writing on literature related to the sacrament of penance, especially his examinations of the *Manuel des Péchés* (pp. 5-15) and of Robert Mannyng's *Handlyng Synne* (pp. 27-63). These essays illustrate two aspects of the tradition of study I am writing about, one the interest in identifying the "form" of a work—what kind of piece it purports to be in relation to earlier works performing a somewhat similar social and literary function, in this case, penitential manuals—and also where specific locutions in the work under study had their origins, whether in earlier theological treatises, ancient or medieval rhetorics, Latin or earlier vernacular penitential manuals, or elsewhere. Robertson developed, in this early work, an instinct that served him well later, that of looking at the continuities between vernacular pieces and Latin "sophisticated" writing, either in a literary or an administrative mode, whether ecclesiastical or civil. He never assumes that the Latin pieces are, by nature, "sophisticated" and learned or that the vernacular ones are only pieces of vulgar pleasantry (see pp. 224-31). This beginning with penitentials also served him well later in his examination of Chaucer, as most of Chaucer's ecclesiastical tales turn on questions of whether clerics administer the sacrament of penance authoritatively or corruptly. That question, to some extent, even undergirds the tales by contemplatives. It is not accidental that he began his Chaucer courses with a thorough examination of the Parson's penitential manual as a Canterbury tale.

As every student of Robertson knows, the first great shift in his methodology came with his arrival at Princeton in 1946; his reading of *La Renaissance du XIIe Siècle: Les Écoles et l'Enseignement* by Paré, Brunet, and Tremblay; and his work with Bernard F. Huppé, 1946-50, a fellow faculty member at Princeton. Robbie often spoke of the wonderful times he and Huppé had together in the late 1940s while trying to formulate a new methodology for reading medieval literature rooted in the practices of medieval modes of interpretation, especially of the Bible. From those discussions came the approach to medieval literature commonly labeled "exegetics," and from them also came their two joint publications: the 1951 *Piers Plowman and Scriptural Tradition* and the 1963 *Fruyt and Chaff: Studies in Chaucer's Allegories*. These were not, in my mind, great pieces of critical interpretation, but they *were* steps toward forming a methodology.

At about the same time came the pieces in this book referring medieval poems and works of art to exegetical theory or exegesis itself, such as the pieces on Marie de Frances's Prologue to the *Lais* (pp. 64-67), *La chanson de sainte Foy* (pp. 107-11), Jaufré Rudel's *Amors de terra lonhdana,* as well as several essays from this period contained in *Essays in Medieval Culture*, especially "The 'Heresy' of the Pearl,"

"The Pearl as a Symbol," "The Doctrine of Charity in Mediaeval Literary Gardens: A Topical Approach through Symbolism and Allegory," "Historical Criticism," and "Some Medieval Literary Terminology, with Special Reference to Chrétien de Troyes" (cf. p. 162 in this volume). Robertson's evolving approach to medieval texts depended, in my view on three assumptions: 1. That medieval poetry, though its surface was largely fiction, should be studied for deeper levels of meaning in somewhat the same way that the medieval Bible was studied by its interpreters; 2. That the *allegories of things* and the *allegories of words* discovered by biblical exegetes could be used to assist in penetrating to "deeper" iconological meanings in serious poetry like Dante's or *Piers Plowman*; and 3. That the fundamental concern of poetic writing, like the fundamental concern of biblical writing as Augustine understood the matter, was to encourage charitable love and condemn its selfish alternative. The same assumptions applied to the interpretation of art, and Robertson learned a great deal from the great iconological interpreters of his own and earlier times, especially from Émile Mâle and Erwin Panofsky.

All three of the interpretive assumptions listed above were, in the fifties, highly controversial, but the first is largely supported by what medieval poets and interpreters of poetry say about how they go about their business, and this book's essay on Marie de France's Prologue as well as *Mediaeval Culture's* essay on Chrétien's terminology support this view, as do numerous later critical writings by, for example, Dante, Mussato, Boccaccio, Petrarch, and Richard Du Bury. That does not mean that medieval pieces on what poetry is and how to read it may not have been, on occasion, flimflam designed to expand the importance of the creator's own work. However, efforts to read medieval texts systematically on four levels do not often appear in interpretations that come to us from the 12th to 15th centuries, and Robertson largely abandoned the effort to do four-fold interpretation after his work on *Piers Plowman* (though the Rudel piece in this book contains some of the approach). Anyone who wishes to watch the methods according to which medieval critics contemplated a heavy-duty text from their own time should go to the dozen and more 14th- to 16th-century commentaries on Dante, to Petrarch's and Boccaccio's readings of their own and other works, and to a gloss like that on the French *Roman de la Rose*-like poem, *Les Echecs Amoureux*. By the time Robertson wrote *A Preface to Chaucer*, he had come to a much more nuanced view of how the reconstruction of medieval biblical meanings plays into the work of medieval poetry than is to be found in his early experiments in this direction. However, he remained proud of his early experiments with taking medieval poetic theory seriously and basically supported their general tenor.

The second assumption, that the allegories of things and the allegories of words discovered by biblical exegetes could be used to assist in penetrating to "deeper" levels of meaning in serious poetry like Dante's or *Piers Plowman*, is illustrated in the essay "Why the Devil Wears Green" (pp. 159–61) and in etymological allegories that appear everywhere in English medieval and renaissance writing from Chaucer's "Tale of Melibee" to Spenser's *Faerie Queene*. Such an etymological allegory appears in Professor Robertson's interpretation of, for example, the name Octovien to mean Christ in *The Book of the Duchess*. The assumption seems to me to have gradually come to be broadly accepted in medieval studies, the primary dispute remaining being how insistently to employ these techniques to determine metaphorical meaning, whether only in interpreting clearly fabulous stories and situations, where secondary meanings are assumed, or also in treating verisimilitudinous stories and poetic histories.

The third assumption, that the fundamental concern of poetic work, like the fundamental concern of all biblical writing, as Augustine understood the matter, was to encourage charitable love and condemn its selfish alternative, does not work as well. It ought not to become a ruling hermeneutic principle in the interpretation of poetry just because St. Augustine said that was how the Bible should be interpreted. Few medieval poetic theorists refer to the hermeneutic of charity. Robertson sometimes seems to suggest such a unitary interpretive strategy, and his critics certainly thought he said as much. If much medieval interpretation moves toward a celebration of divine love and a condemnation of selfishness, it may be because the pattern of the culture was integrated around the opposites of divine and selfish love in a way that often demanded that one interpret in accordance with the dominant values of the culture. However, it is hard to argue that the battle and war poems of Bertran de Born admonish one to follow divine charity, in any standard understanding of it. Dante clearly believed that Bertran had not followed such love (see *Inferno* 28), and Robertson himself sometimes said that not all medieval poetry fulfilled Augustinian biblical purposes. He once told a group of which I was a part that medieval poetry forwards all kinds of loves—"come live with me and be my love" and every other dimension of love possible to sinners and saints.

Robertson's interest in the hermeneutic of charity led him to question productively what he called the myth or the fantasy of courtly love, the literary apotheosizing of adultery and sexual yearning as a major feature of many of the central literary texts from the 12th century on. He reinterpreted important parts of Chrétien's *Cligès*, Andreas Capellanus, and Chaucer using this assumption. Indeed, this revisionist work is pretty generally recognized as providing a tenable scholarly entrance to love literature in the period after the publication of the John Benton's 1960s essays on the Aquitanian courts from which "courtly love" was said to spring,[1] and of F. X. Newman's *The Meaning of Courtly Love* in 1968.

Robertson appeared to be abandoning two paradigmatic approaches to literature, and in doing so caused much controversy. The *first* of these was the philological, historical method with which he began, though he regarded his reconstruction of the iconological resources and language games of medieval poetry as an extension of the work of historical philology and literary genetics.[2]

---

1. Cf. "Chretien's *Cligès* and the Ovidian Spirit" in *Essays in Medieval Culture* but first published in *Comparative Literature* 7 (1955): 32-42; cf. work on Andreas Capellanus in this volume (pp. 130-58), and on Chaucer, especially "Chaucerian Tragedy," (pp. 70-106, later revised from its *ELH* version in *Preface to Chaucer* in a form that answered the animadversions of some of its original critics. Cf. John F. Benton, "The Evidence for Andreas Capellanus Re-examined Again," *Studies in Philology* 59 (1962) and "The Court of Champagne as a Literary Center," *Speculum* 36 (1961).

2. For an exploration of this point, see Paul A. Olson, "Review of Negotiating the Past: The Historical Understanding of Medieval Literature by Lee Patterson," *MLQ* 49 (1988), 386-395.

The *second* was the New Criticism that grew up in the 1930s as an extension of Southern agrarianism and I. A. Richards's work, which emphasized the close reading of texts in a self-referential way, independent of authorial intention and of the historical circumstances of the work being read. Though some New Critical interpretations—for example, of John Donne's work—relied on historically reconstructed nuances, they often seemed indifferent to the question of whether words, phrases, or iconic configurations seemingly understandable in the 20th century might have carried quite a different burden in their own time. Historical scholarship often appealed to authorial intention as a guide to a work's meaning. By the early 1950s, Robbie sometimes appealed in his essays to authorial intention, but by the mid-fifties, he began to cite Wimsatt and Beardsley, arguing that his difference with these New Critics was that they tended to ignore the meanings of words and phrases *as they meant to their original audiences*—that they did not complete the job of historical semantic reconstruction that the philologists had begun. The job of criticism was not to discover private authorial intention but precisely the full burden of what the language meant historically. Methodologically by the mid-fifties that meant resorting to the classical and medieval commentaries on Ovid and Virgil and the ancient myths that circulated widely in the High Middle Ages as guides to semiology of medieval works that used classical myths. The "exegetical" phase of Robertson's criticism extends through the work in *A Preface to Chaucer* and in this volume is represented by much of the writing extending from pages 64 to 174.

IV

The last stage in Robertson's evolution as a critic comes with his deepening interest in the contextualizing of medieval works in contemporary social and political history. Some of this begins with *A Preface to Chaucer*, in which he undertakes to place Chaucer's works in the context of contemporary exegetical and penitential disputes and the history of Wycliffite debate. However, one need only look at the 1980 essay from *Approaches to Teaching Chaucer's Canterbury Tales* (pp. 224–31 in this volume) to see the new emphasis. There Robbie emphasizes that "Chaucer lived among clerks and administrators familiar with the law" and that an understanding of the legal references, as a clue to the structure of society, is crucial to understanding the Chaucerian métier. At the same time, he emphasizes changes in rural law and custom and in the evolution of industry and trade in the English countryside as clues to understanding the references of Chaucer's commercial and rural tales. The best example of this new mode is probably "Some Medieval Literary Terminology, . . . Some Disputed Chaucerian Terminology" (*Speculum* 52 [1979]: 571–581, also republished in *Essays in Medieval Culture*, pp. 291–304). In this volume, the essays on pages 181 to 223 illustrate the usefulness of the approach, as do the essays on pages 374 to 432; that the approach is productive does not mean that Robertson's findings are definitive, but that the kind of investigation he undertook will have to be refined by future scholars if they wish to understand Chaucer's language at all.

Going beyond the broad legal and administrative references that this new sort of study permitted him to penetrate, Robertson also sought to understand specific topical references to court and government news that appeared especially in Chaucer's later works. His analysis of *Troilus*'s picture of English military and court decay in the 1380s, while the country endured imminent invasion threats from the French or "Argives," relate the work to concerns of his audience among the Knights of the Chamber and his patronage by John of Gaunt (pp. 337–73). Here the meaning of a work begins with its probable meaning to its first audience. This method is equally apparent in Robertson's picture of the "Knight's Tale" as an adumbration of possible new beginnings in European civilization, a work conforming more or less in its idealism to the idealism of the Chamber Knights and the Order of the Passion in the 1390s (pp. 433–56). This late Robertsonian effort to situate Chaucer's works in the immediate history of late 14th-century England as well as in the broader history of European civilization gave Chaucerian works "a local habitation and a name" that completed the task of historical criticism as Robbie understood it. The modus of these latter explorations is a modus that I pursued independently throughout my Chaucerian investigations from my 1957 dissertation under Robertson through my various journal essays on Chaucer and *The Canterbury Tales and the Good Society*.

During the period from the mid-1960s on, Robertson relied heavily on a tradition of sociological analysis that he seldom mentions in his essays: that of Emile Durkheim and his structural functionalist successors. Robbie was always interested in seeing medieval culture as a tangle of routine habitual actions that gave solidarity and meaning to social life. Hence, he was interested in the law and the routines of its administration and its perversion in 14th-century culture, in routine religious observance, and in 14th-century civic ceremonial that appeared from a structural functionalist point of view to be designed to counter anomie and cushion change. The sociological works that were particularly meaningful to him, as he recounted things to me, were George Caspar Homans's *English Villagers of the Thirteenth Century,* whose use of manorial rolls gave Robbie an introduction to tools for understanding the precise language of routine manorial administration; Jerome F. Scott and R. P. Lynton's *The Community Factor in Modern Technology,* which suggested ways of organizing societies to counter anomie and social dislocation; and J. H. van den Berg's *The Changing Nature of Man,* which investigated the relationship between historical changes in how human beings organize themselves into groups and how the individuals in those groups are able to function in their inward and social lives, an analysis that privileges small group societies and social solidarity sustained by customs, rituals, and predictable networks of social support. (Robertson also relied somewhat on the sociology that Ortega y Gasset develops in his *Man and People*, a sociology that argues that the social penetrates into the most minuscule experiences of our lives: for example, the conventions of language or the experience of a handshake; for Robbie, the study of a society is also the study of its linguistic conventions, even those basic to literature.)

v

In *Philosophical Investigations*, Ludwig Wittgenstein argues that "to imagine a language is to imagine a form of life" (PI §19). Setting down this aphorism is for Wittgenstein part of showing that language and ways of doing things are imbedded in—create—one another. One cannot, for example, separate a language game in which the word "slab" commands someone to bring a slab to, say, the construction work that is underway from that construction work. When the philosopher says that "The meaning of a word is its use in the language," he is speaking not only of how the word works with other words in syntactic structures to create meaning at the level of words but of what it does in our various life forms, the various contexts in which it can "act" and what its actions are. That indeed is its meaning. Robbie's quest was to understand the life forms of late medieval and early modern culture and to imagine with as much detail as possible how the words of that culture, particularly the words in poems, and its life forms related. Since in my career I was interested in constructing the cultural usages that went into the use of words in, say, Lakota works like those of Black Elk, I would often discuss method with Robbie. He would wonder why contemporary literary criticism so often attended to how the languages of many contemporary cultures and their life forms were one while we did not attend to how we had to imagine the forms of past life in detail if we were to imagine their languages. He was right to ask the question.

Lincoln, Nebraska
October 2017

Buzones, an Alternative Etymology

By D. W. Robertson, Jr.

Studies in Philology 42:4 (October 1945), pp. 741-744.

In a recent article Dr. J. C. Russell called attention to the word *buzones* used in Bracton's *De legibus* as a popular term to designate certain "greater men of the county" who exercised considerable influence in the county court.[1] This word, Dr. Russell suggested, may be a Latinized development from ME *busi*, "busy." Another possibility, perhaps worthy of consideration, may be seen in the resemblance between *buzones* and OF *buison, buson* < L *būtteo* (*būteōnis*), loosely "a kind of hawk, or falcon."[2] Phonologically, this hypothesis presents no difficulties, but the semantic situation is somewhat complicated.[3] It is understandable that certain powerful men in a thirteenth century community who were able to control the action of others in court should have acquired a popular reputation for rapacity so that they were compared, in popular speech, to birds of prey.[4] But the word *buson* is said by Godefroy to have been used where one might expect *buisart, busart*, "buzzard"; moreover, when applied to a person,

---

1. "Buzones, An English-Latin Hybrid?" *SP* XLII (1945), 19-20.
2. See Meyer-Lübke, *REW*, no. 1423; Wartburg, *FEW*, s. v. *būteo*.
3. The semantic values of OF *buson* have been discussed at length by T. Atkinson Jenkins, "A French Etymology: Fr. *bis*, Ital. *bigio*," *Manly Anniversary Studies*, Chicago, 1923, pp. 351-361.
4. Ecclesiastical writers were constantly accusing the nobility of rapine. Thus, in *Le Mariage des neuf filles du diable* attributed to Grosseteste, ed. P. Mayer, *Romania* XXIX, pp. 63-64, the sin *Ravyne* marries the nobility. This was a very popular story. For a similar attitude, cf. Humbert de Romans, *De eruditione praedicatorum*, Lib. II, Tract. I, *MBP* XXV, p. 496. Confessors were instructed by the Synodus Nemausensis (1284), Mansi XXIV, c. 528, to inquire of "principes, castellanos, & milites, & eorum bajulos . . . de rapinis."

the word in this sense indicated stupidity.⁵ "Stupidity," however, does not suit the context of *buzones* in Bracton; there would have been little point in calling powerful and influential men "stupid."

The connotations of *būteo* seem to have been ambiguous in Medieval Latin; it was used as an epithet to describe both stupid persons and rapacious persons.⁶ Perhaps this variation was due to the fact that the word was used loosely to designate birds of various kinds with quite different characteristics. The common European buzzard is still *buteo vulgaris*, but the Old English equivalent of *buteo* was *cyta*, "kite" (*milvus*, variously *ictinus, regalis, vulgaris*);⁷ and, in recent times, Mistral glosses Provençal *busac, busard*, etc., "*Milan royal*." The kite and the buzzard are birds whose very different characteristics must have impressed themselves forcibly on the mind of the medieval villager. In the sixteenth century, Belon described the buzzard (*buse, busard*) as "l'vn des oyseaux de rapine le plus mal à droit que nul autre que nous cognoissons." The bird is, moreover, "de plus grosse corpulence que les autres especes d'Aigles"; it commits "grand dommage sur les Connins de garennes"; it is "nuisant à touts oyseaux de riviere, tellement que s'il y à quelque butte sur vn estang, il se tient dessus espiant sa pasture: comme aussi sur les hayes le long des villages pour prendre les Poulles, Cocs, & tels oyseaux domestiques, non pas en volant, comme font les autres, mais se departant de quelque haye, se va ieter dessus."⁸ The kite (*milan royal*), on the other hand, "fait vn moult plaisant vol pour le Sacre: qui est cōmunement dedié pour l'esbatmēt & plaisir des grāde Seigneurs"; unlike the buzzard, it is "leger" and flies very high; and although "il fait moult dommage sur les Poulsins par les villages . . . en quelque pais il deliure de charonne," so that "il est deffendu sur peine de grosse amende, de luy faire aucune violence. Cela font ils en Angleterre."⁹ The buzzard, then, is a

---

5. Cf. the discussion in Jenkins, *op. cit.*, pp. 355-356.
6. DuCange, s. v. *busio, butheo*.
7. *TLL*, s. v. *būteo*; *NED*, s. v. *kite*.
8. *Histoire de la Nature des Oyseaux*, Paris, 1555 (UNC Microfilm, no. 4), II, IX, 100. I am indebted to Dr. Urban T. Holmes for calling my attention to this work and for making other valuable suggestions.
9. Ibid., II, XXVI, 129-131.

heavy, awkward, stupid bird that sits on a fence making itself a nuisance not only to other birds, but to men as well; whereas the kite is a light, high-flying bird, valuable for sport and sometimes useful because it eats carrion. Part of this distinction is clearly reflected in English, where *buzzard* is used to indicate "a worthless, stupid, or ignorant person," but *kite* indicates "a person who preys upon others, a rapacious person."[10]

The "grosse corpulence" of the buzzard as compared with the relative lightness and agility of the kite may account for the appearance of the two OF words *busart*, with its connotation of largeness, and *buson*, with the opposite connotation. Let us consider for a moment the proverb cited by Jenkins, "You cannot make a hunting-hawk out of a buzzard." After quoting the form

> Ja de buisot no ferez esprevier

from the twelfth century *Proverbes au Vilain*, he continues:

> In quoting the proverb, the noble bird of the duo is always the ēpervier, "sparrow-hawk," while the ignoble bird, in my next oldest example (Robert of Blois, thirteenth century) is a *buison*; for Gautier de Coincy, he has become a *buisart*; in the *Roman de la Rose*, for Eustache Deschamps and for Jean Marot, he was also a *busart* (*buzart*); but in modern dictionaries the word is always *buse*. Evidently a time came when *buison* was no longer apt for comparison, because it had changed to mean "small" or "young" of the species. By the sixteenth century, the original form buison was known only by written tradition....[11]

It seems to me that it is not necessary to gloss *buison* "buzzard" in the proverb of Robert of Blois as Godefroy does in his dictionary. There it is quoted:

> Ainz ne vis faire de buison
> Bon espervier ne bon faucon.

Compare the English proverb of *ca.* 1300:

10. *NED*, s. v. buzzard, kite.
11. *Op. cit.*, p. 354.
12. *NED*, s. v. kite, buzzard (quoted in part in each place).

> Nultow never late ne skete
> A goshauk maken of a kete,
> No faucon mak of busard,
> No hardy knyght mak of coward.[12]

The kite could be contrasted with the hawk as well as the buzzard although the buzzard perhaps made a more forceful and useful distinction. Moreover, the kite is, in a sense, "small of the species"; and the disappearance of *buison* in the sixteenth century might be accounted for by the adoption of the more distinctive *milan*, not easily confused with *buse, busard*.[13]

To conclude, the Old English equivalent of *būteo* was "kite," a bird which in later times was frequently associated with rapaciousness. Whether or not there was a clear distinction between the derivatives *buson* and *busart* in French, it was probably the rapacious kite rather than the stupid buzzard that the speakers whom Bracton heard had in mind when they spoke of certain "greater men of the county" as *buzones*. Dr. Russell suggested an association between *buzones* and *barones*.[14] French *r* and *z* were considerably less distinct than they are in English,[15] so that the two words were not unlike in sound. The word *buzones* spoken in a context where one would expect *barones* doubtless created an effect which appealed strongly to the Gallic relish for parody. What Bracton attempted to preserve, I think, was a current French joke.

Yale University.

---

13. Belon, *op. cit.*, II, X, 102, carefully distinguishes the *buse* or *busard*, the *bondree* or *goirau*, and the *milan*. There is, *ibid.*, II, XXVII, 132, a rarer *milan noir* to be distinguished from the *milan royal;* but the only other names ascribed to the *milan* are, *ibid.*, II, XXVI, 131, *huo*, or *huau*, formed in imitation of the bird's cry.
14. *Op. cit.*, p. 20.
15. Cf. Schwan-Behrens, trans. Bloch (1923), § 273, rem.; Rosset, *Les Origines de La Prononciation Moderne,* Paris, 1911, pp. 295-296.

The *Manuel des Péchés* and an English Episcopal Decree

Modern Language Notes 60:7 (November 1945), pp. 439-477.

In his recent study of the *Manuel des Péchés*, Dr. E. J. Arnould called attention to a decree appearing in the Constitutions of Bishop Grosseteste, describing it as "un chapitre qui pourrait presque servir de table ou d'introduction à notre *Manuel*."[1] Perhaps the decree in question was, in a sense, actually just such a "table." It runs:

> Quia igitur sine decalogi observatione salus animarum non consistit, exhortamur in Domino, firmiter injungentes, ut unusquisque pastor animarum et quilibet sacerdos parochialis sciat decalogum, id est, decem mandata legis Moysaicae; eademque populo sibi subjecto frequenter praedicet et exponat. Sciat quoque quae sint septem criminalia, eademque similiter populo praedicet fugienda; sciat insuper saltem simpliciter, septem ecclesiastica sacramenta; et hi qui sunt sacerdotes maxime sciant quae exiguntur ad verae confessionis et poenitentiae sacramentum, formamque baptizandi; doceant frequenter laicos in idiomate communi: habeat quoque quisque eorum saltem simplicem fidei intellectum, sicut continetur in symbolo, tam majore quam minore, et in tractatu qui dicitur *Quicunque vult,* qui cotidie ad primam in eccelesia psallitur.[2]

The materials here demanded correspond closely with the contents of the earlier versions of the *Manuel*, and the arrangement of topics is strikingly similar.[3] The decree, however, has a history outside of

---

1. *Le Manuel des Péchés,* Paris, 1940, p. 20. This work was reviewed by Charlton Laird, *Speculum,* XX (1945), pp. 99-103.
2. *Epistolae,* ed. H. R. Luard, Rolls Series, 1861, p. 155.
3. It now seems probable that the *Manuel* originally contained the following sections: (1) the Articles of the Faith, (2) the Ten Commandments, (3) the Seven Sins, (4) Sacrilege, (5) the Sacraments, (6) the Points of Shrift. See Laird, *op.*

Grosseteste's Constitutions of such a character as to make an actual relationship between it and the *Manuel* seem probable.

Grosseteste's statute was not of his own making, but was taken over, as C. R. Cheney has put it, "with only slight retouching," from the Constitutions of Walter de Cantilupe, Bishop of Worcester (1240).[4] The changes made by Grosseteste serve principally to soften the emphasis on confession which appears in the original:

> Sciantque sacerdotes ea, quae exiguntur ad verae confessionis poenitentiae sacramentum. Et quia observatio decalogi necessaria est fidelibus ad salutem; exhortamur in Domino sacerdotes, et pastores animarum, ut sciant decalogum, id est, decem mandata legis Mosaicae, quae populo suo sibi subjecto, frequenter praedicent, et exponant. Sciant quoque, quae sunt septem criminalia peccata, quae populo praedicent fugienda. Sciant autem saltem simpliciter vii ecclesiastica sacramenta, quae sunt. Habeat etiam saltem quilibet eorum fidei simplicem intellectum secundum quod continetur in psalmo, qui dicitur "Quicunque vult," et tam in majori, quam in minori symbolo; ut in his plebem comissam noverint informare.[5]

The demand for priestly knowledge concerning confession here appears at the beginning, as though it were a topic sentence. That an emphasis of this kind was intended is clear from what follows immediately:

> Ut autem sciant sacerdotes, quorum aliqui sunt simplices, pro quibus delictis superioribus sunt poenitentiae reservandae; ut sciant etiam parochianos suos instruere, quomodo debeant confiteri, necnon et eorum conscientias perscrutari, injunctionum etiam diversitates, quia non sanat oculum quod sanat calcaneum, quendam tractatum de confessione fecimus, quem sciri ab omnibus capellanis praecipimus, et etiam observari in

---

cit., p. 100; Arnould, *op. cit.*, pp. 60-106. Professor Laird tells me, however, that in a forthcoming article he will suggest that the original *Manuel* may not have contained the Articles of the Faith. The baptismal ceremony is discussed under the sacraments.

4. *English Synodalia of the Thirteenth Century*, Oxford, 1941, p. 121.

5. Wilkins, *Concilia*, I, p. 669.

confessionibus audiendis, quia longum esset, ipsum in praesenti synodo publicare.[6]

It is unfortunate that Bishop Walter decided not to publish his treatise with his decrees, for it does not survive.[7] Several features of his description of it, however, are pertinent to the present discussion. In the first place, the instructional materials listed do not constitute specifically a list of minimum requirements for catechistical instruction;[8] rather, they are presented as suitable materials for a treatise *De confessione*. Moreover, they are referred to as "*delictis*," a clear indication that the author was interested primarily in sins connected with the various rubrics; that is, he was not concerned, for example, with the abstract theology of the commandments and the sacraments but with transgressions against them. Finally, Bishop Walter wished not only to instruct his priests in the technique of confession, but also to have the priests teach their parishioners how they should confess, and how they should examine their consciences.

Turning now to the *Manuel des Péchés*, we find a book, which, as the title indicates, is concerned with "*delictis*," and which was written to teach laymen "*quomodo debeant confiteri, necnon et eorum conscientias perscrutari*":

> La uertue del seint espirit
> Nus seit eidant en cest escrit,
> A nus les choses ben mustrer
> Dunt hom se deit confesser,
> E aussi en quele manere,
> Qe ne fet mie bon a tere;
> Car ceo la uertue del sacrement,
> Dire le pechié, et coment.
> Tuz pechiéz ne poun recunter;

---

6. *Loc. cit.*
7. Cf. Cheney, *op. cit.*, pp. 42-43.
8. The absence of the Lord's Prayer is a striking illustration of this fact. It was demanded as a primary element of religious knowledge throughout the Middle Ages. E.g. see St. Augustine, *Serrnones, Opera*, Paris, 1679-1700, v, cols. 331, 343, 942; St. Caesarius of Arles, Opera, Maretioli, 1937-, I, pp. 75-76, 890; Rabanus Maurus, *Homeliae* (First Series), Migne, PL, cx, c. 27; Benjamin Thorpe,

> Mes par tant se peot remembrer,
> E les pechiéz amender,
> Qe cest escrit uelt regarder.
> . . . .
>
> Pur la laie gent ert fet,
> Deu le parface, si li plest,
> Qe il vere pussent apertement
> Qant il trespassent, & qant nient.⁹

In other words, not only is the general outline of the *Manuel* very similar to that of Walter de Cantilupe's decree, but the purpose of the *Manuel* is similar to the purpose of the treatise which Bishop Walter had in mind when he wrote the decree. Both treatises may be described as compendia of sins designed to promote the efficacy of confession. On the basis of the available evidence, one may say that the *Manuel* has the appearance of an elaboration for lay consumption of some treatise such as that described by Walter de Cantilupe.

Bishop Grosseteste was not the only churchman to appropriate Walter de Cantilupe's decree. A variant appears in the Constitutions of Bishop Walter de Kirkham of Durham (1255) which differs only slightly from that of Bishop Grosseteste. The Lord's Prayer, the *Ave*, and the Sign of the Cross are added to the list of materials demanded, so that the whole has the appearance of a list of catechistical materials

---

Ancient Laws and Institutes, London, 1840, pp. 397, 445; F. Liebermann, *Gesetze der Angelsachsen*, Halle, 1898-1916, I, pp. 302-304 (I Cnut, 22, 1-6); B. Thorpe, *The Homilies of the Anglo-Saxon Church*, London, 1844, 1846, II, p. 604; A. Napier, Wulfstan, Berlin, 1883, pp. 20-21, 33; Burchard of Worms, *Decretum*, Lib. II, Caps. LXII, LVI, Migne, *PL*, CXL, cols. 637, 651; Adrian Morey, *Bartholomew of Exeter*, Cambridge, 1937, pp. 175, 176; and, in general, F. M. Powicke, *Christian Life in the Middle Ages*, Oxford, 1935, p. 32. The *Ave Maria* was also considered fundamental in the thirteenth century. See H. Leclereq, "Sur la Salutation Angélique," in Hefele et al., *Histoire des Conciles*, Paris, 1907-1938, V, Appendice IV, p. 1747. In 1237, three years before Walter de Cantilupe's statutes were issued, Bishop Alexander of Coventry demanded that every Christian repeat the Lord's Prayer and the *Ave* seven times a day. See Wilkins, I, p. 642. A typical catalogue of the elements of catechistical instruction appears in the famous decree of Archbishop Peckham (1281), Wilkins, II, p. 54. This list is more comprehensive and considerably more general than that of Walter de Cantilupe.

9. Ed. F. J. Furnivall, *EETS OS* 119, ll. 1-12; 113-116. Cf. Arnould, *op. cit.*, pp. 58-59.

rather than that of an outline for confessional instruction.[10] A fourth variant, which is exactly like Grosseteste's except for an unimportant introductory sentence, appears in the Statutes of Bishops Walter and Simon of Norwich.[11] But the most elaborate variant of all forms one of the decrees of Bishop Peter Quivil's Synod of Exeter (1287). It is probably too late to have had any influence on the *Manuel*,[12] but an examination of it may shed some light on the tradition of the decree:

> Omnium mater errorum ignorantia praecipue sacerdotibus est vitanda, qui in populo docendi officium susceperunt, quorum opus in praedicatione et doctrina consistit, ut aedificent cunctos tam fidei scientia, quam operum disciplina. Ne igitur per caecitatis ignorantiam, dum ducatum praestant populo christiano, ambo in foveam delabantur; singulis locorum archidiaconis injungimus, ut diligenter inquirant, qui rectores, vicarii, aut sacerdotes in literatura enormem patiuntur defectum; et postquam eis de hoc constiterit, nobis denunciare quam citius non omittant.
>
> De parochialibus sacerdotibus frequentem assumant experientiam et habeant, an sciant decalogum, id est, praecepta legis Moysaicae, ipsa que subditae plebi exponant, et solicite praedicent observanda. An etiam sciant septem peccata mortalia, ipsaque praedicent populo fugienda. Sciant etiam septem sacramenta ecclesiastica, et qualiter habent conferri, ut supra diximus,[13] unumquodque. Et in articulorum fidei christianorum saltem simplicem habeant intellectum, prout in psalmo, "Quicunque vult," et in utroque symbolo continentur; in quibus plebem sibi commissam tanto tenentur studiosius informare, quanto quilibet, qui fidem catholicam firmiter non crediderit, salvus esse non poterit.
>
> Sacerdotes autem si quos invenerint circa praemissa nimia ignorantia laborare, ipsos protinus suspendant ab officio sacerdotali; maxime a regimine animarum, ad quos quidem divinus

---

10. Wilkins, I, p. 704. Cf. note 8, above.
11. *Ibid.*, I, pp. 731-732.
12. Arnould, *op. cit.*, p. 256, dates the Manuel ca. 1260.
13. The first chapter of the synod, Wilkins, II, p. 130, states that the priests are to have an adequate knowledge of the sacraments, and in the following sections, pp. 131-137, there is an elaborate explanation of what they are to know about each one.

sermo dicitur: "Tu vero scientiam repulisti, et ego te repellam, ne fungaris mihi sacerdotio."

Ut autem quilibet sacerdos, cui animarum cura incumbit, melius sciat et intelligat, qualiter debeat in ipsa versari; praecipimus, quod quilibet, cui parochialis ecclesiae regimen incumbit, quandam summulam plurimum utilem, immo verius necessarium a diversis tractatibus extractam sub compendio (quae summula sub eisdem verbis incipit, quibus et praesens synodus) citra festum S^{ti} Michaelis habeat scriptam, et ipsam sane intelligat, ac ea utatur sub poena unius marcae, loci archidiacono applicandae. Quam si archidiaconus remiserit, et ipsam, vel ipsius partem quandam levari poterit, et recipere praetermiserit, eundem archidiaconum in duabus marcis fabricae ecclesiae Exonensi volumus obligari.[14]

This variant differs from the earlier ones quoted chiefly in that Bishop Quivil was more deeply concerned about clerical ignorance than were his predecessors. It is not clear from the decree whether he had in mind catechistical materials or materials concerned with confession; but unlike Walter de Cantilupe, he published the treatise he wrote to carry out his educational program with his decrees, so that we can readily discover what he meant by examining the treatise.

The prologue to the *Summula,* as Bishop Quivil called his treatise, in good sermon style, develops the theme *Altissimus de terra creavit medicinam* (Ecclus. 38) to form, with a concordance of authorities, the conclusion that the Trinity is a physician, sin is a malady to be healed, and penance is the proper medicine. It then continues:

> Haec ergo ego Petrus, Exoniensis presbyter, intime considerans, et insufficientia presbytorum secularium confessiones audientium compatiens, quorum ignorantium, proh dolor! saepissime sim expertus; praesentem summulam eisdem assigno, ut eam sciant ad utilitatem suam et confitentium.[15]

We see that the treatise was not written to enable priests to enumerate the commandments, sins, and so on by rote;[16] it was a treatise *de*

14. *Ibid.,* II, pp. 143-144.
15. *Ibid.,* II, p. 162.
16. This is the view of Miss Margaret Deanesley, *The Lollard Bible,* Cambridge, 1920, pp. 196-197.

confessione to assist the priests in analyzing the experience of their penitents. Both Walter de Cantilupe and Peter Quivil, then, wrote confessional treatises based on an outline of materials which corresponds closely with the general contents of the *Manuel*, which in turn is a confessional treatise addressed to laymen.

Although the *Summula* is later than the *Manuel*, it probably represents fairly well the type of material traditionally associated with the decree, so that by comparing the two works it is possible to form some judgment as to whether or not an hypothetical association of the *Manuel* with the decree is justifiable. Except for the omission of the sacraments, which Bishop Quivil had already discussed at length, the *Summula* elaborates the topics of the decree in the sequence in which they appear there. For the purposes of the comparison, we may disregard the *exempla* in the *Manuel*, which represent a part of its author's efforts to adapt his material for lay consumption. I append below summaries of two sections of the *Manuel* together with corresponding sections of the *Summula*.

1. The First Commandment

M.

Even if you have committed the worst of sins, renouncing God, you may be forgiven if you ask mercy, as an *exemplum* shows. If you have practiced necromancy or conjured the Devil, you have violated this commandment. If you have used the psalter for divination or looked in a sword or basin, that was great folly. If you have believed in bird omens, or omens of morning meetings, you have been foolish. (There follows an exposition of St. Gregory's six causes of dreams. Cf. *Moralia*, VIII, Cap. XXV, 42, Migne, *PL*, LXXV, c. 827; or, better, *Dialogi*, ed. U. Moricca, Rome, 1924, pp. 309-310, for an *exemplum* from the *Dialogi* follows.) One should not believe in sorcery, speak against the faith, nor believe in the three fates. No mortal sin is forgiven without confession.[17]

---

17. *Manuel*, ll. 923-1314.

S.

Recurrat igitur poenitens ad primum mandatum et solicite videat in seipso, si transgressus fuerit illud. An scil. cultum soli Deo debitum, daemoniis, vel aliis creaturis exhibuerit; scil. faciendo praestigia, id est, recurrendo ad conjurationes, sicut solet fieri pro furto, in gladio, in pelvi, et in nominibus scriptis et inclusis in luto, et impositis in aqua benedicta, et similia; vel recurrendo ad auguria sortiarii, vel si sortiariis pro talibus consuluerit, et daemonibus sacrificaverit, sicut faciant quidam miseri pro mulieribus, quas amant fatue.[18]

2. The Fifth Commandment

M.

One should not slay another for felony without justice, nor put anyone in a prison or other place so that he dies. If you deprive anyone of a limb, you are guilty. If you fail to give to the poor and hungry, you are guilty of spiritual slaughter. False counsel resulting in death is evil. Judgment without mercy is criminal, as an *exemplum* shows. Distracting others from good purposes is spiritual slaughter, and detraction also slays. Evil speaking, as an *exemplum* demonstrates, is to be avoided.[19]

S.

Deinde videndum est, quod si transgressus fuerit quintum mandatum, quod est, "non occides"; sive inani occidendo vel vulnerando, vel praecipiendo; vel voluntarie, scil. occidendo, vel. odiendo usque ad mortem; quia qui odit fratrem suum, homicida est: vel subsidium necessarium subtrahendo, quia si non paveris, occidisti; vel spiritualiter, vel pravum actionis, sive locutionis exemplum.[20]

 I have purposely selected sections in which resemblances exist; that is, correspondences like those indicated above do not appear in all sections of the two books. However, there are other resemblances.

18. Wilkins, II, 162.
19. *Manuel*, ll. 1887-2146.
20. Wilkins, II, 163.

For example, a glance at the section of the *Manuel* on pride will reveal that it consists largely of a list of objects, situations, attributes, and so on about which one is apt to be proud. The second half of Peter Quivil's discussion of the subject runs as follows:

> Habet autem superbia materiam multiplicem; scil. bona naturalia; quando scil. homo superbit ex bonis naturalibus, quae habet; ut ex fortitudine, si est fortis homo; ex ingenio, si est boni ingenii; ex specie, si est pulcher; ex facundia, si sit homo eloquens, ut quidam legistae, et etiam laici, qui loquuntur coram judicibus laicis; vel etiam si habeat bonam vocem. Item ex nobilitate, si est ex magno genere; ex prole, ut si multos, vel plures, vel bonos filios vel filias habet. Habet etiam superbia pro materia bona temporalia; ut quando homo superbit, quia multas habet vel pretioses vestes, domos, vel agros, vel reditus, vel multos homines, vel servientes, vel bonos equos, vel quando praepositus est aliis in temporalibus. Habet etiam superbia de materia bona gratuita, quae sunt ex gratia; ut quando superbit, quia sciens est, vel etiam bonus clericus vel bonus praedicator vel bonus placitator, vel bonus artifex, vel bonus colonus. Vel quando homo superbit propter virtutem; quia credit se bonum esse, et abominabitur peccatores: vel quando superbit, quia habet gratiam hominum; vel quia habet bonam famam, vel dignitatem ecclesiasticum, vel ordinem; et secundum omnes istas diversitates, diversae poenitentiae sunt injungendae.[21]

Many of the details in this passage also appear in the *Manuel*. It is thus possible to say that the same general type of material appears in both works, although the resemblance does not consistently extend to specific details. The *Manuel* is, of course, much longer and far more elaborate than the *Summula*.

To conclude, the *Manuel* resembles two works we know to have been based on the decree in general outline and purpose, and it resembles at least one of these in content. In view of the popularity of the decree, and the estimation in which it was held by English bishops, it seems unlikely that these resemblances were fortuitous. Just exactly where in the history of the decree the *Manuel* arose, it is impossible to

---

21. Wilkins, II, 164.

decide on the basis of the facts now at hand;[22] however, the assumption that the *Manuel* and the decree were related seems a reasonable working hypothesis on which to base further research.[23] It is probable that the decree accounts in part for the popularity of the *Manuel*, whether there is a direct relationship between the two or not.

D. W. Robertson, Jr.
University of North Carolina

---

22. The decree may have appeared elsewhere in church councils, not all of which are at present available. See Cheney, *op. cit.*, p. vi. There is also possibility that it may have appeared in other contexts outside of the councils.
23. I hope to make the resemblance between the *Manuel* and the *Summula* clearer in a study of the literary tradition from which both arose.

Correspondence

Modern Language Notes 61:2 (February 1946), p. 144.

THE MANUEL DES PÉCHÉS. The list of episcopal decrees showing the influence of Walter de Cantilupe's statute on materials of instruction, "*The Manuel des Péchés and an English Episcopal Decree*," *MLN,* LX (1945), 442-443, should be revised, tentatively, somewhat as follows: (1) 1240 Grosseteste (*Epistolae*, ed. Luard, p. 155; cf. Cheney, *English Synodalia*, p. 121); (2) 1240-1243 Norwich statutes (Wilkins, I, 731-732; Cheney, pp. 125-136); (3) 1241-1268 Ely statutes (Cheney, pp. 136-138); (4) 1258-1260 Walter de Kirkham of Durham (Wilkins, I, 704; Cheney, pp. 138-141); (5) 1262-1265 John Gervais of Winchester (*Reg. J. Pontissara*, Surrey Record Society IV, 1915, p. 237; Cheney, pp. 103-108); (6) 1287 Peter Quivil of Exeter (Wilkins, II, 143-144). The appearance of the new edition of the *Concilia* should considerably facilitate an evaluation of this decree and an estimate of its possible influence on the author of the *Manuel*.

D. W. Robertson, Jr.

A Note on the Classical Origin of "Circumstances" in the Medieval Confessional

By D. W. Robertson, Jr.

Studies in Philology 43:1 (January 1946), pp. 6-14.

The famous twenty-first canon of the Fourth Lateran Council of 1215 stipulated that confessors should diligently seek out "*et peccatoris circumstantias et peccati*" in order that they might justly weigh the crimes confessed to them and administer suitable remedies.[1] The necessity for considering such circumstances in the examination of penitents had evidently impressed itself upon Innocent III at some time before the date of the council.[2] In general, statements in other councils and in theological treatises show that the idea became an important one in the pastoral theology of the thirteenth century.[3] By St. Thomas' time, it had become important in

---

1. The text of the decree may be conveniently examined in C. J. Hefele and H. Leclercq, *Histoire des Conciles* (Paris, 1907-1938), V, 1350.
2. In the *Liber poernitentialis* attributed to Pierre de Poitiers and perhaps written shortly before 1215, the following sentence appears: "Nam sicut docet innocentius III, non solum considerande sunt quantitates peccatorum sed et circumstantie peccatorum et peccantium." See Amédée Teetaert, "Le 'Liber Poenitentialis' de Pierre de Poitiers," *Beiträge zur Geschichte der Philosophie und Theologie des Mittelalters*, Supplementband III (1935), p. 321. Teetaert's date for the treatise has been questioned by C. R. Cheney, "La date de composition du 'Liber Poenitentialis' attribué à Pierre de Poitiers," Recherches de theologie ancienne et médiévale, IX (1937), 401-404.
3. E.g., in England, see the Council of London (1200), Wilkins, *Concilia*, I, 505; Constitutions of Richard Marsh (c. 1220), *ibid.*, I, 576-577; Council of Oxford (1222), *ibid.*, I, 595; Anonymous Constitutions of 1237, *ibid.*, I, 659; Synod of Exeter (1287), *ibid.*, II, 134. Cf. the *Rationes penitentie* in the *Bibliotheca*

theoretical theology as well.[4] To guide confessors in their consideration of circumstances, a mnemonic verse was employed, some variants of which ran as follows:

> Quis, quid, ubi, per quos, quoties, cur, quomodo, quando.[5]
> Quis, quid, ubi, quibus auxiliis, cur, quomodo, quando.[6]
> Quis, quid, ubi, cum quo, quotiens, cur, quomodo, quando.[7]
> Quid, quis, ubi, quibus auxiliis, cur, quomodo, quando.[8]
> Quid, ubi, quare, quantum, conditio, quomodo, quando:
>   Adiuncto quoties.[9]

These questions, readily applicable to any given situation, enabled the priest to substitute an easily remembered general principle for the long detailed lists of sins characteristic of the old penitentials, which, in the twelfth and thirteenth centuries, were being abandoned in favor of more concise theological and legal treatises.[10] Such a general principle undoubtedly afforded a much more flexible instrument for interrogation than the cumbersome older lists of specific cases which could not include all of the possibilities of person, incident, and motivation which might confront the confessor. Moreover, the priest could

---

Casinensis, (Monte Cassino, 1873-1894) IV (Florilegium) p. 194. This work is said to have been the first of a series of Dominican treatises on penance inspired by the Lateran Council of 1215. See Pierre Mandonnet, "La Summa de Poenitentia m. Pauli," *Beiträge,* Supplementband III (1935), p. 317. Other instances are mentioned below. In this paper, Wilkins' dates and attributions are used uncritically.

4. All of Quaestio 7, *Summa,* I-II, is devoted to the subject. Cf. also *ibid.,* I-II, 73, 7 for a discussion of the aggravation of sin by circumstances.
5. *Concilium Trevirense Provinciale* (1227), Mansi, *Concilia,* XXIII, c. 29.
6. Constitutions of Alexander de Stavensby (1237), Wilkins, I, p. 645. Cf. St. Thomas, *Summa,* I-II, 7, 3.
7. Robert de Sorbon, *De Confessione, MBP,* XXV, p. 354.
8. Peter Quivil, *Summula,* Wilkins, II, p. 165.
9. S. Petrus Coelestinus, *Opuscula, MBP,* XXV, p. 828.
10. An examination of the first few canons in the Penitential of Theodore, John T. McNeill and Helena M. Gamer, *Medieval Manuals of Penance* (New York, 1938), p. 184, in the light of the verse quoted above will make this point clear. On the rise of newer theological and legal works on penance, cf. Teetaert, *op. cit.,* pp. 312-313.

associate conventional theological divisions of the sins with the questions so that they afforded a frame of reference against which to place his theological knowledge as well as a practical device for spontaneous analysis.[11] To make the questions more useful, detailed explanations of their practical application were included in confessional manuals.[12]

This comprehensive and useful series of questions, which, in the thirteenth century, must have contributed to the efficacy of the confessional and considerably simplified the task of training the

11. Thus a conventional division of the sin of gluttony was associated with circumstances by Alexander de Stavensby, Wilkins, I, p. 645: "Circa ebrietatem et crapulam quaerendum est: circa crapulam attendentur istae circumstantiae. Praepropere, laute, nimis, ardenter, studiose." The dependence of many conventional analyses of types of sin on some conception similar to that of circumstances is obvious and probably did not escape the medieval student. See, for example, St. Augustine's classification of lies (*De mendacio, Opera*, Paris 1679-1700, VI, c. 435) ; St. Gregory's classification of dreams (*Moralia*, Lib. VIII, Cap. XXIV, 42, *PL* 75, c. 827, or *Dialogi*, ed. U. Moricca, Rome, 1924, pp. 309-310) ; or the conventional classification of the sins of lechery (e.g. St. Bonaventura, *De decem preceptis*, Collatio VI, 12, *Opera*, Quaracchi, 1882-1902, V, 527). All of these classifications were widely used.

12. E. g., Robert de Sorbon, *op. cit.*, p. 354; Peter Quivil, *op. cit.*, pp. 165-166. To illustrate the use of the questions, I quote the explanation of the first two from the discussion of Peter Quivil: "Debet igitur poenitens, quid fecerit, non in genere, sed in, quantum potest, specificando confiteri. Quod si commisit adulterium, non sufficit dicere, quod fornicatus est, vel quia lapsu carnis peccaverit; quia sic per generalitatem celaret peccatum suum, nec sic sciret sacerdos, quid ei deberet iniungere; quia major poenitentia debetur adultero, quam simplici fornicatori [cf. the classification of lechery mentioned in the preceding note]: et vere poenitens multum odio habet peccatum, et qui aliquid odio habet, turpissimo nomine illud nominat; et sic debet poenitens vocare peccatum suum, dum tamen verum dicat. Item qui fecit parricidium, non sufficit ei dicere, quod homicidium fecerit. Eodem modo de circumstantiis aliis; ut qui commisit incestum cum sorore sua, non sufficit dicere, quod incestum commisit. Inde videndum est, quis scil. fecit; non tamen ut nominet se proprio nomino, sed statum vel personatum suum exprimere debet, ita scil. dicendo: Ego episcopus, vel ego sacerdos: et sic de aliis ordinibus: vel ego monachus ordinis talis, vel inclusa; quia istae proprietates aggravant peccatum: pejus est enim episcopum, quam simplicem clericum fornicari; pejus clericum, quam laicum; pejus religiosum, quam simplicem secularem: et si forte peccaverit quis existens episcopus, vel sacerdos et sic de aliis non sufficit dicere Ego aliquando sic peccavi." The examples given are, of course, merely illustrative.

multitude of new priests necessary to carry out the great popular religious movement stimulated by Innocent III and the Friars, was not the invention of some twelfth century theologian, but a part of the medieval heritage of Greek and Latin culture. The Greek rhetorician Hermagoras, ranked by Isidore of Seville among the founders of the art,[13] divided the materials of rhetoric into two parts: *thesis and hypothesis*. A *thesis* involves an abstract, general question; whereas an *hypothesis* involves a question concerning concrete particulars.[14] The *loci* of any hypothetical question are seven circumstances, which St. Augustine, who is our authority for this feature of Hermagoras' rhetoric, quoted as follows: *quis, quid, quando, ubi, cur, quem ad modum, quibus adminiculis*.[15] In other words, no hypothetical question, or question involviing particular persons and actions, can arise without reference to these circumstances, and no demonstration of such a question can be made without using them. The history of this concept in Greek rhetoric need not concern us here,[16] for it was through the Latin rhetoricians who imitated Hermagoras that it reached the Middle Ages.

The first of the Latin rhetoricians to make full use of the device was Cicero, who, in the *De inventione* ventured to disagree with Hermagoras regarding the subject-matter of rhetoric. General questions or theses (*quaestiones*), he maintained, are the province of the philosophers; rhetoricians must confine themselves to hypotheses (*causae*).[17]

---

13. *Etymologiae*, II, 2, 1.
14. Georg Thiele, *Hermagoras* (Strassburg, 1893), pp. 27-28. Cf. W. von Christ, *Griechische Literaturgeschichte*, 5 ed. rev. W. Schmid and O. Stählin, (*Müllers Handbuch der Alterthumswissenschaft*), 2 Theil, 1 Hälfte, p. 234. The work of Hermagoras does not survive.
15. *De rhetorica*, ed. Halm, *Rhetores latini minores* (Leipzig, 1863), p. 141. Cf. R. Volkman, *Die Rhetorik der Griechen und Römer* (Leipzig, 1885), p. 36; Thiele, *op. cit.*, p. 37.
16. For general remarks on the subject, see Volkman, *op. cit.*, p. 37; Thiele, *op. cit.*, p. 37 f. The word περίστασις used by Hermagoras is said by Thiele, *op. cit.*, p. 37, to have been borrowed from the Stoics. Cf. Wilhelm Kroll, *Rhetorik*, Sonderabdruck aus Pauly-Wissowa, *Real-Encyclopädie* (Stuttgart, 1937), c. 56.
17. *De inventione*, I, 8. Thiele, *op. cit.*, p. 28, regarded the word *interpositione* in this discussion as a mistranslation of περίστασις.

Although Cicero later altered this opinion,[18] it served to emphasize the importance of circumstances in the *De inventione* and in later works based on it. In the *De inventione* there is a trace of the concept of circumstances in the discussion of means by which the *narratio*, or statement of the case, should be made credible;[19] but it appears most clearly in the section on *confirmatio*. There the circumstances are divided into two parts: attributes of persons and attributes of actions.[20] As attributes of persons he lists "*nomen, naturam, victum, fortunam, habitum, affectionem, studia, consilia, facta, casus, rationes.*" The attributes of actions are of three kinds: those concerning the performance of the action itself, those related to the action, and those consequent upon the action. Only the first of these divisions reflects the system of Hermagoras. Those attributes related to the action itself are "*locus, tempus, modus, occasio, facultas.*"[21] It should be observed that Cicero does not phrase the circumstances as questions.

The distinction between thesis and hypothesis was carried on by Quintilian,[22] who disagreed with the arguments in the *De inventione* by means of which Cicero attempted to eliminate *theses* from the province of rhetoric.[23] Consequently, the circumstances play a much smaller part in the *Institutiones* than in the *De inventione*. However, they are reflected in the discussion of the *narratio*,[24] and appear as *loci argumentorum* under "artificial" proofs. Cicero's twofold division is maintained, and again the attributes fail to take the form of questions.[25]

18. Cf. A. S. Wilkins, ed., *De oratore* (3 ed., Oxford, 1895), I, 60. Cf. *Topica*, 79-80. 19. *De inv.*, I, 29-30; cf. the earlier anonymous *Ad Herennium*, I, 16, and Cicero's later *De partitione oratoria*, 32.

20. I, 34: Omnes res argumentando confirmatur, aut ex eo, quod personis, aut ex eo, quod negotiis est attributum.

21. I, 36-38. Cf. II, 28-42. There is a similar discussion *De partitione*, 34-40. Cf. the definition of *causa* in the *Topica*, 80.

22. *Institutiones*, III, 5, 5-7.

23. *Ibid.*, III, 5, 12-15.

24. *Ibid.*, IV, 2, 52.

25. *Ibid.*, V, 10, 20-52, esp. 23: "In primis igitur argumenta a persona ducenda sunt, cum sit, ut dixi, divisio, ut omnia in haec duo partiamur, res atque personas: ut causa, tempus, locus, occasio, instrumentum, modus et cetera rerum sint accidentia...."

Circumstances assume a major role in the rhetoric of Fortunianus. There the orator is advised to consider them before formulating his *narratio*. They are "*persona, res, causa, tempus, locus, modus, materia.*" Each of these is explained separately.[26] The *narratio*, it is said, should contain "*semina quaestionum,*" and this result is obtained "*si septem circumstantias diligentius viderimus.*" After the *narratio*, or in some other part of the oration, it is possible to use a digression; this too is to be taken "*ex septem circumstantiis.*" [27] Fortunianus asserted that "artificial" arguments may concern materials "*ante rem, in re, circa rem, post rem.*" The *loci ante rem* are the seven circumstances, which are also used to distinguish *differentia in re*.[28]

In the commentary on the *De inventione* by Victorinus, the circumstances appear as questions. Explaining Cicero's account of how the *narratio* should be made credible, he wrote:

> Probabilis, inquit [Tullius], crit narratio, si in ea fuerint illa omnia, quibus solet veritas inveniri; nam in his septem omnis ad fidem argumentatio continetur.

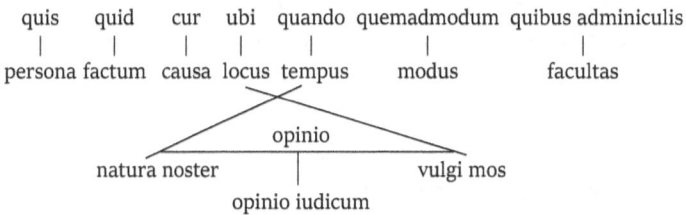

> Septem illa superiora, *quis, quid, cur, ubi, quando, quemadmodum, quibus adminiculis,* omnes artium scriptores tractarunt et in praeceptis suarum artium reliquerunt.[29]

The equivalence of Cicero's substantives with the questions of Hermagoras is here perfectly clear. In his discussion of *confirmatio*, Victorinus asserted that every hypothetical question rests on the circumstances *quis, quid, cur, ubi, quando, quemadmodum, quibus*

26. Halm, *op. cit.*, pp. 102-104.
27. *Ibid.*, p. 113.
28. *Ibid.*, p. 115.
29. Halm, *op. cit.*, pp. 206-207.

adminiculis, but that the first two are of primary importance, the last five being subsidiary to the second. Every argument is to be confirmed, then, from the attributes either of the person or the action. These attributes are discussed separately.[30] The doctrine of circumstances is also reflected in the treatises of Sulpicius Victor and Julius Victor, and the latter lists them as questions.[31]

But the most important discussion of the subject for the later Middle Ages is that in the *De differentiis topicis* of Boethius. Questions, Boethius wrote, are of two kinds: theses, or general questions called *propositiones*, which are not concerned with circumstances of particular persons or events; and hypotheses or specific questions called *causae*, which concern persons, times, actions, or other circumstances. Following the opinion of Cicero in the *De intventione*, Boethius made theses the province of dialectic, hypotheses the province of rhetoric, although dialectic may employ hypotheses to reinforce theses.[32] The *loci* proper to rhetoric are confined to the attributes of the person who is called for judgment and those of the act or statement for which he is to be judged. All arguments either in the defense of the person or for his prosecution must be taken from these materials. Boethius discussed the circumstances — "*quis, quid, cur, quomodo, ubi, quando, quibus auxiliis*" — in detail with illustrations. Thus one of the most influential writers of the early Middle Ages made the seven circumstances fundamental to the arts of prosecution and defense.[33] The fundamental position of circumstances is maintained in the *Disputatio de rhetorica* of Alcuin, which closely follows the *De inventione* in this matter.[34]

---

30. *Ibid.*, pp. 213-231. Cf. pp. 265-269 on *De inv.* II, 28-42.
31. *Ibid.*, pp. 314, 323, 374, 395, 424.
32. Migne, *PL*, 64, cols. 1177, 1205.
33. *Ibid.*, cols. 1212-1213. A slightly condensed version of this discussion appears as a separate treatise, *Locorum rhetoricorum distinctio, ibid.*, cols. 1221-1224. The importance of circumstances in early medieval rhetoric is illustrated by the survival of two separate treatises *De attributis personis et negotiis*, printed by Halm, *op. cit.*, pp. 305-310; 593-595, in addition to that of Boethius mentioned above. Cf. also the anonymous treatise, *ibid.*, pp. 585-586.
34. *Ibid.*, pp. 527, 536-540.

It remains to show that the notion of circumstances was still current among the rhetoricians of the twelfth century so that it was readily available to the theologians of the period. The commentary on the *De inventione* by Thierry of Chartres has not been printed and is, at present, unavailable, but we know that Thierry made use of Boethius, Quintilian, and Victorinus, in addition to the *De inventione*, so that he had the circumstances before him in several places.[35] More direct testimony, however, appears in the *Metalogicon* of John of Salisbury. Following Boethius, John reserved theses for dialectic, leaving hypotheses involving the seven circumstances to the rhetoricians:

> Versatur exercitium dialectice in omnibus disciplinis, si quidem quaestionem habet materiam; sed eam quae ypotesis dicitur, id est que circumstantiis implicatur, relinquit oratori. Sunt autem circumstantie, quas Boetius in quarto Topicorum enumerat, quis, quid, ubi, quibus adminiculis, cur, quomodo, quando.[36]

This passage may represent something of what its author learned from Thierry and Peter Helias under whose tutelage he studied rhetoric.[37] It may be significant that John's list of questions is in the form of the conventional hexameter verse employed by the theologians; the order is not that found in Boethius. Perhaps this mnemonic form was first devised in the schools as a pedagogical device. In the thirteenth century, St. Thomas cited Cicero as his authority for the verse, perhaps confusing either a written gloss on the *De inventione* or a remembrance of some rhetorician's lecture with the text itself.[38]

Since, as Boethius clearly indicates, the circumstances were considered essential in determining the extent of guilt of any accused person, it is natural that they should have been adopted by confessors, whose duty it was to ascertain as accurately as possible the magnitude of each sin confessed to them. Innocent's phrase "*et peccatoris ...*

---

35. The sources of Thierry's commentary are listed by Émile Thomas, "Un Commentaire du Moyen Age sur la Rhetorique de Cicéron," *Métanges Graux* (Paris, 1884), p. 43.
36. Ed. C. J. Webb (Oxford, 1929), pp. 83-84.
37. Cf. *ibid.*, p. 80.
38. *Summa*, I-II, 7, 3.

et peccati" is probably a reflection of the Ciceronian "*personis et negotiis*," and the verses quoted at the beginning of this paper represent attempts to arrange the circumstances in an easily remembered metrical form with variations which may be due either to lapses of memory or personal bias. The second of those quoted, which was used by St. Thomas, may be regarded as the standard form.

A principle of such fundamental importance in both rhetoric and theology was not without literary implications. In his *De eruditione praedicatorum*, written for the Dominican preachers, Humbert de Romans (d. 1277) stated that the preacher needs materials for various kinds of sermons. Not only should he be prepared to deliver the conventional *sermones de tempore* and *sermones de sanctis*; he should also have materials for sermons "*ad omne genus hominum*," and "*in omne diversitate negotiorum*."[39] In other words, he should be able to take into consideration the dominant circumstances of person and action that confront him. Materials for a hundred sermons suited to various kinds of persons and for another hundred suited to various occasions follow in the *De eruditione*.[40] One suspects that the intense interest in the classes and conditions of men evinced by writers of such later doctrinal works as Gower's *Mirour de l'omme* owes much to the notion of circumstances which the thirteenth century confessor borrowed indirectly from Hermagoras of Temnos.[41]

---

39. *MBP*, XXV, 456. Cf. note 30, above.
40. *Ibid.*, XXV, 456-467.
41. I intend to describe a more striking example at length elsewhere.
    It may be observed incidentally that the circumstances were revived by Renaissance rhetoricians. For example, Thomas Wilson, *Arte of Rhetorique*, ed. G. H. Mair (Oxford, 1909), pp. 17-18, made an English verse of them:
    Who, what, and where, by what helpe, and by whose:
    Why, how, and when, doe many things disclose.

    "These places," he continued, "helpe wonderfully to set out any matter...." Italian writers adapted them to historiography. E. g., Francesco Patrizzi, *De historia dialogi X* in *Artis historicae penus* (Basel, 1579), I, 510; and Antonio Viperano, *De scribenda historia, ibid.*, I, p. 510. However, their appearance in Renaissance rhetoric and their possible reflection in the literature of the

period are subjects for separate studies. I owe the above references to Italian historiography to my colleague Mr. A. H. Buford.

In modern times, Thiele, *op. cit.,* p. 38, indicates that at the time he wrote the circumstances were customarily memorized by German schoolboys as a part of their training in composition. Perhaps the "Five W's" of journalism owe something to the Ciceronian tradition. A curious instance of all seven circumstances recently appeared in a popular comic strip, "Don Winslow— U. S. Navy," March 3, 1945. The author, Mr. Frank V. Martinek, informs me that he was not aware of any special source for them. We may conclude that although Hermagoras is little known, his conception of rhetorical *loci* has been astonishingly persistent.

D. W. Robertson, Jr.
A Study of Certain Aspects of the Cultural Tradition of "Handlyng Synne." (Under the direction of George R. Coffman, 1945.)

University of North Carolina Record (1946), pp. 146-147.

The purpose of this study is to sketch the broad outlines of the cultural tradition of Robert Mannyng's *Handlyng Synne* and to place the work in that tradition. It is demonstrated that *Handlyng Synne* may be described as a confessional inquiry showing the systematizing influence of late medieval theology, detached from the immediate environment of the actual ceremony of confession so as to form a general guide to its performance without emphasis on satisfaction, and embellished with *exempla* to make it attractive. A probable relationship is indicated between the *Manuel des Pechiez*, of which *Handlyng Synne* is a translation, and a recurrent English episcopal decree; and a relationship is established between the last section of *Handlyng Synne* on shrift and a sermon by William Peraldus. In general, this study demonstrates that *Handlyng Synne*, both in general and in details, is far more conventional that had hitherto been supposed.

The Cultural Tradition of *Handlyng Synne*

By D. W. Robertson, Jr.

Speculum 22:2 (April 1947), pp. 162-185.

Although a work as complex as *Handlyng Synne* is obviously not a product of any single tradition, it is possible, I believe, to isolate in the general background of Mannyng's book a single literary type which to a large extent determined not only the general character of the materials which Mannyng used, but also his peculiar disposition of those materials. In other words, it may be shown that neither the principles of selection employed by the author nor his system of organization were fortuitous; rather, they resulted from adherence to a well established convention which had been developed to implement certain definite aims of the medieval Church. One's attitude toward the problem of where such a convention should be sought is necessarily determined by the conception of the purpose and general character of *Handlyng Synne* which he obtains from an examination of the text itself.

Perhaps the most widely accepted conception of this kind is that which appears in Professor J. E. Wells' *Manual of the Writings in Middle English*. There *Handlyng Synne* is included among works of religious instruction described as 'comprehensive,'[1] so that one is led to regard the book as an encyclopedia of religious instruction. Certainly Mannyng's work is more comprehensive in character than are the shorter vernacular works dealing with the sins alone or with the commandments alone, but the inference — for which, incidentally, Dr Wells should not be held altogether responsible — that it is therefore an

---

1. Chapter VI, pp. 333-373.

encyclopedia will not bear close examination. An encyclopedia should certainly include some account of all of the basic elements of the faith with which a layman was expected to be acquainted, but *Handlyng Synne* does not elaborate the two most fundamental elements: the Creed, and the Lord's Prayer. Nor does it contain the *Ave,* which was also of primary importance in lay education during the thirteenth and fourteenth centuries.[2] Moreover, the conception of *Handlyng Synne* as a comprehensive work does not lead to fruitful investigation. Comparison with other works similarly regarded, like the *Cursor Mundi* or the *Aʒenbite of Inwit*, only emphasizes the fact that these works are all actually very unlike both in content and technique.

Another commonly adopted attitude is that *Handlyng Synne* is essentially a 'collection of stories.'[3] Although it is undoubtedly true that Mannyng was deeply interested in the 'talys' with which he attracted his audience, it is also true that his stories are always used to illustrate a point of doctrine. They are *exempla* in function as well as in tradition; that is, the stories are not told simply as entertaining narratives, but are subordinate to the doctrine which they illustrate. Mannyng himself tells us in his prologue that he is writing for 'lewde men' who like to hear 'talys and rymys,' but he also says that his purpose is didactic.[4] The convention of using stories to influence the unlearned had been well established at the time he wrote. Jacques de Vitry, recognizing that such people are 'moved more, indeed, by external examples than by profound truths [*sententiis*]',[5] had used *exempla* in sermons with spectacular success; and their employment had contributed no little to the effectiveness of the great revival of popular preaching and instruction carried out by the Dominicans.[6] Étienne de Bourbon had found them 'of value to all men, and to all estates, and to any material; and to dissuasion from every evil; and to persuasion, encouragement,

---

2. On the importance of the Creed, the Lord's Prayer, and the *Ave,* see 'The *Manuel des Péchés* and an English Episcopal Decree,' *MLN,* LX (1945), 441, note 8.
3. E.g. see W. H. Schofield, *English Literature from the Norman Conquest to Chaucer,* London, 1906, p. 413.
4. The relevant lines from the prologue are quoted below.
5. T. F. Crane, *The Exempla of Jacques de Vitry,* London, 1890, p. xli.
6. Cf. J. R. H. Moorman, *Church Life in England in the Thirteenth Century,* Cambridge, 1945, p. 79.

and advancement toward every good; in every place and time....'[7] The use of *exempla* in *Handlyng Synne* does reflect an important literary tradition, but this tradition does not explain either the structure of the book or the character of the doctrine which it contains.

The title *Handlyng Synne* and Mannyng's own statement that his book concerns 'al that toucheth dedly synne'[8] suggest that the work might be conveniently regarded as a treatise on sin related in some way to the many other treatises on the subject produced during the Middle Ages. Assertions that *Handlyng Synne* is related to the most famous of these treatises, the *Summa de vitiis* of William Peraldus, have not been lacking.[9] Unfortunately, there is very little actual similarity between *Handlyng Synne* and the *Summa*. Peraldus did not accord separate treatment to the commandments and sacraments, but the sections on these subjects in *Handlyng Synne* are certainly of great importance. Moreover, those sections of the two works which do correspond in general subject matter differ markedly in method. There is little resemblance between Peraldus' learned lists of 'authorities' arranged systematically under such topics as 'those things which serve to make a given sin detestable,' 'the various divisions of a sin,' 'the sins that follow a given sin,' 'the remedies for a sin,' and Mannyng's enumeration of commonplace manifestations of sins in everyday life, usually enunciated without benefit of 'authority.' In short, even a cursory examination reveals that *Handlyng Synne* and the *Summa* are structurally very different. It is entirely possible, however, that the section of *Handlyng Synne* dealing specifically with the sins does contain reflections of the tradition represented by the *Summa*. But that tradition does not account either for the structure of the book as a whole nor for the specific way in which its materials are presented. In general, then, it may be said that most of the attitudes toward the text

---

7. A. Lecoy de la Marche, ed., *Anecdotes Historiques d'Etienne de Bourbon*, Paris, 1877, p. 12. The nature and history of the *exemplum* have been admirably treated by J.-Th. Welter, *L'Exemplum dans la Littérature Religieuse et Didactique du Moyen Age*, Paris, 1927.

8. *HS*, l. 27.

9. See G. R. Owst, *Preaching in Medieval England,* Cambridge, 1926, pp. 289-290 (note). For another similar view, see below, note 86.

of *Handlyng Synne* which have hitherto been developed have not resulted in a classification of the book which leads to a rational account of its historical significance.

Perhaps the failure to classify *Handlyng Synne* may be attributed in part to a misunderstanding of the relationship between it and its immediate source, the *Manuel des Péchés*. Although this relationship still awaits clarification, we are beginning to discover that *Handlyng Synne* is less of a 'free adaptation' than has been supposed.[10] Whether Mannyng made radical alterations in his source or not, even Dr Furnivall's text of the *Manuel* shows sufficient parallelism between the two works to warrant a tentative assumption that they belong to the same general type. The class to which the *Manuel* belongs has long been apparent. It is true that there have been those who wished to describe it as a 'comprehensive encyclopedia of theological knowledge,'[11] or as 'a satire on the failings and vices of English men and women of all classes of society,'[12] but others have recognized it as something more specific, a manual for the use of penitents.[13] One prominent English scholar, writing at the turn of the century, described the *Manuel* as a work 'intended to be of practical use to persons preparing for confession,' and implied that *Handlyng Synne* was written for the same 'practical purposes,'[14]

---

10. Dr Furnivall, in the original Roxburghe Club edition of Handlying Synne (1862), concluded, pp. xiv-xvii, that Mannyng was an 'adapter' rather than a 'translator.' However, Dr C. G. Laird, who has made a thorough study of the manuscripts of the *Manuel*, will shortly demonstrate that Mannyng followed his source more closely than Dr Furnivall believed. See 'A Program of Departmental Section and Discussion Papers,' *PMLA*, LVIII (1943), Part 2, p. 14.

11. Karl Voretsch, *Einführung in das Studium Altfranzösischen Litteratur,* Halle, 1925, p. 407.

12. Rose Graham in *The Victoria History of the County of Lincoln,* London, 1906, II, 184. The classes of society do play an important part in the *Manuel* and *Handlyng Synne*, as we shall see shortly.

13. Gaston Paris, *Histoire Littéraire de la France,* XXVIII, 182-183; E. Walberg, *Quelques Aspects de la Littérature Anglo-Normande,* Paris, 1936, p. 66. There should be no doubt about the matter now, since the publication of E. J. Arnould, *Le Manuel des Péchés,* Paris, 1940.

14. G. C. Macaulay, *The Complete Works of John Gower,* Oxford, 1899-1902, II, xlvii. A few years later, Miss Hope E. Allen, *RR*, VIII (1917), 451, made the very valuable suggestion that the *Manuel* should be studied in relation to episcopal decrees.

but no one, except Miss Hope Allen and E. J. Arnould, seems to have been aware of the fact that this conception opens up avenues of fruitful investigation which other conceptions do not afford. Even if Mannyng's additions to the *Manuel* involve the engrafting of new traditions not apparent in the original, I think it can be shown that the same basic tradition governs both works. Since no critical edition of the *Manuel* is now available, and Dr. Laird's definitive statement of the evolution of the text has not yet appeared, I shall confine myself here, except for occasional references, to a discussion of evidence for this tradition in *Handlyng Synne*, disregarding the question of whether or not the same evidence always appears in the *Manuel*.

The purpose and general character of the *Manuel* are apparent in the opening lines of the prologue, as it is printed by Dr Furnivall:

> La uertue del seint espirit
> Nus seit eidant en cest escrit,
> A uus les choses ben mustrer
> Dunt hom se deit confesser,
> E ausi en la quele manere,
> Qe ne fet mie bon a tere;
> Car ceo la uertue del sacrement,
> Dire le pechié, et coment.
> Tuz pechiéz ne poun recunter;
> Mes par tant se peot remembrer,
> E les pechiéz amender,
> Qe cest escrit uelt regarder.[15]

The general implications of these lines should be clear to anyone familiar with the confessional procedure of the Catholic Church. In the first place, it is felt that confession should be complete. As one modern authority puts it,

> La confession ne serait pas intégre ou entêre, si, — sans cause excusante, nous le verrons, — on cachait ne fût-ce qu'un seul péché mortel. Et ce manque d'intégrité rendrait la confession nulle et sacrilège....[16]

---

15. Ll. 1-12.
16. J. Bricout, *Dictionnaire Pratique des Connaissances Religieuses* (1925 ff.), II, cols. 421-422.

In order to insure this necessary 'integrity,' it is advisable that the penitent make a thorough examination of his conscience before confession. Various methods are employed for directing and ordering this examination, but the most common of these

> consiste a suivre, un à un, les commandements de Dieu et de l'Eglise, les devoirs des son [i.e., the penitent's] état, les péchés ou les vices capitaux, et à voir, sur chacun, si on a péché par pensée, dar désir, par parole, par action ou par omission.[17]

It is said further that the sins should be memorized and confessed in the order established by the procedure just described. The *Manuel des Péchés,* then, promises to be a guide to assist the penitent in his self-examination before confession. Works of a similar kind are not unfamiliar in the modern Church. For example, there is a guide for penitents in the prayer book known as *The Key of Heaven,*[18] and separate works devoted to this purpose also exist.[19] With these facts in mind, let us turn now to the prologue of *Handlyng Synne*.

If there were a clear-cut statement of purpose in Mannyng's prologue, *Handlyng Synne* would undoubtedly have been properly classified long ago. The opening lines, corresponding in position with the lines quoted above from the *Manuel,* merely state, however, that the author intends to present 'grete' sins 'withoutyn pryuyte.'[20] Dr Furnivall thought the purpose of the book to be revealed in the last five lines of the following passage:

> For lewde men y vndyr-toke
> On englyssh tunge to make þys boke,
> For many ben of swyche manere,
> Þat talys and rymys wyl bleþly here;
> Yn gamys, & festys, & at þe ale,
> Loue men to lestene troteuale;
> Þat may falle ofte to vylanye,
> To dedly synne, or oþer folye;

---

17. *Ibid.,* II, col. 426.
18. New Edition, New York [1926], pp. 164-202.
19. E.g., Rev. Henry Frank, S. T. B., *A Guide for Confession,* Huntington, Indiana, 1945.
20. Ll. 1-12.

> For swyche men haue y made þis ryme,
> Þat þey may weyl dyspende here tyme,
> And þere-yn sumwhat for to here,
> To leue al swyche foul manere,
> And for to kunne knowe þerynne
> Þat þey wene no synne be ynne.[21]

What this passage means, as I interpret it, is that Mannyng wished to attract uneducated laymen from their profane conviviality and to teach them to recognize the true character of actions which they had not thought to be sinful. I believe this to be a subsidiary purpose of the book. Mannyng wished to have his readers recognize their sins, but such recognition was a necessary preliminary to confession. That he had confession in mind is clear in a passage immediately following the rather noncommittal opening lines referred to above:

> Of þyse þan ys my sawe,
> Þe commaundementys of the olde lawe,
> Þyse ten were fyrst vs ȝeuyn,
> *And fyrst we wylyn of hem be shreuyn,*
> *Yn what poyntys þat we falle*
> *Yn opon synne aȝen hem alle.*[22]

It will be remembered that it is still customary for many penitents to begin their self-examination with the commandments. Later in the prologue, when Mannyng turns his attention to his activity as a translator and to the significance of the book he is translating, the fact that he was primarily concerned with teaching laymen what to confess becomes clear. He says there that he has turned a book called *Handlyng Synne* from French into English:

> In þat tyme turnede y þys
> On englyssh tunge out of frankys,
> Of a boke as y fonde ynne;
> Men clepyn þe boke 'handlyng synne.'[23]

---

21. Ll. 43-56. See the Preface to the Roxburghe Club edition, p. iii. Cf. the *Manuel*, ll. 113-116.
22. Ll. 13-18. The italics are mine.
23. Ll. 77-80.

He explains the literal meaning of the French title, *Manuel des Péchés*, and proposes to reveal its significance:

> In frenshe þer a clerk hyt sees,
> He clepyþ hyt 'manuel de pecches.'
> 'Manuel' ys 'handlyng with honde';
> 'Pecches' ys 'synne,' y vndyrstonde.
> Þese twey wurdys þat beyn otwynne,
> Do hem to gedyr, ys 'handlyng synne.'
> And weyl ys clepyd, for þys skyle;
> And as y wote, ȝow shew y wyle.[24]

In the first place, the book may be called *Handlyng Synne* because it shows us that we sin continuously every day; in other words, it shows which of our daily actions are sinful:

> We handel synne euery day;
> In wurde and dede, al we may,
> Lytyl or mochel, synne we do,
> Þe fend and oure flesh tysyn vs þerto;
> 'ffor þys skyle hyt may be seyde
> 'Handlyng synne' for oure mysbreyde;
> ffor euery day & euery oure
> We synne þat shal we bye ful soure.[25]

This is essentially the same idea as that expressed in lines fifty-five and fifty-six quoted above. But the discussion continues, revealing another reason why the book should be called *Handlyng Synne;* it concerns 'handlyng' sin at confession. We should 'handle' our sins carefully in thought, weighing them all, one by one, so that we may rise from them when we confess them:

> Anoþer handlyng þer should be,
> Wyþ shryfte of mouþe to clense þe.
> Handyl þy synne yn þy þouȝt,
> Lytyl & mochel, what þou hast wroght;
> Handyl þy synne to haue drede;
> Noþyng but peyn ys þarfore mede.

---

24. Ll. 81-88.
25. Ll. 89-96.

> Handyl þy synnes, & weyl hem gesse,
> How þey fordo al þy godenesse.
> Handyl þy synnes, & weyl hem euene,
> Elles forbarre þey þe blys of heuene,
> Handyl hem at onys euerychone,
> Noght one by hym self alone:
> Handyl so to ryse from alle,
> Þat none make þe eft falle,
> With shryfte of mouþe, & wyl of herte,
> And a party, with penaunce smerte;
> Þys ys a skyl þat hyt may be tolde
> Handlyng synne many a folde.[26]

Reviewing sins orally at confession is fully as much a kind of 'handlyng' as actually committing them. We should listen carefully when our sins are described to us so that we may 'handle' them in this way:

> Handllyng yn speche ys as weyl
> As handlyng yn dede euery deyl.
> On þys manere handyl þy dedys,
> And lestene and lerne whan any hem redys.[27]

In short, *Handlyng Synne* 'handles' sinful actions so that the reader may 'handle' them in thought and finally 'handle' them at confession. Mannyng's account of the nature and purpose of his book thus corresponds exactly with the intention expressed at the beginning of the *Manuel des Péchés*.

In purpose, then, *Handlyng Synne* resembles the guides for confession still current among Catholic lay readers. Although we should expect considerable difference in specific content between a work produced in the fourteenth century and a similar work produced in modern times, there are nevertheless unmistakable resemblances between *Handlyng Synne* and the section called 'Devotions for Confession' in the modern prayer book. In general, *Handlyng Synne* contains sections on the commandments, the seven sins and the sin of sacrilege, the sacraments, and, finally, the 'points' and 'graces' of shrift. The last

---

26. Ll. 97-114.
27. Ll. 115-118.

section contains general instructions to the penitent arranged under 'points,' some assurances of the benefits of confession which may be called 'graces,' and some closing admonitions — not properly 'graces' — to the effect that the penitent should not be guilty of despair, should not excuse himself, should not minimize his sins, and should not be scornful. The 'Devotions for Confession' begins with some instructions which correspond generally, and in some details, with the last section of *Handlyng Synne*.[28] After some prayers which are prefaced by some explanatory matter, the heart of the treatise begins — the 'Examination of Conscience.'[29] A brief introductory note opens the examination. This is followed by materials based on the commandments, the commandments of the Church, and the seven sins. Further prayers conclude the treatise. The only sections of *Handlyng Synne* for which the 'Devotions' has no corresponding sections are those on sacrilege and the sacraments. However, three of the commandments of the Church in the 'Devotions' are concerned directly with the sacraments,[30] and two of the remaining three have to do with subjects that are treated by Mannyng under sacrilege.[31] On the whole, the general content of the two works is similar.

There are also surprising similarities in detail. *Handlyng Synne* may be said to contain materials of three different kinds: (1) admonitory materials, (2) theological exposition, and (3) *exempla*. The theological exposition and the *exempla* are used to support the admonitions, which form the foundation of the book.[32] A striking-feature of these admonitions is the fact that they are usually introduced with

---

28. *The Key to Heaven*, pp. 157-158. The reader is warned against delaying confession (Cf. Mannyng's second 'point'); he is told that he must be sorrowful (Cf. Mannyng's sixth 'point'); he is admonished to confess '*humbly, simply, sincerely,* and *entirely*' (Cf. Mannyng's fourth, tenth, and twelfth 'points'); and he is cautioned to confess the circumstances of each sin (Cf. Mannyng's third closing admonition).
29. Pp. 164-194.
30. III, IV, VI, pp. 188-190.
31. I, v, *loc. cit.* Cf. HS, ll. 9253-9314; 9315-9332.
32. Not all of the materials in the tradition of the *exemplum* are confined to the stories. For example, the lively description of the little devil Terlyncel, beginning l. 4251, is certainly an *exemplum* although it is not a 'tale.'

conditional clauses, which Mannyng calls 'questions.' The first of these, under the first commandment, appears as follows:

> The fyrst askyng ys yn oure boke,
> '3yf þou euer god forsoke.'[33]

And thereafter the admonitory materials are studded with the expression '3yf þou....' Sometimes there is a whole series of such 'questions' without interrupruption.[34] Again they may occur at the close of a long passage of exposition. For example, after explaining at length the six causes of dreams, Mannyng admonishes:

> 3yf þou telle hem [i.e., dreams], þan mayst þou erre;
> And 3yf þow trow hem, þat ys wel werre.[35]

Sometimes the admonitions are direct, but the 'question' form is predominant. Turning now to the 'Devotions,' we find that the 'Examination of Conscience' consists largely of a list of questions. They are more direct than Mannyng's; the author has used 'Have you ...' rather than 'If you ....' Perhaps the resemblance in form would not be very striking if there were not also resemblances in content. The line regarding faith in dreams just quoted is paralleled in the 'Devotions' by

> Have you given credit to dreams, taken notice of omens, or made any other superstitious observations?[36]

As, for omens, a few lines before the discussion of dreams, Mannyng had warned against believing in the omen of the magpie, that of morning meeting, or the omen of handsel.[37] All of this material appears uuder the first commandment in both works. Other parallels might be cited from the corresponding sections on the other commandments and from those on the various sins, but since my purpose here is merely to establish a working hypothesis as a basis for investigation, and since both *Handlyng Synne* and the *Key* are easily available, I shall forego any further comparison. Both the 'Devotions' and *Handlyng*

---

33. Ll. 153-154.
34. E.g., ll. 3021 if.
35. Ll. 473-474.
36. *Op. cit.,* p. 170.

Synne are essentially lists of questions regarding various commonplace transgressions; and although the medieval work is much longer and more elaborate, covering the sacraments as well as the commandments and the sins, there is nothing unreasonable in a tentative assumption that it may be classed as a confessional manual for laymen embellished with *exempla* and supported by passages of theological exposition. An examination of the relevant literature of penance antedating *Handlyng Synne* should determine the value of this hypothesis.

The lines along which the literature of penance developed in the Middle Ages were largely determined by variations in theological attitudes.[38] In the seventh century, when Theodore of Tarsus came to England, he found that in the Celtic church secret confession had been substituted for the public confession customary among the Romans. Not only was the custom itself well established, but there were also in existence guides or penitentials, as they are called, written to direct confessors in the interrogation of individual peinitents and in the administration of specific penances for each sin confessed to them. Theodore found the Celtic system to his liking and decided to adopt it, a decision which has been said to mark 'a turning point in the history of the Western Church.'[39] The resulting spread in the practice of private confession produced a concomitant spread in the use of penitentials. Since these works were usually unofficial and frequently contradictory, some effort was made to suppress them. In the ninth century, Frankish synods issued orders to burn the existing penitentials so that they might be replaced by orthodox collections of canons. But the tradition of the penitentials persisted, reaching its climax, perhaps, in the enormously influential *Corrector* of Būrchard of Worms, produced in the early eleventh century.[40] When Bartholomew of Exeter wrote in the twelfth century, he still found it appropriate to stipulate that

---

37. Ll. 355-378.
38. The following sketch of the literature of penance necessarily emphasizes only matters pertinent to the background of *Handlyng Synne*.
39. R. H. Hodgkin, *A History of the Anglo-Saxons,* Oxford, 1935, i, 309.
40. Brief accounts of the history of the penitentials may be found in John T. McNeil and Helena M. Gamer, *Medieval Handbooks of Penance,* New York, 1938, pp. 25-50; A. Morey, *Bartholomew of Exeter,* Cambridge, 1937, pp. 168-171.

every priest should have, in addition to other books, a 'canon penitentialis.'[41] Meanwhile, however, theological developments were beginning to make the penitentials obsolete. A new interest in the theoretical aspects of penance was stimulated by its establishment as one of the seven sacraments of the Church by Peter Lombard in the middle of the twelfth century.[42] As the basis for a large part of his discussion Lombard used a treatise *De vera et falsa poenitentia*, which he mistakenly attributed to St Augustine. His use of it in the *Sentences* and the attribution to the most highly venerated of the Fathers led to a widespread interest in the work and in the theoretical discussion it contains.[43] Together with the heightened interest in the theoretical aspects of penance, the twelfth century witnessed a rapid growth in systematic canon law, under the leadership of Gratian. As the theological element in the penitentials became the province of the systematic theologian, so the legal element they contained became the province of the canonist. The theological element, with which we are concerned here, was capable of much systematic improvement by the end of the twelfth century, especially as a result of advances in the theology of the sins. The earlier penitentials contained long miscellaneous lists of transgressions arranged more or less unsystematically under major sins.[44] Later, in harmony with a general tendency

---

Burchard's *Corrector* forms one section of his great *Decretum*. It is carefully described in P. Fournier and G. LeBras, *Histoire des Collections Canoniques en Occident*, Paris, 1931, 1932, i, 368-371. A. Teetaert, 'Le "Liber Poenitentialis" de Pierre de Poitiers,' *Beiträge zur Geschichte des Philosophie und Theologie des Mittelalters*, Supplementband, III (1935), p. 310, note 4, describes the *Corrector* as 'un des traités les plus complets, sir l'administration de la Penitence, que nous a legués le haut moyen Age.'

41. Morey, *op. cit.*, p. 192.

42. Cf. Morey, *op. cit.*, pp. 170-171.

43. For a statement of the importance of the *De vera et falsa poenitentia*, see Dom D. A. Wilmart, 'Un opuscule sur la Confession composé par Guy de Southwick vers la fin du XIIIe siecle,' *Recherches de Théologie ancienne et médievale*, vii (1935), p. 339.

44. For example, the penitential attributed to Egbert of York as printed in part by J. Morinus, *Commentarius historicus de disciplina in administratione sacramenti poenitentiae*, Antwerp, 1682, Supplement, p. 15, contains the following admonition: 'Post haec [certain preliminary questions to be asked of the

toward systematization evident in the development of scholastic methods, the Gregorian analysis of the sins, with some variations, came to be regarded as standard.[45] All specific sins were thought of as arising from seven principal vices, or corruptions of the soul, so that these vices offered a key to the understanding of any particular transgression.[46] Moreover, a means was established for estimating the relative gravity of any given sin based on the degree of consent involved.[47] In the thirteenth century, the confessor's task in making estimates of this kind was further simplified, as I shall show presently, by a convenient guide to the circumstances under which sins are committed; and a general principle, already evident in the penitentials, was employed in the administration of penances.[48] Thus there came into being a highly flexible abstract system much more adaptable to the infinite variation of actual experience than the long but specific lists of crimes and penances in the penitentials.

---

penitent], interroga eum crimina sua quae habet. Hoc est, de superbia, vel sacrilegio, homicidio, & adulterio, falso testimonio, perjurio, mendacio, furto, rapina, ira, avaritia, detractione, & si cum quadripedibus luxuriatus sit, vel incesta commisit.' Certain specific questions follow.

45. Gregory's system may be found in the *Moralia*, Lib. XXXI, Cap. XLV, 87-88; Migne, *PL*, 76, cols. 620-621.

46. An excellent early statement of the theory may be found in Hugh of St Victor, *De sacramentis*, Lib. II, Pars XIII, Cap. I; Migne, *PL*, 176, c. 525. Cf. Wm. of Auvergne, *De vitiis et peccatis*, *Opera*, Orléans, 1674, II, 260. The 'capital' vices were, however, sometimes regarded as major sins, so that theologians found it necessary to emphasize the distinction. See the *Summa sententiarum*, Tract. III, Cap. XVI; Migne, *PL*, 176, cols. 113-114; 'Nec dicitur haec capitalia quod majora sint alijs, cum alia aeque magna sint, vel majora, sed capitalia a quibus oriuntur omnia alia ....'" Cf. St Bonaventura *Comm. in lib. IV Sententiarum*, Lib. II, Dist. XLIII, Dubium III, *Opera*, Quaracchi, 1909, IV, 977.

47. See Peter Lombard, *Sententiae*, Lib. II, Dist. XV, Pars II, Cap. VI-XIII, in Bonaventura, *Opera*, II, 551-553. For an earlier and simpler discussion of a similar character, see St Gregory, *Moralia*, Lib. IV, Cap. XXVII, 48-49; Migne, *PL*, 75, c. 661. The significance of this theory and of the one mentioned immediately above does not arise from their novelty, for they were both old, but from the fact that they became a part of a finely articulated system of theology which achieved surprisingly wide currency in the thirteenth century, reaching its definitive expression in the *Summa* of St Thomas.

48. It was widely held that the penance should be opposite to the crime, e.g., fasting for gluttony. See McNeill and Gamer, *op. cit.*, pp. 44-46, and the discussion in Bishop Peter Quivil's *Summula*, Wilkins, *Concilia*, II, 167.

The great Lateran Council of 1215 offered the impetus necessary to the development of literary types reflecting the theological advances of the preceding century. There it was decreed that every one of the faithful, on pain of minor excommunication, should confess privately to his own priest at least once each year. To set up the necessary machinery for carrying out this program, it was further decreed that the priest should assume the role of a skilled physician to the sinful, and that he should diligently inquire into the circumstances, both of the sinner and the sin, so that he might administer appropriate remedies.[49] The regulation regarding annual confession was repeated or echoed in local councils, sometimes with the recommendation that the people confess at Pentecost and Christmas as well as at Easter,[50] and preachers were admonished to make its implications clear in sermons.[51] At the same time, there grew up, for the use of priests, a new literature of penance. There were, in the first place, learned works of an abstract character in the tradition of the *De vera et falsa poenitentia*, like the *De poenitentia* of William of Auvergne. More pastoral in nature were the so-called *Summae confessorum,* which retained both theological and legal elements in the tradition of the penitentials.[52] Other manuals, specifically intended to enable priests to 'inquire diligently' were issued by bishops and other authorities, sometimes separate works, like the *De confessione* of Robert de Sorbon or the *Summula* of Bishop Peter Quivil, sometimes, especially in the second half of the thirteenth century, as chapters in synodal statutes.[53] In the more

49. C. J. Hefele and H. Leclerq, *Histoire des Conciles,* Paris, 1907-1938, v, 1350.
50. E.g., Constitutions of Richard le Poore (*ca.* 1220), Wilkins, I, 577; Constitutions of St Edmund (1236), *ibid.*, i, 637; Constitutions of Walter de Cantilupe (1240), *ibid.*, I, 669; etc.
51. *Statuta Synodalia Ecclesiae Gerundensis* (ca. 1260), Mansi, *Concilia,* XXIII, ca. 929.
52. These works have been surveyed from a special point of view by J. Dietterle, "Die *Summae Confessorum*," Zeitschrift für Kirchengeschichte, XXIV (1903), 353-374, 520-548; XXV (1904), 248-272; XXVI (1905), 59-81, 350-362; XXVII (1906), 70-79, 166-168, 298-810, 431-442; XXVIII (1907), 401-431.
53. E.g., see the *Statuta Synodalia Claromontensis Ecclesiae,* Mansi, XXIII, cols. 1198-1200; *Statuta Synodalia Cadurcensis,* etc., *ibid.*, XXIV, cols. 988-991; *Synodus Diocesana Herbipolensis, ibid.*, XXIV, cols. 1197-1200.

practical of these works the admonition that the confessor should inquire into the circumstances of sinners and sins was frequently explained by means of a mnemonic verse based on a well established principle of Classical rhetoric:

> Quis, quid, ubi, quibus auxiliis, cur, quomodo, quando.[54]

By having these questions answered, the priest could reach a fair understanding of the degree of consent involved in the sins confessed to him. As we shall see, this device was to have some literary significance. It should be remarked that a further stimulus to the popularity of penitential theory and confessional literature was furnished by the zeal of the Friars, especially the Diominicans, who instituted a whole series of works on penance shortly after the conclusion of the Fourth Lateran Council.[55] Again, in the first half of the century, the theory of the seven sacraments began to reach the level of pastoral practice, so that the importance of penance as a sacrament and the consequent obligation of the ordinary priest with a cure of souls to observe it carefully were more widely recognized.[56] If we are to

54. The origin and use of this verse are explained in 'A Note on the Classical Origin of "Circumstances" in the Medieval Confessional,' *Studies in Philology*, XLIII (1946), 6-14.

55. For a discussion of one of the more important of these, see P. Mandonnet, 'La Summa de Poenitentia m. Pauli,' *Beiträge zur Geschichte der Phil. und Theol. des Mittelalters,* Supplementband III (1935), 525-544. The great popularity of the treatise discussed here was indicated by B. Hauréau *Notices det Extraits,* Paris, 1890-1893, III, 225-226; V, 71.

56. Decrees that priests should know the sacraments and teach their parishioners to observe them became fairly common after 1215. E.g., Constitutions of Richard le Poore (*ca.* 1220), Wilkins, I, 574 (Cf. the London Constitutions printed by R. M. Wooley, *EHR*, XXX (1915), esp. pp. 288-296); Council of Oxford (1222), *ibid.*, I, 593. The Papal Legate, Cardinal Otho, in his constitutions of 1237, named the seven sacraments and ordered the archdeacons to teach the priests to administer them, Wilkins, I, 650. The *Constitutiones Synodales Valentinae Diocesis* (1255), Mansi, XXII, c. 886, order that each priest obtain a certain treatise on the sacraments. A similar warning appears in the *Constitutiones Fratris Arnaldi de Peralta* (1261), Mansi, XXIII, c. 1051. Sometimes the councils themselves issued more or less elaborate explanations of the sacraments. E.g., *Statuta Synodalia Ecclesiae Gerundensis* (ca. 1260), *ibid.*, XXIII, cols. 929-930; *Statuta Synodalia Claromontensis Ecclesiae* (1268), *ibid.*, XXIII, cols. 1186-1203; *Synodus Nemausensis* (1284), *ibid.*, XXIV, cols. 522-526;

assume that the *Manuel* and *Handlyng Synne* are confessional manuals, it is against this background of theological and literary developments that we must consider them. The *Manuel* was produced at a time when enthusiasm for the new theory of the sacraments in general and for the new importance attributed to penance in particular was still high.[57]

As a test preliminary to a more thorough investigation, we may consider whether the complex of traditions just described throws any light on Mannyng's statement in his prologue that he intends to discuss great sins 'withoutyn pryuyte.'[58] Following Gaston Paris, who found the same exception taken in the *Manuel*, I shall interpret *pryuyte* to mean 'secret sin,' [59] and translate Mannyng's phrase 'except for secret sin.' The author of the *Manuel* thought it best to remain silent about certain unusual sins, the very mention of which might introduce his readers to them for the first time; [60] and Mannyng assures us that he will not make any such sins 'oponly kydde,' but warns that they must, nevertheless, be mentioned at confession:

> Of pryuytes speke y ry3t nou3t;
> Þe pryuytes wyl y nat name
> For none þarefore shulde me blame;
> Leuer ys me þat þey be hydde,
> Þan for me were oponly kydde.
> Noþeles þey mote be shreuyn
> 3yf 3yfte of grace shal be 3euyn.[61]

He evidently considered this to be a matter of some importance, for he mentioned it once again at the close of the prologue:

Statuta Synodalia Cadurcensis, etc. (1289), *ibid.*, XXIV, cols. 963-1056. For a particularly fine example in England, see the Synod of Exeter (1287), Wilkins II, 130-137. These decrees and instructions represent an effort to carry out the order in the twenty-seventh canon of the Fourth Lateran Council.

57. Arnould, *op. cit.*, p. 256, dates the *Manuel ca.* 1260.

58. L. 9.

59. *Op. cit.*, XXVIII, 182: 'Les péchés secrets, les "privitez".'

60. Cf. *ibid.*, pp. 182-183, the prologue to the *Manuel*, and especially *MP*, ll. 2538-2540.

61. Ll. 30-36.

> Þarefore may hyt, & gode skyl why,
> 'Handlyng synne' be clepyd oponly;
> For hyt toucheþ no priuite,
> But opyn synne þat called may be.[62]

There are other references to 'secret sin' under the sixth commandment[63] and in section on the sin of lechery.[64]

Turning now to the traditions of penitential literature, we find that Mannyng's caution about mentioning unusual or 'secret' sins together with the accompanying warning that they must be confessed represents an ancient dilemma of the confessor. In the eighth century, the Spanish Visigoth, Bishop Theodulf of Orléans, issued the following in his Capitularies:

> But he who makes confession shall bend his knees with the priest before God and then confess whatever he is able to recall from his youth — his behavior in all particulars. And if he cannot recall all of his misdeeds, or if perchance he hesitates, the priest ought to ask him whatever is set down in the penitential — whether he has fallen into this offense or another. But, nevertheless, not all the offenses ought to be made known to him, since many faults are read in the penitential which it is not becoming for the man to know. Therefore the priest ought not to question him about them all, lest, perchance, when he has gone away from him, at the devil's persuasion, he fall into some one of those offenses which he previously did not know.[65]

Similar warnings appear in the penitentials themselves.[66] Bartholomew of Exeter, for example, admonishes the confessor to explain to the penitent the seven principal vices. But the confessor is warned that in the course of his explanation he should not touch upon 'any sin that may be against nature or otherwise very abominable,' for in doing so he might encourage the penitent to commit some crime he

---

62. Ll. 137-140.
63. Ll. 2038-2040.
64. Ll. 7441-7442; 7575-7584; 8119-8122; 8407-8412.
65. McNeill and Gamer, *op. cit.*, p. 397.
66. Cf. Morey, *op cit.*, p. 170.

had not known about before.[67] In the literature of confession produced in the thirteenth century this idea is constantly reiterated. For example, the following passage appears in a practical manual ascribed to William of Auvergne and in the *De confessione* of Robert de Sorbon:

> Cum repetes à Proximo tuo rem aliquam quam debet tibi, non ingredieris domum eius ut pignus auferas, sed stabis foris, & ille tibi proferet quod habuerit (Deut. 24). With this authority, a certain great clerk of Paris preached that the confessor ought not to inquire of nor examine concerning the sins of the person confessing, miraculously explaining it: Non *ingredieris domum*, that is, the conscience of the sinner; *ut auferras,* that is, so that you elicit; *pignus,* that is, the sins for which his soul is obliged to the Devil, and so on. But he wrongly understood it explaining it in this way. For the confessor may inquire in general. And this is indicated by the expression *rem aliquam;* but he should not inquire of the sins in particular, and by name, lest he lead the person confessing into temptation.[68]

That the 'sins in particular' were 'secret sins' is abundantly clear from the illustrations which appear in the *De confessione*.[69] The same principle of reticence is stated in the *Summula* of Bishop Peter Quivil, where it appears in the course of a long discussion of circumstances:

> Item, moreover, in lechery and in other sins there are many evil devices and many unrightful ways (likewise among married people) which it is disgusting to mention or allude to; however, the penitent ought to confess them precisely, and the priest should hold himself strictly prepared in such things, so that if the penitent does not confess them fully, the priest may inquire about

---

67. *Ibid.,* pp. 204-205.
68. See Wm. of Auvergne, *Opera,* II, 288, and Robert de Sorbon, *De confessione, MBP,* XXV, 354.
69. E.g. *op. cit.,* p. 355: 'Item Confessor debet dicere: Amice, fuisti vnquam osculatus mulieris? sic, Domine: Confessor quaerat vtrum inordinate. Quomodo inordinate? Domine. Hic caveat sibi, confessor, ne descendat ad speciales modos osculandi inordinate: sicut nec descendendum est ad aliquod peccatum contra naturam ne occasionem det vt corruat in peccatum. Sed dicat, quando in Missa, pax sumitur, homines tenent clausem os.' Cf. the parallel treatment of this subject in *Handlyng Synne,* ll. 8119-8124. The corresponding passage in William of Auvergne's treatise, *Opera,* II, 282, is much more explicit.

them. He should not, however, descend to particulars but stop at general terms (so that if the penitent is ignorant [the priest] should not ask him more concerning such things) either with regard to sins against nature or similar sins into which the penitent has fallen.[70]

Secular priests were warned time after time in the church councils against revealing unusual sins at confession. For example, the Constitutions of Richard le Poore (ca.1220) state that

> The confessor should inquire of ordinary sins one by one, but of unusual sins only by circumlocution [a longe], and by circumstances; he shall do this so that the sinner shall not be given new occasion for delinquency.[71]

This admonition is repeated word for word in the Constitutions of St Edmund (1236),[72] with only slight alterations in some anonymous constitutions of ca. 1237,[73] and in Bishop Quivil's Synod of Exeter.[74] Similar warnings appear in continental decrees.[75] Meanwhile, in the *De officiis ordinis* Humbert de Romans offered the following advice to his Dominicans:

> Concerning secret sins, like the sin against nature, one should not inquire [*i.e.*, at confession] except with caution, lest something be made manifest to simple persons which they did not know about.[76]

These examples show beyond any question that Mannyng's concern about *pryuyte* is a reflection of the broad tradition of confessional theory and confessional literature. It is interesting to observe that the

---

70. Wilkins, II, 165-166.
71. *Ibid.*, I, 577.
72. *Ibid.*, I, 637.
73. *Ibid.*, I, 657.
74. *Ibid.*, II, 134.
75. E.g. *Concilium Trevirense Provinciale* (1227), Mansi, XXIII, c. 29; *Concilium Provinciale Moguntinum* (1261), *ibid.*, XXIII, c. 1082; *Statuta Synodalia Claromontensis Ecclesiae* (1268), *ibid.*, XXIII, c. 1200; *Concilium Trevirense* (1277), *ibid.*, XXIV, c. 195; *Synodus Coloniensis* (1280), *ibid.*, XXIV, c. 353.
76. Cap. XLVI, *Opera*, Rome, 1888-1889, II, 363-364.

principle involved is still operative. The section on the sixth commandment in the 'Devotions for Confession' is very brief and general, but it contains an italicized warning to the effect that *'all sins against purity must be carefully examined ...'* and a concluding note urging the gravity and variety of such sins, and the necessity for consulting the confessor 'in a more particular examination.'[77] Like Mannyng before him, the author found it prudent to leave many grave matters unexplained.

Having achieved positive results with our investigation of 'secret sin,' let us turn to another feature of *Handlyng Synne*, the method of proceeding by 'questions.' As I have said, the admonitory portions of *Handlyng Synne* frequently consist of lists of transgressions introduced by conditional clauses with the formula 'ʒyf þou ...' or with some variation of it. A glance at a typical penitential reveals a similar method of procedure. The first five canons of the penitential attributed to Theodore, for example, run as follows:

> 1. if any bishop or deacon or any ordained person has had by custom the vice of drunkenness, he shall either desist or be deposed.
> 2. If a monk vomits on account of drunkenness, he shall do penance for thirty days.
> 3. If a presbyter or deacon [does this] on account of drunkenness, he shall do penance for forty days.
> 4. If [the offense is] due to weakness or because he has been a long time abstinent and is not accustomed to drink or eat much; or if it is for gladness at Christmas or Easter or for any festival of a saint, and he has imbibed no more than is commanded by his seniors, no offense is committed. If a bishop commands it, no offense is committed, unless he himself does likewise.
> 5. If a lay Christian vomits because of drunkenness, he shall do penance for fifteen days.[78]

Introductory conditional clauses like the above are characteristic of the penitentials,[79] but in this specimen they are expressed in the third

---

77. *The Key of Heaven*, pp. 179, 180.
78. McNeill and Gamer, *op. cit.*, p. 184.
79. Cf. the 'Canons Attributed to St Patrick,' *ibid.*, pp. 76-80; 'The Penitential of Finnian,' *ibid.*, pp. 87-97; 'The Penitential of Cummean,' *ibid.*, pp. 101-117; and other penitentials, *ibid., passim.*

person, whereas those in *Handlyng Synne* are expressed in the second. The difference is, of course, due to the fact that the penitentials were intended to describe to priests the various types of sinful activity of which their parishioners were thought to be capable; *Handlyng Synne* was addressed directly to laymen. Nevertheless, the questions in the penitentials are sometimes more direct, as they are in the *Corrector* of Burchard of Worms, where we find the formula 'Hast thou ...' predominant.[80] One small section of the *Corrector*, containing general penitential advice, does employ the formula 'If thou ...' so that the effect is almost that of a miniature of Mannyng's treatment of the seven sins:

> Therefore, if thou has[t] been proud hitherto, humble thyself in the sight of God. If thou hast loved vainglory, take thought lest on account of transitory praises thou lose the eternal reward. If the rust of envy hath hitherto consumed thee ....[81]

On the whole, however, there is one striking difference between the questions in the penitentials and those in *Handlyng Synne*. Those in the penitentials are almost always followed by injunctions of appropriate penances, but Mannyng simply says, in effect, 'If you have sinned in this way, you have sinned greatly,'[82] or, 'If you have sinned in this way, you should confess to the priest.'[83] His emphasis is obviously on the material in the conditional clauses, not on what follows; he seldom mentions specific punishments for the sins he lists, and has little to say of their corresponding virtues.

In the confessional literature of the thirteenth century, which replaced the penitentials, lists of questions covering the sins do appear, and these questions, like those in *Handlyng Synne*, sometimes lack corresponding penitential injunctions. Such lists were designed to guide the confessor in determining the topics about which inquiry should be made. In the treatise ascribed to William of Auvergne, the following questions appear on the sin of pride:

> Brother if you sinned in pride, extolling yourself in heart,

80. See the questions printed *ibid.*, p. 342.
81. *Ibid.*, p. 342.
82. E.g., ll. 347-349.
83. E.g., ll. 1080-1082.

speech, or deed above others on account of your riches, or on account of power, or beauty, or birth, or nobility, or knowledge, or clothes, or popular praise, or what is worse on account of malice glorying in your sins, or on account of your works, or desiring to be praised, or believing yourself to have these things of yourself, or from God on account of your merits, or more than others, or falsely boasting yourself to have, or indeed believing yourself to have merits which you have not.... If you sinned in vain glory, in boasting, in hypocrisy, in arrogance, in presumption, in singularity, in seeking novelty, in disobedience, and if you have done the like.[84]

Not only are the details controlled by the formula 'if you ...' but the conditional clauses are not completed, so little is the author concerned with anything other than the details. No mention is made of penances corresponding to the various misdemeanors. It should be observed also that the faults mentioned are not so concrete as those in the penitentials. The list as a whole, which covers the other six sins and the commandments, as well as the sin of pride, seems to be the result of a loose application of the idea of circumstances to the sins rather than a group of very specific offenses in the manner of Theodore or Burchard. There are other similar lists of questions elsewhere. One further example, from some decrees issued on the continent in 1289, will suffice to illustrate the typical method of proceeding by questions:

> Concerning pride, let [the confessor] ask, if you ever did anything illicit or spoke for the acquisition of human praise or worldly honor; if you ever opposed the truth knowingly, if you knowingly disregarded authority above you, if you ascribed to yourself that which belonged to others, if you boasted about or gloried in knowledge, eloquence, beauty, song, nobility, dignity, or other graces which God gave you. If you condemned another below you, or compared yourself proudly with a superior. If you spoke proud or approbrious words to anyone; and if you struck [anyone] through pride. If, swelling in heart, you contended, disputed, vilified, blasphemed, if you believed the virtues of nature, grace, and fortune which you have to be due to yourself and not

84. Opera, II, 244.

to God, and did not recognize them to be from God; if you passed judgment on others and not yourself; if you usurped and attributed to yourself the praise, and honor, and glory, and judgment which are due to God alone.[85]

Although the questions in these lists are not always in the second person, as they are in the examples above, it is clear that Mannyng's questions resemble them. It is possible, therefore, that an examination of the organization and content of works containing confessional questions may lead to the formulation of further resemblances.

For lack of a better term, I shall call the lists of confessional questions written for priests, together with whatever general instructions may accompany them, *confessional inquiries*. This term should serve to distinguish them from the penitentials and from the *summae confessorum*. It should be emphasized, however, that these inquiries do not always appear as separate treatises, but may be merely chapters or sets of chapters in episcopal constitutions, or sections of larger and more general treatises. The resemblance between the *Manuel* and works of this kind was noticed by Professor Arnould, but he did not pursue the subject very far.[86] In the present discussion, I shall consider a selection of inquiries produced before the fourteenth century that

---

85. *Statuta Synodalia Cadurcensis*, etc., Mansi, XXV, c. 988. The inquiry covers the seven sins. H. C. Lea, *A History of Auricular Confession*, Philadelphia, 1896, I, 370, lists other works of the kind, which he calls 'hideous catechisms of sin.'

86. Op. cit., pp. 49-51. In his chapter on sources, he insists that although the *Manuel* and Peraldus' *Summa* are not analogous works, the *Manuel* leans heavily on the *Summa* with respect to content. I should object to this view generally on the grounds that the *Summa* is essentially a collection of commonplaces so that it is dangerous to assume that parallels between it and later works are indications of source. Specifically, not all of Arnould's parallels are convincing. For example, he says (pp. 200-202) that the account of Gregory's six causes of dreams in the *Manuel* (ll. 1135-1214) must have been derived from the *Summa*, since both accounts contain an introductory remark, some concluding remarks, and an exemplum not found in the original source, Gregory's *Moralia* (Migne, *PL*, 75, c. 827). This argument loses its force when one discovers that the six causes, together with the appendages in the *Summa* and the *Manuel*, appear also in Gregory's *Dialogi* (ed. Moricca, Rome, 1924, pp. 309-311). Moreover, there are far more parallels between the *Manuel* and the tradition of confessional literature than there are between the *Manuel* and the *Summa*, as I shall show presently.

I have found in print. A definitive history of the type would require a painstaking search of manuscript sources at present inaccessible.

On the basis of available evidence, I should say that the inquiry did not immediately assume the rather well developed form it takes in the *De confessione* of Robert de Sorbon, which I shall describe presently. An interesting transitional form appears in the Constitutions issued by Alexander Stavensby, Bishop of Coventry and Lichfield (1224-1237).[87] In addition to some decrees, which make up the first part of the constitutions, Bishop Alexander included two treatises, one of the sins and the other on penance.[88] The treatise on the sins was evidently to be transmitted to the people in sermons, for it begins,

> It is commanded to all priests, when their parishioners are assembled in church on Sundays or on other holy days, that they speak these words, which follow.[89]

What follows is an account of the seven principal vices which makes considerable use of the device of exposition by authorities familiar in academic sermons and treatises. In the treatise on penance there are some instructions concerning confessional interrogation, penance, and absolution. The confessor is referred to the treatise on sin as a guide to use in questioning, so that the two treatises are really interdependent.[90] Of especial interest are the instructions regarding interrogation. After some preliminary material concerning the confessor's approach to the penitent, it is emphasized that special questions should be asked persons of various estates;[91] then there are questions

---

87. Wilkins, I, 640-646. Although we have little evidence to go on, it seems probable that Alexander had been a teacher of theology at Toulouse, where he may have known St Dominic, and later an official in the papal curia. See M. Gibbs and J. Lang, *Bishops and Reform 1215-1272*, London, 1934, pp. 29-30. With such a career behind him, he would have been thoroughly aware of the theological tendencies of his time and of the increasing importance attached to confession.

88. The decrees are printed, *ibid.*, I, 640-642; the treatise on the sins, pp. 642-644; the treatise on penance, pp. 644-646. On this division, cf. C. R. Cheney, *English Synodalia in the Thirteenth Century*, London, 1941, p. 492.

89. Wilkins, I, p. 642.

90. *Ibid.*, I, 644.

illustrating circumstantial inquiry into the sins of lechery and drunkenness. Having furnished examples for inquiry into the circumstances 'of the sinner and the sin,' to use the phrase of Innocent III at the Lateran Council, Alexander supplied the mnemonic verse quoted earlier in this paper and explained each question in it. If all of this material — the survey of the sins and the principle of circumstances — had been integrated into a single illustrative list of questions, the result would have been what I have called a confessional inquiry. Transitional forms of a different kind appear elsewhere. For example, there is a series of questions in some continental decrees published in 1235 which fail to utilize a systematic concept of the sins and so resemble the earlier penitentials in organization.[92]

A more highly developed inquiry occurs in the supplementary treatise on penance ascribed to William of Auvergne, Bishop of Paris (1228-1249).[93] In addition to a full confessional dialogue illustrating the general principles of interrogation;[94] there is a systematic inquiry covering the seven sins and the ten commandments, part of which I have already quoted. It is preceded by a chapter which explains four requisites or 'points' of shrift, admonishes those who fear to confess, attacks presumption and desperation, reprimands those who hesitate to confess because of contempt for the priest, and enumerates the qualities of a good confessor.[95] These matters are all discussed in the last section of *Handlyng Synne*. The two sections together form a

---

91. *Ibid.*, I, 644-645. For example, 'A laicis generaliter quaerendum est de decimis .... A militibus maxime quaerendum est, et ab illis qui sub se habent familias, videlicet pauperes servos, si aliquid ab eis habuerint injuste, quia debent eis restituere.... Circa mulieres, maxime de veneficiis et sorti-legiis.'

92. Mansi, XXIII, cols. 389-395. Cf. cols. 737-744.

93. *Opera*, H, 9.19-247. I do not pretend to know the date of this work. It contains, on p. 237, what may be a reference to the *Summa* of William Peraldus: 'haec invenitur in summa de vitiis....' There are striking resemblances between this treatise and the *De confessione* of Robert do Sorbon. Its authorship, date, and literary relations need investigation. Other works of William of Auvergne are well known to students of medieval philosophy. A biography was published by Noel Valois, Paris, 1880.

94. *Ibid.*, II, 235.

95. *Ibid.*, II, 241-244.

unit which corresponds roughly in content with Mannyng's book, although there is no section on the sacraments. The treatment of the various subjects considered is much more concise in the Latin work than in the English. It is clear, however, that there is at least a vague resemblance in general structure between a portion of William of Auvergne's treatise and *Handlyng Synne*.

A better specimen for comparison is afforded by the *De confessione* of Robert de Sorbon.[96] This work consists of two principal sections, the first of which is an inquiry covering the sins and the commandments systematically, and the second a dialogue like that in the treatise ascribed to William of Auvergne illustrating such matters as the application of circumstances and the avoidance of 'secret sins.' The first section begins with some prefatory remarks which indicate the purpose and content of the inquiry:

> That holy and righteous confession may ensue, three things are necessary to the soul of the penitent wishing to confess his sins. The first is that he diligently think and examine whether he has committed any of the seven criminal sins, which are pride, envy, wrath, avarice, sloth, gluttony, lechery. The second thing which he should do afterward is, indeed, that he should inquire well whether the divine commandments were broken, of which there are ten. The third is that he ought to omit nothing; that is, that (since he cannot recollect and recount all the details of his sins, which because of his sin and negligence in confession, he carries to oblivion) he should recall with lamentation that he has sinned against God in all kinds of sins, that is, in thought, in word, and in deed, to which all sins are reducible.[97]

There follows a confessional survey of the seven sins. The treatment of pride, the first sin, is typical:

---

96. Robert de Sorbon was born in the village of Sorbon, near Rethel, in the Ardennes. In 1253 he founded the famous Sorbonne school at Paris. He became confessor to the King in 1256, and in 1258 a canon of Paris and Chancellor of the University. See Felix Chambon's introduction to the *De consciencia*, Paris, 1903, p. vi. The *De confessione* survives in six Mss and a fragment, a fact which is considered to be indicative of its success. It is printed in *MBP*, XXV, 352-358.

97. *MBP*, XXV, 352.

> First, therefore, he may know if he has sinned in pride in this way: if he has put himself above others in heart or word because of wealth, or because of power, or beauty, or noble birth, or wisdom, or clothes, or popular praise — so that he was more honored or praised among the people — or (what is worse) because of malice, glorying in his own sins or in those of others, or glorying in good works, such as fasting, vigils, prayers, charity, and the like, desiring thence human praise. Item, if he says that the virtues and goods which he has proceed from himself, or from God because of his own peculiar merits, so that God gave him more than others, or boasts falsely that he has some good thing, or believes himself to have good things he does not have. Item, if he was elevated by the beauty of his members, as by that of his eyes, hands, feet, hair, and other members. Item, If because of praise he pretended to be better than he is; or because of the desire for money, as hypocrites do. If he should find all of these things, or any of them in himself, he knows at once that he should confess and say, 'Mea culpa, I have sinned in pride in this way, or in these ways.'[98]

After the section on the sins, a transitional passage leads to the commandments:

> Such ought to be the confession of the holy soul of the penitent, if he has sinned in the manner of any of the seven criminal vices. After these things, he should see if he has sinned against the observations of the Decalogue, transgressions of which are not excused.[99]

Of the first commandment, it is said:

> The first commandment concerns the worship of one God. Whether he [the penitent] adores alien gods; if he believes in one God in a Trinity of Persons, and the other Articles of the Faith, just as Holy Church [requires], which are incarnation, nativity, baptism, passion, resurrection, ascension, and the sending of the Holy Spirit. [And also the] sacraments: baptism, confirmation, penance, Corpus Christi, order, matrimony, extreme unction. He should see then, if he has doubted concerning the faith,

---

98 *Ibid.*, xxv, 352. The resemblance between this passage and that quoted from William of Auvergne above is unmistakable.

99. *Ibid.*, xxv, 353.

or concerning anything that pertains to it. Item, if he has believed in witchcraft, soothsaying, incantations, auguries, dreams, and the illusions of demons, and so on. Item, if he has believed old women to go by night [sc. 'night riders'], and has not exhibited due honor to God.[100]

After a similar treatment of the remainder of the commandments, the first part of the treatise closes with a formula for general confession to cover forgotten sins. If we consider the second half of the *De confessione*, which illustrates the general principles of confession, to be roughly parallel with the last section of *Handlyng Synne*, we find that all of the major sections of the *De confessione* are represented by corresponding sections of *Handlyng Synne*. Mannyng accorded separate treatment to the sacraments, whereas Robert de Sorbon included them under the first commandment. Otherwise the two works are quite similar in structure.[101] There are separate sections on the sacraments in later inquiries, so that we need not assume that there is anything inconsistent with the tradition of the inquiries in Mannyng's inclusion of such a section.[102]

An inquiry which circulated in England in the last years of the century was published by Bishop Peter Quivil in the Synod of Exeter (1287). As I have indicated elsewhere, the *Summula*, as Bishop Quivil called his treatise, should be regarded as a confessional manual. It may be divided into three major divisions concerning (1) the ten commandments, (2) the seven sins, (3) shrift and penance. The sacraments were considered relevant, but were omitted because they had already been treated fully in the decrees which accompanied the

---

100. *Ibid.*, XXV, 353.

101. I do not consider the variation in the order of the sins and commandments to be of major importance.

102. See Lea, *op. cit.*, I, 371. I have not so far succeeded in finding a thirteenth century inquiry in print with a special section on the sacraments. In view of the emphasis placed on the sacraments in pastoral work during the thirteenth century and the widespread desire to impress priest and parishioner alike with their importance, it is reasonable to assume that confessional interrogation concerning the sacraments was frequently emphasized. The confessional was widely used as a medium for lay instruction. On this point, see Moorman, *op. cit.*, p. 78.

treatise.[103] The material on the commandments shows unmistakable evidence of the tradition we have been examining:

> The penitent should therefore recur to the first commandment, and carefully see in himself if it was broken. Whether, that is, he exhibited worship due to God alone to demons or to other creatures; that is, practicing magic such as having recourse to conjurations, as it is customary to do for theft [*i.e.*, for discovering thieves by looking] in a sword, a basin, and in names written and enclosed in clay, and placed in holy water, and the like; or recurring to, auguries of soothsayers, or if he consulted soothsayers for such things, and sacrificed to demons, as certain miserable ones do for women, whom they love fatuously.[104]

The sins are introduced with a metaphor showing the usefulness of the concept of fundamental vices:

> And since the tree of vices with loaded branches can no better be shown than when its root is uncovered, I appraise [it] by turning to its roots. The roots are, indeed, the seven criminal sins which ought frequently to be explained to the people.[105]

The explanation which follows is expository rather than interrogative, but the purpose for which it was used is clear in the context. For illustration, I shall quote only the last half of the section on pride, since the first part merely explains the sins subsidiary to pride in the Gregorian manner:

> Pride has, however, manifold materials: for example, natural gifts; when, that is, a man is proud of the natural gifts which he has, as of fortitude, if he is a strong man; of ingenuity, if he is ingenious; of his appearance, if he is handsome; of his facility in speech, if he is eloquent, as are certain lawyers and even laymen who speak before lay judges, or, indeed, if he has a good voice. Item, of nobility, if he is of great birth; of his children, if he has many or more, or good sons or daughters. He may also be proud of temporal goods; as when a man is proud because he has many or precious clothes, houses, or fields, or income, or many men,

---

103. Cf. *MLN*, LX (1945), 443, note 13.
104. Wilkins, II, 162.
105. *Ibid.*, II, 163.

or servants, or good horses; or when he leads others in temporal wealth. He may also be proud of gratuitous gifts, which are from grace; as when he is proud because he is wise, or, indeed, he is a good clerk or, a good preacher, or a charming person; or a good craftsman, or a good husbandman. Or when a man is proud of virtues, because he believes himself to be good, and has abominated sinners; or when he is proud because he has the good graces of men, or because he has a good reputation, or ecclesiastical dignities, or orders: and according to all these diversities, diverse penances are to be enjoined.[106]

The discussion of the sins closes with the following general instructions:

> The penitent should recur to the particular roots, and to those things which spring from them, and to more, if he knows more. Whence he ought to confess everything into which he has fallen.[107]

At the beginning of the third section of the treatise, there is an analysis of the theory of circumstances which explains in detail a mnemonic verse like the one quoted from Alexander Stavensby. There is a paragraph on sins of the tongue, one on sins of the members, and then a discussion, with a list, of sins a parish priest cannot absolve. There are some instructions on the administration of penances; and, finally, some matters which the penitent should be examined about, such as the Articles of the Faith, belief in the sacraments, and the formulas of the faith.[108] Although much of the material in this section is suited to clerical ears alone, the section is generally analogous with the last section of *Handlyng Synne*, since both deal with the broad principles of effective confession.

Enough evidence has been adduced to show that the confessional inquiries are similar to *Handlyng Synne* in method and structure. They are also similar in purpose, although the inquiries were written for priests and *Handlyng Synne* for laymen. It remains now to determine whether *Handlyng Synne* is similar to the inquiries in specific content. Since it is impossible, for mechanical reasons to reproduce

106. *Ibid.*, II, 163-164.
107. *Ibid.*, II, 165.
108. *Ibid.*, II, 165-168.

all of the texts involved in parallel columns for comparison, I propose to use those sections of the inquiries on the first commandment and on the sin of pride already quoted for comparison with an analysis of the admonitory materials in the corresponding sections of *Handlyng Synne*. I make out thirteen specific admonitions in the section of *Handlyng Synne* on the first commandment.[109] If we allow Robert de Sorbon's general term 'auguries' to stand for Mannyng's three types of omens, only four of these thirteen admonitions are without parallel either in the *De confessione* or the *Summula*.[110] There are, I believe, some forty-one admonitions in *Handlyng Synne* under the sin of pride.[111] Of these, only nine have no parallel in the passages on pride I have quoted from the inquiries.[112] That is, altogether, about seventy-five per cent of Mannyng's admonitory details in two sections of *Handlyng Synne* may be found in a few specimens representing the tradition of the confessional inquiries. One might quarrel with this figure, since opinions may vary about what constitutes an admonition and about what is necessary for a legitimate parallel, and interpretations

---

109. They concern the following topics: (1) forsaking God, (2) necromancy, (3) divination in sword, (4) divination in basin, (5) divination in thumb-nail, (6) divination in crystal, (7) omen of magpie, (8) omen of morning meeting, (9) omen of handsel, (10) dreams, (11) witchcraft, (12) failure to attack heretical opinions, (13) belief in the three fates. The material about lechery at the end is essentially theological exposition designed to show the necessity for confession.

110. The relevant passages have already been quoted. The details peculiar to Mannyng are numbers (5), (6), (12), (13) in the preceding note.

111. The topics, as I see them, are (1) disrespect of superiors, (2) pride in holy life, (3) pride in charity, (4) pride in chastity, (5) pride in lineage, (6) pride in wisdom, (7) pride in beauty, (8) pride in strength, (9) pride in riches, (10) pride in song, (11) pride in power, (12) pride in cunning, (13) pride in horses, (14) pride in hawks, (15) pride in hounds, (16) pride in opinions of others, (17) idea that wit or virtue is due to one's self, not God, (18) boasting of God's gifts, (19) boasting of that which one does not have, (20) blaming others, (21) scorn, (22) hypocrisy, (23) pride in hair, (24) pride in members, (25) pride in clothing, (26) desire for worldly esteem, (27) pride in retinue, (28) pride in halls, (29) proud words, (30) failure of clerks to wear tonsure, (31) blasphemy, (32) thinking ill of God, (33) maintaining evil ways, (34) flattery, (35) chiding, (36) detraction, (37) revealing secrets, (38) foul words in ribaldry, (39) abuse of power, (40) giving to minstrels for praise, (41) pride in wrestling.

112. That is, nos. (14), (15), (30), (34), (37), (38), (39), (40), (41) in the preceding note.

of the texts themselves may differ, but there can be no doubt that the correspondence in detail apparent even from a casual inspection of all of the relevant works, reinforced by similarities of purpose, structure, and method, makes the conclusion that *Handlyng Synne* developed from the tradition of the confessional inquiry inescapable. Whether the author of the *Manuel*, or Mannyng after him, had before him one or more inquiries, or relied merely on a thorough knowledge of the tradition is a matter for further study. What I wish to show is not that any one of the inquiries I have described was an actual source, but that *Handlyng Synne* is essentially an adaptation for lay consumption of materials produced and shaped by the tradition I have described.

It may be objected that there are only general similarities between the last section of *Handlyng Synne* on shrift and the materials in the inquiries. Since the inquiries were addressed to priests, we should not expect to find in them exactly the same kind of materials that we find in a work addressed to laymen. However, the new theology of penance did produce doctrines suitable for lay ears, and it would be natural to suppose that such doctrines might appear in sermons rather than in instructional works for the clergy. That they did indeed appear in this way is evident from the fact that almost every detail in the last section of *Handlyng Synne* is very closely paralleled in a sermon on confession attributed to William Peraldus.[113]

---

113. Arnould, *op. cit.*, pp. 227-229; 233-235, pointed out that the 'points' of shrift and the closing admonitions in the *Manuel*, which Mannyng followed closely, appear in a sermon by Peraldus. He did not find the 'graces' or virtues of shrift in the edition of Peraldus he used (Paris, 1494). However, all of the virtues do appear, along with the 'points' and admonitions, in the corresponding sermon printed among the works of William of Auvergne, II, 154-155. In this sermon, the virtues occur in the midst of a paragraph listing six reasons why confession is commendable. The fifth reason involves the multiplicity of the virtues of confession, and six virtues are explained to support it. Of these, the first four correspond very closely — almost verbally — with the first four in the *Manuel*. The fifth virtue in the sermon appears as two virtues in the *Manuel*, but there is nothing in this version of the sermon to correspond with the seventh virtue in the *Manuel*. The eighth virtue of the *Manuel* corresponds with part of the sixth virtue in the sermon. Perhaps judgment as to whether the sermon was the direct source of the *Manuel* should be suspended until we know more of the sources, literary relationships, and influences of the sermon. Only a relatively small part of the sermon as a whole bears any resemblance to the *Manuel* or to *Handlyng Synne*.

One prominent feature of both the *Manuel* and *Handlyng Synne* remains to be accounted for. As I indicated at the beginning of this paper, the *Manuel* has been described as a work reflecting characteristics 'of English men and women of all classes of society.'[114] And Dr Furnivall's description of the variety of social types represented in *Handlyng Synne* has become famous.[115] It may be demonstrated, I believe, that the reflection of social classes in *Handlyng Synne* is due largely to the conventions of penitential literature. Turning again to the selection from the penitential of Theodore of Tarsus quoted above, we notice that for the same sin — drunkenness — a priest must perform penance for forty days, a monk for thirty days, and a layman for fifteen days. The necessity for such distinctions contributed materially to the length of the penitentials. If one considers further that various classes of people are especially prone to particular sins — merchants to the use of false weights and measures, feudal lords to harsh impositions, and so on — it becomes clear that a good confessor must have found it necessary to consider carefully the social status of his penitents. As Peter Comestor put it,

> Variation in penance is to be considered in accordance with variation of the sinner and of the sin.
>
> Concerning the sinner, indeed, many things are to be observed: profession, dignity, order, age, sex, condition, vows, matrimony, and so on. And according to this greater or lesser penance should be imposed. For greater should be imposed on a monk guilty of fornication than on a cleric, [greater] on a cleric than on a layman, on a bishop than on a simple priest, on a priest than on a deacon, on a deacon than on a subdeacon, on an old man than on an adolescent, on a woman if she has approached a woman than if a man, on a servant if he has violated the bed of his master than if another, on a married than on an unmarried person.[116]

114. See above, note 12.
115. Preface to the Roxburghe Club edition of *Handlyng Synne*, pp. viii-ix. Cf. Wells, *Manuel*, pp. 333-334.
116 *Sententiae de sacramentis,* ed. R. M. Martin O.P., as an appendix to H. Weisweiler, S.J., *Maitre Simon et son Groupe 'De sacramentis'* (*Spicilegium Sacrum Lovaniense,* fasc. 17, 1937), pp. 64*-65*. An account of circumstances of the sin, illustrative of the status of this conception before the adoption of rhetorical circumstances as a guide, immediately follows the above passage.

To facilitate the examination of circumstances of the sinner, illustrative questions were developed, like the ones in the treatise of Alexander Stavensby.[117] As time passed, fairly long lists of such questions were written. The following passage appears in some continental decrees of 1284:

> The priest should ask the person confessing if he was ever tempted to sin, and what the temptation was, and how he resisted it, and thus indirectly the sin of the person confessing, which he was concealing, will appear to him. Item, the priest should ask him if he holds any office, and if he says that he does, he should ask of the circumstances of the office he claims to hold. If he was a regular, [the priest] should ask him especially of the three essential circumstances of the rule, that is, if he obeys his superior in all legitimate and proper things, and whether he is a property owner, and whether he maintains chastity. Item, concerning simony, whether he has received money for that purpose, or if he consented that others received something through simony. Item, whether he talks in places where he should not, and at improper times, and whether he is contrary in the chapter, or speaks against something that is to be ordered or done. Concerning secular clerics, [the priest] should ask whether they indulged in simony for themselves or for others, or whether others did for them. Item, of trade and other things that pertain to avarice and cupidity. Item, of dilapidation [sc. of churches], if he has a church benefice, and whether with money acquired in church affairs he bought any goods in his own name, or in the name of a relative of his, and whether he spent church funds in legitimate and proper ways. Item, whether he participates in divine offices, the nocturnal as well as the diurnal, especially in the church in which he is prelate. Item, of irregularities: item, of the game of dice and bones [*aleorum & talorum*]. Concerning princes, castellans, and knights, and their bailiffs [the priest] should ask whether they made, or had made regulations or precepts against ecclesiastical liberty, and whether they burdened with unrightful tallage the people subjected to them, collected however frequently. Item, of rapine.

---

117. See above, note 91. Cf. the injunction in the *Statuta Synodalia Ecclesiae Constantiensis*, Martène, *Thesaurus*, IV, c. 818: 'Diligenter attendat sacerdos, cujus officii sit confitens. Nam si mercator, vendens, vel emens ad mensuram, prohibendus est ne habeat pondus falsum & falsam mensuram....'

Concerning town merchants and other town officers, the priest should inquire concerning lying, guile, usury, pledges, and barratry, and of unjust weights and measures. Concerning farmers, he should ask of theft, principally concerning tithes and first fruits, *quartas* and *tascas*, and the eradication of boundaries, and of the occupation of the land of others. Item, of the like, also of arson. Concerning mercenaries, ploughmen, servants, shepherds, and similar persons, the priest should inquire whether they have faithfully maintained the works and services imposed on them.[118]

The appearance of a diversity of social types in a confessional manual like *Handlyng Synne* is thus a reflection generally of an old problem of the confessor and specifically of a traditional feature of confessional literature. Circumstances of person, it may be observed, are not without significance for the confessor today. One modern authority, J. Bricout, quoted earlier, recommends that each penitent consider 'les devoirs de son état';[119] and at the end of the inquiry in the *Key of Heaven* there is a note:

> Here, also, masters and servants, husbands and wives, lawyers and physicians, ecclesiastics and magistrates, etc., ought to examine into the sins which are peculiar to their states, and how far they have neglected the duties of their respective callings.[120]

Our initial hypothesis, that *Handlyng Synne* should be considered as a confessional manual, may now be raised to the level of a theory. Much more work needs to be done with such unprinted materials as may survive from the first half of the thirteenth century before one may speak with any confidence of specific sources, or even of the precise status of *Handlyng Synne* among confessional treatises. But I believe that the direction which future research must take is now clear. In purpose, in structure, in method, and in content *Handlyng Synne*

---

118. *Synodus Nemausensis*, Mansi, XXIV, c. 528. Cf. *Statuta Synodalia Cadurcensis*, etc. (1289), *ibid.*, XXIV, cols. 987-988. This passage also appears in Raymund of Pennaforte, *Summa*, Verona, 1744, pp. 434-435. For an account of later inquiries of this type, see Lea, *op. cit.*, p. 371.

119. See above, note 17.

120. P. 194. Cf. the division of the fourth commandment, pp. 173-176, and the note after the ninth commandment, p. 187.

reflects a tradition of penitential literature which had its beginnings in the early Celtic church and reached its highest development, perhaps, in the thirteenth century, when the reformers inspired by Innocent III reshaped it, using for their purposes the theological tools fashioned by Peter Lombard and his disciples.

PRINCETON UNIVERSITY

Marie de France, *Lais*, Prologue, 13-16

Modern Language Notes 64:5 (May 1949), pp. 336-338.

A recent article by Professor L. Spitzer indicates that the Prologue to Marie's *Lais* shows a consciousness on the part of the poet of her rôle as *"poeta philosophus et theologus."*[1] If one accepts this general thesis, it may be possible to clarify lines 13-16 in the light of current exegetical practice. After saying that the ancients deliberately composed their works with a certain obscurity, Marie warns (ll. 13-16):

> Pur ceus ki a venir esteient
> E ki aprendre les deveient,
> K'i peüssent gloser la lettre
> E de lur sen le surplus mettre.[2]

Professor Ewert supplies a literal translation of the Prologue in his notes, where the above passage is rendered:

> so that those who were to come after them and were to learn them, might construe their writing and add to it from their own ingenuity.[3]

If we take *lettre* and *sen* as technical terms, and suppose *surplus* to be a synonym for a third technical term which would be understood in the light of the first two, the translation may be made more precise.

In the schools of the twelfth century a given text was studied on three levels. The process is explained clearly in a recent study of medieval education:

> Elle (*expositio*) comprenait trois sortes d'explications, appelées *littera, sensus et sententia. Littera,* c'était l'explication grammaticale; *sensus,* le sens que donne à premiere vue la *littera*; et *sententia,* l'intelligence profonde de la pensée de l'auteur, le contenu doctrinal.

---

1. *MP* XLI (1943), 96-102.
2. *Lais,* ed. Ewert (Oxford, 1944), p. 1.
3. *Ibid.,* p. 163.

Ces trois explications se suivaient naturellement dans l'ordre où nous les avons énoncées; une fois données toutes trois, l'exégese est parfaite. "Quid enim aliud in lectura queritur quam textus intelligentia, que *sententia* nominatur," dit Robert de Melun.[4]

This method was applied not only in the study of profane authors, but in the study of Scripture as well.[5] Theologians of the period frequently show profound contempt for those who understand only the sense of Scripture and cannot proceed to the *sentence*.[6] It is not impossible that a similar attitude may have prevailed among those whose concern was either the study or the composition of profane texts.[7]

The terms *littera*, *sensus*, and *sententia* suit the context of Marie's prologue with striking appropriateness. The philosophers of olden times wrote with the awareness of the *sententia* which should arise from their texts.[8]

> Pur ceus ki a venir esteient
> E ki aprendre les deveient,
> K'i peüssent gloser la lettre (*littera*)
> E de lur sen (*sensus*) le surplus (*sententia*) mettre.

In other words,

---

4. G. Paré, A. Brunet, P. Tremblay, *La renaissance du XIIe siècle: les écoles et l'enseignement* (Paris, Ottawa, 1933), p. 116. A first-hand description of the process may be found in the *Didascalion* of Hugh of St. Victor.
5. *Ibid.*, p. 228.
6. Thus, for example, Bruno Astensis, *Comment. in Matth.*, Pars IV, Cap. XXII, *PL*, 165, 252: "ut ergo longo vivimus tempore, dimittamus avem et litteram quae occidit, teneamus pullos et ova, id est spiritualem intelligentiam quae vivificat.... Nos enim in civitate Dei, nos in sancta ecclesia harum nuptiarum delicias edimus: illi autem in villa morantur; illi in grosso pane litterae, et rusticano cibo delectantur. In villa enim sunt quicunque extra Ecclesiam sunt."
7. For a late instance of this attitude, see the Prologue to Usk's *Testament of Love*, ed. Skeat, *Chaucerian and Other Pieces* (Oxford, 1897), p. 1.
8. The idea is not far-fetched. Cf. Philosophy's remarks to Boethius, *De consolatione*, I, Pr. V: "Itaque non tam me loci huius quam tua facies movet, nec bibliothecae potius comptos ebore ac vitro parietes quam tuae mentis sedem requiro; in qua non libros, sed id quod libros pretium facit, librorum quondam meorum sententias conlocavi."

so that those who were to come after them and to learn them might gloss the letter or grammatical structure and from the apparent sense determine the doctrinal content.

Perhaps we should inquire into the possible *sententiae* of Marie's *Lais*.

D. W. Robertson, Jr.
Princeton University

Cumhthach Labhras an Lonsa

Modern Language Notes 67:2 (February 1952), pp. 123-125.

One of the most attractive pieces in Miss Knott's *Irish Syllabic Poetry* is a poem describing the lament of an ousel whose mate and nestlings have been destroyed by a herdboy. The speaker regards the mournful bird with sympathy, since his own wife and children have died suddenly, and he too is alone.[1] Stanza 7 of the poem concerns the speaker's religious position with reference to his sorrow:

> A Fhir do chumm an cruinne,
> doiligh linn do leattruime
> na caraid atá rér dtaoibh
> maraid a mná 'sa macoimh.

Mr. Flower's translation sugests that these lines indicate a complaint against God:

> O God that made the whole world thus,
> Alas, thy heavy hand on us!
> For all my friends around are gay.
> Their wives and children live today.

And if we allow *leattruime* its connotation "oppression" this interpretation is almost unavoidable. But we should not expect to find this attitude in either the twelfth or the thirteenth century, and it is possible that the lines actually suggest a profession of faith rather than "grucching."

---

1. Eleanor Knott, *Irish Syllabic Poetry of the Period 1200-1600* (Cork, 1934), 29-30. A translation by Robin Flower appears in his *Irish Tradition* (Oxford, 1947), 80-81. Miss Knott, p. 88, noted that the poem is "a little earlier than our period," indicating, perhaps, the twelfth century; but Mr. Flower made it contemporary with or "perhaps somewhat later" than the work of Donnchadh Mór Ó Dálaigh, who died in 1244.

The word *cruinne* indicates "roundness" or "perfection" as well as "the world," so that the first line quoted may be taken as an assertion of God's Providence:

> O God who made perfection....

To the word *cruinne* the last word of the next line, *leattruime*, seems a deliberate contrast. But the poet would hardly have accused God of oppression immediately after asserting His Providence. Perhaps *leattruime* was meant to suggest not simply "oppression" but that aspect of Providence which sometimes appears oppressive to the limited vision of man—Fortune. Taken in this way the two lines express the conventional medieval contrast between Providence and Fortune with the usual implication of faith in the first of these. In other words, the poem indicates a firm confidence in Providence in spite of an especially disastrous whim of Fortune.

Mr. Flower found themes suggesting the content of our poem in Homer and Virgil, and a similar theme in Shakespeare. But he thought the Irish poem to be a product of personal rather than of literary experience. We may add to his list of analogues an American folksong, "The Lonesome Dove."[2] The bird, as the title indicates, is here a dove which mourns for its lost mate. There is no herdboy, and Death's agent is here "consumption" rather than "sluagh sídh 'na sidhe." But in the American song the profession of faith is unmistakable:

> Bless the words the Lord has given,
> Declares that babes are heirs of heaven;
> There is one thing that cheers my breast
> That my dear Mary's gone to rest.
> For while her dying tongue could move,
> She prayed the Lord for pardoning love;
> She says to me, "My dearest friend,
> Go on be faithful to the end."

---

2. A text is printed by Jean Thomas, *Devil's Ditties* (Chicago, 1931), 162-163. Miss Thomas thinks this song also to be a product of personal experience, "written and set to music by an old mountain preacher ... who had lost his wife and child."

Whatever the personal element in these songs may have been, if we have read the Irish song correctly, they typify the Christian ideal steadfastness in the face of worldly misfortune. A connection between them is not altogether impossible.[3]

D. W. Robertson, Jr.
Princeton University

---

3. Both Irish and medieval elements appear elsewhere in Miss Thomas' collection. For example, "The Bed of Primroses," pp. 176-178, celebrates "a daughter of Daniel O'Connell's" in the framework of a medieval dream vision.

Chaucerian Tragedy

By D. W. Robertson, Jr.

ELH: A Journal of English Literary History 19:1 (March 1952), pp. 1-37.

Chaucer's observations concerning tragedy are well known and have been frequently discussed. But the implications of what he says are sometimes neglected, both in studies of the *Troilus* and in comments on what is called the *de casibus* theme as it appears in later drama. This essay seeks to examine certain of these neglected implications, especially those that concern the philosophical background afforded by the *De consolatione* of Boethius and by other works of a more obviously theological character. It is assumed here that Chaucer, like most of his medieval predecessors, thought of the *De consolatione* as a Christian document and that he considered its philosophical message to be of profound importance. For illustrative purposes, I wish to show that the *Troilus* may be thought of as a typical Chaucerian tragedy, at present confining the implications for later dramatic tragedy to a few incidental allusions.

In the first place, Chaucer found the definition of tragedy which he followed in the Monk's Tale imbedded in a discussion of Fortune in the *De consolatione*. He translated it as follows:

> What other thying bywaylen the cryinges of tragedyes but oonly the dedes of Fortune, that with unwar strook overturneth the realmes of great nobleye? (*Gloss. Tragedye is to seyn a dite of a prosperite for a tyme, that endeth in wrecchidnesse.*)[1]

---

1. II, Pr. 2, ed. Robinson, *Complete Works of Chaucer* (Cambridge, 1933), p. 387. In this paper quotations from Chaucer, except those from the *Troilus*, are from this edition. Quotations from the *Troilus* are from the edition of R. K. Root (Princeton, 1945).

It should be observed that the gloss explains only that the word *tragedy* indicates a special kind of "dite"; it does not elaborate the concept of "dedes of Fortune," which is explained in the treatise itself. In the prologue to his tale, the Monk gives a superficial literary definition of tragedy, elaborating the idea in the gloss just quoted but avoiding the idea of Fortune (1974-1981). Fortune is introduced, however, in the little preface within the tale proper:

> I wol biwaille, in manere of tragedie,
> The harm of hem that stoode in heigh degree,
> And fillen so that ther nas no remedie
> To brynge hem out of hir adversitee.
> 1995   For certein, whan that Fortune list to flee,
> Ther may no man the cours of hire withholde.

Fortune is referred to several times in the course of the individual tragedies, to appear finally in the summation at the close of the last story:

> Tragedies noon oother maner thyng
> Ne kan in syngyng crie ne biwaille
> But that Fortune alwey wole assaile
> With unwar strook the regnes that been proude;
> 2765   For whan men trusteth hire, thanne wol she faille,
> And covere hire brighte face with a clowde.

It is fairly obvious that Chaucer's conception of tragedy is dependent on his conception of Fortune, and that we cannot understand what he meant by *tragedy* unless we understand also what he meant by *Fortune,* and what happens "whan men trusteth hire."[2]

Fortune was regarded in the Middle Ages as a useful designation for an idea which fitted nicely into the scheme of Christian theology. One did not "believe in" Fortune any more than one believed in the goddess Venus; but Fortune, like Venus, was used to express a kind of behavior to which almost everyone is subject. The concept, as a matter

---

2. The importance of the concept of Fortune generally in medieval literature has been amply demonstrated by H. R. Patch, *The Goddess Fortuna in Medieval Literature* (Cambridge, Mass., 1927). However, the implications of *Fortune* in Chaucer's usage are not always immediately clear.

of fact, appears once in the Bible, where we are shown some of the implications of "trusting" Fortune (Isa. 65. 11-14):

> And you, that have forsaken the Lord, and have forgotten my holy mount, that set a table for Fortune, and offer libations upon it, I will number you in the sword, and you shall fall by slaughter: because I called and you did not answer: I spoke and you did not hear: and you did evil in my eyes, and you have chosen the things that displease me. Therefore thus saith the Lord God: Behold my servants shall eat, and you shall be hungry: behold my servants shall drink, and you shall be thirsty. Behold my servants shall rejoice, and you shall be confounded: behold my servants shall praise for joyfulness of heart, and you shall cry for sorrow of heart, and shall howl for grief of spirit.[3]

The *Glossa ordinaria* explains that such persons are those who submit to false doctrines, thinking that everything is governed by changing fortune or the course of the stars.[4] The speaker at the beginning of the *De consolatione* is one among them. He is exiled from his own country in a spiritual sense; he has forsaken God and forgotten the Celestial City, or the holy mount. As Philosophy explains to him (I. Pr. 5):

> For yif thow remembre of what cuntre thow art born, it nys nat governed by emperoures, ne by governement of multitude, as weren the cuntrees of hem of Atthenes; but o lord and o kyng, and that is God, is lord of thi cuntre, which that rejoisseth hym of the duellynge of his citizeens, and nat for to putten hem in exil; of the whiche lord it is a sovereyn fredom to ben governed by the brydel of hym [sc. "reason"] and obeye to his justice.

He has forgotten his true nature and submitted to false doctrine (I, Pr. 5). It is important to observe that Philosophy considers the plight of the speaker to be his own responsibility. He could very well have

---

3. The Bible is quoted here and elsewhere in the paper in the Douay version, which is much closer to the medieval Vulgate than the King James Bible. The latter does not mention Fortune in this passage.
4. *PL*, 113, 1310. Cf. St. Jerome, *Comm. in Is.*, *PL*, 24, 663-664. See also D. W. Robertson, Jr., and B. F. Huppé, *Piers Plowman and Scriptural Tradition* (Princeton, 1951), p. 130.

avoided his distress, since, as she explains, no one is exiled from the Celestial City except through his own volition.

The exile of the speaker is thus not due to chance. One of the false doctrines to which he was subject was a belief in "happes aventurous." Philosophy seeks to show him the "wey" to his "contre" by explaining (V, Pr. 1) that "hap nis, ne duelleth but a voys (*as who seith, but an idel word*), withouten any significacioun of thing summitted to that voys." What appears to be chance is "an unwar betydinge of causes assembled in thingis that ben doon for som oothir thing." That is, those things which appear to happen by chance are actually part of a larger design. Nor does Fortune represent any kind of absolute destiny. Destiny is the operation of providence in particular instances, but there are some things which "surmounten the ordenaunce of destyne" (IV, Pr. 6), notably the free will of man. We cannot say, then, that the victim or "hero" of a Chaucerian tragedy is either the victim of chance or the victim of an inevitable destiny. Like the speaker in the *De consolatione*, he is the victim of his own failure. This failure may come about in various ways, some of which are described at length in the *De consolatione*. If he sets his heart on wealth, dignity, power, fame, physical pleasure, or on any other worldly goods of this kind, he loses his freedom and becomes a slave to Fortune. True freedom is a thing of the spirit which cannot be affected by externals. It is maintained by the reason and lost when reason is abandoned. "Wherefore," Philosophy says (V, Pr. 2), "in alle thingis that resoun is, in hem also is liberte of willynge and nillynge." Thus to be subject to Fortune is to be subject to vices, to wander from the way of the true good in search of false and unreasonable worldly satisfactions. If, on the other hand, a man remains confident in providence, in the essential, though obscure, reasonableness of creation, he can neither be affected by adversity ("evil" fortune) nor by prosperity ("good" fortune). "Whoso it be," Boethius explains (I, Met. 4), "that is cleer of vertu, sad and wel ordynat of lyvinge, that hath put under fote the proude weerdes and loketh, upright, upon either fortune, he may holden his chere undisconfited." Fortune can neither elevate nor cast down the virtuous man, since its gifts are by nature transitory and trivial. Philosophy explains (II, Pr. 1), "thou shalt wel knowe that, as in hir [i.e., Fortune], thow nevere ne haddest ne hast ylost any fair thyng." The evils of adversity are merely apparent, arising from the uncertainty of the reason (II, Pr. 4), "and forthi nothyng is wrecchid but whan thou wenest it." All Fortune, whether "good" or "evil" on the surface, is essentially good (IV, Pr. 7), "so as al fortune, whethir so it be joyeful fortune or aspre fortune, is yeven eyther bycause of gerdonynge or elles of exercisynge of goode folk, or elles bycause to punysshen or elles chastisen shrewes; thanne is alle fortune good, the whiche fortune is certeyn that it be either ryghtful or elles profitable." Specifically, Fortune represents the variation between worldly prosperity and worldly adversity. Reason is able to discern that however superficially disappointing this variation may be, it is due neither to chance nor to destiny, but is a manifestation of the divine will, a function of the chain of love which holds creation together. To love the uncertain and transitory rewards of the world is to subject oneself to their fluctuations. To love God is to acquire freedom and peace of mind.

These formulations are entirely consistent with conventional medieval theology.[5] In the first place, the false goods of the world as described in the *De consolatione* are all objects of cupidity, and the subjection to Fortune in vice described there is sufficiently commonplace to appear, in slightly different terms, in the Parson's Tale (p. 275):

> Ne a fouler thral may no man ne womman maken of his body than for to yeven his body to synne. Al were it the fouleste cherl or the fouleste womman that lyveth, and leest of value, yet is he thanne moore foul and moore in servitute. Evere fro the hyer degree that man falleth, the moore is he thral, and moore to God and to the world vile and abhomynable.

The idea that sin is a departure from reason is also common. The Parson puts this in terms of order. The reason should be subject to God; and "sensuality," or the desire for worldly satisfactions, should be subject to the reason. When the "sensuality" triumphs so that the reason loses sight of what Boethius calls the "verray good," the proper order of things is disturbed so that sin results (p. 279):

---

5. The very wide area of agreement between the *De consolatione* and Augustinian theology has never been systematically explored. Only a few very obvious instances of this agreement are indicated here.

> And ye shul understonde that in mannes synne is very manere of ordre or ordinaunce turned up-so-doun. For it is sooth that God, and resoun, and sensualitee, and the body of man been so ordeyned that everich of thise foure thynges sholde have lordshipe over that oother; as thus: God sholde have lordships over resoun, and resoun over sensualitee, and sensualitee over the body of man. But soothly, whan man synneth, al this ordre or ordinaunce is turned up-so-doun. And therfore, thanne, for as muche as the resoun of man ne wol nat be subyet ne obeisant to God, that is his lord by right, therfore leseth it the lordshipe that it sholde heve over sensualitee, and eek over the body of man. And why? For sensualitee rebelleth thanne agayns resoun, and by that wey leseth resoun the lordshipe over sensualitee and over the body. For right as resoun is rebel to God, right so is bothe sensualitee rebel to resoun and the body also.[6]

Sin, the disturbance of reason through the desire of temporal satisfaction, makes man subject to both "good" and "evil" fortune, that is, to prosperity and to adversity (p. 280):

> Certes, synful mannes soule is bitraysed of the devel by coveitise of temporeel prosperitee, and scorned by deceite whan he cheseth flesshly delices; and yet is it tormented by impacience of adversitee, and bispet by servage and subjeccioun of synne; and atte laste it is slayn fynally.

The Parson is no less certain than Boethius that complaints against "evil" fortune are foolish (p. 289):

> Agayns God it is, whan a man gruccheth agayn the peyne of helle, or agayns poverte, or los of catel, or agayn reyn or tempest; or elles gruccheth that shrewes han prosperitee, or elles for that goode men han adversitee. And alle thise thynges sholde man suffre paciently, for they comen by the rightful juggemeut and ordinaunce of God.

Finally, if the false goods which Boethius describes are typical objects of cupidity, the root from which all evils may be said to spring, the "verray good" which he describes is the object of charity, God Himself;

---

6 Cf. Peter Lombard, *Sententiae*, Lib. II, Dist. XXIV, Cap. IV ff. (Ad Claras Aquas, 1916).

and it is from charity that all virtues arise. Thus the *De consolatione* develops in a systematic way, but in the guise of a philosophical dialogue, the contrast between the two loves, charity and cupidity, which is the cornerstone of medieval theology.[7]

To return now to our definitions of tragedy, it is clear that the subject of a Chaucerian tragedy is not only a man of high degree but also a man who has allowed himself to be elevated spiritually by "good" fortune. Having achieved this eminence, he is beset by "evil" fortune or adversity, before which he falls. Tragedy describes the downfall of "regnes" that are proud, that is of "orders," both internal and external, that are elevated by the vices as symbolized by the chief vice, pride. The tragic "hero" turns from the way and seeks false worldly satisfactions, abandons reason and becomes subject to Fortune. In short, through some sort of cupidity the protagonist loses his free will so that when adversity or "evil" fortune strikes, his doom has a certain inevitability. It may be objected that the tragic protagonist cannot be a sinner, since he is, sometimes treated with sympathy, as he is in the *Troilus*. But in the Middle Ages it was widely recognized that we are all sinners. Moreover, the attitude toward sinners was not necessarily one of unreserved condemnation. The Parson's evident contempt was sometimes modified by a more philosophical attitude. In the *De consolatione*, Philosophy explains that (IV, Pr. 4)

> no wyght nil haten gode men, but yif he were overmochel a fool, and for to haten shrewes it nis no resoun. For ryght so as langwissynge is maladye of body, ryght so ben vices and synne maladye of corage; and so as we ne deme nat that they that ben sike of hir body ben worthy to ben hated, but rather worthy of pite; wel more worthy nat to ben hated, but for to ben had in pite, ben thei of whiche the thoughtes ben constreyned by felonous wikkidnesse, that is more cruwel than any langwyssynge of body.

The pity here advocated is not a sentimental pity, not a desire to eliminate the symptoms of the malady without alleviating the malady itself,

---

7. See "The Doctrine of Charity in Medieval Literary Gardens," *Speculum*, XXVI (1951), p. 24. Systematic theology was developed in the twelfth century as a guide to Scriptural interpretation, which had as its function the discovery of the New Law in the various parts of the Bible.

but a desire to cure it. Theologically, the departure from reason involved in a sin is a corruption of the Image of God. Hence a sinner loses his potentiality as a man and becomes a beast. Philosophy says of sinners that (IV, Pr. 3) "when thei ben perverted and turned into malice, certes, thanne have thei forlorn the nature of mankynde." An avaricious man is like a wolf, a felonious man like a dog, and so on. The loss of potential involved in the destruction of what was thought of as man's essential humanity, his reason, or the divine image, is a pitiable thing. But one does not cure an avaricious man by giving him gold, nor a gluttonous man by giving him food. "What brydles myghte withholden to any certeyn ende," exclaims Boethius (II, Met. 2), "the disordene covetise of men, whan evere the rather that it fletith in large yiftes, the more aye brenneth in hem the thurst of havynge?" In Biblical terms, the effort to destroy appetite by feeding it is figuratively expressed in the water of the Samaritan woman. He who drinks of it shall thirst again. Those who burn with cupidity, whether in prosperity or adversity, are thus pitiable; but the kind of pity desired is exactly the kind exhibited by Philosophy for the speaker in the *De consolatione*. She did not restore his lost dignities, his wealth, or his physical freedom. Instead she gave him spiritual freedom, restoring his essential humanity. She taught him to "laugh at gilded butterflies."

The general pattern of the tragic fall as it was seen in the Middle Ages is vividly described in the opening chapter of the *Policraticus* by John of Salisbury, where the temptations of "good" fortune are discussed. This account includes all of the salient features of the scheme we have described: the worldly temptation, the abandonment of God for the sake of vices, the loss of reason, and the destruction of the divine image. John suggests one additional element, neglect of duty. The tragic protagonist was a man of high degree, a prince or other dignitary. In the Middle Ages, an elevated degree carried with it certain moral obligations. A prince was theoretically a wiser man than any of his subjects, formed of a more refined metal better able to bear the divine image. His fall thus involved an especially disturbing loss of potential and, at the same time, through his neglect of duty, a significant disruption of the earthly hierarchy. John of Salisbury was discussing an actual pattern of behavior, not a "dite." But this pattern, as an examination of the *De consolatione* reveals, is implicit in the statement that tragedy bewails the "dedes of Fortune." The external structure of the "dite" implied for Boethius, and for Chaucer, a very real and significant content. It is to this content and to the artistry and forcefulness with which it is expressed that we should attach primary importance. The overthrow of "regnes that been proude" is a characteristic theme of earlier English literature, from Hrothgar's speech over the sword hilt left by the giants in the earth to Sidney's statement that a tragedy makes "kings fear to be tyrants." And it is a theme firmly rooted in the philosophy of medieval Christianity.

Certain further implications of Chaucer's conception of tragedy may be seen in the Monk's Tale itself, although the little tragedies presented there are not sufficiently elaborated to serve as a very full basis for discussion. The series begins with the fall of Lucifer. This is not a true tragedy, since "Fortune may noon angel dere," but it is a necessary preliminary to the tragedies which follow. Without the influence of Satan, no man would abandon reason and subject himself to Fortune. Satan, in medieval terms, offers to each man the opportunity to exercise his free will, to acquire virtue through resistance or to succumb and move toward a deserved punishment. Satan's actions, incidentally, are all "good" in exactly the same way that the actions of Fortune are, and his temptations are traditionally expressed in terms of prosperity and adversity. Satan cannot avoid the order of providence. The first man to abandon reason and turn away from God under Satan's influence was Adam, whose story appears as the first of the true tragedies. Adam, through "mysgovernaunce," turned away from God and became, as it were, the first fool of Fortune. It is noteworthy that Adam was neither destined to fall nor the victim of an unlucky chance. Traditionally, he had perfect freedom of choice, and his downfall came as a result of his own decision to submit to Eve. The implications of the fall of Adam are very significant, since all tragic protagonists in the Chaucerian sense follow Adam's footsteps. Some of these implications would have been evident to many in Chaucer's audience without any elaboration on his part. For example, the story of Adam and Eve may be taken tropologically as well as literally, so that it not only affords a model for external events in other tragedies but also as a model for events in the mind of the tragic protagonist. These inner implications of the story were well known in the Middle Ages. They are explained at length in St. Augustine's *De Trinitate* (Lib. XII, Cap. 12), in the *Sententiae* of Peter Lombard (Lib. II, Dist. XXIV, Cap. VI ff.), and in many subsequent works.[8] Briefly, Adam, Eve, and the serpent correspond to the higher reason, the lower reason, and the motion of the senses in an individual. The function of the higher reason is wisdom, or *sapientia*, and that of the lower reason is worldly wisdom, or *scientia*. The higher reason, which perceives the laws of God, should dominate the lower reason, which perceives the laws of nature, just as the husband should rule the wife. There is thus an inner marriage within man. Just as the serpent tempted Eve and Eve tempted Adam, so the motion of the senses tempts the lower reason, and this womanly faculty in turn tempts the higher reason. Parenthetically, an individual dominated by the senses or the lower reason is frequently characterized as "effeminate." If the lower reason resists the tempting motion of the senses, the resulting sin is venial. If the lower reason indulges in pleasurable thought ("delectatio cogitationis") when the senses tempt it but the fruit is rejected by the higher reason, the sin is still venial. But the sin is mortal and the individual falls just as Adam fell if the higher reason consents to the temptation or if the lower reason persists too long unchecked in pleasurable thought. In Boethian terms, Fortune is recognized as an illusion which conceals providence by the higher reason, but the lower reason sees Fortune as blind chance or fate. When the

---

8. See O. Lottin, "La doctrine morale des movements premiers de l'appetit sensitif aux XIIe et XIIIe siecles," *Archives d'histoire doctrinale et littéraire du moyen âge*, VI (1931), 49-173. For the common view, see especially pp. 51-53. The three steps of sin correspond to a widespread formula. E.g., see Bede, *In Matt., PL,* 92, 28: "and thus one arrives at sin by three steps: by suggestion, by delight, and by consent." Since the idea of "courtly love" has been introduced in discussions of the *Troilus*, it is not irrelevant to observe at this point that the above pattern is reflected at the beginning of the *De amore* by Andreas Capellanus. When Andreas says that love, by which he means sexual love centered on a single object, proceeds from vision and immoderate thought, he refers to the first two steps: the motion of the senses and the corruption of the lower reason through inordinate pleasurable contemplation. The result "love" represents the corruption of the higher reason as the object of desire is substituted for God. In general, Andreas' familiarity with the theology of his day has been unnecessarily slighted.

higher reason bows to the lower reason, when the pleasurable thought of Eve triumphs, the individual becomes a slave to Fortune, to Satan, or, figuratively, to the God of Love, whom Isidore calls the "demon of fornication." The result is a corrupt inner marriage, an "up-so-doun" condition of the soul which is frequently described in terms of fornication or adultery. The tragic protagonist who through a misdirected worldly love becomes an "unseemly woman in a seeming man" presents a local illustration of the fall of the first and noblest of men.

Finally, two further characteristics of tragedy may be formulated on the basis of the Monk's stories. The definitions of tragedy do not stipulate that the protagonist may not be saved by an ultimate repentance after his fall. The tragedies of "Nabugodonosor" and his son illustrate the two possible alterna- tives here. The first hero was a "proude kyng" who became through his iniquity "lyk a beest." But after his downfall, he "thanked God" and acknowledged His "myght and grace." His son was also "rebel to God," but he died unrepentant at the height of his good fortune. The problem of sympathy for the tragic protagonist is also illustrated. Little pity is wasted on Nero, who seems completely "fulfild of vice," so that when he killed himself in desperation, "Fortune lough, and hadde a game." Cenobia, on the other hand, displays admirable physical competence, virtue, wisdom, generosity, and learning. But her costly array, her dignity, and her power are gifts of Fortune to which she devoted herself, and like all gifts of Fortune, they are unstable. Her loss is obviously the loss of a considerable potential for good, in spite of her devotion to *scientia* for worldly reasons. When the tragic protagonist is treated with some sympathy, the audience can participate in his experiences, sharing, for the moment, his hopes and fears. This kind of participation is desirable at times, for the lesson of a tragedy is the lesson of the fall of man. The more readily we sympathise with the victim, the more easily we may recognize the fact that the fall establishes a tempting precedent for almost anyone to follow. The serpent lurks about us in unexpected places, in a fair face, a sudden honor, or an unforseen misfortune. The tragedian points him out for us; and his work is more effective when he can show him in the guise of commonplace events and superficially attractive individuals.

The following account of the *Troilus* is not intended to be in any sense a complete discussion of the poem; it is, rather, an attempt to show that the poem is a tragedy, whatever else it may be also.[9] The topics discussed, moreover, are treated only in a preliminary way. Chaucer makes it perfectly clear at the beginning that his hero is to be treated sympathetically; that is, Troilus is, as it were, Adam as Everyman rather than Adam as the evil sinner. Adopting the attitude recommended by Boethius, the poet says,

> For so hope I my soule best avaunce,
> To preye for hem that loves servauntes be,
> And write her wo, and live in charite,
I, 50 And for to have of hem compassioun,
> As though I were hire owne brother dere.

The servants of love, already mentioned in line 15, are servants of Cupid, or Satan. Chaucer proposes to describe their "wo" and live in "charite." That is, he will take pity on the followers of the wrong love and seek to maintain the right love in himself. He will "advance" his own soul best in this way, for, as Boethius explained, one should "have pite on shrewes." Love's servants are suitable tragic material, since those subject to cupidity are those subject to Fortune, with whose

---

9. The interpretation advanced here incorporates elements from the very brief but excellent account of the poem by Professor Patch in *The Tradition of Boethius* (New York, 1935), pp. 71-72. It also resembles in some respects the interpretation sugggested by J. L. Shanly, "The *Troilus* and Christian Love," ELH, VI (1939), 271-281. In 1931 Professor Patch published a spirited defense of Chaucer's unity of purpose in the poem, *Speculum*, VI, 225-243. This is an effective answer to those who would consider Troilus' speech on free will and the conclusion of the poem superfluous. Recently, the concept of "courtly love" has introduced a new kind of "dualism" in accounts of the poem, however. See especially A. J. Denomy, "The Two Moralities of Chaucer's *Troilus and Criseyde*," Trans. Roy. Soc. of Canada, XLIV (1950), Ser. III, 2, pp. 35-46. Here it is assumed that Andreas intended to be serious, rather than ironic and humorous, in the first parts of the *De amore*, and that the resulting artificial system was important enough in the fourteenth century for Chaucer to attack it at length. The assumption is reinforced by certain conclusions about Provençal poetry which have by no means been demonstrated. However, the importance of Boethius to an understanding of the *Troilus* has been emphasized again by T. A. Stroud, "Boethius' Influence on Chaucer's *Troilus*," MP, XLIX (1951), 1-9. This article supplies further bibliography.

"dedes" a tragedy is concerned. The literary task of maintaining both a sympathetic attitude and at the same time an attitude which will make clear the protagonist's deviations from the "wey" is a difficult one. If the foolishness of the hero is too apparent, the audience may find his plight irrelevant to themselves. On the other hand, if the departure from reason is not apparent enough, the result will appear to display blind chance or fate rather than providence. Chaucer solves the difficulty by maintaining with fair consistency a sympathetic attitude on the surface, referring at times to his sources or pretended sources for confirmation, or calling attention to the antiquity of his subject. But this sympathy is tempered by a consistent irony.[10] Since critical discussions of the poem sometimes carry the sympathetic attitude to an almost sentimental extreme, the present essay emphasizes the irony, not, however, with the implication that the sympathy does not exist.

Speaking generally, Troilus subjects himself to Fortune in Book I, rises to the false heaven of Fortune's favor in Books II and III, and finally descends to a tropological Hell in Books IV and V. By the close of Book III, he has been distracted by "good" fortune to the extent that he has no freedom left with which to avoid the ensuing adversities. He reaches a point at which there is "no remedie." His doom thus becomes a matter of destiny, or providence, since he loses the power to transcend Fortune. Indeed, it is the function of the "digression" on free will in Book IV to make this point clear and emphatic. The three stages of tragic development — subjection to Fortune, enjoyment of Fortune's favor, and denial of providence — correspond to the three stages in the tropological fall of Adam: the temptation of the senses, the corruption of the lower reason in pleasurable thought, and the final corruption of the higher reason. This correspondence is pointed by the emphasis on Criseyde's external attractions in Book I, by the worldly wisdom developed under the guidance of Pandarus in Book II, and by the substitution of Criseyde for divine grace in Book III. Books IV and V show the practical result of this process: confusion, despair,

---

10. In the article referred to above, Professor Stroud calls attention to the medieval theory of poetry in accordance with which a poem is said to have a surface meaning and an inner meaning, or a *cortex* and a *nucleus*. Cf. "Some Medieval Literary Terminology," *SP*, XLVIII (1951), 669-692. In this instance, I believe that the irony is used to develop the nucleus of the poem.

and death. Troilus becomes one of those who *cry for sorrow of heart* and who *howl for grief of spirit.*

When we first meet Troilus, he is very much aware of the foolishness of lovers: of the labor of winning, of the doubts of retaining, and of the woe of losing (I, 197-203). If his observations had been made on the basis of wisdom rather than as a manifestation of pride, they might have proved useful. But they are made at a religious festival in honor of Pallas, goddess of wisdom,[11] to whom Troilus pays no attention whatsoever. Instead, he and his youthful companions are engaged in looking over the pretty girls who are present, deliberately inviting the temptation of the senses. Troilus is thus guilty of sloth, or neglect of duty, as well as pride, and sloth is traditionally the "porter to the gate" of earthly delights.[12] It should be noticed that he knows very little of Criseyde before he sees her. Whether she is virtuous, wise, agreeable, or in any way reasonable are matters of no importance; what is important is her appearance:

>   Upon cas bifel that thorugh a route
>   His eye percede, and so depe it wente,
>   Til on Criseyde it smot, and ther it stente.
>   And sodeynly he was therwith astoned,
> I, 275 And gan hir bet biholde in thrifty wise.
>   "O mercy, god!" thoughte he, "wher hastow woned,
>   That art so fair and goodly to devise?"

11. Pallas was associated with theoretical arts or wisdom. See Hugh of St. Victor, *Didascalicon*, II, XVIII. There are many examples of *allegoria*, the device of saying one thing to mean another, in the poem. They all point toward the inner meaning or *nucleus*. For this purpose Chaucer uses both figures from classical sources, like Cupid or Pallas, and Scriptural signs, like "night," discussed below. Only a few of these, however, are indicated in the present essay. In connection with the general background of the poem, it is pertinent to recall that Troy was sometime thought to represent the human body and the Trojan horse lechery. See Bernard Silvestris, *Comm. super sex libros Eneidos Virgilii*, ed. Riedel (Gryphiswaldae, 1924), pp. 15-16, 102-103. Chaucer's Troilus is thus, in a sense, a personification of Troy as it was understood by medieval interpreters. The destruction of a man is the destruction of a city when we consider that every man builds either Babylon or Jerusalem within himself and that Babylon is doomed to fall. For a description of the destruction of Jerusalem through lechery, or its transformation into Babylon, see *DeDavid li prophecie,* ed. Fuhrkens (Halle, 1895), ll. 437 ff.

12. See "The Doctrine of Charity," p. 41.

The concluding question was probably about as serious in tone in the fourteenth century as it is now. As Troilus continues to stare, the initial reaction is confirmed, passing from the eye to the heart (I, 295-298), where the effect is so profound that "hym thoughte he felte deyen . . . the spirit of his herte." A famous clerk, describing this process in a pastoral discussion of sin, remarked, "Beauty is introduced through the sight into the soul, where it remains fixed, willy nilly, nor may a man escape from it afterward."[13] The death of the spirit implied in Chaucer's lines was observed by a still older clerk (Ecclus. 9. 7-9): *Look not round about thee in the ways of the city, nor wander up and down in the streets thereof. Turn thy face away from a woman dressed up, and gaze not about upon another's beauty. For many have perished by the beauty of a woman, and hereby lust is enkindled as fire.* The fire alluded to here is remarked several times in the poem (E.g., ll. 436, 445, 449, 490). What Troilus experiences is the motion of the senses stimulated through the eye. The serpent, in this instance, in concealed in the "aungelik beaute" of Criseyde. This is the temptation, the invitation to pleasurable thought and subjection to Fortune.

Troilus reacts to his predicament in exactly the wrong way. In his chamber alone, he makes a "mirour of his mynde," indulging in what Andreas Capellanus calls "immoderate thought upon the beauty of the opposite sex," or in what Peter Lombard speaks of as "pleasurable thought."[14] What he sees in this mirror of Narcissus is Criseyde's "figure." The song he sings is a foreshadowing of the course of his love, typical of those who abandon reason for Fortune. He has tasted the water of the wrong spring, the water of the Samaritan woman, so that the more he drinks the more he thirsts (I, 406) . He is "al steereles within a boot." Petrarch is merely an intermediary for this figure, whose source is Prov. 23. 33-34: *Thy eyes shall behold strange women, and thy heart shall utter perverse things. And thou shalt be as one sleeping in the midst of the sea, and as a pilot fast asleep, when the stern* [i.e., "rudder"] *is lost.* The perverse doctrines

---

13. Humbert de Romans, *Exp. reg. b. Aug., Opera,* ed. J. J. Berthier (Rome, 1888-1889), I, 276.
14. For this mirror, cf. the Merchant's Tale, 1580 ff., and the well of Narcissus in the Romaunt of the Rose.

are evident in the last two stanzas of the Cantus. Troilus gives himself up to the god of love, regards his lady as a "goddess," and resigns his "estat roial" into her hand. This is the neglect of which John of Salisbury warned, and specifically a violation of the wisdom of Ecclus. 9. 2: *Give not the power of thy soul to a woman, lest she enter upon thy strength and thou be confounded.* Troilus has no desire to love Criseyde for her virtue, her potential virtue, or her reason — no desire to take her as a wife. Instead, he wishes to submit to her, to turn the order of things "up-so-doun." The external submission to Criseyde recalls not only Adam's submission to Eve, but also the submission of the reason to the "sensualitee," the wit to the will. The song, however, is an expression of a process that is not actually completed until Book III. But Troilus has already gone so far that no other fear except that of losing Criseyde assails him (I, 463-464). This is the wrong fear that accompanies the wrong love,[15] a fear which takes away Troilus' sense of duty and leads to confusion and despair. In spite of a display of false virtue to capture Criseyde's attention,[16] Troilus soon wishes for death.

The character of Pandarus is a masterpiece of medieval irony. On the surface, he is an attractive little man, wise, witty, and generous. But his wisdom is clearly not of the kind Lady Philosophy would approve, and his generosity is of the type which supplies gold to the avaricious and

---

15. See Hugh of St. Victor, *De sacramentis, PL,* 176, 527. Cf. "The Doctrine of Charity," p. 28.

16. Troilus is at pains to acquire military glory and popular acclaim. His valor and generosity, as well as Criseyde's "honor," should be considered in the light of a principle expressed by Alanus de Insulis in his treatise on the virtues, the vices, and the gifts of the Holy Spirit, ed. Lottin, *Mediaeval Studies,* XII (1950), 20-56. It is explained there (p. 27) on the basis of a distinction from Boethius, *De cons.,* that a virtue must have both its proper "office" and its proper "end." As its end, a virtue must be directed toward God, and the actions in which the virtue is manifest must be performed in charity. The virtues of Troilus are directed toward Criseyde and performed in cupidity, and Criseyde's honor is completely a matter of self-love. It was not uncommon in the Middle Ages to distinguish "true" virtues from "false" virtues. See *Piers Plowman and Scriptural Tradition,* pp. 226-227. The "virtues" of the lover as described ironically by Andreas Capellanus are of the worldly variety. They are illustrated vividly and humorously, for example, in Aucassin's valorous behavior in the upside-down land of Torelore.

dainties to the glutton. In short, he is a sentimentalist and a cynic by turns, for sentimentality and cynicism are but two sides of the same coin. His prototype is Jonadab, *a very wise man*, and the device he uses to bring the lovers together is strikingly like that used by his Biblical predecessor (2 Kings 13). Beneath his superficially attractive surface, his real function is that of intermediary between a victim of *fol amor* and the object of his love. As an intermediary of this kind, he acquires some of the characteristics of a priest. Indeed, there is more than a suggestion in the poem that Pandarus is a blind leader of the blind (I, 625-630), a priest of Satan. It is true that he is not a Mephistophelian figure, in part because the Devil had not yet been romanticised when he was created. He is externally pleasant, somewhat commonplace, and a little unctuous. But this deceptiveness is part of Chaucer's artistry. His "devel," as Troilus once calls him (I, 6923), is convincingly decked out in sheep's clothing. Pandarus' first remarks reveal a witty contempt for "remors of conscience," "devocioun," and "holynesse" (I, 551-560). And when Troilus, with the blind unreasonableness of a typical tragic protagonist, complains against Fortune (I, 837), Pandarus can reply only that everyone is subject to Fortune and that she is by nature fickle (I, 844-854). Neither here nor elsewhere does he ever suggest that it is possible to rise above Fortune. His almost complete lack of scruple is revealed in his offer to get Troilus anyone, even his sister (I, 860-861).

When Pandarus discovers that Criseyde is the object of Troilus' desire, he gives him a little sermon, emphasizing Criseyde's "pitee," a characteristic which she shares with May in the Merchant's Tale. He closes with an admonition to Troilus to repent his earlier remarks about the foolishness of lovers. Like a good priest, he leads his sinner in prayer:

> "Now beet thi brest, and sey to god of love:
> 'Thy grace, lord; for now I me repente
> If I mysspak, for now my self I love;'
> I, 935   Thus sey with al thyn herte in good entente."
> Quod Troilus: "a, lord! I me consente,
> And preye to the my japes thow forgive,
> And I shal nevere more whil I live."

He further admonishes perseverance and devotion, asserting that of the two loves Criseyde is much more inclined toward what is actually the wrong one. In Pandarus' estimation, she would be vicious to engage in celestial love (I, 981-987). In other words, Troilus thus acquires not true humility, but humility before a gift of Fortune, for both loves humiliate just as both loves inflame.[17] He confirms and fortifies his tendency toward pleasurable thought, promising to maintain it. Finally, he obtains assurance of Criseyde's "grace." She will "cure" his appetite by satisfying it. A little appalled by the point to which Pandarus has led him, however, he protests that he desires nothing but "that that myghte sounen into goode." Pandarus' reaction is cynical enough:

> Tho lough this Pandare, and anon answerede:
> I, 1038 "And I thi borugh? fy! no wight doth but so."

That is what they all say. Pandarus is perfectly aware of what Troilus wants, or thinks he wants, and is determined to get it for him. As for Troilus, he falls on his knees, embraces Pandarus, and submits to him completely. "My lif, my deth, hool in thyn honde I ley," he says. His senses have been moved to such an extent that he is willing to place his trust completely in worldly wisdom, in the *scientia* advocated by Pandarus."[18]

Book II is a study in false "curtesie," the Curtesie who leads the lover to the old dance in *The Romaunt of the Rose*, the Curteysie who

---

17. Cf. "The Doctrine of Charity," p. 28.
18. Troilus' behavior in Book I is typical of those who are moved by some false goal, whether in feminine guise or not, to depart from what Boethius calls the "wey" and thus subject themselves to Fortune. The fact that this particular temptation involves the beauty of a woman should not be taken as too much of a limitation. Feminine beauty was thought to typify the attractions of the world generally, and sexual passion was a figure for all the vices. Thus Scotus Erigena, *De div. nat.*, PL., 192, 975-976, wrote: "Whosoever shall look on a woman to lust after her, hath already committed adultery with her in his heart (Matt. 5. 28), obviously referring to the beauty of all sensible creatures as a woman... All vices, in fact, which are contrary to the virtues, and which seek to corrupt nature, are described generally as lechery." Sexual love might be used to describe any form of cupidity, especially when it was carried to the point of idolatry. The temptation of Troilus may thus readily be universalised to include any of the false goals against which Boethius warns.

accompanies Aray and Lust in *The Parlement of Foules*. It consists of nothing more than the corrupted lower reason operating in a sophisticated society. Figuratively, the corruption of the lower reason is the corruption of Eve, and in this book, significantly, Chaucer concentrates attention on the corruption of Criseyde. In doing so, he gives us a vivid picture of "manners" in fourteenth century England. His scenes in the parlor, in the garden, and in the bedchamber combine to form what may be called the first comedy of manners in English. Since what happens in this little comedy reveals a great deal about Criseyde's character, it will repay us to examine it in some detail. It is important to determine whether Criseyde's love, for which Troilus is to suffer the extremity of sorrow, is a "fair thing," or whether it shares the usual deceptive character of Fortune's gifts. At the same time, the book also reveals much about Pandarus, the "friend" in whom Troilus has placed his trust. The book opens on May 3, an unlucky day for Pandarus and for all other followers of Venus, goddess of lechery. For it was on May 3 that Chaucer and his contemporaries celebrated the deeds of St. Helena, who cast down the idol of Venus and set up the Cross in Jerusalem. Pandarus is especially "green" on that day; it was the Cross which finally separated his master, the God of Love, from his first sweetheart, Eve. Pandarus can never enjoy any kind of love himself, but he can suffer the pangs of desire, and he can lead others down the road to what Andreas Capellanus calls "Amoenitas." With many a clever flourish, he proceeds to guide Criseyde. Since Troilus is no Diomede, he must rely on his friend for this service; but once the proper lies have been told to the proper people, once the lady has made her bow to Fortune, he is very willing to cooperate.

The meeting between Pandarus and Criseyde is characterized by a meticulous attention to the social graces. Pandarus finds her with two other ladies, listening to the tale of Thebes, from which she does not seem to learn a great deal. She rises, takes him "by the hond hye," and seats him on a bench, meanwhile beginning some appropriate small talk which gives Pandarus the opportunity to introduce the subject of "love." He is careful to begin his work at some distance from its object, and first asks Criseyde to dance in an effort to undermine the restraint of her widowhood. But she is perfectly aware of the moral obligations of her status:

> II, 117 "It satte me wel bet ay in a cave
> To bidde, and rede on holy seyntes lyves;
> Lat maydens gon to daunce, and yonge wyves."

Widowhood in the Middle Ages bore an analogy to the contemplative life, called the "status viduarum,"[19] and a widow was supposed to look upon her bereavement as an opportunity to renounce the flesh and devote herself to God.[20] At the same time, in pastoral theology, a widow was thought to be not altogether responsible, having, presumably, lost the wise guidance of a husband.[21] Pandarus seeks to take advantage of Criseyde's vulnerable position, and, simultaneously, to remove the inhibitions of her status. He has one advantage. Criseyde is afraid, at this point afraid of "Grekes." As Mr. C. S. Lewis has pointed out, she is almost always fearful,[22] but he does not go on to say that this fear, which is never fully justified, is always the wrong fear which accompanies the wrong love and leads to transgression. In this respect, her fear is like that developed earlier by Troilus, except that it is not centered on a single object, and, in fact, never becomes fully centered in that way. Playing on the present fear of "Grekes," Pandarus finds an opportunity to praise Troilus at some length, preparing the way for his message (II, 157 ff.). Finally, he offers to leave without telling her what he has come for, at the same time repeating his invitation to dance: "let us daunce, and cast youre widwes habit to mischaunce" (II, 221-222). Like that of Curtesie in the *Romaunt*, his invitation has more than one meaning.

Criseyde, overcome by curiosity, will not let him leave. He plans very carefully his next move (II, 267-273), opening this time with

---

19. For the three states of men in the church, see *Piers Plowman and Scriptural Tradition*, p. 20.
20. An early but authoritative statement of this principle may be found in St. Augustine, *De bono viduitatis*.
21. See *Piers Plowman and Scriptural Tradition*, p. 111.
22. *The Allegory of Love* (Oxford, 1936), pp. 185-187. The general tone of these pages is sentimental, but Criseyde's fearfulness is amply shown.

some remarks about good fortune. He who does not make the most of it when it comes is foolish, he says, seeking to tempt her with rumors of prosperity. She remains fearful (II, 134), so that he can safely reveal his message. When he does so, he asserts that Troilus will die if he does not get her. Indeed, he will himself die also, cutting his own throat. "With that the teris burste out of his eyen." All this is obviously a carefully prepared bit of acting. It is followed by a long sentimental lament, which has the desired effect of increasing Criseyde's fear. He is, he asserts, not a "baude"; all he wants is "love of frendshipe," a "lyne" which Diomede also uses with great success later on (V, 185). Criseyde is very much aware of what Troilus and Pandarus actually want: "I shal felen what ye mene, ywis" (II, 387). But after Pandarus has driven his point home with a little false philosophy derived from Wisdom, 2, she pretends shock and astonishment. At this, Pandarus offers to go again, apparently hurt by her suspicions. But she catches his garment and agrees to "save" Troilus provided that she can also save her "honor." Criseyde has a great deal to say on this subject in the remainder of the poem, but the "honor" she seeks to preserve is not any kind of real honor; it is the honor of appearances, a middle class virtue not altogether harmonious with the "aristocratic" qualities some critics have wished to see in her behavior.

To reassure Criseyde, Pandarus offers a little picture of Troilus as he expresses his love. In a "gardyn, by a welle," a typical setting for first steps in idolatry,[23] Troilus confesses his "sins" to the god of love:

> "Lord have routhe upon my peyne
> Al have I ben rebell in myn entente,
> II, 525 Now *mea culpa*, lord, I me repente....

Again, Troilus is depicted lamenting sorrowfully in bed. So enthusiastic does Pandarus wax in his description that he slips a little, revealing the underside of his "process," although the "slip" may be intentional:

> II, 587 " Whan ye ben his al hool, as he is youre;
> Ther myghty god yit grauntne us se that houre."

---

23. See "The Doctrine of Charity," p. 44.

Criseyde's response to this is worth looking at again. She sees what Pandarus has in mind and pretends shock, but he is able to gloss over the situation with very little effort:

> "Nay, thereof spak I nought, a ha!" quod she;
> "As helpe me god, ye shenden every deel."
> "A! mercy, dere nece," anon quod he,
> "What so I spak, I mente nat but wel,
> By Mars, the god that helmed is of steel;
> Now beth nat wroth, my blood, me nece dere."
> "Now wel," quod she, "foryeven be it here."

What Pandarus means by "meaning well" has already been sufficiently revealed. And the oath he swears by Mars has its humor too, for Mars was caught in a trap not unlike that being prepared for Troilus. Criseyde's forgiveness is also interesting in view of the fact that she has never seen Troilus to know him. When she does see him shortly thereafter, the serpent lifts its head again, this time in a somewhat more calculating way. The lady's eyes betray her:

> Criseyda gan al his chere aspien,
> II, 650   And leet it so softe in hire herte synke,
> That to hire self she seyde: "who yaf me drynke?"

When Troilus saw Criseyde, he thought only of her "figure." In addition to his shape, however, she considers his prowess, estate, reputation, wit, and "gentilesse." These things all contribute to a vast self-satisfaction:

> But moost hire favour was, for his distresse
> II, 664   Was al for hire....

Ultimately, her love is self-love of the wrong kind, the kind which seeks the favor of Fortune.[24] The stars have something to do with it (II, 680-686). Criseyde will always be true to herself; she will always seek to escape from the fear of misfortune, no matter what effects her actions may have on others. If Troilus wished to turn the order

---

24. Self-love based on a knowledge of immortality leads ultimately to charity, but self-love based on worldly satisfaction may be thought of as the source of all the vices. Cf. *Piers Plowman and Scriptural Tradition*, pp. 27-28.

of things "up-so-doun" by submitting to Criseyde, she is equally determined that no husband will rule her (II, 750-756). Like the Wif of Bath, fourteenth century cousin of the Samaritan woman, she wants the "maistrie." The mastery of a man like Troilus, a man of prowess and renown, a prince, and a handsome prince at that, would be quite an achievement. The temptation of Criseyde is not unlike the temptation of Eve. Just as Eve was tempted to relinquish her obedience to God and to Adam by prospects of good fortune and dominion, Criseyde is tempted to forsake the obligations of her status for dominion over Troilus.

In the remainder of Book II, we are given some lessons "Messagerie," who accompanies "Foolhardinesse," "Flaterye," "Desyr," and "Meede" in the Temple of Venus (*PF*, 227-228). Pandarus instructs Troilus carefully in the art of writing an effective love-letter in which one says not necessarily what one actually thinks or feels, but what will have the desired effect on the recipient. A tear or two shed in the right places may help. Criseyde, having reluctantly permitted Pandarus to thrust Troilus' literary efforts in her bosom, knows well enough how to write an artfully ambiguous reply. With a quaint little ruse, Pandarus gets her to the window where she may see Troilus again, and again she reacts to externals:

> II, 1266 To telle in short, hire liked al in fere
> His person, his aray, his look, his chere.

Meanwhile, initial success makes the "fir" of Troilus' desire hotter than ever. And Pandarus arranges his little plot to bring the young couple together. The plot involves lying to Deiphebus, to Hector, to Helen, and to Paris, not to mention lying a little also to Criseyde. But Troilus is quite willing to cooperate, to feign sickness like his illustrious predecessor Amnon, so that he and Criseyde may come together, like Adam and Eve still earlier, under cover of lies.[25] When the company is assembled and Troilus' illness is being discussed, Criseyde once more reveals the pride and self-love upon which her "love" for Troilus is based:

---

25. Cf. "The Doctrine of Charity," pp. 25-26.

II, 1592 For which with sobre cheere hire herte lough;
For who is that nolde hire glorifie,
To mowen swiche a knyght don lyve or dye?

This is the love for which Troilus meets his death, the lady for whom he sacrifices his wisdom, his honor, and his obligations to his country. Criseyde is attractive enough externally, witty, graceful, amiable, and, above all, good to look at. But underneath her sentimental appeal, she is self-seeking and vain, an easy victim to the temptations which misled her great mother Eve. At the end of Book II, it is clear that Troilus has allowed his lower reason to be perverted to the ends of his sensual desire. Full of pleasurable thought, he has submitted to the god of love and allowed that god's priest to lead him into the deceit, the lies, and the hypocrisy of perverse worldly wisdom. In Books I and II the first two steps of the Fall, the first great tragedy, find both an internal and an external echo. The serpent has spoken and Eve has lent a willing ear.

In Book III there is a great deal of religious imagery. Literary historians are apt to say that it is "conventional," that it reflects the traditions of "courtly love." One has gone so far as to say that in the fourteenth century love had nothing to do with marriage, that it had a religion of its own which people like Chaucer found acceptable. There is no historical evidence for this sort of thing, however, and there is good reason to doubt that the term "courtly love" as it is usually understood has any validity at all. One distinguished historian has found it necessary to warn his readers that the average knight was "untroubled by the thought that to be truly chivalrous, he must be chronically amorous."[26] In any event, Chaucer certainly does not "accept" the behavior of Troilus. In fact, the religious imagery is intended to suggest the values from which the hero departs, and, at the same time, to furnish opportunity for ironic humor. Much criticism of medieval literature is vitiated by a certain pedantic seriousness on the part of the critics. Specifically, the religious imagery of Book III is used to show the corruption of Troilus' higher reason as he substitutes the "grace" of Criseyde for providence. Once this substitution is made, the fall is

---

26. Carl Stephenson, *Mediaeval Feudalism* (Ithaca, New York, 1942), p. 55.

complete. In the opening scene, both the "religion" and the humor are displayed. Troilus is busily concocting proper speeches to use when Criseyde approaches. But he is not very learned in the seductive arts, a man cut out perhaps for higher things. All he can do when she comes in is to mumble twice "mercy, mercy, swete herte!" But finally he explains that he is all hers, and suggests that now that he has spoken to her, he can do no more. There is nothing left but death. But Pandarus, shedding some well timed tears, digs Criseyde persistently in the ribs:

> III, 115 And Pandare wep as he to water wolde,
> And poked evere his nece newe and newe,
> And seyde: "wo bigon ben hertes trewe;
> For love of god, make of this thing an ende,
> Or sle us bothe at ones, or ye wende."

Criseyde prettily feigns not to understand. But after some preliminaries in which Troilus promises to put himself under her "yerde," and Criseyde stipulates that she will keep her "honour sauf" and at the same time retain the "sovereignete," she assures Troilus that he will for every woe "recovere a blisse." She then takes him in her arms and kisses him. This is a triumph for Pandarus, an event of truly liturgical significance for our little priest, the *elevatio* of his mass:

> Fil Pandarus on knees, and up his eyen
> To hevene threw, and held his hondes hye;
> III, 185 "Immortal god," quod he, "that mayst nat dyen,
> Cupide, I mene, of this mayst glorifie;
> And Venus, thow mayst maken melodie;
> Withouten hond, me semeth that in toune,
> For this miracle, ich here ech belle soune."

God, or at least Cupid, is rapidly drawing matters to what the Wif of Bath would call a "fruitful" eventuality. This is the "miracle" Pandarus had hoped for; soon perhaps he can prepare the way for his communion, a "revel" accompanied by the "melodie" of Venus like that enjoyed by Nicholas and Alisoun:

> "But I conjure the, Criseyde, and oon,
> And two, thow, Troilus, whan thow mayst goon,
> III, 195 That at myn hous ye ben at my warnynge,
> For I ful wel shall shape youre comynge.

Criseyde's "honour sauf," the two young people will, of course, engage in a little light conversation:

> "And eseth there youre hertes right ynough;
> And let se which of yow shal bere the belle
> To speke of love aright," — therwith he lough....

Troilus can walk any time now, and he is very anxious to talk — "how longe shal I dwelle, or this be don?" Evidently the few words spoken earlier were not really enough. There may be some other things to say before he dies, after all. Eleyne and Deiphebus approach, so that Troilus, to keep his "honour sauf," falls to groaning, "his brother and his suster for to blende." This is the son of a king whose country is in danger of destruction by a foreign enemy, a young man, physically strong, well bred, valiant in battle. But he has a fiddle to play too.

When Pandarus and Troilus are alone again, Pandarus decides to confess openly what he has been doing all along. Troilus will not now object. He has become, he says, "bitwixen game and ernest" a "meene" between a man and a woman. This sentimental statement has won for Pandarus many adherents in addition to the one being addressed. But the "game," as Book II abundantly illustrates, was always simply a pleasant and clever device to ameliorate his real intention, to put a "witty" and hence "harmless" face on the matter. The technique is still employed. Now he is serious, however. He admonishes Troilus solemnly and at length to keep his counsel, to treasure Criseyde's reputation. Troilus returns a solemn promise. The surfaces must be kept clean. As for Pandarus' pandaring, why it was only "gentilesse," "compassioun," "felawship," and "trist." To show that he too has these noble virtues, Troilus says that he will be glad to do the same for Pandarus. His sisters, for example, or Helen, might please that gentleman:

> "I have my faire suster, Polixene,
> III, 410   Cassandre, Eleyne, or any of the frape;
> Be she nevere so faire or wel yshape,
> Tel me which thow wilt of everychone,
> To han for thyn, and lat me thanne allone."

Whether any of the "frape" are suitable or not, Troilus is anxious to have Pandarus finish his business. He is thirstier than ever: "Parforme it out; for now is most nede." Morally, Troilus has descended to the level of Pandarus, who, at the outset, offered to get his own sister for Troilus.

After this first exchange of courtesies at Deiphebus' house, Pandarus keeps at his task "evere ylike prest and diligent" to "quike alwey the fir." He is no man to put the fire out as a true priest or a true friend should. In his "messagerie" he shoves "ay on," arranging the proposed conversation at his house. Troilus devises an excuse to explain any absences from his usual haunts. He will be at the temple of Apollo, a god whom medieval mythographers interpreted morally to suggest "truth."[27] But Troilus has long since abandoned any kind of truth. Pandarus invites Criseyde to supper, swearing that Troilus is not at his house (III, 570). Troilus, serving Apollo with diligence, is comfortably ensconced in an attic there, where he can see Criseyde approaching. After supper, when the time comes for her to go home, Fortune intervenes by making it rain. And Criseyde's fear again helps Pandarus; she is afraid of the storm. This storm may well be a literary reminiscence of another storm which sent Aeneas and Dido into a conveniently honorable cave; but storm or no storm, Criseyde knows why Pandarus wishes her to remain. She "koude as muche good as half a world."

Pandarus gets her safely bedded in an inner chamber and goes for Troilus. Still unmindful of Pallas and not very deeply concerned about Apollo, Troilus says a little prayer to "seint Venus." Now that he is ready to go into "hevene blisse," he will need her energies. But another ruse is necessary, another lie to get Troilus honorably into Criseyde's chamber. Never at a loss in such matters, Pandarus devises a little story of jealousy by means of which he succeeds in arousing Criseyde's "pitee" so that she agrees to let Troilus enter. When he kneels by the bed, she somehow fails to ask him to rise; she wants him within reach, sitting beside her (III, 967-973). But unfortunately the two lovers find it necessary to engage in considerable talk, to "speke of love," as Pandarus promised. They are impeded further by Troilus' confusion, which is brought on by his own lies. He is so troubled that he falls "a-swowne." Pandarus, ever ready with the sentimental remedy, tosses him in bed with Criseyde and disrobes him "al to his bare

---

27. See the tables of values for various deities in H. Liebeschütz, *Fulgentius Metaforalis* (Leipzig, 1926), pp. 56-57.

sherte," admonishing Criseyde to "pullen out the thorn." But even after Troilus recovers, more talk ensues before "sodeynly avysed," Troilus embraces Criseyde. Pandarus, at last satisfied that he is no longer needed, offers one bit of parting counsel: "swouneth nat now." When Criseyde perceives Troilus' "trouthe and clene entente," she makes him a joyful "feste." In the resulting "hevene," at a feast which is not exactly the Feast of the Lamb, Troilus appropriately sings a hymn. The hymn is a paraphrase of Dante on the Blessed Virgin Mary, in the original an aspect of the New Song of Jerusalem, but in Troilus' version a song to Cupid, who is ironically called "Charite." It is the grace of Cupid which Troilus praises, a grace which passes "oure desertes," a grace to which, at this time, he can offer only "laude and reverence." His higher reason has now lost sight of providence, of divine grace, and he has turned instead to the "grace" of the world, the "grace" of Fortune. Troilus is no longer a free agent, no longer a man. He is a pawn to Fortune, a star-crossed lover, Fortune's fool. The priest of Satan has led him to his highest sacrament.

But the "hevene" in which Trolius finds himself is not without its qualms, the "doutances" which he foresaw. The blessed are afraid in the midst of their bliss; they find

> III, 1326 That ech from other wende ben biraft,
> Or elles, lo, this was hir mooste feere,
> Lest al this thying but nyce dremes were.

Indeed, things of this kind are dreams, the fleeting appearances which are rounded with a sleep. The lovers are disturbed by the parting of night, a necessary adjunct to the deed of darkness (III, 1422-1442), and they curse the light of day.[28] Parting is torture for them, especially for

---

28. Night was traditionally associated with spiritual ignorance or blindness and with adversity. E.g., see Gregory, *Moralia, PL,* 75, 510 and 563; Alanus, *Distinctiones, PL,* 210, 876; Bernard Silvestris, *op. cit.,* p. 101. Conversely, the day was associated with spiritual understanding or reason. In Bk. III Troilus and Criseyde wish to hide from the light of reason and in doing so invite the night of adversity which descends upon them in Bk. IV. Anagogically, day and night suggest the opposition between Christ, who said "I am the day," and Satan. Both spiritual ignorance and adversity are works of Satan, so that the two "nights" are basically aspects of the same thing. For an early literary use of this convention, see Prudentius, "Hymnus matutinus."

the fearful Troilus (III, 1472-1491). Although he treasures Criseyde's affection more than "thise worldes tweyne," after he has left her, he is far from satisfied. If he was tormented by desire before, he is tormented more than ever now (III, 1536-1547; 1650-1652). As one old moralist put it, "And just as fire does not diminish so long as fuel is applied, but rather becomes hotter and more fervent when more fuel is cast upon it, so also the sin of lechery burns more fiercely the more it is exercised."[29] Pandarus brings the lovers together again occasionally,

> And thus Fortune a tyme ledde in joie
> Criseyde and ek this kynges sone of Troie.

This is the uncertain bliss, the fearful joy for which Troilus has sacrificed his "estat roial." To protect himself, he makes of his own feeling a cosmic force, this time paraphrasing Boethius on divine love, for which he substitutes a generalization of his idolatrous lust (III, 1744-1771). Troilus has made the pleasure he finds in Criseyde's bed the center of the universe, a center that actually rests within himself.

"But al to litel," as Chaucer says at the opening of Book IV, "lasteth swich joie, ythonked be Fortune." Fortune can "to fooles so hire song entune" that they are utterly misled. Troilus is one of these fools. If he called for night and cursed the day, he will now reap the consequences, for Night's daughters "that endeles compleynen evere in pyne" control him. Specifically, the "unwar strook" which unsettles his proud realm appears when he learns that Criseyde is to go to the Greek camp in exchange for Antenor. Thinking of her "honour," Troilus can do nothing to arrest the transaction. In despair he is like a bare tree (IV, 225-231), for the false leaves of vanity have blown away."[30] As he mourns alone in his chamber, he is like a "wylde bole," a beast rather than a man, since he has neglected his reason. He complains bitterly against Fortune, asking "is ther no grace?" He has honored Fortune above all other gods always (IV, 260-268); his subjection to it is complete and self-confessed. He also blames the "verrey lord of love," Cupid, whose "grace" but a short time ago was all-pervasive. Actually, the difficulty is of his own making. "Nothyng is wrecchid but whan thou wenest it."

29. Gérard of Liège, ed. Wilmart, *Analecta reginensia* (Vatican, 1933), p. 201.
30. Cf. "The Doctrine of Charity," p. 26.

Nothing destined him to subject himself to Fortune or to Cupid, but now his reason has lost "the lordshipe that it sholde have over sensualitee." Pandarus offers no real comfort. No person, he says, can "fynden in Fortune ay proprietee." He knows that Fortune is fickle and recommends expediency: he can find Troilus "an other." Moreover, absence, he affirms, "shal drive her out of herte." But Troilus is no mere sinner in the flesh. He is too far gone in idolatry, too much a loyal servant to Cupid to seek solace elsewhere. We may commend him as a "faithful" lover, and indeed his persistence shows a potentiality for devotion; but his is the inverted faith of idolatry which leads him lower than any casual anthologist like Diomede could descend.[31] The only feasible solution seems to him to be suicide, the final act of despair and the consummation of the irremissible sin against the Holy Spirit, against the true love for which he has substituted a false one. Criseyde's condition is almost as bad. With a touch of the comedy of manners developed in Book II, Chaucer shows her beset by her familiar companions, a group of chattering women full of the gossip of her departure. She thinks of herself "born in cursed constellacioun," for like the Wif of Bath, she is subject to the stars. She will do herself to death. Pandarus finds her with her "sonnysh heeris" falling untended about her ears, a condition which may be regarded in a person of her vanity as a "verray signal of martire."

In the process of arranging another meeting between the two lovers, Pandarus discovers Troilus in a temple, full of despair. The frustrated prince laments that "al that comth, comth by necessitee" and that to be lost is his "destinee." This conclusion is followed by a long supporting discussion based on the false reasoning of the speaker in the *De consolatione* and omitting Philosophy's answer. Chaucer's elaborate paraphrase suggests that answer and makes it clear that at this point Troilus has lost his free will almost completely. He can no longer offer any resistance to Fortune, for he has been led by his friendly Mephistopheles to fall into the error of wishing, in connection with his heaven of physical bliss: "Verweile doch! du bist so schön." From now on, he has no real choice. He is a slave to his desire, a victim of

---

31. On the lover's malady as an aspect of idolatry, see *Fulgentius Metaforalis*, p. 71.

his sin. Like old Januarie in the Merchant's Tale, or like Adam himself, Troilus has made a woman's love the controlling feature in his universe. When this love fails, "chaos is come again," a chaos resulting from the universalisation of a selfish passion. Again, Pandarus is of little help. His "wise" philosophy is mere shallow stoicism:

> IV, 1097 "Lat be, and thynk right thus in thi disese:
> That in the dees right as ther fallen chaunces,
> Right so in love ther corn and gon plesaunces."

The old doctrine of "happes aventurous" can afford no real help to Troilus, just as it cannot help the speaker in the *De consolatione*.

The lovers meet once more. Criseyde is so overcome by emotion that she swoons. Thinking her dead, Troilus offers to kill himself in Promethean defiance (IV, 1192 if.). He will conquer Fortune by committing suicide, a device attempted by Nero in the Monk's Tale, "Of which Fortune lough, and hadde a game." Since neither Jove nor Fortune is responsible for Troilus' plight, his defiance is a little hollow. It is especially empty when we consider the character of the lady whom Troilus finds more important than either his country or life itself. When she awakes, she finds a characteristic solution to their mutual problem. If reason fails, something else might help:

> IV, 1242 "But hoo, for we han right ynough of this,
> And lat us rise and streight to bedde go,
> And there lat us speken of oure wo."

Once in bed, Criseyde promises to return in ten days, in spite of Calkas, the Pandarus between the Greeks and the city. Troilus is doubtful, but she engages in a long and verbose promise of fidelity connected with that ancient symbol of fickle Fortune, the moon.[32] Her doctrine is, on the surface, a little better than that offered by Pandarus:

> "And forthi sle with resoun al this hete;
> Men seyn: 'the suffrant overcomth,' parde;
> IV, 1585 Ek, 'whoso wol han lief, he lief moot lete';
> Thus maketh vertu of necessite

---

32. For the moon as a symbol of Fortune's inconstancy, see Simund de Freisne, *Le roman de philosophie*, ed. Matzke, *SATF* (1909), ll. 105 ff.

> By pacience, and thynk that lord is he
> Of Fortune ay, that naught wol of hire recche;
> And she ne daunteth no wight but a wrecche."

Criseyde can quote Scripture and paraphrase Boethius, but it is too late. There is no stopping the "hete" of the fire lighted at the festival of Pallas now. Neither Troilus nor Criseyde has any notion of how to become "lord of Fortune." She knows that "love is thyng ay ful of bisy drede," but this fact is adduced as a reason why Troilus should remain faithful to her, not as something to discourage him from being a "wrecche." The book closes with one final touch of irony. Criseyde explains her love for Troilus:

> "For trusteth wel, that youre estat roial,
> Ne veyn delit, nor only worthinesse
> Of yow in werre or torney marcial,
IV, 1670
> Ne pomp, array, nobleye, or ek richesse,
> Ne made me to rewe on youre distresse;
> But moral vertu, grounded upon trouthe,
> That was the cause I first hadde on yow routhe.
> "Ek gentil herte and manhood that ye hadde,
> And that ye hadde, as me thoughte, in despit
> Every thyng that souned into badde,
> As rudenesse and poeplissh appetit,
> And that youre resoun bridlede youre delit, —
> This made, aboven every creature,
> That I was youre, and shal, whil I may dure."

"Who yaf me drynke?" This is indeed a beautiful little picture of what might have been if Troilus had loved Criseyde for a little more than her "figure" and competence in bed, if he had maintained the integrity of his lower reason and his "moral vertu," and if he had not debased his higher reason. It shows what might have been if Criseyde had actually been interested in "vertu," rather than in "his persone, his aray, his look, his chere." But as it stands, this little picture could not be more false, more distant from the events as Chaucer describes them. Troilus' courtship was hardly "grounded upon treuthe." Both lovers have insisted on an "up-so-doun" relationship directly contrary to reason. And Troilus very carefully renounced his denunciations of "poeplissh appetit." Criseyde can always think of some high-sounding doctrine to rationalize her situation, but she perverts it into so much idle talk. And idle talk cannot now save Troilus from pains "that passen every torment down in helle."

Book V is a picture of the Hell on earth which results from trying to make earth a heaven in its own right. In medieval terms, when the human heart is turned toward God and the reason adjusted to perceive God's Providence beneath the apparently fortuitous events of daily life, the result is the City of Jerusalem, radiant and harmonious within the spirit. But when the will desires one of God's creatures for its own sake, placing that creature above God, the reason can perceive only the deceptive mutability of Fortune, and the result, as one cloud-capp'd tower after another fades away, is the confusion and chaos of Babylon. Troilus has defied the gods and placed Criseyde above them. When adversity strikes, he becomes the "aimlessly drifting megalopolitan man" of the modern philosophers, the frustrated, neurotic, and maladjusted hero of modern fiction. The destiny he brought upon himself by preparing a table for Fortune, by substituting the feast of the flesh for the feast of the spirit, descends upon him. He is hypersensitive, sentimental, a romantic hopelessly involved in a lost cause. In this book Chaucer's ironic humor becomes bitter and the pathos of the tragedy profound.

It is Troilus who leads Criseyde out of Troy to meet the Greek convoy. All he can say at parting is "Now hold youre day, and do me nat to deye." Diomede recognizes the general feature of the situation at once, being an old hand at pulling finches. He takes Criseyde by the "reyne," and for a time the little filly is his, but she has no bridle that will hold her "to any certeyn ende." Like Polonius or Iago, Diomede is a man true to himself: "He is a fool that wol foryete hym selve." Since he has nothing to lose but words, he begins the old game played by Pandarus in Book II, but without circuitous preliminaries. Just as Pandarus requested at first love "of frendshipe," Diomede asks to be treated as a "brother" and to have his "frendshipe" accepted. He will be hers "aboven every creature," a thing which he has said to no other woman before. This is the first time. This is different. And sure enough, by the time they reach the Greek camp, Criseyde grants him her "frendshipe."

She has nothing to lose either and can be thoroughly depended upon to be to her own self true. In the Greek camp, Diomede does not neglect his opportunity: "To fisshen hire, he leyde out hook and lyne." On her "day," when she was supposed to return to Troilus, she welcomes Diomede as a "friend," and is soon lying to save appearances again:

> V, 975   "I hadde a lord, to whom I wedded was,
> The whos myn herte al was til that he deyde;
> And other love, as help me now Pallas,
> Ther in myn herte nys, ne nevere was."

Although she is enticingly ambiguous at the close of their conversation, she gives Diomede her glove (V, 1013). Her fear helps Diomede, just as it helped Pandarus; moreover, Diomede is a man of "grete estat," a conquest to please her vanity. That night she goes to bed

> Retornyng in hire soule ay up and down
> The wordes of this sodeyn Diomede,
> V, 1025   His grete estat, the peril of the town,
> And that she was allone and hadde nede
> Of frendes help. And thus bygan to brede
> The cause whi, the sothe for to telle
> That she took fully purpos for to dwelle.

"Wo hym that is allone." These are the same causes which led her to succumb to Troilus, for she was also fearful and "alone" in Troy, and Troilus was a man of "estat roial." Criseyde has not changed at all. She is beautiful and socially graceful, but fearful, susceptible to sentimental "pite," and "slydynge of corage." When the die is cast and Diomede has what he wants, she says "To Diomede algate I wol be trewe." She meant to be true to Troilus too, but she is actually faithful only to her own selfish desires of the moment. As one of the most distinguished of her critics has said, Criseyde "takes the easiest path."[33] She drifts in the world's winds, a "gilded butterfly." Her beauty is sensuous beauty of the world and her fickleness is the fickleness of Fortune. Neither Criseyde nor Diomede is capable of the idolatry of which Troilus is guilty, of the depths to which Troilus descends.

33. R. K. Root in the introduction to his edition, p. xxxii.

Left in Troy, Troilus curses all the gods together. including Cupid and Venus. But he is still a slave to his cupidity, a "great natural" with no place to hide his bauble. In bed he wallows and turns like "Ixion, in helle," for he has nothing but a pillow "tenbrace." His "lode sterre," substituted for a providence which affords *a way even in the sea, and a most sure path among the waves* (Wisdom, 14.3), has gone. In sleep, he is beset by nightmares, particularly by one in which he seems to fall "depe from heighe olofte," a symbolic revelation of his actual situation. Pandarus gets him off "to Sarpedoun," where singing and dancing are provided. But there is no "melodie" left for Troilus. The Old Song which he once sang in "heaven" has a bitter ring. He spends his time, like a jilted schoolboy, moping over his beloved's old letters. Hastening back to Troy, he hopes to find her there, but in vain. The places where he has seen or enjoyed Criseyde have a perverse fascination for him, and he must visit them again. First, having found an excuse to go into town, he visits her house. When he sees it, he exclaims:

> V, 540 "O paleys desolat,
> O hous of houses whilom best ihight,
> O paleys emty and disconsolat,
> O thow lanterne of which queynt is the light,
> O paleys, whilom day, that now art nyght....

The ironic pun in line 543 is a bitter comment on what it is that Troilus actually misses, and the change from day to night is, ironically again, the fulfillment of his own wish in Book III. The house is a shrine "of which the seynt is oute," the "up-so-doun" church of Troilus' love. Everywhere he goes, he finds memories of Criseyde. He becomes intensely self-conscious, aware of the eye of every passing stranger on the street. Everyone sees his woe:

> Another tyme ymaginen he wolde,
> V, 625 That every wight that wente by the weye
> Hadde of him routhe, and that they seyn sholde:
> "I am right sory Troilus wol deye."

His spirit is the painful focus of creation, protected neither by the "harde grace" of Cupid with which he surrounded it in Book III, nor by his false hopes that Criseyde may return. Each new rationalization leads only to more bitter frustration. On the walls of the city, the very wind itself is a wind that blows from Criseyde straight to him. It blows nowhere else, only where he stands, and as it blows it sighs, "allas, why twynned be we tweyne?" She lurks in the form of every distant traveller, even in a "fare-cart." At last, jealousy adds to his discomfort, and with it comes another nightmare. He tries an exchange of letters, but the letters only make matters worse, for the artfulness of Criseyde's epistolary style is now painfully apparent. One day he sees the brooch he gave her at parting on Diomede's armor. Now his worst fears and Cassandra's prophesy are confirmed: "Of Diomede have ye al this feeste?" (V, 1677). He no longer furnishes the "revel and the melodie "'for Criseyde; his goddess has withdrawn her grace, and there is nothing left now but death. In the depths of despair, Troilus goes out to seek death on the battlefield. His is no heroic defense of the city, no fulfillment of his political obligations, but a quest for revenge and for death to end his woes. This is the ultimate loneliness, a loneliness he has brought upon himself. In so far as the revenge is concerned. Troilus fails, fortunately for Criseyde, but "Ful pitously him slough the fierse Achille."

If Fortune "lough" at the self-destruction of Nero, Troilus can in spirit share that laughter as he rises above Fortune's realm. When the flesh with its cumbersome desires has been left behind, he see the foolishness of his earthly plight. There the "jugement is more clear, the wil nat icorrumped."

> And in hym self he lough right at the wo
> Of hem that wepten for his deth so faste,
> And dampned al oure werk that folweth so
> The blynde lust, the which that may nat laste;
> V, 1825   And sholden al oure herte on heven caste.

The laughter is the ironic laughter with which Chaucer depicts Troilus' "wo" from the beginning, a laughter which he, and Troilus from his celestial vantage point, would bestow on all those who take a sentimental attitude toward such love as that between Troilus and Criseyde. Chaucer adds an admonition to his audience to love Christ, for He "wyl falsen no wight." The wrong love, no matter what form it may take, leads to subjection to Fortune and to the old tragedy of Adam. If a man loves Christ, "lord he is of Fortune ay," a fact of which Troilus and Criseyde, both "payens," were unaware. But neither was willing to use the wisdom by means of which even a pagan like Job might triumph over the world's mutability.

To summarize, Chaucer's *Troilus* follows in its general outlines the pattern of Chaucerian tragic theory. Troilus subjects himself to Fortune by allowing himself to be overcome by the physical attractions of Criseyde. His fall is an echo of the fall of Adam. When his senses are moved, he proceeds to indulge in "pleasurable thought," allowing his lower reason to be corrupted as he cooperates with Pandarus in deceits and lies. Once his object is attained, he substitutes the grace of Cupid as manifested in Criseyde for providence, thus corrupting his higher reason and turning away completely from "love celestial." Not only is his relationship with Criseyde "up-so-doun," but the "regne" of his mind is inverted too. His "capability and godlike reason" are neglected, so that he becomes, like "Nabugodonosor," a "beast, no more." And as a beast, he is completely at Fortune's mercy. There is thus a remarkable logic in the events of Chaucer's tragedy, an intellectual coherence that is rooted firmly in Christian doctrine and Boethian philosophy. The tragedy of Troilus is, in an extreme form, the tragedy of every mortal sinner. The law of the "payens" arises again with each new generation, and it is only with a struggle that any individual can learn to follow the New Law. The "queynte world" continues to have its charms; so great are they, in fact, that

> Evermoore we moote stonde in drede
> Of hap and fortune in oure chapmanhede.

The old words of the prophet are painful in the memory. For the inevitability of providence, which is the inevitability of Chaucerian tragedy, is not especially pleasing to think of when the butterflies seem fair: *And you, that have forsaken the Lord, and have forgotten my holy mount, that set a table for Fortune, and offer libations upon it.* . . . It is not impossible that later tragic heroes may owe their fates, at least in part, to a like inspiration, and that the *de casibus* theme may imply more than the somewhat mechanical fall of men of high estate.

Princeton University

St. Foy Among the Thorns

Modern Language Notes 67:5 (May 1952), pp. 295-299.

In his discussion of the sources of *La chanson de sainte Foy*, Alfaric accuses the poet of taking liberties with the text of Scripture. The offending passage contains some imagery involving trees:

>   Proverbi diss reiz Salamon
>   55 Del pomer qi naiss el boisson
>   Cui clau la spina e·l cardon
>   E·ll albespin in eviron.
>   Achi met flors sus el somjon
>   E pois las pomas de sazon.
>   60 Mal forun li pagan Gascon
>   Qi desconnogron Deu del tron.
>   Lor umbra streins aqest planczon
>   De cui cantam esta canczon,
>   E pres en Deus dolz fruit e bon.

Alfaric remarks that "Le texte visé ne peut être qu'un fragment de dialogue du *Cantique des Cantiques* (II, 1-3)."[1] It could not be derived from the Book of Proverbs, a fact which, the editor says in his note, "montrerait qu'il [i.e., the poet] ne connaît pas très bien ce livre ni le *Cantique des Cantiques*."[2] The poet, however, does not say that he is quoting a passage from the Book of Proverbs, but that he is referring to a *proverbi* of Solomon. The implications of the modern word *proverb* may be misleading here, for a proverb or *parabola* was defined in the Middle Ages as a *similitudo* or figurative expression. Thus Bede, commenting on Prov. 1. 1, wrote: "*Parabolae Salomonis,* etc. *Parabolae* Graece, Latine dicuntur *Similitudines*; quod huic libro vocabulum Salomon ob id imposuit, ut sciremus altius, et non juxta litteram,

---

1. *La chanson de sainte Foy*, ed. E. Hoepffner and P. Alfaric (Paris, 1926), II, 30.
2. *Ibid.*, p. 90.

intelligere quae dicit; in quo Dominum significat per parabolas turbis fuisse aliquando locuturum."[3] When the poet says, therefore, that he is referring to a "proverb" of Solomon, he means simply that he has in mind a figurative expression attributed to Solomon which must be considered for its higher meaning or *nucleus* rather than for its literal meaning or *cortex*. He is not necessarily referring to the Book of Proverbs specifically. It does not follow, therefore, that the poet was ignorant of those books of the Bible attributed to Solomon.

Alfaric goes on to say, in his prefatory discussion, that the poet took further liberties with the Scriptures :

> Le chansonnier applique au "pommier" qui se dresse "parmi les arbres de la forêt" ce qui est dit du "lis" s'élevant "au milieu des épines." Il attribue en outre à Salomon des détails de son cru tels que les "chardons," les "aubépines" et les "fleurs" qui feront place aux "pommes." Or, le texte qu'il utilise appartient à la Bible, il se présente comme une parole divine dictée par l'Esprit Saint. Si le chansonnier garde une telle liberté à l'égard d'un livre canonique, il doit user avec une indépendance encore bien plus grande d'écrits ecclésiastiques qui n'ont pas la même autorité.[4]

The relevant verses in the Canticum read: *Ego flos campi et lilium convallium. Sicut lilium inter spinas, sic amica mea inter filias. Sicut malus inter ligna silvarum, sic dilectus meus inter filios. Sub umbra illius, quem desideraveram, sedi, et fructus eius dulcis gutturi meo.* The editor of the poem adds in his note that the poet has altered the meanings of "shadow" and "fruit" in this passage.[5] But here again it is possible, I believe, to take a somewhat milder view of the poet's activity.

In the first place, the reference to Solomon is not a quotation, not a reproduction of words inspired by the Holy Spirit, but a reference to a *figura* in which the poet is interested. He does not pretend to quote the letter. When almost any figurative passage in the Bible is regarded for its higher meaning, it immediately suggests other

---

3. *Super parabolas Salomonis, PL,* 91, 937. For the New Testament reference, see Matt. 13.13; Mar. 4. 11–12.

4. *La chanson,* II, 30.

5. *Ibid.,* p. 91.

figurative passages of similar import, so that the verses from the Song of Songs alluded to are related under the *cortex* to many other verses in Scripture having to do with trees, flowers, and fruits. It is likely that the poet had in mind some of these other passages as well as the one directly alluded to. The *nucleus* of the passage in the Canticum may be found in the commentary of St. Gregory, where the apple tree represents Christ, or the Tree of Life, and produces nourishing fruit. This passage is not quoted as a "source" for the poem, but as evidence for the character of traditional exegesis with which the poet was probably familiar:

> Ligna sylvestria esui hominum habiles fructus non gignunt; malus vero quod gignit, congrue et salubriter homines edunt. Merito ergo per malum Christus, per sylvestria vero ligna caeteri homines figurantur; quia in solo Christo cibum salutis quoties quaerimus invenimus.[6]

But the *planczon* the poet describes is not Christ; it is St. Foy. The implication is clearly that St. Foy is like Christ, a tree which produces good fruit. The precedent for calling a follower of Christ a fruitful tree is, however, Scriptural, for in Matt. 7. 17 we read: *Sic omnis arbor bona fructus bonos facit, mala autem arbor malos fructus facit.* Those who follow or imitate Christ are fruitful trees which produce good works. The unfaithful and heretical are evil trees which produce evil fruit, or evil works.[7] The poet says that the tree is surrounded by spines, as the lily is surrounded by spines in the Canticum. Since the *lilium inter spinas* of the Bible represents the church, or the members of the church, and the spines are those who "solis verbis Christum confitentur, operibus vero nihil nisi humanas sollicitudines sectantur,"[8] the implication is that St. Foy, although fruitful herself, is surrounded by persons of little faith. Referring again to Matt. 7, we find in verse 16 the question: *Nunquid colligunt de spinis uvas aut de tribulis ficus?* Bede comments: "Nullus sapientium ab haereticis vel infidelibus flagrantiam sanctitatis, aut dulcedinem poterit invenire

---

6. *Super cantica*, PL, 79, 495.
7. Cf. Bede's discussion, PL, 92, 38.
8. St. Gregory, *op. cit.*, 494.

veritatis."⁹ Alfaric calls attention in his note to the relevance of Eccles. 24. 17–20: *Quasi cedrus exaltata sum in Libano*, etc., which refers to the good Christian.¹⁰ We may add that the cedar of Lebanon and the *carduus* are contrasted in 4 Reg. 14. 9 and 2 Par. 25. 18. The poet's final addition, the whitethorn, may be a reminiscence of Bar. 6. 69–70: *Nam sicut in cucumerario formido nihil custodit, ita sunt dii illorum lignei et argentei et inaurati. Eodem modo et in horto spina alba, supra quam omnis avis sedet; similiter et mortuo proiecto in tenebris similes sunt dii illorum lignei et inaurati et inargentati.* In contrast to the thorns and thistles, St. Foy is said to offer flowers first and afterward fruit *de sazon*. In his note on *de sazon*, Hoepffner concludes that "C'est la qualité des fruits qui importe au poète, et non pas le fait qu'ils mûrissent à temps."¹¹ Alfaric translates "de bonne qualité," but calls attention in his note to Ps. 1. 3, where a tree is said to give fruit *in tempore suo*. Considering the character of the imagery being developed, the psalm is probably relevant, for the tree in it represents the Tree of Life, or Christ, like the *malus inter ligna silvarum*. When the tree is Christ, its fruit is the Holy Spirit,¹² and when the tree is an individual living in imitation of Christ its fruit is charity. The phrase *de sazon* thus reinforces the *proverbi* with which the passage begins.

Flowers which lead to the fruit of good works appear in Cant. 7. 12: *videamus si floruit vinea, si flores fructus parturiunt, si floruerunt mala punica.* The flowers are an indication of the fruitful works of the perfect, who nourish those around them:

> Videt etiam si floruerunt mala punica; quia perfectos quosque respicit, et quid utilitatis in proximis habeant, quasi in floribus fructum cognoscit, de quibus bene sequitur: *Ibi dabo tibi ubera mea.* In malis punicis dat Sponso sponsa ubera; quia in perfectis vivit charitas gemina, ex qua dum infirma membra in Ecclesia nutriunt, quasi Christum lactant, quem in minimis suis esse praesentem cognoscunt.¹³

9. *PL*, 92, 38.
10. See Rabanus, *PL*, 109, 929.
11. *La chanson*, I, 264.
12. See St. Augustine on Ps. 1 (Gaume ed.), c. 3.
13. St. Gregory, *op. cit.*, 538.

But the heretics and disbelievers, or the thorny flora around St. Foy, seek to stifle her in their shade. The shadow in Cant. 2. 3 is the Holy Spirit, the shadow of the Tree of Life: "Umbra Christi protectio est Spiritus sancti."[14] The shadow in the poem is obviously an opposite to this one; however, this shadow also has a Scriptural basis, for Scriptural signs tend to have two sides. Thus there are several references in the Bible to an *umbra mortis*. St. Gregory says of one of these, "Per umbram mortis, oblivio debet intelligi; quia sicut mors interimit vitam, ita oblivio extinguit memoriam. Quia ergo apostata angelus aeternae oblivioni traditur, umbra mortis obscuratur."[15] Returning to the poem, we see that the pagans attempted to stifle St. Foy with oblivion, or forgetfulness of God, the opposite of grace or the Holy Spirit. They were men *Qi desconnogron Deu del tron*. But they were not successful, so that God obtained from her sweet and good fruit, the fruit of charity. In fact, she performed the highest act of charity, and in the process she nourished those around her.

In the passage we have considered, the poet employed a device that was not uncommon in the Middle Ages. Related figurative expressions from Scripture were frequently combined so as to make a new *pictura* not apparent on the literal level of the Bible itself. The resulting combination had the advantage of economy of expression combined with a very wide area of connotation.[16] The lines do not reveal either an ignorance of Scripture or a disrespect for its language. On the contrary, the poet's description of St. Foy among the thorns shows not only an easy familiarity with the Bible, but also a knowledge of traditional exegesis. At the same time, his picture is vivid as well as meaningful, the product of no little poetic skill.

D. W. Robertson, Jr.

Princeton University

---

14. *Ibid.*, 495.
15. *Moralia, PL*, 75, 642. Cf. 912, 966, etc.
16. Several examples are given in "The Doctrine of Charity in Mediaeval Literary Gardens," *Speculum*, XXVI (1951), 24-49. For the principle, see p. 35.

Amors de terra Lonhdana

By D. W. Robertson, Jr.

Studies in Philology 49:4 (October 1952): 566-582.

Fifty years ago Carl Appel suggested that the surviving poems of Jaufré Rudel are addressed to the Blessed Virgin Mary rather than to an earthly mistress.[1] But the response to this theory was not satisfactory, so that in 1915 Appel tentatively withdrew it.[2] In the same year, Jeanroy, while acknowledging a "teinte mystique" in the poems, objected to Appel's theory on the grounds that it is "inconciliable avec cette idée, exprimée avec insistance, d'un lointain voyage à enteprendre et avec certaines expressions qui, employées à propos de la reine du ciel, eussent frisé le blasphème." These expressions are *Dins vergier o sotz cortina* (II. 13); *la cambra el jardis* (V. 41); *anc no·m dis ver ni no·m menti* (VI. 29-30).[3] Finally, Jeanroy could not understand why love for the Blessed Virgin should be expressed obscurely. In 1938 Mario Casella considered the poems as expressions of love in terms of Augustinian psychology, but his description of that psychology is insufficiently precise, so that his application is not altogether convincing.[4] A new theory was recently offered by Grace Frank to the effect that the object of the poet's love is not a woman at all, but the Holy Land.[5] This theory provoked an immediate and lengthy response from Leo Spitzer, who alleged certain

---

1. "Wiederum zu Jaufre Rudel," *Archiv,* CVII (1901), 338-349.
2. *Bernart von Ventadorn* (Halle, 1915), LXVIII.
3. *Les chansons de Jaufré Rudel, Cfma,* p. vi. This edition is used in the present study.
4. "Poesia e storia," *Archivo storico italiano,* XCVI (1938), IV, 153-199. The first part of this article, *ibid.,* III, 3-63, is devoted to the poetry of Guillaume IX, which is treated in the same way.
5. "The Distant Love of Jaufré Rudel," *MLN,* LXVII (1942), 528-534.

misreadings in Mrs. Frank's exposition and offered a theory of his own. For Spitzer, the love expressed by Rudel is typical of that he finds in the troubadours generally. It is a love "qui ne veut posséder, mais jouir de cet état de nonpossession, amour-*Minne* contenant aussi bien le désir sensuel de 'toucher' à la femme vraiment 'femme' que le chaste éloignement, amour chrétien transformé sur le plan séculier, qui veut 'have *and* have not.'"[6] In this connection, it should be observed that Jeanroy failed to discover romantic love in the poetry of the troubadours, and indeed, it is entirely inconsistent with the vein of piety which runs through the poetry of Rudel.[7] In reply to Spitzer's essay, Mrs. Frank reasserted her own theory with no little vigor, calling special attention to "the spiritual exaltation and mystical devotion of those who preached the crusades and of those who sought to gain an everlasting life in Paradise by taking part in them."[8] As she points out, it is fairly clear that at least some of the poems are connected with the crusades. The spiritual exaltation to which she calls attention may be worth further exploration.

It is fortunately possible to simplify the problem of the types of love in medieval Christian literature. Any love was thought of as an aspect of one of two opposite loves, charity and cupidity. It was not only possible but desirable to love a woman for her virtue, for her reflection of the Image of God in her actions, or for her potentiality for virtue.[9] This love was an aspect of charity. It was also possible to love

---

6. *L'amour lointain de Jaufré Rudel,* "University of North Carolina Studies in the Romance Languages and Literature," V (Chapel Hill, 1944), p. 2. A. R. Nykl's review of this work, *Speculum,* XX (1945), 252-258, seeks to make the poet's love somewhat more earthy.

7. For Jeanroy's generalization, see *La poésie lyrique des troubadours* (Toulouse, 1934), II, 96.

8. "Jaufré Rudel, Casella and Spitzer," *MLN,* LXIX (1944), 526-531.

9. For the two loves, see St. Augustine, *De doctrina Christiana,* III, 16 (10). A good twelfth century account of the proper love of one's neighbor may be found in Hugh of St. Victor, *De sacramentis,* PL, 176, 529 ff. It has been maintained that the Provençal poets worked out a compromise between the two loves, but a study of St. Augustine's definition will show that this is hardly possible. That the troubadours, or at least some of them, were aware of the distinction is clear in Peire of Auvergne, I, iv, ed. Zenker, p. 735. See Appel's

a woman for her physical attractions, for her wealth, or for her social graces. This love was an aspect of cupidity. Everyone recognized that most men have certain inclinations toward the wrong love where women are concerned, and the accepted solution to this difficulty was marriage. In marriage a legitimate combination of sexual love and charitable love could be effected without difficulty. In a feudal society, we should add, a bond of love was supposed to exist between a vassal and his overlord, a love that extended to his overlord's wife. Sometimes, indeed, the overlord was a lady. This last love was a part of the natural hierarchy of creation, extending from God downward to the lowest creatures and upward through the hierarchy to God. It was, therefore, a charitable love. There is no reason why we should not expect to find expressions of love of all of these types, both good and evil, in a body of poetry as extensive as that of the troubadours. But Jaufré Rudel says that cupidity is opposed to his love (II. 24-25), and, moreover, that his love is formed by God (V. 36-37). It follows, unless we take these remarks as so much decorative rhetoric, that the love expressed in the poems is an aspect of charity. It can be neither straightforward sensual love nor an effete variation of it such as that described by Spitzer.

Mrs. Frank's suggestion that the object of the poet's love is a personification of the Holy Land has a great deal to be said for it, if we consider the Holy Land as "Jerusalem" and give the word its medieval connotations. Interpreted as a word, *Jerusalem* meant "visio pacis," a concept which conveys the notion of that ultimate good which everyone may be said to seek. Taken as a thing, as an actual city, Jerusalem had tropological, allegorical, and anagogical significances. Tropologically, Jerusalem represents the soul suffused with charity and at peace with the world, whatever good or evil fortune it may bring. Allegorically, it is the church of the faithful on earth, and anagogically it is the Celestial City of ultimate peace and security. For most persons individually and at most times socially, Jerusalem is a *terra lonhdana*,

---

comment, *Bernart von Ventadorn,* LXX. That some of them celebrated the delights of the flesh without reference to God or to any other serious philosophical subject is fairly obvious. See Marcabru, XXXVII, ii, iii, ed. Dejeanne, pp. 178-179. It is a mistake, I think, to suppose that the troubadours all wrote about the same thing.

or, in Scriptural terms, a *terra longinqua*, for the world is characteristically Babylonian. The poems of Jaufré Rudel seem to be connected with a crusade, an earthly symbol of man's pilgrimage toward Jerusalem and his struggle against Babylonian, or pagan, iniquity. Thus an expression of love for the Holy Land, not as a place "wo die Zitronen blühn," but as a symbol of man's better destiny, would be appropriate to them. Feminine personifications of Jerusalem in the form of personifications of the Church were common in medieval art,[10] and the Church is personified as the lady of the Canticum, reflections of which appear in Rudel's poems. But the Blessed Virgin Mary was also a sign of the Church Celestial, so that the Canticum was interpreted to apply to her as well as to the Bride of Christ. Indeed, she is sometimes called Jerusalem: "Quid igitur verius Jerusalem quam gloriosa Virgo, in qua pax pectoris et pax aeternitatis?"[11] Mrs. Frank's theory thus has certain points of contact with the older theory of Appel. It is possible that the *terra lonhdana* may be the Holy Land or Jerusalem, and, at the same time, that the poet's love may be the Blessed Virgin. But we must determine whether the poems are consistent in detail with this possibility.

In this connection, it is necessary to determine first whether Rudel regarded his works as "poems" or merely as pleasing songs. Theoretically, a poem in the twelfth century, as distinguished from a mere song, contained two levels of meaning: a more or less obscure *cortex* of surface meaning beneath which lay a *nucleus* of truth. This convention was a standard feature of twelfth century literary education and was extremely widespread.[12] That Rudel did have this convention in mind seems clear from what he says in his poem *No sap chantar qui so non di*. There he says that

    3. *Ni conois de rima co·s va*
        Si razo non enten en si.

The *razo* here is the underlying meaning, the implied "gloss" or *nucleus* which we must understand if we are to enjoy the poem fully:

10. See the remarks of F. J. E. Raby, *Christian Latin Poetry* (Oxford, 1927), 357.
11. Alanus de Insulis, *Elucidatio in Cantica, PL*, 210, 91.
12. The convention is discussed at length in "Some Medieval Literary Terminology, with Special Reference to Chrétien de Troyes," *SP*, XLVIII (1951), 669-692.

> 6 Com plus l'auziretz, mais valra.

On the surface this poem, as we shall see, is paradoxical, employing the conventional device of *aenigma*. To make sure that the reader does not abandon it as a mere play on words, the poet warns:

> 31 Bos es lo vers, qu'anc no·i falhi,
> Et tot so que·i es ben esta;
> E sel que de mi l'apenra
> Gart se no·l franha ni·l pessi.

That is, the poem is so arranged that it has a coherent *razo* beneath the obscure surface, where everything is placed correctly. Lord Bertrand and the Count in Toulouse, we are assured, will find a worthwhile meaning in it. Jeanroy's objection that love for the Blessed Virgin would not be expressed obscurely fails to take into consideration the literary conventions of the twelfth century which are clearly reflected in this poem. Whatever meaning the poem may have is deliberately obscured. There is a strong possibility that the other poems by Rudel which have survived reflect the same convention. They are not altogether clear on the surface. In view of the obvious piety in the poems, it is also probable that the surface obscurity is effected by the use of conventional scriptural imagery. If the assumption that the imagery is for the most part scriptural in origin lends coherence to the poems which they do not display otherwise, we must accord the resulting explanation the status of a reasonable, if not an altogether demonstrable theory.

The first poem in Jeanroy's edition opens with the reference to the effect of spring on the poet. When the nightingale in the leaves gives and receives love, sings joyfully, and regards his mate frequently, when the waters are clear and the meadows smiling with new life, the poet feels great joy in his heart. Traditionally, in many countries and at many times, spring has been regarded as a stimulus to sexual love. But the last stanza of our poem is an admonition to abandon earthly delights:

> E qui sai rema deleytos
> E Dieu non siec en Belleen
> No sai cum ja mais sia pros
> Ni cum ja venh' a guerimen,

> *Qu'ieu sai e crei, mon escien,*
> *Que selh qui Jhesus ensenha*
> *Segur' escola pot tener.*

It is thus probable that the poet had in mind at the outset a kind of love consistent with Christ's teaching. In the Middle Ages spring was a sign of the Resurrection, a promise of the Resurrection of the Just, and a token of the vivifying influence of the Holy Spirit, who, in human terms, is love and joy, "amor et gaudium."[13] Some of these meanings are familiar in the famous hymn of Fortunatus, in which the nightingale also has a place.[14] The observation that the *riu son clar* may be compared with a passage from the *Eructavit* (ed. Jenkins, 1985-1988):

> Li biaus ruz d'icele fontaine
> Qui le siègle conduit et maine,
> C'est la vertuz saint esperite
> Par cui Dex entre nos habite....

The same figure appears in Gautier d' Arras, *Eracle,* 6329-6330,

> Si com li rius de la fontaine
> Sourt et descent de toi [sc. "Biaus sire Deus"].

The fountain is Christ, and the waters are the living waters which renovate the meadow of the church, or more personally, inspire the individual with the proper love.[15] In the light of these conventions, the

---

13. On the Holy Spirit, see Hugh of St. Victor, *De sacramentis, PL,* 176, 229. The significance of spring developed from passages in the Bible like Cant. 2. 11-12, or Matt. 24. 32. See Rabanus, *De universo, PL,* 111, 302-303, for a full discussion, and the remarks of St. Bernard in a sermon, *PL,* 183, 1055-1061. The convention appeared in literature at a very early date. See Minucius Felix, *Octavius,* XXXIV, 10-12.

14 . Raby, *op. cit.,* pp. 92-93. Cf. Strecker, *Cambridger Lieder,* no. 22, pp. 62-63.

15. The meadow is conventional. See Rabanus, *De universo, PL,* 111, 529: "Pratum mystice intellegi potest sancta Ecclesia, vel Scriptura sacra, in quibus flores diversarum virtutum reperiuntur, et pratus spiritalis piis animalibus, hoc est, fidelibus hominibus praeparatur. Unde sponsa in Cantico canticorum dicit: *Flores apparuerunt in terra,* id est, in otio fidei et justitia floruerunt in mundo, crescente Ecclesia. Hine item ipsa doctoribus dicit: *Fulcite me floribus, quia amore langueo;* ac si diceret: consolamini me exemplis seu incipientium, seu terminantium viam salutis, dum adhuc in hujus peregrinationis taedio amore supernae visionis languesco." For the waters in this meadow, see Ecclus. 24. 42, and Rabanus, *PL,* 109, 944.

poet may be thought of as saying, in effect, that the thought of the Resurrection and its promise, and of the vivifying influence of the Holy Spirit on earth fills his heart with joy.

In the second stanza, the poet, inspired by his vision of God's love as suggested by the spring atmosphere, desires to partake of that love. Specifically, he wishes for a friendship which will bring a joy worth more than any other, the joy of the blessed which is the "amor et gaudium" associated with spring. This love is personified as a lady, who, if she regards him favorably, will grant him her love. She is *gras, delgat, e gen* and without any kind of fault, *ses ren que·y descovenha*, and her love is *bon' ab bon saber*. These qualifications are eminently suited to the Blessed Virgin, whose cult was becoming increasingly popular in the twelfth century. Actually, she is the only woman without taint of sin, *ses ren que·y descovenha*. Moreover, she was widely considered to be the most accessible source of the water of grace. St. Bernard went so far as to call her the "aquaeductus" through which this water, arising from the fountain which is Christ, descends to earth.[16] It is most appropriate, therefore, that Rudel, having expressed a desire to partake of God's love, should turn to its most convenient source. He is disturbed both when he is awake and when dreams come to him in sleep. It is then, in his dreams, that he has a marvellous experience, for then he possesses his love, both giving and receiving joy. But the beauty of his love (in dreams) is of little use to him, for no one can help him obtain it when he does not enjoy its sweetness. Sleep is a common sign for contemplation. As the *Allegoriae in sacram Scripturam*, a twelfth century commonplace book, tells us, "*Dormitio* est quies vitae, ut in Cantico: *Ego dormio, et cor meum vigilat*, id est, in contemplatione quiesco."[17] And it is only through contemplation that the poet, or anyone else, may visualize the joys of the celestial realm. The precedent for the amorous imagery involved here is the Bible itself, for the most extended picture

---

16. *In nativitate BMV, PL*, 183, 439-440.
17. *PL*, 112, 913. This work is erroneously ascribed to Rabanus in Migne. Other meanings for sleep are given: torpor, mors, in peccatum cadere, concubitu. None of these is appropriate here. Cf. Alanus, *Elucidatio, PL*, 210, 85, and Honorius, *Expositio in Cantica, PL*, 172, 434.

of the fruition of charity is the Canticum, which was, and still is regarded not only as an epithalamium for the marriage of Christ and the Church, but also as an expression of the joy of the soul united with God. Spiritual joy was commonly described in terms of the marriage bed. Alanus, for example, speaks of it in these terms: "Haec est thalamus Dei, palatium Christi, lectus coelestis sponsi. Ibi sponsa, id est anima, requiescit cum Christo sponso suo."[18] The third stanza of Rudel's poem may be seen as an expression of his vision of celestial love in the New Jerusalem and of his anxiety that the joy thus perceived is remote. The general pattern of thought is traditional. St. Gregory describes it as follows: "Alii vero, a carnalibus vitiis liberi, aut longis jam fletibus securi, amoris flamma conpunctionis lacrymis inardescunt, coelestis patriae premia cordis oculis proponunt, supernis jam civibus interesse concupiscunt. Dura eis apparet servitus, longitudo peregrinationis suae."[19] The idea of a distant voyage to be undertaken is certainly far from inconsistent with the expression of love for the Blessed Virgin.

The fourth stanza indicates that any efforts the poet makes to rush to his beloved are futile. His horse moves so slowly that he almost despairs of reaching her, but he knows that love inspires her to wait for him. This retreat of the lady is appropriate as an expression of the unattainability of the fruition of charity on earth. The horse is a conventional sign for the flesh, whose slow progress through the world here impedes the spirit. [20] Only a realization of the infinite mercy of his lady keeps the poet on the proper path. But, as the fifth stanza reveals, there are reasons why he should happily endure his separation from his beloved, *per so quar vou mo mielhs queren*. This does not mean that he is abandoning his love or his lady, but simply that it is to his advantage to endure separation. The slow progress of the horse through the temporal realm is a necessary purgation before the joy of the next may be realized, "quam purgationem," as St. Augustine observed in an extremely influential discussion, "quasi ambulationem

---

18. *Summa de arte praedicatoria*, PL, 210, 180. For the "chamber of love," cf. the *Eructavit*, ed. Jenkins, ll. 1560-1562.
19. Hom. X in Ezech., PL, 76, 1070.
20. See *Allegoriae*, PL, 112, 916; Gregory, *Moralia*, PL, 76, 588.

quadam, et quasi navigationem ad patriam esse arbitremur."[21] The poet, assured of the mercy of his lady, can pursue this journey in hope. She calls him, accepts him, and turns him to *bon esper*.[22] The poem closes with the admonition already quoted. If one does not follow Christ in Bethlehem, salvation is in doubt, but he who is instructed by Christ follows a sure way. Just as Christ was brought to the world through Mary in Bethlehem, so He may be brought to the poet through Mary, the most beautiful and gracious of women. It is evident, I think, that when the poem is interpreted in some such fashion as this, it becomes a coherent and logically developed statement of sentiments which must have been rather popular in the twelfth century.

The opening of II is very similar to that of I except that attention is centered on *lo rius de la fontana*. The eglantine is blooming, and the song of the nightingale inspires the poet to sing of his own love. His subject is stated specifically at the beginning of the second stanza:

> *Amors de terra lonhdana,*
> *Per voz totz lo cors mi dol ...*

Here the expression *terra lonhdana* may well reflect the Biblical *terra longinqua*, where the distance is that between Babylon and Jerusalem.[23] The love expressed by the poet may well be that of Cant. 2.5 or 5.8: *in amore langueo*. That is, the spring season with its clear streams, flowers, and singing birds suggests the Holy Spirit, the New Law, and the *canticum novum* (Ps. 32. 3, etc.) in which he feels that he should participate. His heart longs for the delights of Jerusalem, where he will experience the joy of love *dinz vergier o sotz cortina*. Jeanroy, as we have seen, objected to this language in a devotional poem. But it, too, is scriptural. The garden appears in Cant. 5. 1 : *Veniat dilectus meus in*

---

21. *De doct.,* I, 10 (10).
22. Gaston Paris, "Jaufre Rudel," *Revue historique,* LIII (1893), 239, note, considered the *bon guiren* of this stanza to be God. P. Cravayat, "Les origines du troubadour Jaufré Rudel," *Romania,* LXXI (1950), 177, contends that it is not God, "mais son suzerain qui va lui permettre de suivre Dieu a Bethléem." But be does not integrate this idea with the remainder of the poem.
23. E.g., see Is. 39. 3; 3 Reg. 8. 41-43, where the expression appears in the prayer of Solomon at the dedication of his temple, which is a common sign of the church, or, anagogically, the celestial city. In Ier. 46. 27, the Lord promises to save his people from a distant land: *Quia ecce salvabo te de terra longinqua.*

hortum suum. Taken anagogically, this verse applies to the joys of the faithful in heaven. To quote Alanus, "*hortum,* id est in coelestem paradisum; quae est hortus deliciarum, quae est vita aeterna."[24] And *cortinas* are a prominent feature of the Tabernacle of Moses (Exod. 36. 8 ff.), which, like the Temple of Solomon, represents the church on any of its various levels. The delights envisaged may be those of the fruition of charity in Jerusalem, *ab dezirada companha.*

In the third stanza, the poet describes his ardor, which is increased by the fact that the power of consummating his love has always been refused. As one authority on the love of charity describes this condition, "Porro amor languor est, dum amans ex desiderii dilatione torquetur, dum sponsi suspirat in amplexus."[25] Meanwhile, there is no woman—neither Christian, Jew, nor Saracen—who is more beautiful than the poet's lady, *ni Deus non la vol.* "Quae pulchra inter mulieres," writes Alanus, "nisi Virgo mater quae prae caeteris privilegiata est donis spiritualibus, mater est Dei sacrarium Spiritus sancti, sigillum virginitas, speculum humilitas?"[26] The grief to be cured by his love, the poet says, is sharper than a thorn. Charity cures those discomforts which are usually symbolized by a thorn: sin, the pain of sin, and eternal torment.[27] Finally, the poet sends his poem to those about to depart on a crusade.[28] A crusade, as I have already suggested, is a concrete expression of the armed pilgrimage which constitutes a Christian life.[29]

24. *Eluc. in Cant., PL,* 210, 84; Cf. Honorius, *Expos. in Cant., PL,* 172, 431. Cf. the *Eructavit,* ll. 1540-1545. Gardens are discussed at some length in "The Doctrine of Charity in Medieval Literary Gardens," *Speculum,* XXVI (1951), 24-49.

25. Petrus Blesensis, *De amicitia Christiana,* LXIII, ed. Davy (Paris, 1932), p. 570. Cf. St. Bernard, *Sermones in Cantica, PL,* 183, 1026.

26. *Eluc. in Cant., PL,* 210, 49. Manna, among other things, means "beatitudo coelestis," an appropriate reward for one who gains the love of man's best mediator, as she was thought to be. See *Allegoriae, PL,* 112, 995.

27. For various meanings of *spina,* see Alanus, *Distinctiones, PL,* 210, 951-952.

28. See Grace Frank, "Distant Love," pp. 530-531.

29. Conventionally, the good Christian is an exile in the world. See Bede, *PL,* 93, 52; Hugh of St. Victor, *Didascalicon* (ed. Buttimer), III, XIX, p. 69; Peter Lombard on Ps. 118. 19, *PL,* 191, 1054. For a discussion, see Marc Bloch, *La société féodale* (Paris, 1939, 1940), I, 138. Specifically, he travels from Babylon, the country of his exile, to Jerusalem, his true home. This journey is directed by

In III, the poet tells us that around him there are enough *del chan essenhadors*—meadows and gardens, trees and flowers, birds singing in the sweet season. The song of creation pictured here is similar to that described by the author of the *Eructavit* (ll. 2047 ff.). The New Song of the New Man, the song of praise sung by those who follow the lesson of the Resurrection is suggested by the new season. But the song itself remains tantalizing for one who languishes for the consummation of his love. To the poet, as he says in the second stanza, those loves which permit one to give and to receive joy, mere earthly loves, that is, are as pipes to shepherds or as flutes to children, mere playthings. The consolations of earthly desires seem trivial. He knows that his lady has good will toward her lover who is in *greu logau,* in the wilderness of a world which is to be used rather than to be enjoyed for its own sake. He is frequently troubled because he does not have that which his heart longs for, an object, he implies, which brings no merely transitory satisfaction. The language of the third stanza is based on the feudal conception of Jerusalem as a castle, dominated by a tower, the "palatium Christi." The castle, as Rudel laments, is *luenh*. However, good counsellors, perhaps good priests or other *sapientes*, tell him that he will die unless love comes to him from his lady there. The death referred to is not physical, but spiritual, the death which Christ conquered on the Cross and which no one else may conquer except by following Him. In the fourth stanza, those who dwell in the castle are said to be all *senhors*, the least of them courteous and loyal. This is a familiar means of expressing the transcendent virtue of those who achieve the celestial kingdom, of those who are said to "reign with Christ." In spite of the distance from the tower and the danger of death, the poet is confident that his lady is aware of his good thought and hope, which here probably represent the first two of the theological virtues. As for the third, charity, his heart, as he goes on to say in stanza five, is always with her, for otherwise it has neither root nor crown. The tree image implied here is an exegetical

---

charity. See Peter Lombard on Ps. 64, *PL,* 191, 581. To cope with the adversities of the way, the pilgrim is conventionally a *miles Christi*. The pilgrimage may be significant on any of the three higher levels of meaning.

and poetic commonplace. A good man is a good tree, rooted in humility and crowned with the fruits of charity.[30] Without the love of the Queen of Heaven, the poet would have neither the root of the tree nor the leaves and fruit. When he is asleep, in contemplation, his spirit is always with his beloved. But he languishes because the love he bears her is not fulfilled. At the same time, he knows that the virtue of patience will eventually lead him to his joy.

In the Canticum, the impatience of the lover is expressed in the verse (2. 5) *Stipate me malis, fulcite me floribus, quia amore langueo.* Usually, the flowers are taken to mean faith and the fruits good works. Languor of this kind is said to be healed by the example of those zealous in faith and works.[31] This principle may account for the somewhat puzzling message of the poet's lady in the sixth stanza:

> "Amicæ," fa s'elha, "gilos brau
> An comensat tal batestau
> Que sera greus a departir,
> Tro qu'abdui en siam jauzen."

Ordinarily, the activities of the *gilos brau* in an earthly affair would be no cause for rejoicing, but in this instance, the *gilos* may be *zelotes*, perhaps the crusaders themselves, whose *batestau* or *militia* is not only pleasing to the lady but a source of comfort to the lover. It affords the example of faith and works necessary to relieve his languor. But nevertheless, as the last stanza asserts, the poet is sorrowful that he does not possess his lady in an appropriate place, the *terra lonhdana* of his true home. His bitterness is not so profound, however, that one little kiss would not heal his heart completely. The meaning of this kiss may be inferred from the comment of Honorius on Cant. 1. 1 : *Osculetur me osculo oris sui*:

> Tropologia autem haec est. Fidelis anima sponsa Christi cogitans ubi fuerit, ubi erit, ubi sit, ubi non sit, scilicet quod in originali et actuali peccato fuerit, quod in tremendo judicio Dei erit, quod in vanitatibus saeculi sit, quod in aeterna beatitudine non sit gemens et

---

30. See "The Doctrine of Charity," p. 27.
31. See note 15, above. Cf. Honorius, *PL,* 172, 387-388; St. Bernard, *PL,* 183, 1025 ff.

tremens dicit: Osculetur me osculo oris sui. Ac si dicat: Ille qui in mea carne in dextera Patris sedet, meus advocatus, justus Judex me de peccatis dolentem, de judicio suo trementem, visitando osculetur, et pace signo amicitiae quam proprio ore poenitentibus promisit, me osculetur.[32]

Honorius considers the situation on the basis of the figure of the bride seeking the bridegroom, whereas in the poem the figure is that of the lover seeking the Queen of Heaven, but the underlying thought is very similar. The kiss the poet seeks is the kiss of peace which promises eternal rest. Since the desire for this rest is his malady, he needs no learned physician to cure him. To recapitulate, the song of the poet is an echo of the *canticum novum* of charity, inspired by the thought of the Resurrection. In the sterile ways of the world, he longs for a satisfaction that is more profound than the transient delights around him. His lady, the Blessed Virgin Mary, is merciful, but he cannot attain his desire on earth. Jerusalem is distant, and his spirit will die if he does not reach it. All those there are *senhors*. The poet through faith, hope, and charity hopes to assure the mercy of his lady for himself, and he is encouraged by the example of the faithful and charitable around him. One kiss, one promise of amnesty, would cure his languor. Then he too might enjoy the delights of the *terra lonhdana* as a *senhor* in the castle of Heaven.

If the contemplation of the Resurrection symbolized by spring is enjoyable, so also are the trials and adversities which make the ultimate benefit of that Resurrection possible. Figuratively, these adversities may be expressed as "winter." Thus Alanus defines *hiems* as "tentatio" or "adversitas."[33] Temporal adversity, as Boethius points out, is necessary to the development of virtue,[34] and virtue is necessary to salvation. Poem IV takes up the theme of temptation and its value. The flowery time of summer is pleasant, but winter is even more enjoyable, for in winter, or in conflict with temptation and adversity, the poet knows that greater joy is due him. Through this conflict, as

---

32. *PL*, 172, 360-361. Cf. the *Eructavit*, ll. 1570-1572.
33. *Distinctiones, PL*, 210, 810.
34. *De consolatione*, IV, pr. 7.

he goes on to say in the second stanza, his worth is restored. "Itaque ut aurum ignibus," to quote a very early statement of a theme which still echoes in Milton, "sic nos discriminibus arguimur." [35] Nevermore, Rudel says, will he go elsewhere or seek the conquests of others, for now he knows of a certainty that he who awaits in patience is wise, whereas he who becomes impatient is foolish. That is, he will not seek the satisfaction or accomplishments of men on earth, for he knows that God rewards the patient pilgrim who does not succumb to temptations. He was, as he says in the third stanza, long uncertain of himself. But he was never so far gone in the wrongful sleep of immersion on the world that fear, probably the fear of God, did not awaken him.[36] His lady, in the fourth stanza, is said to hold him in honor because of his return to the true way. He sends praise to her, and to God, and to those who in the Celestial City have attained their desire. There he will remain (in spirit) and there find his satisfaction. In familiar terms, *inhabitem in domo Domini in longitudinem dierum*. Stanza five contains an assertion of security in the face of the *lauzenjador*, the scornful liars who would lead him astray. Never was he further from the wrong love. This love may force those wiser than himself into self-deception, but he knows that the *fin amors* which he has in his own heart, in this instance charity, never betrayed anyone.[37] The temptation from which the poet derives his strength is referred to specifically in the sixth stanza, where a common figure of clothing is used:

> *Mielhs mi fora jazer vestitz*
> *Que despolhatz sotz cobertor.*

The *vestimentum* involved here may be that described by Alanus as follows: "Dicitur status innocentiae et immortalitatis, unde in Apoc.: *Beatus qui vigilat et custodit vestimenta sua. Ille servat vestimenta*

---

35. Minucius Felix, *Octavius*, XXXVI, 8-9. Cf. Milton's comment on "a fugitive and cloistered virtue."
36. For the evil sleep, see above, note 17. The poet plays on the two meanings of sleep in VI. One sleep is the sleep of the flesh, the other the sleep of the spirit. Various subsidiary meanings may be derived from these two basic meanings.
37. This sentence is not intended to imply that *fin amors* always means charity in the poetry of the troubadours. A poet is apt to call any kind of love he happens to be celebrating *fin amors*.

sua qui gravioribus peccatis se non maculat."[38] When he lost his innocence temporarily through a relapse into sin, not necessarily the sin of *luxuria*, the *lauzenjador* derided him, and he is sorrowful because of his fall. One thing, as he says in the seventh stanza, troubles him. He wonders concerning the truth of the belief that the sister (i.e., Mary) will forgive him for that which the brother (i.e., Christ) would not. Mary is, as the *Eructavit* puts it, one "Qui Deu seroiz et file et mere." But he feels that no one has enough natural wisdom, as opposed to that wisdom which is a gift of the Holy Spirit, to avoid going astray in some fashions: *Septies cadet justus et resurget*. Mary, the well of mercy, will forgive those transgressions which no man may avoid. Finally, the poet concludes that his song will be understood in the month of April, at Easter. And he himself is fortunate for having discharged himself of a foolish burden. The burden he has lost is sin, the wrong love which tempted him in the adversity of winter. With the coming of spring, the time of the Resurrection when the New Law of charity triumphed over the old love of cupidity, his song will be understood; for he himself has undergone a like transformation celebrated in his song. And the hope that inspired him was the thought of the mercy of Mary, the sister of Christ and the mother of Christ, who brings Christ to the hearts of the faithful just as she brought Him to the world. If we wished to state the theme of this poem in a few words, we might well use those of St. James: *Beatus vir qui suffert tentationem, quoniam cum probatus fuerit accipiet coronam vitae.*

Poem V opens with a contrast between spring on earth and the eternal spring of the New Jerusalem. When the days are long in May, the month of Mary we might observe, the poet is pleased by the song of distant birds. Birds representing the souls of the faithful praise God around the Tree of Life, which is Christ in the distant Jerusalem.[39] In the second stanza, the poet refers specifically to his Lord, Christ. He is a true lord, through whom he will see his distant love. But for one benefit which he obtains from this lord, he also obtains a twofold evil, for every grace which strengthens his love makes him doubly anxious to be united with his beloved. The pilgrimage to which he refers is the

---

38. *Distinctiones, PL*, 210, 999-1000. Cf. St. Martin of Lyons, *PL*, 209, 383.
39. For these birds, see "The Doctrine of Charity," p. 35.

pilgrimage of the spirit, which he wishes to make under the auspices of the Queen of Heaven and with her approval. When he has made this pilgrimage, as he says in the third stanza, he will be filled with joy to seek *per amour Dieu, l'alberc de lonh*. And if it pleases God, he will be lodged near his beloved. If he does see her, he will be sad and joyous to part with her again, sad because of the separation, but joyous because of the visit. There are many routes from here to there, but the poet cannot predict his own destiny. That is in the hands of God. In stanza five, he returns to the contrast between Heaven and earth. He will never enjoy any other love except his distant love, for he knows no woman better or more noble, near or far. Her virtue is so pure that for her sake he would gladly be called captive in the land of the Saracens. In one sense, this land is simply the Babylon of the world, wherein every good Christian should recognize himself as a prisoner until the time of release comes.[40] He asks that God, who created everything and gave him his love, may give him the power—for he has the will—to see his distant love truly, so that the chamber and the garden will always be a palace to him. In other words, he wishes for the power to maintain his spiritual joy, to keep the Celestial City before him as his home always. The garden is the garden already mentioned in II, and the *camera* is probably the "thalamus Dei" mentioned by Alanus, or the "chambre celee" of the *Erucravit*, a place of ultimate rest and security. The poem closes with a lament for the fact that the poet's love is still unfulfilled. It is well said that he is avid in his distant love, for no other love pleases him. But that which he desires is denied him, for his sponsor (at baptism) dedicated him to a love which may not be fulfilled on earth. The poem concludes with a mock reprimand to the person who committed this dedication.

Poem VI, whose bright and joyful tone has frequently been noted, belongs to the tradition of Christian riddling poetry.[41] In this instance, the riddle involves the nature of the poet's love, and the obscurity

---

40. On the two kinds of captivity to which human beings are subject, see Alanus, *Sententiae, PL,* 210, 242. Cf. Hugh of St. Victor, *Adnot. in Ioelem, PL,* 175, 360-361.
41. The beginning of this tradition is discussed by Professor B. F. Huppé in a study of Caedmonian poetry now being prepared.

hinges on the fact that love for the Blessed Virgin is altogether a different kind of thing from love for another human being, although the two loves have some things in common. The second stanza states that the poet has never seen his love and does not know what good will come to him because of his affection. The reward for his devotion, of course, is something which he cannot predict. In the third, he says that joy strikes him in such a way as to dry up his flesh and to make his body thin. For, he implies, this is not a love of the flesh which thrives on fleshly vigor. No other joy strikes him so powerfully, and no other blow makes him languish in this way. So strong a reaction to an earthly passion would not be proper, and, moreover, he is spiritually fortified to the extent that nothing else could move him. The fourth stanza states that he never sleeps so sweetly (in outward absorption in the pleasures of the world) that his spirit is not with his beloved; nor does he ever give himself up to sorrow (because of worldly affliction) to the extent that his spirit leaves her. He is, that is, a man to whom the fluctuations of Fortune are trivial in the light of his supreme purpose. When he awakens (from the sleep of contemplation), all the sweetness of his love departs. He knows, as he says in the fifth stanza, that he has never taken joy of his beloved (in the earthly sense of joy), that she will never take joy of him (in the same sense), nor make any promise to him in her own person. She speaks neither truly nor falsely to him, a statement which means simply that she does not speak to him at all, and he does not know whether she ever will. From the vantage of an earthly lover, all this is strange and seemingly self-contradictory, but if the signs are regarded as signs, and the pieces in the puzzle are put down with the proper side up, the underlying *razo* emerges. Terms like *love*, and *joy*, and *sleep* have two sides in the Middle Ages, and the poet is at liberty to use either side he pleases in fashioning the obscure *cortex* of his poem. In the final stanza of this poem, Rudel returns to his opening statement about poetry, which we have already considered.

    This examination of the surviving poems of Jaufré Rudel has shown that Appel's interpretation is not inconsistent either with the content or with the imagery of the poems, at least not necessarily so. Jeanroy's chief objections to that theory disappear when the poems are considered in the light of twelfth century poetic theory and commonplace Christian symbolism. The lady whom Rudel addressed may very well have been the Blessed Virgin Mary, and the *terra lonhdana,* which romantic poets of the last century found dreamily appealing, may be the Celestial Jerusalem, a city of considerably more importance in the history of our civilization than the hazy realm of some North African Dido.

Princeton University

The Subject of the *De Amore* of Andreas Capellanus

D. W. Robertson, Jr.

Modern Philology 50:3 (February 1953), pp. 145-161.

The present discussion seeks to reopen the question of the nature of the love discussed in the *De amore* of Andreas Capellanus. Most studies of this work and of literary works thought to be related to it assume the existence of something called "courtly love," although definitions of this concept vary enormously, and great difficulties have been encountered in attempts to account for the origin of whatever it is that is so designated.[1] It is possible that the concept is altogether misleading.[2] In any event, I wish to show here that Andreas' statements about his own book in the closing paragraphs of the *De amore*, the evidence of the preface, and the general discussion of love in the first five chapters of Book I all point to the conclusion that Andreas was not concerned with what has been called "courtly love" at all.[3] These portions of the book should be sufficient to show the nature of Andreas' actual subject. For the purpose of this demonstration it will be necessary to introduce a rather

1. A convenient summary of older theories concerning "courtly love" may be found in Urban T. Holmes, *A History of Old French Literature* (New York, 1948), pp. 170-73. For more recent developments see Theodore Silverstein, "Andreas, Plato, and the Arabs," *MP*, XLVII (1949), 117-26.
2. I have made suggestions to this effect elsewhere. See "The Doctrine of Charity in Mediaeval Literary Gardens," *Speculum*, XXVI (1951), 36-39; "Some Medieval Literary Terminology," *SP*, XLVIII (1951), 691; "Chaucerian Tragedy," *ELH*, XVIX (1952), 23-24. Cf. R. J. Schoeck, "Andreas Capellanus and St. Bernard of Clairvaux," *MLN*, LXVI (1951), 295-300.
3. Other parts of the book will be examined in subsequent articles. A few references to the latter sections appear below.

elaborate discussion of twelfth-century ideas concerning love and friendship and of some commonplace theological principles. When Andreas' statements are projected against this background, it will be seen, I think, that what he actually says is quite in harmony with statements by writers of recognized orthodoxy and, moreover, that Andreas had one virtue conspicuously lacking in some of his modern interpreters: a sense of humor.[4]

Andreas incorporated a very specific statement of intention in Book iii of the *De amore* as his closing address to the reader, or to "Walter," for whom the book is said to have been written.[5] It begins as follows: "Haec igitur nostra subtiliter et fideliter examinata doctrina, quam tibi praesenti libello mandamus insertam, tibi duplicem sententiam propinabit."[6] The word "sententia" as it is used here indicates the higher meaning or doctrinal content of a work as opposed to its surface meaning, and this higher meaning is said to be "double."[7] Professor Parry's translation of this passage reflects a very widespread attitude toward the *De amore*, but it does not do full justice to what is said: "Now this doctrine of ours, which we have put into this little book for you, will if carefully and faithfully examined seem to present two different points of view."[8] Andreas says nothing

---

4. See R. Bossuat, *Li Livres d'amours de Drouart la Vache* (Paris, 1926), p. 2. Generally, potentialities for humor in the Middle Ages are neglected by literary scholars. The observation of C. T. Flower, *Introduction to the Curia Regis Rolls* (London: Selden Society, 1943), p. 5, deserves profound consideration: "In the middle ages men were very practical and found little use for sentiment; in their spare moments they were humorists rather than romantics."

5. The theory that "Walter" is fictitious seems to me most reasonable. Another "Walter" appears as one of the disciples who interrogate Ailred of Rievaulx in the *De spirituali amicitia*. Evidence adduced below, although not intended to indicate "sources," shows at least a probability that Andreas was familiar with this work. Walter is presented in the preface as a young man who has been moved by "love" and who finds difficulty in holding the "reins." In i. 1, it is said that this condition arises after "immoderate thought." We may take Walter as a representative of those youths about to embark on the quest of love .

6. Ed. Trojel, p. 358.

7. For this use of the word *sententia* see "Some Medieval Literary Terminology," pp. 686-87.

8. *The Art of Courtly Love* (New York, 1941), pp. 210-11.

about different points of view, however. He says rather, "This our carefully and faithfully tested doctrine, which we enjoin to you inserted in this little book, will present for you a double lesson." The word "sententiam" is singular, not plural, so that it implies a single lesson with two sides. And Andreas goes on to describe exactly this kind of lesson. Love of the kind Walter wished to have explained was described in the first part of the treatise (i.e., in the first two books); and a careful reading of the work will show (1) that this love leads to the delights of the flesh but (2) that it alienates the lover from the grace of God, from the approval of good men, and from honor in the world.[9] Having said this, Andreas turns at once to the last part of the book, in which, since he wished to do something for Walter's "utility," he rejected this love.[10] The last part of the book is thus simply an application of the double lesson of the first part, suitable to anyone for whom the author has any concern. That is, we are told that the grace of God, the approval of the just, friendship, honor, and so on, are preferable to a concentration on delights of the flesh which can lead only to frustration and damnation. In Andreas' closing discussion there is nothing to show that he considered the last part of his book to be inconsistent with the first part or that he was aware of two different "points of view." He does warn us to read his book

---

9. Trojel, pp. 358-59: "Nam in prima parte praesentis libelli tuae simplici et iuvenili annuere petitioni volentes ac nostrae quidam in hac parte parcere nolentes inertiae artem amatoriam, sicut nobis mente avida postulasti, serie tibi plena dirigimus et competenti ordinatione dispositam delegamus, quam si iuxta volueris praesentem exercere doctrinam, et sicut huius libelli assidua tibi lectio demonstrabit, omnes corporis voluptates pleno consequeris effectu, Dei tamen gratia, bonorum consortio atque virorum laudabilium amicitia iusta manebis ratione privatus, tuamque famam non modicam facies sustinere iacturam, nec facile huius saeculi consequeris honores."

10. *Ibid.*, p. 359: "In ulteriori parte libelli tuae potius volentes utilitati consulere, de amoris reprobatione tibi nulla ratione petenti, ut bona forte praestemus invito, spontanea voluntate subiunximus et pleno tibi tractatu conscripsimus." The "utility" of a work arises from the conclusions which may be drawn from it. See the explanation in the *Livre d' Enanchet,* ed. W. Fiebig ("Berliner Beiträge z. rom. Philologie," Vol. VIII [1938]), p. 2, and, in general, Edwin A. Quain, S.J., "The Medieval Accessus ad auctores," *Traditio,* III (1945), 215-64. In Book iii of the *De amore,* Andreas elaborates these conclusions but does not change either his matter or his intention.

with care, and he does reject, not "courtly love," but what he calls the "works of Venus," or "worldly delight."

It is probable that the love described in the first two books of the *De amore* is the same as that rejected in the last book. This probability is strengthened by the fact that in the preface, where Andreas announces his subject, he also speaks of the love he is concerned with in terms of "Venus."[11] If this love is rejected in the third book, it is also rejected in the preface, albeit in a light and humorous vein: "Quamvis igitur non multum videatur expediens huiusmodi rebus insistere, nec deceat, quemquam prudentem huiusmodi vacare venatibus, tamen propter affectum quo tibi annector, tuae nullatenus valeo petitioni obstare; quia haec clarius novi, quod docto in amoris doctrina cautior tibi erit in amore processus, tuae, prout potero, curabo postulationi parere."[12] The prudent man, which is as much as to say the man who can distinguish between good and evil, will not engage in the kind of pursuit encouraged by Venus; and some knowledge of what that pursuit actually involves should make anyone cautious. To understand what Andreas means by Venus and her works, however, we cannot rely on our own conception of the classics. We must consider these things as they were thought of in the twelfth century. At that time Venus would suggest certain contexts in Virgil and Ovid and certain definite interpretations of those contexts which were not irrelevant to commonplace theological ideas. The principles justifying the use of the classics in a Christian society had been laid down by Augustine and Jerome,

---

11. Andreas employs the expressions "Veneris iacula" and "Veneris ... servituti." There may well be some word play in the epithet "venerande amice," which has puzzled commentators on Andreas. The figure of "hunting" may also have been suggested by Venus in Ovidian contexts. In the *Ars amatoria* the lover, who is under the auspices of Venus, is compared with a hunter, and the word *venare* is used to describe his quest (i. 45-46, 89, 253-54). In the twelfth century, Arnulf of Orléans comments: "*Scit bene venator,* quaerenda et poteris invenire si tantummodo ames. Quod ostendit a simili per venatorem et piscatorem et per aucupem." See F. Ghisalberti, *Arnalfo d'Orléans* ("Mem. del r. instituto Lombardo di sc. e lett.," Vol. XXIV [1932]), p. 167. Andreas uses all three of these figures in the course of his work. In *Met.* x, Venus recommends a hunt for timid game. This hunt is, by implication, contrasted with the hunt of Diana; for, according to *Amores* iii, 2. 31-32, Diana hunts "fortes ... feras."

12. Trojel, p. 2.

who based their conclusions on interpretations of Exod. 3:22, 12:35; and Deut. 21:10-14.[13] To make classical poetry useful, however, the allegorical interpretation of poetic fables, begun in ancient times and introduced as a Christian practice by Fulgentius, was elaborated.[14] The pagan gods and goddesses became figures for physical or moral concepts which could be related to Christian ideas.[15] It will repay us, therefore, to make a rather thorough investigation of what the word *Venus* implied in the twelfth century.

There is a rather full description of Venus in the commentary on the first six books of the *Aeneid* by Bernard Silvestris, a work which probably represented academic traditions of some standing at the time it was written, and which enjoyed a wide and lasting popularity.[16] Since the material is presented in an abbreviated style, it may be quoted here in full; but for the same reason it will require elaboration and explanation if we are to understand it. There are, we are told, two Venuses:

> Veneres vero legimus duas esse, legitimam et petulantiae deam. Legitimam Venerem dicimus esse mundanam musicam, i.e., aequalem mundanorum proportionem, quam alii Astream, alii naturalem iustitiam vocant. Haec enim est in elementis, in sideribus,

---

13. Cf. Quain, pp. 223-24. The medieval use of the passage from Deuteronomy is illustrated by Rabanus *De cler. inst.*, *PL*, CVII, 396. The passage from Exodus was more influential. See Rabanus, *ibid.*, 404; Scotus *De div. nat.*, *PL*, CXXII, 723-24; Baudri de Bourgueil (ed. Abrahams), No. ccxxxviii, ll. 121-26; Peter of Blois, Epist. xci, *PL*, CCVII, 286; Alanus de Insulis *De arte praed.*, *PL*, CCX, 180; John of Salisbury *Policrat.* vii. 2, and Webb's note. Cf. M. Grabmann, *Die Geschichte der scholastischen Methode* (Freiburg im Breisgau, 1911), II, 123, and the references there.

14. Cf. "Some Medieval Literary Terminology," pp. 673-77. An excellent brief introduction to the allegorical method appears in the commentary *Super Thebaiden* attributed to Fulgentius (ed. Helm), pp. 180-81. For Augustine's approval of the adaptation of pagan stories for Christian purposes, see *De ordine* i. 8 (24).

15. For the physical and moral values of the pagan deities see Augustine *Contra Faustum* xx. 9, where some examples are given. Medieval commentaries on Virgil and Ovid furnish ample illustration of the practice. Some illustrations are quoted below.

16. It was echoed, for example, in the *Policraticus* by John of Salisbury and was used rather extensively by C. Salutati in *De laboribus Herculis*. Professor J. B. Reese informs me that it is echoed in the *D. gen. deorum* of Boccaccio.

in temporibus, in animantibus. Impudicam autem Venerem, petulantiae deam, dicimus esse carnis concupiscentiam quia omnium fornicationum mater est.[17]

Andreas is obviously concerned with the "petulantiae deam," but her significance can be appreciated fully only as she is contrasted with the more attractive Venus. The idea of "mundana musica" is probably derived from the general discussion of the subject near the beginning of the *De musica* of Boethius.[18] But the good Venus is obviously a moral as well as a physical concept. Astrea, who appears in the cosmological opening of Ovid's *Metamorphoses*,[19] furnishes the notion of justice but does not afford us a picture of cosmic love. Today we are likely to turn to Empedocles or Lucretius for discussions of love as a cosmic force. However, in the twelfth century, such a discussion might have been found in the popular *De consolation* of Boethius. Here the same love which governs the stars and the elements is said to hold people joined by a holy bond, to govern chaste marriages, and to give laws to friends. Unfortunately, mankind in general does not abide by this love.[20] Boethius' love is obviously a kind of "natural justice." The poetical, or philosophical, concept of love in Boethius has a counterpart in traditional Christian theology, for in Augustine's *De genesi ad litteram*

---

17. *Comm. super sex libros Eneidos Virgilii*, ed. Riedel, p. 9. In the subsequent discussion, the good Venus is also called "mundi concordiam."
18. *PL*, LXIII, 1171-72.
19. i. 150.
20. ii. meter 8: "Quod mundus stabili fide / concordes variat vices, / quod pugnantia semina / foedus perpetuum tenent, / quod Phoebus roseum diem / curru provehit aureo, / ut, quas duxerit Hesperos, / Phoebe noctibus imperet, / ut fluctus avidum mare / certo fine coherceat, / ne terris liceat vagis / latos tendere terminos, / hanc rerum seriem ligat / terras ac pelagus regens / et caelo imperitans amor. / Hic si frena remiserit, / quicquid nunc amat invicem, / bellum continuo geret / et, quam nunc socia fide / pulchris motibus incitant, /certent solvere machinam. / Hic sancto populos quoque / iunctos foedere continet, / hic et coniugii sacrum / castis nectit amoribus, / hic fidis etiam sua / dictat iura sodalibus. / O felix hominum genus, / si vestros animos amor, / quo caelum regitur, regat!" The expression "pulchris motibus" relates the subject being discussed here to the same author's "mundana musica." For the connecting idea, see Augustine *De musica* i. 3, where music is defined as the science of moving well. This idea is given a cosmic force, *ibid.* vi. 17.

we are told that there is a force in created things which determines their behavior, so that the elements act as they should and living beings reproduce in accordance with their species.[21] In the twelfth century, this force was described as a "vestigium divinae caritatis."[22] Man alone among creatures had the power to abandon the natural love appropriate to him, which was charity. That is, man found himself in harmony with the love which governs creation when he himself loved God and creatures for the sake of God. He was then, poetically speaking, living under the auspices of the good Venus. When, through the exercise of free will, he abandoned this love, he obtained, to replace it, exactly what Bernard Silvestris calls the "petulantiae deam": *concupiscentia carnis*. This love is described as a malady, but as a malady necessary to perpetuate the race after the loss of reason.[23] After the Fall,

21. (Gaume ed.) ix. 16 (32): "Omnis iste naturae usitatissimus cursus habet quasdam naturales leges suas, secundum quas et spiritus vitae, qui creatura est, habet quosdam appetitus suos determinatos quodammodo, quos etiam mala voluntas non possit excedere. Et elementa mundi hujus corporei habent definitam vim qualitatemque suam, quid unumquodque valeat vel non valeat, quid de quo fieri possit vel non possit. Ex his velut primordiis rerum, omnia quae gignuntur, suo quoque tempore exortus processusque sumunt, finesque et decessiones sui cujusque generis. Unde fit ut de grano tritici non nascatur faba, vel de faba triticum, vel de pecore homo, vel de homine pecus."
22. Ailred of Rievaulx *Speculum charitatis* i. 21, PL, CXCV, 524-25. I quote the beginning of this rather long discussion: "*Quod in omnibus creaturis quoddam vestigium divinae charitatis appareat*.... Porro si omnem creaturam a prima usque ad novissimam, a summa usque ad imam, a summo angelo usque ad minimum vermiculum subtilius contempleris, cernes profecto divinam bonitatem, quam non aliud dicimus, quam ejus charitatem; non locali infusione, non spatiosa diffusione, non mobile discursione; sed substantialis praesentiae stabili et incomprehensibili in se permanente simplicitate omnia continentem, omnia ambientem, omnia penetrantem, ima superis conjungentem, contraria contrariis, frigidia calidis, siccis humida, lenibus aspera, duris mollia, concordi quadam paci foederantem: ut in ipsa creaturae universitate nihil adversum, nihil possit esse contrarium; nihil quod dedeceat, nihil quod perturbet, nihil sit quod ipsam universitatis pulchritudinem decoloret, sed in ipsius ordinis tranquillitate, quem ipsi universitati praefixit, cuncta quasi tranquillissima quadam pace quiescant." In chapters 22 and 23 it is explained that man finds his true rest in God, not in the satisfactions of the flesh. Cf. the same author's *De spirituali amicitia*, PL, CXCV, 667.
23. Augustine *De gen. ad litt.* xi. 32 (42): "Hoc ergo amisso statu, corpus eorum [i.e. Adam and Eve] duxit morbidam et mortiferam qualitatem, quae inest

good and evil grow together in the field of the world, and both good and evil may be said to reside in the vice of concupiscence. When it is controlled properly, it is a just means of perpetuating the species, but it can be controlled only through grace.[24] In itself it is the burden man must bear for his original transgression: the "law of the members," the "law of the flesh," the "law of sin," or the Old Man. In the Augustinian theology of the twelfth century, it was the *fomes peccati,* or original sin.[25] Loosely, it may be equated with cupidity, the love of one's self or of any other creature for its own sake.[26] Bernard's definition thus presents a contrast between the source of all the good in the world of man, which is charity, and the source of all evil in that world, which is cupidity. It cannot be emphasized too strongly that in the twelfth century, as in any century dominated by Augustinian thought, good

---

etiam pecorum carni, ac per hoc etiam eumdem motum quo fit in pecoribus concumbendi appetitus, ut succedant nascentia morientibus."

24. The proper function of concupiscence is described in the *De planctu* of Alanus de Insulis, *PL*, CCX, 454, where Venus is used as a figure: " ... Venerem ineffabili scientia peritam, meaeque [i.e., Nature's] operationis subvicariam in mundiali suburbio collocavi, ut meae praeceptionis sub arbitrio, hymenaei conjugis, filiique Cupidinis industria suffragante, in terrestrium animalium varia effigiatione desudans, fabriles malleos suis regulariter adaptans incudibus, humani generis seriem indefessa continuatione contexeret, Parcarumque manibus intercisorum injurias repararet." The power to control fallen Venus or concupiscence so that it may be useful may be obtained only through grace or, specifically, through baptism. See Peter Lombard *Sententiae* ii. 31. 1: "Sed licet remaneat concupiscentia post baptismum, non tamen dominator et regnat sicut ante; immo per gratiam baptismi mitigatur et minuitur, ut post dominari non valeat." After baptism, however, the reason must exert itself to keep concupiscence in its place. In the *De planctu* what we have described as the good Venus appears as Genius. See C. S. Lewis, *The Allegory of Love* (Oxford, 1936), p. 362.

25. See Peter Lombard's discussion, largely based on Augustine, *Sententiae* (Ad Claras Aquas, 1916), ii. 30. 1-10. The doctrine of original sin was refined somewhat in the latter Middle Ages. It is important to avoid modern conceptions of this subject in the examination of works written during the twelfth century.

26. See Ailred of Rievaulx *Speculum charitatis, PL*, CXCV, 513. In the *De spirituali amicitia, PL,* CXCV, 667-68, the fact that cupidity replaced cosmic love of the good Venus in the Fall is elaborated in some detail. The pattern of Bernard's definition of the two Venuses is clear in this discussion.

and evil were matters of love.[27] The most influential treatise on friendship produced in the century, the *De spirituali amicitia* of Ailred of Rievaulx, contains a vivid account of how man abandoned cosmic love or charity in the Fall to have it replaced by cupidity.[28] If Andreas was concerned with the evil Venus as she was described by Bernard Silvestris, he had in mind some thing much more profound than anything usually associated with "courtly love." It will help us to understand the two Venuses if we relate them to the concept of nature. Bernard's definition makes it clear that the good Venus is a function of nature, but there is a strong tradition of common parlance which makes the other Venus "natural" also. This difficulty is resolved for us in a discussion centering on Eph. 2:3 in the *Sententiae* of Peter Lombard. The authority being quoted is Augustine:

> Quadam iustitia Dei in potestatem diabolic traditum est genus humanum, peccato primi hominis in omnes originaliter transeunte et illius debito omnes obligante; unde omnes homines ab origine sunt sub principe diabolo. Unde Apostolus [Eph. 2:3]: *Eramus natura filii irae*; natura scilicet ut est depravata peccato, non ut est recta creata ab initio.[29]

The good Venus is a part of nature "ut est recta creata"; but the nature of man became corrupted with original sin, so that the second Venus is a function of nature "ut est depravata peccato." As the state of man now is, we are conceived in sin. The relation of the evil Venus

---

27. See, for example, the *Liber de spiritu et anima,* attributed to Alcher of Clairvaux, *PL*, XL, 813: "Nec aliunde bonum est, si bonum est, cor humanum, nisi quod bene amat quod bonum est. Nec aliunde malum est, si malum est, nisi quod male amat quod bonum est. Omne enim quod est, bonum est: sed in eo quod male amatur tantum vitium est." Cf. the *De substantia dilectionis*, erroneously attributed to Augustine, *PL*, XL, 843-44: "Unus fons dilectionis intus saliens, duos rivos effundit: alter est amor mundi, cupiditas; alter est amor Dei, charitas. Medium quippe est cor hominis, unde fons amoris erumpit: et cum per appetitum ad exteriora decurrit, cupiditas dicitur; cum vero desiderium suum ad interiora dirigit, charitas nominatur. Ergo duo sunt rivi, qui de fonte dilectionis emanant, cupiditas et charitas: et omnium malorum radix cupiditas, et omnium bonorum radix charitas." Cf. "The Doctrine of Charity in Mediaeval Literary Gardens," p. 24.

28. See the reference in n. 26 above.

29. iii. 20. 2.

to sin is expressed by Bernard when he calls her "mater omnium fornicationum," for *fornicatio* was conventionally used as a designation for any deliberate departure from the Law of God, or, that is to say, for any act against created nature.[30] The manner in which the vices follow the evil Venus is vividly described for us in the *De planctu naturae* of Alanus de Insulis.[31] To follow the evil Venus is to abandon reason and to corrupt the Image of God in man, to become, as it were, worse than a beast. It is man's duty to control concupiscence, not to follow it, and thus to restore his original nature.[32] Obviously, the hunt of the evil Venus is not something a prudent man would be willing to undertake, and a little knowledge of what the hunt involves should make any prospective hunter cautious.

We should expect some of the characteristics of the evil Venus to appear in the definition of love at the beginning of the *De amore* if Andreas actually had any of her wider connotations in mind. On the

---

30. Rabanus Maurus uses as a basis for this figure the fact that *fornicatio* in the Bible is frequently a synonym for *idolatria*. *PL.* CVII. 811: "Cum enim tam assidue idolatriam fornicationem Scriptura dicat ... quis dubitet omnem malam concupiscentiam recte fornicationem vocari, quando anima, neglecta superiore lege, qua regitur, inferiorum naturarum turpe voluntate, quasi mercede, corrumpitur?" Cf. *Glossa ordinaria, PL,* CXIV, 95: "Non enim fornicatio est tantum stupri, sed generaliter quae a lege Dei aberrare facit"; Augustine *De sermone Domini in monte* i. 12 (36).

31. *PL,* CCX, 476: "Vides enim qualiter homines originalis naturae honestatem bestialibus illecebris inhonestent, humanitatis prIvilegialem exuentes naturam, in bestias, morum degeneratione transmigrant, Veneris in consequentia affectus proprios consequentes, gulositatis vorticibus naufragentes, cupiditatis vaporibus aestuantes, alis superbiae ficticiis evolantes, invidiae morsibus indulgentes, adulationis hypocrisi alios deaurantes." Considering the fact that "Venus" here represents *concupiscentia carni,* or original sin, I see nothing "non-Augustinian" here or elsewhere in this work. Both the content and the technique have Augustinian precedent. Students of the work, interested in the vagaries of its *cortex,* have neglected the central traditions of Christian thought.

32. The Image of God, corrupted at the Fall, can be restored only through charity. See Ailred *Speculum charitatis, PL,* CXCV, 512. On the duty of man, cf. Hugh of St. Victor *Didascalicon* i. 5 (ed. Buttimer, p. 12): "Omnium autem humanarum actionum seu studiorum, quae sapientia moderatur, finis et intentio ad hoc spectare debet, ut vel naturae nostrae reparetur integritas vel defectuum, quibus praesens subiacet vita, temperetur necessitas."

surface, the definition is straightforward enough: "Amor est passio quaedam innata procedens ex visione et immoderata cogitatione formae alterius sexus, ob quam aliquis super omnia cupit alter ius potiri amplexibus et omnia de utriusque voluntate in ipsius amoris praecepta compleri."[33] But at least one medieval reader found in it something beyond its surface meaning. Albertanus of Brescia gave it a prominent place in his discussion of the difference between charity and cupidity. Since the original text of Albertanus is not available in a modern edition, I quote the medieval Italian translation:

> Et ama ogn'uomo con dritto amore, e non con perverso; perciò che l'amor diritto e detto carità, secondo che io t'ò detto di sopra. E un altro amore si può appellare cupidità, del qual tratto Gualtieri, e difinillo così: l'amore è una passione inata che move del vedimento e del temperamento e pensamento della forma dell'altro sexo, cioè all'uomo della femina, e la femina, dell'uomo; per la quale altri desidera tutte le cose altrui, e per voluntà dell'uno e dell'altro compiere tutti comandamenti di cotale amore. Et anche de'amare gli uomini in bene e non in male.[34]

Albertanus states that Andreas wrote concerning cupidity and that his definition is a definition of cupidity. Moreover, he seems to regard the definition as a condemnation of cupidity clear enough to warrant the immediate conclusion that a man should love "in bene" and not "in male." It can be shown, I think, in terms of commonplace medieval ideas, that Albertanus was completely justified in this treatment of the definition.

The functions of the good Venus among men, as Boethius describes them, are to hold together men joined by a holy bond, to unite people in chaste matrimony, and to join friends. Human beings who are joined in these ways are united by the force which holds together the elements. In nature as it was created, spiritual friendship implementing the second precept of charity was natural, and the creation of

---

33. Trojel, p. 3.
34. *Dei trattati morali Albertano de Brescia,* ed. F. Selmi (Bologna, 1873), pp. 203-4; cf. Trojel, pp. xxxix-xl, where a small portion of the original is quoted. On the use of the name "Gualterius" for the author of the *De amore* see Trojel, pp. xxxix-xli.

Eve as a companion to man was a stimulus to it. After the Fall, however, men joined themselves to one another under other auspices, being motivated not by charity but by concupiscence or cupidity. Ailred of Rievaulx's description of false unions motivated by concupiscence bears an unmistakable resemblance to the definition of Andreas:

> Verum amicitiae carnalis exordium ab affectione procedit, quae instar meretricis divaricat pedes suos omni transeunti, sequens aures et oculos suos per varia fornicantes; per quorum aditus usque ad ipsam mentem pulchrorum corporum, vel rerum voluptuosarum inferuntur imagines: quibus ad libitum frui, putat esse beatum; sed sine socio frui, minus aestimat esse jucundum. Tunc motu, nutu, verbis, obsequiis, animus ab animo captivatur, et accenditur unus ab altero, et conflantur in unum: ut inito foedere miserabili, quidquid soeleris, quidquid sacrilegii est, alter agat et patiatur pro altero; nihilque hac amicitia dulcius arbitrantur, nihil judicant justius: idem velle, et idem nolle, sibi existimantes amicitiae legibus imperari.[35]

If this description is stripped of its value judgments, it will be seen to contain exactly the pattern of the definition in the *De amore*. The lover is stimulated first by his senses; he forms an image or series of images involving his beloved in his mind, then he proceeds to join himself with his beloved in a bond formed in accordance with the "laws of friendship" or the "precepts of love." The pattern of behavior indicated here was not an unfamiliar one in the twelfth century, for Ailred's description was imitated in the *Liber de amicitia*, which carried the authority of Augustine's name, although it was not written by him, and in the *De amicitia Christiana* of Peter of Blois.[36] The general plan of Andreas' definition might very well have suggested to Albertanus a familiar concept of carnal love, together with the various implications of that love which I have suggested.

The terminology of Andreas' definition is quite different from that of Ailred. Although it does not contain any explicit value judgments, it does contain certain terms which have definite implications of value.

---

35. *De spirituali amicitia, PL,* CXCV, 665.

36. *PL*, XL, 833; M.-M. Davy, *Un Traité de l'amour du XIIe siècle* (Paris, 1932), p. 130.

In the first part of the definition there is a progression indicated by the terms *visio, cogitatio, passio*. Since Andreas elaborates each one of these in the discussion which follows the definition, we are justified in attributing some significance to them. The subject of the definition suggests a well-known biblical verse involving the concept of vision used in a similar context (Matt. 5:28) : "Ego autem dico vobis, quia omnis qui viderit mulierem ad concupiscendam eam iam moechatus est eam in corde suo." But the Bible was not read alone in the Middle Ages, as it is read now; it was read with a gloss. The commentaries on this verse furnish both the pattern of behavior in the first part of the definition and the term *passio*. Bede, for example, has this to say: "Qui viderit mulierem et ejus anima fuerit titillata, hic propassione percussus est; qui autem delectationi consensum praebuerit, de propassione ad passionem transit; et sic tribus gradibus pervenitur ad peccatum, suggestione, delectatione, consensu."[37] He who looks at a woman in a certain way is open to "suggestion." If the suggestion is accepted and is pleasurable, the result is *propassio*. And if the reason consents to the delight, the result is *passio*. Augustine, borrowing a little Egyptian gold from Cicero, had defined *passio* as a "motus animi contra rationem," and pointed out that beasts are incapable of this kind of motion, since they lack reason.[38] The consent of the reason implied by Bede is, as it were, an unreasonable act of the reason or, to put it in another way, a corruption of the reason. The correspondence between the steps of sin as described by Bede — "suggestio," "delectatio," "consensus" — and the steps in Andreas' definition — "visio," "immoderata cogitatio," "passio" — is evident. Bede, however, goes on at once to make a general statement to the effect that the process represents the steps toward sin, not toward adultery or fornication in particular, but toward any sin. The sexual act implied by the sense level of the passage was taken to represent sin in general.[39] If sin in general is meant, we may well inquire as to what we should understand

37. *PL*, XCII, 28. Cf. Rabanus, *PL*, CVII, 811; Paschasius Radbertus, *PL*, CXX, 247-48. The ideas expressed by these writers are basically Augustinian; see Augustine *De sermone Domini in monte* i. 12 (33-36) .
38. *Civ. Dei* viii. 17.
39. The quotations in n. 30 above are from comments on this verse .

by *mulierem*. Scotus furnishes the logical answer: "*Qui viderit mulierem ... mulierem videlicet appellans generaliter totius sensibilis creaturae formositatem.... Omnia quippe vitia, quae virtutibus contraria sunt, naturamque corrumpere appetunt, generali libidinis vocabulo solent appellari.*"[40] The false sensual beauty of the world, first apparent to man when Eve looked around her after eating the fruit, may be represented as the beauty of a woman. And all the vices which seek to corrupt nature may be spoken of as *libido*. The three steps in Andreas' definition thus correspond to the three steps which lead to the confirmation of cupidinous desire of any kind. If the definition is read with the implications of its terms in mind. therefore, it is seen to condemn that which it defines. We have not, however, exhausted the implications of the terms.

The progression from suggestion and delight to *passio* represents the pattern of the Fall of Adam, a pattern which every mortal sinner was said to follow.[41] Various accounts of this procedure were circulated in the Middle Ages, but the most prominent is that of Augustine, which appears in the *Sententiae* of Peter Lombard.[42] Adam, Eve, and the serpent are said to represent, respectively, the higher reason ("superior rationis portio"), the lower reason ("inferior rationis portio"), and the motion of the sense ("sensualis motus animae"). When the individual is properly oriented, there is a "marriage" between the higher reason (Adam) and the lower reason (Eve), so that the higher reason is in a position to protect the soul from bestial motions. The senses offer the lower reason "fruit," or tempt it. If the lower reason accepts the fruit, the result is "delectation cogitationis," or pleasure of thought concerning the attractiveness of the fruit. We may justly compare this with Andreas' "immoderata cogitatio," which, in

---

40. *D. div. nat., PL,* CXXII, 975-76.
41. The connection between Matt. 5:28 and the story of the Fall is made by Augustine in *De sermone Domini in monte* i. 12 (34): "Tria ergo haec [i.e., *suggestio, delectatio, consensus*], ut dicere coeperam, similia sunt illi gestae rei quae in Genesi scripta est, ut quasi a serpente fiat suggestio et quaedam suasio; in appetitu carnali, tanquam in Eva, delectatio; in ratione vero, tanquam in viro, consensio...."
42. The summary here given is based on *Sententiae* ii. 24. 6-13. Cf. "Chaucerian Tragedy:' pp. 10-11, and the references there.

his extended description of it, may certainly be characterized as "pleasure of thought." When the lower reason has accepted the fruit, it offers it to the higher reason. If the higher reason accepts the fruit, the individual falls, just as Adam fell before him. In this account, the higher reason is that part of the reason which perceives the Laws of God, and its end is *sapientia,* or wisdom. When it accepts the fruit from the lower reason, it turns away from God. Moreover, an important part of its function is to guide the lower reason so that it will not accept the fruit in the first place, or, if that is impossible, to see that it does not retain it too long. The lower reason perceives the laws of the world, and its end is *scientia.* The higher reason should see to it that *scientia* is directed toward the fulfilment of God's Laws and not toward the satisfaction of the senses.[43] A mortal sin is the corruption of a marriage, since the "mulier" becomes dominant over the "vir" when the higher reason submits to the lower reason. It is customary in Augustinian parlance, moreover, to speak of this submission as *fornicatio*. To return now to Andreas' definition, we see that the "visio" he speaks of, probably suggested by Matt. 5:28, corresponds with the "suggestio" of Bede and with the "sensualis motus" of Augustine. Andreas' "immoderata cogitatio" is the equivalent of the "dilectio" of Bede or of the "delectatio cogitationis" of Augustine. Finally, the *passio* in Andreas' definition implies the consent of the higher reason, or, figuratively, submission to Eve in an adulterous relationship. In this instance, Andreas' "subtiliter et fideliter examinata doctrina" presents very clearly the double lesson he described for us, although, as he also said, a careful reading of what he says is necessary. Albertanus was amply justified, I think, in considering the definition as a kind of argument condemning cupidity.

    Andreas does not lard his definition with the kind of deprecatory language that we have seen in Ailred's description of the same thing. And, indeed, in some of the subsequent discussion Andreas seems to praise the love he is speaking of. But, as we shall see, beneath this

---

43. On *sapientia* and *scientia,* cf. *Sententiae* ii. 24. 4-5; iii. 25. 1. It is possible to speak of the lower reason figuratively as *sensualitas* (see ibid. ii. 24. 13). This fact accounts for some of the elaborations of the theme "reason and sensuality" in the Middle Ages.

praise there is always an implied condemnation, just as there is an implied condemnation in the definition. The literary device employed here was well known in the Middle Ages. It was called "irony." To quote Isidore of Seville, the source of many medieval commonplaces, on the subject, "Ironia est, cum per simulationem diversum quam dicit intellegi cupit. Fit autem cum laudamus quem vituperare volumus, aut vituperamus quem laudare volumus."[44] One result of irony is humor. When we see that Andreas is actually describing love with his tongue in his cheek, condemning it when he seems to praise it, we can understand the laughter of Drouart la Vache. If a literary precedent is needed to account for this irony, we may find it without any difficulty in Andreas' acknowledged classical master, Ovid. Ovid had praised love and its "precepts" with wit and sarcasm in the *Ars amatoria* and had subsequently written a treatise on the remedies of love without retracting anything — "nec nova praeteritum Musa retexit opus." Andreas follows the same general pattern, except that his *ars* is much more profoundly ironic than Ovid's and his *remedia* are thoroughly Christian. He would have found ample precedent for the ironic treatment of Venus and her works in the tenth book of the *Metamorphoses*, a work which was regarded as a consistent condemnation of the improper love of *temporalia*, with implied praise of the proper love of the Creator.[45] The first two books of the *De amore*, are, as it were, a Christian *Ars amatoria* in which the author takes full advantage of the various traditions of love and friendship developed by his

---

44. *Etymologiae* (ed. Lindsay) ii. 21. 41; cf. Martianus Capella *De nuptiis* (ed. Eyssenhardt) v. 523.

45. See Arnulf of Orléans in Ghisalberti. p. 181: "*Intencio* est de mutacione dicere, ut non intelligamus de mutacione que fit extrinsecus tantum in rebus coporeis bonis vel malis sed etiam de mutacione que fit intrinsecus ut in anima, ut reducat nos ab errore ad cognitionem veri creatoris. Duo sunt motus in anima unus rationalis alter irrationalis: rationalis est qui imitatur motum firmamenti, qui fit ab oriente in occidentem, et e contrario irrationalis est qui imitatur motum planetarum qui moventur contra firmamentum. Dedit enim deus anime rationem per quam reprimeret sensualitatem, sicut motus irrationalis VII planetarum per motum firmamenti reprimitur.... Vel intencio sua set nos ab amore temporalium immoderato revocare et adhortari ad unicum cultum nostri creatoris, ostendendo stabilitatem celestium et varietatem temporalium."

Christian predecessors. Andreas would have found ample justification for using sexual love as a figure for something much more profound in the Bible, in the Fathers, in theological works, and in the humanistic learning of his time. His definition of love is, on the surface, objective and noncommittal, as though he were simply complying with a friendly request to explain love to a prospective lover. But this superficial earnestness conceals, like a kind of trap, the implications we have described. The humor of the definition arises with the growing realization that Andreas is pulling "Walter's" leg.

Following the definition, there is an extended elaboration, the first part of which is devoted to the fact that the lover is always fearful. The same subject is treated in Book iii, where this fear is described as a kind of foolishness. It is one thing to say that the lover's fear is foolish, as Andreas does in Book iii, but quite another thing to demonstrate the foolishness without calling attention to it openly. This is exactly what Andreas does in the first discussion of the subject. The idea that love is fearful is used to support the statement: "Quod amor sit passio, facile est videre."[46] If we neglect the connotations of *passio* and translate it "suffering," we miss the point; but if we recognize the fact that *passio* implies an act contrary to reason, we have little trouble in following the course of the argument. To make the point of unreasonableness, or foolishness, apparent, Andreas says first, "antequam amor sit ex utraque parte libratus, nulla est angustia maior." The lover is in a very uncomfortable situation before he attains his desire. What happens to him afterward? Does he find peace of mind in fulfilment? "Postquam etiam amor utriusque perficitur, non minus timores insurgunt." He is just as uncomfortable as he ever was, if not in a worse condition. The anxiety of love is increased by success, for, as Andreas says, it is worse to lose a thing gained than to lose a thing merely hoped for.[47] Clearly, a love which involves a continuous and incurable anxiety is not very reasonable. Meanwhile, the fact that cupidity is always accompanied by fear, no matter how "successful" it may be, is a commonplace. There are

---

46. Trojel. p. 4.
47. Cf. "Chaucerian Tragedy," p. 28, where this principle is illustrated.

two fears which are associated with the two loves. The fear of God leads to wisdom and charity, but cupidity is always accompanied by the fear of earthly misfortune.[48] And charity, as all writers on the subject insist, leads to the "requiem" which all men seek, not to the foolish uneasiness of Andreas' lover. It is impossible, of course, to demonstrate that Andreas' lively description of the uneasy lover is humorous, but at least it is evident that the description cannot be a serious recommendation to acquire *passio* and that what is actually said is not inconsistent with traditional Augustinian doctrine, however innocently conciliatory toward "Walter" it may appear to be on the surface.

In the remainder of chapter 1, Andreas emphasizes the fact that *passio* is inborn. It does not arise from any action, but only from immoderate thought; for when a man sees a woman shaped to his liking, "statim eam incipit concupiscere corde."[49] The more he thinks of her, the more he burns with love, until he begins to think of her members and to desire to exploit their full potentialities. Then he begins to take action which will lead to this kind of exploitation. Thus love is born "ex vision et cogitatione" and comes from within. Moreover, a truly immoderate contemplation is necessary, since a moderate thought will not remain in the mind. This argument, in the first place, simply elaborates the implications of the definition. For the development of *passio* it is necessary either that the higher reason consent to the temptation of the lower reason, so that "plena voluntas perficiendi" arises, or that the higher reason allow the lower reason to dwell on the beauties of the fruit.[50] For either eventuality, "delectatio cogitationis" is absolutely necessary. No matter how the "sensualis motus" may be moved, *passio* cannot follow unless the individual contemplating the object of his desire *moechatus est iam in corde suo*. As a chapter heading in Gregory's *Moralia* puts it, "Cogitatio immunda

---

48. Cf. "The Doctrine of Charity," p. 28.

49. The language here echoes Prov. 6:25. The entire passage, 6:23-35, is relevant, for it describes the same kind of departure from wisdom that Andreas describes.

50. See Lombard *Sententiae* ii. 24. 9-12. In effect, Andreas requires that the lover's sin be mortal.

non inquinat cum pulsat, sed cum per delectationem subjugat."[51] One interesting consequence of Andreas' remarks is that the lover himself is responsible for his own inborn love. Neither fortune nor destiny has anything to do with it, and for the lover to blame anyone or anything except himself for his condition is, in terms of the *De amore*, an absurdity.[52] If "Walter" becomes a lover by virtue of prolonged lascivious thought, his resulting uneasiness will be entirely self-engendered.

Chapter 2, "Inter quos possit esse amor," begins by limiting love to members of opposite sexes. It is possible to consider the works of Venus without limiting them in this way, but Andreas follows the example of Ovid[53] and the limitations established by the definition. To have done otherwise would have deprived him of much amusing play on the relationship between love and marriage and of opportunities to relate his materials to the Adam and Eve story. The reasoning he uses to support his restriction is the familiar rationalization to the effect that love is "natural." A French poet who wrote about five years before the composition of the *De amore* has his lovers, with whose iniquity he is thoroughly familiar, say,

> ... n'est pechiez de luxure
> de tot est humainne nature.[54]

Andreas says, as if to praise love: "Nam quiquid natura negat, amor erubescit amplecti."[55] As usual, however, there is a certain irony in his

---

51. *Moralia.* xxi. 6, *PL*, LXXVI, 192.

52. Theologically, the underlying principle here is that the individual alone is responsible for his sins, so that no excuses are valid. See the *De vera et falsa poenitentia, PL*, XL, 1126. This work, which was probably written in the eleventh century, was attributed to Augustine and carried wide authority in the twelfth century. Literary lovers are notorious for their complaints against Fortune.

53. In the *Ars amatoria* Ovid does not consider irregularities (see ii. 683-84). In the *De planctu* where the development of the evil Venus is carried on without the limitation of Matt. 5:28 and the tropological meanings of the Fall are not fully exploited, concupiscence has a wider range.

54. *De David li prophecie,* ed. Fuhrken (Halle. 1895), ll. 1153ff. This poem, which was written in 1180, contains many of the basic conventions developed by Andreas. The vice *Luxure* is used with its full figurative implications. The poet makes it responsible for the Flood and shows how it destroys the City of Jerusalem (the human heart). He also develops the Idea of "virtues" which accompany *Luxure*.

55. Trojel, p. 7.

logic, for the statement is perfectly true if the meanings of "natura" and "amor" are arranged correctly: "Quidquid natura [ut est recta creata ab initio] negat, amor [caritas] erubescit amplecti." The love which Andreas has in mind is not charity, so that we shall have to put this in another way: "Quidquid natura [ut est depravata peccato] negat, amor [cupiditas] erubescit amplecti." When we are familiar with these two senses of "nature" and "love," as Andreas' readers undoubtedly were, the statement can mean only that love as Andreas describes it is a feature of man's corrupted nature. Again, this apparent praise of love is not very favorable under the surface. To perceive this fact is, I think, to perceive a joke, specifically a joke on those who use the familiar rationalization.

Andreas proceeds to a further characterization of lovers, elaborating an idea we have seen in Ailred of Rievaulx: "nichilque hac amicitia dulcius arbitrantur, nichil judieant justius ... sibi existimantes amicitiae legibus imperari." The lover, Andreas says, wishes above all to fulfil the "mandata" of love as he finds them in treatises on the subject, a reference, perhaps, to the *Ars amatoria* and the *Amores*.[56] In any event, the lover finds nothing better in life than the satisfaction of his concupiscence: "In amantis ergo conspectu nil valet amoris actui comparari, potiusque verus amans cunctis exspoliari divitiis vel omni eo, quod humano posset excogitari ingenio, sine quo quis vivere non potest, penitus privari eligeret quam sperato vel acquisito amore carere."[57] The kind of concentration on the sexual act envisaged here may not seem altogether strange to readers of certain modern psychiatric writings, but in the Middle Ages it could have been nothing but ludicrous. Persons like Andreas' lover are described with cynical humor in the *Lai dou lecheor* and in the *Du C.* of Gautier Le Leu.[58] To suppose that Andreas, who

56. Arnulf of Orléans, ed. Ghisalberti, p. 167, says of the *Ars amatoria*, "Intencio sua est tractare de amore dando precepta et regulas."
57. Trojel, p. 7.
58. For the *Lai dou lecheor*, see G. Paris, "Lais inédits," *Romania*, VIII (1879), 64-66. Mortimer J. Donovan, *RR*, XLIII (1952), 81-86, sees the poem as a literary satire. But it is certainly also a social satire. See the discussion by C. H. Livingston, *Le Jongleur Gautier Le Leu* (Cambridge, Mass., 1951), pp. 234-35. The text of *Du C.* is printed, *ibid.*, pp. 238-49. The idea that a certain kind of "courtesy" has a singularly crude beginning was not uncommon. See "Chaucerian Tragedy," pp. 18 ff. Some MSS of the *De amore* describe the book as a "liber amoris et curtesie." See Trojel, pp. xxiv, xxx. If "courtesy" is thought of as it is described in the *Lai dou lecheor*, the term *amour courtois* is not

was a court chaplain, could seriously recommend that anyone place the sexual act above everything else requires a remarkable stretch of the historical imagination. In any event, he certainly does not do so in this chapter, for he proceeds to develop at once a familiar principle of Christian philosophy. He who concentrates his efforts on the attainment of any one of the false goods of the world, as Boethius assures us, loses all of them, including the one he seeks:

> Qui divitias, inquit, petit penuriae fuga, de potentia nihil laborat, vilis obscurusque esse mavult, multas etiam sibi naturales quoque subtrahit voluptates, ne pecuniam, quam paravit, amittat. Sed hoc modo ne sufficientia quidem contingit ei, quem valentia deserit, quem molestia pungit, quem vilitas abicit, quem recondit obscuritas. Qui verum solum posse desiderat, profligat opes, despicit voluntates honoremque potentia carentem, gloriam quoque nihil pendit. Sed hunc quoque quam multa deficiant, vides; fit enim, ut aliquando necessariis egeat, ut anxietatibus mordeatur, cumque haec depellere nequeat, etiam id, quod maxime petebat, potens esse desistat. Similiter ratiocinari de honoribus, gloria, voluptatibus licet; nam cum unumquodque horum idem quod cetera sit, quisquis horum aliquid sine ceteris petit, ne illud quidem, quod desiderat, apprehendit.[59]

This is exactly the kind of concentration Andreas ascribes to his lover, and love leads to its own destruction in poverty. For the sake of his love, the lover undergoes all sorts of perils, is contemptuous of death itself, scatters his wealth, and reduces himself to poverty. With poverty come torturing thoughts, melancholy, and loss of love. For, as Ovid says in the *Remedia amoris*, "Non habet unde suum paupertas pascat amorem."[60]

---

inappropriate to describe the love which Andreas satirizes. There was, however, another kind of courtesy of less humble origin.

59. *De cons.* iii. pr. 9. For the importance of this idea to John of Salisbury, see Hans Liebeschütz, *Mediaeval Humanism in the Life and Writings of John of Salisbury* (London, 1950), p. 33.

60. Trojel, p. 8; *Rem. am.* 749. Ovid stresses the fact that women desire wealth. *Ars. am.* i. 419-20, and that wealth is necessary to the lover, *ibid.* ii. 276-78. On the incompatibility of avarice and lechery cf. the *super Thebaiden* attributed to Fulgentius (ed. Helm), p. 185: "Ad ultimum duellant fratres, id est auaritia et luxuria, et mutuo se perimunt...." In proverbial terms, one cannot have a cake and eat it too.

In his customary way, Andreas enforces this principle with a little ironic logic. By way of what appears to be encouragement, the lover is urged to avoid prodigality so that he may retain enough of his patrimony to pursue his beloved. When riches decrease, love decreases also. For this kind of love is always increasing or decreasing, unlike that love which Jerome in a famous dictum described as true: "Amicitia quae desinere potest, nunquam vera fuit."[61] Andreas advises "generosity" to keep his love from decreasing, but at the same time suggests that the sources of wealth are not inexhaustible, particularly when one devotes all his efforts to love. The lover's situation is not made any more pleasant by the closing statement: "amans nihil sapidum ab amante consequitur nisi ex illius voluntate procedat."[62] When the lover can no longer elicit a voluntary response through his "generosity," his cause is lost. As a matter of fact, there is no such thing as generosity for an unworthy purpose,[63] so that the so-called "generosity" of the lover is always prodigality, as Andreas himself assures us in Book iii.[64] The lover cannot avoid prodigality and hence must necessarily suffer the consequences which Boethius, and Andreas, envisage for him. What appears to be fatherly advice to the eager young disciple is thus actually an ironic assurance that he will come to a bad end. In true friendship, poverty is a virtue,[65] but Andreas' love shares both the qualities of lecherous love and the qualities of what Ailred calls "amicitia mundialis":

> At amicitia mundialis, quae rerum vel bonorum temporalium cupidine parturitur, semper est plena fraudis atque fallaciae; nihil in ea certum, nihil constans, nihil securum; quippe quae semper cum fortuna mutatur, et sequitur marsupium. Unde scriptum est [Eccl. 6: 8]: *Est amicus secundum tempus, et non permanebit in*

---

61. *PL*, XXII, 335; cf. Prov. 17:17.

62. Trojel, p. 9.

63. A virtue must have both "officium et finis." If an action is directed toward an improper end, it cannot be virtuous. See the treatise on the virtues and vices by Alanus de Insulis printed by O. Lottin, *Mediaeval Studies*, XII (1950), 27; cf. Augustine, *Contra Julianum* iv. 3 (21); and *Civ. Dei* xix. 25.

64. Trojel, pp. 320-21.

65. *De spirituali amicitia, PL*, CXCV, 688-89; *Liber de amicitia*, col. 840.

die tribulationis. Tolle spem quaestus, et statim desinet esse amicus. Quam amicitiam quidam versus ita eleganter derisit [Ovid *Ex Pont.* iii]:

> Non est personae sed prosperitatis amicus,
> Quem fortuna tenet dulcis, acerba fugat.[66]

It may truly be said that this love does nothing against the corrupted nature of man. Like the vices, it is nourished on wealth,[67] and it leads its adherents to an ultimate bitterness and frustration, for, no matter how anxiously they seek to avoid "prodigality," they cannot escape losing both their wealth and the object of their desire.

At the beginning of the *Ars amatoria*, Ovid speaks of the lover's pursuit in terms of hunting, fishing, and fowling. Andreas uses the hunting image in the preface. In chapter 3, the lover becomes a fisherman, thanks to a convenient definition in the *Etymologiae* of Isidore of Seville. Isidore's definition falls into two parts, since he recognized the difference between true and false friendship: "Amicus per derivationem, quasi animi custos. Dictus autem proprie: amor turpitudinis, quia amore torquetur libidinis: amicus ab hamo, id est, a catena caritatis; unde et hami quod teneant."[68] The first part of this definition, which concerns true friendship, is echoed by writers on that subject. Thus Ailred wrote: "Porro amicus quasi amoris, vel, ut quibusdam placuit, ipsius animi custos dicitur; quoniam amicum meum amoris mutui, vel ipsius animi mei oportet esse custodem, ut omnia ejus secreta fideli silentio servet...."[69] But Andreas uses, instead, the second part, since he is concerned not with the "custodian of the soul" but with the "amator turpitudinis":

---

66. *De spirituali amicitia*, col. 666. Cf. *Liber de amicitia,* col. 834; Davy, pp. 134 ff. The basic attitude here attributed to Ovid is significant.

67. See B. Silvestris *In Aen.*, p. 99: "Vitia enim in carnem plurimum viuunt, dum opulentiam, quia materiam sui, inveniunt." Chaucer, on the basis of similar ideas, in *PF,* 260 ff., pictures Venus sporting with "hire porter Richesse." Andreas' statement concerning his own experience does not show salacious inclinations on his part. On the contrary, it calls attention to the fact that he is not in a position to indulge in the malady he describes because he has given up, or presumably given up, the pursuit of wealth as a part of his office. Cf. the remarks to the same effect in chap. 4.

68. Ed. Lindsay, x. 4-5.

69. *De spirituali amicitia*, col. 663; cf. *Liber de amicitia,* col. 832.

> Dicitur autem amor ab amo verbo, quod significat capere vel capi. Nam qui amat, captus est cupidinis vinculis aliumque desiderat suo capere hamo. Sicut enim piscator astutus suis conatur cibiculis attrahere pisces et ipsos sui hami capere unco, ita vero captus amore suis nititur alium attrahere blandimentis totisque nisibus instat duo diversa quodam incorporali vinculo corda unire vel unita semper coniuncta servare.[70]

Here Isidore's "catena caritatis" is changed to suit twelfth-century ears, becoming the somewhat less ambiguous "cupidinis vinculis." We have already seen the idea of mutual captivity brought about by "allurements" in Ailred: "Tunc motu, nutu, verbis, obsequiis, animus ab animo captivatur ... ut inito foedere miserabile," and so on. Andreas' discussion of the subject "unde dicatur amor" thus serves merely to emphasize the fact that he is talking about the libidinous love of the Old Adam. At the same time, his remarks may have contributed to the cynical jocularity of such expressions as Chaucer's "To fisshen hire, he leyde out hook and lyne." But the crowning irony of Andreas' innocent little etymology is that, as a result of careful preparations, the fisherman is himself caught. To catch another on love's hook is to hook one's self as well, to be caught, like Mars with Venus, in a ridiculous servitude.

Chapter 4 concerns the effects of love. In the first part of it, we are told that love makes men virtuous. A lover, for reasons we have seen, cannot be avaricious: "Divitiis alitur luxuriosus amor." Love makes the ugly man handsome, the lowly man noble: the proud man humble. The lover becomes, like Chaucer's Squire, "lowely, and servysable." Moreover, love actually makes the lover chaste; for, after he has centered his attention on one woman, he can hardly contemplate embracing another. How love does these things is amusingly illustrated in the dialogues, where for example, a lover's ugly legs and feet become, as he describes them, a part of "divinam naturam"; lovers from the lower

---

70. Trojel, p. 9. Andreas may have been thinking of Ovid as well as of Isidore's definition. See *Met.* iv. 182 ff., and Arnulf of Orléans. p. 210: "Quae quidem virtus prava consuetudine illicita fervoris quasi cathena constringitur." This gloss echoes Fulgentius *Mit.* ii. 7: "Quae quidem uirtus corrupta libidine turpiter catenata fervoris constrictione tenetur." For this captivity as a theological idea, see Augustine *De sermone Domini in monte* i. 12 (36).

ranks of society openly ally themselves with "true nobility" of character; and so on. To understand the irony of the passage fully, however, it is necessary to take into account the fact that in the Middle Ages the distinction between true and false virtues was widely recognized.[71] Chastity for an unworthy purpose was something quite different from the virtue of chastity. The very vices themselves were sometimes said to masquerade as virtues.[72] Moreover, Andreas was not the first writer to associate "virtues" with the activities of the corrupt Venus. Ailred of Rievaulx finds false virtues in false love:

> Falso sibi praeclarum amicitiae nomen assumunt, inter quos est convenientia vitiorum. ... Unde colligitur eos amicitiae falso nomine gloriari, fallique ejus similitudine, non veritate fulciri. Verumtamen cum in hac tali amicitia, quam vel libido commaculat, vel avaritia foedat, vel incestat luxuria, tanta ac talis experiatur dulcedo: libet conjicere, quantum habeat suavitatis illa, quae quanto honestior est, tanto est securior; quanto castior, tanto jucundior; quanto liberior, tanto felicior.[73]

It is profitable to the sinner to keep the surfaces clean. In the light of these observations, we should have no difficulty in judging the tone of Andreas' exclamation: "O, quam mira res est amor, qui tantis facit hominem fulgere virtutibus tantisque docet quemlibet bonis moribus abundare!"[74]

These virtues are so attractive that Andreas himself would follow the wonderful guidance of Love if it were not for certain other considerations:

> Hoc ergo tuo pectori volo semper esse affixum, Gualteri amice, quod, si tali amor libramine uteretur, ut nautas suos post multarum procellarum inundationem in quietis semper portum deduceret, me suae servitutis perpetuo vinculis obligarem. Sed quia inaequale pensum sua solet manu gestare, de ipsius tanquam iudicis suspecti non ad plenum confido iustitia.[75]

---

71. See n. 63 above, and "Chaucerian Tragedy." p. 16, n. 16.
72. E.g. see *De David li prophecie*, ll. 121 ff.
73. *De spirituali amicitia*, col. 665.
74. Trojel, p. 10. Cf. *Lai dou lecheor*, ll. 71-92.
75. *Loc. cit.*

The other considerations seem on the surface to be a trivial matter having to do with weights, but they involve actually a direct contrast between the justice of Love (Venus) and the justice of God. In scriptural language, the justice of God which he expects man to imitate is expressed in terms of equal or just weights.[76] To deal with just weights is to obey the Law of God, or to act charitably.[77] To do anything else is to sin, for sin is conventionally defined in the twelfth century as "omne dictum, vel factum, vel concupitum, quod fit contra legem Dei."[78] To follow the justice of love is therefore to suffer the consequences of sin. The idea is further elaborated in the nautical imagery. The sea was often taken as a sign of the world, or of life in the world, wherein we are guided to a safe harbor through faith.[79] Venus, however, leads her followers to shipwreck, as she does in the authoritative account of Fulgentius: "Hanc etiam in mari natantem pingunt, quod omnis libido rerum patiatur naufragia, unde et Porfirius in epigrammate ait: 'Nudus, egens, Ueneris naufragus in pelago.'"[80] Andreas explains to his young friend that to follow love is to forsake the justice of God and to invite perdition. But he puts the matter subtly. You go ahead and be a lover, he says in effect to Walter, but you will excuse me if the thought of certain little matters makes me hesitate to follow you.

Augustine says that we do not reach the lowest degradation of the human soul at once; we reach it by degrees, through the operations of the senses and the lower reason. When the reason turns completely away from God and recognizes nothing as divine except those images

---

76. See Lev. 19:35-37; Deut. 13:16; Job 31:5-6; Prov. 11:1, 16:11, 20:23; Ez. 45:9-11; Amos 8:4-8; Mic. 6:9-12. See also, on the first of these passages, *Glossa ordinaria, PL*, CXIII, 353: "Stateras quoque divinas, et mensuras divinas, justas habeamus; id est, leges divinae Scripturae sancte et justa custodiamus." It should be remembered that *fornicatio* stands for any departure from the Law of God.
77. See Radulphus Flaviacensis, *MBP* (ed. 1677), XVII, 177. For the popularity of this commentary on Leviticus see C. Spicq, *Esquisse d'une histoire de l'exégèse latine* (Paris, 1944), p. 125.
78. Augustine, quoted by Peter Lombard *Sententiae* ii. 34. 1.
79. See Alanus de Insulis *Distinctiones, PL*, CCX, 850-51. This work is a repository of exegetical commonplaces of long standing.
80. *Mit.* ii. 1.

of corporeal things which it derives from the senses, then the soul commits fornication, sinning against its own body.[81] Acts of fornication of this kind lead to a confirmed idolatry, in which the corporeal image becomes more important than anything else either in heaven or on earth. Andreas informs us that to be a really good lover it is necessary for a man to reach this stage of enduring idolatry. It is not enough to proceed at times from immoderate thought to the hunt of Venus. To be a good lover, a man must put the sexual act above all other earthly things, fix his mind on one single object of concupiscence, and never deviate from his position. Only then can he be a true follower of Venus, a man who is, as we have seen, worse than a beast. In chapter 5, those persons who are unfit for this final consummation of concupiscence are eliminated from the ranks of true lovers. First old persons are rejected. Although they may be able to perform the act of love, they can do so only with difficulties which prevent them from developing an enduring *passio*. For them, the solaces of the world are reduced to food and drink. Those who are old will recognize the fact that this leaves little room for enthusiasm. Boys under fourteen and girls under twelve are unfit for the same reasons they were considered unfit for marriage.[82] The necessary element in marriage was consent, but boys and young girls were thought to be too irresponsible to make this consent surely and fully. If they could not marry, neither could they engage in an inverted marriage. For, as Andreas says, boys are never constant.[83] Without the full consent of the higher reason, there can be no idolatry. Similarly, a blind man can perform the sexual act, but he cannot indulge in the necessary immoderate thought, since he cannot see the physical world and hence cannot idolize it. By "blind" men we may understand all those who cannot see the world as Eve saw it when she ate the forbidden fruit. Finally, those who are too voluptuous are, like boys, unable to confine themselves to a single object. Even though a man of this kind may think immoderately of a woman and accept from her what Andreas ironically and suggestively calls "fruit," he wanders from one female to another without discrimination. Men of this type are, Andreas

---

81. See *De Trinitate* xii. 10; cf. Andreas in Book iii, Trojel, p. 318.
82. Peter Lombard *Sententiae* iv. 36. 4 .
83. Trojel, p. 12. For the same reason, boys were excluded from true friendship. See *De spirituali amicitia*, cols. 676-77; *Liber de amicitia*, cols. 836-37.

says, like beasts without reason: "Sed nos credimus, asinis comparandos; ea namque solummodo natura moventur, quae caeteris animantibus homines ostendit aequales, non vera, quae rationis differentia nos a cunctis facit animalibus, separari."[84] An animal may be lecherous, but, as Augustine says, he cannot develop a *passio*, for he has no reason to corrupt. On the surface, all Andreas says is that the true lover must have neither the incapacities of age or blindness nor the instability which results from youth or a superabundance of animal spirits. In other words, he must have three qualifications: an adequate sensual appetite, the ability to engage in immoderate thought, and reason. Andreas seems to praise the lover because of his reason; he must have his full share of that part of his nature which distinguishes him from the beasts. But the ironic implication beneath these seemingly matter-of-fact assertions is that the lover needs his human nature only so that he may corrupt it in a *passio*. A lover, that is, is worse than an old man, a blind man, a boy, or an ass can be.

When the opening chapters of the *De amore* are examined in the light of theological, philosophical, and literary conventions prevailing in the twelfth century, two conclusions emerge. First, it is evident that Andreas employs the literary device of irony and, second, that, if we take this irony into account, there is no doctrinal inconsistency in the *De amore* as a whole. In the search for conventional ideas underlying Andreas' work, it is not necessary to go beyond the central traditions of Christian thought. The necessary materials may be found in such thoroughly commonplace works as the *De spirituali amicitia* of Ailred of Rievaulx, which was written under the inspiration of Bernard of Clairvaux; the *Sententiae* of Peter Lombard, which was a standard text; the *De consolatione* of Boethius, which was one of the most popular books of the Middle Ages; and the commentary on the *Aeneid* by Bernard Silvestris, which inspired humanistic thinkers from John of Salisbury to Salutati. The subject of the *De amore* is *fornicatio* used with its full connotations as the opposite of *caritas*, and Andreas does nothing except condemn it. His lesson is exactly what we should expect from a chaplain in a great feudal court, and it differs hardly at all from the lesson of the *Eructavit* or from what must have been the

---

84. Trojel, pp. 13-14.

lesson of the vernacular paraphrase of Genesis plus gloss, also written for Marie of Champagne.[85] Modern accusations that Andreas was an "insincere" priest with a lecherous eye are without foundation in his work. His only apparent weakness, a sense of humor, did not become a weakness in Christian thought until some three hundred years after he wrote. When the gods were assembled to see Mars, who here represents "virtue" in medieval glosses, caught with Venus in a net of illicit furor, "superi risere, diuque haec fuit in toto notissima fabula caelo." The fable was still current in the twelfth century, and Andreas also laughed, tempering and deepening his laughter with the memory of another kind of celestial laughter (Ps. 2:4): "Qui habitat in caelis irridebit eos, et Dominus subsannabit eos." Theories to the effect that Andreas and the great poets who took up his themes were swayed by scurrilous Albigensian doctrines, by Arabic or Andalusian cults of sensuality, if such indeed existed, or by obscure neo-Platonic heresies are little short of ridiculous. There is no evidence that the medieval poet thought it a kind of poetic duty to give up his patrimony and pay homage to the Count Bougars de Valence. Finally, the term "courtly love" is appropriate to label the love described by Andreas only if it is also appropriate to indicate the activities of Eve and Adam at the Fall.

Princeton University

85. The Bible was thought to condemn only cupidity and to commend only charity. See Augustine *De doctrina Christiana* iii. 10 (15).

Why the Devil Wears Green

Modern Language Notes 69:7 (November 1954), pp. 470-472.

The summoner of Chaucer's Friar's Tale rode out under a "grene-wode shawe" like a hunter "evere waityng on his pray." But there he met another hunter:

> And happed that he saugh bifore hym ryde
> A gay yeman, under a forest syde.
> A bowe he bar, and arwes brighte and kene;
> He hadde upon a courtepy of grene,
> An hat upon his heed with frenges blake. [1]

That the green hunter confesses himself to be "a feend" does not disturb the impenitent summoner, who has sworn to be his "brother." To his credit, the gentleman from "fer in the north contree" was a man of "softe speche" with whom "daliance" seemed pleasant. But the devil's green garment has been taken as a kind of unheeded warning, since it is said to suggest the Celtic underworld. Thus R. M. Garrett, writing of *Sir Gawain*, observed, "The color green connects the Knight with the Celtic underworld. Chaucer's Friar's Summoner should have taken warning at the color of the devil's clothes, but pride closed his eyes."[2] But even after the summoner learns the yeoman's identity he shows no sign of taking warning. The friar probably wished his exemplary summoner to look as much as possible like a true "brother" of the devil. Chaucer and his Friar may or may not have been familiar with the verdure of the Celtic underworld. But there was a clear and well known non-Celtic authority for dressing the devil in green

---

1. *Canterbury Tales,* III (D) 1379-1383, text of F. N. Robinson, *The Complete Works of Geoffrey Chaucer* (Cambridge, Mass., 1933), p. 108.
2. "Sir Gawayne and the Green Knight," *JEGP*, XXIV (1925), 129. Cf. J. R. R. Tolkien and E. V. Gordon, *Sir Gawain and the Green Knight* (Oxford, 1930), p. 86: "... gren was a fairy colour, and suitable for such a being as this knight, whose Green Chapel was nothing else than a fairy mound."

clothes, and as they appear here, these clothes are if anything the opposite of a warning.

One of the most distinguished humanists of the mid-fourteenth century was Pierre Bersuire. He translated Livy, composed a moralization of the Bible, a Scriptural dictionary, a commentary on Ovid, and a moralization of the natural world which generally follows the organization of Bartholomew de Glanville's *De proprietatibus rerum*. Personally, he was a friend of Petrarch and of the poet whom Petrarch called, somewhat extravagantly, "the only poet among the French," Philippe de Vitry.[3] One chapter of his great encyclopedia is devoted to the color green. As we should expect, this color has meanings both "in bono" and "in malo."[4] But in the course of his discussion Bersuire points out that green is a pleasant color so that beasts like it and are attracted to green places. Hunters who seek beasts in such places dress in green so as not to forewarn their victims and so as to appear pleasant themselves. This fact suggests the techniques of that old hunter, the devil:

> Venator ergò diabolus, scilicet hypocrita, solet vestes virides, id est, honestam conversationem induere, ut praetextu exterioris honestatis, possit bestias, id est, simplices ad se attrahere, & dum insidias malitiarum suarum non praecavent, ipsos decipere & fraudere. Ideò bene dicitur Matt. 7. *Attendite vobis à falsis Prophetis, qui veniunt ad vos in vestimentis ovium, intrinsecus autem sunt lupi rapaces.*[5]

The Friar's devil clearly fits this description. He is a hunter dressed in green seeking his prey "under a forest syde." His cheery welcome, his very polite "deere brother," and his courteous and frank replies to the summoner's inquiries give him a sufficiently "green" air, just the

---

3. For Bersuire see F. Ghisalberti, "L'*Ovidius moralizatus* di Pierre Bersuire," *Studi romanzi*, XXIII (1933), esp. pp. 15-25; J. Engels, *Etudes sur L'Ovide moralisé* (Groningen, 1945), 23 ff.

4. For the principle, see Augustine, *De doctrina Christiana*, II, 16 (24). In his Scriptural dictionary Bersuire usually arranges the "good" and "bad" meanings of the signs he explains separately.

5. *Opera* (Coloniae Agrippinae, 1730, 1731), II, 543.

kind of protective coloration needed to attract his fellow worker the summoner.[6] I suggest that it may well have been Bersuire's account or one like it rather than memories of Celtic myth which dressed Chaucer's devil in a green coat.

D. W. ROBERTSON, JR.
Princeton University

---

6. It should be pointed out that the Green Knight is not quite comparable to the green devil. In the first place, he is not a hunter. On the evil reputation of hunters in the Middle Ages, see Rudolph Willard, "Chaucer's Text that Hunters 'ben nat Hooly Men,'" *University of Texas Studies in English*, XXVI (1947), 209-251, and Muriel Bowden, *A Commentary on the General Prologue to the Canterbury Tales* (New York, 1949), pp. 109-110, 116-117. Cf. Bersuire, II, 424, in a discussion of deserts: "ibi tamen sunt aucupes, & venatores, id est, daemones." Again, the Green Knight not only wears green; he is green. That is, there is no discrepancy between himself and his clothing. We might more readily compare the Friar's devil with the Yeoman of the General Prologue, but current opinion views him favorably. Thus Miss Bowden, p. 88, calls him "a sound and likable fellow."

A Further Note on *Conjointure*

Modern Language Notes 70:6 (June 1955), pp. 415-416.

Recently (*MLN*, LXIX [1954], 180-181) Professor W. A. Nitze reaffirmed his view that the word *conjointure* in Chrétien's *Erec*, v. 14, reflects the *iunctura* of Horace, *Ars poetica*, 240 ff. This view may indeed be correct, but it is possible that the verses in Horace, like those in Philippe Mouskés' description of grammar, may refer to the arrangement of words rather than to the ordering of plot elements.[1] Thus a modern French translation of Horace by F. Richard interprets the relevant lines as follows:

> Je prendrais dans la langue courante les éléments dont je façonnerais celle de mes vers: si bien que tout le monde croirait pouvoir en faire autant, mais verrait à l'expérience que les efforts pour y réussir n'aboutissent pas toujours: tant a d'importance le choix et l'arrangement des termes, tant peuvent prendre d'éclat des expressions empruntées au vocabulaire ordinaire![2]

The interpretation underlying this translation, which has been, perhaps, most forcefully stated by Professor Rostagni,[3] is supported by the use of *iunctura* in vv. 46-48: "in verbis etiam tenuis cautusque serendis / dixeris egregie notum si callida verbum / reddiderit iunctura novum." There are, however, those who support the view assumed by Professor Nitze that in 240 ff. Horace was referring to subject matter

---

1. My phrase "elements of composition" in "Some Medieval Literary Terminology," *SP*, XLVIII (1951), 670, n. 7, was followed by a reference to Quintilian, who said (*Inst.* 9. 4. 22) : "In omni porro compositione tria sunt genera necessaria: ordo, junctura, numerus." In 9. 4. 32 he explains, "Junctura sequitur. Est in verbis, incisis, membris, periodis."
2. "Classiques Garnier" (Paris, 1950), II, 277.
3. *Ars poetica* (Turin, 1930), pp. 69-70. Cf. A. S. Wilkins, *The Ars Poetica of Horace* (London, 1939), pp. 382, 383.

and not to language.[4] There is, it seems to me, no way of knowing with certainty how Chrétien would have regarded the passage.

The word *conjunctura* in Alanus probably rests ultimately on a concept like that expressed by Hugh of St. Victor, *Didas.*, 1. 9 (ed. Buttimer, p. 16), in accordance with which any artificial (as distinguished from divine or natural) creation is either "digregata coniungere" or "coniuncta segregare." Elsewhere (3. 4, p. 54) Hugh refers specifically to works of poets: "vel etiam diversa simul compilantes, quasi de multis coloribus et formis, unam picturam facere." The idea here seems to me quite similar to that of Alanus who said that poets compose "ut ex diversorum competenti conjunctura, ipsius narrationis elegantior pictura resultet." Both writers may owe something to Horace's "ut pictura poesis," and it is possible that they may have been influenced by "series iuncturaque." Professor Nitze's judgment in this matter certainly deserves respect. But the relationship between Chrétien's *conjointure* and Alanus' *conjuctura* seems to me clearer than that between either of them and Horace's *iunctura*.

D. W. Robertson, Jr.
Princeton University

---

4. With the translation quoted above compare that of Leon Hermann, "Collection Latomus," VII (Brussels, 1951), p. 29.

The Book of the Duchess

D. W. Robertson, Jr.

In: *Companion to Chaucer Studies,* ed. Beryl Rowland (New York: Oxford University Press, 1968), pp. 332-340. Updated bibliography in Revised Edition, 1979, pp. 409-413.

The Book of the Duchess is an elegy for Blanche, Duchess of Lancaster, who died of the plague on September 12, 1369. At that time her husband the Duke, John of Gaunt, was campaigning on the continent, whence he did not return until November 3. He established an annual memorial service to be held each year at St. Paul's, London, arranged for a tomb for Blanche and for himself to be erected there, and endowed two chantry priests to sing masses daily. As we learn from Froissart, Blanche was an extremely attractive young woman, and at the time of her death she was among the highest ranking ladies at the English court. Chaucer's poem was probably (although not certainly) used in connection with one of the annual services, perhaps in 1374, when the Duke was able to attend for the first time. In any event, the poem should be thought of as a part of a ceremony of considerable dignity and national importance held for members of the royal and Lancastrian households and great men of London.

Briefly, as the poem opens, the speaker, echoing the words of Froissart, describes himself as being overcome by "sorwful ymaginacioun" and unable to sleep. After reading the Ovidian tale of Seys and Alcyone (somewhat altered to suit the purposes of the poem), he is enabled to fall asleep. In a dream he awakens at dawn to hear birds singing a "solempne servise." His chamber is decorated with scenes from the story of Troy, which appears in the windows, and the "text and glose" of the *Roman de la rose,* which appears on the walls. Riding out, he witnesses the beginning of a hunt, led by "th'emperour Octovyen." After being led by a whelp through an earthly paradise, he finds a beardless Black Knight under an oak. The Knight sings a tuneless lament for his deceased beloved that the dreamer apparently overhears. But the dreamer, feigning ignorance, questions him at length. He discovers that the Knight has lost his "bliss" in a chess game with Fortune. In youth he gave himself up to love and idleness, saw his lady, and was overcome by her beauties and virtues. These are described at length in what has sometimes been called the "elegy proper." When he approached her first, awkward and ashamed, she would have nothing to do with him. "Another yere," when she realized his good intentions, he was granted mercy and thereafter lived under her "governaunce." On further questioning, he admits that his lady is dead. The "hert-huntyng" is over, the king rides to a "long castel" on a rich hill wherein a bell strikes twelve, and the dreamer awakens. The poem contains many echoes of fashionable French poetry, and is enlivened by touches of humor.

Modern discussions of the poem usually follow, in general outline, the account of G. L. Kittredge (1915), wherein the Knight, identified as the bereaved John of Gaunt, is described as being a "finished gentleman," whereas the dreamer is naive, full of "childlike wonder," and "stupefied by long suffering." Kittredge regarded love as "the only life that became the gently nurtured" so that "submission to the god [of Love] was their natural duty" (p. 63). He felt that the dream itself was "near to the actual phenomena of dream life." Following this general outline, H. R. Patch (1939) called the dreamer a "poor dolt" (p. 29) and described the poem in colorful terms, saying that it is "full of the high frivolity of Courtly Love." Kittredge's views were repeated by H. S. Bennett (1947), but he also expressed some dissatisfaction with the poem. It is, he said, structurally faulty, containing much that is "derivative and crude," and lacking in "profound emotion or any piercing thought" (p. 36). Adverse criticism also appeared in the discussion of J. S. P. Tatlock (1950), where the poem is said to be repetitious and dilatory, and the dreamer, who is here not Chaucer, indifferent to "human reality" (p. 30). The dreamer continued to suffer in the discussion of

Kemp Malone (1951), where his lack of awareness is said to be an inconsistency on Chaucer's part. Malone also asserted that Chaucer was forced to turn the marriage of John of Gaunt (the Black Knight) into "an extra-marital love affair for the sake of the conventions of courtly love" (p. 40). The dream, he said, is "realistic."

Kittredge's "naive" dreamer has not lacked defenders, however, and the integrity of the poem has been vigorously supported. James R. Kreuzer (1951) denied the dreamer's naivete altogether, refusing to identify the dreamer and the speaker (pp. 544-5). The dreamer's lack of awareness, he explained, was "consciously contrived" to enable him to administer a cathartic remedy. In a long and carefully wrought article, B. H. Bronson (1952) elaborated the idea of the dreamer's "tact," at the same time describing the Knight and Blanche as ideal "courtly lovers." Here the Knight acts as a "surrogate" for the dreamer. His description of Blanche is both his own (i.e., the Duke's) and Chaucer's. However, D. S. Brewer (1953), calling attention to the public presentation of the poem and to its "conventionality," warned that it was not "a private outcry of grief nor a private consolation" (pp. 44-5). Brewer considered the humor of the poem to be largely unintentional and the portrait of Blanche to be archetypal. With some similar misgivings about Chaucer's own participation, Donald C. Baker (1955) made the description of the lady the work of a "peer" (John of Gaunt) rather than of the poet, since the expression of such noble grief was, he asserted, beyond the comprehension of the poet-dreamer. The poet's inadequacy as a personal eulogist was also emphasized by Stephen Manning (1956), but at the expense of the dreamer once more, who is said to be characterized by "nonpareil dullwittedness." In a later article (1958) Manning's dreamer still displays "customary stupidity," and the portrait of Blanche is said to show the influence of the troubadours and of the traditions of "courtly love."

Professor Malone's observations on extra-marital "courtly love" were answered elaborately by John Lawlor (1956), who maintained that such love, stemming from the traditions of the *Roman de la rose,* could exist between married persons, especially in England, and that Chaucer halted his account of the love affair at its highest point, which is not marriage but the acceptance of the lover (p. 631). This is, Lawlor assures us, the "highest earthly good," a good that the Knight has enjoyed but that the dreamer, whose love is unrequited, has not. In a briefer and more recent statement of his thesis (1966), the same author, using a hint from Bronson, makes the poet a "substitute figure for the real mourner." The dreamer is further exculpated by W. H. French (1957), for, it is said, the song he overheard might well be taken simply as a conventional lyric without specific personal application. In Charles Muscatine's treatment of the poem's style (1957), the dreamer is a lover, but the realism or "factualism" of the dream itself is seriously questioned. R. M. Lumiansky (1959) maintained, however, that the narrator in the poem suffered from bereavement, not love-longing, and that he, Alcyone, and the Knight are united in grief. An extended argument is presented to show that the poem consoles both the dreamer and the Knight. But the dreamer was severely criticized once more by Dorothy Bethurum (1959), who found him obtuse, a failure as a lover, and ignorant of currently fashionable classical lore. He was defended once more by Joseph E. Grennen (1964) for his deft "psychological maneuvering" that reflects conventional treatments of *cardiaca passio*. Finally, in a carefully reasoned article, J. Burke Severs (1964) maintained that the speaker's condition at the opening was not due to unrequited love, and that the dreamer never speaks as a lover. He, speaking for Chaucer, keeps the Black Knight talking until he can face his sorrow "in plain utterance."

These are the principal variations on the pattern of interpretation established by Professor Kittredge. The questions that have concerned scholars most are (1) whether the speaker at the opening suffers from unrequited love or from grief as a result of bereavement; (2) whether the dreamer is naive, or even awkward, or, on the other hand, courteous and considerate; and (3) whether the consolation is well applied, and if so how it is applied. Some of the works mentioned above, especially those of Bronson, Lawlor, Lumiansky, and Severs, contain elaborate treatments of the third question that cannot be summarized adequately in a few words. In addition to the works mentioned above, there have been at least two extensive critical appreciations of the poem in recent years, one by Donald C. Baker (1958), using "archetypal imagery," and one by Georgia Ronan Crampton (1963). These read a little like pleasant afternoon lectures on abstract paintings, although the tendency to treat Chaucer's poem as a work of modern expressionism is by no means confined to these two essays.

There have been a number of efforts to explain specific details in the poem. John M. Steadman (1956) suggested that the "whelp" might be a symbol of marital fidelity, calling attention to dogs in Alciati's *Emblemata,* in Pierius' *Hieroglyphica,* and on late medieval funerary monuments. Beryl Rowland (1962) suggested that the "twelve ferses" may constitute a reference to the signs of the Zodiac, and that the chess game in the poem might be a variant of the standard game. She also suggested (1963) that the "round tour of yvoyre" used in the description of the lady might refer to an ivory chess piece. Turning to the "whelp," the same author (1965) found that Chaucer never commends dogs, and that the whelp may be a kind of nightmare feature of the dream hunt that acts to split the dreamer into two parts (Black Knight and interrogator). James I. Wimsatt (1967), in a careful and detailed article, has shown that the description of Blanche contains definite suggestions of the Blessed Virgin Mary.

The general formulation established by Professor Kittredge was abandoned altogether by D. W. Robertson, Jr. (1962), who considered the "courtly love" that plays such a large part in the usual discussions to be, as it is there used, an irrelevant modern fantasy. In this account, the Black Knight is said to be no literal reflection of John of Gaunt, but the erring will of the speaker that sees the loss of the lady as the loss of a gift of Fortune, while the dreamer represents the reason. The dream thus contains a dialogue between what may be considered as two parts of the same person (pp. 463-5) who represents the mourners for Blanche. B. F. Huppé and Robertson (1963) sought to interpret the entire poem in the light of medieval literary theory, offering interpretations of many of its details on the basis of traditional iconography. Here the Knight is not the Duke but a kind of alter-ego of the dreamer, expressive of grief over the loss of Blanche as a merely physical object of desire. The details in the description of Blanche are said to reflect conventional imagery, chiefly Scriptural in origin, and to point to her spiritual virtues. Some features of this explanation were elaborated in an essay by Robertson (1965) in an attempt to place the poem in its historical setting. Chaucer's poem is here said to be consistent with the conventional themes of funerary consolation as they are implicit in *The Consolation of Philosophy* and explicit in the Mass for the Burial of the Dead. Its surface humor is attributed to the chivalric character of the audience and to the underlying idea that Chaucer had no desire to cultivate grief on an occasion of hope and inspiration. The speaker typifies the initial sorrow of all of the mourners for Blanche. The Knight and the dreamer are not "characters" but exemplifications of attitudes, so that the Knight may be dismissed as soon as the theme of the poem becomes clear. That is, "if the virtues of the Duchess were an inspiration to reasonable and noble conduct in life, her memory should continue to inspire such conduct," not the helpless sorrow of the speaker at the opening, nor the bitter grief of Alcyone, who has no hope, nor the sloth of the Man in Black, who has lost his "bliss" to Fortune and does not understand the implications of the lady's virtue, even after he has described them in his own words.

It is obvious that further contributions to our knowledge of the poem must rest on an intensive study of primary materials. We have hardly begun to understand the French sources. As the late Rosemond Tuve demonstrated in her study of *Allegorical Imagery* (1966), we may need to revise considerably our general estimate of even such well-known works as the *Roman de la rose,* which is mentioned explicitly in Chaucer's poem. Again, we know very little about the meaning of the dream vision as a poetic form; it is, in any event, certainly not conducive to dream "realism" of the kind envisaged by Kittredge and Malone. Again, we are largely ignorant of the conventions of Gothic iconography as they were manifested in fourteenth-century England. Finally, there are many traits of style, attitude, and demeanor in the England of Edward III that remain obscure. Simple readjustments of the ideas set forth in the secondary sources above without careful attention to primary materials may fatten our bibliographies, but they will not contribute substantially to our knowledge of Chaucer's work, nor to any real appreciation for it.

BIBLIOGRAPHY

Baker, Donald C. "The Dreamer again in *The Book of the Duchess*," *PMLA*, LXX (1955), 279-82.

———. "Imagery and Structure in Chaucer's *Book of the Duchess*," *SN*, XXX (1958), 17-26.

Bennett, H. S. *Chaucer and the Fifteenth Century*. (Oxford History of English Literature, II, pt. 1.) Oxford, 1947.

Bethurum, Dorothy. "Chaucer's Point of View in the Love Poems," *PMLA*, LXXIV (1959), 511-20.

Brewer, D. S. *Chaucer*. London, 1953. Rev. 2nd ed. London, 1960.

Bronson, Bertrand H. "*The Book of the Duchess* Re-opened," *PMLA*, LXVII (1952), 863-81.

Crampton, Georgia Ronan. "Transitions and Meanings in *The Book of the Duchess*," *JEGP*, LXII (1963), 486-500.

French, W. H. "The Man in Black's Lyric," *JEGP*, LXVI (1957), 231-41.

Grennen, Joseph E. "*Hert-Huntyng* in the *Book of the Duchess*," *MLQ*, XXV (1964), 131-9.

Huppé, Bernard F., and D. W. Robertson, Jr. *Fruyt and Chaf: Studies in Chaucer's Allegories*. Princeton, 1963.

Kittredge, G. L. *Chaucer and his Poetry*. Cambridge, Mass., 1915.

Kreuzer, James R. "The Dreamer in the *Book of the Duchess*," *PMLA*, LXVI (1951), 543-7.

Lawlor, John. "The Pattern of Consolation in *The Book of the Duchess*," *Speculum*, XXXI (1956), 626-48.

———. "The Earlier Poems," in *Chaucer and Chaucerians: Critical Studies in Middle English Literature,* ed. D. S. Brewer. London, 1966. pp. 39-64.

Lumiansky, R. M. "The Bereaved Narrator in Chaucer's *The Book of the Duchess*," *TSE*, IX (1959), 5-17.

Malone, Kemp. *Chapters on Chaucer*. Baltimore, 1951.

Manning, Stephen. "That Dreamer Once More," *PMLA*, LXXI (1956), 540-1.

———. "Chaucer's Good Fair White: Woman and Symbol," *CL*, X (1958), 97-105.

Muscatine, Charles. *Chaucer and the French Tradition: A Study in Style and Meaning*. Berkeley, 1957.

Patch, Howard Rollin. *On Rereading Chaucer*. Cambridge, Mass., 1939.

Robertson, D. W., Jr. *A Preface to Chaucer: Studies in Medieval Perspectives*. Princeton, 1962.

———. "The Historical Setting of Chaucer's *Book of the Duchess*," in *Mediaeval*

Studies in Honor of Urban Tigner Holmes, Jr. Chapel Hill, N.C., 1965. pp. 169-95.
———. See under Huppé, Bernard F.
Rowland, Beryl. "The Chess Problem in Chaucer's *Book of the Duchess*," *Anglia*, LXXX (1962), 384-9.
———. "'A Round Tour of Yvoyre'," *N&Q*, X (1963), 9.
———. "The Whelp in Chaucer's *Book of the Duchess*," *NM*, LXVI (1965), 148-60.
Severs, J. Burke. "The Sources of 'The Book of the Duchess'," *MS*, XXV (1963), 355-62.
———. "Chaucer's Self-Portrait in the *Book of the Duchess*," *PQ*, XLIII (1964), 27-39.
Steadman, John M. "Chaucer's 'Whelp': A Symbol of Marital Fidelity?" *N&Q*, III (1956), 374-5.
Tatlock, J. S. P. *The Mind and Art of Chaucer.* Syracuse, New York, 1950.
Tuve, Rosemond. *Allegorical Imagery: Some Mediaeval Books and Their Posterity.* Princeton, 1966.
Wimsatt, James I. "The Apotheosis of Blanche in *The Book of the Duchess*," *JEGP*, LXVI (1967), 26-44.

During the years since the above was written over thirty notes, articles, and chapters in books have been devoted to the *Book of the Duchess,* only a few of which can be mentioned here to illustrate variety of opinion. "Courtly love" has been less popular, although John Gardner (1977) seeks to revive it, praising Chaucer for his "psychological realism" and calling the poem a "celebration of earthly love." The character of the dreamer still causes difficulty. Perhaps we should remember that Chaucer was well-known to his audience, some of whom were his superiors, so that, not being a pompous man, he avoided taking himself too seriously, although he had important things to say. The serious side of the dreamer is emphasized in two Boethian interpretations. The first, by Michael D. Cherniss (1969), shows parallels between the dialogue in the poem and the first two books of the *Consolation.*

Cherniss maintains, however, that the Knight is not consoled (See lines 566, 1301). Charles P. R. Tisdale (1973) compares the relation between the dreamer and the Knight with the "two parts of the same person" ascribed by Jean de Meun to the speakers in the *Consolation,* and discusses the significance of Boethian "imagination." However, "comic," "stupid," or "foolish" dreamers still abound.

In an article reflecting current interest in number symbolism Russell A. Peck (1970) says that the Knight is led to recount acts of "memory, intellect, and love," and that his likeness (the Trinity within) is restored in his "marriage." He discusses other numbers as well. A rhetorical interpretation by Robert M. Jordan (1974) explains that the poem is discontinuous rather than "organic," so that consistent characters are not to be expected. There have been "psychological" interpretations, although these are usually remote from the poem and from fourteenth-century life and thought, notably by John Norton-Smith (1974), who discusses the curative effects of objectified dreams. John M. Fyler (1977) adopts the views of Amis in the *Roman de la rose* to show that the Knight and Blanche represent Golden Age innocence.

Edward I. Condren (1971) on the basis of the eight years' malady seeks to date the poem in 1377, and John H. Palmer (1974) presents evidence to show that Blanche died in 1368.

BIBLIOGRAPHY

Baker, Donald C. "The Dreamer again in *The Book of the Duchess*." *PMLA,* 70 (1955), 279-82.

———. "Imagery and Structure in Chaucer's *Book of the Duchess*." *SN,* 30 (1958), 17-26.

Bennett, HS. *Chaucer and the Fifteenth Century.* Oxford History of English Literature, II, pt. 1. Oxford: Oxford Univ. Press, 1947.

Bethurum, Dorothy. "Chaucer's Point of View in the Love Poems." *PMLA,* 74 (1959), 511-20.

Brewer, D.S. *Chaucer.* 1953. Rev. 3rd ed. London: Longmans, 1973.

Bronson, Bertrand H. "*The Book of the Duchess* Re-opened." *PMLA,* 67 (1952), 863-81.

Cherniss, Michael D. "The Boethian Dialogue in Chaucer's *Book of the Duchess*." *JEGP,* 68 (1969), 655-65.

Condren, Edward I. "The Historical Context of the *Book of the Duchess*." *ChauR*, 5 (1971), 195-212.

Crampton, Georgia Ronan. "Transitions and Meanings in *The Book of the Duchess*." *JEGP*, 62 (1963), 486-500.

French, W.H. "The Man in Black's Lyric." *JEGP*, 66 (1957), 231-41.

Fyler, John M. "Irony and the Age of Gold in the *Book of the Duchess*." *Speculum*, 52 (1977), 314-328.

Gardner, John. *The Poetry of Chaucer*. Carbondale: Southern Illinois Univ. Press, 1977.

Grennen, Joseph E. *"Hert-Huntyng* in the *Book of the Duchess*." *MLQ*, 25 (1964), 131-39.

Huppé, Bernard F., and D.W. Robertson, Jr. *Fruyt and Chaf: Studies in Chaucer's Allegories*. Princeton: Princeton Univ. Press, 1963.

Jordan, Robert M. "The Compositional Structure of the *Book of the Duchess*." *ChauR*, 9 (1974), 99-117.

Kittredge, G.L. *Chaucer and His Poetry*. Cambridge, Mass.: Harvard Univ. Press, 1915.

Kreuzer, James R. "The Dreamer in the *Book of the Duchess*." *PMLA*, 66 (1951), 543-47.

Lawlor, John. "The Pattern of Consolation in *The Book of the Duchess*." *Speculum*, 31 (1956), 626-48.

———. "The Earlier Poems." In *Chaucer and Chaucerians: Critical Studies in Middle English Literature*. Ed. D.S. Brewer. London: Nelson, 1966, pp. 39-64.

Lumiansky, R.M. "The Bereaved Narrator in Chaucer's *The Book of the Duchess*." *TSE*, 9 (1959), 5-17.

Malone, Kemp. *Chapters on Chaucer*. Baltimore: Johns Hopkins Univ. Press, 1951.

Manning, Stephen. "That Dreamer Once More." *PMLA*, 71 (1956), 540-41.

———. "Chaucer's Good Fair White: Woman and Symbol." *CL*, 10 (1958), 97-105.

Muscatine, Charles. *Chaucer and the French Tradition: A Study in Style and Meaning*. Berkeley: Univ. of California Press, 1957.

Palmer, John H. "The Historical Context of the *Book of the Duchess*: A Revision." *ChauR*, 8 (1974), 253-61.

Patch, Howard Rollin. *On Rereading Chaucer*. Cambridge, Mass.: Harvard Univ. Press, 1939.

Peck, Russell A. "Theme and Number in Chaucer's *Book of the Duchess*." In *Silent Poetry*. Ed. A. Fowler. New York: Barnes & Noble, 1970, pp. 73-115.

Robertson, D.W., Jr. *A Preface to Chaucer: Studies in Medieval Perspectives*. Princeton: Princeton Univ. Press, 1962.

———. "The Historical Setting of Chaucer's *Book of the Duchess*." . In *Mediaeval Studies in Honor of Urban Tigner Holmes, Jr.* Ed. J. Mahoney and J.E. Keller. 1965. Rpt. New York: Russell & Russell, 1976, pp. 169-195.

———. See under Huppé, Bernard F.

Rowland, Beryl. "The Chess Problem in Chaucer's *Book of the Duch*ess." *Anglia*, 80 (1962), 384-89.

———. "'A Round Tour of Yvoyre'." *N&Q*, 10 (1963), 9.

———. "The Whelp in Chaucer's *Book of the Duchess*." *NM*, 66 (1965), 148-60.

———. *Blind Beasts: Chaucer's Animal World*. Kent, Ohio: Kent State Univ. Press, 1971, pp. 161-65.

Severs, J. Burke. "The Sources of *The Book of the Duchess*." *MS*, 25 (1963), 355-62.

———. "Chaucer's Self-Portrait in the *Book of the Duchess*." *PQ*, 43 (1964), 27-39.

Steadman, John M. "Chaucer's 'Whelp': A Symbol of Marital Fidelity?" *N&Q*, 3 (1956), 374-75.

Tatlock, J.S.P. *The Mind and Art of Chaucer*. 1950. Rpt. New York: Gordian Press, 1966.

Tisdale, Charles P. "Boethian 'Hert-Huntyng': The Elegiac Pattern of the *Book of the Duchess*." *ABR*, 24 (1973), 356-80.

Tuve, Rosemond. *Allegorical Imagery: Some Mediaeval Books and their Posterity*. Princeton: Princeton Univ. Press, 1966.

Wimsatt, James I. "The Apotheosis of Blanche in *The Book of the Duchess*." *JEGP*, 66 (1967), 26-44.

———. "Machaut's *Lay de Confort* and Chaucer's *Book of the Duchess*." In *Chaucer at Albany*. Ed. Rossell Hope Robbins. New York: Burt Franklin, 1975, pp. 11-26.

Chaucer Criticism

D. W. Robertson, Jr.

Medievalia et Humanistica 8 (1977), pp. 252-255.

*A*side from a few illustrations, Donald R. Howard's *The Idea of the Canterbury Tales* relies almost exclusively on secondary sources.[1] That is, the author has read a great deal of scholarship and criticism but has done very little original research, displaying only rarely first-hand information about fourteenth-century English society, its intellectual traditions, or its literary conventions. In Chapter I, in fact, he renounces historical interpretation, to concentrate instead on what *The Canterbury Tales,* as he puts it, *is,* and on the "mind" of Chaucer. Nevertheless, he does not hesitate to tell us from time to time what "medievals," as he calls them, thought about things, deriving this information from a selection of secondary materials. At the outset, an analysis of the Ellesmere portrait of Chaucer leads to the conclusion that the disproportionately small horse, and Chaucer's small legs, emphasize the head and torso to show that "the man and the poet loom over the fictional pilgrimage." Thus, as we learn in Chapter II, it is important to know the "idea" Chaucer had in mind when he wrote. The *Tales* reflect the idea of the pilgrimage, which is obvious enough, and they are, moreover, comic. For the idea of comedy Professor Howard uses the fourth-century definition of Evanthius, which he found in Cunliffe (1912). Except for some discussion of Dante, later medieval statements about comedy are disregarded. Comedy is said to imply "espousal of the world," an idea with which John of Salisbury might have agreed, but with the additional idea that this represents an unfortunate subjection to Fortune, or to

---

1. Donald R. Howard, *The Idea of the Canterbury Tales* (Berkeley: The University of California Press, 1976).

Providential ill consequences.[2] But in Chaucer, Professor Howard assures us, the morality arises from the *Tales* as a whole, so that the basic idea he had in mind was that of "the book," although he concluded his book with another "book," the Parson's sermon.

The style of the "book" of the *Tales* is discussed in Chapter III, where we learn, without much astonishment, that although Chaucer related events in the past, he often used the present tense to create a sense of immediacy. Another stylistic device described is a "sense of obsolescence," especially in contrasting ideals thought to be characteristic of the past with a more reprehensible present. This is a common device of satirists and moralists, but Professor Howard does not examine events during Chaucer's lifetime to determine whether in this instance there was any basis for Chaucer's attitude. There is a diffuse discussion of irony, but again without any reference to medieval ideas about irony and its techniques. Part of the "idea" of the Tales is said to be "the search for the world," whose attractions are vividly revealed, especially in the "ideal" love portrayed in *Troilus*.

The "search" is examined further in Chapter IV on "Memory and Form," where it is described as being carried out on a "pilgrimage through the world," which is a part of the "idea" of the *Tales*. But the pilgrimage is a memory of past experience, and, in this connection, a rather obscure argument is developed to show that the pilgrims in the General Prologue fall into "mnemonic groups." The author does not seem to be familiar with modern memory systems of the kind used by stage performers and card players. The tales themselves can be thought of as occupying a single day in a "symbolic" sense. But the individual tales "discredit each other." The form of the whole is that of a "memory," here compared, again obscurely, with circular designs like those of the so-called rose windows in cathedrals. This "form," we are told, also has a "structure," described in Chapter V. That is, the tales are arranged in pairs, like the Knight's Tale and the Miller's Tale, the latter discrediting the former, the Miller's Tale and the Reeve's Tale, the latter discrediting the former, and so on. This "binary" arrangement, with its "breaks" between the various fragments or groups, is

---

2. *Policraticus,* 3.8, ed. Webb, 1.190-199.

said to form the basis of an "interlace" structure somewhat like that attributed by Professor Vinaver to certain romances. There follows a rapid and superficial survey of the tales, partly designed to show this structure, concluding with the Manciple's Tale, which leads us back to the General Prologue as we seek to remember the character of the Manciple. Thus, the "interlace" is "circular" before we reach the final "book" of the Parson's Tale. The "themes" said to be the basis for the interlace are things like Fortune, food, money, sex, "quitting," and so on. These are four subjects and a device, not themes. There are actual themes in the tales, like the foolishness of submission to Fortune, the ill effects of Mars and Venus (taken figuratively), the advantages of wise old age and the disadvantages of cultivating the old age of the Pauline Old Man, and so on; but these are disregarded, or even denied. However, we are offered one final analogy for the interlace structure, the labyrinth used for symbolic pilgrimages on cathedral floors. The final chapter discusses two tales of special significance, those of the Pardoner and the Parson, with emphasis on the former, which is treated with passionate expressionism, making it sound a little like a modern horror film with intense psychological realism. In general, the author is stubbornly obtuse to stylistic history and the perspectives it affords. The Parson's Tale is said to shed new light on the previous "book," so that we are forced to reflect once more on the tales we have read.

The above summary is a simplification of a diffuse and often verbose argument that almost continuously adduces complexities. It is designed, as your reviewer understands it, to enable the reader to become vicariously involved in the "book" of the *Tales*, so that reading it becomes an emotional experience somewhat like that provided by a novel, and it will undoubtedly appeal to those who relish experiences of this kind. In the course of the argument there are some dubious statements, some historical and some concerning the text. For example, we are told that chivalry was "obsolescent" and that Chaucer would have thought it to be so. From the perspective of history it is true that chivalric ideals would soon weaken and almost disappear, but Chaucer would not have known this. He and his friends were not familiar with mass warfare. Men like Clanvowe and Stury, not to mention Chaucer himself, would have thought the function of chivalry to be something like that of a modern defense establishment, and although they may well have thought that it had declined in England, they could observe without too much difficulty that it had begun to flourish in France. The Yeoman, who is dressed as a forester, is said to wear a "warlike costume." Although a reeve in the fourteenth century is by definition a manorial servant elected from among customary tenants, we are told that there were "no serfs" among the pilgrims. It is quite possible also to think of the Miller and the Plowman as serfs, remembering that the social distinction between freemen and serfs was becoming blurred in the late fourteenth century. The Plowman's concern for his neighbors suggests strongly that he was a traditional manorial servant elected from among bondmen, and not a hired worker from outside a manor. If we accept this view, then the Parson, his brother, must have been a man of servile origin freed by his education.

The pilgrims are said to represent a "cross-section" of English society. This commonplace of criticism is true only in a very general way, for there are many gaps in the "cross-section." There are no bishops, abbots, archdeacons, or chaplains, although the last were very numerous and often unruly. There are no great magnates, officials of the royal household (except for Chaucer himself, who is not so identified), obstreperous local lords, like the notorious Lord John Fitzwalter of Essex[3] or the almost indestructible Sir Matthew Gurney of Somerset,[4] no stewards or other members of lay courts, no royal justices, apprentices at law, local lawyers, or filacers, no coroners, borough officials, city apprentices, and so on. Many familiar figures are, in fact, missing, and the problem of why Chaucer selected the groups he did

---

3. See Elizabeth Chapin Furber, *Essex Sessions of the Peace 1351, 1377-79*, Essex Archaeological Society Occasional Publications, 3 (1953), pp. 61-62, 82-90.

4. Isobel D. Thornley and T. F. T. Plucknett, eds., *Year Books of Richard II: 11 Richard II* (Ames Foundation, Cambridge, Mass.: Harvard U. Press, 1937), pp. xiii-xvi and 170-174. In spite of his extortions and other felonies, Gurney was named on commissions of the peace and of oyer and terminer in 1381-85 and on peace commissions again in 1388-92. He became a member of King's Council under Henry IV, and died in 1406 at the age of 97.

has never been faced squarely; it has simply been obscured by a convenient generalization. The pilgrims are also said to be "types," but if this means that they are "typical," it is an absurdity. Chaucer himself is called a "bourgeois," although as a royal squire with war service he was very clearly a gentleman.[5] He is said to have served as a J. P., as though this were an occupation. It is true that he was named on commissions of the peace, but this does not mean that he ever attended sessions, and if he did they would have not taken much time and would have been remunerative only if he had been unscrupulous, as his Franklin evidently was.

With reference to the text, the "end" sought by Palamon and Arcite in the Knight's Tale is said to be marriage, although neither Palamon's oath to make war on chastity all his life nor Arcite's dedication to wrathful passions sounds much like an anticipation of marriage. In this connection, critics of the tale often pay little attention to the text, which does not fit their theories, and the present discussion is no exception. The miller's daughter in the Reeve's Tale, who "thikke and well ygrowen was, / With kamus nose, and eyen greye as glas, / With buttokes brode, and breestes round and hye," is said not to be "sexually desirable," except perhaps for her hair. The urgent exclamation of Nicholas in the Miller's Tale — "for deerne love of thee, lemman, I spille" — is called "courtly love parlance," although Henry of Lancaster's use of it, as he describes it in his *Les Seyntz Medicines,* can hardly be called "courtly," and similar expressions were doubtless used by persons of all ranks. The Franklin's Tale is treated reasonably, if superficially, but the Franklin himself is described as a "genial country squire," as though he might have just emerged, country-fresh, from the pages of Mr. Fielding. It may be an exaggeration to say with one authority that the sheriff's tourn after 1388 became little more than "an instrument

---

5. Cf. N. Denholm-Young, *Country Gentry in the Fourteenth Century* (Oxford, 1969), p. 24. The word *bourgeois,* unless it means simply residents of boroughs and cities, makes little sense in fourteenth-century terms. Many members of the higher nobility had residences in London. London merchants were sometimes knighted, and many more of them would have been knighted if the Crown had had its way.

of extortion,"[6] but there is enough truth in it, not to mention, in addition, examples of extortionate sheriffs earlier, like Robert Hacche and William Auncel of Devon,[7] to make our very wealthy and self-indulgent Franklin look more than a little suspicious.

To say that the "form" of *The Canterbury Tales* is a memory is to do little more than to place it in the very large class of narratives in the past tense, and the construct of a circular interlace pattern is not very convincing, in spite of recent tendencies among literary critics to try to make almost any work of literature operate like *Finnegan's Wake*: by "a commodious vicus of recirculation." Before we can talk about form and structure in Chaucer's work with any real conviction we shall need to devote much study to the history of classical forms in the Middle Ages, frequently transformed into modes, first in Latin literature and then in the various vernaculars. But this kind of study has hardly begun. In the present work Chaucer's wit, humor, and vigor suffer because of a failure to appreciate the specific relevance of what he had to say to fourteenth-century English life. More importantly, although the author does make notable concessions to Chaucer's moral ideals, he does not take them seriously enough to provide the necessary vantage for a humorous stance. Finally, it is unfortunate that Professor Howard did not devote more of his considerable energy and intelligence to primary research. It is to be hoped that university presses will in the future demand more such research, and the intelligent use of it, from their authors and that their assigned readers will be more alert to the need for it. If they do not do so, much Chaucer criticism is likely to remain frothy and insubstantial.

---

6. I. S. Leadam and C. S. Baldwin, eds., *Select Cases before the King's Council 1213-1482* (Selden Society, Cambridge, Mass.: Harvard U. Press, 1918), lxxxvi. On sheriffs generally, see lxxxiii-lxxxix.

7. Bertha Haven Putnam, ed., *Proceedings before the Justices of the Peace in the Fourteenth and Fifteenth Centuries* (Ames Foundations, London, 1938). For Hacche, see pp. 63, 73-74, 76--77, 80; for Auncel, pp. 74-75, 77-78. See further, N. Neilson, *Customary Rents* in *Oxford Studies in Social and Legal History,* II (1912), pp. 140, 147-148; Helen M. Cam, *The Hundred and the Hundred Rolls* (London, 1930), 67-85, 106. For an amusing endorsement of the corruption of sheriffs by local lords, see John Smyth, *The Lives of the Berkeleys* (Bristol and Gloucester Archaeological Society, 1883), I, p. 307.

"And for my land thus hastow mordred me?": Land Tenure, the Cloth Industry, and the Wife of Bath*

by D. W. Robertson, Jr.

The Chaucer Review 14:4 (1980), pp. 403-420.

Embedded in the Wife's Prologue are various statements concerning transfers of land and wealth that may be indicative of her legal status. She is sometimes thought of as a freeholder under the common law, or, alternatively, as a borough tenant. I should like to suggest here that she was probably thought of in Chaucer's time as a rural clothier, and that her Prologue may indicate further that she was a bondwoman. Although the social distinction between freeholders and villeins was disappearing in the later fourteenth century when social status in rural communities depended on wealth rather than on legal distinctions, and when increasing numbers of villeins were more wealthy than some of their neighboring freeholders, unfree status would have been consistent with the iconographic overtones of the Wife's character.[1] I believe that Chaucer was careful about such matters and hope to demonstrate further instances of this concern.

---

* I am grateful to Professor J. R. Strayer for reading this paper in an earlier form and making useful suggestions about legal matters. Any errors remaining are, however, my own. My colleague Gail Gibson also furnished valuable references and criticisms. Robinson's text of Chaucer is used in this article (*The Works of Geoffrey Chaucer*, ed. F. N. Robinson, 2nd ed. [Boston: Houghton Mifflin, 1957]).

1. For some of these overtones, see the present author's *A Preface to Chaucer* (Princeton Univ. Press, 1972), pp. 317-31, and the further observations in

Whether the conclusion concerning status is found acceptable or not, however, the following discussion should help to shed some light for Chaucerians on the character of the late medieval cloth industry, afford an explanation for the Wife's concern about land, and suggest a reasonable explanation for her obvious and even ostentatious wealth.

With reference to her first three "good" husbands, who were "riche and olde," she says, "They had me yeven hir lond and hir tresoor" (204), so that she held these husbands "hooly" in her hand, and pleased them only for her "profit" and "ese" (211-224). Nevertheless she complains, as if to all three of them in one person,

> "why hydestow, with sorwe,
> The keyes of thy chest awey fro me?
> It is my good as wel as thyn, pardee!"
>
> (308-310)

And she further asserts that her husband (sc. husbands) cannot be "maister of my body and of my good," and will forego one of them. Indeed, she charged for her services, demanding "raunson" for them (411), and endured their lust for "wynnyng" (406), thus converting her Pauline "marriage debt" (153) into a means of prostitution, apparently for the sake of ostentatious dress, a common target for moral censure both in prose and verse during the fourteenth century (cf. ParsT, 932-34). There is a seeming inconsistency here, for if her husbands had given her their land and wealth, why did she need access to their chests (used to keep cash and documents, since there were no banks)? Is her claim that the money is hers valid? Or is she simply reflecting the "Theophrastian" opinion that a wife will always claim "half part" of her husband's goods (MerchT, 1299-1300)?

Before seeking to answer these questions, we might review very briefly a few points of English law. In the first place, no one "owned" land. He or she held it of someone else in some sort of tenure; and the person of whom it was held, traditionally a "lord," although in the

---

"Simple Signs from Everyday Life in Chaucer," to appear in *Signs and Symbols in Chaucer's Poetry*, ed. John P. Hermann and John J. Burke (Univ. of Alabama Press).

complex tenurial relationships of the late Middle Ages not necessarily a person of higher status, in turn held it of someone else, the ultimate lord being the king. Those who held directly of the king were called "tenants in chief" of the crown. But the king did not "own" land either, so that we can say that there was no such thing as the "ownership" of land in medieval England. In France there were "lordless" or "alodial" lands, but not in England. An individual might be "seised" of land, which meant that he occupied it either in person or through someone else; or a manorial lord might be "seised" of land occupied by his tenants, the terms of whose occupancy and rights of inheritance were governed by local custom, or, at times, by special grant. Under the circumstances, unlike personal property such as beds, robes, drapes, cups, silverware, gold and silver, pots, pans, other kitchen utensils, kerchiefs, stocks of wood, etc., land could not be devised or willed to someone else. There were exceptions in burgage tenure in some towns, where land could be devised even to a person who was neither a direct nor a collateral heir, and among villeins on some manors.[2]

In spite of this situation, land was the most secure and popular form of investment, and even merchants, after accumulating cash from trade, often exchanged it for land or purchased landed estates for retirement. Land was then evaluated not for features like pleasant views, flower gardens, proximity to beaches, schools, churches, or markets, but for the annual income that might be expected from it. That is, medieval documents do not ordinarily evaluate land in terms

---

2. For the general principles in the paragraph above, see A. W. B. Simpson, *An Introduction to the History of the Land Law* (Oxford Univ. Press, 1961), and S. F. C. Milsom, *Historical Foundations of the Common Law* (London: Butterworth's, 1969). For wills of land in burgage tenure, see Simpson, *Introduction*, p, 14. Some idea of the variety of borough customs may be formed by glancing through Mary Bateson, *Borough Customs*, Selden Society 18 (1904) and 21 (1906). A few boroughs restricted devise. See M. de W. Hemmeon, "Burgage Tenure in Medieval England," *LQR*, 27 (1911), 44-46. Histories of individual towns sometimes contain more thorough information. For a good recent bibliography, see the list of works cited in Susan Reynolds, *An Introduction to the History of English Medieval Towns* (Oxford: Clarendon Press, 1977), pp. 202-23. For villein wills, see Cicely Howell, "Peasant Inheritance Customs in the Midlands 1280-1700," in *Family and Inheritance*, ed. Jack Goody, Joan Thirsk, and E. P. Thompson (Cambridge Univ. Press, 1976), p. 120.

of sale price, but indicate that such and such land was worth so much a year. And when sale prices were determined, they were often awkwardly managed, although during the fifteenth century a purchase price amounting to twenty years' income became common.[3] During the fourteenth century, tenants in need of cash might be expected to make sacrifices, and there were land brokers in London, like Sir John Philpot, ready to arrange transactions.

Free land might be held in "fee simple," like the land acquired by the Sergeant of the Law (GP 319), and such land had the advantage of liquidity because, with some exceptions on certain manors, it was freely alienable. But it was not highly suitable for the formation of estates, since collateral heirs could claim an interest in it, so that some landholders in the late Middle Ages sought to convert tenures in fee simple into tenures in fee tail, usually tail male, so that a male heir could not alienate it but was forced to retain it for his own male heir.[4] On the other hand, especially after the fifteenth century had begun to show its own economic peculiarities, there were those who sought to avoid the restrictions of entailments. Under the common law, primogeniture was the ordinary rule where male heirs were concerned except that in Kent and here and there elsewhere the custom of "gavelkind" prevailed, in accordance with which all sons shared equally in an inheritance. In some boroughs and in villein tenure on some manors "borough English" prevailed, in accordance with which the youngest son inherited.[5] Under the common law, females might inherit in instances where there was no male heir; and if there were more than

---

3. Barbara Harvey, *Westminster Abbey and its Estates in the Middle Ages* (Oxford: Clarendon Press, 1977), pp. 197-98. Appendix IV of this work contains a record of the Abbey's purchases. During the second half of the fourteenth century, the price £66 13s. 4d. or 100 marks seems to have been curiously appropriate for a wide variety of holdings. See nos. 19, 20, 26, 27, 28, 30, 33, 36, 40, 43, 44. It was a convenient round sum, but it could purchase over 100 acres or a mill. Cf. the evaluations placed on the holdings of Margery Haynes, below. These, however, included chattels.

4. Kenneth B. McFarlane, *The Nobility of the Later Middle Ages* (Oxford: Clarendon Press, 1973), pp. 270-74.

5. On peasant inheritance customs, see Rosamond Jane Faith, "Peasant Families and Inheritance Customs in Medieval England," *AgHR,* 14 (1966), 77-95.

one, land, or even a manor house,[6] and other tenurial rights, like the right to take the profits of a hundred courts,[7] were divided equally among them. If the land given to the Wife by her "good" husbands was land subject to the common law, it must not have been encumbered by reversions, remainders, or entailments, for the marriages were without issue and she says that she retained it after they died (630-31), in effect buying her fifth husband with it, just as her good husbands had purchased her when they were old; and then, finally, she implies that she recovered it. All this would have been a little awkward.

Under the common law, a principle of "Baron et Femme" (not completely abolished until 1935) operated,[8] in accordance with which all a wife's holdings both in land and personal property, including cash, vested in her husband. A husband could not rightfully alienate his wife's land without her consent, but he could dispose of personal property as he pleased. But the Wife of Bath must not have been subject to this rule, since the "tresoor" of her old husbands was attractive to her, and she managed, apparently without too much difficulty, to make extravagantly expensive pilgrimages (GP 463-67). That is, if their cash had vested in them immediately after their marriage, there would have been little point in their offering it to her in the first place. Moreover, she says that since they had given her their land she could govern them as she pleased, demanding "gaye thynges fro the

---

6. For a description of a manor house made necessary by the fact that it was to be divided equally between two daughters who inherited it, see Marion K. Dale, *Court Rolls of Chalgrave Manor 1278-1313*, Bedfordshire Historical Record Society, 28 (1950), xxxi-xxxii. The house with its grounds and outbuildings to which Sir Nigel de Loring retired after many campaigns in the field still sounds attractive.
7. For a striking example, see Helen M. Cam, *Liberties and Communities in Medieval England* (New York: Barnes & Noble, 1963), p. 127.
8. J. H. Baker, *An Introduction to English Legal History* (London, 1971), pp. 258-59. The rule that a husband could not alienate his wife's lands was strictly enforced at Nottingham. See W. H. Stevenson, *Records of the Borough of Nottingham* (London: Her Majesty's Stationery Office, 1882), I, 83, 123-25. Under the common law, however, a wife could not act against her husband, so that if he did alienate her land she was obliged to wait until his death before she could seek to recover it in court. See Donald W. Sutherland, *The Assize of Novel Disseisin* (Oxford: Clarendon Press, 1973), p. 112.

fayre" (221) and chiding them unmercifully. Under the common law, she had no claim to any of the contents of any husband's "chest." To continue for a moment with matters of common law, if a husband survived his wife, he was entitled to only half of her land during his lifetime "by Curtesy of England" (abolished as to fee simple in 1925), provided, as the old authorities said, that "a cry was heard within four walls," i.e., that a living child had been born of the union. It did not matter whether the child survived.[9] A widow, regardless of the dower specified "at church door," where in the Sarum Rite a husband endowed his wife with all his worldly goods, could claim only a third of her husband's holdings in land during her lifetime.[10] Meanwhile, under the common law a wife could incur debts only as an agent of her husband, not on her own behalf. The attitude of the royal courts was well expressed by Chief Justice Charleton of the Common Bench in 1388: "A writ of account was never maintainable against a woman, because a man would not have such a writ enseled in the chancery against any woman, and it is the folly of a man that he should deliver any money to a woman for her to account for it."[11] But widows in burgage tenure sometimes (but not in all boroughs) inherited all their husband's holdings, including tenements, shops, and manufacturing facilities, and could be expected, with the aid of children, apprentices, and servants, to carry on the trade.[12] And widows in customary

---

9. Simpson, *Introduction*, p. 66. Professor Donald W. Sutherland, who generously read and commented on this article after it had been submitted, informs me that Simpson is here misleading, since husbands usually enjoyed all holdings of their deceased wives for life "by Curtesy."

10. *Ibid.*, p. 65, and Baker, *Introduction*, pp. 146-47. However, a widow received half in Kent and in the boroughs of Ipswich, Nottingham, and Torksey. The general limitation to a third makes the argument advanced by Cecile Margulies, *MS* (1962), 210-16, concerning the Wife's acquisitions from her first husbands, questionable. The Sarum ceremony is now conveniently available in R. P. Miller, *Chaucer: Sources and Backgrounds* (New York: Oxford Univ. Press, 1977), pp. 374-84.

11. *Year Books of Richard II: 12 R II*, ed. George F. Deiser (Ames Foundation, 1914), pp. 164-65.

12. For examples in the cloth industry, see Barbara McClenaghan, *The Springs of Lavenham* (Ipswich: W. E. Harrison, 1924), p. 18, and, in the fifteenth century, Gladys A. Thornton, *A History of Clare, Suffolk* (Cambridge Univ. Press, 1928), pp. 181-82.

(servile or villein) tenure often entered the holdings of their deceased husbands, sometimes even alienating them on their own behalf after they had remarried.[13] In other words, there were some ways in which women in burgage or servile tenure enjoyed more freedom than their legal and (often but not always) social superiors. The evidence of the Wife's Prologue so far adduced makes one of these alternatives almost a certainty.

To continue with the Prologue, however, there are no references to land in connection with the fourth husband, the "revelour." Both he and the Wife were young, and their difficulties matters of jealousy rather than of tenure or of access to cash. We do know that she went on one of her costly pilgrimages to Jerusalem during this marriage, so that she must have had access to cash without selling her favors. In fact, her husband died at her return (495), an indication that he had managed the trade during her absence. She was happy to be rid of him and was niggardly with his funeral expenses, an indication, perhaps, that he had made no will or that he had little or nothing to dispose of in his own name. To her fifth husband, Jankyn, the Oxford student and parish clerk with legs and feet "clene and faire," she gave, as we have seen, "al the lond and fee" she had accumulated. Here "fee" probably means "heritable interest," and not simply "wealth." Under the common law, this gift would not have affected Jankyn's rights during her lifetime except his right to alienate without her consent. In any event, having grown old and having under some kind of jurisdiction guaranteed his inheritance, she naturally becomes suspicious that he may be awaiting her demise with some impatience in order to enjoy the profits of her land for himself and to attract a younger wife, perhaps with legs and feet like his own.[14] Hence her complaint,

> "And for my land thus hastow mordred me?"
>
> (801)

---

13. Edward Britton, *The Community of the Vill* (Toronto: Macmillan of Canada, 1977), pp. 20-24.
14. Cf. M. M. Postan's "marriage fugue" as described by J. Z. Titow in *Essays in Agrarian History*, I (Newton Abbot, 1968), p. 45.

But since Jankyn lost his benefit of clergy when he married a widow,[15] her suspicions about his ultimate intentions if not of his murderous inclinations were probably correct. His clergy would not have protected him from being hanged or outlawed if he had indeed murdered her, and all his lands, held in any form of tenure, as well as his chattels, would have escheated to the crown, a fact that adds a certain sting to the complaint. He might have been able to purchase a royal pardon, but this procedure would have been risky unless he had an influential patron. However, the accusation worked, seasoned with a little sentimental appeal (802), and the Wife recovered her control over her land, presumably including the "fee," and wealth (814), as well as a kind of "maistrie" she had not quite succeeded in obtaining over her first four husbands, the first three of whom complained bitterly, while the fourth had a wandering eye. If the land was free land, or even if it was held in burgage tenure in some boroughs, Jankyn was left with the dubious prospect of "Curtesy of England," and this only if he was successful at literal "engendrure."

In so far as "engendrure" is concerned, there is no indication in her Prologue that the Wife had succeeded in literal obedience to the commandment to "wexe and multiplye," having in mind as she did her own gloss on this text,[16] as well as her own view of the nature of the "fruyt of mariage" (114). We may assume, therefore, that the Wife's recovery of her fee effectively removed any temptation Jankyn might have suffered. Perhaps a glance at the nature of land transfers under the common law will provide further clues as to the kind of tenure she enjoyed. Traditionally, seisin of land was transferred by a formal ceremony called "livery of seisin" in the presence of witnesses who could testify that the ceremony had been properly carried out. Since the testimony of witnesses was becoming subject to vicissitudes of one kind or another, livery was often supplemented by a written charter. Jankyn, a parish clerk like Absolon in the *Miller's Tale*, could probably make a "chartre of lond" (3327). Charters were more secure if they were indentured; that is, two copies were made on either half of a skin

---

15. Pollock and Maitland, *The History af English Law,* 2nd ed. (Cambridge Univ. Press, 1952), I, 445.
16. Cf. *A Preface to Chaucer,* pp. 322-23.

that was cut apart on a jagged line and a copy given to each party. If the two parts fit, the charter was considered valid. But charters could be stolen or forged, and the most secure method of transfer was by "fine" that involved a fictitious lawsuit and the inscription of a triple indenture, the one at the bottom of the skin, or the "foot," being left as a court record. Surviving "feet of fines," as they are called, are important historical records.[17] In view of the Wife's adversary relationship with her husbands, only the last of these methods would have been completely safe. But it is difficult to imagine her undertaking the necessary legal procedures to acquire seisin from her first three husbands, to transfer such seisin to Jankyn, and finally to recover it, for under the common law a husband could not transfer land directly to his wife, nor a wife to a husband, and neither could be the heir of the other, since in this matter they were "one person." But there were ways of circumventing these restrictions. Thus the establishment of joint tenure between husband and wife through a final concord would insure a life estate to the survivor, although the Wife speaks of "gifts" rather than joint tenancies.

Possible explanations are available for the gifts or transfers. The first three husbands might well have enfeoffed the Wife with land or tenements of one kind or another, perhaps as a pre-condition of marriage, although if they took part in the trade, as the Wife's pilgrimages suggest that they did, and as the fourth husband almost certainly did, it is difficult to see how they lost control over their monetary wealth or tangible goods. Again, the Wife may have enfeoffed Jankyn with her tenements through a third party, and then later persuaded him to re-enfeoff her, again through a third party, perhaps this time with a final concord for security. No such procedures are mentioned in the text, but Chaucer may have thought that his audience would assume them. The assumption, sometimes made, that Jankyn's loss of control was simply an informal or personal arrangement does not account for the implications of "lond and fee," and hardly removes the tempting prospect that young man once had before him. And in all of the above instances in which the husband took part in the trade, a kind of joint

---

17. Simpson, *Introduction*, pp. 112-17.

tenure would have been implied during life with a strong social bias in favor of the husband. Again, if charters or other documents were involved in any of the land transactions mentioned in the Prologue, why does Chaucer fail to mention them? In the *Merchant's Tale,* where free holdings were involved, Januarie urges May to make charters granting her all his heritage (2171-75).

Boroughs varied enormously in character, administration, and custom. The tenements in a borough might be partly or entirely under manorial, baronial, ecclesiastical, or royal jurisdiction, and customs might vary in different parts of a single borough. In some, alienation was restricted by *retrait lignager,* or by the right of a kinsman to a kind of option to purchase.[18] Most boroughs contained adjacent arable lands that could be alienated separately, but ordinarily the most prosperous burgage tenants held little arable. Rents from burgage tenements could be traded in themselves, their value ranging from 6d. to £4, but on the average between 5s. and 10s. Tenants held for life, by long lease, at will, remainder in fee, and "by Curtesy of England," the most common type of holding being by long lease.[19] It is unlikely that in a town near Bath rents would fall in the upper range of the above figures, and if the Wife depended on holdings such as these for three pilgrimages to Jerusalem, not to mention lesser journeys hardly undertaken with much penitential abstinence, her holdings must have been so extensive as to strain credulity. Her complaint, moreover, mentions "land," not tenements, messuages, shops, stalls, or rents. There is a reference to "hous and lond" (814) suggesting a single residence and holdings in land.

Finally, it has become conventional to assume that the Wife's place of origin "biside Bathe" implies the parish of St. Michael's "juxta Bathon," where there are said to have been weavers. But this is a conjecture, and Chaucer's phrase could just as well imply any village near Bath or simply a birthplace, as does the name "Alicia Bathe" in the records of Castle Combe mentioned below. E. M. Carus-Wilson indicated over twenty years ago that the Wife of Bath should be thought of as

---

18. Hemmeon, "Burgage Tenure," *LQR,* 26 (1910), 344. This article appears in two sections of Vol. 26 and in one section of Vol. 27 of the *Review.*
19. *Ibid.,* 26 (1910), 336-40.

a "west-country clothier,"[20] participating in an industry that was expanding in the region using rural labor, mostly female,[21] and creating substantial wealth for its "managerial" participants, the clothiers. One of the most striking features of the rising cloth industry was its rural character. Thus R. A. Donkin tells us that "the most significant development was the gradual shift in the distribution of cloth-making away from the old-established towns and towards a much larger number of smaller places, many in fact mere villages. The gilds of textile workers in the older centres naturally tried to monopolise manufacture, but in the end they failed."[22] And R. E. Glasscock, writing specifically about the fourteenth century, says that "cloth-making was spreading rapidly in the rural areas made possible by the spread of the fulling mill, and encouraged by urban entrepreneurs who, free from the restrictions of town gilds, could produce cloth more cheaply in rural areas."[23] It should be added that gilds were becoming wary about women in the trade, and that they ordinarily enjoyed great power in town governments. It seems quite likely that Chaucer and his audience were well aware of these trends, and that most members of the audience would have concluded immediately that the Wife's prosperity was the result of her participation in the thriving rural cloth industry, not as a mere weaver, a proper companion for haberdashers, carpenters, dyers, and makers of tapestries in parish fraternities, but as a clothier, and certainly not as the holder of a large portion of the tenements in

20. "Trends in the Export of English Woolens in the Fourteenth Century," *EcHR*, 2, ser. 3 (1950-51), 177. This is an extremely important article by the foremost authority on the late-medieval English cloth industry.

21. A good literary example of an ordinary worker from another region and a later period is afforded by Mak's wife in the Wakefield *Second Shepherd's Play*. The same play contains in the complaint of the Second Shepherd (ed. Cawley, lines 55-108) a picture of hierarchical inversion under the Old Law as it perennially manifests itself similar to that so strongly recommended by the Wife. The solution, implicit in the Wife's Scriptural citations and explicit in the play (lines 710ff.) is the same in both instances.

22. In H. C. Darby, *A New Historical Geography af England before 1600* (1973; rpt., Cambridge Univ. Press, 1976), pp. 113-14. Cf. Edward Miller, "The Fortunes of the English Textile Industry during the Thirteenth Century," *EcHR*, 18 (1965), 64-82.

23. In Darby, *Historical Geography*, p. 170. Cf. McClenaghan, *Springs*, p. 6.

a suburb of Bath. But is what we are told about land transactions in the Wife's Prologue consistent with customary (unfree) tenure? Land in customary tenure, in which a holding did not involve seisin on the part of the tenant, was transferred in manorial courts,[24] where each transfer or entry might involve a fine set by the court that was profitable for the lord. In many areas customary tenure had become in effect "copyhold" tenure, so named because the tenant kept a copy of the court record involving his land for himself. But copyhold tenure, which remained distinct from freehold tenure until 1925, did not alter the legal status of the copyholder in the Middle Ages. That is, a "native" or villein of his or her lord remained a native or villein. So long as the manorial steward, who presided over the court for his lord, maintained his rents, land transfers involving new entry fines were advantageous. An example will illustrate these principles more vividly than an abstract discussion.

Before we turn to the example, one more question that probably arose in the minds of Chaucer's audience, at least momentarily, should be considered. Why were the good old husbands willing to give up all their land and wealth in order to marry Alisoun? It is true that older men often find the prospect of fresh young wives attractive, as the tales of the Miller and the Merchant sufficiently indicate, just as older women sometimes long for "Housbondes meeke, yonge, and fressh abedde." Perhaps the first of her husbands succumbed to a lure of this kind. But to account for two more in succession in this way, especially in a society in which a woman's treatment of her husband was likely to be well-known, and in which most persons were practical rather than romantic, is to strain the imagination. There were ways of satisfying "human needs," as we now like to call them, that did not demand the kind of sacrifice contemplated by young Aurelius in the *Franklins Tale*. We should expect, therefore, that the Wife had something more profitable than her "propre yifte" (103, 608) to attract these old men,

---

24. The observation of Thornton, *Clare*, p. 108, that "a great part of the business of the manorial court was in witnessing the transfer of unfree land" reflects a common situation, although on many manors minor temporary land transactions among servile tenants were often not recorded or even brought before the court if they did not interfere with rents and services.

in spite of her obvious confidence in its powers. It did not, we notice, occupy the exclusive attention of her fourth husband, who "hadde a paramour" (454). But he married her nevertheless, probably to gain access to something else. That Chaucer does not tell us specifically what this "something else" was probably results from his very characteristic technique of indirection, allowing the audience just sufficient information to puzzle them a little before the answer dawns on them. The solution to this problem, as well as to the legal problems adduced above, may become apparent in our example.

The example in question is that of a native of her lord or bondwoman at Castle Combe in Wiltshire. First, by way of background, a rental of the manor in 1340 reveals the presence of a fulling mill on an acre of land held by a free tenant, John Daniel, who paid an annual rent of 20s. for it, but like all the other free tenants except one, a miller who held a virgate of land and a grain mill, he was a tenant "at the will of the lord," whose holding did not pass to his heirs.[25] In 1352 the lord abandoned the cultivation of his demesne for his own use and commuted the obligations of the customary tenants (villeins, natives, bondmen) to money rents.[26] In the seventies one Thomas Touker (a

---

25. For the rental, see G. Poulett Scrope, *History of the Manor and Ancient Barony of Castle Combe in the County of Wilts* (London, 1852), pp. 146-51. Oddly, one of the free tenants, a miller (p. 147), owed light agricultural services and a rooster and three hens on the Feast of St. Martin (11 Nov.) if he had a wife, or one rooster and one hen if he had no wife. He was also obliged to serve as reeve if elected, although this obligation, like the agricultural services and the chickens, was usually a villein obligation. But see Harvey, *Westminster Abbey*, p. 108.

26. Scrope, *Castle Combe*, pp. 81-82. For the benefit of students of literature unfamiliar with agricultural manors, it may be appropriate to explain that such manors were frequently, but not always, divided into demesne lands cultivated for the benefit of the lord of the manor (who might be resident, resident occasionally, or non-resident), who might consume or sell their produce, or do both, and the lands of his tenants, free or servile, or both. Villein tenants traditionally owed "customary" services (determined by local manorial custom) on the lord's demesne, such as plowing, harrowing, sowing, weeding, reaping, harvesting, stacking hay, etc. Such services were usually divided into "works," each work consisting of one-half a day's labor, the number of works owed in a year being determined roughly by the size of the tenant's holding, although other factors might intervene. Tenants with large holdings sometimes employed workers, who might be local cottagers

name meaning "fuller") took over the fulling mill and became one of the first clothiers in Castle Combe. The industry prospered in the area,

> or itinerant laborers, to perform their works. Villeins also paid rents, ordinarily less than those paid by free tenants but ordinarily about the same if the value placed on their works was added to them. In addition to their work on demesne lands, villeins might be required to perform a variety of miscellaneous services, like carting, carrying messages, spreading straw in manor houses, providing horse shoes or plow irons (if they were smiths), etc. They paid for agistment (pasturing pigs in the lord's park), repaired roads, and took their grain to the lord's mill. Some owed gifts of eggs, chickens, honey, fish, rushes, or other produce at specified times of the year. They might be required to attend the manorial court (which met traditionally "from three weeks to three weeks," but often less frequently in practice) and to act, if elected by the court, as one of the manorial servants: as reeve, messor (an office that varied depending on the character of the manor), plowman, miller, butcher, ponder, baker, dairy maid, etc. The number and nature of such offices varied from place to place. Those from more prosperous families might serve as jurors or ale-tasters. The extent and nature of villein obligations depended on a number of factors: the difference in area between demesne land and customary land, climate, soil, proximity to the sea, to marshes, or to rivers, etc. Some free tenants owed minor services like mending park fences or supervising villein workers. The salient feature of late-medieval England was its diversity, and, after the middle of the fourteenth century, its propensity for change. It is very difficult to generalize about "the medieval English peasant" during the years of Chaucer's maturity.
>
> Diversity extended to land measurements. The following observations are suggestive rather than definitive. A *knight's fee* contained four, five, or, at times, eight *hides* or *carucates* of anywhere from 120 to 160 acres. In the north, a *bovate* was one-eighth of a hide; in the south, a *yardland* or *virgate* was one-fourth of a hide. One-fourth of a yardland was called a *ferling*. The word *acre* originally meant almost any strip of arable land. A traditional acre (except in Cornwall) is four *perches* wide and forty perches long (or a strip of similar area but of different dimensions), but perches varied locally from the *King's perch* of sixteen-and-a-half feet. A quarter of an acre is a *rood*. On many manors the *virgate*, which actually ranged in size from ten to sixty-eight acres, was the standard by which holdings were measured; that is, tenants were said to hold one or more virgates, a half virgate, a quarter virgate, or a *cotland* consisting of five acres more or less, or combinations of these units. There is thus no way of "defining" a virgate, for even if we are told that on a certain manor it consisted of thirty acres (a common measurement), unless measured acres are specified we still do not know its size. Moreover, English soils varied in friability, productivity, and suitability for various crops, sometimes on a single manor and very markedly in different parts of the country.
>
> After the Black Death, there was an increasing tendency on the part of many lords to abandon the cultivation of their demesne lands for their own

and continued to do so in the fifteenth century.[27]

Our bondwoman, Margery Haynes, appears together with a list of her holdings in a manorial extent of 1454.[28] First, as the widow of Edward Walcote, known as Jones, she held a tenement and a virgate of land in customary tenure for which she owed a rent of 10s., the obligation to serve as reeve or other official (or to pay a fine for not serving when elected by the court), and heriot (an obligation to the lord at the tenant's death, usually consisting of his best horse in servile tenure or a horse with trappings in free tenure, or in either instance a fine agreed upon between the tenant and the steward). Several virgates on the manor were said in the extent to contain 24 acres, so that we may assume that Margery's was of about this size, allowing for some flexibility in the meaning of *acre* and remembering that virgates might vary in area on a single manor. Margery is also listed, as the widow of William Haynes, her first husband, among the servile cottagers. In

---

use, leasing those lands and substituting money rents for customary services and obligations. There was a general desire, both on the part of lords and on the part of agricultural workers, for ready cash. Hence, the leasing of demesnes by the lords and the demand for wages by the day and better food allowances on the part of agricultural workers, who were stimulated by opportunities for day work in industries, like the cutlery trade at Thaxted in Essex, or, above all, by the cloth industry generally, but especially in the west country around Bristol, in Suffolk, in Essex, and in various towns like High Wycombe (Bucks) on the road between London and Oxford. For the last, see L. J. Ashford, *The History of the Borough of High Wycombe* (London, 1960), pp. 40-41. The results were a breakdown of traditional manorial communities, many of which had been closely knit cooperative groups, with a consequent decline in mores, rising wages and prices, and a largely unsuccessful effort to control them on the part of the government through the justices of the peace. Meanwhile, after about 1360, on many manors families whose ancestors had occupied the same land for many generations disappeared, replaced by new tenants with larger holdings, interested chiefly in profit, a development that hardly cemented community solidarity. It it probably impossible to understand Chaucer's characters very well without keeping these general trends in mind, as well as their specific consequences, which are still being explored by historians.

27. E. M. Carus-Wilson, "Evidences of Industrial Growth on Some Fifteenth-Century Manors," in her *Essays in Economic History* (London, 1962), II, 159-63. The account of Castle Combe in these pages, based on new research, supplements that of Scrope for the period in question.

28. Scrope, *Castle Combe*, pp. 203-21.

this category, ordinarily the most humble of all on agricultural manors, she held a cottage in South Street where she resided for 2s. In addition she held a close with a dovecote (probably the old manorial dovecote) and an adjacent "solo" or workshed for 4s. 6d., a tenement in the gatehouse of the manor at the market with an adjacent curtilage or garden for 20d., and a larger cottage near the cemetery for 4s. 10d. But her most important holding, still as a servile cottager, was a plot of three acres serving as a "milling-place." It contained three mills: a grain mill, a fulling mill, and a mill called a "Gyggemille" (a gig mill for teaseling cloth). As the extent puts it, "de eadem Margeria molendina sumptibus suis propriis sustentabit." Accompanying the mills was what must have been a large cottage in West Street, perhaps the original residence, valued at 5s. rent. For the mills and cottage together she paid 19s.10d., since a milling place was rated at 14s.10d., or about the equivalent of a virgate of land in accordance with manorial custom. In this respect manorial custom failed to account for industrial development, since the three mills, as we shall see, produced an income far greater than that from a virgate of agricultural land. It is of incidental interest that two other servile cottagers, both male, held fulling mills. One paid 20s. for a mill and a cottage; the other paid 21s. for his mill, a cottage, and a parcel of land.

Margery's first husband died in 1435, leaving at his death chattels valued by his friends and relatives appointed by the court to make an inquest at the enormous sum of 3,000 marks (£2,000), or twice what Aurelius in Chaucer's *Franklin's Tale* was worth. But the homage of the manor (the men obliged to attend court) — as Scrope, the historian of Castle Combe and editor of its documents, suggests — "liable to similar imposts and naturally desirous to mitigate their rigour,"[29] testified that after debts, funeral expenses, and charitable bequests (like that of £20 for the fabric of the church and bell tower of Castle Combe) had been paid, the remainder would amount to only 200 marks. In any event, in 1436 the court imposed an entry fine of £40 so that Margery could retain the remainder of her husband's goods. Her son Thomas, apparently of age, was granted £43 12s. 4d. for his own

---

29. *Ibid.*, p. 223.

use, £ 26 for his father's burial and anniversaries, and 60s. for the repair of a mill. This last grant suggests that he may have been associated with his mother in the trade. But it is noteworthy that the widow, not the son, was regarded as the heir to the business. Shortly thereafter Margery married Edward Jones, who brought his virgate and tenement with him, and she was fined what looks like a wildly extravagant merchet (fee for permission to marry, only 6s. 8d. elsewhere in the court rolls of Castle Combe, and often much less than this on agricultural manors in the fourteenth century), combined with an entrance fee, amounting altogether to £ 100. Scrope observes sagely that, in spite of these fines, "she appears to have offered a tempting prize." Indeed, Jones became fairly prosperous, for in 1439 we find him paying £10 5s. 7d. for some of the goods left in the confiscated estate of a deceased rector, including a silver gilt goblet, two silver cups, a dozen spoons, a silver belt, a feather bed, and other less luxurious items.[30]

However that may be, Jones did not gain immediate control of his new wife's holdings. In fact, he found it necessary to pay a fine of £60 in 1442 for a part of Margery's holdings, one of the cottages now being called a "shopa." And by this time the holdings included fishing rights at Gatecombe and Longbridge. Scrope and E. M. Carus-Wilson disagree on the nature of this fine, the latter stating that it was an addition to the £40 already paid to make up the £ 100 demanded at the time of the marriage.[31] But this is still a very large sum. The relationship between Margery and her husband was apparently satisfactory for a time, and the records suggest a form of joint tenancy. But in the following year we find Margery again paying £60 in the manorial court "ut possideat bona sua mobilia, pannos laneos, lanum [sic], mader pro tincturis, ac tenementa et molendina sua quae reputantur valere die obitus sui mille marcas."[32] Jones may have died, although his name appears in a court record of 1453.[33] It is noteworthy that the steward and his court had the usual difficulty in placing an evaluation

30. Pp. 224, 228.

31. *Loc. cit.*

32. *Castle Combe*, p. 225, note.

33. *Ibid.*, pp. 245-46. It is possible that this may have been the son of the original Edward Jones.

on the holdings, but they were now once more firmly in Margery's hands, where they remained, as we have seen in the manorial extent of 1454. To conclude our story, Margery died in 1455. Her holdings passed to her son, Thomas Haynes, a reliable man who served as bailiff in 1457-58, for an entry fee of only £4. Perhaps the court felt that the substantial fines already charged were almost enough. Happily, Thomas was manumitted in 1463 for £20.

Looking back over these events, we can see that Margery was a singularly wealthy woman, in spite of being a bondwoman. Her mills undoubtedly supplied a generous income, and the fulling mill and gig mill must have been especially profitable, since they would serve the needs of some of her fellow clothiers as well as her own. The documents indicate, as we have seen, that she had facilities for dyeing as well as for fulling and teaseling, and the further fact that she owned a stock of wool suggests that some of the tenements listed among her holdings were occupied by servants, mostly female, in addition to her two French man-servants, working at the various steps in cloth manufacture.[34] One can almost visualize the fulled red and white broadcloths, colors favored by her lord, Sir John Fastolf, who supplied cloth for uniforms, stretched out in strips four-and-a-half or six feet wide and seventy-two feet long on frames equipped with tenterhooks near the stream that ran through the village, which was situated in a narrow valley, awaiting their turn at the gig mill and the finishing ministrations of the shearers. Or we may imagine Margery standing before her cottage with one of her French servants chatting with the royal ulnager (an inspector of cloths) as cartloads of cloths folded and tacked by women make their way laboriously out of the village toward the highroad. The cloths of the Wife of Bath (at least in the imaginations of Chaucer's audience) would have been destined for Bristol, a thriving cloth port in the late fourteenth century. Chaucer, who was not a "realist," affords us no descriptions of the Wife's daily business concerns, but it is likely that most members of his audience needed no reminders and were thoroughly familiar with the sight of women

---

34. For the French manservants, see Carus-Wilson, *Essays*, II, 163. The process of cloth manufacture is described in her classic article, "The Woolen Industry," in *The Cambridge Economic History of Europe,* II (1952), 379-81.

sorting, carding, and spinning. They had seen weavers at their looms, heard the clatter of fulling mills, and experienced the unpleasant odors of dye vats. Through open doorways they had seen the look of concentration on the faces of shearers poising their long blades over cloths laid out on tables as they labored to create an even nap. To return to Castle Combe, it is likely that some of the women listed as cottagers in the manorial extent who were less fortunate than Margery, although one held a dyehouse, worked for Margery and other clothiers to pay their rents and sustain themselves. One of them, amusingly enough, called herself "Alicia Bathe." The dovecote probably provided food for Margery's table as well as profits substantially beyond its rent of 4s. 6d. And the fishing rights, much coveted in the Middle Ages when fish was an extremely popular food, not merely Lenten fare, had similar advantages. Castle Combe boasted good trout.

The example of Margery thus clarifies the probable nature of the Wife's land transactions and demonstrates the peculiar attractiveness of her land to her husbands. We are not told what facilities she had as a clothier. But the basic holding that made prosperity in cloth-making possible was ordinarily a fulling mill. Chaucer's audience might well have envisaged a dyehouse and other facilities, including work-sheds, but they may have spontaneously imagined also poor cottagers laboring at home, or even more substantial persons who preferred the daily wages of industry to the smaller and less certain monetary rewards of agricultural labor. A "milling-place" might be small in area, but the cash flow to be expected from it would have been far greater than that from many acres of agricultural land, or from a large number of borough tenements. It was probably this, rather than that other busy "milling-place" she mentions, that attracted her old husbands whose desire to increase their wealth made them willing to give their land and treasure to have access to it, and, where Jankyn was concerned, to fortify his patience with an elderly wife who was, to borrow a phrase, "ful of hoker and of bisemare." Whether the first husband brought her the cloth business or whether she inherited it we do not know, and the question is not important. The fact that the first three husbands were rich by country standards need not surprise us. Many villeins, especially those experienced as reeves, were able to take up holdings left vacant by the series of pestilences after 1349 and to manage them well, or to take over demesnes or parts of demesnes abandoned for rents by their lords. Throughout most of England, individual peasant holdings were growing larger. Thus there were bondmen who had more to offer than Edward Jones brought to Margery, and the general regard for land as an investment would have made these holdings tempting to the Wife. Finally, if the Wife's pilgrimages puzzle us, chevage, or the fine paid by a villein to leave the manor, was often light. It amounted to 20*d.* at the most at Castle Combe, where it was often less, and this would have been a very small preliminary expense for a trip to Cologne, Rome, or Jerusalem. Chaucer's picture of Alisoun's wealth, wandering, and intense interest in fleshly satisfaction is a caricature designed to exemplify certain concomitant trends in his society. In so far as wealth is concerned, the trend indicated is accurate, for by the early sixteenth century a clothier, like Thomas Spring of Lavenham, might be many times wealthier than either Margery Haynes or the fictitious Wife of Bath.[35]

It is probably quite safe to conclude that Chaucer meant his audience to think of the Wife of Bath as a rural clothier from the west country and quite possibly as a bondwoman. The assumption that she was a free tenant either under the common law or under borough custom offers legal difficulties in explaining her land transactions and her ability to control her holdings after marriage. However, when we think of the Wife of Bath, we must resist the temptation that so often presents itself to literary historians to locate her in space and time rather than as something in the minds of Chaucer's audience. She is in effect a series of clues whose significance depends on the experience, the attitudes, the expectations, and the ideals of those who heard them. There is no real reason to think that either Chaucer or the members of his audience had any special prejudice against unfree tenants,[36] but

---

35. McClenaghan, *Springs*, pp. 49, 73-78, 86-88. Thomas was lord of many manors in Suffolk and Norfolk, two in Essex, and one in Cambridgeshire. He also held other lands and tenements. His tomb still stands in Lavenham Church, and one may visit the Lady Chapel he provided and see the tower to which he made generous contributions.

36. Cf. my article, "Some Disputed Chaucerian Terminology," *Speculum*, 52 (1977), 571-81.

in view of the nature of the Wife's Prologue, the first part of which is a kind of mock Lollard "lay sermon" in which she elevates the flesh and deprecates the spirit at the expense of the New Law and of St. Paul especially, the implication that she was a bondwoman would have been singularly appropriate in the light of Gal. 4, 22ff., where it is said, "But he who was of the bondwoman, was born according to the flesh," and "we are not the children of the bondwoman, but of the free: by the freedom wherewith Christ has made us free." This commonplace distinction, which would have been familiar to even the most unlettered among Chaucer's listeners, may indeed be the basis for the Clerk's figure of the "secte" of the Wife of Bath, whose adherents in avid pursuit of fleshly satisfactions flourish because the "gold" or wisdom in them is corrupted by the "brass" of Venus, so that they cannot like Griselda (originally a poor cottager) sustain the "sharpe scourges of adversitee" with which Christians were said to be providentially tested. Chaucer's portrait probably represents, as I have sought to show elsewhere,[37] a satire on the acquisitiveness of some of his contemporaries, the disruption of traditional hierarchies, the breakdown of established communities, and a concomitant decline in mores, all attributable in part, and especially in certain areas, to the rise of the cloth industry. In this connection, it may not be irrelevant to point out that the court at Castle Combe discovered bordellos in the village in 1416, 1419, and 1424,[38] a surprising multiplicity of such facilities in a small community, where some apparently shared the general outlook of the Wife of Bath. It cannot be emphasized too strongly that, although Chaucer's humorous satire is basically moral[39] and displays a learned use of traditional

37. See note 1, above, and the article "Chaucer and the 'Commune Profit': The Manor," to appear in a *Festschrift*.

38. *Castle Combe*, pp. 235, 236, 237. The first of these is said to have been in operation for five years "ad grave nocumentum." The proprietor was fined only 20d., but he was ordered to desist or pay a much larger fine.

39. Moral analysis of what we should call psychological, social, political, and economic problems is characteristic of the late Middle Ages, and is a Classical inheritance modified by specifically Christian ideals. I believe that a failure to recognize this fact and to face its implications has led to distortions and to stubborn misunderstandings, not to mention a neglect of much of Chaucer's humor, for the perception of the ridiculous depends on departures from accepted values. An illustration of the general principle is afforded by the

materials from a wide variety of sources, it is directed toward specific conditions and problems of his own time and place. Unless we come to understand more about these conditions, we can hardly appreciate the "relevance" of what he had to say to the immediate interests and concerns of his audience. We shall miss also the skill and agility with which he wields his satiric weapons.

Princeton University

---

list of books recommended to Charles VI by Philippe de Mézières. It emphasized the Scriptures and service books first, the *Ethics* and *Politics* of Aristotle, the *De regimine principum* of Aegidius Romanus, which was very popular in England, and included Augustine's *City of God* and the *Policraticus* of John of Salisbury, with which Chaucer was familiar and which stresses the need for community integrity based on virtue. It is very probable that Chaucer's audience was spontaneously responsive to concepts like the distinction between spiritual servitude among "sons of the bondwoman" and what they regarded as true freedom. Cf. Chaucer, ParsT, 149: "... wel oghte man have desdayn of synne, sith that thurgh synne, ther as he was free, now is he maked bonde." The Wife is appropriately followed in the Tales by the Friar and the Summoner, who, far from furnishing a mere interlude in "the marriage group," illustrate the corruption of the administration of God's mercy and justice through a literal-minded desire for wealth and fleshly satisfaction of exactly the kind advocated with inadvertent ludicrousness by the Wife. Philippe's Order of the Passion, based firmly on moral grounds, was very influential at the English court. See J. J. N. Palmer, *England, France and Christendom* (Chapel Hill: Univ. of North Carolina Press, 1972), pp. 187-90. Chaucer's own admiration for one of Philippe's "evangelists," Otto de Cranson, is obvious and needs no comment.

Chaucer and the "Commune Profit": The Manor

D. W. Robertson, Jr.

Mediaevalia 6 (1980), pp. 239-259.

In the introductory stanzas of *The Parliament of Fowls* Chaucer tells us that Scipio Africanus, that exemplar of chivalry and bitter enemy of lecherous self-indulgence,[1] informs his namesake of the sad fate of "brekers of the lawe" and "likerous folk," of the kind that "Massynisse" might have become without the elder Scipio's guidance, having first assured him that if he seeks "commune profit" and guides others to do so he will come to a place of bliss and bright souls. It has long been recognized that a love for "commune profit" of the kind manifested, for example, in Griselda's judgments of the people in the *Clerk's Tale* (431), as distinct from self-love, is synonymous with, or in the present instance highly suggestive of, Christian charity. It has not so often been recognized, however, that in the context of Chaucer's society this ideal not only had immediately practical applications but that its application was viewed as a matter of some urgency, regardless of how we might wish to view the situation in modern terms. First of all, "brekers of the law" and "likerous folk" had a great deal in common in the fourteenth century, whether the law involved was moral law or positive law. Violations of the moral law were conventionally regarded as departures from reason,[2] and when Sir John Stoner, Chief Justice, observed, referring to the laws of

1. See the quotation from Petrarch's *De Viris Illustribus* in Aldo S. Bernardo, *Petrarch, Scipio and the "Africa"* (Baltimore, 1962), pp. 17-18.
2. See, e.g., Geoffrey Chaucer, "The Parson's Tale," in *The Works of Geoffrey Chaucer*, ed. F. N. Robinson, 2nd ed. (Boston, 1957), p. 234, ll. 259-68. (All line references are to this edition.) The idea is a consistent medieval commonplace.

England, that "ley est resoun,"[3] he was merely repeating a commonplace. Thus those who broke either the moral law or the law of the land in its various forms violated reason to produce disorder, or what Gower and some of his Elizabethan successors would call "division."[4] The unhappy consequences of disorder in England after the plagues of 1349 and 1369, whether in the court (where King Edward turned away from a concern with the community of the realm for a more leisurely life of hunting and dalliance with Alice Perrers, and Richard was unable to cope adequately with increasing French aggressiveness) or in the countryside (where traditional social ties and the hierarchies they formed were being disrupted by the economic activities of enterprising individuals and sometimes by downright revolt) were plain for everyone to see.

The widespread loss of interest in "commune profit" in late-fourteenth-century England is a large topic, and it will be possible to consider it here only with reference to manorial communities, and even there only very briefly. A "manor" in fourteenth-century usage could be a great many different things, and not all "manors" had as their chief function agricultural production. In fact, it is not actually very useful to talk about "the decline of the manor" in the late Middle Ages, since some of its features survived into the present century, and some were not totally obliterated by the Agricultural Holding Act of 1923. It is possible to discuss changes in manorial life and organization, however. If we eliminate for convenience "manors" that were chiefly country residences, those that included a great many borough tenants, special purpose manors like the Black Prince's stud farm of Macclesfield in Cheshire,[5] or large free tenements within manors that

---

3. Bertha Haven Putnam, *The Place in Legal History of Sir William Shareshull* (Cambridge, 1950), p. 105. Sir John was the father of Edmund Stonor, whose surviving correspondence *(The Stonor Letters and Papers, 1290-1483,* ed. Charles Lethbridge Kingford, Camden Society, 3rd ser., Vol. 29 [London, 1919]) affords specific glimpses of the activities of a fourteenth-century sheriff. Edmund's grandson was the ward of Thomas Chaucer, who was a friend of the family.

4. See John Gower, *Confessio Amantis,* Prologue, ll. 881 ad fin. The relationship between inner and outer disorder was a commonplace.

5. See H. J. Hewitt, *Mediaeval Cheshire,* Chetham Society, NS 88 (Manchester, 1929), pp. 52, 56.

could themselves be called "manors,"[6] we can say that manors fell roughly into three types. First, some employed an "open field" system on which the lands of the tenants were divided into strips distributed over two or more fields or *seisone* (which might or might not exactly coincide) used for crop rotation. These might or might not contain demesne lands (which might be relatively large or relatively small), sometimes scattered in strips among the strips of the tenants (though not in Kent, and probably not in Sussex) and sometimes separate from them. Other manors, especially in Devon, Cornwall, parts of Somerset, Hereford, Shropshire, Lancashire, the West Riding of Yorkshire, Cumberland, and Durham, employed an "infield-outfield" system where the "infield" was regularly cultivated, but the "outfield," divided into strips on poor land, was cultivated only once in every few years. Finally, there were some manors on which the holdings consisted of separate farmsteads, especially in Devon and Cornwall, and a few manors were all demesne.[7] We should remember that the tenure of land was tenure, not "ownership," and that there were no lordless lands in England.

On manors of the first type especially, the scattered holdings on two or more fields subject to crop rotation[8] demanded community cooperation in the various tasks of the agricultural year. Generally wheat and rye were sown in the fall, and oats, barley and peas in the spring. Livestock were allowed on the stubble of wheat and barley after harvest, but the fields were temporarily fenced after sowing.[9] The regular

---

6. For an example, see M. T. Pearman, *A History of the Manor of Bensington* (London, 1896), p. 33. Large freeholdings became more common late in our period.
7. For a demesne manor see Eleanor Searle, *Lordship and Community: Battle Abbey and Its Banlieu* (Toronto, 1974), esp. pp. 268-70. For another example in Hampshire, see J. S. Drew, "Manorial Accounts of St. Swithun's Priory, Winchester," in *Essays in Economic History,* ed. E. M. Carus-Wilson, Vol. II (London, 1962), p. 15.
8. A series of essays on field systems in various parts of England is available in A. R. H. Baker and R. A. Budin, eds., *Studies of Field Systems in the British Isles* (Cambridge, 1973). In some areas the climate permitted only a single crop.
9. There is some evidence for an alternation between grass and arable at intervals of several years in Sussex on relatively poor soil, but the manor involved did not employ an open-field system. See Searle, *Lordship and Community,* pp. 273-75.

routine here implied was, it is said, eventually disrupted by the widespread cultivation of turnips in the nineteenth century.[10] Meanwhile, the community spirit of open-field manors, uncorrupted by turnips, has often been remarked by agricultural historians.

But before we consider manorial communities we should remember that manors varied enormously in lordship and tenure. Thus manors held of the Crown in "ancient demesne" were somewhat different from other manors. They might have very elaborate peasant hierarchies, but their tenants had special rights.[11] Manors might be managed locally by resident lords or their families, or administered by resident bailiffs, "servientes" or sergeants (whose duties might or might not be identical with those of bailiffs), and in some instances by monks. Clerks, canons, rectors of parishes, monastic obedientiaries, priors, abbots, cathedral chapters (monastic or secular), bishops, merchants, lawyers, large freeholders, groups of self-perpetuating trustees, members of the royal household, minor noblemen, and great lords could all be lords of manors. Most individuals in these groups could also be small tenants on the manors of others. To cite an extreme example, the great London merchant Sir John Philpot held seven acres in villein tenure on a manor held by Robert Braybrook, Bishop of London,[12] although he was

10. See Arthur G. Ruston and Denis Witney, *Hooton Pagnell* (New York, 1934), pp. 181-82. The propaganda efforts of Turnip Townshend after 1730 were not immediately successful.

11. Modern writers often refer vaguely to the "well-known" privileges of tenure on lands in ancient demesne. For a specific analysis, see Sir William Holdsworth, *A History of English Law,* 3rd ed. (London, 1923), III, 263-64. For a just complaint in 1394 concerning violation of the privileges by the abbot of Abingdon (Berkshire), see I. S. Leadam and J. F. Baldwin, eds., *Select Cases Before the King's Council, 1243-1482,* Publications of the Selden Society, Vol. 35 (London, 1918), pp. ciii-civ and 82-85. Practical implications of tenure on ancient demesne are discussed by K. C. Newton, *The Manor of Writtle* (London, 1970), pp. 86-91.

12. See T. F. T. Plucknett, ed., *Year Books of Richard II: 13 Richard II* (Cambridge, Mass., 1929), pp. xxxii-xliii, 122-28. After Sir John's death the resident tenants obtained the fee in the manorial court of the bishop. The Common Bench refused to hear the case of Sir John's heir, who sought recovery, observing (p. 123), "In many manors there is the custom that those who are neifs and villeins shall inherit, and that their heirs shall have their lands after their death, and that they may have an action within the manor to claim the fee simple, and so also those who hold at will."

by no means a poor cottager. Lords of manors might have obligations to the Crown directly, indirectly through the sheriff, or both, or to another lord, secular or ecclesiastical. Their contact with their tenants might be intimate and direct, occasional, or distant through an intermediate official. A lord might hold a "home manor," with or without a series of nearby manors he visited frequently, and he might also hold distant manors he seldom if ever visited.[13] Professional stewards who could manage a number of manors were in some demand in the later fourteenth century, constituting a substantial body of literate laymen. Tenants might be either free or unfree by birth (except in Kent, where a man was born free), although by the time of Chaucer's maturity this distinction often had little to do with the size of his holdings, his obligations for them (which often went with the land), or his social status. There were, of course, numerous families of small servile tenants tied to their holdings who survived long after the fourteenth century. Both free and servile tenants owed a surprising variety of obligations, often met not by the nominal tenants themselves but by leaseholders, who were sometimes prospective heirs and sometimes not,[14] or by servants of the tenants or of their leaseholders. The complexities of land tenure in the later fourteenth century are baffling. The tranquil prospect of forest, field, meadow, and stream concealed an enormously complex series of hierarchical and peer group tenurial relationships. Nevertheless, the inevitable seasonal routine of agrarian labor, the medieval

---

13. John Smyth observed of Thomas III Lord Berkeley, "In the course of his whole life I seldome observe him to continue one whole yeare togeather at any one of his houses, but having many furnished hee easily removed (without removing)" *(The Lives of the Berkeleys* ..., Vols. I and II of *The Berkeley MSS.,* ed. John Maclean [Gloucester, 1883], I, 301).

14. Subletting or transfer of land among villein tenants had been taking place since the twelfth century. See C. N. L. Brooke and M. M. Postan, eds., *Carte Nativorum,* Northamptonshire Record Society, Vol. 20 (Oxford, 1960), esp. p. xlix. Cf. M. M. Postan, "The Chronology of Labour Services," in W. E. Minchinton, ed., *Essays in Agrarian History,* Vol. I (Newton Abbot, 1968), p. 76; Marian K. Dale, ed., *Court Roll of Chalgrave Manor, 1278-1313,* Publications of the Bedfordshire Historical Record Society, Vol. 28 (Streatley, Beds, 1950), pp. xxiii-iv, and, for a complex example, p. 15; R. H. Hilton, *Social Structure of Rural Warwickshire in the Middle Ages,* Dugdale Society Occasional Papers, No. 9 (Oxford, 1950), p. 19. An example from the manor of Palgrave, Suffolk, in 1357 appears in J. Z. Titow, *English Rural Society* (London, 1968), p. 163.

respect for the idea that a man should be judged by his peers, and the further tendency to inculcate group responsibility whenever possible forged tightly knit communities. These communities were threatened during the later fourteenth century by disruptive influences, which, although mild by modern standards, were sufficient to cause much concern among those interested in furthering the "commune profit."

Community integrity is especially apparent on manors employing the "open field" system, although there is no reason to suppose that it did not exist on manors of other types, and even, we may add, in towns.[15] Basic attitudes supporting community integrity were furnished by the Church, and local churches were active community centers that might in some instances be subject to a certain amount of administrative control in manorial courts.[16] Confessors warned lords against unjust tolls and tallages, which were considered to be sinful, and peasants were enjoined to perform their duties faithfully and to avoid transgressions.[17] The hierarchical or "feudal"[18] character of society generally, combined with the popularity of verbal contracts of all kinds, ranging from borrowings of plows or horses among peasants to marriage and even land transactions, lent the ideal of "fidelity" or "truth," usually thought to be dependent on faith in God, an especial importance. Thus a guide for manorial lords, the *Seneschaucy,* warns that "The lord ought to be fair in word and deed, he ought to love God and honesty, and he ought to hate sin, wrong, and wickedness."[19] Another manual, *The Rules of*

---

15. See, e.g., the general remarks of J. S. Furley, *City Government in Winchester from the Records of the Fourteenth and Fifteenth Centuries* (Oxford, 1923), p. 147. On what was regarded as the moral basis for community integrity, see Susan Reynolds, *An Introduction to the History of Medieval Towns* (Oxford, 1977), p. 136.

16. An instance is cited by Sidney O. Addy, *Church and Manor* (London, 1913; rpt. New York, 1970), pp. 270-71.

17. See, e.g., *Robert of Brunne's "Handlyng Synne,"* ed. Frederick J. Furnivall, Early English Text Society, OS 119, 123 (London, 1901, 1903), p. 70, ll. 2445-634. Cf. Chaucer, "The Parson's Tale," *Works,* p. 252, ll. 750-64, 773-76.

18. S. F. C. Milsom *(Historical Foundations of the Common Law* [London, 1969], p. 8) observes acutely that "feudalism was not a system," but a word used to describe a society organized by dependent tenures.

19. Dorothy Oschinsky, *Walter of Henley and Other Treatises* (Oxford, 1971), pp. 291-92.

Robert Grosseteste, urges the lord, "Admonish all your household often that all who serve you should endeavor to serve God and to serve you loyally and diligently, and that in order to do the will of God they ought to do your will and pleasure in all things; in all things, that is, that are not against God."[20] Walter of Henley's *Husbandry* commands, "If thy people fall into the danger of thy courtes, see that they be amercied by their peeres. And if your owne conscience telle yowe that they bee to hyghe amercied, moderate it soe that you bee not reproved for it heare nor before God."[21] Actual manorial lords varied in character, some being petty tyrants in the countryside,[22] but there are examples of lords who sought to behave in accordance with the prevailing ideals. In his recent study of the manors of the Duchy of Cornwall John Hatcher observes that the estates of the Black Prince there "were governed with a degree of benevolence that far exceeded the feudal obligations of a lord to his tenants, and with a spirit of charity often wanting in the administration of many ecclesiastical estates at this time."[23]

Perhaps it will be helpful to recall the general nature of manorial courts, bearing in mind that local variations were common. In the first place, except in areas of early Danish influence and sometimes in the south, the shires of England were divided into hundreds, originally administered by bailiffs, although by Chaucer's time many hundreds were held privately by lords who acted as royal agents.[24] Hundred courts met during the terms of Easter and Michaelmas, and at these meetings, or at one of them, what was called the "View of

---

20. Oschinsky, pp. 398-99.
21. Oschinsky, p. 311. Students of manorial court rolls are familiar with numerous instances in which fines against an individual are mitigated or forgiven entirely *quia pauper.*
22. See, e.g., the description of John Somery in R. H. Hilton, *A Medieval Society* (London, 1966), p. 42.
23. John Hatcher, *Rural Economy and Society in the Duchy of Cornwall, 1300-1500* (Cambridge, 1970), p. 127; cf. pp. 116, 117, 128.
24. In Kent and in the Rape of Hastings in Sussex there were "lathe courts" sharing some functions of hundred courts and county courts. See Elinor Joan Courthope and Beryl E. R. Formoy, eds., *Lathe Court Rolls and Views of Frankpledge in the Rape of Hastings,* Sussex Record Society, Vol. 37 (Lewes, 1934), esp. pp. xv-xxiii.

Frankpledge" was held. The rural male non-gentry and non-clerical population over the age of twelve was divided into groups of four to thirty men headed by a tithingman or "chief pledge" who reported their behavior to the jurors of the hundreds, although in some areas in the south "tithings" were territorial. In any event, members of tithings were mutually responsible for each other's behavior. Tithingmen paid "chevage" at court, either for failure to attend or as a regular fee, and they were frequently amerced for failure to report offenses.[25] During the later fourteenth century major offenders were reserved for the Justices of the Peace or for the itinerant justices of jail delivery, although courts on manors in ancient demesne could try civil cases and felonies.[26] Manorial lords frequently had the right to hold the View, so that their courts became in effect hundred courts as well as courts devoted to manorial business, and chief pledges often became important members of their courts.[27]

A manorial court met traditionally "from three weeks to three weeks," although in actual practice meetings were often irregular or less frequent. A court might meet in the lord's hall, in a church, or in some other place. Usually the presiding officer was the lord's steward, who might pronounce judgments at the View, but who could not interfere with the nomination of manorial servants, like the reeve, and who was not supposed to raise the fines imposed by "affeerors," or men elected for the purpose from among the tenants or appointed by the reeve.[28] The courts established bylaws or customary regulations

25. Hundred courts continued to meet in the twentieth century in some areas. See F. J. C. Hearnshaw, *Leet Jurisdiction in England,* Publications of the Southampton Record Society, Vol. 3 (Southampton, 1908), p. 255.
26. For a convenient record of a court with a View, see Titow, *English Rural Society,* pp. 169-72. A list of articles of inquiry at the View appears in Titow, pp. 189-90. Such articles might vary from time to time and from place to place.
27. On the estates of Crowland Abbey the tithingmen, who might be free or unfree, represented the "whole homage" in the manorial courts, executed court injunctions, undertook inquisitions, and elected the manorial servants: reeve, bailiff, collector, hayward, ale-tasters, etc. The tithingmen were responsible for the behavior of those elected. See Frances M. Page, *The Estates of Crowland Abbey* (Cambridge, 1934), pp. 67-70.
28. An extortionate steward might find himself before the royal justices. Thus at the View on the manor of Edgeware held annually on May 1, the tithingmen

for both the agricultural and disciplinary management of the manor, recorded land transactions, and imposed fines for trespasses (*transgressiones*) involving such things as straying animals, failure to clean ditches, obstructing roads, boundary infringements, failure to perform customary works properly, poaching, encroachments on the lord's garden (often by boys), carrying off wood or thorns, improper gleaning, harboring strangers (who might commit crimes), refusal to return borrowed goods, minor debts, minor assaults, defamation, eavesdropping, failure to raise the hue, improper raising of the hue, fornication (among bondwomen), and so on. It used to be said that "the action of the courts was nothing but a concealed form of taxation" and that bond tenants were "girdled round with a net of feudal offenses."[29] Modern writers, assuming, perhaps, that love is free, still complain bitterly about *leyrwite* or *lecherwite,* the fine imposed on bondwomen (except on ancient demesne) for fornication or extramarital pregnancy; but in general it is now common to regard manorial courts with some appreciation for the community cooperation they entailed.

An early indication of this more appreciative tone appears in John Booth's introduction to the Durham Halmotes: "The orders made at the court for the common weal of the vills, and which affected the relation of the tenants toward each other, show a keen appreciation for the benefits arising from cooperation."[30] In their classic study, *The Open Fields,* the Orwins discuss at length the spirit of "democracy" and community responsibility at the manorial court of Laxton, which they clearly regard with more favor than the modern situation where rural communities are governed by paid officials and the only power

---

    chose three men for the office of reeve from whom one was selected by the lord or his steward. But in 1392 the tithingmen refused to nominate the man preferred by the steward, John Brook. Brook fined them 20s. He also doubled some affeerments decided upon by the regular affeerors selected by the reeve. He was distrained by the sheriff and brought before the King's Bench. See G. O. Sayles, ed., *Select Cases in the Court of King's Bench,* Publications of the Selden Society, Vol. 88 (London, 1971), pp. 87-88.

29. G. W. Kitchin, *The Manor of Manydown* (London, 1895), pp. 17-18.
30. W. H. D. Longstaffe and John Booth, eds., *Halmota Prioratus Dunelmensis,* Surtees Society, Vol. 82 (Durham, 1889), p. xxv. Examples are offered on the following pages.

of the resident lies in his vote.[31] Professor Homans observed that "in English villages of the Middle Ages, cooperation in farm work was the basis of village life."[32] It has become clear that decisions regarding changes in field systems, usually from two fields to three fields, were made by the community as a whole.[33] Professor W. O. Ault, who has studied manorial or village bylaws carefully and extensively, stresses the fact that they involved matters "of mutual profit and concern to all the 'shareholders' in the agrarian enterprise, be their status free or servile, and whether they be landlord or tenant."[34] Moreover, by-laws were frequently established in the manorial court itself not by the lord or steward but by the free and customary tenants together.[35] As for leyrwite, those who have no experience with small communities of persons whose sustenance depends on the mutual efforts of the entire group do not appreciate either the immediate social consequences of fornication, which easily leads to violence, or the economic burden imposed by illegitimate children who may not have adequate families to support them. In any event, the fines imposed were usually small. It has been said that these fines were roughly equivalent to *merchet,* or license to marry, which the lord presumably lost as the result of fornication,[36] or that the lords lost a bondman through

---

31. C. S. Orwin and C. S. Orwin, *The Open Fields,* 2nd ed. (Oxford, 1954), pp. 173-74.

32. George C. Homans, *English Villagers of the Thirteenth Century* (Cambridge, Mass., 1942), p. 81.

33. See Homans, p. 56, for an example, and, for a general statement, Joan Thirsk, "Field Systems in the East Midlands," in Baker and Budin, *Studies in Field Systems,* p. 232. For a complex example, see Joan Wake, "Communitas villae," *English Historical Review,* 36 (1922), 406-13.

34. W. O. Ault, "Village By-Laws by Common Consent," *Speculum,* 29 (1954), 394.

35. W. O. Ault, *Open-Field Husbandry and the Village Community,* Transactions of the American Philosophical Society, NS, Vol. 55, Pt. 7 (Philadelphia, 1965), pp. 40-54.

36. Page, *Estates of Crowland Abbey,* p. 133. Merchet varied a great deal, probably in relation to the land involved. Ada E. Levett *(Studies in Manorial History* [Oxford, 1938], pp. 237-38) regarded it as a registration fee. The relationship between merchet and land is convincingly argued by Eleanor Searle, "Seigneurial Control of Women's Marriage: The Antecedents and Function of Merchet in England,» *Past & Present,* 82 (1979), 3-43.

fornication, since bastards were free.[37] But the facts do not offer very good support for either of these theories. Thus on the manors of the prior of Durham in 1366 two women were amerced 6d. each for leyrwite, and, at the same time, 12d. each for merchet. On these same manors much higher fines (2s.) were imposed for fornication with a chaplain or adultery.[38] At Wakefield male offenders might be flogged through the marketplace,[39] although this may have been done under the jurisdiction of the archdeacon, since it was the standard penalty in ecclesiastical courts. The usual fine for bondwomen was 6d. or 12d., about the same as for breach of the assize of ale, but on at least one Crowland manor after 1349 the fine seems to have been 5s., or enough to purchase a modest brass pot at a fair. Male offenders and freewomen were at the tender mercies of summoners, archdeacons, and rural deans (whose jurisdictions corresponded roughly with the hundreds). A man might have to pay considerably more than his female companion.[40] The usual fines for bondwomen were ordinarily no greater than those imposed for defamation (verbal assault), and, considering the basic economic and social environment, they were neither unwarranted nor especially burdensome. Moreover, they were probably supported by the communities in which they were imposed.

On an ordinary open-field manor with a demesne there was a staff of servants elected or appointed from among the unfree tenants. These might include, in addition to the reeve, a hayward or *messor,* an autumn reeve, plowmen, shepherds, swineherds, cowherds, gooseherds, millers, butchers, smiths, carpenters, dairy maids, brewers, ponders, gardeners, and so on, depending on the economy of the manor and on the extent to which outside labor was hired for manorial services.

---

37. R. H. Hilton, "Peasant Movements in England Before 1381," in *Essays in Economic History,* II, 76.

38. *Halmota Prioratus Dunelmensis,* pp. 60, 125, 26, 27. Cf. W. O. Ault, ed., *Court Rolls of the Abbey of Ramsey and of the Honor of Clare* (New Haven, 1928), p. 196.

39. J. W. Walker, ed., *Court Rolls of the Manor of Wakefield,* Vol. V: *1322-1331,* Yorkshire Archaeological Society Record Series, Vol. 109 (Leeds, 1945), p. vii. Here the fines for leyrwite were variously 4d., 6d., and 12d.

40. See Page, *Crowland Abbey,* pp. 59, 373-74, 388, 416.

The duties of these servants varied considerably from manor to manor. At times an obligation to serve in one of these capacities if necessary went with the tenure of a holding, or with that of a type of holding. Bond tenants with large holdings often owed extensive work services on the demesne lands in addition to rents, fewer services being demanded of smaller tenants, although rents and services among the same type of tenants might vary widely on the same manor, a fact that probably had something to do with the character of the land held. Free tenants, even substantial ones, often owed customary services in addition to their rents, and these might vary from supplying plows, mending park fences, or supervising harvests to furnishing a squire, or someone who could pass as a squire, for a certain number of days to a bishop. The community of the manor was linked to that of the shire by the reeve and by free tenants who attended county courts or performed jury services at the behest of the sheriff (except on ancient demesne), and by reeves and their committees of three others who reported to the jurors of royal justices.

We may conclude without too much exaggeration that the community of the manor, or of the vill or township where several manors shared a vill or where there was more than one vill on a manor was, in spite of the complexities of tenure, fairly well integrated, bound together by mutual interests both in agricultural production and in keeping the peace. Strenuous efforts were made to suppress contentiousness or "discord."[41] But the plagues of 1349 and 1369 dealt a severe blow to community organization in many areas. Matters were not improved by French pillaging in the south during the later seventies, Scottish raids in the north, heavy taxes, the misbehavior of English soldiers at home, and raiders from Cheshire in neighboring shires.[42] Meanwhile, the statutes of laborers were insufficient to curb a new spirit of enterprise in industry, especially in cloth-making, that

41. Sometimes all the members of a group or vill were fined for the intransigence of anyone of them. Thus a bylaw of Houghton (Ramsey Abbey) stipulated that if any customary tenant entered the grain of another to destroy it, all customary tenants would be fined 6d. each (Ault, *Court Rolls*, pp. 254, 259).

42. Cf. Mary Margaret Taylor, ed., *Some Sessions of the Peace in Cambridgeshire in the Fourteenth Century,* Cambridge Antiquarian Society, Octavo Publications, No. 55 (Cambridge, 1942), p. xvii.

attracted people of all kinds from the countryside. There is probably no simple explanation for the Revolt of 1381, although it is clear that it did represent a breakdown in community spirit and integrity.

The effects of the Black Death of 1349 varied from place to place, and it is difficult to determine whether subsequent unrest represented delayed reaction or was due to other circumstances. The manors of the Black Prince in Cornwall show few traces of relaxation of manorial discipline,[43] perhaps in part because of the wisdom of the Prince's council and in part because of the proximity of an established tin-mining industry that had for some time permitted an interchange between agrarian and industrial labor.[44] On the Cambridgeshire manors of Crowland Abbey no very disastrous social consequences resulted immediately,[45] and on the manor of Alciston (Battle Abbey) the disruption was slight and temporary.[46] On the other hand, on the manor of Manydown (Hampshire), a number of holdings fell into the hands of the lord (the prior of Winchester), and there was no real recovery until the 1360s.[47] At Cuxham (Oxfordshire), more than half of the half-virgates (holdings of about 15 acres) were untenanted in 1352, although by 1355 all the holdings were taken, sometimes by temporary tenants, and by 1377 the tenurial structure had settled down.[48] At Forncett (the earl of Norfolk), about a quarter of the free holdings and more than half of the customary holdings were unoccupied during the period from 1376 to 1378.[49] Members of the higher

---

43. Hatcher, *Rural Economy*, p. 136.
44. It is true that the tin market suffered immediately after the plague but recovered later in the century. It may be relevant that a large number of tenants held leased lands that were granted to the highest bidder every seven years, thus introducing what Hatcher calls a "free market" element into the agrarian economy.
45. Page, *Crowland Abbey*, pp. 89, 120-25.
46. Judith A. Brent, "Alciston Manor in the Later Middle Ages," *Sussex Archaeological Collections*, 106 (1968), p. 95.
47. Kitchin, *The Manor of Manydown*, pp. 61-63.
48. P. D. A. Harvey, *A Medieval Oxfordshire Village: Cuxham*, Oxford Historical Series, 2nd ser. (London, 1965), pp. 136-38.
49. R. H. Hilton, *The Decline of Serfdom* (London, 1969), p. 34. Page (*Crowland-Abbey*, pp. 152-53) notes a scarcity of tenants beginning in the 1390s.

nobility seem to have retained their incomes more or less by leasing their demesnes.[50] The evidence is spotty, and it is difficult to draw firm conclusions. Many historians still maintain the view advanced by J. E. Thorold Rogers that the effects of the plague were economically beneficial.[51]

If economic conditions improved generally,[52] several factors contributed to a breakdown in community life, a loosening of traditional *mores,* and a rise in crime. When demesnes were leased on a large scale and the size of individual holdings increased, as they did in many areas, the old organization centering around the manorial servants disappeared and customary works were replaced by higher rents. A demand for hired labor was created, stimulating rising wages attractive to those still settled in traditional manorial communities.[53] In

50. G. A. Holmes, *The Estates of the Higher Nobility in Fourteenth-Century England* (Cambridge, 1957), pp. 114-17. A decline in income in the 1380s seems to have been common. On some manors like Cuxham profits declined markedly. They were £34/12/6 in 1343-44, but when the manor was farmed during 1361-68 it brought only £20/0/0, dropping to £18/10/0 in 1395-1400. See Harvey, *Medieval Oxfordshire Village,* pp. 94-95.

51. J. E. Thorold Rogers, *A History of Agriculture and Prices in England, 1259-1793,* Vol. I (Oxford, 1866), p. 61. Cf. J. Z. Titow, "Some Differences between Manors and Their Effects on the Condition of the Peasantry in the Thirteenth Century," in *Essays in Agrarian History,* I, 39, n. 2; F. R. H. Du Boulay, *An Age of Ambition: English Society in the Late Middle Ages* (London, 1970), p. 34. The last notes "a stronger competition for women and a more civilized attitude toward them." Cf. Elizabeth Chapin Furber, ed., *Essex Sessions of the Peace 1351, 1377-79,* Essex Archaeological Society, Occasional Publications, No. 3 (Colchester, 1953), p. 6.

52. The evidence concerning prices is conflicting and probably needs more detailed study. Efforts to control prices were notoriously unsuccessful in some areas. Striking examples are given by Nora Ritchie, "Labour Conditions in Essex in the Reign of Richard II," in *Essays in Economic History,* II, 91-111. At Nottingham in 1395 the tithingmen made blanket condemnations of bakers, butchers, fishers, taverners, poulterers, tanners, shoemakers, cooks, hostelers, weavers, fullers, shoemakers, and dyers for overpricing. See William H. Stevenson, ed., *Records of the Borough of Nottingham,* Vol. I (London, 1882), pp. 269-73. On the other hand, prices of consumables are said to have risen until the seventies and then to have declined until about 1390. See E. H. Phelps-Brown and Sheila V. Hopkins, "Seven Centuries of the Prices of Consumables, Compared with Builders' Wage-Rates," in *Essays in Economic History,* II, 183.

53. The leasing of demesnes proceeded unevenly and at varying terms. Castle Combe (Wiltshire) was leased to the tenants collectively for £5 in 1352:

some areas the plague and the events of subsequent years merely added impetus to a process that had already been under way,[54] but in any event, there was a very marked new spirit of individual initiative at the expense of community integrity in the countryside, often accompanied by an increase in trespass and violence. At Warboys (Ramsey Abbey) unrest is especially evident in the sixties, in the mid-seventies (generally a gloomy and depressed period), and in the eighties after the Revolt.[55] This situation seems to have been fairly typical,[56] although some counties were more lawless than others. On some manors substantial free tenants became so powerful by the nineties that they could not be distrained for fines in their manorial courts.[57] Meanwhile the spiritual leadership of small communities suffered from the same difficulties as those that affected laymen. The errant behavior of chaplains especially became a real problem in the countryside.[58] Almost everyone wanted cash instead of payment in kind,

---

see E. M. Carus-Wilson, "Evidence of Industrial Growth on Some Fifteenth-Century English Manors," in *Essays in Economic History*, II, 159-60. At Thaxted (Essex), except for a few acres of mowing, demesne work for the tenants ceased in 1362, so that the manor had a monetary economy: see Newton, *Thaxted*, p. 25. For phases of leasing at Marley (Battle Abbey), see Searle, *Lordship and Community*, p. 324. The new farmers became prominent members of the community: see F. R. H. Du Boulay, *The Lordship of Canterbury* (New York, 1966), pp. 140-42 and 197. Leasing was stimulated in the fifties, the sixties, and then again in the eighties. For the leasing policies of Thomas IV Lord Berkeley, see Smyth, *The Lives of the Berkeleys*, II, 5-6, although here reeves were still being chosen at manorial courts in the early seventeenth century.

54. See Marjorie Morgan, *The English Lands of the Abbey of Bec*, 2nd ed. (Oxford, 1968), pp. 115-17.
55. J. A. Raftis, *Warboys* (Toronto, 1974), pp. 220-21; and see Edwin B. DeWindt, *Land and People in Holywell-cum-Needingworth*, Pontifical Institute of Mediaeval Studies, Studies and Texts, 22 (Toronto, 1972), Ch. iv.
56. See the cases in *Halmota Prioratus Dunelmensis*, pp. 36-37 and 145-47. During the sixties tenants became sensitive about being called "natives" or "rustics" (i.e., serfs). Thus in 1364 in the village of East Raynton a tenant could be fined the enormous sum of 20s. for calling another a *neif* (*Halmota Prioratus Dunelmensis*, p. 33).
57. Page, *Estates of Crowland Abbry*, p. 149; J. A. Raftis, "An English Village After the Black Death," *Mediaeval Studies*, 29 (1967), 175.
58. See Elisabeth Guernsey Kimball, ed., *Rolls of the Warwickshire and Coventry*

and agricultural workers often demanded day work instead of employment by the year,[59] sought generous food allowances on working days, or where feasible took advantage of increasing opportunities for industrial work. For example, a town developed at Thaxted, so that by 1381 it housed 79 cutlers, as well as smiths, brewers, carpenters, and other tradesmen,[60] a situation that probably stimulated high agricultural wages on the manor.[61] Plowmen seem to have been especially difficult to retain except at very high wages.[62] Perhaps the most disruptive industry insofar as the agrarian labor market was concerned was the textile industry. Cloth-making had spread over the countryside during the thirteenth century, and fulling mills were erected in comparatively remote areas. After 1353 the cloth-making industry began to flourish, and exports increased steadily until 1369. But the upward trend resumed after the plague of that year, beginning in about

---

Sessions of the Peace, 1377-1397, Dugdale Society, 16 (1939), p. lxxviii. On the impoverishment of chantries after 1350 see K. L. Wood-Legh, *Perpetual Chantries in Britain* (Cambridge, 1965), p. 93. Chaplains were frequently indicted for assault, rape, theft, and even murder: see E. G. Kimball, ed., *Rolls of the Gloucestershire Sessions of the Peace 1361-1398,* Transactions of the Bristol and Gloucester Archaeological Society, Vol. 62 for 1940 (Kendal, 1942), pp. 65, 66, 72, 75, 78, 87, 115-16, 117-18, 119, 122-23, 124-25, 130, 154. See also Rosamund Sillem, ed., *Records of Some Sessions of the Peace in Lincolnshire, 1360-1375,* Lincoln Record Society, 30 (Hereford, 1936), pp. 4-5, 160; E. G. Kimball, ed., *Records of Some Sessions of the Peace in Lincolnshire 1381-1396,* Vol. I, Lincoln Record Society, Vol. 49 (Hereford, 1955), p. 74; Vol. II, Lincoln Record Society, Vol. 56 (Lincoln, 1962), pp. 37, 46; Charles Gross, *Select Cases from the Coroners' Rolls, A.D. 1265-1413,* Publications of the Selden Society, Vol. 9 (London, 1896), pp. 52-53, 69, 93-94, 124. Vicars and rectors were not above similar kinds of activity, and even a bishop, Henry of Wakefield (Worcester), whom Chaucer undoubtedly knew as Keeper of the Wardrobe and Treasurer, found himself indicted for rape. It is not actually surprising that ecclesiastics suffered from community disruption as well as laymen.

59. Cf. Ritchie, "Labour Conditions," p. 93.
60. K. C. Newton, *Thaxted,* pp. 20-23.
61. Ritchie, p. 95. Prices were generally high in the area.
62. Ritchie, p. 98. At Marley (Battle Abbey) plowmen received £1/17/0 in 1309-22 with a grain allowance; but by 1384-85 they were getting £3/0/0 with grain (Searle, *Lordship and Community,* p. 308).

1379 and reaching a peak in the mid-nineties, to the great detriment of Flemish and Italian manufacturers.[63] By that time Essex and East Anglia enjoyed a brisk business in the manufacture of worsteds,[64] while Bristol became a flourishing port for the export of woolens. The trade not only offered opportunities for poor cottagers to supplement their incomes, but enabled more enterprising persons to become comparatively prosperous by working at or supervising the work of others in one or more stages in the process of cloth-making. Chaucer's Wife of Bath offers an exaggerated example of success of this kind,[65] and her *mores* characteristically show little concern either for the "commune profit" or for traditional ideals of order.

If we are to understand the "manorial" characters in the *General Prologue,* not to mention others in the tales, we should view them against the perspective of events during Chaucer's lifetime as well as in terms of the traditional Christian attitudes he embraced. Certain characteristics of these figures, not immediately apparent to us, would have been transparent to members of Chaucer's audience, who we may safely assume were men about the royal court and their friends and were thoroughly familiar with manorial administration. Since Chaucer shows little sympathy for figures who are chiefly interested in money, other tangible assets, or lecherous self-satisfaction, we may safely assume that his ideas about manorial life, like his ideals concerning chivalric life, were conservative, and that he viewed the disruption of manorial communities for selfish ends with disfavor.

63. E. M. Carus-Wilson, "Trends in the Export of English Woolens in the Fourteenth Century," *Economic History Review,* 2nd ser., 3 (1950-51),162-79. This is an extremely important article.

64. Furber, *Essex Sessions,* p. 2.

65. E. M. Carus-Wilson ("Trends," p. 177) calls her properly "a west-country clothier." Bath was convenient to the export town of Bristol. The prominence of women among clothmakers in Yorkshire evidently gave rise to a certain amount of male envy. See Herbert Heaton, *The Yorkshire Woolen and Worsted Industries,* Oxford Historical and Literary Studies, Vol. 10 (Oxford, 1920), pp. 38-39. A similar situation may have prevailed elsewhere. For further information on the Wife and the cloth trade, see D. W. Robertson, Jr., "'And for my Land thus Hastow Mordred Me?': Land Tenure, the Cloth Industry, and the Wife of Bath," *Chaucer Review,* 14 (1980), 403-20.

The first "manorial" character we meet in the *Prologue* is the Yeoman,[66] clearly a manorial servant, a forester whose presence as the Knight's only servant on his pilgrimage is an indication of his humility. We are not told much about him, just enough to exemplify the character of his lord. The Franklin is, however, described in more detail.[67] In the treatise *The Manner of Holding Courts* (1342) the word *franklin* is used for a freeholder who owes homage and fealty, a heriot consisting of an accoutred horse, and the wardship of his son.[68] Homans points out that such men owed suit at hundred courts,[69] and the evidence indicates that they attended county courts as well.[70] Chaucer's Franklin is a man of this kind who has expanded his holdings in the flourishing land market of the second half of the century to become a "worthy vavasour" and who has, at the same time, won for himself profitable offices in the shire. His expensive Epicurean tastes and his ostentation mark him as a self-seeking enemy of the old order. It is quite likely that Chaucer's audience would have seen the Wife of Bath as an essentially rural character whose substantial profits in the cloth industry enabled her to take very expensive pilgrimages[71] for amusement rather than for penance, and to dress ostentatiously in expensive coverchiefs and hose of fine scarlet. Both the Franklin and the

---

66. I have discussed the significance of the word *yeoman* in "Some Disputed Chaucerian Terminology," *Speculum*, 52 (1977), 577-78. Here it may be added that it is used to describe members of a peasant aristocracy of prominent villeins on the manor of Littleport (Ely) in F. W. Maitland and W. P. Baildon, *The Court Baron*, Publications of the Selden Society, Vol. IV (London, 1891), p. 113. An example is afforded by one in 1324 who was a chief pledge, a constant juror, an affeeror, and a reeve. He held seven tenements. Cf. DeWindt, *Holywell*, pp. 159-60. Manorial yeomen were not freemen in the fourteenth century.

67. I have sought to examine the Franklin's career and his *Tale* in "Chaucer's Franklin and his Tale," *Costerus*, NS 1 (1974), 1-26.

68. Maitland and Baildon, *The Court Baron*, pp. 103-04.

69. Homans, *English Villagers*, pp. 248-50.

70. See William Henry Hart, *Historia et Cartularium Monasterii Sancti Petri Gloucestriae*, Rolls Series [No. 33] (London, 1863-67), III, 77.

71. Pilgrimages to Jerusalem were especially costly and could be afforded only by the wealthy. See Dorothy Owen, *Church and Society in Medieval Lincolnshire* (Lincoln, 1971), p. 125.

Wife were undoubtedly intended as amusing caricatures of persons whose views are dominated by a spirit of enterprising self-interest.

The Miller in the *Prologue* is a less elaborately drawn figure than the miller in the *Reeve's Tale,* but his gross physical features, reserved for low characters in the contemporary International Style, suggest strongly his villein status. His sword, his speech, and his wrestling (with its obvious iconological overtones) make him a striking if exaggerated exemplar of the contentiousness that plagued agrarian communities after 1349.[72] It would be possible to amass a great deal of material concerning reeves, who were important manorial officers upon whose efficiency and loyalty the welfare of the manor often depended, since they, together with the bailiffs who supervised them, were responsible for agricultural management, production, the buying and selling of livestock, produce, and supplies, and the rendering of annual accounts.[73] In addition, they sometimes appointed members of the staff of servants and accounted for customary works. Complaints about reeves vary from trivial misbehavior[74] to inefficiency,

---

72. His behavior was criminal and might have brought him before the royal justices. See Bertha H. Putnam, *Proceedings Before the Justices of the Peace ... Edward III to Richard III* (Cambridge, Mass., 1938), p. 112.

73. The agricultural manuals devote considerable attention to reeves. See the *Seneschaucy* (ca. 1275) in Oschinsky, pp. 275-81. Walter of Henley emphasizes the need for loyalty among reeves (Oschinsky, p. 340). On the manors of the prior of St. Peter's, Gloucester, an elaborate treatise was provided that the reeve and the hayward were supposed to read, or have read to them, at least once a month outlining their duties in detail. See Hart, *Historia et Cartularium ... Gloucestriae,* pp. 213-21. There is a full if somewhat skeptical discussion of reeves in J. S. Drew, "Manorial Accounts," pp. 12-30. N. S. B. Gras and E. C. Gras (*The Economic and Social History of the English Village: Crawley, Hampshire, A.D. 909-1928* [Cambridge, 1930; rpt. New York, 1969]) print a long series of reeves' accounts. For the fourteenth century, see pp. 239-93. They observe (p. 24) "few instances of malfeasance of office." An excellent example with a convenient glossary from the late fourteenth century is provided by N. W. Alcock, "An East Devon Manor (Bishop's Clyst) in the Later Middle Ages," *Devonshire Association Reports and Transactions,* 102 (1970), 176-87. The privileges of reeves appear often among manorial bylaws. See W. D. Peckham, trans. and ed., *Thirteen Custumals of the Sussex Manors of the Bishop of Chichester,* Sussex Record Society, Vol. 31 (Cambridge, 1925), p. 122.

74. A late-thirteenth-century reeve was accused of being "too long at the fair" — "*nimis diu ad nundinas de Worth.*" See R. B. Pugh, ed., *Court Rolls of the*

theft, and even extortion.[75] Chaucer's reeve, with his calculating efficiency, is at once a thief and a man who knows how to keep his fellow tenants in fear of him.[76] He shows no interest whatsoever in "commune profit"; on the contrary, he exploits his community for his own profit. Chaucer is obviously not seeking to describe a "typical reeve," but to exemplify the worst qualities of reeves who have no real fidelity either to their lords or to their communities.

Finally, a word should be said about the Parson and his brother the Plowman. If they are brothers literally, they are clearly both members of a peasant family. The peace rolls of the later fourteenth century reveal a surprising number of criminal parsons,[77] and many took advantage of opportunities to find comparatively easy and remunerative tasks in London. Chaucer's Parson, who is content with a small "suffisaunce," and who exhibits real concern for his parishioners, is an ideal figure who comments unfavorably by implication on numerous less worthy members of his calling. The obvious concern of his brother the Plowman for the welfare of his neighbors contrasts sharply with the self-seeking of many of his kind, who left their fellow-tenants and sought high pay at daily labor. Generally speaking, the loyalty of Chaucer's characters and their interest in community obligations were matters that would have registered at once in the minds of his audience, and this audience would also have been aware of criminal behavior in speech and deed that often escapes modern critics. It is time, I think, that Chaucerians began to consider not only the literary and intellectual traditions that underlay Chaucer's attitudes, but also the specific significance of those attitudes in his own society. It was, after all, this

---

Wiltshire Manors of Adam de Stratton, Wiltshire Record Society, Vol. 24 for 1968 (Devizes, 1970), p. 86.

75. E.g., Morgan, *Abbey of Bec,* pp. 65-66; Page, *Crowland Abbey,* p. 75; Putnam, *Proceedings,* p. 79.

76. For an example of a reeve whose trespasses were concealed by his fellow tenants until after he left office, probably because they feared him, see P. D. A. Harvey, *Manorial Records of Cuxham* (London, 1976), p. 669.

77. E.g., Putnam, *Proceedings,* pp. 50-52, 80, 120, 213; Sillem, *Records ... 1360-1375,* pp. 55, 205, 209; Kimball, *Records ... 1381-1396,* I, 9, 33, 37; Kimball, *Rolls, Warwickshire and Coventry,* pp. 96-97. These are simply examples.

relevance that made his work vivid and often amusing to his own contemporaries. Departures from reason, whether that reason is moral or legal, are often ludicrous in a society where reason rather than feeling is considered to be the natural guide for conduct. The poet's delineations of greed, either for land or money, or even for the Pardoner's coveted wool, cheese, wheat, and imaginary jolly wenches can be ludicrous and at the same time comment trenchantly on events in his own time.

Princeton University

The Intellectual, Artistic, and Historical Context

D. W. Robertson, Jr.

In: *Approaches to Teaching Chaucer's Canterbury Tales,* ed. Joseph Gibaldi (New York: Modern Language Association of America, 1980), pp. 129-135.

I believe that an advanced or graduate course including Chaucer's *Canterbury Tales* should introduce students to a variety of primary materials useful to an understanding of that text, should recommend only such secondary materials as are based firmly on primary research or that help to control the use of primary materials, should place Chaucer's work in a cultural tradition that extends from classical antiquity through the early decades of the eighteenth century, and should lead finally to an appreciation of Chaucer's techniques for making what he had to say vivid, attractive, and meaningful to his own special audience. The tendency to read Chaucer from a "modern" point of view, a point of view, incidentally, that has changed considerably during my lifetime, results in distortions, leads to cultural deprivation which should not be an educational goal, and makes the *Tales* less attractive to students, who can supply this point of view spontaneously and need no instruction in its application. Students, both graduate and undergraduate, do enjoy learning something about a different and now remote culture with its own ideals, spontaneous attitudes, and, not least, sense of humor. With reference to the last, much of what is now frequently taught about the *Tales* reduces some of the most witty and humorous passages to solemn nonsense. Humor results from departures from reason, and unless we have clear ideas about what Chaucer and most of his contemporaries thought to be true and reasonable, we cannot perceive his humor.

During the last thirty years, it has become possible to develop a number of new approaches to the *Tales,* partly as a result of scholarly progress in other fields. It is now possible to offer students significant insights into the principal intellectual traditions that underlie the attitudes in Chaucer's writings as well as insights into the application of those attitudes to the rapidly changing social and economic conditions of the later fourteenth century — conditions that affected persons in all walks of life. Basic to any reasonable grasp of these attitudes, both traditional and contemporary, is some knowledge of the Bible, its exegesis, and the principles derived from exegetical study in what is loosely called "theology," although the more technical ramifications and speculations of academic theology are probably of small relevance to the study of Chaucer. As a preliminary grounding in these traditions, a knowledge of the Latin Fathers, especially Augustine, whose works found a prominent place in almost all fourteenth-century libraries of any consequence, is essential. A familiarity with standard medieval works like the commentaries of Peter the Lombard on the Psalms and the Pauline Epistles, known together as the *Major glossatura,* and the *Glossa ordinaria* is necessary as an approach to the later exegetical tradition, while these works were themselves standard references throughout the later Middle Ages. In the late fourteenth century there was also a revival of interest in the spiritual writings of the twelfth century, in part stimulated by the Franciscans. Ancillary material is available in letter collections, in treatises, and in a variety of miscellaneous writings on special subjects, as well as in sermons. These last often afford insights into popular attitudes, figurative conventions, conventional thought structures, and, where fourteenth-century English sermons are concerned, into the application of traditional attitudes to contemporary problems.

It has been said that early Christian writers embraced "the best traditions of Classical philosophy." The classical influence was maintained in medieval schools, where Cicero, Seneca, Vergil, Ovid, Horace, Statius, Lucan, and other Latin authors were carefully studied with special attention both to their eloquence or literary technique and to their wisdom, chiefly moral. In considering the relevance of these authors, especially the poets, to the study of Chaucer, however, it is necessary to become familiar with the attitudes developed toward them in the Middle Ages and to study the works of medieval mythographers and commentators. We are now fortunate to have available both reprints of earlier editions of such works and new editions of others, as well as some valuable secondary guides and studies. One work that illustrates vividly the adaptation of classical thought for Christian purposes is *The Consolation of Philosophy* of Boethius, which exerted a profound influence on English writers from the Old English period to the mid-eighteenth century. It is not strange that the *Consolation* and Saint Gregory's *Moralia* on Job were two of John of Salisbury's favorite works and that both were often found in fourteenth-century English collections. The influence of Boethius was especially powerful in Europe during the years following the Black Death, when themes from it appeared frequently in English wall painting. All serious students of English literature should, if only in a detached way, accord the *Consolation* a sympathetic understanding without quarreling with its metaphysical principles, which are developed for a moral purpose, or suggesting that it is somehow "pagan." It would also be especially helpful if students could have access to the standard medieval commentaries of William of Conches and Nicholas Trivet. Meanwhile, we now have available in English translations two of the most useful guides to medieval educational practice, the *Didascalion* of Hugh of Saint Victor and the *Metalogicon* of John of Salisbury, as well as a good recent book by Nicholas Orme (1973) on educational practice in English schools in the Middle Ages.

Scriptural and classical texts, together with their medieval interpretations, provided fruitful sources of imagery, conventional descriptions, and patterns of action in medieval literary texts. Thus, knowledge of the Bible and the classics provides not only a philosophical basis for understanding the *Tales* but also a background for studying Chaucer's literary techniques. Sometimes a series of scriptural passages acquired special medieval connotations. For example, a series of them, first used by William of Saint Amour, became associated with attacks on the fraternal orders, and these are reflected in unmistakable fashion in Chaucer's portrayals of friars. Chaucer was neither the first nor the last poet to make use of these materials, some of which he undoubtedly found in earlier works like the *Roman de la rose,* now available in a good English prose translation by Charles Dahlberg (1971) and well treated in a number of secondary studies, although it is still systematically abused by advocates of "courtly love" or "sensualistic naturalism." It is extremely important to seek to understand not only literary works, like the *Roman,* that Chaucer knew and used extensively but also the literary traditions that such works represent. There is a close connection, for example, between the *Roman* and the Latin literature that developed in the monasteries and cathedral schools of the twelfth century and provided both the *Roman*'s authors with ironic and satiric techniques. Again, the "form" of this poem, the Dream Vision, represents a fusion of classical and Scriptural traditions that took place in the twelfth century, a fusion that gave the poem and others like it special connotation and helped to assure their widespread appeal. Where medieval commentaries on medieval authors are available, like those on Dante, for example, they should be treated with respect and not dismissed as irrelevant in the light of our own supposedly superior knowledge.

Much the same sort of influences that shaped both the techniques and the general content of literary works is also evident in the visual arts of the Middle Ages. Emile Mâle's great study of religious art in France, the first volume of which has recently appeared in a new translation with supplementary notes (Princeton Univ. Press, 1978), is, in spite of certain limitations, a basic guide to the meaning of medieval religious art. Since Raimond van Marle's *Iconographie de l'art profane au Moyen Age et la Renaissance* (1931–32) other special studies have provided similar analyses of "nonreligious" art that now enable the student of Chaucer often to find significant imagery common to the visual arts and to Chaucer. In addition, changes in style during the course of the Middle Ages, which were sometimes fairly rapid, are more clearly evident visually than they are textually.

Research in the other arts is frequently rewarding, both in the illumination of details in Chaucer's text and in leading to an understanding of his general outlook. Thus, some knowledge of medieval music, both in its basic theory — as illustrated in the treatises of Augustine and Boethius and in a series of subsequent medieval treatises — and in its actual practice, can be very rewarding. The usefulness of a knowledge of medieval astrology, cosmology, medicine, and logic has been amply demonstrated.

Chaucer lived among clerks and administrators familiar with the law. A distinguished legal historian has recently observed that the actual structure of a society, the nexus of commonplace relationships that is frequently taken for granted and not much discussed, is most readily discernible in its laws and their application. Thus, students of *The Canterbury Tales* should find a study of law useful in evaluating the behavior of Chaucer's characters. There are now available good editions of some of the relevant Year Books, an excellent selection by G. O. Sayles of cases from the King's Bench, some fine editions of rolls of the Justices of the Peace, coroners' rolls, borough court records, records of courts with the View of Frankpledge, and manorial court records. The Civil Law has been less thoroughly studied, but there are studies that offer good introductions to the work of the ecclesiastical courts, like R. H. Helmholz, *Marriage Litigation in Medieval England* (1974). Meanwhile, a new edition of the synodal decrees of English bishops is under way. Finally, there is a good study of the laws of war by M. H. Keen. More generally, we now have a good brief history of English law in J. H. Baker, *An Introduction to English Legal History* (2nd ed., 1979), and some special studies that shed light on the development of law during the fourteenth century.

Among the changes that took place during Chaucer's lifetime were those in the organization of the royal administration. Since Chaucer was closely associated with the Chamber and had frequent dealings with the Exchequer, we need to know something about administrative history to understand his daily concerns. In this connection, it is important that we study the characters of Chaucer's associates, some of whom probably made up the membership of the audience he usually addressed. The recent publication of the works of Sir John Clanvowe is especially welcome. Medieval political theory offers another field of fruitful inquiry although such theory in Chaucer's time represented a Christian modification of the ethical principles of Aristotle's *Politics* and was not in the modern sense "political." John of Salisbury's *Policraticus,* which Chaucer knew, forms a useful introduction, and the *De Regimine Principum* of Aegidius Romanus was popular in the later fourteenth century. Fourteenth-century court "politics" itself, which was partly a matter of rivalries among magnates domestically and friction between followers of reformers like Philippe de Mézières on the one hand and advocates of the recovery of English power on the Continent on the other, surely influenced Chaucer's attitudes. He was also undoubtedly cognizant of events in what has been called "the turbulent London of Richard II."

England in the fourteenth century was still basically an agrarian society. During recent years a great many manorial documents, in addition to the court rolls mentioned above, have become available, and there are some extremely useful regional histories, histories of estates, and studies of individual manors. These often shed a great deal of light on the significant changes in English society after the Black Death, some of which undoubtedly disturbed Chaucer and his associates and influenced his treatment of rural characters. In fact, it is probably impossible to understand what he was saying about them and why he was saying it without some understanding of contemporary developments. While rural society was changing, certain industries and trades were undergoing changes as well, and there have been good specialized studies of the cloth industry, the wool trade, and the wine trade, as well as general studies in social and economic history. Developments in rural society and in trade and industry affected towns, some of which were also deeply affected by relations with foreign powers. There is a good recent general *Introduction to the History of English Medieval Towns* by Susan Reynolds (1977), and there have been useful studies of individual towns.

In view of the presence of ecclesiastics in the *Tales*, students also need to know something about diocesan administration and the characters of English bishops. Further, the basic ideals and the actual conditions of cathedrals, regular and secular, of monasteries, of nunneries, and of friaries familiar to Chaucer's audience but no longer familiar today need further study on the part of Chaucerians. Ecclesiastics of all varieties were deeply affected by the same social changes that affected the rest of society, and Chaucer's attitude toward these religious figures, in the light of traditional ideals, has a great deal to do with their appearance in the *Tales*. For example, the persistence of certain of William of Saint Amour's accusations against the friars is explicable only in part as a result of literary tradition. Finally, ecclesiastical records often include wills, which afford excellent clues to the value placed on a variety of material possessions as well as indications of the nature of private devotion.

It should be emphasized, I think, that all the various areas of investigation suggested above are interdependent. Thus, one can learn a great deal about friars and monks, for example, from the study of towns, and since some towns had close connections with agricultural activity, the study of one sector of society can hardly be carried out without the study of the other. Similarly, statements by bishops and other ecclesiastical authorities sometimes reflect the figurative conventions discernible in both literature and the visual arts. There is a sense, indeed, in which the various "fields" of modern research may be misleading since society itself was an integrated whole.

In the above remarks, I may have omitted certain "fields," but I have sought to show that Chaucerians still have a great deal to learn and that those wishing to deepen their understanding and appreciation for Chaucer's writings still have a great deal to do. There is plenty of room left for hard work, for the excitement of discovery, and for the satisfactions of real accomplishment. Teachers of advanced and graduate Chaucer courses should, I think, offer their students every opportunity to enjoy the possibilities that lie before them.

Editor's Note: For another view of D. W. Robertson's "program" of reading in the Middle Ages, see his anthology, *The Literature of Medieval England* (New York: McGraw-Hill, 1970). Its introduction discusses medieval life and ideals, medieval astronomy and astrology, the medieval Bible, the character of medieval literature, and the literature of medieval England. Its twelve chapters are devoted to early Celtic literature in Britain, early Anglo-Latin literature (Gildas, Bede, Boniface, Alcuin, et al.), Old English literature, later Celtic literature in Britain, later Latin literature in Britain (John of Salisbury, Geoffrey of Monmouth, et al.), medieval literary theory (John of Salisbury, Dante, Boccaccio, Richard de Bury, Bernard Silvestris, Nicholas

Trivet, William of Conches, et al.), French literature in England (Marie de France, Jean Froissart, et al.), songs and short poems in Middle English, the English medieval romance *(Sir Gawain and the Green Knight* and Malory's *Morte d' Arthur), Piers the Ploughman,* Chaucer, and early English drama.

Hugh of St. Victor's *Didascalion* appeared in an English translation by Jerome Taylor (New York: Columbia Univ. Press) in 1961. John of Salisbury's *Metalogicon* is available in a translation by Daniel M. McGarry (1955; rpt. Gloucester, Mass.: Peter Smith, 1962). *The Statesman's Book* (trans. John Dickinson, New York: Knopf, 1927) includes Books 4, 5, and 6 and selections from Books 7 and 8 of John of Salisbury's *Policraticus;* the volume entitled *Frivolities of Courtiers and Footprints of Philosophers* (trans. Joseph B. Pike, Minneapolis: Univ. of Minnesota Press, 1938) also offers selections from Books 7 and 8 as well as the first three books of the *Policraticus.* For translations of other works mentioned in the essay, see the appropriate bibliographical listings for, among others, Vergil, Ovid, Boethius, Augustine, Dante, Guillaume de Lorris and Jean de Meun, and Emile Mâle.

Religion and Stylistic History

D. W. Robertson Jr.

In: *Theolinguistics,* ed. J. P. van Noppen (Brussels: Vrije Universiteit Brussel, 1981), pp. 215-229.

Bishop John A.T. Robinson begins his *Honest to God* with the statement that the Bible speaks of a God "up there". Most of us, he says, have substituted for this God who is "above" a God that is somehow "out there" since, because of the spatial structure of the universe, there is no special virtue in being "up". That is, we no longer believe in what the Bishop calls a "three-decker universe" wherein Heaven is spatially "up", earth in between, and Hell "down". In order to save God from disappearing altogether, since "out there" is, astronomically speaking, no better than "up there", Bishop Robinson seeks to locate God "in the depths", not in the depths of the physical universe, but in the depths of the personality. He tells us that "personality is of ultimate significance in the constitution of the universe", and that "in personal relationships we touch the final meaning of existence as nowhere else".

Now I have no wish to quarrel with Bishop Robinson, nor, for that matter, with his critics. I should like to point out, however, that St. Paul, whose language seems to trouble the Bishop, had no word at all for "personality", and that the concept represented by that word would have been incomprehensible to him. It does not exist in either Greek or Roman antiquity, and it is not used, except in a very rudimentary form in discussions of the Persons of the Trinity, either by the Fathers of the Church or by the theologians of the Middle Ages. The word *personalities* in scholastic Latin means simply the quality of being a person as distinct from a thing. It is not until the late eighteenth century that the word *personality* in English comes to mean the peculiar combination of attributes which make up one individual as distinct from another; and expressions like the "force of personality" do not become current until the nineteenth century. Bishop Robinson's "personality" is something even more recent than this. It represents a kind of totality of the essential peculiarities of the individual, an essence of his peculiar being. And this is a concept derived from modern psychology. In other words, Bishop Robinson wishes to take God down from "up there", draw Him in from "out there", and locate Him in what amounts to a distinctly modern invention. As I said, I do not wish to quarrel with this procedure. I do object, however, to Bishop Robinson's criticism, or implied criticism, of St. Paul. The difference between St. Paul's God "up there" and Bishop Robinson's God "in the depths" is essentially, I suspect, a difference in style. If we have an awareness of stylistic change, perhaps we can, without too much difficulty, appreciate both Bishop Robinson's location for God and St. Paul's location for God.

What is meant by stylistic change?

If we look at a painting by Monet and compare it with one by Matisse, we are aware at once of a profound difference in something called "style". Perhaps we may call the first impressionistic" and the second "expressionistic". The words *impressionism* and *expressionism* are difficult to define, but they are nevertheless useful, since paintings by a great many other artists may be seen to be either like the one by Monet, or, in some respects at least, like the one by Matisse. Since a few painters — Picasso for example — demonstrate during their careers a variety of styles of this kind, we are likely to think of them in much the same way that we think of styles in ladies' hats. They seem to be mere fashions that undergo almost annual alterations, and we are inclined to attribute to them no very profound significance.

However, if we take a somewhat larger view — stand off, as it were, at some distance from the shifting panorama of artistic styles — a number of rather interesting features emerge. In the first place, the great rapidity with which styles have changed since the early nineteenth century, let us say, between the time of Delacroix's great painting of "Liberty, Guiding the People, the 29th of July, 1830", and the development of abstract painting in the early twentieth century, is not characteristic of earlier periods. For example, what is called the

"Gothic style" emerged during the second half of the twelfth century and persisted, with various changes, well into the fifteenth century. It is true that there are marked variations in this style at certain periods, like the mid-fourteenth century, for example, but its general characteristics are recognizable, at least in Northern Europe and England, throughout the period. Again, if we maintain our distance, it is possible to see that although surface changes since the early nineteenth century have been frequent and spectacular, the various modern styles are, in a sense, all outgrowths of romanticism. That is, there are attitudes in romantic painting and poetry that may be said to anticipate various developments in the arts since. Realism, impressionism, expressionism, surrealism, and abstract expressionism all betray romantic origins. The modern period, in spite of the fact that a painting by Constable, with its delight in cloud formations and landscapes, does not much resemble a painting by Kandinsky, is not so fragmented as it seemed at first glance.

Keeping our stand at a distance, we may notice something else. The various styles we see in painting are not confined to painting alone. In the Romanesque period, for example, (roughly the period of the late eleventh and early twelfth centuries), it is easy to demonstrate analogies between manuscript illumination and sculpture. The same disregard for spatial rationality, the same emphasis on more or less rigorous frontal poses in the representation of holy personages, and the same taste for "monsters" of various kinds, appears in both. Again, in the early Gothic period, both statues and manuscript illustrations show the human figure, transfixed, as it were, in a long s-curve. As the style changes toward the close of the period, an increasing verisimilitude appears in both painting and sculpture, and the s-curve tends to disappear. If we extend our gaze a little farther, we may notice rather striking similarities between the style of the manuscripts and statues and that of the architecture of the cathedrals. Similary, in our own period, there are certain obvious analogies between modern music, like that of Stockhausen. and certain forms of abstraction in painting. The more we study the stylistic characteristics of a given period, in fact, the more obvious it becomes that they are extremely pervasive, affecting human expression in a great variety of forms.

In the visual arts, style is usually discussed in terms of space, time, the verisimilitude with which objects are represented (if objects are represented at all) ordering principles of one kind or another, and the nature of the reality to be communicated. This last consideration leads us from the study of style proper to the study of iconography, or meaning in the arts. Taken together. these considerations touch upon some very fundamental matters indeed, matters that have an importance for beyond the history of art. For example. Bishop Robinson, whom we quoted at the outset, was disturbed by what he regarded as spatial conceptions in the Bible. St. Paul seemed to imply, in effect, that things get better the farther "up" you go. But Bishop Robinson, who lives on a sort of accidental planet out on one arm of a huge whirling galaxy, no longer knows whether any direction should be called "up", and he finds the interstellar spaces somewhat forbidding in any event. If we turn our attention to medieval Christian art for a moment, however, I think we can show that we need not actually be concerned about St. Paul's feeling that God is a Being toward Whom we must "ascend", since the "ascent" involved has nothing whatsoever to do with the interstellar spaces. Moreover, St. Paul was not, as Bishop Robinson seems to suspect, speaking metaphorically. He meant what he said.

When religious art in the West ceased to imitate classical models and developed a distinctive style of its own, one of its most striking features was its lack of regard for spatial continuity. In painting, no real effort is made to achieve depth. That is, an illumination is usually made up of a pattern of flat surfaces without any attempt at rounding in the figures and with no spatial depth at all. The space is rigorously two-dimensional, and the flat surfaces are in fact sometimes arranged in such a way that their placement one before the other is almost deliberately irrational, sometimes the representation fails to be coherent even in two dimensions. This situation is not confined to the visual arts. For example, when St. Augustine describes the Cross for devotional purposes in terms of the description of charity found in Ephesians 3. 17-18, he says,

> "Thus 'rooted and founded in charity', we may be able 'to comprehend, with all the saints, what is the breadth, and length, and height, and depth,' which things make up the Cross of Our

Lord. Its breadth is said to be the transverse beam upon which the hands are stretched, its length extends from the ground to the crossbar, and on it the whole body from the hands down is affixed; its height reaches from the crossbar to the top, where the head is placed; and its depth is that part which is hidden beneath the earth".

St. Augustine had before him the words *breadth, length, height,* and *depth,* but he nevertheless produced a two-dimensional figure. No account at all is made of the thickness of the Cross in the direction of the observer. The same situation prevails generally in medieval art until the last phase of the Gothic style finally merges into the style of the Renaissance with its perspective and spatial coherence.

If we consider time in late classical and medieval art, we shall find a similar situation. Characteristically, the Romanesque artist arranges his figures in fairly symmetrical patterns that seem to be governed by geometry. These patterns have the effect of "fixing" the figures so to speak, so that they cannot move. Motion, that is, would destroy the pattern and ruin the picture. A similar effect was achieved in late antiquity by establishing figures in a rhythmic relationship to one another across a flat surface. In early Gothic art the figures are fixed in that long rhythmic s-curve mentioned earlier, which has the effect of making them completely static. That is, medieval artists were not at all concerned to show something just happening as we look at it; nor were they interested in anything just about to happen. Perhaps this situation may be made clearer if I quote a description of realistic art from an historian of the art of the nineteenth century. "An artist", he says, "who is concerned to represent every event strictly in the coloring of its time, sees both past and present happening as transient things, as things that have happened once and will never happen in precisely that way again." But if we look at a medieval religious painting it soon becomes obvious that the actions depicted are not literal actions at all. They are symbolic actions that refer us, not to events in history, but to abstract events that have a validity at any time, events that in a way go on happening over and over again. Just as the space of the painting is not the space of the observer, so also the time element in the painting is not a part of the time-scheme in which the observer moves as a physical being. Space is nullified by the flat surface, and time is stopped, and, we might say, eternalized, by the symbolic content of the action.

An illustration may help to clarify these points. The typical Gothic Nativity scene shows Mary lying on a couch with her head on the observer's left looking away from the scene presented. Joseph is usually placed at the observer's right. In the center of the picture the Christ child lies on an altar, and behind him stand the ox and the ass, sometimes nibbling at the crib. This configuration persists throughout most of the thirteenth century without much change. No effort at all is made to "humanize" the figures. Mary shows no maternal affection, the child is not "cute" or "cuddly," and the picture seems on the surface to be entirely without emotional content. Certainly, the human figures are not "personalities", and they do not, on their two-dimensional surface, show any potentiality for interacting with one another. The scene is fixed in a space and time of its own, usually against a background of gold leaf, and is devoid of realistic representation. It is not an attempt to reproduce an actual scene at all. What, then, is its function?

The location of the Christ child on the altar at the upper center of the picture is intended to suggest the Sacrifice of the Crucifixion and the Sacrament of the Eucharist, which unites the members of the Church into a single community. The ox and the ass are the Jews and the Gentiles, who, in the Sacrament of the Altar become one in the Church of the Faithful. That is, the event depicted is something that happens first of all within the heart of anyone who becomes a convert to Christianity, or who pauses to meditate thereafter on the significance of his conversion. Christ is, as it were, born anew in every new Christian, and born again whenever that Christian achieves new insight into the significance of his faith. At the same time, the picture represents, on a larger scale, something that took place whenever Mass was said in any medieval church. In effect, what is actually represented is a series of abstract ideas, objective realities not limited by time and space at all.

Later on, after perspective had been introduced in the early Renaissance, representations of Nativity become more human, and the space around them becomes more rational. The figures communicate with one another and begin to develop sentiments. By the time we reach the eighteenth century, in fact, the sentiments become more important than the abstract idea in the picture, until finally we are left with not much more than feeling. But, to return to the Gothic original, as we have seen, the space and time of our picture are completely artificial. Within this artificial space, the Christ Child is located in the upper center of the picture. But this does not mean that at the Nativity itself, considered as an historical event, the Christ Child was actually placed on an altar higher than Mary and Joseph, and the Gothic artist did not mean that the beasts, as a matter of history, nibbled at the crib. The placement of the Child has no relation to photographic reality; it is intended instead to express a value judgement. Christ is the high center of the picture, the focus of our attention, and the most important object in it. To put this more specifically, the arrangement of objects in the picture is hierarchical. And this sort of arrangement is typical of Gothic art as a whole. Statues are arranged in hierarchical fashion around the portals of the cathedrals, the personified virtues, and sometimes the Saints, stand with the vices under their feet, the figure of Christ in Judgement appears at the top of painted or sculptured scenes with the unjust below Him on His left and the just below Him on His right. But none of these arrangements has any real relation to actual space. They are not even "metaphorical." That is they are a reflection of a real hierachical universe of values which has no relation to the continuum of space and time in which we live.

Our Gothic picture is thus not a representation of an historical reality, but it is, nevertheless, a representation of something that was thought of as being very real indeed, and was, in fact, easily available to anyone in everyday experience. Although the fact is sometimes difficult for us to understand, it is nevertheless true that many of our ancestors, both in antiquity and throughout the Middle Ages, firmly believed in the objective reality of what we would call abstractions. For Plato wisdom was not something that could be touched or measured, but it was something very real, whose presence or absence made an enormous difference in the way in which people behaved. I do not imagine that Homer, as he wandered out among his household grapevines in the evening, believed the Pallas Athena might suddenly appear before him and teach him how to formulate his verses. But Homer probably not only believed in but actually loved Wisdom, a wisdom perhaps with a larger dash of cunning in it than Plato's wisdom, but wisdom nevertheless. St. Paul tells us that "the invisible things of God" are clearly seen, "being understood through the things that are made." These invisible things are the object of faith, a belief in things unseen, and this faith is closely allied with reason, not an enemy of it as it became later. The reason involved is the same reason by means of which Plato and Cicero had been able to perceive the reality of virtue.

One of the most popular books of the Middle Ages and the Renaissance was *The Consolation of Philosophy* of Boethius. It was first translated into English under the supervision of King Alfred the Great, who admired it enormously. It was among the favorite books of John of Salisbury, who was one of the greatest English humanists of any age. Later on, it was translated by Geoffrey Chaucer, and still later by Queen Elizabeth I. There are echoes of it in Shakespere and in Alexander Pope. What is it about? The best introduction to it was writen by Jean de Meun in the thirteenth century for a translation he made for Philip the Fair of France. Jean points out, first of all, that all things tend toward the good. In this respect, however, man differs from other things, since he has free choice and his course is not predetermined. The true good of man lies in the real or the intelligible because man is a reasonable creature. But those goods perceived by the senses rather than by the understanding impress him first, and he is misled into deserting his proper good in favor of the tangible goods that impress the senses. He must therefore be taught to distinguish reasonably between the two kinds of good and to know which kind he should enjoy. Most men, Jean says, go astray in this respect, enjoying things of the wrong kind. And this causes their lives to be full of bitterness. For tangible things are transitory and mutable and cannot be enjoyed without sorrow. Among all the books ever written, Jean assures his royal patron, the *Consolation* is the best one for teaching the distinction between true and false good, for showing what things are to be enjoyed, and for demonstrating how other things are to be used. The "true goods" that Boethius recorrmends for our enjoyment are, of course, what St. Paul calls "the invisible things of God". These things were just as real to Boethius and to his audience as the depths of the personality are to Bishop Robinson. If we cannot understand this reality we shall not only fail to understand St. Paul; we shall also find it impossible to understand Chaucer and Shakespeare and a great many other men whose work deserves our very respectful attention.

When St. Paul places God "above," then, he does not do so in a spatial sense at all. He places him above in a hierarchy of *invisibilia*. Let us listen for a moment to St. Augustine, who was a profound student of the New Testament, describing two ways of seeking God, one through the senses and the other through 'the understanding:

> "For when the one God of gods is thought of, even by those who recognize, invoke, and worship other gods, either in Heaven or on earth, he is thought of in such a way that the thought seeks to attain something than which there is nothing better or more sublime. Since men are moved by diverse goods, some by those which appeal to the bodily senses, some by those which pertain to the understanding of the mind, those who are given to the bodily senses think that God of Gods to be either the sky, or that which they see shining most brightly in the sky, or the world itself. Or, if they seek to go beyond the world, they think of something luminous or infinite, or with a vain notion shape it in that form which seems best to them, perhaps thinking of the form of the human body, if they place that above others .... Those, however, who seek to know what God is through the understanding, place Him above all things mutable, either visible and corporal or intelligible and spiritual."

As this discussion continues, St. Augustine rejects the idea of placing God among sensible objects at all, moving from the concept that God is life itself to the higher concept that God is an immutably wise life, or Wisdom itself. He moves, that is, up the steps of a hierarchy of abstractions to the highest abstraction he can conceive. In studying this passage, however, we should remember two qualifications. First of all, the idea of Wisdom was something that had long been celebrated in antique philosophy and literature. It was, in St. Augustine's time, a familiar concept that had a vivid and immediate significance. When modern neo-positivist philosophers say that words like *wisdom* have no actual referents and are not meaningful, they actually mean that such words are not meaningful to them. We must come to understand that a concept may be very meaningful at one point in history and not meaningful at another. The second qualification is that St. Augustine did not mean to limit God by calling Him wisdom. As he says elsewhere, God is ineffable and cannot be defined. The important point is that God, for St. Augustine, was something to be sought at the top of a conceptual hierarchy.

Perhaps it is legitimate to ask the question, "Why did St. Paul and St. Augustine place God at the top of an hierarchy of abstractions?" The answer is simply that they wished to be understood. The real universe of abstract values, as distinct from the physical universe, was a part of their inheritance. It constituted a pattern of thought, or, if you will, a stylistic convention that would make what they had to say comprehensible to their contemporaries. There is nothing especially naïve or primitive about the convention, and St. Augustine is able to use it with an enormous amout of skill and precision, so that the implications of what he has to say are sometimes very profound and still quite useful.

Moreover, the abstract hierarchy of St. Paul and St. Augustine, described rather inadequately by Bishop Robinson as a "three-decker universe," persisted for a very long period of time, outlasting a number of drastic changes in man's conception of the physical world. One of the last great descriptions of the hierarchy, a description that, as we shall see, contains the seeds of its destruction, appears in Pope's *Essay on Man*. Here it is described as the "Great Chain of Being":

> See, thro' this air, this ocean, and this earth,
> All matter quick, and bursting into birth.
> Above, how high progressive life may go !
> Around, how wide ! how deep extend below !
> Vast chain of being, which from God began,
> Natures aethereal, human–(angel, man),
> Beast, bird, fish, insect! what no eye can see,
> No glass can reach ! from Infinite to thee,
> From thee to nothing !

Here we may notice. aside from the somewhat Rococo style of the presentation. an emphasis on the physical content of the hierarchy. The progression God, angel, man, beast, bird, fish, insect, and so on to microscopic and sub-microscopic beings constitutes a confusion of the intelligible world and the tangible world in the same general system.

In much the same way, Pope describes virtue in terms of the passions, or, that is, "psychologically", instead of using abstractions for the purpose. Medieval writers, like Alanus de Insulis, for example, describe Nature in an hierarchical fashion, but they do not place it in the same hierarchy with the world of the intelligible without transforming it into an intelligible realm also, a realm sometimes described as "the Book of God's Work", a book wherein one might find "sermons in stones, and good in everything". What happens to the hierarchy of the intelligible, in other words, is that it becomes a kind of extension of the hierarchy of the tangible.

Speaking of the hierarchy in art in accordance with which ideal forms were considered to be superior to actual forms, an hierarchy that lasted until the eighteenth century, the art historian quoted earlier remarks that it "contrasts with the bourgeois-democratic hunger for facts, which is so well explained by a saying of Dr. Johnson's. 'I had rather see the portrait of a dog than all the allegories you can show me'. The bourgeois wants to know what's all about". The "hunger for facts" mentioned here, was in part responsible for the exploitation of the natural world in nineteenth-century art, a world that seemed to be gradually slipping away before advancing industry, and to new forms of religious expression. First of all, since ideal forms were no longer considered appealing, natural forms were substituted for them. Thus Caspar David Friedrich, in 1808, painted a Crucifixion against a spectacular natural setting to show that Nature should be regarded as "God's House". A very similar attitude underlies much of the poetry of Wordsworth, who found that God was somehow closer in humble and rustic surroundings among men whose domestic affections were still unspoiled. If nature could no longer be made a part of the divine order by giving it a conceptual significance, perhaps it could be consecrated by sentiment, so that we may be made to hear in it "the still, sad music of humanity".

In 1807 Schelling wrote, "Like anyone else whose work lies in the sphere of mind, the artist can only follow the law which God and

Nature have written upon his heart; he can follow no other. Nobody can help him; he can only help himself". Since the "heart" of the artist is of primary importance and his impulses must spring from it rather than from the past or from the work of others, it is not surprising that in the course of time man, a natural being, should come to replace God. This is exactly what happened in the mid-nineteenth century. The same spirit that turned the Cathedral of Notre Dame in Paris into a Temple of Reason, tempered, perhaps, by certain conceptions derived from Hegel, produced Chenevard's painting for the Paris Exposition of 1855. The artist said that he wished to make a dogma of reason and a God of man. The picture contained Oriental and Nordic deities as well as the Sages of the Apocalypse. Zoroaster, Confucius, Homer, and the Prophets of the Old Testament all find a place. Ptolomy, Alexander, and Caesar are represented, as well as Charlemagne, and, below, the great men from the Renaissance to modern times, including Napoleon and George Washington. At the top center looking upward is an enormous semi-nude figure which represents Christ in part, but in a larger sense is the deity of humanity. Below is a chaos representing not Hell, but death and rebirth. With a few additions this non-sectarian, non-rational scheme might well serve to ornament the United Nations Building in New York. Much the same kind of attitude moved the Saint-Simonists to think that by properly organizing the forces of industry and by emancipating both the poor and the flesh in a kind of religion of human love they could create the Kingdom of God on earth. In a more popular sense, these ideas found expression in the great international exhibitions of the century, the predecessors of our own World's Fairs. Man was felt to be a creature whose science would soon conquer the world and whose love would bring the world together in one great community. Humanitarian love became in one form or another the great religion of the century.

Humanitarian love offered to the nineteenth-century mind, just as it offers to Bishop Robinson, a new freedom from what were thought of as the restrictions of the past. At the same time, however, it was frequently an expression of loneliness. As the great French sociologist Durkheim showed, *anomie*, or the lack of social norms, leads to despair. Loneliness became one of the great themes of nineteenth-century art.

The Crucified in Friedrich's painting described earlier is a lonely figure in the solitude of a mountain top seen against the rays of the setting sun as they spread over a vast and lonely sky. No Marys comfort Him and no angels hover above Him. Artists found themselves alone, strangers in an alien society, and it was not difficult to see that a great many other people felt the same way. Among the most moving lines in Coleridge are those from *The Ancient Mariner*:

> Alone, alone, all, all alone,
> Alone on a wide sea !
> And never a saint took pity on
> My soul in agony !

The solitary figure, alone in a broad landscape, became a favorite theme in painting, and lonely Byronic heroes, the direct ancestors of existential anti-heroes, a favorite type in fiction. The theme of isolation which emerges clearly for the first time in Rousseau grows stronger as we approach the twentieth century.

Impressionism offered for a time a kind of private heaven, a dreamworld of light, color, and merging forms, where no strong lines separated the figures into isolated units. If man could not merge with his environment and with his fellow-men in actual life, the impressionistic paintings of artists like Renoir provided a private world where he could do so. The bolder line and harsh colors of expressionism appeal to another private world, the world of expressed frustrations, Our greatest expressionist. poet, T. S. Eliot, regarded art generally as a release of the artist's private frustrations, and his poetry undoubtedly provided a similar emotional release for many of his readers. If we look at the nineteenth and twentieth centuries as a whole, we can discover an increasing tendency toward subjectivity. The space of Heidegger's universe is a subjective space objectified, and it is this subjective space regarded as an object, the space of the personality, that becomes the space of abstract art. Paul Klee, who was a very devout man, regarded his paintings as a defence against a sorrowful and irrational world, a world that acquired validity only when it was re-created. Other abstractionists thought of their work as having a definite religious significance. Theo van Doosburg wrote in 1916, "To discover the beautiful is nothing else than to discover the universal. That universal is the divine", Mondrian said that in his abstractions he sought to "manifest purely the universal that is present in everything. It is identical with that which is unveiled in the past under the name of Divinity, and which is indispensable to us, to poor human beings who must find an equilibrium for ourselves, for things in themselves are opposed to us, and the matter which is further outside of ourselves fights against us".

Considering these developments, it is not surprising that Bishop Robinson should locate God "in the depths of the personality", and that he should wish to remove traditional restrictions on conduct that may be regarded as impediments to love. He quotes St. Augustine, who says, "Love and do what you will", but he omits to tell us that here St. Augsutine means for us to love God, the highest Wisdom, and our neighbors as ourselves, and then do what we will. The abstract world of St. Paul and St. Augustine became entangled with the concrete world of visible things. As a somewhat irrational extension of the visible world, it then disappeared altogether. Nature, which had at first seemed benign and appealing to the romantics became first amoral, as it is in John Stuart Mill's famous essay, and then a part of an absurd and inimical universe. Man himself as an isolated individual became more important. But as revolutionary movements destroyed his traditional communities, he sought consolation in universal brotherhood. When the impracticality of this goal became apparent, if not altogether conscious, he retreated into himself. He had nowhere else to go. Reality became a matter of what Bishop Robinson calls "personal relationships". This is, incidentally, not an isolated development, but a part of the style of the times. A non-religious philosopher, Ortega y Gasset, says that reality is "my life", not life alone, but life with "the others".

To conclude, I must confess that I have used Bishop Robinson as a device to get at something else. I have, as I said at the outset, no theological quarrel in mind, either with Bishop Robinson or with his critics. What I do wish to emphasize is that it is possible to develop a certain sympathetic understanding for the stylistic conventions of any period. If we are able to do this with reference to the great periods of the past, whole new worlds of satisfying study become available to us. St. Augustine was among the world's greatest thinkers and it is a shame to neglect his writings simply because we do not wish to make the effort to learn something about the language of his style. Similarly, we can learn much from Erasmus, from Hooker, from Locke, and from the great writers of the nineteenth century. Much of what at first seems strange, uninteresting, or downright absurd in their writings will become clear and stimulating if we approach them with some knowledge of their stylistic conventions. It is at times very difficult to avoid reading our own conventions into the past, but the effort to avoid doing so can lead to very satisfying results. We are urged on every hand to be tolerant of those around us, regardless of race or creed. Let us also be tolerant or even more than tolerant, of those men in the past who worked very hard to shape our history and our tradition.

Simple Signs from Everyday Life in Chaucer

D. W. Robertson, Jr.

In: *Signs and Symbols in Chaucer's Poetry,* ed. John P. Hermann and John J. Burke Jr. (Tuscaloosa, AL: University of Alabama Press, 1981), pp. 12-26 & 208-215.

Perhaps it would be helpful at the outset if I explained my title or "theme," somewhat in the fashion of a good medieval preacher, although I have never, in spite of my reputation, sought to rival a good preacher. The title, "Simple Signs from Everyday Life in Chaucer," falls into three parts: "Signs," "Everyday Life," and "Chaucer," which I shall discuss in that order, including under "Chaucer" some brief observations about the poet, his audience, and his work. I regret that I do not have time for more *exempla,* since these, as any good preacher knows, are more entertaining than anything else. But to begin with the word *sign,* I should like to say at the outset that I do not care much for disputes about terminology, which strike me as being pedantic. However, I think that Chaucerians should use as much medieval terminology as possible, recognizing the fact that medieval authors except for scholastic theologians tended to use terms rather loosely. But modern terms tend to carry with them connotations in a universe of discourse alien to that of the Middle Ages. The term *sign* has the advantage of being current in the Middle Ages and being very loose at the same time, allowing me considerable freedom, since a *sign* is simply something that signifies something else. *Signs,* as Saint Augustine tells us,[1] may be either words or things, or even actions, some of which are literal and some of which

---

1. *De doctrina Christiana,* 1.2.2; 2.1-4; 2. 16, 40. Cf. Peter Lombard, *Sententiae,* 1.1.1.

are figurative. The word *iconography,* borrowed from art history, implies the identification of objects represented, or the study of literal signs, whereas *iconology,* borrowed from the same discipline, is concerned with meanings.[2] Many persons, myself included, use *iconography* to mean both, a simple and convenient stratagem. The word *symbol* has the disadvantage of bearing connotations in modern art and literature consistent with an expressionistic style, so that it can sometimes be misleading when used in connection with styles different from expressionism, and I think that C. S. Lewis was wrong in adducing such symbols in the Middle Ages.[3] Finally, although medieval writers used the terms *types* and *antitypes,* the word *typology* is late and not generally current in the Middle Ages. As I have sought to show elsewhere,[4] the juxtaposition of types and antitypes in accordance with what was called *allegoria* in scriptural exposition usually implied a moral or "tropological" meaning, so that the mere juxtaposition of Old and New Testament events or even fictional or current events with scriptural events carried out for its own sake, without

2. Cf. Erwin Panofsky, "Iconography and Iconology," in *Meaning and the Visual Arts* (New York, 1955), pp. 26–54.
3. *The Allegory of Love* (Oxford, 1936), ch. 2. A modern "symbol" is not the same thing either as a sacrament or as a figurative attribute. It is, rather, in Crocean terms, an intuitively perceived inner reality based on feeling that can be expressed only as a symbol. We are inclined to think of many of the ideas implied by figurative signs as "abstractions." But the idea that generalized concepts of all kinds are derived from the observation of a series of related particulars is Aristotelian and did not profoundly influence European thought until after the thirteenth century. Even then, "abstractions" were often treated as external realities whose existence might be discovered through experience. Generally speaking, "reality" has moved rapidly inward since the late eighteenth century. The term "personified abstractions" applied to certain figures in works like the *Roman de la Rose* is misleading, a fact clearly indicated by our tendency to think of them as "psychological" even when some of them, like *Bien celer,* are clearly strategic rather than "psychological." They actually belong to a moral rather than to a psychological realm. One of the last great English works to employ allegory in the ancient manner is Pope's *Rape of the Lock,* where the sylphs and gnomes represent outer realities that may or may not be reflected in Belinda, depending on her choice of whether she harbors an "Earthly Lover" (3.144) in her heart or maintains "good sense" and "good humour" (5. 16, 30).
4. "The Question of 'Typology' and the Wakefield *Mactacio Abel,*" *American Benedictine Review,* 25 (1974), 157–73.

further implication, was not a common medieval practice, in spite of some observations in a recent book.[5] Altogether the word *sign* thus has distinct advantages, although I have no wish to be pedantic about this, nor to condemn anyone for using the other terms mentioned, especially since I have used all of them myself.

A sign, like a word, may mean one thing to one individual and something else to another, for no two of us have exactly the same experience. But members of a given culture often employ figurative signs that mean roughly the same things to many other individuals in that culture, although a sign may have a more profound or more emotionally charged meaning to some than to others, depending on differences in experience, education, and intelligence; and there may be some who fail to perceive some figurative signs, or who take them literally.[6] "Meanings" do not exist in words, events, or things, but in the individuals who perceive them, where they have a certain regularity because of custom. Since people are constantly changing, both within generations and from one generation to the next, "meanings" change constantly. It is also true that the meaning of a sign may be very different from that of its referent. For example, the printed word *tiger,* even burning brightly in the forests of the night, does not alarm me, but an actual untethered tiger in my vicinity would suggest immediate evasive action. Similarly, a broiled lobster on a plate before me

---

5. Earl E. Miner, ed., *Literary Uses of Typology* (Princeton, 1976), Preface, where *typology* becomes synonymous with *allegoria* in its exegetical sense, from which *types* and *antitypes* are actually derivative, and comes perilously close also to embracing the sacraments.

6. As Boethius sagely observed, *Consolatio,* 5. pr. 6, "omne quod scitur non ex sua sed ex comprehendentium natura cognoscitur." On conventional figurative signs in the Middle Ages, see E. Mâle *L'Art religieux du XIIIe siècle* (Paris, 1923), Introduction, ch. 1. It was generally thought that a failure to understand figurative signs in the Scriptures was extremely reprehensible. See Saint Augustine, *De doctrina Christiana,* 3.5.9. The idea persisted throughout the Middle Ages. Cf. Erasmus, *Enchiridion,* 3. With reference to poetry, the same author observes (*Enchiridion,* 14) that it may be better to read a poetic tale allegorically than to read the Scriptures literally. Petrarch and Boccaccio recognized the fact that some might fail to understand figurative signs in poetry. See C. G. Osgood, trans., *Boccaccio on Poetry* (rpt.; New York, 1956), pp. 58–62 (*Genealogia deorum gentilium,* 14.12.).

might produce one kind of meaning if I were hungry and quite another meaning if I had just eaten three of them. To put this in another way, the universe of discourse is made up of arbitrary signs, and these are not identical with the universe itself. Both shift with time and circumstance. The study of signs is thus difficult and poses many problems.

In recent years many scholars have become occupied with the study of figurative signs. Not all of them, incidentally, are "Robertsonians," since such studies, especially in the visual arts,[7] long antedate my own efforts, and students of Renaissance literature, some of whom have never heard of me, now sometimes pursue the subject with avidity. Signs from scriptural texts and their commentaries, from classical texts and their commentaries, or from mythographic writers, from astrology, from music, from early medieval texts, like the *Psychomachia* of Prudentius, from texts widely used in schools, like the *De nuptiis* of Martianus Capella, or the *De planctu Naturae* of Alanus, from popular vernacular texts like the *Roman de la Rose,* and from representational conventions in the visual arts, including the drama, have all been studied, and their presence traced in Chaucer's poetry. There is still a great deal of this sort of thing to be done. In many instances we do not understand earlier texts very well, and in others we lack readily available primary sources since many commentaries both on the Scriptures and on the classics remain unpublished, and others, especially from the late Middle Ages, have been lost. Moreover, much evidence from the visual arts has been destroyed by religious or rationalist zeal, or simply by the ravages of time. We are thus often forced to adduce traditions rather than sources, but in any event it is necessary to exercise extreme care to become familiar with available primary sources and to avoid speculation as much as possible. Rosalie Green of the Index of Christian Art has recently issued a very stern warning concerning undisciplined iconological studies,[8] and it would

---

7. A pioneer study now often neglected is A. Goldschmidt, *Der Albani-Psalter* (Berlin, 1895).

8. "Iconography and Delusion," delivered 23 Nov. 1976 at the Courtauld Institute, London. She is preparing a book on the subject of iconographic research for which she is likely to propose extremely high standards. Cf. the recent study by Peter Hyland, "Number Symbolism in *The Canterbury Tales*: Some Suggestions," *The Annual Reports of the Faculty of Arts and Letters, Tohuku University,* 26 (1976), 1–11.

not be difficult to compile a long list of highly dubious interpretations of figurative signs in Chaucer studies, some of them ostensibly relying on primary materials.

Turning now to my second topic, "Everyday Life," I should like to assert first of all that this was Chaucer's primary concern and that he hoped that his work would be beneficial in a practical way. But this hope was probably tempered somewhat by a realization that passionate zeal is not productive and involves an undesirable submission to Fortune. That is, for the most part he seems to have taken his own advice in "Truth":

> Tempest thee noght al croked to redresse,
> In trust of hir that turneth as a bal.

He did not usually employ figurative signs and other forms of indirect language for merely decorative or what we might call "literary" purposes, but to comment, frequently in a humorous way, on the mores of his own time. Throughout the Middle Ages, but especially after the middle of the twelfth century, figurative devices of all kinds, combined with other devices like specious argument and irony,[9] were often used for humorous moral comment. Since we cannot hear Chaucer reading, we probably miss a great deal of his humor, especially various kinds of ironic intonation. However, we can probably rely on the advice of Boncompagno of Signa quoted by John F. Benton: "Irony is the unadorned and gentle use of words to convey disdain and ridicule. If he who expresses irony may be seen, the intention of the speaker may be understood through his gestures. In the absence of the speaker, manifest evil and impure belief indict the subject.... It is nothing but

---

9. Specious argument was much relished as a source of irony in the Middle Ages. See, for example, my "Two Poems from the Carmina Burana," *American Benedictine Review,* 27 (1976), esp. 45–60; "Chaucer's Franklin and his Tale," *Costerus,* n.s., 1 (1974), esp. 12–17; Roy J. Pearcy, "Investigation into the Principles of Fabliau Structure," in Paul G. Ruggiers, *Versions of Medieval Comedy* (Norman, 1977), esp. pp. 97–100. J. A. W. Bennett, *Chaucer at Oxford and Cambridge* (Toronto, 1974), p. 83, refers justly, I think, to "that delight in specious argument for its own sake which characterizes the later fourteenth century," although Chaucer uses it for satiric comment on the speaker. For an amusing example from everyday life, see the hypothetical defense offered by a manorial tenant for stealing fish in F. W. Maitland and W. P. Baildon, *The Court Baron,* Selden Society, 4 (1891), 54–55.

vituperation to commend the evil deeds of someone through their opposite, or to relate them wittily."[10] To the modern mind a basic moral stance and humor, like Ovid's majesty and love, do not readily go together; but in the Middle Ages even scriptural materials could be used humorously since they afforded a background of rationality or "pure belief" that could be used to comment on ludicrous speech or behavior,[11] a fact that has misled certain staid and serious readers of more recent times to invent such things as "the religion of courtly love," or to find "pagan values" (whatever they are) in medieval texts presented before reasonably orthodox audiences. Where Chaucer is concerned, the monitory raised finger and the prayer beads in the Hoccleve portrait, combined with his early reputation as a "philosopher," are probably sufficient indications of the basic attitude we should expect from him.

Chaucer's moral comment, although based on certain Christian principles that are not difficult to recover, even though literary scholars are sometimes reluctant to pursue their implications, was directed toward specific fourteenth-century English problems, and I think that it is time we paid more attention to these problems. Chaucer did not write "for all humanity," or "for all time," but for a specific audience that had immediate everyday concerns. The indirection he employed lent his comments a certain incisiveness, making them more entertaining and hence more effective than the more direct criticisms of his friend Gower. The evidence of the visual arts, music, and literature itself, not to mention overt statements by writers like Boccaccio and Petrarch, suggest strongly that sophisticated medieval audiences

10. "Clio and Venus: An Historian's View of Medieval Love," in F. X. Newman, ed., *The Meaning of Courtly Love* (Albany, 1968), pp. 28-29, 37. If a fairly orthodox audience is being addressed we can be reasonably certain that the definition is valid. Professor Benton, for example, believes that it "deserves a place at the beginning of every edition of [Chrétien's] *Lancelot*." Along with the quotation from John of Salisbury in note 12 below it might well have a place at the beginning of every edition of Chaucer.

11. The first part of the Wife of Bath's Prologue offers an excellent illustration, but the technique flourished long before Chaucer. See the article on the *Carmina Burana* mentioned in note 9 above, and for another striking illustration the Old French play, *Courtois D'Arras*. For Chaucer, see also Gail Gibson's article in this volume.

were not, like modern audiences, passive, awaiting technical operations on their feelings and vicarious thrills, but active and alert, perceiving the activities of the poet before them (who was often beneath them in rank) with a certain detachment, and demanding that he supply substantial food for thought in a diverting manner. I think that we often fail to realize the rather curious effects of mass culture in modern times and to discount those effects when we study earlier literature. The earlier attitude is well described by Erasmus, who wrote in a letter to a friend,

> "Horace thought that advice given jocularly had no less effect than that given seriously. 'What forbids,' he exclaims, 'that anyone speak the truth with a smile?' This fact has not been overlooked by the wisest men of antiquity who have preferred to express the most salutary principles of conduct in the form of laughable and childish fables, because the truth, a little austere in itself, adorned with the attraction of pleasure penetrates more easily into the minds of mortals."

Erasmus goes on to cite Saint Augustine's *De doctrina Christiana* for the appearance of similar principles in the Scriptures.[12] Chaucer was thus fulfilling an ancient tradition when he read his Tales with a certain subtle indirection. But he also had in mind the immediate interests of his audience.

Much of Chaucer's figurative language was readily available, however, in "everyday" sources and was not in itself very obscure. The visual arts offer some fairly simple examples. Thus the significance of the Marriage at Cana, the implications of which are so blatantly disregarded by the Wife of Bath, were explained in part in an inscription on a stained glass window at Canterbury,[13] a "gat-tothed" wife appears

---

12. Letter to Martin Dorp (no. 337, 1515) often printed in early editions of *The Praise of Folly*. For a similar use of Horace (*Sermonum*, 1.1.24–25) with the conclusion that "nothing forbids telling the truth with a laugh and representing in fabulous narratives, which philosophy does not reject, that which may be prejudicial to morals" see John of Salisbury, *Policraticus*, ed. Webb (Oxford, 1909), 8.11.753a. Cf. Richard de Bury, *Philobiblon*, ed. A. Altamura (Naples, 1954), 13. 15–25, and Chaucer, Cook's Prologue, 4356.
13. Mâle, *L'Art religieux*, pp. 186–97, and Bernard Rackham, *The Ancient Glass of Canterbury Cathedral* (London, 1949), p. 63 and pl. 19.

in an illustration for the *Roman de la Rose*,[14] cloistered monks leaving their cloisters to signify inconstancy appear in Gothic statuary,[15] wrestlers were used in marginalia to signify discord,[16] and so on. Since Chaucer was once appointed Clerk of the King's Works, an office that involved the maintenance of royal buildings and their decorations as well as the arrangement of pageantry, we can assume that he was familiar with a wide variety of representations in the visual arts. But it is also possible to find figurative signs in everyday sources that are neither "literary," exegetical, nor visually representative. For example, the pilgrimage of the spirit, now often adduced in connection with the larger thematic structure of *The Canterbury Tales,* appears vividly represented in an early fourteenth-century legal document, a charter written for the foundation of a chapel, which begins as follows:

> "How many and how great are the tempests of the inner man, the foes of peace, wherein the exile of this world abounds, experience, the effective revealer of doubts, daily makes manifest. I, therefore, Roger de Martivallis, archdeacon of Leycestre, and lord of Nouesle, wishing, with the Lord's consent, to make ready for myself in the desert of this world, a straight path, whereby under the guidance of divine grace, amid the powers of darkness, I may more easily be able to come to that place where I may deserve after toil to receive the wages of true recompense ..."

and so on concerning the chapel first planned by Roger's father, Sir Anketin de Martivallis, knight.[17]

Here are the storms of the inner man that Chaucer urges us to calm in "Truth" by avoiding trust in Fortune, the "exile" of Boethius at the

---

14. Reproduced from a MS in the Princeton University Library in my *Literature of Medieval England* (New York, 1970), p. 479.
15. E.g., Charles Rufus Morey, *Mediaeval Art* (New York, 1942), pl. 112.
16. See my *Preface to Chaucer* (Princeton, 1962), p. 243 and fig. 39.
17. George F. Farnham and A. Hamilton Thompson, "The Manor of Noseley," Transactions of Leicestershire Archaeological Society, 12, pt. 2 (1921–22), 242. For another example, see the description of the "garden of the Church" in Bishop Bransford's visitation notification of 1339, printed by R. M. Haines, *The Administration of the Diocese of Worcester in the First Half of the Fourteenth Century* (London, 1965), p. 85 (n. 3).

beginning of the *Consolation,* the desert or "wilderness" of this world in Chaucer's *House of Fame,* elaborately and competently explained by B. G. Koonce,[18] and reflected in other ways as the realm of the Fox in the Nun's Priest's Tale or as the "wilderness" that is no home in "Truth," the straight path that is the alternative of the "croked wey" recommended by the Old Man in the Pardoner's Tale, and, finally, the movement toward the Celestial Jerusalem that the Parson urges us to follow through penance at the close of *The Canterbury Tales.* I call attention to these things simply to indicate that a great deal of material we so laboriously seek out in learned and literary sources is actually a part of the everyday language of the time, at least among the literate. Chaucer was not always obscure to his contemporaries when he is obscure to us. Meanwhile, I think we should also notice that the archdeacon refers to experience as the revealer of those tempests that disturb the inner man and destroy his peace. Within the terms of their own means of describing human nature medieval people were very practical, and we do them a disservice when we substitute our own "psychological" terminology for theirs. Not only is the practicality of that terminology rather dubious, but it is out of context in their very different society.[19]

Turning now to the third division of my theme I should like to discuss Chaucer, his audience, and his work, and, finally, to illustrate the importance of simple signs from everyday life to our understanding of what he wrote. First of all, it is now clear that Chaucer was a gentleman and, as the positions he held reveal, something of a clerk, and not, as is frequently said, a "bourgeois," except in the sense that he

---

18. *Chaucer and the Tradition of Fame* (Princeton, 1966), pp. 125-29.
19. Theoretical psychology is essentially a feature of the modern universe of discourse (not necessarily of "the nature of things") which is unsuited to the study of authors whose analysis of human conduct is basically moral. The fragmentation of modern theoretical psychology into "schools" does not speak well for its credibility, and modern practical psychology must face social and cultural circumstances entirely different from those of the Middle Ages and, consequently, entirely different kinds of people. On this last point Dr. J. H. van den Berg of the University of Leiden has been insisting for some time. See most recently his *Divided Existence and Complex Society* (Pittsburgh, 1974).

lived for a long period in London, which might be called a "bourg."[20] He was also a "court man" who served the king and certain members of the royal family in a variety of ways. He was a royal squire and not a knight, probably because he was insufficiently wealthy or unwilling, for many persons sought to avoid knighthood and its obligations. He was thought sufficiently distinguished to be named on peace commissions, but this fact does not indicate that he ever actually sat as a Justice, and there is no record that he ever received any pay for that office, although it is true that Justices of the Peace often served without payment. He served once in Parliament, although this was not a great distinction, and frequently on government commissions, often for the Chamber, with which he seems to have been closely associated. He was Controller of the Customs in London, an office that brought him in close contact with the Exchequer, and he held the important office of Clerk of the King's Works for a reasonable period. His son, Thomas, also a squire, received numerous grants from John of Gaunt and the king, and in the year of his father's death became sheriff of Oxfordshire and Berkshire. He married the daughter of a knight, and his daughter, Alice, was married in succession to two earls.

Chaucer's audience, as Derek Pearsall has recently suggested, probably consisted of "household knights and officials, career diplomats and civil servants," men like "Clifford, Clanvowe, Scogan, Hoccleve, Usk, Gower, Strode."[21] This rather miscellaneous list could easily be expanded to include chamber knights like William Neville, who was Clanvowe's close friend, Peter Courtenay, Richard Stury, Philip la Vache, William Beauchamp, and John Montagu, who became Earl of Salisbury in 1397. We know something about some of these men, and since, as I suggested earlier, meanings exist in people rather than in words, it should be helpful to Chaucerians to learn all they can about them. For Chaucer was a successful poet whose skills as an entertainer probably account for the respect paid him by both supporters of

---

20. See F. R. H. Du Boulay, "The Historical Chaucer," in Derek Brewer, *Geoffrey Chaucer* (London, 1974), p. 37. Cf. my "Some Disputed Chaucerian Terminology," *Speculum*, 52 (1977), 572.
21. "The *Troilus* Frontispiece and Chaucer's Audience," *Yearbook of English Studies*, 7 (1977), 73-74.

Richard II and supporters of Henry IV. It would be absurd to attribute attitudes to Chaucer that would have been either offensive or incomprehensible to his audience. In the first place, a number of these men were lords of manors, thoroughly familiar both with problems of manorial administration and with the rapid changes in manorial economy and society in many areas after the first outbreak of the Black Death. They had considerable experience with yeomen, reeves, millers, plowmen, dairy maids, franklins, and poor cottagers like the widow in the Friar's Tale or Griselda before her marriage. They knew knights and merchants in variety, sergeants at law, both royal and ordinary, physicians, clothiers like the Wife of Bath, clerks, and a wide variety of ecclesiastics. Some had seen extensive military service, and a number had obvious literary or cultural interests. Gower was a successful poet in three languages; Clanvowe was the author of a graceful Chaucerian poem and of a stern moral treatise; Usk, secretary to London's controversial reforming mayor, John of Northampton, wrote a Boethian treatise on love; and Montagu was praised for his verse (which does not survive) by Christine de Pisan. Strode was not only a distinguished Oxford logician but probably also the author of a poem, now lost. He undoubtedly appreciated keenly the amusingly specious arguments advanced by some of Chaucer's characters. Stury owned a copy of the *Roman de la Rose;* Beauchamp had a university education; and there were probably a number of well-educated clerks and ecclesiastics in the audience.

Some of these men were keenly interested in social and ecclesiastical reform, and, in fact, have been accused, falsely I think, except for a temporary lapse on the part of Usk, of being Lollards.[22] Let me

---

22. The standard article on this subject is W. T. Waugh, "The Lollard Knights," *Scottish Historical Review*, 11 (1913–14), 55–92, who regarded Lollardry among persons of rank with general skepticism. A more favorable attitude toward possible Lollardry among Chamber knights was advanced by K. B. McFarlane, *Lancastrian Kings and Lollard Knights* (Oxford, 1972), part 2. McFarlane also corrected certain errors of fact in Waugh's account and added new biographical information. He may, however, see "Lollardry" (specifically sympathy for Wyclif's doctrines) in reforming attitudes having other origins. Thus Du Boulay, "The Historical Chaucer," p. 46, observes that "it remains possible that as a group they showed in exaggerated form the sentiments felt by many orthodox contemporaries." On Clanvowe, see V. J. Scattergood,

consider some examples.[23] Sir Lewis Clifford, after an early military career, was made squire of the Black Prince in 1364 with an annuity of £40, increased to a hundred marks in 1368 and to £100 when he was knighted. I might observe in passing that the Black Prince was on the whole an efficient and charitable administrator of his landed estates.[24] Clifford fought in Spain in 1367, in France in 1377, and in Brittany in 1378. John of Gaunt, who led this last unsuccessful venture, made him one of his executors. Between 1370 and 1372 he married Eleanor, daughter of John, Lord Mowbray of Axholme and Joan of Lancaster. Their daughter later married Philip la Vache. Clifford was made Knight of the Garter in 1377 and became a royal knight in 1381. Joan of Kent granted him custody of Cardigan Castle in 1378.

The Works of Sir John Clanvowe (Totowa, N.J., 1975). Clifford's membership in the Order of the Passion, which envisaged a new crusade, and the participation of Clanvowe and Neville in a crusade are hardly consistent with Wyclif's teachings. A worldly person might hurl the epithet "Lollard," which was originally a term of opprobrium, at any unworldly person. See my *Chaucer's London* (New York, 1968), pp. 152, 211. The word "Lollard" was apparently applied to followers of Wyclif by Henry Crump, Regent in Sacred Theology at Oxford, in 1381, an act that led the Chancellor of the University, Robert Rigg, to charge him with breaking the peace. See the discussion in Joseph Dahmus, *William Courtenay* (University Park and London, 1966), ch. 6. We may compare the tone used by Henry of Wakefield, Bishop of Worcester, in a pastoral letter of 1387 concerning followers of Wyclif in his diocese wherein he speaks of "quidam tamen eterne dampnationis filii Antichristi discipuli et Machomete sequaces instigatione diabolica conspiratori in collegio illicito et a iure reprobato nomine seu ritu Lollardorum confederati." See W. P. Marett, *A Calendar of the Register of Henry of Wakefield, Bishop of Worcester, 1375-1395*, Worcester Historical Society, n.s., 7 (1972), 150. Harry Bailey's remark, "I smelle a Lollere in the wynd" (Man of Law's Tale, Epilogue, 1173) is probably indicative of his own worldliness and rude speech rather than of any weakness on the part of the Parson, who is idealized in the General Prologue in highly conventional terms. As John Barnie indicates, *War in English Medieval Society* (Ithaca, 1974), p. 103, English reverses during the seventies and eighties "were explained as a punishment visited by God on the sins of his people." A moral stance among responsible courtiers and officials was thus to be expected.

23. The information here is derived from the studies of Waugh and McFarlane mentioned in the previous note unless otherwise indicated.

24. See John Hatcher, *Rural Economy and Society in the Duchy of Cornwall* (Cambridge, 1970), p. 127.

He served her faithfully until her death and was made one of her executors. In about 1385 or a little later he joined the Order of the Passion founded by Philippe de Mézières, who had been chancellor to the famous crusading leader Peter of Lusignan and who, in his later years, dedicated himself to the moral reform of European chivalry and the establishment of peace between France and England, preferably through a royal marriage, for which Sir Lewis conducted negotiations between 1391 and 1396, after 1392 as a member of the Royal Council. Literary scholars will remember Philippe as the author of the liturgical drama, "Figurative Representation of the Presentation of the Virgin Mary in the Temple."[25] Clifford befriended Eustache Deschamps during a mission to France in 1385 and 1386, and brought back with him that author's little poem in praise of Chaucer. He and Stury were among the executors of the Duchess of York, who left him, in 1392, her book of Vices and Virtues. This has been a very brief sketch, but enough to show that Clifford was among the most trusted and reliable members of the court, a distinguished knight in the field in his youth and a wise and discreet counsellor in his maturity, sufficiently pious to be deeply interested in the Order of the Passion and rigorous enough in his views to be branded with the unsavory epithet "Lollard."

Among his friends were Sir John Clanvowe and Sir William Neville. Clanvowe had begun his career as a knight bachelor serving under Humphrey de Bohun V of Hereford between 1363 and the earl's death in 1373. During this period he fought under Sir John Chandos, who was one of the great exemplars of English chivalry, wise as well

---

25. Printed by Karl Young, *The Drama of the Mediaeval Church* (Oxford, 1933), 2:225-45; for a translation, see Robert S. Haller and M. Catherine Rupp, O.S.M., *Figurative Representation of the Presentation of the Virgin Mary in the Temple* (Lincoln, Nebraska, 1971). Documents for the Order of the Passion have been published by Abdel Hamid Handy, "Philippe de Mézières and the New Order of the Passion," *Bulletin of the Faculty of Arts, Alexandria University,* 18 (1964), 1-104; Philippe's *Songe du vieil pèlerin* has been edited by G. W. Coopland (Cambridge, 1969), and the same editor has published (with a translation) *Philippe's Letter to Richard II* (Liverpool, 1975) urging Richard to join the Order. The standard biography of Philippe is N. Jorga, *Philippe de Mézières, 1327-1405, et la croisade au XIVe siècle* (Paris, 1896). For the influence of Philippe's order in England, see J. J. N. Palmer, *England, France, and Christendom* (London, 1972), pp. 181, 186-91, 198.

as worthy. Together with Neville, Stury, and Philip la Vache he commanded a group of 120 men during Gaunt's Breton campaign of 1378. The king made him a knight of the Chamber in 1382. Like Clifford, he was one of the executors of Joan of Kent, who seems to have gathered around her a group of men interested in reform. When England seemed certain to be invaded by the French in 1386, he and Neville went to Essex and Sussex to prepare defenses. In his later years he served on the Council. On 17 October 1391 he died near Constantinople. He and Neville had participated in a crusade in Tunisia during the previous year. Neville, who was with him in his last days, died of grief two days later.

Neville was a Chamber knight after 1381, and served on the Council. His later reputation for "Lollardry" stems from the fact that he sought the custody of the heretic Nicholas Hereford at his castle of Nottingham "because of the honesty of his person." Others apparently agreed with this estimate, however, for Nicholas recanted and became, during 1395-96, Chancellor of St. Paul's Cathedral. We may remember that Cecily Champain's release of Chaucer for all claims of rape or other actions against him filed before Bishop Sudbury in the Chancery was witnessed not only by William Beauchamp, the royal Chamberlain, but by Clanvowe and Neville as well. Considering the character of these witnesses, we can be fairly sure that Cecily had no real claims.[26]

The most distinguished members of Chaucer's audience were probably men like these. Perhaps we should occasionally ask ourselves rather simple questions like the following: What would Clanvowe have thought of Neville if, while arranging the defenses of the southern coast in 1386, he had become infatuated with a widow simply by

---

26. The usual modern allegations rest on the unfounded assumption that the recognizance by John Grove of 2 July 1380, two months after Cecily's release of Chaucer, represented hush money supplied by the poet. For the documents, see Martin M. Crow and Clair C. Olson, *Chaucer Life-Records* (Oxford, 1966), pp. 343-47. If Chaucer had raped Cecily or anyone else, it is probable that he would have been forced to purchase a pardon, as Henry of Wakefield was forced to do for this offense, to be presented before the King's Bench. Rape was a felony punishable by death. Du Boulay, "The Historical Chaucer," p. 46, lists the modern tendency to see Chaucer as a rapist among "rash dramatizations" concerning the poet's life.

looking at her, had shown immediate suicidal tendencies, had forgotten his obligations to the kingdom, and had feared nothing except the possible reluctance of the lady? Those who think that Troilus is an admirable character should recall that Englishmen regarded themselves as inhabitants of New Troy[27] and that their realm was in serious danger of foreign invasion at the time Chaucer completed his poem. French incursions on the south coast had caused unrest for many years and had given rise to serious doubts about English chivalry, concerning which Peter de la Mare complained bitterly in Parliament in 1377, alleging that chivalry and other virtues were being neglected in favor of vice. It has even been suggested that a failure to defend the coast properly was one of the causes of the revolt of 1381.[28] The idea that Chaucer's audience could have regarded Troilus with any real sympathy borders on the absurd; it is most probable that the character was

27. Cf. *Chaucer's London*, p. 2. The idea was still current in 1605, when the story of Brutus was reenacted in a pageant by Anthony Munday, *The Triumphes of Re-United Britannia*. See David M. Bergeron, "Civic Pageants and Historical Drama," *Journal of Medieval and Renaissance Studies*, 5 (1975), 103-04.

28. Eleanor Searle, *Lordship and Community: Battle Abbey and Its Banlieu* (Toronto, 1974), p. 345. In 1377 there were raids along the south coast, assaults on the Isle of Wight and Yarmouth, and Rye and Hastings were burned. At Southampton the burgesses petitioned the king in 1376 to take the town into his own hands and to assume its defenses. Henry Yevele, whom Chaucer undoubtedly knew, was commissioned in 1378 to build a new keep for the city. There were further invasion scares in 1383 and in the period between 1385 and 1388. See Colin Smith, *Medieval Southampton* (London and Boston, 1973), pp. 127-28. J. J. N. Palmer observes, *England, France, and Christendom*, p. 5: "Almost every parliament of the 1380s made plaintive reference to the innumerable enemies surrounding the kingdom: all of them rich, powerful and active; all intent on the utter destruction of the country; all inseparably bound together by firm alliances; and all possessing separate and highly dangerous advantages over their isolated and dismayed opponent." On the general invasion scare of 1386, see ibid., ch. 4. In view of the conventional association of England with Troy and the actual situation in which England found itself at the time Chaucer wrote his poem, the usual romantic, sentimental, psychological, or "courtly love" interpretations now fashionable among academic critics amount to nothing more than accusations that Chaucer and his friends at court were frivolous and irresponsible, and these are hardly supported by the facts as we know them. But such interpretations have little or no support in the text, which, as its closing stanzas clearly indicate, should be read as a warning.

intended as an exemplary warning to the men of New Troy. Certainly, no one in Chaucer's audience would have sought to excuse Troilus on the ground that he was a "courtly lover." There is absolutely no evidence to show that either Chaucer or any member of his audience had ever heard of "courtly love"; and we might say exactly the same thing about "psychological realism." The figurative signs in the poem, insofar as we can identify them, its classical mythography, its scriptural and doctrinal echoes, and its reflections of Boethian philosophy all suggest that Troilus is an example to be avoided. And the historical circumstances under which the poem was written strongly reinforce this impression. Chaucer's good reputation both as a man and as a literary craftsman was probably not achieved by sentimental or "sophisticated" endorsements of human weakness. Rather, he could be counted upon to ridicule foolishness with good-natured philosophical detachment wherever it might appear in his society, although, except for Harry Bailey and perhaps Hodge of Ware,[29] he generally refrained from attacking individuals.

And this observation brings me to *The Canterbury Tales*. Chaucer's technique of portraiture in the General Prologue reflects a medieval tendency to identify individuals in terms of attributes. That is, for example, we identify Saint Peter as he stands among other saints in sculpture or illumination by the fact that he carries keys; we can recognize Saint Paul as a miller grinding the grain of the Old Law to produce the flour of the New; John the Baptist is dressed in the garments of the wilderness; and so on. Similar techniques had been used by both Ovid and Prudentius, and by their imitators. We can observe a similar tendency in everyday life. Thus a bailiff attending a manorial court might be fined for not carrying his rod, the attribute of his office, or a hayward for not carrying his horn.[30] Trespassers placed in the stocks were often adorned with objects to show the nature of their crimes, a whetstone being placed around the neck of a slanderer or a liar, for example, to show that he was like the deceitful "sharp razor" of Psalm 51.[31] Or a trespasser might be paraded through the

---

29. For Hodge, see *Chaucer's London*, p. 104.
30. Frances M. Page, *The Estates of Crowland Abbey* (Cambridge, 1934), p. 77.
31. *Chaucer's London*, p. 47.

streets, like the false physician, who, it is said, in 1382 rode backward through London carrying not only a whetstone but two urinals, fore and aft.[32] There is a strong element of humor in these punishments, for trespassers were thought to find the ridicule of the community discouraging. A number of the characters in the Prologue and the subsequent Tales are, legally speaking, trespassers; others are guilty of extremely dubious practices. Are their portraits literal and "realistic," or does Chaucer gather together his little collections of attributes to create figures very like grotesques? Are the characters actually "typical"? The same questions apply to many of the figures in the Tales, especially since the Tales often elaborate the significance of the attributes mentioned in the Prologue, serving, in effect, as additional attributes of the speakers.

There is only one way in which we can reasonably answer these questions, and that is by a careful study of everyday life in the later fourteenth century. Before illustrating this point, however, I should like to discuss briefly Chaucer's technique. At the beginning of the Prologue to the Tales he says that he will tell us who his characters were, indicate their "degree" in society, and describe their "array," a subject that includes their horses and their trappings. In practice, he includes direct observations about virtues or vices, significant attributes of complexion or physiognomy, significant actions, like the Miller's wrestling, and observations about what the various figures love. The "ideal" characters — the Knight, the Clerk, the Parson, and the Plowman — love intangibles, whereas the others love more tangible goods, ranging from little dogs and fancy dress to lands, robes, expensive foods, jolly wenches, and money. Chaucer is especially hard on figures who pretend to higher station or greater wisdom than they actually have. Thus his Sergeant of the Law, who seems wise, apparently knows all the cases since the Conquest and all the statutes by heart, a manifest impossibility, which means that he pompously refers to nonexistent authorities. Similarly, the list of authorities known to the Physician probably indicates simply that he overawed his patients with

---

32. *Chaucer's London*, p. 106. Cf. Ruth Melinkoff, "Riding Backwards," *Viator*, 4 (1973), 153–76. In this article it seems to me that attacks against the Old Law as it appears among Christians are sometimes mistaken for literal attacks against Jews.

what sounded like authoritative citations in connection with his ministrations. Henry Fielding was by no means the first author to discover that vanity and hypocrisy are excellent sources of the ridiculous. It is true that Chaucer assumes a good-natured and self-effacing attitude, and does not hesitate to make fun of himself as he does, for example, in the Prologue to Sir Thopas or in his dream visions, a fact that has, I think, misled some readers into sentimentalizing or "humanizing" his characters and to oversimplifying the idea that he presents himself as a naive persona. The group for which Chaucer probably wrote was a tightly knit community in which everyone knew everyone else, and in which, as we have seen, many were above Chaucer in degree. They were thoroughly familiar with the poet's actual attitudes, so that remarks like the mild comment on the Monk's desire to abandon his cloister, "I seyde his opinion was good," are actually examples of antiphrasis, or explicit irony, reinforced in this instance by the subsequent comments, including, "How shal the world be served?" But this is more than antiphrasis, or saying the opposite of what is meant; it probably provoked laughter from Chaucer's friends. If instead Chaucer had made a directly pejorative comment he would have sounded much more like his friend moral Gower, and his audience might well have been bored rather than amused. The criticism of inconstant monks was still there, and Chaucer's humor does not either temper it or diminish it in any way; if anything, it makes it more incisive. Our bold lover of fat swans, as well as of other kinds of flesh, riding on an ostentatiously decorated horse, represents an increasingly common kind of monastic weakness in the later fourteenth century. One historian has observed that after 1350 the relaxation of the Benedictine Rule in matters of occupation and diet had become common, so that many monks liked luxurious dress, kept greyhounds, and were frequently outside the cloister.[33] But this situation represents a considerable decline from conditions earlier in the century,[34] largely due to economic

---

33. Douglas Jones, *The Church in Chester 1350–1540*, Chesham Society, 3d ser., 7 (1957), 35–36.
34. E.g., see the Archbishop's injunctions to the monastery of St. Peter's Gloucester (1301) in William Henry Hunt, *Historia et cartularium monasterii Sancti Petri Gloucestriae*, 3 (Rolls Series, 1867), esp. lxiv (on dress), lxii (on behavior

factors that resulted in a reduction in monastic population,[35] and a general decline in mores. But some monks were poorly fed, not all monks were degenerate, and it would be unfair to say that Chaucer's monk is "typical." He is, rather, an exaggerated picture indicating a trend that was evident during Chaucer's lifetime and that eventually led to monastic dissolution. Here, as elsewhere, Chaucer was deeply interested in and genuinely concerned about developments that were taking place in his own society.

One other feature of Chaucer's technique is, I think, sometimes neglected. Most of the Tales, the exceptions being the Clerk's Tale, the Second Nun's Tale, the Parson's Tale, and, possibly, the Knight's Tale,[36]

---

outside the cloister), lxvii (on sporting dogs, reserved for the abbot alone). Abbots and priors sometimes entertained noblemen by hunting with them on their estates and thus had need of dogs.

35. On population decline see Jones, *The Church in Chester,* p. 11. And for the same problem in the south, cf. Eleanor Searle and Barbara Ross, *The Cellarer's Rolls of Battle Abbey, 1225–1513,* Sussex Record Society, 65 (1967), 15. Abbeys found difficulty in supporting their many visitors in midcentury. See H. J. Hewitt, *Mediaeval Cheshire,* Chetham Society, 2d ser., 88 (1929), 128. For decay of monastic fare elsewhere, see Marett, *Calendar,* p. 160. Monastic houses were generally less well supported after the middle of the fourteenth century. See Dorothy Owen, *Church and Society in Medieval Lincolnshire* (Lincoln, 1971), p. 53. Abbots, like lay lords, often resorted to the device of leasing their demesnes after the Black Death, and there was a natural tendency for them to engage in profitable worldly enterprises.

36. The "literacy of the nobility" in the later Middle Ages is still an obscure subject, perhaps because literacy, like other characteristics, varied enormously from one nobleman to another. For an illustration of the kind of books that might be treasured by a member of the higher nobility, see the evidence from the will of Eleanor de Bohun, Duchess of Gloucester (1399), cited by K. B. McFarlane, *The Nobility of Late Medieval England* (Oxford, 1973), p. 236. Among her books were Psalters, one glossed, a copy of the Golden Legend, St. Gregory's *Cura pastoralis,* a book of decretals, a book of French history, and a French Bible. For the complete list, see N. H. Nicolas, *Testamenta Vetusta* (London, 1826), pp. 147–48. The will of Alice, Lady West, the wife of a knight, leaves to her daughter-in-law all her books in Latin, English, and French (McFarlane, p. 137). Women may have been more bookish than men. In any event, there is some evidence for a general revival of interest in the classics among laymen during the later fourteenth century. Chaucer's Knight may represent an "ideal" in this respect, just as he does by his campaigns under Peter of Lusignan, his worthiness, his wisdom, and his humility.

are adorned with learned allusions like those in the Wife's Prologue, reflections of doctrine, and various kinds of eloquence that would have been completely beyond actual persons in the degrees of the fictional speakers. In other words, the Tales represent Chaucer still talking to his audience about his fictional narrators, and this is also true of his more worthy characters, whom he treats with approval. I do not think that anyone in the audience would have missed this point as Chaucer stood before them, taking advantage of opportunities to imitate local dialects, as in the Reeve's Tale, or to render speeches or descriptions with humorous emphasis. The fact that both he and his audience had first-hand knowledge of the groups represented by the various characters, as well as of the pressing issues of the day, probably lent his oral delivery an effectiveness we cannot now recover. The audience knew, for example, with reference to the Miller, how dangerous contentiousness could be in local communities, and something about the steps taken to control it.[37] A more detailed knowledge of daily life should

---

37. In general, violence as a manifestation of social disruption seems to have become frequent around 1360, again in the mid- to late seventies, and again after the revolt of 1381. See E. B. Dewindt, Land and People in *Holywell-cum-Needingworth* (Toronto, 1972), ch. 4; J. A. Raftis, *Warboys* (Toronto, 1974), pp. 216–21, and idem, "An English Village After the Black Death," *Mediaeval Studies*, 29 (1967), esp. 163–65. The records of the Durham Halmotes show a temporary unrest in 1360 and then after 1378 cases of beating and drawing knives become more frequent. See W. H. Longstreet and John Booth, *Halmota prioratus Dunhelmensis*, Surtees Society, 82 (1889), 36–37, 145, 146, 147. A few measures illustrating efforts to prevent contention may be listed here from this source. It was forbidden to call a man a "rustic" or a "native" (pp. 33, 40–41, 141), to call a woman a "whore" (p. 144), to defame another in any way (pp. 151–53), to permit a stranger to start a fight (p. 147), to raise knives or clubs (p. 154), to play at dice (p. 166), to arrange football contests between villages (p. 171). Women were especially restrained from shrewish speech (pp. 144, 169, 171). Eavesdropping, false raising of the hue and cry, and harboring strangers were common transgressions. Fornication and adultery (thought to give rise to contention) could bring fines in local courts to bondwomen, although men and free women were left to the mercies of the ecclesiastics. A man guilty of fornication might be whipped around his parish church or market place, or, if he persisted in fornication with the same woman, might be forced to marry her. See R. H. Helmholz, *Marriage Litigation in Medieval England* (Cambridge, 1974), pp. 172–75, 182. Cf. the Harley lyric beginning "No mai no lewed lued libben in londe."

not only help us to understand what Chaucer was saying but also afford us some helpful clues about how he probably said it.

I should like to use one pilgrim as an example — the Wife of Bath — who has frequently been seen as a champion of women and their rights, although it is doubtful that Chaucer's audience would have seen her in this way. Rather, like the Monk, she represents a new and distinctive feature of fourteenth-century life, again treated with humorous exaggeration. Chaucer tells us that she was a clothier or cloth-maker:

> Of clooth-makyng she hadde swich an haunt,
> She passed hem of Ypres and of Gaunt.

This business, in which the English had indeed begun to surpass the Low Countries, has made her very wealthy. In church, we are told with humorous exaggeration, she wears almost ten pounds of expensive coverchiefs. Kerchiefs were among a woman's most prized possessions, as we learn from their careful distribution in wills.[38] Her hose were made of the most expensive of all woolens, scarlet, dyed with kermes.[39] Pilgrimages to Jerusalem were extremely expensive, available only to the wealthy,[40] but the Wife has been three times, as well as to Boulogne, which was not very far, Cologne, St. James of Compostella, and Rome. Her "wandering by the way" confirms our suspicion that these journeys, like the present one to Canterbury, have not been undertaken with much penitential fervor. Pilgrimage was sometimes enjoined as penance for adultery,[41] a fact that lends a certain irony to the Wife's peregrinations.

To return to the cloth industry,[42] the manufacturer of woolens, as distinct from linens, worsteds, or local coarse cloth, began to flourish

---

38. E.g., see the wills printed by Marett, *Calendar*, pp. 15, 25–27.
39. On dyes, and kermes in particular, see Eleanora Carus-Wilson, "The Woolen Industry," in *The Cambridge Economic History of Europe* (1952), 2:375–77.
40. Cf. Owen, *Church and Society*, p. 125.
41. C. R. Cheney, *Medieval Texts and Studies* (Oxford, 1973), p. 354.
42. Except where indicated the following information about the cloth industry is based on the article in The Cambridge Economic History cited in note 39 and on E. M. Carus-Wilson, "Trends in the Export of English Woolens in the Fourteenth Century," *Economic History Review*, 3d ser., 2 (1950–51), 162–79;

in the north of England in the late thirteenth century, and by the fourteenth century fulling mills and dyeing vats became common features of manors in the area. Dyeing, which required considerable skill in the mixing of dyes and the application of mordants, as well as a tolerance for strong odors, which sometimes moved communities to restrict dyers to isolated spots, was usually undertaken by men. The wool was sorted, beaten, and washed. It was then carded and spun. After spinning, warp threads were sized and wound to make them about thirty yards long, and the wool was spooled on a bobbin. After it was woven, the cloth was fulled, either by being trodden in a tub with fuller's earth by three strong men (known variously as fullers, walkers, or tuckers), or by being treated in a fulling mill operated by water power. The cloth was then tentered, or stretched to exact size on a frame to which it was attached by tenterhooks. Once dried, it was teaseled, or brushed with the dried heads of *Dipsacus fullonum,* which have hooked barbs, to raise the knap. It was then sheared, a delicate process, with long flat shears before being brushed, folded, and tacked for shipment. Except for dyeing, fulling, and shearing, this work was ordinarily done by women. In the course of time, many women became masters of the trade, supervising the work of others. We should imagine the Wife of Bath as the master of a shop, becoming wealthy through the labors of other women, employed either in the shop itself or in the countryside, dealing effectively at the same time with dyers, fullers, or shearers to whom her products were sent for processing. She was hardly a liberator of women, although some women eagerly sought higher income in industrial employment, even though it meant long hours of hard work. The prosperity of female masters, the quality of whose products was sometimes said to be questionable, caused some uneasiness among male masters of the trade, who sought to restrain their activities by guild regulations at the close of the century.

After the Black Death various industries were attracting workers from agricultural manors, bringing about a demand for hired

---

E. M. Carus-Wilson and Olive Coleman, *England's Export Trade, 1275–1547* (Oxford, 1963); Herbert Heaton, *The Yorkshire Woolen and Worsted Industries,* Oxford Historical and Literary Studies, 10 (Oxford, 1920).

agricultural labor that in turn created a demand for higher wages by the day.[43] Workers wanted not only better pay but better food, and were naturally not much interested in the closely knit organizations of the manorial communities in which they worked or in the customary laws by which they were governed. A new spirit of enterprise was abroad in the realm, a fact that has led one historian to characterize the later fourteenth century as an "age of ambition."[44] Among the growing industries the cloth industry was especially spectacular. After an interruption brought about by the Black Death it recovered in about 1353, so that between that time and 1369 exports of woolen cloths rose from less than 2,000 cloths a year to 16,000. There was a lull in the industry between 1369 and 1379, reflecting a general depression in English trade, but after that, except for another lull during the period of widespread panic and confusion resulting from threats of invasion between 1385 and 1388, the industry expanded rapidly. By the early nineties England was exporting 40,000 cloths, or half as much wool in the form of cloth as in the form of raw wool. Prosperity encouraged shady practices, however, and in 1390 clothiers from the west country, which had become the new center of the industry, became notorious for selling poorly dyed and sheared cloths, folded and tacked so that their defects were not visible. English merchants who sold them abroad were sometimes subjected to violent treatment.[45] Bristol became the chief port for the export of cloth. The Wife thus represents a new kind of wealth in a new area whose prosperity was accompanied, incidentally, by a spread of heresy.

---

43. See the important article by Norah Ritchie, "Labour Conditions in Essex in the Reign of Richard II," in E. M. Carus-Wilson, ed., *Essays in Economic History* (London, 1962), 2:91–111. On the stimulus to wages provoked by the cloth industry, see A. R. Bridbury, *England and the Salt Trade in the Middle Ages* (Oxford, 1955), p. 36–37.
44. See F. R. H. Du Boulay, *An Age of Ambition: English Society in the Late Middle Ages* (London, 1970). A concomitant phenomenon was, naturally enough, higher prices. E.g., see the blanket condemnations of various tradesmen for overcharging at Nottingham in 1395 and 1396 in W. H. Stevenson, *Records of the Borough of Nottingham* (London, 1882), 1: 296–73, 317–19.
45. L. F. Salzman, *English Trade in the Middle Ages* (Oxford, 1931), pp. 337–38.

It is not surprising that Chaucer, who admired those who loved "common profit" and who remembered the relatively tranquil, closely knit communities of his youth, should have devoted considerable attention to a clothier, and, to make his point more trenchant, chosen a female clothier for illustration. No one in the audience would have failed to recognize the Wife as a greedy exploiter of female labor who could be expected to enjoy a sense of mastery over men as well as over women. If Chaucer had been a modern realist he might well have given us a detailed picture of the cloth industry, but he was instead a medieval moralist who could reasonably expect his audience to know a great deal about that subject. Instead, therefore, he developed the implications of the activities of the Wife and those like her, using for his purpose the theme of marriage suggested in the General Prologue and the parallel between the Wife's five husbands and the five false husbands of the unconverted Samaritan woman, who were understood to represent the senses.[46]

However, as a general framework he employed a variation of another late medieval development, a practice M. M. Postan is said to have described as "the marriage fugue,"[47] which was becoming fairly common in the countryside. That is, landless young men eagerly sought out relatively wealthy widows to marry. After marriage the young men naturally awaited the demise of their wives so that they could obtain younger ones, "fressh abedde." But they often had to wait until they were themselves advanced in age before their unsatisfactory spouses died, so that when they did marry the position was reversed, and it was the women's turn to seek wealthy husbands. Women are said to have sometimes run through two or three husbands in this manner, and this is exactly what the Wife has done. In effect, like the wife in the Cook's Tale, she "swyved for her sustenaunce" in youth, albeit under the cover of marriage. Thus she wore out three "good" old wealthy husbands before succumbing to a young man who presented difficulties because he was unfaithful. But he too passed when she was old. Even then, she overcame her fifth wise husband, a clerk

---

46. Cf. *A Preface to Chaucer*, p. 321.
47. Cited by J. Z. Titow in *Essays in Agrarian History* (Newton Abbot, 1968), 1:45.

who should have known better,[48] in an amusing echo of the Fall of Man. Marriages of this kind were naturally not conducive either to domestic tranquility or to genuine sexual satisfaction, which was considered especially desirable among women (who had not yet learned any curious nineteenth-century attitudes toward the subject),[49] although, as Henry of Lancaster tells us, women of lower station were more desirable in this respect than others, being less restrained.[50] It is not surprising that the Wife displays sexual uneasiness and a keen appetite indicative of frustration.

In a general way, the Wife represents a humorous caricature of the pursuit of worldly satisfaction in defiance of traditional values that was growing in fourteenth-century society. To make the point as vividly as possible, Chaucer creates what might be called a "Babylonian" situation. To illustrate this point I might quote a passage from the most influential late medieval commentary on the *Aeneid,* describing Carthage:

> "In this city [Aeneas] found women ruling and Penos serving, for in the world there is such confusion that libido reigns and virtues, which we understand by Penos, strong and stern men, are suppressed; and thus the man serves and the woman rules. Thus in the divine books the world is called 'Babylon,' that is, confusion."[51]

The Wife, deaf to spiritual understanding, becomes a fairly obvious figure of the flesh rampant, with overtones recalling the unconverted Samaritan, the Old Whore in the *Roman de la Rose,* Ovid's Dipsas,

---

48. Clerks who married widows were declared bigamus and denied benefit of clergy. See Pollock and Maitland, *The History of English Law,* 2nd ed. (Cambridge, 1952), 1:445.
49. See the amusing cases testing male impotence, cited by Helmholz, *Marriage Litigation,* pp. 88–89, and the belief cited by Benton, "Clio and Venus," p. 32, to the effect that women enjoy twice the pleasure experienced by men in intercourse.
50. See the discussion by Barnie, *War in English Medieval Society,* p. 63.
51. J. W. and E. F. Jones, *The Commentary on the First Six Books of the Aeneid of Vergil Commonly Attributed to Bernardus Silvestris* (Lincoln, Neb., 1977), p. 12.

and the Synagogue. She neglects the sacramental implications of the Marriage at Cana, glosses the New Law with the Old, turns Saint Paul upside down by reading him "carnally," turns so-called antifeminist clichés, actually attacks directed against venereal inclinations in men, against her old husbands, and in her tale promises that those who allow the flesh, or the wife, to rule will find satisfaction for their "worldly appetite" in an essentially illusory earthly paradise.[52] Her tale is followed by two vivid illustrations in which those "children of wrath"[53] the Friar and the Summoner humorously illustrate the corruption of spiritual offices for money. As we learn from the Clerk, a great many persons, failing to follow Griselda in obedience to the operation of Providence, belong to the Wife's "sect,"[54] and it is to them that we owe the confusion or "Babylon" of the world.

52. The nature of this paradise is well illustrated in the Merchant's Tale.
53. The Wife, who is a vivid representation of Old Law attitudes characteristic of "the children of wrath" (Eph. 2:3) represented in her Prologue by Mars, provokes a wrathful quarrel between the Friar and the Summoner, who are also, in Old Law fashion, blind to spiritual realities and interested primarily in material gain. The Friar, who, as we learn in the General Prologue, cares nothing for the repentance of those who come to him for confession, but only for their money, amusingly suggests that summoners repent. And the Summoner, a minister of God's "wrath" or justice, wrathfully tells a tale illustrating the folly of exactly the kind of wrath from which he suffers. The two tales are comic and exaggerated revelations of the corruption in the administration of God's mercy and justice in a society where many are, like the Wife, interested only in the satisfaction of the senses, or private rather than common good. The activities of men like the Friar and the Summoner could lead only to widespread impenitence, compounding the problem.
54. The "sect" of the Wife should probably be seen as a comment on the widespread pursuit of greater profits and more ostentatious self-indulgence becoming manifest among both the laity and the clergy after the Black Death, which disrupted established communities and led to a breakdown in mores. For some fairly typical examples among ordinary people see Rosamund Sillem, *Records of Some Sessions of the Peace in Lincolnshire, 1360–1375*, Lincoln Record Society, 30 (1936), 21 (case of Robertus Raulyn), 173–74 (case of Hugo Beaumares and similar cases), 198–99 (case of Henricus Souter). Concerning the last, cf. G. O. Sayles, *Select Cases before the Court of the King's Bench*, 7 (Selden Society, 1971), 61–62. It would be possible to cite many similar cases from other areas, including the boroughs. The rolls reveal numerous erring ecclesiastics, especially chaplains, but even a bishop might stray. Thus Bishop Henry of Wakefield was indicted for extortion and even rape.

The basic moral ideas are, of course, not new with Chaucer. But the scriptural and doctrinal materials in the portrait of the Wife add considerably to its humor and sharpen its satiric point. She is neither a "personality," a "realistic portrait," nor a "typical example" of the female clothier. She typifies instead a new spirit of self-aggrandizement and a new kind of wealth that were disrupting traditional values cherished by Chaucer and by most of his audience, and, at the same time, destroying traditional communities based on a concern for the "common profit." Conditions in the cloth industry afforded an especially vivid illustration, but the same sort of thing was evident elsewhere, if on a smaller scale.[55] I suggest that it was this situation, not the literary portrait for its own sake, that was the focus of Chaucer's attention and the principal interest of his audience. Further, I think that unless we learn to understand the immediate relevance of Chaucer's work to the everyday life of his times, we shall run the risk not only of formulating undisciplined interpretations, but also of failing to appreciate his real craftsmanship in making what he has to say vivid and entertaining. If it is objected that everyday life is not the true subject of literary study, which should concern itself with aesthetics, I can only reply that in the humanities there may be some virtue in the study of humanity itself.

See Elizabeth Gurnsey Kimball, *Some Warwick and Coventry Sessions of the Peace, 1377–1397*, Dugdale Society, 16 (1939), 105–06, and Sayles, *Select Cases*, 7:53–54. Some local lords were notorious. For example, Lord John Fitzwalter of Essex regularly practiced extortion, illegal distraints, and outright theft. See Elizabeth Chapin Furber, *Essex Sessions of the Peace, 1351, 1371–79*, Essex Archaeological Society, Occasional Publications, 3 (1953), 61–62. There were obvious reasons why Chaucer and his audience at court should be concerned about moral decline.

55. E.g., see Norah Ritchie's observations, "Labour Conditions," p. 95, on the effects of the flourishing cutlery trade at Thaxted.

Chaucer and Christian Tradition

D. W. Robertson, Jr.
Princeton University

In: *Chaucer and Scriptural Tradition,* ed. David Lyle Jeffrey
(Ottawa: University of Ottawa Press, 1984), pp. 3-32.

I. Introduction

The medieval use of Scripture and scriptural tradition generally—that is, of the Bible and its accessory literature and commentary—can only be understood adequately when the textual materials are contextualized within the relevant social history of medieval Christian tradition. This becomes particularly apparent when we consider the case of Geoffrey Chaucer. Chaucer was eminently a 'textual' man, but he was preeminently a moral, social, and political man, a statesman committed to the ethical well-being of his community, and it was these concerns which directed—even dictated—his attention to scriptural tradition.

Medieval European Christianity was not primarily a metaphysical system, a superstitious regard for the supernatural, a chimerical escape from the burdens of existence, nor an authoritarian and oppressive set of shackles imposed on the "innocent" and "natural" freedoms of humanity. It is true that during the thirteenth century a metaphysical system, based on Aristotle and largely, though not entirely, academic, did develop; that a hope for a better life hereafter was often inculcated, although medieval people devoted far more attention to ways of facing the problems of this life than they did to dreams about the next; and it is also true that Christian thought, although humane, was not characterized by the kind of sentimental humanitarianism that grew up during the later eighteenth century and has since come to dominate modern thought. "Man," wrote St. Augustine, "is a great thing, made in the image and likeness of God, not in that he is encased in a mortal body, but in that he excels the beasts in the dignity of a rational soul." But he went on to quote with approval the warning of Jeremiah, "Cursed be the man that trusteth in man."[1] Man's great gift, and the "image of God" within him, was reason, and when he abandoned it for the sake of passion, he lost his "likeness," becoming something other than a man. Our fellow men are to be loved, he thought, not for themselves, but for the virtues reflected in them, or for the source of those virtues, God.

Christians inherited from Antiquity a mode of thought, not so much a "system" as a fundamental attitude, that envisioned the existence of "intelligible" (intangible) realities, whose existence was available to the reason but not immediately to the senses, calling them for their own purposes after St. Paul "the invisible things of God." Although these are to be understood, as St. Paul said (Romans 1:20), "through the things that are made," they are not "abstractions" derived from observing the qualities of concrete particulars, or from "experiment upon things seen"; they are rather external realities, "natural" in their own right. Among them were the virtues, which were the gift of God's grace, available to those who loved them and Him. And God was Himself the apex of a hierarchy of such realities. The efficacy of the virtues, when they were reflected in men, was thought to be a matter of common experience, for they protected men from the ill consequences of their "natural" inclinations.[2] Thus St. Augustine was able to say, quite reasonably under the circumstances, that every Christian has an obligation in his "pilgrimage" through the created world "to comprehend the eternal and spiritual" by his observation of "corporal and temporal things." Such things, as Hugh of St. Victor was to put it later, are "the voice of God speaking to man."[3] The Trinity was

---

1. *On Christian Doctrine*, 1. 22. 20.
2. That is, such inclinations were "natural" after the Fall, although not "natural" to man as he was created. The words "Nature" and "natural" as applied to man are thus ambiguous.
3. *On Christian Doctrine*, 1. 4. 4.

a mystery, difficult to comprehend, but faith did not involve a mystical leap into the realm of the "supernatural." Most educated Christians regarded "magic" as an illusion. The miracles of Christ and his Saints were not magical, but were manifestations of God's grace. The idea of the "supernatural" was introduced into Europe by the scholastic philosophers in the mid-thirteenth century.[4] To confuse a sense of the reality of the "intelligible" with ordinary superstition, as Cain does in the Wakefield *Mactacio Abel*,[5] is to demonstrate both irrationality and what St. Augustine calls "the crime of malevolence." However we, with an entirely different universe of discourse, may wish to evaluate this old mode of thought, we must seek at least to understand it if we wish to understand those who shared it, their behavior, and the products of their culture.

Although medieval thinkers were able to make Christian beliefs and attitudes rationally coherent, medieval Christianity was not a "system" but essentially a way of life supported by ideals that, because of human weakness, were not often observed consistently. No one expected that they would be, but everyone was urged to seek, and if possible to find, the grace made available to him through Christ to wish to do what he should do. Human beings were expected to be sinners, and the fact that a man was a sinner did not make him either a "pagan" or a "hypocrite" (unless he professed innocence); it simply implied that he was among those whom the great crusading bishop Adhemar de le Puy called *exsules filii Evae*. Rousseau had not yet made humanity basically innocent, and common experience taught that left to himself man might well anticipate Freud's "polymorphous perverse infant." Christianity was cherished because it had what we should call beneficial psychological, economic, social, and political functions, restraining people from the immediate satisfaction of their physical appetites or worldly ambitions at the expense of others, and concerning them with the welfare of their communities. It was an "ecologically

---

4. See Johann Auer, "In wieweit ist im 13. Jahrhundert der Wandel des Begriffs "Supernaturalis" bedingt durch den Wandel des Naturbegriffs ?" in *La filosofia della Natura nel Medioevo* (Milan, 1966), pp. 331–49.

5. Ed. A. C. Cawley, *The Wakefield Pageants in the Towneley Cycle* (Manchester, 1958), p. 8, line 297.

sound" feature of medieval culture.[6] Its basis was the Bible regarded in a certain way, a way indicated in the writings of the Fathers of the Church that were often thought of as a necessary extension of the scriptural text.

As time passed and the structures of medieval society changed, emphases on various principles of Christian thought changed also, along with "styles" in the arts and in literature itself. A verbal statement may be quoted with approval for centuries, but the "meaning" of the statement, which is something that exists not in words but in people, changes as societies and people change, and may indeed vary from place to place at a given time in different "cultures." When we talk about "semantic change" we are actually talking about changes in people and their ways of doing things. Ways of doing things changed more rapidly during the Middle Ages and varied more from place to place than most people suppose, and it is wrong to use the word *medieval* as though we were talking about a static culture without sharp local differences. Nevertheless, certain principles, varying in their implications for different communities, remained constant.

St. Augustine, pausing to consider cultural diversity in a discussion of the *mores* revealed in the Old Testament, observed that

> "Some, as it were somnolent, who were neither in the deep sleep of folly nor able to awaken in the light of wisdom, misled by the variety of innumerable customs, thought that there was no such thing as absolute justice but that every people regarded its own way of life as just. For if justice, which ought to remain immutable, varies so much among different peoples, it is evident that justice does not exist."

There is nothing new, we notice, about the lure of "situational ethics," and the fact of cultural diversity has long been recognized. But St. Augustine continues,

> "They have not understood, to cite only one instance, that 'what you do not wish to have done to yourself, do not do to another'

---

6. I refer to human ecology, although the general attitude that the world was to be "used" for the sake of God probably contributed to reasonably sound "ecological" practices.

(cf. Matt. 7: 12, Luke 6:31) cannot be varied on account of any diversity of peoples," and he goes on to call attention to "charity (or the love of God and of one's neighbor for the sake of God) and its most just laws."[7]

The catechism of Queen Elizabeth I, composed many years later in a different world, contains the statement: "My duty towards my neighbor is to love him as myself: And to do to all men as I would they should do unto me." And Alexander Pope, still later, could write in his *Essay on Man* that "all Mankind's concern is Charity," adding that "where Faith, Law, Morals all began, / All end, in Love of God and Love of Man." St. Augustine is in fact typical of the whole "Christian era" in regarding charity, or love, as the basic message of the Scriptures. Its implications vary from place to place and from time to time, so that each generation requires new verbal elaborations to make it vivid and understandable.

The general outlook we have briefly sketched, except for the Christian addition of the "laws of charity," is an adaptation of classical attitudes in Pythagorean and Platonic traditions, and it continued to influence European thought, with some exceptions especially toward the end of the period, down through the early eighteenth century, providing a certain cultural continuity. Before considering the variety of ways in which it was applied, it may be useful to inquire into the literary assumptions that accompanied it. St. Augustine advised his friend Licentius to keep his poem on Pyramus and Thisbe, but to arrange it in such a way that it would praise divine love,[8] and he defined a fable as a lie composed for utility and delight.[9] He thought that figurative language made truths hidden beneath its surface more pleasant and memorable when they were discovered with some effort, and that such discovery aided in the comprehension of the intelligible.[10] These

---

7. *On Christian Doctrine*, 3. 14. 22.
8. *On Order*, 1. 8. 24.
9. *Soliloquies*, 2. 10. 18 and 19.
10. *On Christian Doctrine*, 2. 6. 7–8. Cf. 4. 8. 22, and Letter 50. 7. 13 to Januarius: "And in like manner, whensoever illustrative symbols are borrowed, for the declaration of spiritual mysteries, from created things ... this is done to give the doctrine of salvation an eloquence adapted to raise the affections of

views are reflected in numerous statements about the usefulness of fabulous narratives from the early Middle Ages to the defenses of poetry written by Petrarch, Boccaccio, and Salutati.[11] In general, therefore, although there are in the Middle Ages many explicitly doctrinal poems and narratives, there are many others whose doctrine is concealed beneath a pleasing surface. The tendency among scholars, eager to find support for "enlightened modern attitudes" in medieval literature, to read such works literally has led to some curious interpretations. Some figurative language, like "the sleep of folly," or the "light of wisdom" in the passage from St. Augustine quoted above, is more or less inherent in the general intellectual posture, and some of it, more obscurely derived from "the things that are made" or from classical sources often requires research to discover. The following very brief survey should help to explain why students of Chaucer should be interested in scriptural and patristic materials, and at the same time introduce some of the more important general sources for such study.

II. *Militia est vita hominis super terram*

Turning now to the general changes in medieval culture that led to varying emphases on "the laws of charity"—and here we shall content ourselves with a very brief account, ignoring many variations and emphasizing the close of the period—we find that Christianity in the earlier Middle Ages stressed the abandonment of superstitious worship (of various kinds from locality to locality) and pagan ritual, and the importance of controlling violence. Thus St. Caesarius of Aries, whose eloquent and effective sermons enjoyed wide circulation, especially since they were sometimes confused with the sermons of St. Augustine, pointed to the evils of sacrilege, homicide, adultery,

---

those who receive it from things seen, corporeal and temporal, to things unseen, spiritual and eternal." See the Rev. J. G. Cunningham, *Letters of St. Augustine* (Edinburgh, 1872), I, 215. A more eloquent and striking statement of this principle, since it involves amatory imagery, may be found in St. Gregory's Preface to his commentary on the Canticle of Canticles.

11. See D. W. Robertson, Jr., *A Preface to Chaucer* (Princeton, 1962), pp. 337-65.

false testimony, theft, rapine, pride, envy, avarice, wrath, drunkenness, and detraction.[12] Similar transgressions likely either to disturb the peace or to lead to disturbances of the peace were emphasized in the Old German *Beichten,* which were probably influenced by the sermons.[13] Peace could not be maintained without the motivation supplied by faith, so that an effort was made to see to it that everyone knew the Paternoster and the Creed; and the *abrenuntiatio* at Baptism often included specific renunciation of pagan beliefs.[14] As St. Gregory's famous letter to Mellitus indicates, Augustine of Canterbury was urged not to destroy pagan temples but to transform them into churches.[15] In much the same way the songs of the pagans were transformed. Aldhelm is said to have composed verses in English in order to lead his listeners "to health by interweaving among the foolish things, the words of Scripture," and our first English poet of record, Caedmon, sang songs of great skill and subtlety to his vernacular audience.[16] The vanity of worldly ease and glory and the necessity for the wise man to maintain his *militia* are celebrated in short poems like "The Wanderer" and "The Seafarer"; and longer poems, in military ("epic") terms, from *Beowulf* and the "Christian Epics" to *The Song of Roland,* portray the struggle to maintain wisdom and to combat vice, stressing the dangers of fraternal discord. The *Psychomachia* of Prudentius, which affected iconography in the arts for centuries, and the *Beatus* page of the St. Albans Psalter reflect a common concern. This general idea persisted throughout the Middle Ages, and is well illustrated, for example, in a letter by Elizabeth's faithful and long-suffering counsellor William Cecil to Nicholas White in 1570.

12. Sermo 169 in *Opera,* ed. D. G. Morin (Maretioli, 1937), I, 684. There are similar lists in other sermons. It is not difficult to find a similar emphasis in St. Gregory's account of the armies of the vices in *Moralia,* 31. 45. 87–88, *PL,* 76, cols. 620–21.
13. See Franz Hautkappe's dissertation, *Uber die altdeutchen Beichten und ihre Bezeihungen zu Casarius von Arles* (Munster, 1927).
14. E.g., see W. Braune, *Althochdeutsches Lesebuch,* 9th ed. (Halle, 1928), p. 170.
15. Bede, *Ecclesiastical History,* 1. 30.
16. See B. F. Huppé, *Doctrine and Poetry* (New York, 1959), p. 69, and Chapter IV. For an account of Aldhelm's life and work, see W. F. Bolton, *A History of Anglo-Latin Literature* (Princeton, 1967), pp. 68-100.

Cecil, we should notice, loved the virtues "settled in" his friend, and he himself was armed against the "darts and pellets" of the world by faith. His words paraphrase St. Paul:

> I do contynue and will not desist to love hartily the honest virtues which I am persuaded are settled and rooted in you, and so will, except you make the change. I am as you have known me if not more tormented with the blasts of the world, willing to live in calm places, but it pleaseth God otherwise to exercise me, in sort as I cannot shun the rages thereof, though his goodness perserveth me as it were with the targett of his providence, from the dangers that are gaping uppon me. *Vita hominis est militia super terram.* I use no armour of proofe agaynst the darts or pellets, but confidence in God by a cleare conscience.[17]

During the later Middle Ages it was thought that one achieved strength for this battle through the sacrament of confirmation.

III. *Deus caritas est*

Local strife by no means disappeared during the early twelfth century, as the successful preaching of St. Norbert, who sought to calm it, well illustrates. But a new *militia Christi* arose with the establishment of the crusading orders, directed against paganism in the Holy Places across the sea, first with the transformation of the Order of the Knights of the Hospital of St. John of Jerusalem into a military order (1113) and then with the establishment of the Knights of the Temple of Solomon (1118), whose aims and ideals were set forth in a rule under the aegis of St. Bernard, providing the foundation for the European cult of chivalry. The ascetic ideals of these orders and the demand for self-sacrifice in chivalric doctrine illustrate once more the fact that the two kinds of *militia* could be combined. One was an inspiration to the other, and both were inspired by love. More settled conditions generally, especially within the confines of monastic and cathedral schools, permitted renewed attention to the central doctrine of Christian belief, love.

---

17. Thomas Wright, *Queen Elizabeth and her Times* (London, 1838), II, 364–65.

The Canticle of Canticles, upon which the most influential and distinguished commentary had long been that of St. Gregory the Great, received new attention. Five commentaries on this book were produced in the ninth century, one in the tenth century, six in the eleventh, and thirty-three by writers who died between 1115 and 1215.[18] Of the last, six treated the Bride as the Blessed Virgin, whose cult developed steadily during the century, so that in 1198 Odon de Soliac, Bishop of Paris, added the *Ave* to the Paternoster and the Creed as formulas to be recited daily by Christians.[19] Among the authors of the commentaries were such distinguished figures as St. Bernard, Alanus de Insulis, Honorius of Autun, William of St. Thierry, Hugh of St. Victor, Richard of St. Victor, and Ailred of Rievaulx, whose commentary, unfortunately, has been lost. Meanwhile, treatises on love, both human and divine, proliferated, and included the extremely influential transformation of Cecero's *De amicitia* into a work *On Spiritual Friendship* by Ailred of Rievaulx, and the same author's *Mirror of Charity.* Abelard had written a love story, *The History of My Calamities,* to illustrate the vulnerability of sexual love to the whims of Fortune (Providential justice misunderstood), a theme still flourishing in Chaucer's *Troilus* and in Shakespeare's *Romeo and Juliet,* and he explores the possibility of its transformation into divine love.[20] This last possibility, elaborated by Ailred,[21] was to have far-reaching consequences in the works of Dante and Petrarch, in Castiglione's *Courtier,* where it received a "Platonic" decor, and even in Elizabethan sonnet sequences.[22]

Tags from the Canticle had long been used to illuminate Latin poems, like the famous "Levis exsurgit Zephirus" from *The Cambridge Songs,* which concludes with an echo of Cant. 3:1. Spring in the Canticle is the *tempus putationis,* or time of penance during Lent, and the

---

18. John C. Gorman, S. M., *William of Newburgh's Explanatio sacri epithalamii in matrem sponsi* (Fribourg, 1960), pp. 42-43.

19. H. Leclercq, "Sur la Salutation angélique," in C. J. Hefele and H. Leclercq, *Histoire des Conciles* (Paris, 1907-38), V, App. IV, p. 1747.

20. See D. W. Robertson, Jr., *Abelard and Heloise* (New York, 1972), pp. 99-118.

21. *PL,* 195, cols. 659-702.

22. See the forthcoming study of sonnet sequences now in preparation by Thomas P. Roche, Jr.

contrast between the burgeoning of the earth, the mating of the birds and animals, with the penitential duties of the Christian or the scholarly duties of the schoolboy moved by another love became a popular subject for song, and there is indeed a reflection of this theme at the opening of *The Canterbury Tales,* whose pilgrims are, presumably, setting out on a penitential journey. In the schools of the twelfth century new poetic material was provided by a renewed interest in the Classics, especially in the poetry of Ovid. Although both St. Caesarius and Rabanus had warned against hearing "wicked" or "lecherous" songs,[23] a warning that continued to echo in later confessional manuals, masters in the schools, like Hildebert du Lavardin, and their students who learned Latin and plainsong simultaneously,[24] became especially interested in Ovid, not because he was regarded as a "lecherous poet," but because he was read as a "mocker of light loves," offering vivid and amusing illustrations of their consequences. Mythographers like "the Third Vatican Mythographer," and commentators like Arnulf of Orleans both summarized traditional teachings and offered aid to new students seeking moral instruction in the Classics. If a verse from Ovid could serve Alanus de Insulis as a "theme" for a sermon,[25] and if Ovid could offer useful quotations for a commentary on the Canticle,[26] there was no reason why he could not serve as a model for schoolboys, most of whom were in any event thoroughly familiar with sexual activity, partly because of a lack of privacy and squeamishness in medieval homes, and partly because they came from a prevailingly agricultural environment. A kind of Ovidian wit, reinforced by scriptural allusions, flashes through some poems in the *Carmina Burana,*[27] while others explore various amorous inclinations and

---

23. Caesarius, *Opera,* I, Sermo I, pp. 10-12; Rabanus, *Homeliae* (First Series), *PL,* 110, col. 34. The homilies of Rabanus often reflect the sermons of Caesarius.
24. Cf. Nicholas Orme, *English Schools in the Middle Ages* (London, 1973), p. 63. Song was an aid in learning Latin pronunciation.
25. See Marie-Thérèse d'Alverny, *Alain de Lille: Textes inédits* (Paris, 1965), pp. 136-37.
26. See the commentary by Thomas the Cistercian, *PL,* 206, cols. 22-862.
27. E.g., see D. W. Robertson, Jr., *Essays in Medieval Culture* (Princeton, 1980), pp. 131-50.

experiences, usually suggesting, if only by mentioning Venus, the ill consequences of her delights. The basically Ovidian inspiration and clerical wit that many of these poems display also appears in the famous *De amore* of Andreas Capellanus.[28]

If love, which as St. Augustine said, "moves the pilgrim's feet" in the road of this life, was a popular subject in the schools, it was also a popular subject in vernacular literature. The troubadours explored its ramifications in crusading songs like those of William IX of Aquitaine, who was famous for entertaining his military followers in songs often reflecting Ovidian techniques, or Marcabru, who castigated noblemen for indulging in adulterous affairs while their obligations demanded a struggle against the inroads of the pagans, or Jaufré Rudel, who found the Blessed Virgin, of whom he spoke rather openly in amatory terms reminiscent of the Canticle, an inspiration to valor overseas. A kind of Ovidian wit even permeated the romances that were beginning to vie with the "feudal epics" in popularity.[29] As the cult of chivalry developed it became obvious that faith to one's overlord, an aspect of faith in God,[30] could not be maintained except by a tie of love, a tie that naturally extended in court circles to the overlord's wife and to the ladies of his court. As John of Salisbury said, discussing the need for love between the prince and his subjects, "That battle wedge that is bound by a tie of love is not easily broken."[31] But the greatest enemy of military effectiveness, he said, was luxury,[32] which leads to the weaknesses of lust.[33] Conventionally, the *militia Veneris* was the worst enemy of any form of that *militia* that is a part of every man's obligation, whether in chivalric enterprise or in the conduct of life.[34] Chrétien's Erec has to learn to subdue his venereal preoccupations before

---

28. Cf. Robertson, *Preface,* Chapter V, and *Essays,* pp. 257-72.
29. Cf. Robertson, *Essays,* pp. 173-201.
30. See John of Salisbury, *Policraticus,* 6. 9, who argues that a man who cannot keep faith with God cannot keep faith with his overlord.
31. *Ibid.,* 4.3.
32. *Ibid.,* 6. 11.
33. *Ibid.,* 8. 6; cf. 8. 15.
34. See Robertson, *Preface,* pp. 408-10.

he can set out on his quest for wisdom, and in Chaucer's *Parliament* the speaker is taught by that model of valor and chastity Scipio Africanus[35] to link "brekers of the lawe" and "likerous folk."[36] The Blessed Virgin, the highest and most striking exemplar of chastity, now being adorned with increasing frequency with imagery from the Canticle, was especially venerated by St. Bernard.[37] She was celebrated in some of the most beautiful Latin sequences ever written, and she became increasingly an inspiration to chivalry and courtesy as well as an object of popular devotion.[38] Geoffrey of Monmouth's King Arthur, the model for English chivalric *pietas,* carried her image on his shield and called to her as he rode into battle, foreshadowing that later model of chivalric reform in a decadent "Arthurian" court, Sir Gawain in *Sir Gawain and the Green Knight.* Toward the close of the thirteenth century the last of the great troubadours, Giraut Riquier, addressed her in moving terms, and in his final song, "Be'm degra de chantar tener," he realized that through their pride and malice, "far from the commandments and love of our Lord," Christians had been cast out of God's Holy Place across the sea. The holy *militia* had failed because of "disordered will," so that Christians, raging at one another, should be driven into the earth. The song concludes with a prayer to Mary:

> Dona, Maires de caritat,
> acepta nos per pietat
> de ton filh, notra redeptor,
> gracia, perdon, et amor.

35. The hero of Petrarch's *Africa* was, like his Laura, noted for chastity and his discouragement of lechery in Massinissa.
36. By Chaucer's time many schoolboys in England were reading a poem called Cartula *(PL,* 184, cols. 1307-14), recommending love for Christ and condemning worldly love, Including prominently at the outset "the filth of carnal love." See Orme, *op. cit.,* pp. 104-5. Bishop Bradwardine's *Sermo Epinicius* delivered in 1346 to celebrate English victories against the Scots and French attributed the defeat of the French, among other things, to their' 'militia Venens," calling them "milites Epicuri." See the edition of H.A. Obennan and J.A. Weisheipl, *Archives d'histoire doctrinale et littéraire du moyen age,* 33 (1958), 323-24.
37. See the attractive and useful volume, *Saint Bernard et Notre Dame,* edited by P. Bernard (Abbaye de Sept-fons, 1953).
38. See the reference in note 19, above.

Notable men, still moved by what were then regarded as Christian ideals of military valor, turned to her in fourteenth-century England. Sir John Chandos, famous for valor and wisdom, wore a surcoat embroidered with her image; that image often adorned English swords and breastplates, and Garter Knights bore it on their right shoulders during Divine Service.[39] Visual testimony of the devotion of Richard II survives in the Wilton Diptych. The beauty and grace of the Virgin were widely heralded, and it was natural that Chaucer should surround another inspiration to chivalric conduct, Blanche of Lancaster, with her imagery,[40] having written, presumably, one of his earliest surviving poems, the "ABC," for her devotion to Mary. Later on, he would close his great poem shadowing the failure of English chivalric ideals with a prayer to the Trinity for defense against both visible and invisible foes and to Jesus for mercy.

> For love of mayde and moder thyn benigne!

This is no mere rhetorical flourish, no empty convention, but in the context of its time a powerful appeal for a redirected love that might free Chaucer's contemporaries from the attacks of "invisible enemies" of the kind that produced the "disordered will" of Giraut's Christian crusaders, and that brought Troilus (and Troy) to destruction. The success of enemies within invited attacks by visible enemies without.

As European governments grew more complex and written documents multiplied in their administrations, there were new demands for "practical" literacy among lay officials.[41] In England, the rise in the number of such documents was especially impressive during the reign of Henry II, who was himself notable for his love of learning.[42] M. T.

---

39. Edmund Walerton, *Pietas Mariana Britannica* (London, 1879), pp. 41-46. I wish to thank my colleague Gail M. Gibson for calling my attention to this volume.
40. James I. Wimsatt, "The Apotheosis of Blanche in *The Book of the Duchess*," *JEGP*, 66 (1967), 26-44.
41. See the stimulating and useful book by M. T. Clanchy, *From Memory to Written Record* (Cambridge, Mass., 1979).
42. W. L. Warren, *Henry II* (London, 1973), p. 208. On documents, see Clanchy's table, *op. cit.*, p. 44. Feeling that he lacked time to read all of St. Gregory's *Moralia*, Henry had Peter of Blois compile a compendium on Job known as the *Gregorianum* (*PL*, 207, cols. 777-92), so that he could master it quickly.

Clanchy writes that "an educated layman in 1300 ... like Henry de Bray was probably familiar with some writing in three literary languages (Latin, French, and English)."[43] John of Salisbury, following (but modifying) the *Institutio Traiani* attributed to Plutarch, held that there are four things that should be inculcated in rulers of commonwealths: "a reverence for God, self-discipline, the learning of officials and those in power, the affection of their subjects, and their protection."[44] The learning of officials, and this means administrators of all degrees, was an important matter for John, who thought that all learning had as its end the promotion of charity.[45] Among officials, he thought avarice, an aspect of the love of the tangible, to be the worst of vices,[46] and this idea was to become more important with the passage of time and the increasing complexity of both secular and ecclesiastical administration. The "political" theory of the day (actually a part of moral theory, as it had been in Aristotle's *Politics*) was based on the assumption that the commonwealth was an integrated whole whose health depended on the virtue of all of its members, including the prince. "If, then, everyone were to labor in self-cultivation," John said,

> "and were to regard external things as alien to him, the state of individuals and of the whole would straightway become the best, virtue would flourish and reason would rule, with mutual charity everywhere prevailing, so that the flesh would be subjected to the spirit and the spirit would, in complete devotion, become as a servant to God."[47]

A new aggressiveness inspired by a love for wealth gained by peaceful but underhand means was beginning to replace the aggressiveness of the sword, in spite of clerical attacks on it.

How were the literate able to learn "the laws of charity"? As Clanchy notes, "The sacred Scriptures, which had dominated literate

---

43. *Op. cit.*, p. 86. For Henry de Bray, see *The Estate Book of Henry de Bray*, Camden Third Series, 27 (1916).
44. *Policraticus.* 5. 3.
45. *Ibid.*, 7. 11.
46. *Ibid.*, 8. 5.
47. *Ibid.*, 6. 29. Cf. Aegidius Romanus, *De regimine principum*, 1. 2. 10 (Rome, 1607), p. 72. This work was extremely popular in fourteenth-century England.

culture since before 1066, still stood in pride of place, of course, but they were surrounded and overlaid from the twelfth century onwards by the glosses and summaries of the schoolmen."[48] Among the summaries of the schoolmen the most important was the *Four Books of Sentences* of Peter the Lombard, produced in Paris around the middle of the century. This was largely a series of selected quotations from the Fathers (and some of their notable successors) arranged in systematic fashion so as to form a work of easy reference suitable at the same time for systematic study. It remained, in fact, a basic theological textbook for many years and a standard introduction to the Scriptures.[49] Students of theology gained their reputations by lecturing on it and writing commentaries on it. It remains, with some few exceptions, the best source for standard doctrines during the later Middle Ages. Patristic opinions became available also in a variety of glosses. The most important of these, which often accompanied the scriptural text in the margins, was the *Ordinary Gloss,* now usually attributed to the "school" of Abelard's old enemy Anselm of Laon.[50] Lombard's *Commentaries on the Psalms of David* offered a verse by verse account of all the Psalms with quotations from Jerome, Augustine, Chrysostom, Cassiodorus, Alcuin, and Remigius of Auxerre.[51] More influential, however, was his great *Collection in All the Epistles of St. Paul,*[52] which contained "questions" of the kind used later in the *Sentences.* These two glosses together were called the *Major Glossatura* since they provided a much more thorough treatment than the *Ordinary Gloss.* There were other commentaries, treatises, and sermon collections that afforded materials useful to an understanding of the sacred

---

48. *Op. cit.,* p. 259.
49. In the Preface to his *Laws of Ecclesiastical Polity* Hooker observed that among the Reformed, Lombard had been replaced by Calvin as a standard reference, implying that the "unreformed" were still using him.
50. A partial version is available in *PL,* 113 and 114, cols. 9-752. Migne attributed it (falsely) to Walahfrid Strabo. This edition omits some books and often gives only the beginning and conclusion of a gloss available elsewhere in *PL.*
51. *PL,* 191, cols. 55-1296. The great *Ennarationes in Psalmos* of St. Augustine, however, retained its prestige, and was much admired by Boccaccio and Petrarch. Meanwhile, the commentary by St. Ambrose was often consulted.
52. *PL,* 191, cols. 1297-1696; 192. cols. 9-520.

text, not to mention sermons delivered in churches, and the writings of the Fathers themselves continued to be copied and made available in libraries. For the entire Middle Ages the standard introduction to what we should call the "method" of scriptural study was St. Augustine's *On Christian Doctrine,* supplemented at times by *On the Education of Clerics* by Rabanus Maurus, which often repeats whole passages from St. Augustine. The twelfth century produced another such guide, the *Didascalicon* of Hugh of St. Victor (who was often hailed as "the second Augustine") which became, like the works just mentioned, a standard school text.[53] For perspectives on scriptural history, the *Scholastic History* of Peter Comestor, also a standard text, is useful for commonplace historical opinions. The influence and popularity of *The Consolation of Philosophy* of Boethius (who was venerated as a saint), which had been adapted for English readers by King Alfred, continued to grow, and a very influential commentary on it was provided by William of Conches, who had assisted in the education of King Henry II of England.[54]

Were laymen interested in works of this kind? Henry II was an avid reader, and other noblemen shared his enthusiasm for books. The Beaumont twins, Robert and Waleran (b. 1104), are said to have astonished Pope Calixtus and the Cardinals with their learning at the age of 15 during a conference at Gisors. In Britanny, Abelard, whose father, he says, had some knowledge of letters, encouraged his education; and he abandoned his inheritance for learning. Many younger sons of noblemen went to school, seeking clerical careers. Preachers like Robert of Arbrissel, St. Norbert, and St. Bernard were astonishingly popular. Not all noblemen could read and write Latin as Henry de Bray could, but even those who did not often had access to the new learning. Thus Baudoin of Guisnes, who was knighted by Thomas of Canterbury, was not a "mute auditor" of theological writings, but listened eagerly to readings in the Scriptures, demanding not only the

---

53. Ed. C. H. Buttimer (Washington, 1939) and available in an annotated English translation by Jerome Taylor (New York. 1961).

54. *PL,* 198, cols. 1053-1722. All Chaucerians should, of course, have a first-hand familiarity with standard texts used in the schools during Chaucer's time if only to acquire an understanding of prevailing attitudes.

literal but the spiritual sense. He enjoyed disputation with his clerks and had translations made, including one of the Canticle of Canticles, along with a gloss on the text. His library contained a variety of books, including the Life of St. Anthony, a work on physics, a work on the nature of things, books of noble deeds, songs, and fabliaux.[55] It is true, however, that his son preferred stories about Roland, Oliver, and King Arthur, and romances.[56] Generally, the literary abilities and tastes of noblemen in the twelfth century are difficult to assess, but modern historians may have been over-cynical about this matter. Clanchy, referring to the next century, observes somewhat acerbically that

> "by and large the knights of thirteenth-century England, and their families too, probably had a wider and deeper knowledge of language than those historians who have adopted a patronizing tone towards them because they were not highly literate."[57]

Among vernacular writers in England we should include Marie de France, who probably belonged to a noble family and who indicates in the Prologue to her *Lais* that she could translate Latin. Her *Lais* were said, by a somewhat prejudiced contemporary observer, to have been especially popular among the ladies. They were undoubtedly designed to produce lively discussion and varied interpretation among the members of their audience. and they are, as might be expected, largely concerned with varieties of love.

---

55. Lambert d'Ardres, *Chronicon* (Paris, 1855), pp. 173, 175. Baudoin was a vigorous man. After the death of his wife, Chrétienne, in 1177, he developed a taste for virgins, and there were said to have been 33 children at his funeral. Lambert, who was a priest, laments his lechery but does not call him either a "pagan" or a "courtly lover," either of which would have been an absurdity. Looking at the matter calmly, however, we can see that Baudoin did not have to be spectacularly lecherous to produce some twenty-odd children in twenty-odd years. Nor were lecherous inclinations confined to men. See the account of the Countess Yde de Boulogne, *ibid.*, 205, 207.
56. *Ibid.*, pp. 215, 217.
57. *Op. cit.*, p. 261.

IV. *Altissimus de terra creavit medicinam*

Chaucer's *Canterbury Tales* concludes with a sermon on penance. Perhaps a brief glimpse of historical developments will assist our understanding of why this arrangement was appropriate. In the first place, it was widely held that the Old Law was a law of strict justice, but that the New Law fulfilled the Old with charity, so that under Christ the law of justice became a law of justice tempered with mercy, not to everyone, but to those who are repentant, or, to put it in another way, to men of good will. Thus St. Augustine said, "the mercy of God is never to be despaired of by men who truly repent."[58] How does one "truly repent"? It was clearly necessary for the Church to devote special attention to the penance of its members and to provide formal means for its expression. In the early Roman church confession was public, but in the Celtic church secret confession to a priest rather than public confession was customary, and "Penitentials," or long lists of sins and crimes, were compiled along with the penances to be administered for each.[59] When Theodore of Tarsus came to England, he decided to continue the Celtic system he found there, a decision that had profound repercussions throughout Western Christendom, for under his influence the custom of private confession spread throughout Europe. Penitentials, which emphasized penances to be imposed—and these were often severe—were not uniform, a fact that gave rise to complaints about injustices, so that some Frankish synods sought to abolish them. They continued to be used, however. In the early eleventh century Burchard of Worms produced a kind of standard Penitential, his famous *Corrector*, which was widely circulated and continued to be influential for many years.[60] This, like its predecessors, has little schematic organization and contains no account of general

---

58. *Enchiridion*, 65.

59. For accounts of these works, see John T. McNeill and Helen M. Gamer, *Medieval Handbooks of Penance* (New York, 1938), pp. 25-50, and Adrian Morey, *Bartholomew of Exeter* (Cambridge, 1937), pp. 168-71.

60. This work is described at length in P. Fournier and G. Le Bras, *Histoire des collections canoniques* (Paris, 1931, 1932), I, 364-421.

principles to be followed in questioning penitents and in estimating the gravity of their sins.

During the later eleventh century there developed an interest in the general theory of penance. Certain basic guidelines were set forth in a treatise *On True and False Penance* which seemed so reasonable and authoritative that it was attributed to St. Augustine,[61] and it is usually printed among the Appendices to his works in modern times. Principles from this text were incorporated in Lombard's *Four Books of Sentences*. In the early Middle Ages little differentiation was made between sacraments and sacramentals, but Lombard described a series of seven sacraments, all of which could be said to have been established by Christ, and penance was among them. A decisive impetus to the spread of the new doctrines concerning the sacraments and penance especially was provided by the decrees of the Fourth Lateran Council of 1215, as the reactions of local bishops clearly indicate.[62] The Profession of Faith at the opening of the Council endorsed, for the first time officially, the doctrine of transubstantiation, and the decree on penance demanded that everyone participate in Communion at least once a year.[63]

The decree itself is worth quoting:

> Every one of the faithful of either sex [*utriusque sexus*], after he arrives at the age of discretion [i.e., seven years], should confess all of his sins faithfully in private, to his own priest, at least once

---

61. For the importance of this work see Dom D. A. Wilmart, "Une opuscule sur la confession composée par Guy de Southwick vers la fin du XIe siècle," *Recherches de théologie ancienne et médiévale,* VII (1935), p. 339. Cf. Morey, *op. cit.,* p. 71.
62. E.g. in England, see David Wilkins, *Conciliae Magnae Brittaniae et Hiberniae* (London, 1737), I, 593, 650. For the Continent, see G. D. Mansi, *Sacrorum Conciliorum ... Collectio* (Paris, 1903-27), 23, cols. 929-30, 1051, 1186-1203; 24, cols. 903-1056. Dates and attributions in Wilkins should be checked in C. R. Cheney, *English Synodalia in the Thirteenth Century* (London, 1941). English episcopal statutes offer many interesting insights into the life of the times.
63. For the Profession of Faith, see Hefele and Leclercq, *op. cit.,* V, 1325. The decree on the Eucharist was echoed in episcopal statutes throughout the thirteenth century. One bishop, Peter Quivil of Exeter, urged his priests to explain the doctrine of Transubstantiation to laymen with *exempla,* reasoning, and miracles. See Wilkins, *op. cit.,* II, 133.

in the year, and should seek to fulfill the penance enjoined to him before men, receiving reverently at least at Easter the sacrament of the Eucharist, unless, indeed, on the advice of his own priest, for some rational cause, he should abstain from taking it at that time. Otherwise, if he is alive, he should be denied entrance in the church [i.e., suffer minor excommunication]; and if he is dead, he should be denied a Christian burial.[64]

Here the requirements for an annual participation in the Sacrament of the Altar and annual confession are combined, for it was thought participation in the former might be inefficacious, or even noxious, if the individual were in a state of sin. However, it was recognized that the proper administration of penance would require considerable skill on the part of priests, and the decree went on to urge that the priest be discreet and cautious

> "so that in the manner of a skilled consecrated physician, he may administer wine and oil to the wounds, diligently inquiring of the circumstances, both of the sinner and of the sin, by means of which inquiry he may prudently judge how he should counsel the sinner and what kind of remedy he should apply, using varied evidence in curing the sick."[65]

If the decree were to be properly implemented, an enormous program of clerical and lay education would be necessary. With reference to the latter the Council had already recognized the need for more efficacious preaching, observing that "the food of the word of God is known to be most necessary" for the Christian people, "for even as the body is nourished by material food, so is the spirit nourished by spiritual food," so that bishops should appoint "preachers to assist them profitably in the office of preaching, men powerful in deed and word, who shall visit the people committed to them in their places ... and edify them by word and example."[66] We may recognize in the distinction between "material" and "spiritual" food a prevailing theme in *Piers*

64. Hefele and Leclercq, V, 1350.
65. Cf. Chaucer's *Parson's Tale* (ed. Robinson), lines 958-80. Cf. D. W. Robertson, Jr., "A Note on the Classical Origin of 'Circumstances' in the Medieval Confessional," *SP*, 43 (1946), 6-14.
66. Hefele and Leclercq, V, 1340.

Plowman, and in the demand for preachers "powerful in deed and word" a foreshadowing of Chaucer's Parson. In England the most famous response to this demand was the decree of Archbishop Peckam (1281) specifying a series of sermons on seven topics that would assist parishioners in an understanding of their penitential obligations. Preachers were to explain the following subjects four times a year: (1) the fourteen articles of the faith, (2) the Commandments, (3) the two precepts of charity, (4) the seven Works of Mercy, (5) the seven capital sins and their progeny, (6) the seven virtues, (7) the seven Sacramental graces. They were to do this simply and clearly without any "fantastic elaboration."[67]

Generally the response to the Council was astonishing. Bishops both in England and on the Continent echoed it in their Constitutions, sometimes supplying manuals of instruction for their priests to enable them to become skilled physicians.[68] Meanwhile, the Council repeated a decree of the Third Lateran Council, which now acquired a new significance, that there should be a master in every Cathedral Church to teach grammar and other subjects to the local clergy and to "other poor scholars" free of charge, and that there should be a master of theology in every metropolitan church.[69] Insofar as the Eucharist is concerned, enthusiasm for its efficacy became widespread, leading eventually to the establishment of the Feast of Corpus Christi with its attendant processionals, sometimes under guild auspices, and to the cycles of mystery plays.[70] In addition, the necessity for confession to be complete and circumstantial stimulated the production of confessional manuals both in Latin and in the vernaculars. One such manual by the Lincolnshire scholar William de Montibus, written before the Council but resembling a miniature "Parson's Tale," became a standard school text in the fourteenth century.[71]

67. Wilkins, II, 54.
68. See Cheney, *op. cit.,* pp. 40-43, and Robertson, *Essays,* pp. 116-25.
69. Hefele and Leclercq, V, 1341.
70. See most recently V. A. Kolve. *The Play Called Corpus Christi* (Stanford. 1966). esp. pp. 44-49.
71. See Orme, *English Schools,* pp. 103-4. The text is by the Lincolnshire scholar William de Montibus (d. 1213). *PL,* 207, cols. 1153-56.

It had been customary to compose sermons for special social groups known as *sermones ad status*. Society was, as John of Salisbury insisted, an interrelated whole, somewhat like the human body, and its health depended on the proper functioning of all of its parts, or on the virtues of all of its members and, since society was hierarchical, on the fidelity of each member to his superiors and the charitable treatment of inferiors. Fidelity was ideally insured by love, for, as St. Augustine had said, Christ binds His Church (Christian society), which is His body, "which has many members performing diverse offices, in a bond of unity and charity."[72] To endanger this bond was to offend against "the laws of charity." The "diverse offices" exposed men to various temptations, some peculiar to each office. The great Cardinal Jacques de Vitry preached special sermons to prelates, to priests in synods, to regulars, to scholars, to pilgrims and crusaders, to merchants, to farmers and craftsmen, to servants, to virgins, and to widows.[73] Similarly, in his manual for Dominican preachers, Humbert de Romans, fifth Master of the Order, presented his followers with materials for one hundred such sermons, ranging from "*ad omnes homines*" to "*ad mulieres meretrices*."[74] Manuals of confession were sometimes organized in the same way, suggesting that priests inquire of their penitents specifically concerning the obligations of each group. For example, of monks, whether they have observed the rule; of priests concerning simony, the proper expenditure of church funds, and the observance of the offices; of merchants concerning cupidity; of lords and their officers concerning unjust tallages; of burgesses concerning lying, guile, usury, pledges, barratry, and unjust weights and measures; of agricultural laborers concerning theft, tithes, the eradication of boundaries, encroachments on the lands of others, and of faithfully maintaining their works and services.[75] It is not often recognized by historians that oppressive lords,

---

72. *On Christian Doctrine*. 1. 16. 15.

73. T. F. Crane. *The Exempla of Jacques de Vitry* (London, 1890), p. xxxix.

74. *Maxima bibliotheca veterum patrum* (Lyons, 1677), 25, pp. 456-67. Cf. Lecoy de la Marche, *La chaire française au moyen âge* (Paris, 1886), p. 341.

75. E.g. see Mansi, 24, col. 528; cf. cols. 987-88.

greedy merchants, and slothful peasants were alike violators of fidelity, and that confessors questioned them on these matters and required penances for them. However, surveys of the social order like that near the beginning of *Piers Plowman* or that in the General Prologue to *The Canterbury Tales* probably owed a great deal to the habit of thought engendered both by preachers and by confessors in their attention to specific social groups.

Humbert de Romans was, as indicated above, a Master of the Dominicans, and Archbishop Peckham was a Franciscan. The Friars, especially the Franciscans and Dominicans, helped enormously, both in their theoretical studies and in their pastoral work, to implement the decree of the Lateran Council. The Dominicans arrived in England first in 1221, establishing a convent at Oxford. Their numbers increased rapidly, and by the end of the century Blackfriars in London, with its great church two hundred and twenty feet long, was well established and had close connections with the royal court, which it retained throughout the next century. The Franciscans' great London church Greyfriars, even larger than Blackfriars, adorned with marble columns and a marble floor not entirely consistent with Franciscan ideals of poverty, did not arise until the next century, but meanwhile the order had established itself in towns throughout England. Bishop Grosseteste, who lectured to the Franciscans at Oxford, was impressed by their zeal, and they won the hearts of townsmen with their evangelical fervor and popular preaching, which often included the employment of songs.[76] They became active in such civic matters as the construction of waterworks for towns, and the wealthy who wished to reward them often resorted to use of enfeoffments, stimulating the growth of that arrangement.[77] Their contribution to the style and content of the Middle English lyric can hardly be exaggerated, and

---

76. See David L. Jeffrey's study, *The Early English Lyric and Franciscan Spirituality* (Lincoln, Nebraska, 1975). On Franciscan literature generally, see John V. Fleming, *An Introduction to Franciscan Literature of the Middle Ages* (Chicago, 1977).

77. J. H. Baker, *An Introduction to English Legal History* (London, 1971), p. 130, and A. W. B. Simpson, *An Introduction to the History of the Land Law* (Oxford, 1961), p. 164.

they also exerted an influence on the development of the vernacular drama.[78] Unfortunately the Friars did not agree on basic doctrinal matters, and they quarreled among themselves. Meanwhile, under the leadership of William of St. Amour at Paris a controversy between the Friars on the one hand and the "secular" clergy on the other, sometimes aided by traditional regulars, raged in the universities and spread to popular literature, especially in the later fourteenth century when the Friars had become very influential, very numerous, and often seemingly more interested in their own wealth than in the souls of the people. They became rivals of the secular clergy rather than their supporters, and were accused of standing on street corners like so many Pardoners, preaching for monetary contributions, and of offering easy penances for money. These activities, it was alleged, diverted funds from parish priests and their churches.[79]

Although some Friars, like Nicholas Trivet, who wrote a very full commentary on *The Consolation of Philosophy,* had "humanistic" leanings, many persons regarded Friars as being "enemies of poetry," at least of the humanistic variety. Chaucer was influenced by the *Roman de la Rose,* which espoused the cause of William of St. Amour, and probably by Boccaccio, as well as by anti-fraternal preaching and writing in England, the latter well exemplified in the *Philobiblon* of Richard de Bury. And it is undoubtedly true that the Friars were subjected to the same kind of pressures and temptations in late medieval England that affected the population as a whole. Chaucer's tales of the Friar and the Summoner do not leave us much to choose from between the abuse of penance on the part of the Friars and the administration of canonical correction on the part on the secular hierarchy. It is true, nevertheless, that the *animus* against the Friars still echoes in the pages of Erasmus, St. Thomas More, and Rabelais. There are still faint echoes in Shakespeare.

78. See David L. Jeffrey, "Franciscan Spirituality and the Rise of Early English Drama," *Mosaic,* 8 (1975), 17-46.

79. Another complaint involved the zeal of the Friars in the profitable business of burying the dead. See, for example, F. M. Powicke and C. R. Cheney, *Councils and Synods with Other Documents Relating to the English Church,* II, Part II (Oxford, 1964), pp. 1255-64.

The sermons delivered by the Friars in their hall churches, designed more for preaching than for liturgical ceremonies, were often enlivened by *exempla* or entertaining and instructive stories as well as by adaptations of popular songs or by lyrics composed for the purpose. Exemplary narratives or descriptions became common in popular sermons during the thirteenth century,[80] and in the fourteenth century the tendency toward increasingly specific and sometimes localized exemplification became a feature of both verbal and visual art, producing an impression of "realism," although *verisimilitude,* a term current at the time, would be a better word for it.[81] Jacques de Vitry had said that in addressing rustics the preacher should use such "corporal and palpable things" as they knew most frequently "by experience," since they are more moved by "external examples" than by profound doctrines.[82] Etienne de Bourbon, a Dominican, found them to be valuable, however, in addressing men of "all states."[83] As time passed the Friars became famous for their stories, although some of their opponents, like Wyclif, thought them to be more entertaining than edifying and objected to their use. In *The Canterbury Tales* Chaucer's characters frequently either grossly misinterpret the *exempla* they use or amusingly disregard their implications, creating a humorous effect that may reflect the inept use of stories among preachers, fraternal and otherwise. And the tales told by the less worthy of his pilgrims often cause them to comment inadvertently on themselves as they are described in the General Prologue. On the other hand, it is but a step from an elaborate *exemplum* to a Canterbury Tale, except that the Tale conceals its *sentence* under what Petrarch called a "veil" of fiction, instead of employing an elaborate moralization at the close. The technique of the "fabulous narrative" was by no means new in the fourteenth century, but Chaucer's heavy dependence on various kinds of

80. For the history of the *exemplum* see the monumental study by J.-T. Welter, *L'exemplum dans la littérature religieuse et didactique du moyen âge* (Paris, 1927).

81. Cf. Robertson, *Essays,* pp. 99, 222, 232.

82. Crane, *op. cit.,* p. xlii.

83. A. Lecoy de la Marche, *Anecdotes historiques d'Étienne de Bourbon* (Paris, 1877), p. 12.

exemplification was a feature of the general "style" of his time, and it allowed him opportunities for especially incisive satire. There is thus a sense in which the character of Chaucer's literary artistry owes something to the Lateran decree and its effects.

The more obvious literary consequences of the decree are not difficult to detect, especially in England. M. Dominica Legge, in her study of Anglo-Norman literature, wrote that it produced "a remarkable series of manuals, treatises, and encyclopedias of religious knowledge designed for the laity, or for the parish clergy who were to prepare them for confession,"[84] adding that "all sorts of people wrote these books, from an archbishop and an earl to a chaplain and a friar." They include St. Edmund's *Merure de Seinte Eglise,* clearly influenced by the decrees of Bishop Richard Poore of Salisbury, who was among the first English bishops to respond to the recommendations of the Council in his own statutes.[85] The *Merure* survives in numerous Anglo-Norman, Latin, and English manuscripts, and it contains the lyric Carleton Brown called "Sunset on Calvary."[86] The manual of confession called the *Manuel des péchés* attributed to William of Wadington enjoyed a fairly substantial audience. Its English adaptation, Robert Mannyng's *Handlyng Synne* has become famous in modern times for its skillful use of *exempla*. A more popular work was the *Lumere as lais* based on the *Elucidarium* of Honorius of Autun and the *Sentences* of Peter the Lombard, indicating once more an interest on the part of laymen in problems of doctrine. Grosseteste's *Chasteau d'Amour,* probably directed to a noble audience, is an indication of the same kind of interest. For other works in the same tradition, which extends into the next century, Legge's chapter "The Interdict and the Fourth Lateran Council" forms a useful guide.[87] The "earl" she mentions was Henry of Lancaster, father of Chaucer's Blanche, whose *Seyntz Medicines* describes his own penitential experience, and offers, at the same time a

---

84. *Anglo-Norman Literature and its Background* (Oxford, 1963), p. 106.
85. For Poore's interest in penitential material and a general discussion of the sources of his statutes and their influence, see Cheney, *English Synodalia,* Chapter III.
86. *English Lyrics of the Thirteenth Century* (Oxford, 1933), no. 1, p. 1.
87. Legge, *op. cit.,* pp. 206-42.

remarkable illustration of the effects of the new penitential doctrines on a distinguished layman. There is, in fact, a close relationship between literature describing the need for penance and devotional literature, as W. A. Pantin has observed.[88] True penance was inspired by love, not by fear. Love for Christ and the Virgin and sympathy for their sufferings at the Crucifixion, portrayed in many English lyrics, was thus a very proper inspiration to contrition, the basis for true penance. Among thirteenth-century English works the *Ancrene Wisse,* which contained sections on Confession, Penance, and Love, including an account of the seven sins, became, as Geoffrey Shepherd said, a "manual of counsel" cherished by "many gifted Englishwomen and Englishmen of the last medieval centuries."[89] The spirituality of the twelfth century, as the *Merure* of St. Edmund also demonstrates, blended well with the new doctrines following the Lateran decree, and the latter undoubtedly contributed to the renewed interest in the former, which grew as the Middle Ages progressed toward the Renaissance.[90] The "medicine" of the new pastoral theology was thus in part a logical development of the doctrines of love that flourished in the twelfth century, and it helped to reinforce and preserve them.

V. *Non veni pacem mittere, sed gladium*

During the thirteenth century the population of England, as of Europe generally, experienced rapid growth, possibly as a result of the increasing consumption of meat.[91] The vills of England and the manorial organizations associated with them (for vill and manor did not always coincide) became integrated into tightly knit communities whose social interests were supported by centers of two kinds, the local courts

---

88. *The English Church in the Fourteenth Century* (Cambridge, 1955), pp. 248-50.
89. *Ancrene Wisse: Parts Six and Seven* (Manchester, 1972), p. ix.
90. See Giles Constable, "The Popularity of Twelfth-Century Spiritual Writers in the Late Middle Ages," reprinted from *Renaissance Studies in Honor of Hans Baron* (Florence, 1971).
91. Vern Bullough and Cameron Campbell, "Female Longevity and Diet in the Middle Ages," *Speculum,* 55 (1980), 317-25.

and the parish churches. Speaking generally, the courts were of three kinds: manorial courts representing the community of the manor; honor courts to which freemen had access in some areas; and the county court with its subsidiaries in the hundreds or on manors which enjoyed the "View of Frankpledge." The towns had courts of various kinds of their own, differing somewhat from locality to locality. The county court represented the community of the shire, which was the *patria* of its inhabitants.[92] These were all social, and sometimes "political," as well as legal institutions. There were also less popular ecclesiastical courts administered by bishops, archdeacons, and rural deans.[93] But the local social center for all ranks of society was the parish church whose parson or vicar shared in the agricultural life of the community in rural areas and was closely associated with guilds and fraternities in the towns. He sponsored processionals (where he was not being superseded by the Friars), pilgrimages to local shrines and holy places, which often had the atmosphere of community "picnics," and the celebration of festivals, including the popular festivities on St. John's Eve ("Midsummer Night"), commemorating the passing of the Old Law, represented by "witches" or fairies, and the coming of the New, and on Maundy Thursday, all of which have left their literary traces in such works as Adam de la Halle's *Le jeu de La feuillée* and *The Tournament of Tottenham*. As some of the liturgical plays and many of the cyclic plays reveal, medieval religious festivities were not necessarily "solemn" in the modern sense, and we should not assume that the reverence for Christian attitudes implied a somnolently serious attitude. The Good Lord was to be served with joy.

In the countryside many agricultural families had occupied the same lands for generations. There was a close tie between families and the lands they tilled, and manorial communities depended for their

---

92. For the community of the shire generally. see Helen M. Cam. *Liberties and Communities in Medieval England* (New York, 1963), pp. 245-47; and on county courts in the fourteenth century, see J. R. Madicott. "The County Community and the Making of Public Opinion in Fourteenth-Century England." *TRHS*, Fifth Series, 28 (1978), pp. 27-43.

93. See Jean Scammel. "The Rural Chapter in England from the Eleventh to the Fourteenth Century," *EHR*, 86 (1971), 1-21.

welfare on close ties between lord or manorial steward and tenants acting to further their mutual interests.[94] As the population grew, the necessity for the full use of all economic resources, both physical and human, became evident. "Assarts," or newly cleared lands, expanded the arable areas, new towns or vills were established, and in the parish churches the new teachings concerning the sacraments brought even closer ties between a man and his church, and, consequently, between a man and his fellow communicants. Bishops appointed confessors, including Friars, to circulate in the parishes during Lent to hear confessions and to remind folk of the evils of transgressions against their neighbors or lapses in fidelity. The churches supplied the ideals that fostered mutual interest in communities and sought to deter self-aggrandizement at the expense of neighbors or of the community as a whole, assisted by manorial customs, royal laws enforced at the "View," borough regulations, and guild regulations. In the towns merchants developed a keen sense of local patriotism, a jocular and humorous but nevertheless sincere manifestation of which may indeed survive in *Havelok the Dane,* which is easily envisioned as entertainment for a festive gathering of fishmongers at Grimsby. Close ties developed between merchant guilds, or groups of prominent individual guilds, and town governments. Many guilds were outgrowths of parish fraternities when groups of persons engaged in the same trade attended the same parish church, and such fraternities or guilds sought to control the moral as well as the commercial behavior of their members, to settle differences among them, and to provide for aged and impoverished members. When a man looked from the fields toward a town or village, the steeples or towers of the churches that met his eye did not represent something separate from the ordinary conduct of his affairs, but an integral part of his community life. His ancestors and those of his friends, close relatives, and neighbors rested there. The fragmentation of modern life, demanding separate demeanors

---

94. The community spirit of manorial life has often been commented on, especially on open field manors. See, for example. C. S. and C. S. Orwin. *The Open Fields,* 2nd ed. (Oxford. 1954), pp. 173-74, and, more recently, W. O. Ault, *Open Field Husbandry and the Village Community, TAPS,* New Series. 55.7 (1965). pp. 40-54.

for different groups and occasions (multiple "personalities") was as yet unknown.

The fourteenth century witnessed a series of events that severely strained community relationships of all kinds. The disastrous crop failures of 1315-1322, accompanied by human and cattle disease, dampened the rise in population, led to spectacularly high prices for grain, and encouraged crime in the countryside.[95] The prevailing intellectual attitudes of the time suggested a need for penance and moral reform, and Archbishop Reynolds of Canterbury ordered the clergy to go barefoot on processionals carrying the Sacrament and the sacred relics, ringing bells and chanting the Litany, urging the people to atone for their sins, and to devote themselves to prayer, fasting, and the performance of good works.[96] The economy generally seems to have recovered fairly well from this disaster, or series of disasters, but royal taxation and the activities of voracious and unscrupulous purveyors and local commissioners of array (some of whom apparently outdid Shakespeare's Falstaff) during the early years of Edward III certainly represented a burden, especially on the poor, as a poem on the subject indicates:

> Unquore plus greve a simple gent collectio lanarum,
> Que vendre fet communement divicias earum.[97]

The poem goes on to complain about the scarcity of coinage, so acute that many were unable to sell their cloth, grain, pigs, or sheep. For one historian these things all represented a very serious situation, reaching a peak in the years 1336-1341, when many thought that the people would rebel.[98] Another, however, has pointed out that although taxation was sometimes disastrous locally, the economy as a whole,

---

95. The situation has been studied by Ian Kershaw, "The Agrarian Crisis in England in 1315-22," in R. H. Hilton, *Peasants, Knights, and Heretics* (Cambridge, 1976), pp. 85-132.
96. *Ibid.*, p. 89.
97. Isabel S. T. Aspin, *Anglo-Norman Political Songs* (Oxford, 1963, rpr. N.Y., 1971), X. 5. 21-22. Cf. the Harley lyric "Ich herde men upon mold make muche mon."
98. J. R. Madicott, *The English Peasantry and the Demands of the Crown, 1294-1341*, Past and Present Supplement I (1975).

as wool exports indicate, remained vigorous, and that the nation as a whole did not share the economic woes of the government.[99] Whatever we may conclude about this period, when the Exchequer "seal of the green wax" became an object with which to terrorize simple people,[100] and a sensitivity to taxation developed which was to hamper foreign policy and lead to "tyrannical" measures in the next reign, a disaster of devastating proportions struck the land in 1348-49, the Black Death, which, according to some estimates, wiped out between a third and a half of the population, although its effects were not uniform throughout the country.[101]

Chaucer was only a small boy in London when this happened, but he must have witnessed some of the devastation and panic and heard harrowing tales about it during his early youth, especially since plagues were recurrent, in 1354, 1361, 1369, and again in the seventies. In the countryside the "wrath of God" was felt keenly, inspiring a new interest in themes from *The Consolation of Philosophy* which began to appear with increasing frequency in wall paintings in parish churches, along with representations of St. Christopher, whose influence was thought to be helpful in protecting potential victims of the disease. Barbara Harvey observes that on manors "the family sense of association with a particular holding, which had been so marked a feature of rural society in the early Middle Ages, weakened; indeed, in some places it almost disappeared."[102] This effect was sometimes delayed until after the plague of 1361, or even later, so that Cecily Howell,

---

99. A. R. Bridbury, "Before the Black Death," *EcHR*, Second Series, 30 (1977), 303-410.

100. The green seal of the Exchequer was still a frightening object many years later, since its appearance on a document could be used to extort money from illiterate persons who recognized it but could not read. See the Wakefield play of the Last Judgment, ed. David Bevington, *Medieval Drama* (Boston, 1975), p. 647, lines 283-84, although the editor's note misconstrues the word *green*.

101. On some manors the effects were not serious. See, for example, Judith A. Brent, "Alciston Manor in the Later Middle Ages," Sussex Archaeological Collections, 106 (1968), 89-102. Cf. Francis M. Page, *The Estates of Crowland Abbey* (Cambridge, 1934), pp. 120-25.

102. *The Estates of Westminster Abbey in the Late Middle Ages* (Oxford, 1977), pp. 318-19.

examining inheritance customs in the Midlands, writes that "there was a sharp decline in hereditary continuity between 1350 and 1412."[103] As families disappeared, peasant holdings increased in size, and landlords seeking ready cash began to lease their demesne lands on a large scale and to substitute money rents for customary services on villein holdings generally. Naturally, these developments tended to encourage a new kind of landholder chiefly interested in making profits beyond his rent without regard for the maintenance of the land and its buildings,[104] but it also tended to increase productivity on the larger holdings that could be managed more efficiently.[105] However, the new situation weakened community ties. A new spirit of personal ambition, stimulated by rising wages as the demand for agricultural labor increased, developed throughout the realm. And plagues seem to have been followed by significant rises in crime, especially after 1361.[106]

A further decline is evident in the social functions of local courts. The shires except in the north and the south where somewhat different procedures were followed, were divided into "hundreds," traditionally supervised by bailiffs under the sheriff or by manorial lords who held the "View of Frankpledge." The population was divided into groups called "tithings," originally groups of ten (although the numbers varied), including everyone reaching the age of 12 except women, members of the clergy, noblemen, and wealthy freeholders presumably

---

103. "Peasant Inheritance Customs in the Midlands, 1280-1700," in Jack Goody, Joan Thirsk, and E. P. Thompson, *Family and Inheritance* (Cambridge, 1976), p. 127.
104. Cf. E. M. Holcrow, "The Decline of Demesne Farming on the Estates of Durham Cathedral Priory," *EcHR,* Second Series, 7 (1955), pp. 351-54.
105. Cf. Howell, *op. cit.,* p. 139. D. L. Farmer, "Grain Yields on the Winchester Manors in the Later Middle Ages," *EcHR,* Second Series, 30 (1977), 555-56, finds a substantial increase in productivity after 1381.
106. E.g., see J. A. Raftis, "An English Village After the Black Death," *Med. Stud.,* 29 (1967), 163-64. Cf. the same author's *Warboys* (Toronto, 1974), p. 220. The conditions described here were widespread. John Bellamy, *Crime and Public Order in the Later Middle Ages* (London and Toronto, 1973), p. 6, reports that "in 1362 there was a great clamour about the committing of felonies and trespasses and the excesses of officials." There were said to be congregations or warlike vagabonds in Staffordshire and many felons abroad in Devon. The chronicler Knighton reported a wave of theft in 1364.

under the jurisdiction of their lords. The members of these "tithings" under one or two "chief pledges" were responsible for one another's behavior, and the pledges insured their appearance at court, where minor offenses ("trespasses") were tried. The mobility of agricultural workers after the Black Death tended to disrupt the frankpledge system, injuring another form of mutual responsibility among neighbors, although some landlords continued to maintain it throughout the fifteenth century and a few even later.[107] The government, meanwhile, sought to control wages and prices in the Ordinance of Labourers of 1349 and the Statute of 1351. In 1352 the Keepers of the Peace were given power to enforce the Statute, and this function was later assumed by the Justices of the Peace. The activities of the Justices diminished the importance of the shire courts, but efforts to control wages and prices were not successful. An especially good harvest in 1375 brought agricultural prices down, but there was no corresponding decline in wages, a fact that stimulated parliamentary agitation.[108] A more determined effort to control wages may have been partly responsible for the Revolt of 1381.

The royal courts generally had been suffering from a failure to observe an ordinance of 1346 that stipulated that the royal justices execute the laws for rich and poor alike, that they should take no robes and fees from anyone except the King, and no gifts beyond food and drink of small value. In spite of it magnates frequently retained justices and sergeants on a regular basis, a fact that led to widespread discontent. The judicial process was being corrupted on a large scale, affecting not only justices of assize and jail delivery, but also justices of the peace and local sheriffs, not to mention the central courts themselves. Chaucer's Sergeant of the Law with his "fees and robes," and his extensive holdings in land held in fee simple, which were readily alienable, together with his companion the Franklin, who had been both a sheriff and a justice of the peace, with his own extensive lands and epicurean tastes, and capacity for offering lavish entertainment to influential men of the county, are vivid exemplifications of this

---

107. See D.A. Crowley, "The Later History of Frankpledge," *BIHR*, 48 (1975), 1-15.
108. A. R. Bridbury, "The Black Death," *EcHR*, Second Series, 26 (1973), 584-85.

corruption. The situation undoubtedly contributed to the unrest that burst forth in 1381, for the rebels displayed special *animus* against lawyers.[109] The connection between the corruption of justice and the revolt was pointed out at the Parliament of 1381 (November) by Sir Richard de Waldgrave, the speaker for the Commons, a distinguished Suffolk knight whose career is said to have resembled that of Chaucer's Knight. He had been associated with Joan of Kent, who was surrounded by men who showed a strong interest in reform, and served as a Knight of the Household and as a member of the Council.[110] It is quite likely that Chaucer knew him. He said in effect that maintenance and embracery were so common in the countryside that no justice could be done.[111]

To return for a moment to the manors of England, which functioned as the basis for the national economy, the disruption in local communities we have discussed was further aggravated by the development of industries that offered wages by the day and hence ready cash of a kind that could not be obtained on traditional holdings. Here local conditions determined what trades were most attractive. In Cornwall the proximity of agriculture and tin mining had been beneficial to both, creating a ready market for produce and maintaining a demand for land.[112] But this situation, assisted by the system of seven-year leases on the lands of the Duchy and the enlightened policies of the Black Prince and his council, was unique. As new trades developed elsewhere the effect was to cause agricultural workers to demand higher wages by the day for labor in the fields that could most readily be obtained from the new class of leaseholders with extensive

---

109. See J. R. Madicott, *Law and Lordship: Royal Justices and Retainers in Thirteenth and Fourteenth Century England,* Past and Present Supplement 4 (1978). Cf., on commissions of oyer and terminer, Richard W. Kaeuper, "Law and Order in Fourteenth-Century England: The Evidence of Special Commissions of Oyer and Terminer," *Speculum,* 54 (1979), 734-84. For the connection between judicial corruption and the Revolt, cf. Madicott, pp. 61-64.

110. See J. S. Roskell, *The Commons and their Speakers* (Manchester, 1965), p. 127.

111. Madicott, *Law and Lordship,* p. 64.

112. John Hatcher, "A Diversified Economy: Later Medieval Cornwall," *EcHR,* Second Series, 22 (1969), 208-27. See also the same author's detailed study, *Rural Economy and Society in the Duchy of Cornwall* (Cambridge, 1970).

holdings on manors.¹¹³ At the same time, trade attracted many people away from the land. The cutlery trade at Thaxted in Essex offers a good example that has been studied in detail.¹¹⁴ But the most rapidly developing industry was the cloth industry which spread to rural areas where convenient streams for fulling mills were readily available and where tradesmen would not be restricted by guild regulations.¹¹⁵ The last factor is in itself a manifestation of the general tendency to seek to avoid community obligations for the sake of profit. Even persons in villein tenure who held fulling mills might become wealthy in an industry that relied heavily on cheap labor, mostly female, readily available in the countryside. It is not surprising that one of Chaucer's most spectacular characters who vehemently attacks accepted views of hierarchy and glorifies wealth should be a female clothier. At the same time, tradesmen in the towns, motivated by the growing general desire for money, were making what authorities both royal and civic regarded as outrageous profits, often by dubious means.¹¹⁶

The ecclesiastical hierarchy was not immune from the temptations that beset other members of society. As we have seen, the Friars were becoming wealthy, and in many instances greedy and unscrupulous, and archdeacons and their officials, never popular, were becoming more and more burdensome to their communities. The Black Death impoverished parishes and monastic communities and left many small chapels in the countryside without support. In her study of the church in Lincolnshire Dorothy Owens writes that "the rolls of the justices of the peace for 1360 and 1375 are full of accusations of theft and violence committed by chaplains." But such accusations were confined

---

113. See Elizabeth Chapin Furber, *Essex Sessions of the Peace, 1351, 1377-79*, Essex Archaeological Society, Occasional Publications, 3 (1953), p. 68.
114. Norah Ritchie, "Labour Conditions in Essex in the Reign of Richard II," in E. M. Carus-Wilson, *Essays in Economic History*, II (London, 1962), 91-111.
115. This situation is discussed at length in an article on the Wife of Bath by the present author soon to appear.
116. To cite an illustrative example, one Henry Souter of a town in Lincolnshire is said to have bought all the shoes made by William Brid and his men for 5½d. a pair on 11 Oct. 1372 and then, on 28 March and later during the next year sold them for 8d. a pair "to the serious oppression of the people." See Rosemund Sillem, *Records of Some Sessions of the Peace in Lincolnshire, 1360-75*, Lincoln Record Society, 30 (1936), pp. 198-99.

neither to Lincolnshire nor to those years.[117] Moreover, similar offenses were committed by other members of the hierarchy. Parsons were not all like Chaucer's Parson. Thus in 1372 the Parson of Rothwell with others stole crops of 5 acres valued at 5s. an acre at Cuxwold. Shortly thereafter Walter the Parson of Scoter harbored a female felon and raped her, extorted 6s. 8d. from a man, stole 20 pigs belonging to the Abbot of Peterborough, and 19 other pigs, and assaulted a man. In 1375 another Parson is said to have stolen a black bull belonging to the Master of the Temple.[118] In the same year the Parson of Witton in Norfolk is said to have raped a man's wife and stolen goods worth 20s.[119] These are merely illustrative cases, and it would be possible to compile substantial lists of vicars and clerks accused of similar offenses. To judge from the peace rolls, ecclesiastical officials were often given to extortion. The extortionate practices of archdeacons and their officials were notorious,[120] but others were also accused of similar offenses. The Dean of Manly is said to have extorted £20 in the wapentake of Manly, and he excommunicated one Henry of Walsham, forcing him to pay £10 and later threatened to kill him.[121] The Registrar of the Bishop of Winchester was brought before the King's Bench for a series of extortions.[122] And Henry of Wakefield, Bishop of Worcester,

---

117. *Church and Society in Medieval Lincolnshire* (Lincoln, 1971), p. 133. Cf. during the period 1355-59, E. G. Kimball, *Sessions of the Peace for Bedfordshire,* Bedfordshire Histoncal Record Society, 48 (1969), pp. 52, 55, 57, 57-8, 63; and the same author's *Rolls of the Gloucestershire Sessions of the Peace,* Transactions of the Bristol and Gloucestershire Archaeological Society, 62 (1942), pp. 65, 66, 72, 75, 78, 87, 115, 115-16, 117-118, 119, 122-23, 123, 124-25 (in which instance the chaplain broke into a man's house, raped his wife, and stole goods valued at 10s., but the Dean of Hawkesbury, having discovered this misdeed, extorted 26s. 8d. from him for adultery, for which he in turn was indicted, as he was in a later case of extortion), 130, 154. Chaplains seem to have especially enjoyed raping wives and stealing the husband's goods, sometimes, indeed, taking the wives with them also.

118. Rosemund Sillem, *op. cit.,* pp. 55, 205, 209.

119. Bertha Haven Putnam, *Proceedings before the Justices of the Peace in the Fourteenth and Fifteenth Centuries* (Ames Foundation, 1928), p. 120.

120. E.g., see Margaret Aston, *Thomas Arundel* (Oxford, 1967), pp. 92-94.

121. Kimball, *Lincolnshire,* II, Lincoln Record Society, 56 (1952), p. 157.

122. G. O. Sayles, *Select Cases before the Court of the King's Bench,* VII (Selden Society, 1971), pp. 82-83.

whom Chaucer undoubtedly had known at court where he had been Keeper of the Wardrobe and later Treasurer of the Exchequer, was indicted, together with his suffragan, for extorting money for consecrating chapels and altars.[123] The same bishop was brought before the King's Bench for an especially unsavory double rape. He is said to have raped a young woman twice and subsequently raped her mother whom he abducted along with goods valued at 40s.[124] Monastic estates were subject to economic strains, relaxed discipline, and a dwindling population of monks. The necessity to glean as much profit as possible from their tenants naturally encouraged increasingly worldly concerns.[125] It is not surprising that the author of *Piers Plowman* should have envisioned the ecclesiastical hierarchy succumbing to the charms of Lady Meed or questioned the possibility of finding the true priesthood of God on earth, or that Wyclif should have doubted the rights of sinners in the hierarchy to spiritual dominion. But of more importance was the fact that the most cherished social center of English communities, the parish church, was suffering from moral decay. This does not mean that all parishes everywhere lacked good shepherds. It does mean that enough of their clergy were corrupt to give rise to uneasiness and a growing desire for reform.

After 1369 the "Sword of Castigation" was considerably assisted by the French and their allies, and the period between that date and the nineties was one of gloom and disillusionment, creating demands for reform. To put this in another way, the years of Chaucer's maturity during which he produced his major works were haunted by memories of former glories in an atmosphere of what appeared to be almost continuous deterioration.[126] Edward III had been spectacularly

---

123. E. G. Kimball, *Some Warwickshire and Coventry Sessions of the Peace, 1377-97*, Dugdale Society, 16 (1939), pp. 105-6.

124. Sayles, *Select Cases*, VII, 53-54.

125. Chaucer's Monk well illustrates the prevalent weaknesses of monks in this respect, but this does not mean that he is "typical."

126. It has been vigorously argued that the economic effects of the Black Death were ultimately beneficial and that the new spirit of enterprise was basically healthy. See, for example, F. R. H. Du Boulay, *An Age of Ambition: English Society in the Late Middle Ages* (London, 1970). But the actual process

successful as a military leader, often compared with King Arthur, and the Order of the Garter had become the most prestigious chivalric center in the West. But after the Plague bereft Edward of his Queen in 1369 he began to spend more and more time on his estates, hunting and enjoying his unedifying relationship with Alice Perrers. A brief look at just some of the succeeding events in the perriod should help us to understand the general mood. There were disastrous floods in 1370, followed by a series of plagues. The French adopted a strategy of avoiding confrontation on the battlefield, so that Gaunt's march through France, from Calais to Bordeaux, although it represented a military feat of astonishing proportions and helped to demoralize the enemy, produced no famous victories to hearten the people at home. Overseas trade, especially the cloth trade, suffered a depression from which it did not recover until 1379. The Black Prince, who was the hope of English chivalry, died in 1376, and in that year the town of Southampton asked the government to take over its defenses. Edward III died in 1377, leaving a minor, Richard II, to assume the crown. The south coast was heavily attacked by the French, including the towns of Hastings, Rottingdean, Dartmouth, and Plymouth. Rye was burned, and the Scots attacked in the north. The city of London was hastily fortified. Meanwhile, the French were making headway in Gascony. In 1378 Gaunt unsuccessfully attacked St. Malo, returning home in disgrace. In the next year the expedition of John of Arundel, who is said to have abducted nuns as companions for his followers, was destroyed in a storm at sea. In 1380 Thomas of Woodstock unsuccessfully invaded France, Spaniards attacked the south coast, and Winchelsea was taken by the French. The unsuccessful efforts of the government to defend the south coast were probably a contributing factor to the unrest that broke forth in the "Peasants' Revolt" of the following year. As M. M. Postan has explained, the actual facts of the revolt do not support the traditional picture of

---

> must have appalled contemporaries whose ideas of value were traditional and who had no means of rationalizing the kind of behavior that produced a new kind of wealth for individuals and at the same time denied financial support for chivalric action abroad.

a "working class revolt against oppression."[127] The moral outrage of John Gower probably represents a widespread reaction at court. In 1382 an earthquake rocked London (ominously) during the trial of Wyclif. In the following year the Bishop of Norwich launched his unsuccessful and misdirected crusade (probably reflected in the portrait of Chaucer's Squire). The court was torn by factionalism, and an unsuccessful attempt was made to kill Gaunt in a tournament in 1385 while a great French fleet was assembling to attack England. The threat of invasion created panic throughout the realm during the next year, and some lords, complaining about the decay of chivalry, threatened to depose the King.

The continuing influence of the Lateran decree was probably stimulated by the general decline in *mores* that accompanied social change in the fourteenth century in England, as well as by natural disasters and setbacks overseas. The century produced numerous manuals for priests, religious instruction books for laymen, and devotional works, the last probably made more popular in part by disillusionment with the ecclesiastical hierarchy. There was at the same time, as Pantin indicates, a rise in lay literacy especially in the towns, providing a ready and often eager audience.[128] There were reform movements at court.

---

127. M. M. Postan, *The Medieval Economy and Society* (Berkeley and Los Angeles, 1972), p. 153.

128. *Op. cit.,* Chapters IX, X, XI. It is not difficult to detect the influence of the decree in works of a more "literary" character as well. If *The Canterbury Tales* closes with a sermon on penance, the B and C Texts of *Piers Plowman* conclude with the complaint that the Friars have "enchanted" the people and "plastered" them easily (or in C given them an opiate for their "wounds") so that they do not fear sin. That is, Chaucer reminds his audience of basic principles whereas Langland assumes a desire for the proper administration of the Sacrament. The latter also attributes the difficulty to the Friars, whereas Chaucer, although he attacks them on similar grounds in the General Prologue, finds similar kinds of corruption throughout the fabric of society, perhaps taking a fairer view. The works of the *Pearl* poet show somewhat less striking but nevertheless obvious traces of the same influence. That is, *Pearl* praises that "innocence" (or freedom from sin) that is restored through penance; *Purity* praises chastity, or the maintenance of proper love; *Patience* recommends patient obedience to authority (Cf. Chaucer's *Clerk's Tale*); and *Sir Gawain* not only celebrates the fortitude necessary to the *militia Christi,* but closes with a recommendation for penance (represented by the wearing of the girdle) when that fortitude is weakened through "cowardice and covetousness."

Chaucer, who was probably associated closely with the Chamber, and clearly sympathetic with men like Sir Lewis Clifford, Sir John Clanvowe, and Sir Richard Sturry, all of whom were accused (falsely) of being "Lollards" because of their interest in reform,[129] read the revised version of his first great poem, *Troilus,* to a court audience at a time when "New Troy" seemed about to be invaded by its enemies. The fact that modern critics, swayed by attitudes stemming from the literary traditions of the late eighteenth century, should have turned this poem into a lament over the "tragic beauty of human love" or "courtly love" is one of the ironies of history. As the ending of the poem clearly indicates, and as the Boethian reflections throughout the poem, not to mention the structural use of the traditional three steps in the progress of sinful conduct, imply,[130] it is a clear warning against the substitution of self-indulgent passion for chivalric self-sacrifice of the kind that had been demanded ever since the ideals of chivalry were first developed in the twelfth century. English reverses during this period, as John Barnie tells us, "were explained as a punishment visited by God on the sins of his people."[131] If Chaucer had read the poem modern readings have attributed to him he would have disgraced himself before his friends. At about this time Clifford began to show an interest in the Order of the Passion founded by Philippe de Mézières, who had been Chancellor to the great crusading leader Peter of Lusignan. Philippe attributed the decline of chivalry to pride, avarice, and luxury

---

129. Du Boulay observes in his essay "The Historical Chaucer" in Derek Brewer, *Geoffrey Chaucer* (London, 1974), p. 46, that "it remains possible that as a group they (the "Lollard Knights") showed in exaggerated form the sentiments felt by many orthodox contemporaries." K. B. McFarlane's argument for actual Lollardy in *Lancastrian Kings and Lollard Knights* (Oxford, 1972), Part II, seems to me, except in one instance, unconvincing. The interest in Crusading evinced by Clifford, Clanvoe, and Nevill, for example, is hardly consistent with literal Lollard views. And Clanvoe complains openly in his moral treatise that persons who refrain from worldliness are called "Lollards."
130. Cf. Robertson, *Preface,* pp. 477. The pattern is adumbrated in Book I, which emphasizes the first step; the second step is exemplified in Book II, and the third, the abandonment of reason, in Book III. The whole procedure is decorated with the kind of wit that had characterized literate attacks on Venerian pursuits since the twelfth century.
131. *War in Medieval Society* (Ithaca, 1974), p. 103.

(whose tutelary spirit was Venus), reflecting a variation on the traditional three temptations that brought down Adam and that Christ overcame in the wilderness,[132] and hoped to unite the French and English in a new crusade against the Turks, strongly urging that Christians not fight among themselves. If Christians were to escape the sword of God's wrath a new *militia* was required, both against vices at home and against physical attacks on Christian territory. The idea was an old one, but the implications were new. Philippe had a very strong and genuine influence on both the French and English courts.[133] Chaucer's open admiration for one of his ambassadors, Oton de Grandson, is well known, and he made the fictional Knight of his *Tales* a participant in some of Peter of Lusignan's campaigns.[134] The principles of ordered social life laid down by John of Salisbury had by no means been forgotten. Philippe urged Charles VI to read the *Policraticus* as well as St. Augustine's *City of God*,[135] and when Sir Arnold Savage, who supervised the election in which Chaucer obtained his seat in Parliament and who served as executor for his friend Gower, addressed Parliament himself as speaker in 1401, he pointed out that the new king was indeed a rich man, as well as being a man of sense and humanity, for he had the greatest treasure that any king may have, "le coer de son poeple."[136]

To literate persons at court, of whom there were many during the

---

132. *Sentences,* 2. 21. 5.

133. See J. J. N. Palmer, *England, France, and Christendom* (London, 1972), pp. 186-91.

134. It has been alleged that the Knight is suspect because he fought under one of Peter's pagan allies, and this allegation has found its way into a popular school text. However, John of Salisbury insists that it does not matter if a Christian knight fights under a pagan, so long as he maintains his faith. See *Policraticus,* 6. 9. It is clear that Chaucer knew this work.

135. For a summary of Philippe's recommendations to the king, see G. W. Coopland, ed., *Philippe de Mézières, Le Songe du vieil pèlerin* (Cambridge, 1969), II, 18-20.

136. See Roskell, *op. cit.,* p. 362; *Rotuli parliamentorum,* III, 456a. Under "sense" and "humanity" the Speaker referred to the competence of Henry's ecclesiastical and lay associates.

time that Chaucer was writing *The Canterbury Tales,* it must have seemed that "charity and its most just laws" were being blatantly disregarded throughout the kingdom by individuals of all ranks, and that "the love of money" was disrupting communities, great and small. The inherited ideals of the past were being abandoned for the sake of personal gain, and the institutions they had brought forth were being systematically corrupted for money. And all this was happening while England was losing its holdings overseas and the frontiers of Christianity were being attacked by pagans. It was obvious that a new *militia* was required involving the patience, constancy, and fortitude necessary to face disaster with equanimity and to maintain the coherence of English society. New lessons in love, like those afforded by *The Consolation of Philosophy,* seemed desirable to shift men's affections away from "sensible" goods toward those goods that are "eternal and spiritual." Boethius was a potent supporter of Augustinian ideals of responsibility and of freedom from that slavery of the spirit that subjects men to the whims of Fortune. Finally, if the wrath of God were to be appeased, the clear remedy was penance, and through it a new dedication to "the common profit." Chaucer had translated Boethius for his friends and patrons, and had written *Troilus,* further enforcing the contemporary relevance of Boethian ideas. In *The Canterbury Tales* he offered trenchant and amusing criticisms of the weaknesses of social groups, along with vivid reminders of the ideals that were being disregarded. He begins with the Knight's jocular portrayal of the evil effects of the concupiscible and irascible passions and the desirability of harmony with "the fair chain of love"; and he closes with a very salutary sermon on the practical means of achieving that harmony on the "way" to what Christians regarded as their "home," from which, as Boethius had reminded them, they can be exiled forever only by themselves. It is not the purpose of this essay to examine patristic and scriptural materials in the *Tales* specifically, but simply to suggest that Chaucer's narratives would have been impossible without the traditions of patristic and scriptural teachings as they were adapted and elaborated to meet the needs of medieval life. To understand Chaucer it is, I believe, important to discover as much as we can about those traditions, so that we can recognize them when Chaucer employs them; and, at the same time, to discover as much as we can about the actual lives of people living in his time, so that we can understand the relevant application of those traditions. Otherwise, we shall be in no position to account for his success nor to appreciate the craftsmanship he employed in saying what he wished to say vividly and effectively to his own audience.

The Wife of Bath and Midas

D. W. Robertson, Jr.
Duke University

Studies in the Age of Chaucer 6 (1984), pp. 1-20.

It is frequently helpful to consult Chaucer's sources to see first how he has managed them for his own purposes, or allowed his characters to manage them, or both, and then to consider the alterations made in the original. When the sources are scriptural or classical or are well-known medieval works, like the *Roman de la Rose*, we can assume that the members of Chaucer's audience, or at least many of them, remembered a great deal about the original and its implication, that alterations or gross misinterpretations would have been obvious to them, and, moreover, that these changes would often have produced smiles and even laughter among them. The story of Midas from Ovid's *Metamorphoses* (lines 1-193), introduced by the destruction of Orpheus at the hands of frenzied Thracian women, and the Wife of Bath's use of it have been examined perceptively, but in a rather general sense.[1] I should like here to examine these matters in more detail, since it seems to me that the story of Midas is reflected in the Wife's progress as she relates it in her *Prologue* and that it echoes in the *Tale* itself, forming a sort of theme that unfolds as the narrative progresses. In the development of the last point I shall advance an interpretation of the *Tale*, not altogether a new one, I confess. But I believe that some attention to the *Roman de la Rose*, long recognized as being significant because of the Wife's

---

1. Judson Boyce Allan and Patrick Gallacher, "Alisoun Through the Looking Glass: Or Every Man his own Midas," *ChauR* 4(1970):99-105.

obvious kinship with La Vieille,[2] will make the interpretation more cogent and enhance our appreciation for the wider significance of the story of Midas.

At the close of the Wife's *Prologue* the Friar laughingly comments on her "long preamble of a tale," a remark probably intended to suggest that her mental processes resemble the pace of the slow and easy "amblere" on which she is mounted. Neither her spurs nor the whip added by the Ellesmere illustrator seems to have been of much avail. The Summoner, irritated by the Friar's remark (for he is a rival of the Friar in seeking monetary gain from the people, corrupting the administration of God's justice for gain just as the Friar corrupts the administration of God's mercy for gain), responds (*WBP* D 837-39):

> "What! spekestow of preambulacioun?
> What! amble or trotte? — or pees! or go sit doun!
> Thou lettest oure disport in this manere."[3]

Women like the Wife, who enjoyed "compaignye in youthe" before her first marriage and who could not refuse "a good felawe," were useful to summoners, as the Friar reveals in his *Tale*. It is significant, however, that the "trot" is the conventional pace of an old woman in a hurry; hence the expression "old trot." Old women like the Wife do not move very fast. The Summoner is a despicable character, and his interference produces a promise from his rival to tell uncomplimentary

---

2. The Wife, of course, begins her *Prologue* by quoting La Vieille. M. S. Luria's observation, in *A Reader's Guide to the Roman de la Rose* (Hamden, Conn.: Archon, 1982), p. 84, that "the Wife of Bath is quite simply inconceivable without the antecedent conceptions of Jean de Meun in the *Roman*" seems quite just; further support for it will be offered below. For La Vieille's "sect" or "school" see the *Roman,* ed. Langlois, lines 13,475-13,498, or Charles Dahlberg's translation (Princeton, N.J.: Princeton University Press, 1971), p. 232. The idea is imitated by Boccaccio in *The Corbaccio*. See the translation by Anthony K. Cassell (Urbana: University of Illinois Press, 1975), p. 331 n. 223. It is fairly obvious that Chaucer must also have had La Vieille in mind when he had his learned Clerk refer to the Wife's "secte."

3. References and quotations, with some alterations in punctuation and spelling for clarity, are from Robinson's second edition of Chaucer's works (Boston: Houghton Mifflin, 1957).

tales about summoners,[4] so that even Harry Bailly, who is not exactly a penetrating character, says that the two ecclesiastics are behaving like "folk that dronken been of ale." But why did Chaucer place the Wife on an "amblere"? Had he seen wealthy female clothiers so mounted? Or is this, like much else in the Wife's *Prologue* and *Tale,* a literary echo?

The Wife begins her *Tale* with some humorous remarks about the unrestrained lechery of friars, remarks perhaps not altogether unwarranted,[5] though rather ironic in view of her own self-confessed worship of Venus and her gifts. She then introduces her protagonist, a "lusty bacheler,"[6] or young knight bachelor, riding "fro river," a phrase that implies a quest for venereal pleasure when the context supports such an interpretation, as it does in this instance, as well as the literal act of hunting for waterfowl, hawk on wrist, along a river.[7] For he meets a "mayde," whom he rapes at once, in spite of a legal death penalty for the deed.[8] King Arthur, at the plea of the queen and her ladies, turns his felon over to them for judgment, an action that does

---

4. This was not a difficult task, for summoners were notoriously corrupt. Cf. Brian L. Woodcock, *Medieval Ecclesiastical Courts in the Diocese of Canterbury* (Oxford: Oxford University Press, 1952), pp. 49, 111. In 1378 their extortionate practices provoked a parliamentary complaint. See *Rotuli Parliamentorum* (Record Commission, 1783), 3:43.
5. Cf. D. W. Robertson, Jr., *Chaucer's London* (New York: Wiley, 1968), pp. 192-96.
6. In the twelfth century Étienne de Fougères, who was chaplain to Henry II, complained: "Haute ordre fut chevalerie, / Mes or est ce trigalerie. / Trop aiment dance et balerie / Et demener bachelerie." See his *Le Livre des manières,* ed. J. Kramer, *AARP,* Vol. 39 (1887), lines 585-89. It is quite possible that *bachelerie* still had the connotations he suggested. Etienne was probably influenced by John of Salisbury, who severely condemned the kind of chivalric behavior exemplified in Chaucer's Squire.
7. See D. W. Robertson, Jr., *A Preface to Chaucer: Studies in Medieval Perspectives* (Princeton, N.J.: Princeton University Press, 1962), pp. 190-94, 209, 446; and D. W. Robertson, Jr., *The Literature of Medieval England* (New York: McGraw-Hill, 1970), p. 363, and the accompanying illustration.
8. Rape was a felony, like other felonies punishable by death in Chaucer's England. The ordinary penalty under the common law was hanging (left dangling without benefit of a trapdoor or a knot at the base of the skull), but other means of execution, including beheading with an ax, burial alive, and drowning were used under various borough jurisdictions. Chaucer may have thought beheading appropriate for a knight.

not comment very favorably on either the chivalric leadership or the administration of justice in England.⁹ The queen defers judgment, sending her knight off on a quest to discover "What thyng it is that wommen moost desiren" in order to save his life. At this point in the narrative we can anticipate that there will be one judgment — that of the queen — though Chaucer has another — that of the knight — in store for us. As a kind of prologue to these, he allows the Wife to suggest still another — that of Midas — though she omits the actual judgment and deals only with its consequences.¹⁰ This does not mean, of course, that either Chaucer's audience or the modern reader should forget about the actual judgment. It is quite likely that Chaucer's audience did not.

At this point I should like to digress for a moment to remind modern readers that in the later Middle Ages, and, indeed, even in the later sixteenth century, it was common to associate "wife" or "woman" with the flesh or sensuality.¹¹ This does not mean that actual women were thought to be necessarily either weak spiritually or without virtue. Among Chaucer's characters Constance and Saint Cecilia, as well as Griselda, who was regarded as an actual woman,¹² are good

---

9. One can hardly imagine a felony being transferred from King's Bench to a group of court ladies; indeed, although Alice Perrers for a time served on the council and may have intervened in court cases, the idea is laughable.

10. The importance of the theme of judgment in the Wife's *Tale* is emphasized by Allen and Gallacher in "Alisoun Through the Looking Glass."

11. See Robertson, *A Preface to Chaucer,* pp. 61-62, 69-75.

12. Thus Philippe de Mézières, in his *Letter to Richard II* of 1395, refers to "the authentic chronicle of the said Marquis of Saluzzo and Griselda his wife, written by that learned doctor and sovereign poet, Master Francis Petrarch." See the translation and edition of G. W. Coopland (New York: Cambridge University Press, 1976), p. 42. Philippe used the story, having first urged his readers to take the fruit and disregard the chaff, and echoing Petrarch's explanation (also used by Chaucer) in *Le Livre du sacrament de mariage et du reconfort des dames mariées*. See E. Golenistcheff-Koutouzoff, *L'Histoire de Griseldis en France au XIVe et au XVe siècle* (Paris: Droz, 1933), p. 156. In his own explanation Chaucer says that "sith a womman was so pacient / Unto a mortal man ..." (*ClT* E 1149-50). In other words, Griselda and her husband are exemplary rather than allegorical characters. Their relationship may resemble that between the faithful soul and God, but this does not mean that Griselda is the faithful soul or that Walter is God.

illustrations. Nevertheless, to live *muliebriter* was to live "softly" or "effeminately" with a concentration on fleshly comforts and satisfactions, these and related connotations being a classical inheritance reinforced among Christians by accounts of Eve's disobedience like that, for example, in Chaucer's *Parson's Tale* (I 321-35) and by tendencies to associate her with a kind of hedonistic weakness. To be truly "manly" was to act *viriliter,* or virtuously, facing trials and temptations, whether of the flesh or of the spirit, cheerfully and patiently in accordance with the precepts of charity. In some Hispanic circles this is still what is meant by "machismo," in spite of popular notions that this characteristic has something to do with violence. In her *Prologue* the Wife makes herself an exemplar of the disobedient flesh or sensuality in terms of both scriptural and classical imagery. As we shall see, she does not regard women very highly in her *Tale,* and I think that we can evaluate what she says more justly if we keep the figurative connotations of "wife" or "woman" in mind. Perhaps I should stress once more that these are "figurative" connotations, not to be taken too literally and applied as a stereotype, as John Knox may have done in his *First Blast of the Trumpet Against the Monstrous Regiment of Women,* which made him a despicable figure to that very "virile" lady, Queen Elizabeth I of England.

Returning to the *Tale* itself, we find that the knight roams far and wide seeking an answer to the royal question, only to find a variety of opinions not very complimentary to women. The Wife herself agrees at least partly with that opinion advanced by some that women have a weakness for flattery and attentiveness. Others say that women, no matter what they do, dislike being reprimanded or corrected, an idea that, as we shall see, probably derived from the advice of Amis in the *Roman de la Rose.* Others affirm that women like to be held trustworthy and capable of keeping secrets, though the Wife, having confessed that she betrayed the secrets of her old husbands, comments that "we wommen konne no thyng hele" and illustrates this point by mistelling the story of Midas, omitting the first part, altering the betrayer of Midas's secret so as to blame his wife rather than his barber, who whispered it into a hole in the ground, and the reeds, which whispered it again when they grew in the spot where the secret was buried. The Wife omits the reeds altogether. "Redeth Ovide," the Wife says, and that is very good advice indeed, for, as Judson B. Allen and Patrick Gallacher have pointed out, "she has mistaken the moral tone of her exemplum."[13] In fact, this is putting it rather mildly, for she has misinterpreted it completely and changed it in order to do so. Through a bit of masterful Chaucerian irony, however, the actual implications of what she says are not very different from those of the original.

To see this, we must examine Ovid's story. As he explains, Midas, who rescued and then wined and dined Silenus, the foster-father of Bacchus, first betrayed his foolishness by requesting as a gift from grateful Bacchus the power to turn everything he touched into gold. Bacchus granted the gift, but Midas found that his food turned to gold so that he could not eat and that wine mixed with water turned to molten gold when it touched his lips, so that he narrowly avoided the fate of Crassus (*TC*, 3.1390-91), with whom Chaucer compared him. This turn of events may be said to illustrate the rather commonplace idea that miserliness prevents other fleshly satisfactions, even proper nourishment.[14] In any event, when Midas in desperation again solicited the aid of Bacchus, he was offered a cure. He could bathe himself in a fountain at the source of the river Patoclus, afterward famous for the gold found in it, and there wash away his sin — a remedy that would have had rather obvious connotations to medieval readers.

Yet when he had accomplished this cure, Ovid assures us, Midas remained stupid — *pingue sed ingenium mansit* — or, somewhat more accurately, heavy and dull of understanding. True, he abandoned his passion for wealth, but instead of living in moderation, he devoted

---

13. Allen and Gallacher, "Alisoun Through the Looking Glass," p. 101. The authors go on to quote the moralization by Giovanni del Virgilio, which, though useful, pays insufficient attention, I believe, to the Ovidian context of the story.

14. Cf. the remark of the Third Vatican Mythographer in G. H. Bode, *Scriptores rerum mythicarum Latini tres Romae nuper reperti* (Cellis, 1834; reprint, Hildesheim: Georg Olms, 1968), line 227: "Midas, that is, one called 'knowing nothing,' for a miser is so stupid that he does not know how to benefit himself." This is echoed by Thomas Walsingham, *Archana Deorum*, ed. Robert A. van Kluyve (Durham, N.C.: Duke University Press, 1968), pp. 161-62. In his chapter on how "Epicureans never attain their goal" *(Pol.* 8.24), John of Salisbury observes that "the miser hungers in the midst of wealth." Cf. Panofsky's remark on Poussin's painting, quoted below.

himself to the half-goat Pan, the god of nature and the ruling deity of Arcadia, and took up his habitation in caves. As Ovid tells us elsewhere, the Arcadians lived like beasts,[15] for they devoted themselves to immediate fleshly satisfactions, usually unavailable, we remember, to misers. Leaving Ovid for a moment, we observe that what this meant in medieval Christian terms was that Midas began following the "law of kinde," as Chaucer calls it in *The Book of the Duchess,* or that of the Age of Nature between the Fall and the imposition of the Law of Moses,[16] when, as Paul says (Rom. 5:13), "sin was not imputed." Everyone could do what he pleased without being called a "sinner," and as an act of self-defense men began arranging themselves in hierarchies and establishing laws, which would not be necessary if everyone behaved reasonably. We shall consider this concept later. Meanwhile, to return to Ovid, in whose works Christians could find many ideas parallel to their own, Pan grew proud, and, while singing songs to soft nymphs and playing on his pipes made of reeds held together with wax — the transformed Syrinx, who was turned to reeds in her effort to escape the unwelcome attentions of the half-goat — boasted that his music was superior to that of Apollo, god of truth and wisdom.

The mountain god Tmolus heard of this boast and decided to hold a musical contest between Pan and Apollo, where a judgment could be made about the merits of the two melodies. There Pan played on his seductive reeds, and Apollo played with great artistry upon his beautifully decorated lyre. Tmolus and all those assembled save Midas alone held the music of Apollo to be superior. For his foolish judgment Apollo

15. *Fasti* 2.289-92. Cf. the quotation from Samuel Butler in Erwin Panofsky, "Et in Arcadia ego," in *Meaning in the Visual Arts* (New York, 1955), pp. 297-98. Panofsky accuses Ovid of neglecting the music of Arcadia, but Ovid certainly does not do so in the story of Midas.

16. This was a commonplace idea. See, e.g., Thomas Wimbleden in his famous sermon "Redde racionem villicacionis tue," ed. Nancy H. Owen, *MS* 28(1966): 178. The "law" of the chaotic time between Adam and Moses that produced the Flood and the Tower of Babel resulted from a self-protective desire to establish hierarchies in human societies. Their governance was modified first by the rigorous law of Moses and finally by the New Law of Christ. The continued existence of hierarchies was thought to be made necessary by "natural" regressions toward the Law of Nature after the Fall or in the direction of the Law of Moses unfulfilled by the New Law, either of which might produce tyranny.

caused Midas to grow the ears of a "slow-stepping ass" (*lente gradientis aselli*). The *asellus,* parenthetically, as distinct from the *asinus,* designated a small ass or colt noted not only for its figurative "deafness," as in the proverbial expression echoed by Horace (*Epist.* 2.1.199-200), "scriptores autem narrare putaret asello / fabellam surdo" but also in classical parlance for its use as an exemplar of lecherous persons. The Wife, of course, shares these characteristics.

It is not surprising, therefore, that she says nothing about all this, confining herself to a misrepresentation of what Ovid says afterward. This does not mean, however, that either Chaucer or many in his audience were ignorant of the entire story, for Ovid was a common schoolboy text. Indeed, it is highly probable that the "slow-stepping ass" offered the suggestion for the Wife's "amblere." Chaucer could hardly have presented a wealthy west-country clothier mounted on a small ass without creating a very clear absurdity, but he could put her on a slow-stepping "amblere" and then include a suggestive discussion of her "preamble." It is generally true that we can say of the pilgrims to Canterbury "by their mounts ye shall know them," or at least something significant about them. We can, in fact, attribute to the Wife the ears necessary to convert her mount.

Be that as it may, the judgment of Midas was a famous event duly celebrated in later European art, albeit in a somewhat indirect manner. Thus around 1630, Gaspard Poussin completed two paintings, companion pieces. The first showed Midas washing his face in the Patoclus to get rid of his first gift from Bacchus, and the second placed a tomb in the midst of Arcadia topped by a skull, perhaps reflecting Paul's (Rom. 5:14) "but death reigned from Adam unto Moses." Erwin Panofsky observed that "the two compositions thus teach a twofold lesson, one warning against a mad desire for riches at the expense of the more real values of life, the other against a thoughtless enjoyment of pleasures soon to be ended."[17] Later on, the romantics changed the meaning of the expression *et in Arcadia ego* into a nostalgic recollection of youthful pleasures, indicating that they had once been in Arcadia themselves.[18] Indeed, the desire to escape from civilized restraints

---

17. Panofsky, *Meaning in the Visual Arts,* p. 312.
18. Ibid., p. 319, and illustration no. 94.

into Arcadias of various kinds seems to be perennial. The Garden of Deduit in the *Roman de la Rose,* reflected in January's garden in Chaucer and in many other places, still lures us.

In this connection it is significant that the Wife, as she describes her career in her *Prologue,* has undergone exactly the progress of Midas. That is, in her youth she devoted her efforts to the acquisition of wealth, perhaps early in her life with the connivance of summoners, but certainly in her marriages to her old husbands. But she abandoned all of this wealth when she was forty for the joys promised by the legs and feet "so clene and faire" of the twenty-year-old Jankyn. Significantly, this is exactly the reverse of the progress of one of her chief mentors and predecessors, La Vieille in the *Roman de la Rose,* who tells us that in her youth she wasted her energies in the pursuit of pleasure but learned when older and wiser to use her favors to acquire wealth.[19] Chaucer's alteration of Jean de Meun, to whom we shall return shortly, in this respect was clearly influenced by the fact that he had Midas in mind. In her early career the Wife follows the teaching of La Vieille but not her example. Ultimately, she claims to have satisfied both her lust and her avarice by recovering the land she abandoned to gain Jankyn's solaces, thus embracing both of Midas's weaknesses at once. That this is a perilous course is well illustrated by the fates of her old husbands, who were both avaricious and lecherous. In Ovidian terms it does not speak well for her *ingenium,* and in terms of English law her specific stratagem was impossible if we regard her as a freeholder.

We have not yet examined the part of Midas's career that the Wife does use, and here we return once more to Ovid. In shame poor Midas sought to conceal the disfigurement wrought upon him by Apollo, but it was revealed indirectly by his barber, who discovered it. Unable to keep the secret of his master's disgrace, he whispered it into a hole in the ground and there buried it. Some "sly reeds," as James Joyce called them in one of his lyrics, grew up in the place and whispered the buried words, thus revealing them. The soft, complaining sound of the reeds into which Syrinx had been transformed had first suggested to Pan the possibility of using them to make his instrument, or "syrinx."

---

19. Langlois, lines 12, 761-12,835, Dahlberg, trans., pp. 222-23.

Actually, therefore, just as the inadequacies of Pan were betrayed by his "syrinx," so also was Midas betrayed by the same agency. This is another way of saying that devotees of the "music" of Pan are betrayed by it, becoming in Boethian language "asses to the harp," having ears, but because of a certain dull bestiality becoming deaf to the harmonies of truth and wisdom.[20]

The Christian parallel to this idea is not obscure. In Matthew 13, when Christ was asked by his disciples why he spoke in parables, he replied in part (13:13-15):

> Therefore do I speak to them in parables: because seeing they see not, and hearing they hear not, neither do they understand. And the prophecy of Isaias is fulfilled in them, who saith: By hearing you shall hear, and shall not understand: and seeing you shall see, and shall not perceive. For the heart of this people is grown gross, and with their ears they have been dull of hearing, and their eyes they have shut: lest at any time they should see with their eyes, and understand with their heart, and be converted, and I should heal them.

Apollo, we may recall, was not only a god of prophecy, revealing the past, the present, and the future, but the god of healing. As Phoebus he also enabled those who could see to see. Meanwhile, it is significant that hearing and sight are coupled in the scriptural passage, and I believe that a failure to see has much to do with subsequent events in the Wife's *Tale*.

Before pursuing this topic, we should consider briefly what the Wife does with the story of Midas, to show that women can conceal nothing. In her version the wife of Midas, her own invention, discovers her husband's long, hairy ears, goes down to the mire, and there "booms like a bittern," urging the quiet waters not to reveal the secret. She has little to fear from the waters, but the bittern, as the article on the bird in the eleventh edition of *Encyclopaedia Britannica* explains, has a very "loud and awful voice," so that it is quite unlikely that any further revelations were necessary to spread her message abroad. Who,

---

20. For the image in Boethius, see *Cons.* 1 pr. 4 in Robinson, p. 323. This became a popular figure in the visual arts.

we should ask, was the "wife" of Midas? The solution I am about to suggest may be somewhat easier to understand if we recall that under the laws governing real property in England a husband and wife were regarded as a single person, so that, for example, a husband could not confer lands on a wife, and a wife could not confer lands on her husband. A man might give a woman lands as a precondition of marriage, but he could not do so after the marriage took place. If we recall further the figurative connotations of "wife" referred to earlier, we may conclude that Midas was betrayed by his sensuality, though the Wife herself does not understand this, having made herself into a kind of exemplar of the sensuality and at the same time "deaf" to any wisdom that may be implied in a text. As Richard Hoffman observed,

> "Since, as we have seen, the Wife of Bath — even more than the Samaritan woman before her — was similarly deaf to the words of Christ and the New Law [and, we might add, to the words of Ovid], but most responsive to the fleshly Old Song of Pan, she too may be characterized with the ass's ears of Midas."[21]

That is, in effect, the Wife is both Ovid's Midas and her own "wife" of Midas, and she has been talking about herself without knowing it. In this respect she resembles her predecessor La Vieille, who does not understand her own exempla.[22] The Wife's resemblance to these figures gives her, figuratively, those long, hairy ears of the classical *asellus* bestowed by Ovid on Midas, quite in keeping with her own deafness and lechery. Her voice, meanwhile, like that of the ass or that of Midas's wife, is by no means subdued. In short, she is herself quite sufficient to transform her "amblere" into a kind of image of Ovid's "slow-stepping ass."

Having pretty thoroughly explored the shortcomings of those who "hearing ... hear not," Chaucer now turns his attention to those who "seeing ... see not," exemplified in the person of the Wife's protagonist, the young knight. In terms of Christ's words in Matthew, if a person cannot hear the message of wisdom, he cannot see either, remaining, as it were, blind, like January, for example, who is still blind

---

21. Richard I. Hoffman, *Ovid and the Canterbury Tales* (Philadelphia: University of Pennsylvania Press, 1967), pp. 147–48.

after he recovers his sight, or Almachius, or other characters who like Chauntecler "wynken" when they should see. Our young knight, having discovered no consensus among those he has consulted to discover "what women most desire," turns homeward. On the way he encounters more than twenty-four ladies "upon a daunce," a rather fetching sight under ordinary circumstances, reminiscent of the "women enowe" dancing about the Temple of Venus in *The Parliament of Fowls,* who are there, Boccaccio says, because such sights "incite much when seen by the libidinous."[23] The knight's libido has cooled somewhat because of the impending court decision, and he approaches the ladies seeking wisdom (line 994) rather than more immediate satisfactions. And indeed he discovers an opportunity to exercise it, for the dancing ladies vanish, and there instead is a single woman, "a fouler wight ther may no man devyse." Allen and Gallacher observe that "it is obvious that the loathly lady is the Wife's surrogate, her representation."[24] But so are the "more than twenty-four ladies." That is, they represent the Wife of Bath as she might have been seen by her avaricious old husbands, a kind of paradise of earthly delights not unlike January's May, offering a round of solaces, not to mention the profits of her fulling mill. Just as the ears of the lecherous may find the seductive music of Pan attractive indeed, leading to a realm where "no sin is imputed" and one may do as one pleases quite freely, so those seeking wisdom at the feet of Apollo may find it contemptible. We have not witnessed a magical transformation, no miracle, but simply a shift in point of view. The best discussion of the Wife's "miracles," I believe, appears in Robert P. Miller's *"The Wife of Bath's Tale* and Medieval Exempla,"[25] in which a series of exempla illustrates the point

---

22. See Chauncey Wood, "La Vieille, False Love, and Boethius," *RLC* 51(1977): 336-42.
23. Boccaccio *Teseida,* ed. A. Roncaglia (Bari: Laterza, 1941), p. 418. On Boccaccio's notes, here quoted, see Robert Hollander, "The Validity of Boccaccio's Self-Exegesis in his *Teseide," M&H,* n.s., 8(1977):163-83. However, the point in question is clear enough without consulting Boccaccio.
24. Allen and Gallacher, "Alisoun Through the Looking Glass," p. 103.
25. Robert P. Miller, *"The Wife of Bath's Tale* and Mediaeval Exempla," *ELH* 32(1965):442-56. Cf. the conclusions reached by Bernard S. Levy, "The Wife of Bath's Queynte Fantasye," *ChauR* 4(1970): 117-22.

that whether something appears to be fair or foul depends entirely on the point of view, or more specifically on whether it is regarded with the fleshly or with the spiritual eye, with the senses or with the understanding. Our knight has, in effect, seen Duessa unclothed.

The old hag has a close cousin in the Synagogue as it was used in medieval art to represent Old Law carnality, rather than a specifically Jewish place of worship. She appears quite attractive in her representation on the west portal of Strasbourg Cathedral, as indeed she should, for in medieval Christian terms she has attracted many followers and indeed appeals to almost all men and women, as do all those "false" or "partial" goods described in *The Consolation of Philosophy* of Boethius. She may also be made to appear foul and old, however, as she is in Philippe de Mézières's *Figurative Representation of the Virgin Mary in the Temple*,[26] where she is "an old woman ... with a worn-out tunic reaching to the ankles made of plain-colored cloth, and a torn black mantle." Like the Wife of Bath, whose Old Law carnality is fully revealed in the little sermon she delivers at the beginning of her *Prologue,* she is a comic figure, for Philippe makes allowance for laughter at the point in his presentation where she is expelled from the scene. In the same way the Wife's stubborn foolishness must have produced laughter in Chaucer's audience.

Midas, who had unseeing eyes as well as deaf ears, could well see the difference between Pan's fragile instrument of reeds and wax and the elaborately decorated lyre of Apollo, or that between the half-goat and the magnificent figure of the god of Truth. The Wife's protagonist, like Midas, remained "fat-headed" even when the nature of what he had been pursuing was revealed. This time he acted out of fear rather than lust, and his fear led him to seek salvation from the same source from which he had sought it before. In the Wife's narrative he promises to reward his newly perceived mentor for assisting him, granting her anything she requires if she can offer a solution to his problem before nightfall. In effect he has once more allowed his senses to overcome his understanding. She in turn offers to satisfy the queen,

---

26. I quote Robert S. Haller's translation (Lincoln: University of Nebraska Press, 1971), p. 9.

whispering her solution to his problem in his ear. The two proceed together to the court, where the queen, together with "Ful many a noble wyf and many a mayde," not to mention a "wise" widow, sit to render judgment. The knight presents the hag's solution to these justices assembled, averring (lines 1038-40):

> "Wommen desiren to have sovereynetee
> As wel over hir housbond as hir love,
> And for to been in maistrie hym above."

This doctrine comes straight from the advice of Amis in the *Roman de la Rose*,[27] that cynical adversary of Reason who proceeds to remind his amorous disciple of the Golden Age, when all men were equally wealthy and men and women loved each other freely and naturally, before fraud, sin, misfortune, pride, covetousness, avarice, envy, and other vices created lordship and property. As Amis had described it elsewhere, the Golden Age was a time of flowers and idleness, a paradise of sensual delights like the Garden of Deduit or Pan's Arcadia. This is, of course, a distortion of the Golden Age as it was conventionally understood, a paradise of spiritual rather than sensual delights typified by Eden before the Fall.[28] Since the loss of this age, Amis says, women are not what they used to be, so that if a lover finds his beloved unfaithful, he should be blind to that fact and not chide her; he should neither mistrust nor reproach her but freely allow her to do as she pleases. If she beats or reviles him, or even pulls out his nails, he should not complain. If he takes another mistress, he should conceal the fact or beg for mercy if his fault is detected, using flattery and caresses, including sexual solaces. He must not boast about his beloved and must pamper her when she is ill. But, Amis adds, women are so

---

27. Lines 9443ff. For the whole passage see Langlois *Roman*, trans. Dahlberg, pp. 170-77. Cf. Luria's summary in *A Reader's Guide*, pp. 102-103. I have omitted a few details for the sake of brevity and recommend the original.

28. See the excellent discussion in John Fleming, *The Roman de la Rose* (Princeton, N.J.: Princeton University Press, 1969), pp. 145-54. The "worldly" version of the Golden Age is more or less natural among "worldly" people. It is not surprising, therefore, that when old Gonzalo in jest envisages a new Golden Age on the newfound isle Antonio should respond, "All idle — whores and knaves."

changeable that they are as hard to hold as is an eel caught by the tail in the Seine. In other words, women are pleasure-loving and fickle and desire always to have complete sovereignty, not unlike the women described in Pope's *Epistle to a Lady,* whose ruling passions are "the Love of Pleasure and the Love of Sway." These strictures, Amis says, do not apply to good women who govern themselves with virtuous restraint, a principle with which Pope would have agreed; unlike Pope, however, who celebrated a virtuous woman, Amis says that, although he has tested many, he has never found one virtuous.

Jean de Meun did not expect his readers to disregard the ironic implications of what his "characters," if we may call them that, said. It is clear on reflection that Amis is actually complaining about conditions that in many respects parallel conditions in Arcadia in his own Golden Age, actually the Age of Nature, when everyone did as he pleased before either the civil constraints of "lordship" or the spiritual constraints of the Law of Moses were established. As Paul aptly puts it (Rom. 3:20), "By the law is the knowledge of sin." Unfortunately, the "knowledge of sin" is not very helpful, and the Old Law was harsh and literal, remaining so until the New Law brought grace and a motivation to do the right thing and tempered justice with mercy to the repentant. Amis, however, finds himself in a world in which women are unrepentant sinners and recommends that men behave in the same fashion to protect themselves. Just as La Vieille believed that women are "naturally" promiscuous[29] and that there are no good men, so Amis finds men "naturally" promiscuous and believes that there are no good women. Both urge that one follow his or her "natural" inclinations in full freedom.

To return to the *Tale,* we find that the ladies of the court agree with the hag's teaching as it is repeated by the knight (lines 1043-45):

> "In al the court ne was ther wyf, ne mayde,
> Ne wydwe, that contraried that he sayde."

Clearly there were no "good women" there, only devotees of Pan who wished to behave "naturally" and did not hesitate to echo the

---

29. Langlois *Roman* 13,875-966, trans. Dahlberg, pp. 238-39; cf. lines 13,265-82, trans. Dahlberg, p. 229.

judgment of Midas, or, rather oddly, the teachings of Amis. The old hag, naturally delighted with this decision, immediately calls attention to her bargain with the knight and demands marriage as her reward, freely admitting that she is foul, old, and poor. What is worse, she also demands to be the knight's "love." The knight, who has actually been under her dominion ever since he went riding "fro river," is loath to accept his "wife" or "love" as he now perceives her, albeit without any real understanding. In other words, he has not yet recovered his amorous desire, and he says, with ironic truth, that she will be his damnation, adding (lines 1068-69):

> "Allas! that any of my nacioun
> Shoulde evere so foule disparaged be!"

As a matter of fact, persons of all ranks and estates in England had very clearly been pursuing wealth or Epicurean satisfactions, or both together, for some time. A glance through the Rolls of Parliament, the Statutes of the Realm, the Peace rolls, and borough court records will easily reveal the unpleasant facts, as indeed will a study of Chaucer's *General Prologue* to the *Tales*. It is almost as if justice in England had degenerated into the sort of thing represented by the decision of the queen and the assembled ladies as the Wife envisages them.

After a secret and at least on the knight's part woeful wedding, the couple retire to bed, where the husband continues his lamentations and maintains his distance from his bride. Discomfited, the bride inquires whether the treatment she is getting is the "lawe of Arthures hous"; it is certainly not the law as seen by the queen and her ladies. She adds that she not only is his wife and his love but she saved his life, a dubious claim, since she, in her other guise, endangered it in the first place. In his reply the knight complains that she is loathly, old, and of low lineage, characteristics that he should have recognized much earlier in his career. For this complaint, however, he receives a long and salutary lecture echoing, so to speak, the lyre of Apollo, but his mentor knows that because of his Epicurean inclinations he will not be able to understand its implications.

To his objection concerning her "kynde," or lineage, she replies that inherited lineage is worthless, since true nobility is a matter not of lineage but of virtue, citing correctly the views of some distinguished authorities like Dante and Boethius to make her point, a point also made, we may remember, in Chaucer's *Gentilesse* and illustrated vividly in the person of Griselda, who, we might observe, would have given small credence to the hag's conception of what women most desire. The doctrine, however, is conventional, frequently used to illustrate the point that persons of high estate have a special obligation to be virtuous, as part of their responsibility in governing others. She continues by praising voluntary poverty, using some well-known commonplaces to support her argument, and concludes by reminding her husband that the elderly should be respected, presumably because long experience has made them wise. All of this is followed by an amusing and, insofar as the knight is concerned, confusing non sequitur (lines 1217-18):

> "But natheless, syn I knowe youre delit,
> I shal fulfille youre worldly appetit."

Perhaps we should pause for a moment to consider why this is a non sequitur. If true nobility rests on virtue, then a noble person restrains his or her worldly appetites out of consideration for his or her fellows or sisters in whatever kind of community he or she belongs. A failure to discover women practicing such restraints, we remember, led Amis to the conclusion that there are no good women. Nor can one fulfill worldly appetites by willingly embracing poverty, like some obedient nun immured in a convent, as the very popular and somewhat "revolutionary" French poet Colardeau once movingly, but not very thoughtfully, demonstrated.[30] Finally, an old person like our old hag, however experienced she may be, is not an attractive object for a young man's sexual appetites, even though he may respect her for reasons that are, in the present circumstances of the marriage bed, irrelevant. For Chaucer's audience as for Shakespeare's, and even indeed for the Puritan audience of Marvell's "To His Coy Mistress," an error in logic by a speaker constituted a joke, a fact often missed by modern readers taught to rely on their feelings so that they tend to

---

30. See D. W. Robertson, Jr., *Abelard and Heloise,* ed. Norman Cantor (New York: Dial, 1972), pp. 207-14.

be serious-minded. More than an error in logic is here involved, however, for the old woman has, in effect, echoed both the music of Apollo and that of Pan. Which will the young knight choose?

Having heard all of this, the knight is confronted by a choice. He can choose between having his new wife, or what seems to him to be his new wife, either foul and old and faithful or young and fair but unreliable. This is also a choice described by Amis in his account of the jealous husband. Having cited "The Golden Book of Theofrastus" from Jerome's treatise *Against Jovinian* on the inconveniences of marriage, Amis complains that if a wife is both well-to-do and beautiful "everyone will run after her ... until in the end they will have her," a fact of which the Wife as she describes herself in her *Prologue* took full advantage. But if she is ugly, he adds, "she wants to please everybody," a conclusion that leads to the further observation that any woman, beautiful or ugly, can be led astray. Since the world is full of tyrants like the jealous husband, even though the ideal situation would be a return to Golden Age conditions where what might be called "the Franklin's Solution" (much hailed by modern Chaucerians) prevails,[31] the lover has no recourse but to submissiveness and deliberate blindness based on the assumption that there are no good women.

Our lover, however, has no need to pretend to be blind, for, as we have seen, submission to the music of Pan causes one to become both deaf and blind. The old woman has promised him that she will satisfy his worldly appetite, and, having no wish to argue with her, he leaves the decision up to her and freely grants her the sovereignty or "maistrie" she so strongly covets. Having acquired this, she promises to be both fair and good and (lines 1255-56)

> obeyed hym in every thyng
> That myghte doon hym plesance or likyng.

As R. P. Miller very appropriately remarks concerning the Wife:

> In her scheme the delights presented to the sensual will (or *worldly appetite*) are true; the vision of clerks produces the

---

31. Lines 9,421ff., trans. Dahlberg, pp. 169-70. On the Epicurean character of this "solution," see Robert P. Miller, "The Epicurean Homily on Marriage by Chaucer's Franklin," *Mediaevalia* 6(1980):151-79.

illusions. Her hero, then, is saved because he has joined the ranks of those who have achieved the state of mind in which, as Vincent of Beauvais described it, "that which is truly foul seems to them fair, and that which is harmful seems to them delightful."[32]

When sensuality dominates the reason, in other words, it can do no wrong. The queen's justice has succeeded only in returning her knight to the condition he suffered before he raped the maiden, and the Wife has inadvertently explained the nature of the marital bliss into which she led young Jankyn after she (an old woman) had obtained "al the soveraynetee."

Chauncey Wood says, regarding the misuse of exemplary stories by La Vieille, who is, like Horace's *asellus* or the Wife herself, deaf, that "this kind of literary joke is a delightful ornament if and when observed."[33] The Wife's misuse of the story of Midas is, indeed, a delightful ornament devised by Chaucer for the Wife's *Tale*. It evokes memories of *The General Prologue* and the Wife's long "preamble," lending added significance to both, and at the same time forms a thematic background for events in the *Tale* subsequent to its introduction. Moreover, once we have discovered the Wife's omissions and alterations in the story of Midas, we can also share in the laughter with which Chaucer's audience must have greeted the judgment of the queen and her ladies and the persistent foolishness of the protagonist. Instead of berating his wealthy female clothier as Gower might have done, Chaucer allows her to expose herself, for all the characters in her *Tale* except for the wronged maiden, who does not appear in person, are, in one way or another, reflections of the idea she represents, little images of the Wife dressed in new guises. Her solution to the problem of the tomb and skull in Arcadia, briefly glimpsed by her knight, is an old one: simply grow very long ears and blear the eyes so that the message of these omens cannot be heard and they become invisible. In times when most persons thought that they had immortal souls whose destinies were of some importance, the implications of these unpleasant presences were much more profound than

---

32. Miller, *"The Wife of Bath's Tale* and Mediaeval Exempla," p. 456.
33. Wood, "La Vieille," p. 341.

they might be today. The memento mori in its various forms, from early lyrics like "Death's Wither-Clench" to Poussin's painting, was designed not to encourage "Arcadian" attitudes like those expressed by the "riotours" in the second chapter of Wisdom but to induce repentance, for which Chaucer provided some sound instruction in the last of *The Canterbury Tales*.

The Probable Date and Purpose of Chaucer's *Troilus*

D. W. Robertson, Jr.

Medievalia et Humanistica. 13 (1985), pp. 143-171.

I.

Although it has long been customary to assign a date for Chaucer's *Troilus* during the period 1380-86, preferably toward its close, most Chaucerians have devoted little attention to events in England during that time. Since the poem was probably read before a court audience, some of whom, as Derek Pearsall has indicated, were men who were not only deeply interested but directly involved in those events,[1] we can hardly dismiss the historical situation as being irrelevant.

Generally speaking, it is safe to say that English prestige declined steadily after about 1370, that fears of invasion from abroad reached a kind of climax in 1385 and 1386, and that this situation was widely held to be the consequence of moral decline that led providentially to adversities,[2] an understandable attitude among men who were, like Chaucer himself, deeply moved by attitudes found in *The Consolation of Philosophy* of Boethius. The interests and attitudes of the time undoubtedly had much to do with the shaping of Chaucer's great poem, and unless we can share them, at least in imagination, we shall deprive ourselves of an opportunity to appreciate it. Unless we understand, if only in a general way, the purpose for which it was devised

---

1. See Derek Pearsall's perceptive and cogent article "The *Troilus* Frontispiece and Chaucer's Audience," *YES* 7 (1977), esp. pp. 73-74.
2. See, e.g., John Barnie, *War in Medieval English Society* (Ithaca. 1974), pp. 28, 103, and the sermons cited below.

and very carefully crafted, we can hardly appreciate the literary stratagems designed to fulfill it. In the following pages I shall discuss the relevant historical events, some basic attitudes, a few literary stratagems, and finally and very briefly the poem itself.

Concerning the probable character of the audience, Pearsall, in the article referred to above, argues that it included "household knights, career diplomats, and civil servants." Chaucer's own diplomatic missions were carried out under the auspices of the Chamber, which also came to serve eventually as the center of social activity at court, and may have been at least in part responsible for such activity at the time the poem was written.[3] Although the Chamber after 1356 no longer served as an administrative office for royal lands, it became increasingly important for its services on "the king's secret business," so that instead of the three Chamber knights in 1377, there were eleven by 1385, and seventeen in 1388. Richard often employed these men on his Council and rewarded them with lands and offices.[4] They included old followers of Prince Edward and friends of Princess Joan, who gathered about her a group of men interested in reform, and who for this reason have become known as "Lollard Knights," although their sympathies were probably more closely allied with the ideals of Philippe de Mézières than with those of John Wyclif.

It will suffice to mention a few of them and to supply some relevant facts about them, concentrating on the years before 1387. First, Sir Lewis Clifford, perhaps the godfather of Chaucer's son Lewis but in any event a close friend, had been both a squire and knight under Prince Edward, was a Garter Knight in 1377 and became a royal knight in 1381. He was among those appointed to remain with Princess Joan during Richard's foray into Scotland in 1385; and he, his son-in-law Philip la Vache, a Chamber Knight from 1378, Sir John Clanvowe, William Beauchamp, and many others were given livery of mourning for her after her death in August 1385. Clifford was one of

---

3. The social importance of the Chamber at a somewhat later date has been discussed by Richard Firth Green, *Poets and Princepleasers* (Toronto, 1980), chap. 2.
4. See the discussion by J. H. Tuck, *Richard II and the English Nobility* (London, 1973), pp.62-85.

her executors. He is said to have joined Philippe de Mézières's Order of the Passion whose aim was to establish an international crusading movement based on peace between France and England and governed by a strict moral discipline, either in 1385 or shortly thereafter. Clifford was abroad on diplomatic missions in late 1385 and early in 1386, bringing home with him on his return Deschamps's poem in praise of Chaucer.[5] The French poet had attended a peace conference in 1384.[6] Clifford's second mission was probably made in connection with John of Gaunt's forthcoming crusade, to which we shall return in a moment.

William Beauchamp, the younger brother of Thomas Beauchamp, Earl of Warwick (1339-1401), is said to have had a university education. He was Chamberlain between 1378 and 1381, and in May 1380 he, Sir John Clanvowe, Sir William Neville, and two prominent London merchants went with Chaucer before Bishop Sudbury, the Chancellor, to witness Cecily Champain's release of Chaucer from charges of rape or other trespasses.[7] His interest in the estate of his deceased friend John Hastings, Earl of Pembroke, led to a famous legal dispute, but it was not discreditable to him.[8] Chaucer probably accompanied him on a mission to Calais in 1387. Sir John Clanvowe, a Chamber Knight since 1382, was to write a transparently Chaucerian poem inspired partly

---

5. Information about some of the Chamber knights is available in W. T. Waugh, "The Lollard Knights," *Scottish Historical Review* 11 (1914): 55-92; and in Kenneth McFarlane, *Lancastrian Kings and Lollard Knights* (Oxford, 1972). McFarlane is, I think, too quick to attribute "Lollard" views to these men. Cf. F. R. H. Du Boulay, "The Historical Chaucer," in Derek Brewer, ed., *Geoffrey Chaucer* (London, 1974), pp. 45-46; D. W. Robertson, Jr., "Simple Signs from Everyday Life in Chaucer," in John P. Hermann and John J. Burke, Jr., eds., *Signs and Symbols in Chaucer's Poetry* (University, Alabama, 1981), pp. 18-19; and Paul Strohm, "Chaucer's Fifteenth-Century Audience and the Narrowing of the Chaucer Tradition," in Roy J. Pearcy, ed., *Studies in the Age of Chaucer* 4 (1982):9-13.

6. J. J. N. Palmer, *England, France and Christendom* (London, 1972), pp. 33, 37, 228. The subject of Chaucer's connections with French poets is now being explored by James I. Wimsatt.

7. See Martin M. Crow and Clair C. Olson, *Chaucer Life-Records* (Oxford, 1966), pp. 343, 347.

8. R. Ian Jack, "Entail and Descent: The Hastings Inheritance," *BIHR* 38 (1965): 1-11.

by *The Parliament of Fowls,* and partly by the Knight's Tale, as well as a moral treatise, *The Two Ways,* possibly for the child of a friend or an ecclesiastic engaged in elementary teaching.[9] He was, like Clifford, busy abroad in connection with arrangements for Gaunt's crusade in the early part of 1386. Also like Clifford, he was one of Joan of Kent's executors. His friend William Neville, a very close companion, had been a knight of King Edward's household and a Chamber Knight after 1381. Toward the close of their careers they participated together in Louis of Bourbon's unsuccessful crusade.

Among the knights closely associated with Princess Joan was Sir Richard Stury, who was ransomed along with another royal squire, Geoffrey Chaucer, after Edward's campaign of 1359. Whereas Chaucer brought only £16 to his captors, Stury, who was praised for his bravery by Froissart, was worth £50. He became a Chamber Knight some time around 1371 and thereafter served frequently on diplomatic missions. Unfortunately, at the "Good Parliament" of 1376, where he served as *prolocutor,* he reported to the king that the Commons were seeking to depose him, and for this indiscreet exaggeration he was banished from the court and lost the friendship of Prince Edward, who was sympathetic with the reformers. The court and Princess Joan soon forgave him, however, and in 1377 he was engaged in peace negotiations with the French, seeking a marriage between young Richard and a French princess, in company with Guichard d'Angle (d. 1380), who was one of Richard's tutors and a friend of both Oton de Granson and Deschamps. With them was Geoffrey Chaucer, probably in a clerical capacity.[10] Stury, who headed a commission of walls and ditches of which Chaucer was a member in 1390, was an active diplomat and member of the Council until his death in 1395. His literary interests are attested by the fact that he owned a copy of the *Roman de la rose* (BL MS Royal 19 B XIII), one of Chaucer's favorite books. Sir John Montagu, a royal knight after 1383 and heir to the earldom of Salisbury through his uncle, was closely associated with these men and was a

---

9. These have been edited with an introduction by V. J. Scattergood, *The Works of Sir John Clanvowe* (Totowa, N.J., 1975). The conjecture about the purpose of the treatise is my own.

10. *Life-Records,* pp. 49-53.

poet in his own right, admired for his work by Christine de Pisan, a lady of ready if not always astute moral sensibilities.

It is fairly safe to assume that one or more of these men formed a part of the audience who assembled to hear Chaucer read his poem. We should also include John Gower and Ralph Strode, the Oxford logician who had become Common Pleader for the City of London, since both are mentioned at the close of the poem. And if the date about to be suggested is credible it would not be rash to include John of Gaunt and some of those planning to accompany him in Spain, including Chaucer's son Thomas. We should also expect some ecclesiastics like Thomas Rushook, Richard's confessor, who was transferred from Llandaff to Chichester in 1385; clerks of both the royal and Lancastrian households; and ladies, including Philippa Chaucer, with their handmaidens. (The apology to the ladies toward the close of the poem implies their presence.) We have no means of knowing how large the audience was, but we can be fairly certain that it was requested for a specific social occasion, attended by persons of some prominence, that might involve at least five days of festivities. It is unlikely that Chaucer wrote anything very extensive without considering the possibility of an occasion for its public delivery; and it seems very likely that a friend, or group of friends, seeking to help him increase his prestige, asked him to prepare what he had written for presentation at a specific time and place.

II.

Before speculating about the occasion and the individual or individuals responsible for Chaucer's appearance, I shall review briefly certain aspects of events in England that contributed to a loss of national prestige. As George Holmes has well described them, English fortunes had been gloomy before the Good Parliament of 1376.[11] King Edward had not kept a firm hand on his government during the last years of his reign, and with the transition to the new reign matters were not much improved, especially from a military point of view. The

---

11. *The Good Parliament* (Oxford, 1975), pp. 21-62.

Aquitaine won by Edward in the Treaty of Bretigny was drastically reduced by French forces under du Guescelin in 1372, and in the early summer of 1373 he retook much of Brittany. The English response, a naval expedition led by the king, lasted only a few weeks, although a force led by Sir John Neville of Raby took and held Brest, which was besieged. In March 1373 Sir William Montagu, Earl of Salisbury, failed to relieve the siege. In July Gaunt undertook his famous march from Calais to Bordeaux but did not relieve Brittany, perhaps because he thought Aquitaine more important. During 1374 and 1375 the French outmaneuvered the English both diplomatically and militarily, so that when the Good Parliament met the lords had no successes to proclaim, there was a very real threat of attack on the coasts by Castilian naval forces, and Charles V was readying his own naval forces to be used on the expiration of a truce. Indeed, in 1377 the French captured Rye, burned Lewes, overran the Isle of Wight, and burned Hastings.[12] The Scots massacred a gathering at a fair at Roxburgh, and the Duke of Anjou successfully invaded Gascony. In that year Peter de la Mare, a protege of Edmund de Mortimer, Earl of March, who was once more speaker for the Commons in Parliament, complained that English chivalry had once been "most energetic, ardently desirous of great enterprises, each man eager to perform great deeds of arms, one above the other," but, he lamented, it is now "together with all other virtues placed behind; vice is praised, advanced, honored, and not at all chastised" (*RP,* 3:24). We should notice that "chivalry" is here regarded, as it is in Chaucer's description of his Knight, as a virtue, not as a form of outmoded and empty panoply. Memories still lingered of King Edward's cultivation of chivalric virtue in the Order of the Garter and in tournaments to stimulate the courage and dedication of his followers that had produced such obvious success abroad.[13] The new reign with its child king had nothing to compare with it.

---

12. See C. F. Richmond, "The War at Sea," in Kenneth Fowler, ed. *The Hundred Years War* (London, 1971), pp. 115-16.
13. The connotations of the word *chivalry* were still very much like those associated with the good knight by John of Salisbury, *Policraticus,* 6:2-19. Attitudes toward it varied, however. See Barnie's discussion, *War in Medieval English Society,* chap. 3.

In the following year Gaunt besieged St. Malo, but probably because of the negligence of the Earl of Arundel in preparing a mine the siege had to be abandoned, a fact that sullied Gaunt's reputation. Castilian galleys attacked Cornwall and burnt the town of Fowey, and it became evident that the government was in serious financial difficulties. In 1379 Sir John Arundel, the Marshall, after the south coast had been ravaged by his own troops, set out for Brittany (according to Walsingham's gossip taking with him nuns seized as companions for his men), only to have his fleet, his troops, and himself, not to mention the alleged nuns, destroyed in a storm. The Scots attacked in the north in 1380. Thomas of Woodstock conducted a great raid from Calais to Brittany, encouraging the disheartened Commons to levy the now-famous poll tax. It was well intentioned enough, designed as a substitute for the old levies of a tenth and a fifteenth that had demanded a fixed sum from each locality and had now become inequitable; but it was so poorly administered that it precipitated the Great Revolt of 1381, which had clearly been brewing before the allegations in Parliament in 1377 concerning "counsellors, abettors, and maintainers in the country," who for their own profit had used "exemplifications out of the Book of Domesday" to cause villeins to refuse their customary services, to menace ministers of their lords, and to gather in "great routs" threatening force (1 R II 7, *SR,* 2:3; cf. *RP,* 3:21).

In his remarkable address to Parliament in 1381 *(RP,* 3: 100-101) Sir Richard Waldgrave, the Speaker, painted a depressing picture of the state of the kingdom, urging that "if the government of the realm is not within a short time amended, the realm itself will be completely lost." He spoke of the "outrageous number of familiars" in the household and of corruption in the courts, including the Chancery, the King's Bench, and in the Exchequer. There were, he said, outrageous numbers of quarrels and maintainers (probably referring in part to those who were profitably encouraging villeins to abandon their services) who were like kings in the country so that right and loyalty were made to hardly anyone.[14] In language reminiscent of

---

14. For the general situation, see J. R. Madicott, *Law and Lordship,* Past and Present Supplement 4 (1978). Edward and his Council had ordained in 1346 (*SR,* 1:303-6) that justices "do equal law and execution of right to rich and poor

Archbishop Mepham,[15] he complained of "the purveyors for the said household of the king and of others," referring to the higher nobility, who "pillage and destroy the people,"[16] and of the "subsidies and tallages" levied to their great distress. The ministers of the king and of others, he said, commit "grievous and outrageous oppressions"; great treasure was levied for the defense of the realm, but the people were nevertheless "burned, robbed, and pillaged" by their enemies from abroad, and no remedy was provided.[17] These things and others, he said, had moved the "lesser commons" to riot and make mischief, and he warned that greater mischiefs might ensue. This was a

---

without having regard to any person," that justices disregard royal letters or other letters contrary to right and justice, that they take fees and robes from no one except the king, that they should counsel great and poor alike, and that they should take no gifts "except meat and drink, and that of small value." The justices of assize were to inquire of "sheriffs, escheators, bailiffs of franchises, and their under ministers, and also of ministers, common embracers, and jurors in the county, of the gifts, rewards, and other profits which the said ministers do take of the people to execute their office, and for making array of panels, putting in the same suspect jurors and of evil fame, and of maintainers, embracers, and jurors that do take rewards against the parties, whereby losses and damages do come daily to the people, in subversion of the law." Justices were required to take an elaborate oath to fulfill the terms of the ordinance. As Madicott shows, however, the ordinance was not well observed.

15. *Speculo regis Edwardii III*, ed. J. Moisant (Paris, 1891), who attributed the two "recensions" he published to Simon Islip, although they are now usually attributed to Mepham and dated ca. 1330. On the traditional character of the complaints in this work, see G. L. Harriss, *King, Parliament, and Public Finance in Medieval England* (Oxford, 1975), chap. 5.

16. Edward had issued what has been called "the principal statute of the Middle Ages on the subject" of purveyance in 1362. See Harriss, *King, Parliament*, p. 376. This provided that purveyors for the household now be called buyers, that the prices paid be those of nearby markets, that indentures be used instead of wooden tallies on which the persons, quantitites, and prices should be clearly recorded, that no menace be used, no bribes taken, and that a commission be appointed in every county to inquire into abuses. Similar rules applied to the purveyors for the households of magnates. The statute was unfortunately not well observed. Waldgrave's complaint in some ways resembles the petition of the clergy in 1377. See Dorothy Bruce Weske, *Convocation of the Clergy* (London, 1937), pp. 72-73.

17. Cf. Eleanor Searle, *Lordship and Community: Battle Abbey and Its Banlieu* (Toronto, 1974), p. 345.

thoroughly reputable analysis.[18] Running through it is the theme that greed and self-interest were corrupting the administration of justice at home and, at the same time, weakening the defense of the realm against its enemies abroad.

Jealousies and factions began to make themselves apparent at court, while the situation abroad deteriorated. When the Revolt shook the kingdom, Gaunt, whose magnificent house in London, the Savoy, was destroyed, had been negotiating with the Scots, who treated him with respectful deference and even offered to assist him when Henry Percy sought to prevent his return to England. A bitter quarrel resulted, resolved only when Percy made a formal apology in Parliament. In 1382 Philip van Artevelde acknowledged Richard to be king of France, but the forces he assembled against the French were annihilated and he was himself killed. In October Bishop John Gilbert told Parliament that England had never been in greater danger of invasion. Brigandage was rife in the country, and many ships were destroyed off the northern coast. The disastrous crusade of Bishop Despenser of Norwich in 1383 and Richard's failure to assist him after his initial success hardly improved matters, and in 1384 Philip of Burgundy took control of the Netherlands but left Ghent its municipal freedom. England was fast losing its Continental allies and with them the protection of its trade.

At home factionalism grew at court, and morale was shaken by the quick temper of the young king and by his clear tendency to place his personal interests above the common profit of the realm. He was preoccupied with his favorites, the most prominent of whom was the youthful Robert de Vere, Earl of Oxford, who was spoiled by the king and easily moved to jealousy. He was undoubtedly responsible for suborning a Cannelite friar to accuse John of Gaunt before the king of

18. We might add that lesser ecclesiastics were increasingly suffering excommunication for failure to pay subsidies. See J. Donald Logan, *Excommunication and the Secular Arm in Medieval England* (Toronto, 1968), pp. 54-57, and the table on p. 68. As the peace rolls reveal, impoverished chaplains were turning to crime. There was, meanwhile, a growing tendency toward oligarchical government in the towns, causing discontent among lesser tradesmen. As R. B. Dobson has observed, *The Peasants' Revolt of 1381* (London, 1970), p. 13, the. "traditional description of the 1381 rising as a 'Peasants' Revolt' ... is in itself deceptive."

seeking to kill him and seize the kingdom. This incident occurred at the Salisbury Parliament, where Richard told the Earl of Arundel to "go to the Devil" when he criticized the government of the realm. De Vere probably hoped that Richard's quick temper would move him to precipitous action against Gaunt. Indeed, the king is said to have gone into a tantrum and to have thrown his hat and shoes out the window, and Thomas of Woodstock, betraying an equal lack of self-control, is said to have drawn his sword and threatened to kill anyone who called his brother a traitor.[19] Gaunt was able to calm the king. But de Vere tried again early in 1385, this time by arranging a meeting of the Council at Waltham, where he hoped to have Gaunt accused, tried, and executed for treason by suborned justices. But the Duke heard of the plot and refused to attend; instead, he confronted Richard at Sheen with an appropriate military following. The two were finally reconciled by Princess Joan, who brought them together at Westminster, Richard having meanwhile drawn his sword before Archbishop Courtenay when he, together with some members of the Council, sought to reprimand him, as they met on barges on the Thames, for plots like that against Gaunt.

III.

Since *Troilus* is usually assigned to the latter part of the period 1380–86, it will repay us to examine the last two years in some detail, including events in the lives of Chaucer and his family. In France Charles VI assembled a great fleet for the invasion of England and sent 1,600 men under Jean de Vienne to aid the Scots, planning a simultaneous attack on England from the south and the north. These actions produced widespread consternation in England, leading to preparations to defend the coast, to the requisition of convoys for the wine fleet, and to a depression in the rising cloth trade that lasted until 1388.[20]

---

19. A vivid account of these events is given by Sydney Armitage-Smith, *John of Gaunt* (London, 1904; repro N.Y., 1964), pp. 382–87.

20. On the cloth trade, see E. M. Carus-Wilson, "Trends in the Export of English Woolens in the Fourteenth Century," *EcHR* 2 Ser. 3 (1950–51):174. As she puts it, "These were years of panic and confusion in England."

The Chancellor, Michael de la Pole, realizing that the realm lacked financial resources for aggressive action, had been pursuing a determined peace policy toward France since 1383.[21] He now saw that policy collapsing before his eyes, while the "war party" at court, led by the Earls of Buckingham and Arundel, became more and more restive. Pole now resorted to an unsuccessful effort to raise scutage, which had not been levied for fifty years, to finance a campaign led by the king in Scotland. Richard summoned Gaunt, who led the largest force, to meet him at Newcastle on March 24.

Near York the king's half-brother, John Holland, killed young Richard Stafford, the son of the earl, in a quarrel. Richard was a royal favorite, and the king angrily avowed that he would treat Holland like any other felon, much to the distress of Princess Joan; but Holland fled into sanctuary at Beverley. As the army of almost 12,000 men crossed the border,[22] Richard, in a somewhat feeble imitation of Edward III, created two new dukes (his uncle the Earl of Cambridge became Duke of York, and his uncle the Earl of Buckingham, Thomas of Woodstock, the Duke of Gloucester) and knighted various other persons. The Scots and their French allies, confronted by much larger forces than their own, prudently retreated northward without a confrontation. Although Richard's articles of war had forbidden attacks on religious,[23] he burned two monasteries and would have burned a third had not Gaunt intervened. The army reached Edinburgh without a battle, and de Vere urged the king to return home, which he did. It is not surprising that Walsingham, echoing a charge at least as old as the *Aeneid*, said that the court circle was made up of "knights of Venus rather then of Bellona."[24] (Walsingham is a good source for popular gossip, or for propaganda spread by interested magnates,[25] and this

---

21. See Palmer, *England, France and Christendom*, chap. 3.
22. Armitage-Smith, *John of Gaunt*, pp. 295, 437-9. For the numbers, however, see Palmer, p. 60.
23. *Black Book of the Admiralty*, ed. Sir Travers Twiss (Rolls Series, 1871), 2:453.
24. Quoted by May McKisack, *The Fourteenth Century* (Oxford, 1959), p. 438. On the *miles amoris*, see D. W. Robertson, Jr., *A Preface to Chaucer* (Princeton, 1962), pp. 408-10.
25. Cf. Anthony Goodman, "Sir Thomas Hoo and the Parliament of 1376," *BIHR* 41 (1968):145.

probably represents fairly widespread opinion in the countryside.) In November de Vere was made Marquis of Ireland, and the Chancellor hoped to collect sufficient funds from a ransom for John of Blois, the claimant to Brittany, to finance his projected campaign in that country.

The French fleet was prevented from sailing by an action taken by the town of Ghent, which distracted the forces drawn up along the coast. Meanwhile, the news of the Portuguese victory at Aljubarotta, assisted by English archers, had reached England before Parliament met in October. The Commons, dissatisfied with Pole's management of the royal revenues and alarmed by invasion threats, was now prepared to listen favorably to Gaunt's proposals for a crusade in Spain, rejected earlier in favor of Despenser's crusade. A few days before the opening of Parliament Chaucer was appointed to a commission of the peace from Kent. Among his fellow justices was Sir Arnold Savage, who once accompanied Gaunt on a peace mission. He had been a member of the royal household since Richard's accession, his mother having acted as nurse to the young king. He had been knighted in Scotland. To anticipate a little, he was sheriff of Kent at the time of Chaucer's election to Parliament in 1386. Such elections were not "democratic" in the modern sense, and the sheriff himself, often dominated by any interested magnates, determined the outcome. There is no evidence that Chaucer was a prominent Kentish freeholder, and it is a fair assumption that his election resulted from favorable action on the part of someone of higher rank. Sir Arnold, who probably had some literary interests since he was later to act as executor for John Gower,[26] probably found such action congenial. He is said to have later joined Gaunt's crusade.

When Parliament met in October 1385, the government was heavily in debt, the people were not in the mood for heavy taxation, the successes of Edward III on the Continent were now nostalgic memories, clouded by the realization that the advantages he had gained had somehow faded away, and the country seemed hardly capable of

---

26. On Sir Arnold Savage, see J. S. Roskell, *The Commons and Their Speakers* (Manchester, 1965), pp. 139, 362. His famous address to the commons is recorded *RP,* 3:456.

defending itself. It was fairly easy to conclude that through "evil counsellors," or household extravagance and corruption, Richard, abetted by his favorites and the chancellor, had frittered away both the moral and the financial resources of his kingdom. Among his "extravagances" was a grant made to Chaucer under the signet (endorsed by de Vere) allowing him to appoint a permanent deputy at the wool wharf.[27] A bill introduced by the Commons demanded, among other things, that controllers and other customs officials perform their duties in person and not by deputy, and the entire bill was endorsed by the king. Michael de la Pole did nothing about it and, in fact, was probably responsible for having it removed from the rolls of Parliament. His action, or inaction, was largely responsible for his impeachment in 1386.[28] Chaucer and his friends probably knew that this bill was pending some time before Parliament met, and that it would eventually be implemented. The appointment to the peace commission probably resulted from their desire to increase his prominence in anticipation of an eventual loss of his position. In any event, Parliament granted a modest subsidy on the basis of the concessions represented in the bill, and approved Gaunt's crusade in Spain. Neither Richard nor his chancellor wanted a direct confrontation with France, and it is likely that for Gloucester and Arundel, Gaunt's venture represented positive and potentially fruitful action. It is possible also that Richard and his favorites were happy to have Gaunt out of the country, although in 1389, when de Vere was out of the way, Richard was anxious to have him back, and even assumed his livery when he returned. Meanwhile, those actively seeking peace with France may have thought that a diversion in Spain might help negotiations with the French, as indeed Gaunt's initial success in Asturias seemed to do. Meanwhile, however, the situation on the Continent was not improving, for Ghent capitulated to the French in December, assuring French control of the Low Countries.

27. *Life-Records,* pp. 168-69. Although de Vere endorsed the petition, he may have been urged to do so by someone else.
28. For the ordinance of 1385, omitted from the rolls of Parliament for that year, and for the Chancellor's neglect of it, see J. J. N. Palmer, "The Impeachment of Michael de la Pole," *BIHR* 42 (1969), esp. pp. 96-97, 100.

Some indication of the possible source of influence in assisting Chaucer is provided by the fact that on February 19, 1386, John of Gaunt personally supervised the admission of Philippa Chaucer, along with his son Henry of Derby (the future Henry IV) and certain other members of his family, including two sons of Philippa's sister Katherine Swynford, into the fraternity of Lincoln Cathedral. (Gaunt was lord of the castle at Lincoln and a patron of the cathedral, protecting its rights in the town.) Henry Percy, perhaps as a gesture of friendship, joined in the same year, and King Richard and Queen Anne joined in 1387 during their ramblings.[29] By the time of Philippa's admission to the Lincoln fraternity it had probably already been decided that Chaucer's son Thomas would accompany Gaunt on his crusade, where he evidently performed well, for the Duke granted him an annuity for life dated at Bayonne in 1389. During February John Holland agreed to furnish three chaplains for his victim Richard Stafford and was restored to favor. He allowed himself to be overcome by the charms of Gaunt's daughter Elizabeth, however, seduced her, quickly married her, and as a new member of the Lancastrian family, so to speak, was made Constable of the expeditionary force.[30] Meanwhile, Gaunt had obtained a papal bull endorsing his crusade and providing plenary pardons for all those who sided with him. The crusade was proclaimed publicly at St. Paul's on February 18, 1386, and the new bishop of Llandaff, William of Bottlesham, and John Gilbert, bishop of Hereford, roamed through the country preaching it, assisted by Carmelite friars. On Saturday March 25 at an elaborate ceremony of farewell, Richard presented gold crowns to King John of Spain, as Gaunt styled himself, and Queen Constance, who set off soon afterward toward Plymouth with their two remaining unmarried daughters and, probably, with an impressive entourage of household ministers, participants, and well-wishers.

29. J. W. F. Hill, *Medieval Lincoln* (Cambridge, 1948), p. 258 and note 4.
30. He was lavishly rewarded on his return to England and subsequently treated with great generosity by the king, who made him Duke of Exeter in 1397. He participated in a rebellion to restore Richard after his deposition and was beheaded on orders from the Countess of Hereford in 1400.

Meanwhile, diplomatic negotiations with the French continued. In February Richard lavishly entertained Leo of Armenia, who was seeking to establish peace between England and France so they could unite in a crusade against the Turks, whose threat to Christian territory was becoming steadily more alarming. The negotiations led to an agreement whereby Richard would meet King Charles and Philip of Burgundy on the Continent in March, and Richard granted Leo an annuity of £1,000.[31] Charles and Philip proceeded to Bologne, but Richard failed to arrive at Calais, since Michael de la Pole could not convince the French that Gaunt should be allowed to pursue his aims in Spain. Fears of invasion were by no means over in England, and in the spring, commissioners of array were sent to the southern counties, and the ports and the town of Calais were fortified. Military activity lapsed for a time in France, probably because of the illness of the Duke of Burgundy. A truce with Scotland, which had been deserted by Jean of Vienne, who did not like living conditions there, was signed on June 27, removing at least for a time the military threat from the north. But shortly after the departure of John of Gaunt in early July the French buildup on the coast resumed, and by September there was assembled the largest invasion fleet ever seen in Europe, with some 30,000 men and elaborate equipment for establishing footholds on the English coast. It was compared by one writer with the fleet that attacked Troy,[32] a comparison, as we shall see, that was not inappropriate. At some time during this period Clanvowe and his friend Neville were sent to help organize the defense of the south coast, where unpaid soldiers were being troublesome. The king, meanwhile, was rather ostentatiously disregarding the French and devoting his attention to de Vere's preparations for departure for Ireland, showering privileges and benefits on his favorite, who did not in fact depart.

Chaucer was elected to Parliament in September. By the time it met he had probably made arrangements to give up his residence at

---

31. See Palmer, *England, France and Christendom*, pp. 68-69. The material following relies heavily on this study, which sheds new light on the events of 1386 and on the motivation of Richard and his uncles.

32. Ibid., p. 74.

Aldgate, and on October 15, during the session, he gave his testimony at the Scrope-Grosvenor trial, an event that has led to a great deal of discussion about his assertion that he was "del age xl ans et plus armez par xxvii ans," which affords evidence of his approximate date of birth.[33] The trial actually allowed him to appear before a prominent gathering and, in addition, to make a favorable impression on the Scropes, one of the most prominent families in England.[34] John of Gaunt and his followers had given their testimony (in favor of the Scropes) at Plymouth before their departure for Spain, and it is quite possible that the Duke arranged for Chaucer to testify. At Parliament the Commons was ready to join the "war party" at court, demanding the dismissal of Michael de la Pole, whose diplomacy had clearly failed and who had prevented the reforms passed in 1385 from being implemented. After being threatened with deposition at Eltham, where he had retired from Parliament, Richard returned and acceded to the new demands. Pole was replaced by Bishop Thomas Arundel, the brother of the earl,[35] and the new treasurer was Gaunt's friend Bishop John Gilbert. Gloucester and the Earl of Arundel were now in effective control of the government. Petitions were introduced in Parliament complaining about the behavior of Richard's friend the London merchant Nicholas Brembre. The Commons also asked that the statute concerning fees and robes for justices be reissued,[36] a subject recalled by Chaucer in his description of the Sergeant of the Law, who had often been a justice of assize:[37] "Of fees and robes hadde he many oon."

33. *Life-Records*, p. 370.
34. Sir Richard had fought at Crecy in 1346 and in other campaigns under Edward. He accompanied Gaunt on his march to Bordeaux in 1373 and was appointed Steward of the Household on Richard's accession. He served as Chancellor in 1378-80 and again in 1381-82. During 1385-88 he was a trier of petitions in Parliament. His son William, who was to serve as Gaunt's Seneschal in Aquitaine and who became the first Earl of Wiltshire in 1397, and his son Stephen were also prominent. Richard was in Gaunt's retinue in Scotland, and William was one of Gaunt's executors.
35. Bishop Arundel's connections and his political career between 1386 and 1397 are discussed by Margaret Aston, *Thomas Arundel* (Oxford, 1967), chap. 12.
36. See note 14, above.
37. Cf. Richard W. Kaeuper, "Law and Order in Fourteenth-Century England," *Speculum* 54 (1979):734-84.

The Commons complained also that lands seized by escheators were regranted before the injured parties could bring their cases to court, and that when they sought a remedy they found that those to whom their lands had been regranted had letters of protection (*RP,* 3:222-23). Richard replied, rather ineffectively, that such persons should seek a remedy from the chancellor, although the practice was in violation of Edward's statute on the subject of escheators (*SR,* 1:367-68). (Richard had a deplorable habit of regranting newly escheated lands to his favorites.) The Commons further asked, again echoing Edward's statute against fees and robes, that no prorogations be granted in cases involving land, causing justice to be delayed. It is clear that while the lords were thinking nostalgically of Edward's conquests abroad, the Commons was thinking nostalgically about his justice. In December Chaucer was deprived of his position at the Customs House, an eventuality he had probably been anticipating for some time. Considering Richard's obvious extravagance in the use of the signet or secret seal for grants made to his household favorites,[38] it seems unlikely that Chaucer would have regarded his own dismissal from what had become a merely nominal office with much resentment.

To extend our glance, very briefly, into the following year, we find that Richard spent some ten months in his "gyrations," during which he obtained legal opinions concerning the legality of the acts of the October Parliament and returned to London only to precipitate what amounted to a civil uprising and the "Merciless Parliament" of 1388, which succeeded, by very crude means indeed, in removing what many regarded as his "evil counsellors" and establishing a short-lived government by Council. Chaucer was not to obtain another lucrative office until after Richard declared himself of age and resumed power on May 3, 1389. In July, this time under the Privy Seal, a warrant was issued naming him Clerk of the Works, an office more eminent than any he had held before.

Chaucer's personal reaction to the October Parliament of 1386 has aroused some discussion. It has, for example, been plausibly argued

---

38. This provoked a complaint in Parliament in 1387 (*RP,* 3:247). Cf. Tuck, as cited in note 4, above.

that his account of the Trojan Parliament in which Antenor is ransomed for Criseyde *(Troilus,* ed. Robinson, 4:141-217) is a reflection of his discouragement at the decisions affecting him.[39] But the analogy between the two parliaments is not very convincing. There was no Hector in the English Parliament to oppose the proceedings, which under the circumstances were understandable enough. And in the Trojan parliament Hector is just as blind as anyone else to the behavior of Antenor; he simply objects that Trojans do not sell women, chivalrously fulfilling his obligation to protect Criseyde incurred immediately after her father's defection *(Troilus,* 1: 117-23). There is no evidence that King Priam is being either recalcitrant or threatened by his own noblemen, and it can not be seriously argued that Criseyde is promoting the chivalry of Troy, as, for example, Blanche of Lancaster had once done in England. The frequent assertion that the comparison between the spread of the "noise of people" and the spread of fire in straw is an allusion to Jack Straw is not very convincing either, since the "lesser commons" did not attend parliament in England and were not well represented there. The implication seems to be rather that if Troy lacked wise leadership its people were likely to act unwisely, just as the senses are likely to rebel if a man is not governed by reason. The unwise leadership began when the Trojan court welcomed Helen, in effect abandoning Pallas for the sake of Venus. Troilus has done exactly the same thing, and at this point has been "burning" for some time. The action of the Trojan parliament is in effect suicidal, and is parallel with the immediate reaction of Troilus, who, having been misled by his senses, calls on Death to destroy him, foolishly cursing Fortune, whom he says, again foolishly, he has always worshipped above all other gods. Readers of *The Consolation of Philosophy* or, for that matter, of Chaucer's poem "Fortune," should be fully aware of the dangers of this kind of blind devotion, and it is quite likely that many in Chaucer's audience found Troilus ridiculous, if not laughable. It would be difficult to think of Chaucer reacting to his dismissal in a manner in any way resembling the reaction of Troilus.

---

39. See John P. McCall and George Rudisill, "The Parliament of 1386 and Chaucer's Trojan Parliament," *JEGP* 58 (1959):276-88.

Again, it is not easy to think of an appropriate date in 1387 to which we could assign the probable delivery of Chaucer's poem, unless we make the unlikely assumption that Richard asked for it while engaged on his travels or during the turbulent period after his return to London. Troy is under siege as Chaucer describes it, and a similar situation existed in England almost at any time between 1377 and the close of 1386. The French, for reasons not well understood, abandoned their invasion plans in December of that year. It is true that in the same month the Council at Amiens determined to renew the effort in 1387, but as it turned out King Charles had only the resources to send some forces into Spain to oppose Gaunt. The Scots attacked in 1388, enjoying a victory at Chevy Chase, but that seems a very late date for the poem. The year 1386 seems more promising than either 1385 or 1387. Gaunt's preparations for departure and the festivities connected with it would have provided a suitable occasion. Specifically, the days before and including that of the "coronation" ceremony arranged by Richard suggest a likely date, although a later date at Plymouth while the expedition was waiting to set forth is another possibility. John of Gaunt, clearly concerned about Chaucer's family, was most propably involved in arrangements for presenting the poet in a favorable light before persons of eminence so that he might find something to replace his income at the Customs House, and in this effort he probably found Chaucer's friends at court ready to cooperate. I do not mean to suggest that Chaucer suddenly composed a long poem for a specific occasion, but that he put the finishing touches on a poem he had been working on for some time at the request of someone who knew about it.

IV.

Before turning to the poem itself I shall discuss its general relevance to England, the kind of ideals we may safely assume to have been held by Chaucer's friends at court and, very briefly, some points concerning literary technique. First, the English, influenced by traditions stemming from Geoffrey of Monmouth's *History of the Kings of Britain*, regarded themselves as inheritors of the traditions of ancient Troy.

"Britain" was the realm established by "Brutus," the great-grandson of Aeneas, or as Chaucer called it in his poem addressed to Henry IV, "Brutes Albion," and London was often called "New Troy." The fall of Troy thus served as a kind of perpetual warning, especially against following the example of Paris, the young Trojan prince who chose Venus over the busy life of Juno or the wise contemplation of Pallas.[40] Paris is made to say with unwitting irony in Ovid's amusing Epistle (*Heroides*, 16:48-49), "One of the seers said that Ilion would burn with the fire of Paris." Chaucer, in effect, makes Troy burn with the fire of Troilus. Gower, who uses the commonplace association of England with Troy in *Vox clamantis*, complains, near the close of his poem attacking the evils of his time in England, that his country "who was once holy is becoming the goddess Venus herself."[41]

That idleness and lecherous self-indulgence were inimical to chivalric endeavor, reflected in Walsingham's remark about Richard's court quoted above, appealed strongly to the medieval mind, and indeed, had antecedents in both Virgil and Ovid. Thus, in a sermon preached at St. Paul's in May 1375, Bishop Brinton of Rochester, having explained that those who wish others to be subject to them should be ruled by reason themselves, said further that the honor of a king depends on military power, sane counsel, clerical wisdom, and the just rule of the people, quoting, with reference to the first, John of Salisbury on the oath of a soldier. He went on to say that the English under Edward were once victorious in war, but because of their sins, God, who "was once an Englishman," had receded from them. (The sins he had in mind were those of idleness and lechery.)[42] And in the following year, in a sermon praising the recently deceased Prince Edward,

---

40. Cf. ibid. and D. W. Robertson, Jr., "The Concept of Courtly Love as an Impediment to the Understanding of Medieval Texts," in F. X. Newman, ed., *The Meaning of Courtly Love* (Albany, N.Y., 1968), p. 11; *Chaucer's London* (New York, 1968), pp. 2-4, 150, 167, 178, 221-22; "Simple Signs from Everyday Life in Chaucer," p. 212 n. 27; and David Anderson, "Theban History in Chaucer's *Troilus*," in *Studies in the Age of Chaucer* 4:133.

41. For the context of this observation, see *Major Latin Works of John Gower*, trans. Eric W. Stockton (Seattle, 1962), pp. 284-86.

42. *The Sermons of Thomas Brinton, Bishop of Rochester*, ed. Sister Mary Aquinas Devlin, O.P., Camden Third Series 85 (1954), pp. 46-48.

he said, "What is surprising, therefore, if the English are unfortunate in war, when in England everywhere reign lechery, adultery, and incest, so that few, and especially lords, are content with their wives."[43] In 1346 Bishop Bradwardine, in a famous sermon celebrating English victories, vigorously castigated the French for being soldiers of Cupid and Venus, attributing their defeat at least partly to this fact. The fruit of their lechery, he said, was "a stinking and intense burning."[44] Chaucer's repeated references to the "fire" that burns Troilus are singularly appropriate. In short, the virtue of chivalry and devotion to Venus were traditionally regarded as being incompatible.[45]

John of Salisbury insists repeatedly throughout the *Policraticus,* a book that Chaucer knew, that self-indulgence and the pursuit of Venus undermine not only military valor but the general efficacy of a prince, using the Terentian braggart soldier as an exemplar for ridiculing the weaknesses of his own contemporaries in England. And in the popular commentary on the *Aeneid* attributed to Bernard Silvestris, the Trojan horse is used as a figure for *luxuria* that brings with it all the other vices.[46] Troy burned because its leaders led it to desert Pallas for Venus, and it seemed possible that New Troy might burn in the same way for what were thought of as essentially the same reasons. Since the days of Marcabru, moreover, venereal preoccupation had been thought of as one of the worst deterrents to crusading zeal. Hence the attention accorded it by Philippe de Mézières in *Le songe du vieil pelerin* (1:52-56), where Luxure describes her baleful influence under her mistress Venus.

Chaucer was able to add depth and authority to his poem by suggesting various kinds of what might be called "analogies" or, to use a medieval term, "similitudes," many of which are implied rather than

---

43. Ibid., pp. 346-7; cf. pp. 338-39. For the underlying philosophical principle, see Boethius, *Cons.* 3:m. 5.
44. The passage is quoted in English in "The Concept of Courtly Love," p. 6.
45. Cf. the account and the references in *A Preface to Chaucer,* pp. 108-10. The account of *Troilus* in the pages below draws on the discussion in this work and is not inconsistent with it.
46. *The Commentary on the First Six Books of the Aeneid of Vergil,* ed. J. W. and E. F. Jones (Lincoln, Neb., 1977) pp. 102-3.

stated. Eugene Vinaver has called our attention to the use of anology in romances, where one episode may be made to recall and comment upon a much earlier episode in the interwoven fabric of the narrative.[47] Chaucer's shorter narrative made this technique impractical. But he could and did suggest a number of analogies simultaneously, appealing to the memories of a reasonably literate and sophisticated audience well grounded in the classics and the Scriptures.

First, there is an obvious analogy within the poem itself between the macrocosm represented by Troy and the microcosm represented by Troilus. The fall of Troy and the fall of Troilus take place simultaneously, and the carefully traced fall of the man offers an explanation and a paradigm for the fall of the city. A similar device had been used in the commentary on the *Aeneid* just mentioned, where Troy is made through "moralization" a figure for the human body in order to emphasize the moral causes of its destruction. John of Salisbury had used the analogy between a man and the commonwealth the other way around, to emphasize the interdependence of all of society's "members" or groups and the necessity for reason and wisdom on the part of the ruler, and the further necessity for an interest in the welfare of the whole on the part of the individuals making up the "members." This is a fruitful similitude rather than an "organic theory of the state."[48] The same kind of analogy is adduced by Gower in the Prologue to his *Confessio Amantis* (945-62), begun at a time roughly contemporary with *Troilus*. In Chaucer's poem, while Pandarus, who protected Paris from Menelaus while Pallas was still guiding Troy,[49] is busily encouraging Troilus in his self-destructive passion, his brother Calchas is assisting the Greeks in their efforts to destroy the city. And while Antenor, presumably, is seeking the same end, his sister Trojan Antigone helps to bring about the aid of Criseyde in the destruction of Troilus.

---

47. Eugene Vinaver, *The Rise of Romance* (Oxford, 1971), chap. 6.
48. A similar device was employed by Bishop Brinton in his sermon "On Unity," *Sermons*, pp. 109-17.
49. Cf. Boccaccio, *Genealogie deorum gentilium libri,* ed. V. Romano (Bari, 1951), 1:304.

A concentration on the microcosm facilitated the development of further analogies from a variety of sources, of which I shall here mention only a few. For example, frequent allusions to ideas and doctrines from *The Consolation of Philosophy*, which Chaucer had probably been translating at about the time he was fashioning his poem, suggest that Pandarus is in part an inverted Lady Philosophy, whose part Stoic and part Epicurean teachings represent, as Philosophy says (1:pr. 3), "cloutes ... out of my clothes," used to induce Troilus to embrace worldly joys rather than to forego them for the sake of his people.[50] Again, his assiduousness in urging Troilus on recalls the Terentian parasite who affixes himself to Epicureans in the pages of the *Policraticus* (especially Bk. 3). Chaucer can also evoke such analogies for a single episode. For example, the ruse Pandarus arranges to bring Troilus and Criseyde together in Deiphebus's house (2:1513-26) is reminiscent of that employed by Jonadab, "a very wise man," to bring together the ill-fated Amnon and Thamar (Douay, 2 Kings, 13). There are, of course, analogies in fourteenth-century life, and these are in some ways the most important of all, since the "background" analogies simply reinforce them by calling forth implications arising from associations in the minds of the audience, made pleasurable by recognition. Thus Pandarus is a counselor to a prince, in fact the only member of Troilus's retinue we meet in the poem. His destructive aid recalls the "false counsellors" who urge princes to follow their own inclinations rather than the dictates of wisdom, vigorously condemned in Chaucer's Melibeus and often said to be busy about the English court. Again, Pandarus leads Troilus in prayer and causes him to beat his breast in contrition for his sins against the God of Love (1:932-38) as though he were a priest. (Bishop Brinton had complained bitterly about confessors who failed to correct the sins of magnates guilty of adultery or other similar transgressions.)[51] Pandarus actually offers to help Troilus if he wants his brother's wife (1:676-79) and, after progress has been made with his own niece, acts to "quike alwey the fir" that burns him (3:484).

50. Cf. Alan Gaylord, "Uncle Pandarus as Lady Philosophy," *PMASAL* 46 (1961):571-95; and John P. McCall, "Five-Book Structure in Chaucer's *Troilus*," *MLQ* 23 (1962):279-308.

Troilus is in some ways another Paris, or a transformation of Paris into a similitude of Troy itself. Although less aggressive than either his brother or his rival Diomede, he repeats his brother's unfortunate choice; and just as Helen betrayed Paris for Deiphebus, whom she in turn betrayed to the Greeks, so Criseyde betrays Troilus for Diomede. As Mary-Jo Arn has indicated,[52] the theme of betrayal is introduced early in the poem when Pandarus refers to Oenone's Epistle to Paris in the *Heroides* (1:652 ff.), hardly tempered by his observation that even if he, like Oenone, cannot cure his own frustrated love, he can advise Troilus and will not restrain him even if he wants Helen, with whose character he seems to have been familiar. This action suggests that in a sense he is once more "assisting" Paris in a new guise.

An ominous background to the poem is afforded by both direct and indirect allusions to Theban history and legend, most explicitly in the story of Niobe, which Pandarus characteristically misapplies; in Criseyde's "Romance of Thebes" (2:106), with its story of Amphiarus whose implications (WB Prol. 740-46, "Mars," 245 ff.) Pandarus does not wish to face; and in Cassandra's interpretation of Troilus's dream. The Theban material in the poem, suggestive of the ill consequences of civil or fraternal strife, not, as we have seen, unknown in the English court, has been ably examined by David Anderson,[53] and a few details will suffice here. In the Knight's Tale Chaucer shows Palamon complaining about Juno, whom Boccaccio calls the "dea de' matrimonii," angry at Thebes "per gli adulterii da Giove, suo marito, commessi con le donne tebano," because she "hath destroyed wel ny al the blood / Of Thebes." Juno was also said to be inimical to Troy after the judgment of Paris, as well she might be, and the behavior of Troilus and

---

51. Brinton, *Sermons,* Sermon 51, p. 245.
52. "Three Ovidian Women in Chaucer's *Troilus:* Medea, Helen, and Oenone," *ChauR* 15 (1980):6-9. The citations of Classical story by Pandarus are almost uniformly inept, commenting humorously on what he is trying to say.
53. See note 40, above.
54. *Teseida,* ed. A. Roncaglia (Bari, 1941), pp. 446, 383. Cf. Boccaccio, *Genealogie,* p. 438; and the Third Vatican Mythographer in G. H. Bode, *Scriptores rerum mythicarum Latini tres Romae nuper reperti* (repr. Hildesheim, 1968), 1:166.

Criseyde can hardly have pleased her.[55] Nevertheless, Pandarus, after having suggested "That in the dees right as their fallen chaunces, / Right so in love ther come and gon plesaunces," hardly an idea pleasing to Juno, continues ineptly to console Troilus by saying, in connection with Criseyde (4:1116-18),

> blisful Juno, thorugh hir grete myght,
> Shal, as I hope, hir grace unto us sende.
> Myn herte seth, "certayn, she shal nat wende."

And Criseyde later (4:1538) amusingly invokes Juno in connection with her sworn intention to return to Troy. It may be that Chaucer thought of Hecuba as the daughter of King Dymas of Thebes. Ovid, immediately after his account of Ceyx and Alcyone, calls her a child of Dymas (*Met.* 11:761), identified by one mythographer as a king of Thebes.[56] But whether or not Troilus shares the "blood of Thebes," he does share with the Thebans a neglect of Juno, and is hardly kind to Pallas, Apollo, or Diana. Criseyde and Diomede both have connections with the ill-fated "Seven against Thebes." She, the daughter of Argia (Chaucer's "Argyve"), is the fruit of a Chaucerian union between Calchas and the wife of Polynices, who corrupted the wife of Amphiorus with the "Brooch of Thebes." This also makes her first cousin to Diomede, the son of Argia's sister Deiphyle. Finally, if Trojan Antigone is Criseyde's niece, her deceased husband must have been a Chaucerian younger brother of Laomedon, the father of Priam, Anchises, Antenor, and Antigone. (Antigone, as we shall see, also had her difficulties with Juno.) It is difficult to escape Anderson's conclusion that "Chaucer added the specter of Thebes to the background of *Troilus* to underscore an implicit theme of the poem, namely that one fallen city may serve as a warning to another not yet fallen. As Thebes should have been to Troy, so Troy should be to England."

55. Second Vatican Mythographer in Bode, 1:143; cf. Anderson, "Theban History in Chaucer's *Troilus*," p. 131.
56. First Vatican Mythographer in Bode, 1:63. The same source, p. 64, affords authority for Apollo's courtship of Nisa, daughter of Admetus, mentioned in Pandarus's account of Oenone's letter. Nisa may have appeared in a gloss on the Epistle, in an Italian translation, or even in the text itself, which is problematical. Cf. Boccaccio in Roncaglia, *Teseida*, p. 390.

Vinaver makes a further point about the romances of Chrétien de Troyes that may be valid for *Troilus* as well, as Ida Gordon has suggested.[57] He tells us that the French poet "lets the characters enact a line of argument that happens to interest him, no matter what kind of characterisation, real or unreal, may emerge as a result."[58] Since the analogies to which we have called attention determine the patterns of action to be followed by the characters, Gordon is probably correct, although Chaucer does maintain a reasonable verisimilitude in contemporary terms, Criseyde is widely hailed as a "complex" character, and the motivations of Pandarus have been difficult to explain. But the problems are not so grave as they at first seem. Troilus is a prince distracted from his obligations by a self-indulgent passion, and such princes were not unknown in the fourteenth century. Criseyde, who has a very good opinion of herself (2:746-49) and is rather vain, is easily impressed by a man obviously above her in station who wishes to take advantage of her. She can, moreover, readily cite salubrious doctrines in all sincerity without understanding their relevance to her own conduct, a not uncommon trait. And Pandarus is not unlike familiar gnathonic persons who attach themselves to their betters, as he does both in his defense of Paris and in his eagerness to satisfy the appetites of his prince.

One further point about Chaucer's technique is, I think, often misunderstood because of a change in taste. In spite of his ultimate seriousness of purpose, Chaucer, again like Chrétien, delights in teasing his audience; and he very seldom writes at any length without a smile. He had undoubtedly read and thoroughly digested John of Salisbury's elaboration of an Horatian maxim (*Satires*, 1:1.23-24) in the *Policraticus* (8:11): "Nothing prevents one from speaking the truth with a smile and from illustrating in fabulous narratives that which may be detrimental to good morals." John is about to relate the story of the widow of Ephesus, and the point is illustrated once more in his obvious admiration for the *Eunuch* of Terence, skilfully used in the argument of *Policraticus* 8 to show that tyrants are actually Epicureans. The basic

---

57. "Characterisation in Chaucer's *Troilus and Criseyde*," in W. Rothwell et al., *Studies in Medieval Literatures and Languages in Memory of Frederick Whitehead* (New York, 1973), pp. 118-19.

58. Vinaver, *Rise of Romance*, p. 30.

principle was known even to Harry Bailly, who says in the Prologue to the Cook's Tale (4355), "A man may seye ful sooth in game and pley," although he is himself, being something of an Epicurean, slow to grasp the "sooth" of what he hears.

To return to John of Salisbury, we find him innocent of the idea that a tragedy should be solemn. He had read Boethius, rather than Aristotle, who told him that tragedies portray the downfall of men of high estate who foolishly, and hence from a medieval point of view amusingly, subject themselves to Fortune and suffer the Providential consequences. Thus John was able to write of those who abandon the obligatory "warfare" of "the life of man upon earth" (Job 7:1; 2 Cor. 10:4) as mere players subject to the whims of Fortune as they act out "the comedy or tragedy of this world" (*Pol.* 3:8). Such players are "comic" because their actions are ludicrous, even though the consequences may be providentially "tragic" or disastrous. Even Shakespeare, later, often made his tragic protagonists ridiculous and introduced comic scenes into his tragedies, not as "relief" but as witty thematic reinforcements. The change in taste exemplified in Joseph Wharton's attack on wit and his assertion that the sublime and the pathetic, which are solemn matters, are the true subjects of poetry had not yet taken place. In Chaucer's day wit still reigned.

V.

As we have seen, *Troilus* was most probably written at a time when England was in danger from invasion from abroad, and quite possibly at a time when hopes were raised for a remedy in the crusade of the Duke of Lancaster. Meanwhile the king and his ministers, not to mention ordinary merchants and peasants, seem to have been guided more by immediate self-interest than by consideration for the welfare of the realm. Chaucer set out to show how "invisible foes," as he calls them at Troy, make possible the destruction of a commonwealth by "visible foes" without, using a negative example to make the positive appeal at the close of his poem more poignant. The example is the story of Troilus, and it will repay us to glance briefly at his behavior as a prince and as a chivalric leader.

When we first meet Troilus he is attending the festival of the Palladium, the sacred image of Pallas, who was regarded in the Middle Ages as the goddess of wisdom, a virtue recognized as being of special importance in a prince or knight, who should be, as Chaucer puts it elsewhere, worthy and wise. Pallas is said to have protected Troy until the Palladium was stolen by Diomede.[59] This brings us a further analogy, since it was Diomede who in effect stole Troilus's image of Venus, Criseyde, plunging the young prince into self-destructive wrath under the inspiration of the "Herynes," who lead him to the "angry Parcas," ministers of destiny. Instead of dutifully paying homage to Pallas, whose festival was traditionally celebrated at Athens, by holding philosophical conversations,[60] Troilus and his young followers are idly, and I use this word advisedly,[61] "beholding ay the ladies of the Town." Thus Troilus, foolishly defying Venus when, as Chaucer says, "Th'eschewing is only the remedye,"[62] is practically inviting the arrow of Cupid. As he makes fun of lovers for their labor in winning, their uneasiness in keeping, and their woes and pains at losing, at the same time he is indicating his own condition and his own fate.[63]

---

59. *Remigii Autissiodorensis commentum in Martianum Capellam,* ed. Cora E. Lutz (Leiden, 1962), 1:183; Boccaccio, *Genealogie,* p. 465; Thomas Walsingham, *Archana deorum,* ed. R. A. van Kluyve (Durham, 1968), p. 189.

60. See Guillaume de Conches, *Glosae super Platonem,* ed. E. Jeauneau (Paris, 1965), p. 71; and Jeauneau's *"Lectio philosophorum,"* (Amsterdam, 1973), p. 239.

61. On idleness and Venus, see Ovid, *Rem. am.,* 135-68; and for a discussion, Robertson, *Preface,* p. 92 and note 69.

62. See B. F. Huppé and D. W. Robertson, Jr., *Fruyt and Chaf* (Princeton, 1963), p. 112 and note 16. The basic idea is Pauline.

63. Troilus's reference to the labor in winning, fear in keeping, and sorrow in losing reflect the *De miseria humanae conditionis* of Innocent III (1:15). The first part of this chapter is paraphrased by the Man of Law in the prologue to his Tale (99-119), although that worthy fatuously goes on to describe the joys of the wealthy, abandoning Innocent's characterization of their miseries of which the predicament Troilus describes is paramount. Its application to lovers by Troilus associates them with the avaricious, treated at length in Innocent's Second Book, which contains chapters on avaricious princes and justices (3-5). Troilus's blindness is discussed at length in a forthcoming study by Chauncey Wood. On lust and avarice, see the closing remarks below.

An analogy for this action is a bit of wisdom from Ecclesiasticus (9:7-9): "Look not around thee in the ways of the city, nor wander up and down into the streets thereof. Turn away thy face from a woman dressed up, and gaze not upon another's beauty. For many have perished by the beauty of a woman, and hereby lust is enkindled as a fire." He sees Criseyde, her image (Cupid's arrow) sticks to his "hertes botme" bypassing his reason as it usually does, so that he abandons his companions, not to mention Pallas, and retreats to his chamber, where, having defied Ovid's precept (*Rem. am.,* 579) "beware of solitary places!" he begins to burn. He soon resigns his "estaat royale" to her, repeating in effect the Judgment of Paris, so that he ceases to worry about either the siege or his own salvation. He actually decides that death is the only solution to his problem, and he prays to Criseyde, whom he has seen only once and that briefly, and concerning whose character he is completely ignorant, to have mercy on him and save him from "the death." This is silly enough, but when Pandarus comes and offers assistance, Troilus first tells him to go away, for he will die. Love, he says, has overcome him, and his burning desire is so great

> That to be slayn it were a gretter joye
> To me than kyng of Grece ben and Troye.

These are truly deplorable sentiments in a prince whose nation is under attack, and we can well imagine how Chaucer's audience would have regarded their own companions substituting "France" and "England" for "Grece" and "Troye." We can rest assured, moreover, that this commonplace analogy did occur to them, and that they recognized in Troilus an extreme exemplification of what some of them, in one way or another, had been doing. Since Troilus has no wish to marry, he is reduced to either inaction or subterfuge.

Pandarus is ready to supply the subterfuge, in spite of his own amorous difficulties. He can help, he says, even if Troilus loves Helen, and he advises Troilus not to weep like Theban Niobe. Niobe's seven sons and seven daughters were shot down by Apollo (wisdom or truth) and Diana (chastity) after she defied their mother, Latona, a goddess of wisdom. If anything, this reference emphasizes the foolishness of angering any of these deities, or disregarding the virtues they represent, a point emphasized once more, and again inadvertently and hence amusingly, when Pandarus says that although Troilus may suffer pains as sharp as those suffered by "Ticius in helle," he can still be of assistance. Tityus became a common figure for insatiable libido, for which naturally there is no cure, for he attempted to rape Latona, was shot down by Apollo and Diana, and sent to hell where he suffers the eternal torment of having his liver (Pandarus's "stomak" was thought to be the seat of libido in women) gnawed by "volturis." Having explained that Fortune's wheel always turns and Troilus may yet rise upon it, but omitting the obvious consequence that he will also fall if he rises upon it, Pandarus generously offers in true gnathonic fashion, to get his own sister for him if he wants her Having discovered that it is his niece, Criseyde, rather than his sister, for whom Troilus burns, he leads him in prayer to Cupid and asserts that if Criseyde does not love in accordance with "natural" love, by which he means what would have been regarded as "natural" after the Fall when human nature was corrupted, rather than "celestial" love, he will hold it a vice in her.

Having grown hotter through encouragement, Troilus prays to Venus for help, although, amusingly, it is the business of Venus to make the fire hot (a fact abundantly evident in the *Roman de la rose),* and, falling upon his knees before his parasite, entrusts his life and death to him, saying, "fy on the Grekes alle!" as though the attack on the city did not matter. He becomes like a lion on the battlefield and friendly and gentle to everyone at home, not to save or encourage his countrymen, but to make an impression on Criseyde. This is almost an echo of Bradwardine's accusation, in the sermon referred to above, that the French, subjecting themselves to Cupid and Venus, seek "a name upon earth" so that "they may be loved by foolish women." The witty satire of this book has been generally neglected in favor of more sentimental and serious concerns.

In the second book, an amusing reflection of contemporary court manner somewhat exaggerated for effect, Pandarus and Criseyde seek to maneuver themselves into a situation where Troilus can have his will and Criseyde can preserve her "honor," which would suffer if a secret and illicit affair became known. Pandarus paints for her little pictures of Troilus discussing military strategy in "the paleis garden, by a welle," playing idly at darts, and mournfully confessing his sins to the God of Love; or in his bedchamber groaning for love. The military strategy was obviously not the subject uppermost in his mind, although Criseyde, who is flattered, disregards this obvious implication. When she sees him from a window with his battered helm and shield she is impressed by his prowess, his high estate, his reputation, but more than anything else by the fact that his distress is all for her. She argues with herself about the most profitable course she could take, but determines not to take another husband who might be dominating or unfaithful, and is clearly impressed both by her own attractiveness and by the exalted station of her lover. She hears the song of Antigone, who, the mythographers tell us, thought herself to be more beautiful than Juno, so irritating that deity that she turned her hair into serpents, a punishment later mitigated by having her transformed into a stork.[64] But Criseyde is impressed by the song praising love rather than Junonian marriage, and the later picture of her tearing her "ownded" hair may be reminiscent of this suggested analogy as well as being, along with the hand-wringing, a signal of *tristitia,* or worldly sorrow. When she grants Troilus "love of friendship" the young prince is gladder than if someone had given him "a thousand Troys," again an indication of his lack of any sense of chivalric or princely obligation, what we today might describe as "social conscience." The fire "of which he brente" becomes even hotter. Pandarus develops his plot to bring the two together, invovling lies to Deiphebus, to Helen, to Criseyde, and a feigned illness on the part of Troilus. I need not print out that none of the actions in this book has much to do with "chivalrie, trouthe, honour, fredom, and curtesie," although they do illustrate false virtues that resemble these virtues on the surface. Our word for simulated virtue is hypocrisy.

Book III is a comic account of the activities of Venus, "plesaunce of love," who is invoked at the outset, along with a brief account of the activities of Jove that so offended Juno and some veiled hints of divine

---

64. Bode, 1:55, 63, 98.

love. As Troilus lies in bed at Deiphebus's house, Criseyde and Pandarus appear, and she, quite properly, asks him for "lordship," which is the last thing he has in mind. He asks to be under her "yerde" or dominion, and in fact he plays, from a medieval point of view, a curiously feminine role in the subsequent narrative, consistent with the commonplace idea that passion makes men effeminate. Criseyde says that if he will keep her "honor" (meaning her reputation) she will receive him into her service, providing he will have no sovereignty in love, thus reversing her original proper request. When Pandarus offers to bring the couple together to "speke of love," as he laughingly puts it, Troilus is overjoyed, but he groans to deceive Helen and Deiphebus entering from the garden, to which Pandarus has cleverly led them. Improper aims lead to worldly stratagems, or, as they are now called, "cover-ups," and under the guidance of Pandarus Troilus becomes adept at them.

When he and Pandarus are alone, the latter seeks to excuse his pandaring, asking that Troilus keep everything secret, since if anyone knew what he had done it would be considered "the werste trecherie." Chaucer's audience knew, of course, and could hardly have escaped making that judgment themselves and the further observation that the "treachery" was not only condoned but encouraged by Troilus. Pandarus also warns against boasting and lying, although it is clear that he is himself a skilled liar. Troilus swears secrecy and promises to serve Pandarus as a slave forever, calling his action "nobility, compassion, fellowship, and trust," and offering to get Pandarus his sister Polyxena, his sister Cassandra, or Helen, or "any of the frape" if he wants one of them.[65]

Thus our prince offers to become an unscrupulous pander himself, as well as a parasite to a man beneath him in status. He devises the stratagem of pretending to be preoccupied with the problem of the siege, in which he has no real interest, at the temple of Apollo when he is actually with Criseyde. The virtues of wisdom and truth, represented by Apollo, are once more carelessly defied. For

---

65. The "frape" are by no means uniform in character. Polyxena's moving death, in the course of which she seeks to preserve her virgin modesty, is described by Ovid, *Met.*, 13:441-80.

by lying to Criseyde Pandarus gets her to his house, although she, a kindred spirit, is clearly aware of the lie. Pandarus, however, needs still another lie to bring the lovers together. Troilus, after lurking in a "stewe," feels compelled to say a prayer to Venus, whom he promises to serve until he dies. This self-dedication to idleness and lust is hardly propitious either for himself, for Criseyde, or for the people of Troy, whose "Hector the Second" is thus abandoning them. The amusing ineptitude of the prayer constitutes a kind of witty comment on the speaker, for it is hardly propitious for what he has in mind. He mentions Venus's unsuccessful love for Adonis, the love of Jove for Europa, which had disastrous consequences, the love of Mars for Venus, which led to his great embarrassment, the frustrated love of Phebus for Daphne, and the love of Mercury for Herse, which provoked the wrath of Pallas. He even calls on Diana, who is unlikely to find his enterprise agreeable, and he finally addresses the Fates, ministers of destiny, who shape the ends of all those who lose their free will through passion, including, of course, Troilus himself (5:1-7). There can be little doubt that this ridiculous performance produced laughter in the fourteenth century.

Criseyde, always full of good doctrine, lectures Pandarus at length on the fleeting character of worldly joys and her lover on the evils of jealousy. The young prince faints in confusion and is thrown in bed by Pandarus, actions that further detract from his princely dignity. Even more conversation is necessary before the two lovers subside into the uneasy heaven of Venereal bliss where, unfortunately, both feel that their delights may be mere dreams or in any event transitory. Criseyde has just pointed out that they are transitory by nature, although it is amusing that neither she nor her lover shows any sign of recognizing this fact. Next morning Troilus thanks Pandarus for having rescued him from "Flegetoun, the fiery flood of helle," a river, as a popular mythographer says, "signifying the fires of wrath and cupidity with which human hearts are inflamed,"[66] passions later to be elaborated by Chaucer in his portraits of Arcite and Palamon in the Knight's Tale. But Troilus immediately finds himself back in this river, urging Pandarus

---

66. Third Vatican Mythographer, Bode, 1:176.

to arrange a new assignation because, as he says, "I had it never half so hote an nowe." This constitutes a witty comment on the "rescue."

The unquenchable fire was thought to be one of the disadvantages of lust, not a plaintive comment on the human condition. Thus the plight of Tityrus was thought to illustrate the fact that "when the action is once performed it is not enough for lust, for it always breaks out again."[67] The idea had been elaborated by John of Salisbury, who said, echoing Terence (*Eunuch,* 2:3),

> The touch of the bodies of others, and the more ardent appetite for women is next to insanity. Whatever any of the senses attempt is game and play compared with those things brought about by this frenzy. From it we desire, we are wrathful, we are passionate, we are worried, and after our pleasure has been fulfilled we inflame ourselves again through a certain dissatisfaction, seeking to do that, when we repeat it, leaves us once more dissatisfied. [*Pol.* 8:6].

These points are well illustrated in the remainder of the poem. Although we may feel compassion for those who suffer from spiritual maladies of this kind, as Chaucer says he does at the outset (1:47-51) and as Boethius urges us to do (*Cons.* 4:pr. 4), they are especially dangerous in persons of responsibility and trust, upon whose integrity the welfare of others depends. Chaucer observes, "And thus Fortune a tyme led in joie / Criseyde and eek this kinges son of Troye."

Troilus has abandoned his reason, a fact driven home by his ridiculous corruption of one of the meters of *The Consolation of Philosophy* (2:m. 8; *Troilus,* 3: 1744-71), in the course of which he substitutes his own list for the divine love of the original, so that he and his beloved are "Fortune's fools." Hence, as Chaucer assures us in the Proem of Book IV, Fortune blinds fools who listen to her song. Troilus has cursed the day, and the Muses are now the Furies, daughters of Night, together with Mars, the god of wrath and war.[68] The season places the sun in Leo, so that the malignant "dog days" afford a background to the events described.

67. Ibid., 1:177.
68. See R. E. Kaske, "The Aube in Chaucer's *Troilus*," in R. J. Schoeck and Jerome Taylor, eds., *Chaucer Criticism,* Vol. II: *Troilus and Criseyde and the Minor Poems* (Notre Dame, 1961), 2:167-79.

Parliament makes the exchange we have already discussed, and Troilus like a wild bull butts his head against the wall of his chamber, wishing that Fortune had killed his father, or his brothers, or even himself rather than depriving him of Criseyde's solaces. This reaction is not only ignoble but treasonable. He can neither support Hector nor carry Criseyde away by force for fear of ruining her reputation and of adding to the ignominy brought upon Troy by Paris, in whose footsteps he has been surreptitiously treading. Soon he is meditating in a temple where, in despair, he confuses simple and conditional necessity in such a way as to defend the proposition that "al that comth, comth by necessitee." This conclusion eliminates moral responsibility along with free choice. Finding Criseyde in a swoon and thinking her dead, he draws his sword to kill himself, thinking thus to defy the gods and Fortune in particular and demonstrating little princely fortitude.

Criseyde recovers in time to prevent this act, thanks Venus for their narrow escape, and suggests they go to bed, where the relief from their difficulties is only temporary. She promises to return to Troy within ten days, calling attention to her father's covetousness and the possibility of peace, concerning which there had been almost continuous negotiations (as there had been between the English and the French). She convinces her lover that they should not "steal away," for such an action would dishonor them, and people would accuse him of "lust voluptuous and coward drede," as though Troilus had not already demonstrated these qualities. They should, she says, "make a virtue of necessity," quoting Boethius, and remember that Fortune overcomes only wretches. As for herself, Criseyde says, rather amusingly, that she loved Troilus only for his "moral vertu, grounded upon trouthe," and because his reason always bridled his delight.

The Fates, ministers of destiny, rule over the last book. Diomede wins Criseyde's "friendship" by the time the two have reached the Greek camp. Chaucer devoted considerable time to the torments of Troilus, to his bitterness, his frustration, his isolation from his fellows, and to his gradual realization of Criseyde's unfaithfulness. Having scorned Pandarus's Ovidian advice in Book IV (400-27) to find another love, Troilus now disregards the further Ovidian advice to destroy old letters (*Rem. am.,* 718-22) and to avoid places where he has enjoyed Criseyde (*Rem. am.,* 725-26). Toward the close Chaucer remarks that Fortune "Can pull awey the fetheres brighte of Troye / Fro day to day, til they ben bare of joye."

The city suffers the fate of Troilus. After the treacherous slaying of Hector by Achilles, Troilus becomes convinced of Criseyde's defection to Diomede, and goes out to fight not to protect the town, but to seek vengeance on Diomede and his own death. When he has achieved the latter and his spirit has ascended above the mutable realm of the elements, he looks down, laughs at those who wept for his death, and damns all "oure wil that folweth so / The blynde lust, the which that may nat laste." This, Chaucer assures us, is the end of Troilus's worthiness, of his royal estate, of his lust, and of his nobility. He urges the "yonge fresshe folkes" in his audience not to love the transitory attractions of the world, but to love Christ, who will not betray them, and concludes with a prayer to the Trinity to defend himself and his countrymen from visible and invisible foes.[69] The visible enemies were at the time threatening to strike, and unless the invisible enemies within were conquered, they might well succeed. The prayer closes with a plea to Jesus to make "us," meaning the English, worthy of His mercy for the love of Mary, who was not only a source of compassion because of her humanity but the traditional sponsor of English chivalry and an appropriate mentor for a crusade.[70]

Chaucer's *Troilus* offers a vivid example of the degrading and ultimately disastrous consequences when a man of noble estate and great physical valor, but little fortitude, places his own private will, misled by the attractiveness of ephemeral satisfactions, above what was traditionally called "the honor of God and the common profit of the realm." When Chaucer enjoins the youth of the realm to abandon "worldly

---

69. Chaucer's contrast between the love of worldly vanity, typified by lust, and the love of Christ may have reminded many in his audience of a widely used school text, the *Cartula* (*PL,* 184:1307-14), which elaborates this theme. On its use in schools, see Nicholas Orme, *English Schools in the Middle Ages* (London, 1973), pp. 104-5. If and when this boyhood reminiscence occurred, it was probably pleasant.

70. Geoffrey of Monmouth's Arthur, widely emulated in England during the fourteenth century, carried an image of the Virgin on his shield. Garter knights wore her image on their shoulders during ceremonials. For the Wilton Diptych as a work commissioned in anticipation of a joint French and English crusade, see *England, France and Christendom,* pp. 205, 242-44.

vanyte," he generalizes his lesson, for Venus is a goddess of *luxuria* as well as of *concupiscentia carnis*, in its narrower sense, and the idolatrous lust for a woman had long been a figure typifying any concupiscent passion. Chaucer hints strongly at this principle in his ironic praise of love as being something far better than avarice (3:1373-93) immediately after Criseyde has given Troilus the Brooch of Thebes, and the idea was strongly suggested earlier in Troilus's formulaic criticism of lovers before he saw Criseyde. The fate of Crassus (3:1373-93) and, presumably, all of his imitators forced to drink molten gold, is actually similar to the fate of Troilus and of Troy. Chaucer undoubtedly had in mind the extortionate abuses that King Edward had vainly sought to remedy and that Sir Richard Waldgrave and his successors among the Commons in Parliament had later sought to remedy,[71] as well as the sexual behavior of the chivalrous. He was seeking a renewed dedication on the part of his audience, couched in terms then most likely to be appealing, however they may strike us now, stressing the obligation of the English to set their love where it would lead neither themselves nor their countrymen to the burning destruction that had devastated old Troy, and to behave, as reason then demanded, with due reverence for wisdom and its restraints, now represented by *Sapientia Dei Patris,* or Christ, rather than by Pallas.

In the atmosphere of England in the mid-1380s it is not unlikely that many in his audience were inspired by what he had to say and renewed their own dedication. He had, after all, neither castigated them directly as a preacher might have done, nor cast any aspersions on particular individuals. He had simply urged them, with a great deal of wit and learning, to love as they should not only for their own welfare, but for the welfare of England. A new dedication would have been especially appropriate, in just these terms, for those about to set out for Spain with the Duke of Lancaster.

---

71. For a more detailed account of later parliamentary complaints, see my forthcoming "Chaucer and the Economic and Social Consequences of Plague," to appear in the Papers of the Fifteenth Annual Conference of CMRS, SUNY Binghamton.

Who Were "The People"?

D. W. Robertson, Jr.

The Popular Literature of Medieval England, ed. Thomas J. Heffernan (Knoxville, TN: University of Tennessee Press, 1985), pp. 3-29.

The term *popular literature* is actually not very specific, and it quite naturally suggests for the period of the late Middle Ages "vernacular" literature, or where England is concerned, literature in Middle English. It may well be argued that even where Middle English works are translations or adaptations from Latin, AngloNorman, or French they are still "popular" by virtue of the language in which they are written. However, M.T. Clanchy has recently suggested that it was often "the most sophisticated and not the most primitive authors who experimented with vernaculars," so that "we should not be misled by the prefatory apologies in vernacular works, or by their unusual orthography, into thinking that they were composed by the less educated."[1] Today we often associate popular literature with unlettered folk, or, alternatively, with best-selling books, the most popular of which at the moment are romances written for women, cook books, diet or exercise books, or books on sexual techniques. Except for certain books falling under the general category "religious instruction," like *The Prick of Conscience,* for example, and perhaps certain songs and carols, it would be difficult to describe Middle English works generally as being popular in this sense. It is probably fair to say that there was no popular literature in the modern sense in late medieval England and except for certain religious beliefs held in common, it lacked a "mass culture." For this reason, it should be

---

1. M.T. Clanchy, *From Memory to Written Record in England, 1066-1307* (Cambridge, Mass.: Harvard Univ. Press, 1979), p. 170.

helpful to know something about the various kinds of audiences that did exist at the time.

No one who studies English dialects or local customs, social, legal, or, to use a rather inappropriate modern term, "political,"[2] can escape the conclusion that England was a highly diversified country during the late Middle Ages. Each shire had its own distinctive customs, and some shires, like Kent in the south or Cheshire in the north, had their own peculiar laws and organizational structures. The same principle holds, perhaps to an even greater extent, for English towns. The national economy was basically agricultural, but agricultural procedures varied enormously with soil and climate, and with other features like proximity to the coast, proximity to waterways, the availability of pasture, or even proximity to towns that sheltered a preponderant population of tradesmen, as not all towns did. Proximity to active mining areas, like the tin mines of Cornwall, might also have a marked effect on manorial practices and agricultural prosperity. Areas of "open field" agriculture, sometimes regarded as being "typical," were actually extremely diversified, for manorial customs varied from manor to manor. Manors under the lordship of large ecclesiastical or monastic organizations were generally more closely supervised than those under lay jurisdiction, even when these were controlled by "liberties," like the Duchy of Lancaster; and, finally, the relationship between lord and tenant was determined in part by whether the lord was resident, occasionally resident, or nonresident, with his jurisdiction in the hands of stewards or local bailiffs.

Much depended also on the character of the lord and his relationships with other lords in the vicinity. Land in the hands of the Crown, or in "ancient demesne," enjoyed access to royal legal jurisdiction, and lands in the hands of lords who enjoyed liberties were sometimes subject to local jurisdiction for offenses that would ordinarily be referred to royal courts. Other factors that influenced manorial communities were the proportion of free and unfree tenants, the absence of one of these classifications, the proportion between demesne and tenant

---

2. Governmental structures were for the most part customary and had nothing to do with "political theory," which was then ultimately moral theory.

lands, susceptibility to inclement weather, whether flood or drought, and, finally, the little understood local variation in the effects of plague or murrain. Tenants in some areas, moreover, were more exposed than those in others to mistreatment by extortionate sheriffs, bailiffs, summoners, archdeacons, rural deans, or diocesan officials. Again, some areas suffered more than others from the activities of royal purveyors or purveyors acting for noblemen, from the itinerant jurisdiction of the marshall and his court, from the intervention of the Court of the Admiralty, or from the depredations of soldiers moving to and from the coast or awaiting departure in the neighborhood of ports,[3] or from raiders from France or Castile. We should I think understand that agricultural workers or "peasants" were not by any means all alike, that their immediate interests were not the same throughout the country, and that they did not constitute "the masses" of the time. Community interests were still very strong, and manorial communities tended to arrange themselves in hierarchies. The easy generalizations of Marxist and post-Marxist rhetoric should be restrained when we think about them.

It is true that many agricultural workers underwent extreme hardship during the early years of Edward III,[4] and that the plagues, murrains, droughts, and floods of the second half of the fourteenth century (not to mention the wars) produced a great deal of suffering. On the other hand, plague left many survivors with larger holdings that could be more efficiently managed, encouraging a new prosperity resulting from greater productivity. At the same time a shortage of labor inconvenienced landlords who were forced to pay higher wages, while artisans in towns demanded higher prices or engaged in the production of substandard goods. People and their attitudes not only varied from place to place; they also varied in time.

---

3. See the parliamentary complaint in the third year of King Richard (3 R II), *Rotuli Parliamentorum* (Record Commission, 1783, hereinafter *RP*), 3:80.
4. The situation is discussed at length by J.R. Madicott, *The English Peasantry and the Demands of the Crown,* Past and Present Supplement, vol. 1 (1975). It is reflected in an Anglo-Norman poem printed by Isabel S.T. Aspin, ed., *Anglo-Norman Political Songs* (Oxford: B. Blackwell, 1953), no. 10. There is an excellent analysis of the poem in G.L. Harriss, *King, Parliament, and Public Finance in Medieval England to 1369* (Oxford: Clarendon Press, 1975), pp. 250-52.

For these reasons the question, Who were the people? is very difficult to answer, but a few details may be helpful. The "peasantry," with whom we shall begin, included not only free and unfree tenants of manors but miscellaneous agricultural workers (including Welshmen in border areas) who could be hired legally by the year, like those, for example, compelled by the Statute of Laborers to bring their implements to town and offer their services publicly where everyone could see and hear (so that landlords could not offer wages beyond the statute).[5] Both manorial lords and tenants with larger holdings after the great plague could afford to hire workers of this sort. There were also cottagers or small artisans on many manors who worked for more prosperous tenants. A manor might contain tenants who held only a portion of a virgate,[6] a virgate, more than one virgate, or several virgates. This matter is also complicated by the fact that a nobleman (or noblewoman) or a merchant might hold tenements under the manorial lord operated by local families. In any event, by the later fourteenth century, social status on a manor generally depended on wealth rather than legal status, so that a bondman might have a higher status in the manorial community than many of his free neighbors. It is also true that a tenant might hold both free and unfree lands since rents and services were often attached to the land rather than to the person. In the years preceding the Great Revolt of 1381 (which involved ecclesiastics and minor noblemen as well as villeins, of whom there were none in Kent), there is evidence that some villein tenants were withdrawing their services. In 1377 it was alleged in Parliament that they were the victims of "Counsellors, Maintainers, and Abettors in the Country, which hath taken Hire and Profit of the said Villaines and Landtenants, by Color of certain Exemplifications made out of the Book of Domesday of the Manors and Towns where they have been dwelling, and by virtue of the same Exemplifications, and their evil Interpretations of the same, they affirm them

---

5. For the statute, see *Statutes of the Realm* (London, 1810-28, hereinafter, *SR*), 1:311-16.
6. For a discussion of the word *virgate* and related terms, see D.W. Robertson, Jr., "'And for my Land thus Hastow Mordred Me?': Land Tenure, the Cloth Industry, and the Wife of Bath," *Chaucer Review*, 14 (1980), note 26, pp. 418-20.

to be quite and utterly discharged of all Manner Servage, due as well of their Body as of their said Tenures, and will not suffer any Distress or other Justice to be made upon them; but do menace the Ministers of their Lords of Life and Member, and, which more is, gather themselves together in great Routs, and agree by such Confederacy, that everyone shall aid other and resist their Lords with strong Hand."[7] In the following year there was a complaint that many agricultural laborers had gone to "vills, boroughs, and towns" and there "become artificers, mariners, or [surprisingly] clerks," making it difficult to keep lands in cultivation.[8] This sort of exodus apparently continued throughout the remainder of the century in spite of efforts on the part of the justices of the peace to stop it, for the temptation of ready cash afforded by wages by the day was very great.[9] Villeins on manors generally held the offices of ordinary manorial servants at stipends fixed by manorial custom and were elected by the manorial court. That is, the reeve, carter, shepherd, ponder, oxherd, butcher, dairymaid, and, at times, the miller or other regular servants of the manor (whose offices varied from manor to manor) were now demanding higher stipends. The examples afforded by hired laborers, or by laborers turned "artificers, mariners, or clerks" probably stimulated them to demand what was regarded as "outrageous and excessive Hire," so that a statute seeking to control them was passed in 1388.[10]

On many manors landlords, who were also interested in ready cash, commuted the labor services of their villeins for cash in the form of higher rents, or leased their demesne lands, often the most productive on the manor, so that labor services were no longer of interest to them. At the same time efforts on the part of lords to maintain the traditional work obligations of villeinage were ultimately doomed

7. 1 R II c. 6, *SR*, 2.2; cf. *RP*, 3.21.
8. *RP*, 3.46; cf. Nora Ritchie, "Labour Conditions in Essex in the Reign of Richard II," in E.M. Carus-Wilson, ed., *Essays in Economic History* (London: E. Arnold, 1954-1962), 2:93.
9. See, for example, the parliamentary complaint of 1391, *RP*, 3:296.
10. 12 R II 4, *SR*, 2:57. Generally, "reform" statutes were passed in the first year of Richard's reign, when he was too young to be responsible and there was, in any event, a generally conciliatory policy on the part of the government; and in 1388 when the Appellants were in control. Richard was much less concerned about abuses than Edward had been during his best years.

to failure, and this fact was becoming more and more obvious.[11] A rather amusing petition in the parliament of 1393-1394 complained that some religious had avoided the statute of Mortmain by arranging to have their villeins marry women holding free lands so that such lands might be inherited by the sons of villeins and, concomitantly, fall into the seizin of religious houses.[12] One can imagine the good brothers furbishing their more prosperous villeins to make them attractive to the ladies in prospect. Considering the agricultural economy as a whole, one should not assume that later fourteenth-century peasants were generally very poor persons gaining a mere subsistence in lamentable circumstances. The "spirit of enterprise" sometimes said to be characteristic of the age[13] extended to agricultural communities, often at the expense of community spirit and mutual cooperation, a fact that troubled the moralists of the age, but, nevertheless, at least from a rigorous economic point of view, seems a promising development, although the promise was not fulfilled in the fifteenth century, when real wages declined generally.

An ordinary peasant lived in a "long house," a rectangular structure, one end of which, containing perhaps two chambers, sheltered the tenant and his family while the other was used for his beasts. A more prosperous family might have a separate building for farm animals, placed at a right angle to the dwelling so as to form a kind of courtyard, and some tenants boasted two or three residential buildings. Although in a few areas these houses may have been of stone, ordinarily they were walled with wattles and clay set within a timber framework.[14] The resultant walls were not very sturdy and, as the

---

11. The matter is actually somewhat complex. See, for example, Barbara F. Harvey, *Westminster Abbey and Its Estates in the Middle Ages* (Oxford: Clarendon Press, 1977), chs. 9, 10.

12. *RP*, 3:3.19

13. See especially F.R.H. Du Boulay, *An Age of Ambition: English Society in the Late Middle Ages* (London: Nelson, 1970).

14. See most recently J.G. Hurst, "The Changing Medieval Village in England," in J.A. Raftis, ed., *Pathways to Medieval Peasants* (Toronto: Pontifical Institute of Mediaeval Studies, 1981), esp. pp. 38-44. Cf. Sarah M. McKinnon, "The Peasant House: The Evidence of Manuscript Illuminations," in the same volume, pp. 301-9.

coroners' rolls reveal, could be broken down by a determined robber, or by persons inside seeking to escape pursuit. Surrounding the house or houses was a tract of land, usually rectangular, with a short side on the lane. This might contain four or five acres more or less, affording room for a garden of vegetables and herbs, some fruit trees, and a small pasture. In some instances several families along a lane shared a common pasture at the rear of their tenements bordered by a service lane. Poor cottagers lived in smaller houses, perhaps with the "bower and hall" divided by a hanging. The animals might be cows, pigs (especially in Cheshire), sheep, goats, and fowl, and occasionally horses or oxen. Not infrequently a peasant wife brewed ale, which she sold, but each new batch was supposed to be judged by the local ale-taster, who also kept a watchful eye for violations of the assize and on some manors saw to it that the lord received a portion of each brew. Violations of the assize of ale had to be reported to the bailiff of the hundred or to the manorial court if its lord held the "View."[15]

Before the ill effects of plague (which varied from place to place) weakened traditional manorial communities there was a considerable amount of cooperation among manorial tenants, free and unfree, practically necessitated by overpopulation. This did not entirely disappear in the later fourteenth century, although some tenants were clearly more interested in making money than they were in the welfare of their fellows. The tenants elected their own jurors or "affeerors," who imposed fmes in the manorial court. They determined in cooperation with the lord and his steward the customs of the manor, reached decisions about such matters as alterations in manorial field systems, and cooperated in keeping the peace. In accordance with the frankpledge system, male tenants of twelve years or more who were neither ecclesiastics nor persons under the direct jurisdiction of noblemen were divided into groups or "tithings," ideally of ten (although the number varied), presided over by a chief tithingman, who was bound to report transgressions by any of his men at the View.[16] The whole

15. For the Assize of Bread and Ale, see *SR*, 1:199-200, 201-4.
16. For articles of the View, which might vary somewhat from place to place, see *SR*, 1:246-47.

tithing could be fined for a transgession by any one of them; indeed, the whole vill or township might be fined in severe cases or on occasions when the tithingmen had failed to report transgressions of which they were clearly aware. The behavior of one's neighbors was thus a matter of some interest to everyone. Anyone being attacked or molested was required to raise the "hue and cry" so that the perpetrator might be seized by his neighbors. Those who raised the hue falsely or who failed to raise it when they should have done so could be fined. Transgressors might find "pledges" among their neighbors to guarantee payments of fines or future good behavior. On some manors the tenants might be divided into rather rigorous hierarchies, depending on the kind of tenure they held and on the size of their holdings.[17] Although these hierarchies often became fictions when demesnes were leased, they were replaced by hierarchies depending on wealth.

The peasant diet has received much attention, and here one must allow for considerable local variation, although the widespread impression that peasants for the most part ate little more than gruel is probably erroneous. The gardens referred to above, not to mention the livestock, probably afforded ample supplements of vegetables, eggs, milk, cheese, and some meat, like the "seynd bacoun" of Chaucer's abstemious dairymaid. Food offered at "boonworks" when tenants assisted at the lord's harvest varied from place to place. Thus gruel might be served on some manors, but at Stoneleigh Abbey workers received a small white wheaten loaf, four eggs, pottage, sometimes cheese, and ale.[18] At Waltham in Essex a worker was given at dinner (in the early afternoon) bread and ale, pottage, a dish of either pork or mutton, or a dish of fish and some herrings. In the evenings he had bread, ale, and herrings or milk and cheese.[19] At Stretham, a manor of the Bishop of Chichester in Sussex, a bond tenant received wheaten bread and ale for breakfast; at dinner wheaten bread, soup, beef and mutton or other meat of two kinds and cheese; and for supper a wastel (gateau),

---

17. E.g. see K.C. Newton, *The Manor of Writtle: The Development of a Royal Manor in Essex, c. 1086–c. 1500* (Chichester: Phillimore, 1970), pp. 40–52.
18. R.H. Hilton, ed., *The Stoneleigh Leger Book,* Dugdale Society (Oxford: Oxford Univ. Press, 1960), p. 103.
19. Ritchie, "Labour Conditions," p. 97.

a drink, two herrings, and cheese.[20] There is no reason to think that agricultural workers generally suffered from a lack of protein, even in those areas where their bread was made of oats, in the fourteenth century. After the great plague they often demanded better food as well as higher wages. By modern standards they may have been somewhat injudicious in asking for white bread, as they sometimes did.

The most important centers of social activity for agricultural workers were the church and the manorial court. Unfortunately, we have little first-hand evidence of parish entertainments in the fourteenth century.[21] Writers on morals like Robert Mannyng may complain about dances in the churchyard, beauty contests, and "summer games," but such complaints are often traditional so that it is difficult to determine whether they reflect current activities. It would be safe to assume, however, that parish priests organized pilgrimages to nearby shrines, which, in accordance with late-medieval attitudes toward decorum on "religious" occasions, might be very pleasant without being scandalous. There were processions on Rogation Day governed by similar prepuritanical standards, and festive celebrations on major holy days, probably with an element of pageantry. Itinerant friars interlaced their sermons with songs and stories,[22] some of which modern scholars would call folk tales, and weddings offered occasions for community celebration. Less decorous forms of entertainment, organized by the men of the vill, might give rise to difficulties. Thus in 1381 a football (soccer) game produced a "fray" between men of two villages under different lordships in Durham, and the prior's tenants were heavily fined in court.[23] Dice playing had been forbidden in one

---

20. W.D. Peckam, ed. and trans., "Thirteen Customals of the Sussex Manors of the Bishop of Chichester," Sussex Record Society, no. 31 (Cambridge: W. Heffer and Sons, 1925), pp. 106-8. This customal was completed in 1374.
21. See Alexandra F. Johnston, "Parish Entertainments in Berkshire," in *Pathways to Medieval Peasants,* pp. 335-37.
22. See John V. Fleming, *An Introduction to the Franciscan Literature of the Middle Ages* (Chicago: Franciscan Herald Press, 1977), ch. 4; and David L. Jeffrey, *The Early English Lyric and Franciscan Spirituality* (Lincoln: Univ. of Nebraska Press, 1975), chs. 5, 6.
23. W.H.D. Longstaffe and John Booth, eds., *Halmota Prioratus Dunelmensis,* Surtees Society, no. 82 (Durham: Andrews and Co., 1889), p. 171.

of the prior's vills in the previous year.[24] A statute of 1388 stipulated that no "servant of husbandry" carry a "buckler, sword, or dagger," but have bows and arrows to use on Sundays and holy days, and that such servants leave all "playing at Tennis or Football, and other games called Coits, Dice, Casting the Stone, Kailes [skittles], and other such importune Games."[25] We may assume that such games had been popular and that archery gradually came to replace them, although statute law, in spite of being proclaimed at county courts and marketplaces, was notoriously ineffective until the fifteenth century. Other opportunities for entertainment were afforded at fairs, where professional singers, dancers, and prostitutes might well be found among the merchants in their stalls. In the late fourteenth century there were still large fairs at St. Ives and Stourbridge, as well as lesser ones elsewhere. Local marketplaces probably afforded occasion for discussion of current events and the exchange of witty tales, not to mention songs airing current grievances.

Meetings of the manorial court, theoretically "from three weeks to three weeks," but often less frequently, gave everyone an opportumty to gain new insights into the character and behavior of his neighbors as well as to observe their land transactions of various kinds and to effect his own. Trespasses and other grievances were aired, including failures to clean ditches (which might become dangerous if blocked), digging in or otherwise obstructing highways, and failure to pay debts.[26] Licenses to marry were granted, and fines were imposed on women of villein status for fornication, pregnancy out of wedlock, or adultery. Occasionally young men were warned about illicit affairs; a Durham tenant was warned, for example, in 1380 not to keep a certain Katerina within the vill nor to come with her to a suspect place on pain of a heavy fine.[27] Among the various trespasses against the lord were allowing children to raid his orchard, pasturing

---

24. Ibid., p. 166.

25. 12 R II 6, *SR*, 2:57.

26. For an illustration of debt cases on one medieval manor (Writtle), see Elaine Clark, "Debt Litigation in a Medieval English Vill," in *Pathways to Medieval Peasants*, pp. 247-79.

27. *Halmota Prioratus Dunelmensis*, p. 166.

beasts on his land, or taking thorns,[28] an event immortalized, so to speak, in the lyric "The Man in the Moon."[29] There were frequent cases of defamation, or verbal assault. For example, on the estates of Crowland Abbey a man was fined 2s. for saying to a villein that he wished he would burn.[30] It was, in effect, illegal to call a woman a prostitute or a man a robber.[31] A woman could not lightly be called a witch,[32] although it was considered worse to call a man a thief than for him to call her a whore,[33] probably because theft might be a felony punishable by hanging if the perpetrator were found guilty before royal justices. The punder, who impounded stray beasts, must have often aroused the ire of negligent tenants, so that in a Durham vill it was a trespass to insult him.[34] The Durham court also forbade calling a tenant a "native" (villein) in 1364 on pain of 20s., and in the following year began fining tenants for calling their fellows "rustics."[35] Women were especially prone to use abusive language.[36] In the vills of Durham shrewish women seem to have become a problem after 1378.[37]

---

28. See W.O. Ault, ed., *Court Rolls of the Abbey of Ramsey and of the Honor of Clare* (New Haven: Yale Univ. Press, 1928), p. 206 and note; and *Halmota Prioratus Dunelmensis,* p. 86.

29. Carleton Brown, ed., *English Lyrics of the Thirteenth Century* (Oxford: Clarendon Press, 1932), no. 89. The speaker offers to get the hayward ("hedgeguard") drunk, take from him the "wed" or token payment the moon-man has given him and with it placate the bailiff.

30. Frances M. Page, *The Estates of Crowland Abbey: A Study in Manorial Organization* (Cambridge: Cambridge Univ. Press, 1934), p. 143.

31. W.O. Massingberd, trans., *Court Rolls of the Manor of Ingoldmells in the County of Lincoln* (London: Spottiswood, 1902), pp. 19, 42, 53, 93.

32. Ault, *Court Rolls,* p. 256.

33. See F.W. Maitland and W.P. Baildon, eds., *The Court Baron,* Selden Society, no. 4 (London: B. Quaritch, 1891), p. 133.

34. *Halmota Prioratus Dunelmensis,* p. 42.

35. Ibid., pp. 33, 40, 40-41, 141.

36. Page, *Estates of Crowland Abbey,* p. 139, and J.A. Raftis, *Warboys: Two Hundred Years in the Life of an English Village* (Toronto: Pontifical Institute of Mediaeval Studies, 1974), pp. 250-51.

37. E.g., see *Halmota Prioratus Dunelmensis,* pp. 144, 154, 169, 171.

At the court of Carshalton in Surrey, five women were accused in 1393 of being "communes garulatores, ad grave nocumentum patrie."[38] Occasionally a woman might become sufficiently obstreperous to beat a man.[39] Generally, manorial courts sought to keep the peace as best they could and to prevent contentiousness among neighbors. When courts were held, food was sometimes served, and the occasion was social as well as legal. The various cases and judgments undoubtedly produced much discussion, some of it amusing.

The question of peasant literacy is a difficult one. Clanchy contends that reeves, who were required to make fairly elaborate accounts annually to a steward or auditor and were admonished not to alienate anything without a writ, might have been able to read;[40] but P.D.A. Harvey has pointed out that reeves' accounts at Cuxham were compiled by clerks, probably from wooden tallies simply labeled with drawings (not unlike labels used to mark bundles of some government documents) and kept by the reeves.[41] It has also been noted that some peasants had seals and conveyed land by charter.[42] Ada E. Levett noted that villeins at St. Alban's Abbey frequently conveyed lands by charter, registered wills, some of which (unlike wills made by freeholders under the common law) conveyed lands, and that they sometimes held copies of records describing their holdings.[43] The fact that peasants of villein status often sought and obtained for a fee permission to send off their sons to acquire sufficient education to enter the clergy suggests strongly, moreover, that small schools for boys conducted by

---

38. *Court Rolls of the Manor of Carshalton,* Surrey Record Society, 7, no. 2 (London: Roworth, 1916), p. 38.
39. *Halmota Prioratus Dunelmensis,* p. 101.
40. Clanchy, *From Memory to Written Record,* p. 32.
41. *Manorial Records of Cuxham,* Oxfordshire Record Society, no. 50 (1976), pp. 37–40. For labels on bundles of documents, see Hubert Hall, *The Antiquities and Curiosities of the Exchequer* (New York: A.C. Armstrong, 1891), pp. 54–58.
42. Clanchy, *From Memory to Written Record,* pp. 34–35.
43. "The Court and Court Rolls of St. Alban's Abbey," *Transactions of the Royal Historical Society,* 4th ser., vol. 6 (1924), pp. 68, 71–72.

priests, chaplains, monks,[44] or canons were probably more numerous in rural areas than has been generally supposed, for the boys in question had probably shown some aptitude in elementary instruction. This may well have included, in addition to some psalms, "Cato," the *Liber parabolum* of Alanus de Insulis (*PL*, 210.581-94), the *Cartula* (*PL*, 184.1307-14), the *Facetus* on good manners, and Bishop Grosseteste's *Stans puer ad mensam*.[45] Some peasants, especially reeves, who traditionally acted as pledges for those elected to parliament, guaranteeing their attendance, probably attended sessions of the shire courts, and in the general round of social activities that accompanied such sessions may have been exposed to some "literary" entertainment. Meanwhile, it is undoubtedly true that peasant mothers often sang to their infants or children,[46] or told them stories, about which we know very little, although there is reason to believe that they may have included ghost stories.[47] And men in the countryside, like men anywhere else, probably relished jocular stories, or, as folklorists call them, "merry tales."

If we turn to the more prosperous towns, especially to chartered boroughs with their own governments, the "literary" situation immediately improves, and here we find a ready audience for songs, romances, plays, and for popular works of religious instruction, which were numerous and varied, ranging from simple creed or confessional formulas to much more elaborate works of doctrine or spirituality, not to mention informative or instructive works that we should be inclined

---

44. For a monastic school, see H.P.R. Finberg, *Tavistock Abbey: A Study in the Social and Economic History of Devon* (Cambridge: Cambridge Univ. Press, 1951), p. 224. Some boys became priests; "others," Finberg tells us, "appear later as burgesses, portreeves, and members of parliament."
45. Cf. Nicholas Orme, *English Schools in the Middle Ages* (London: Methuen, 1973), esp. pp. 103-4, 146-49.
46. See Carleton Brown, ed., *Religious Lyrics of the Fourteenth Century* (Oxford: Clarendon Press, 1924), no. 28. This and related songs involving the Christ child are probably variants of a popular lullaby.
47. The peace rolls reveal that in Lincolnshire two men lurked in a churchyard covered with a white sheet, and then attacked one John Lockwood and his servant when they came to see who was there. See Elisabeth G. Kimball, *Some Sessions of the Peace in Lincolnshire 1381-96,* Lincoln Record Society, no. 56 (Hereford: Hereford Times 1962), p. 235.

to call literary.[48] *The Canterbury Tales* contains a reworked saint's legend, an elaborate moral treatise bv Albertanus of Brescia, and a sermon (or treatise) on penance.[49] But Chaucer was fortunate in having a court audience that included noblemen, ecclesiastics, clerks, and officials about the royal court.[50] These are, of course, "people" too, although their tastes were not exactly "popular." Audiences in lesser towns were somewhat less sophisticated and less responsive to various kinds of literary subtlety. Perhaps a few brief remarks about boroughs and their inhabitants may be helpful.

A borough was, as H.P.R. Finberg wrote, "a place where the tenements were held in burgage tenure,"[51] or for rents without services, although the terms under which various persons held could and did vary,[52] and in some boroughs there were remnants of heriot, fealty, and alienation and entrance fees.[53] By population the largest towns were London (about three times as large as the next largest town),

---

48. For works dealing primarily with spiritual guidance, see P.S. Joliffe, *A Check-List of Middle English Prose Writings of Spiritual Guidance* (Toronto: Pontifical Institute of Medieval Studies, 1974). If we were to add to this list works in verse and related works not included in Joliffe's rather rigorous classification, the volume of survivals would be impressive indeed. Some citizens of towns had sufficient training to appreciate similar books in French or Latin, and the same thing might be said of some noblemen.

49. The distinction between a sermon and a treatise, or what we should call a treatise (for the medieval term was looser), is a hazy one, for a lengthy exposition could readily be excerpted for use as a sermon. The Parson's Tale itself omits the Commandments, a fact of which the Parson is clearly aware; see *The Works of Geoffrey Chaucer*, ed. F.N. Robinson, 2d ed. (Boston: Houghton Mifflin, 1957), lines 956-57. Some penitential treatises also included treatments of the Sacraments.

50. See, for example, Derek Pearsall, "The *Troilus* Frontispiece and Chaucer's Audience," *Yearbook of English Studies*, 7 (1977): 73-74.

51. *West-Country Historical Studies*, (New York: A.M. Kelly, 1969), p. 105.

52. The best concise account is M. de W. Hemmeon, "Burgage Tenure in Medieval England," *Law Quarterly Review* 26 (1910): 215-30, 331-48; and ibid., 27 (1911): 44-59. For a very detailed account of tenurial arrangements in Bristol containing frequent comparisons with other boroughs, see E.W.W. Veale, ed., *The Great Red Book of Bristol*, Bristol Record Society, vol. 2, pt. 1 (1931).

53. See Hemmeon's book, *Burgage Tenure in Medieval England* (Cambridge: Harvard Univ. Press, 1914), pp. 59-60.

York, Bristol, Coventry, Plymouth, Norwich, Lincoln, and Salisbury. Coventry was a monastic town, the largest of some thirty such towns in England and a thriving commercial center. Town governments varied a great deal, for, as J.S. Furley wrote, "in the Middle Ages ... there was no uniformity; the system of government in a town depended on its individual history."[54] Borough customs, involving such matters as inheritance, the treatment of felons, and so on, varied from place to place.[55] In some boroughs primogeniture was the rule, as under the common law (except in Kent); in others, "borough English," in accordance with which the youngest son inherited, prevailed. Wives ordinarily took over the shops and tenements of their deceased husbands, whereas under the common law they were entitled to only a third of their husbands' lands for life, except in Kent, where they received half for life, or for so long as they remained single and did not become pregnant.[56] And many borough tenants, like many villein tenants, had the right to will or devise their holdings to others, a privilege denied free tenants under the common law. Chartered boroughs or towns with their own courts and governments tended to have a great deal of civic pride and to be very jealous of their privileges.[57]

Beverley affords a good example of a large agricultural town, in this instance dependent on the raising of oxen, cows, pigs, horses, and sheep, supported in common pastures, although sheep were allowed to wander about the town. It was governed by twelve "keepers"

---

54. *City Government in Winchester* (Oxford: Oxford Univ. Press, 1923), p. 1.
55. See Mary Bateson, *Borough Customs,* Selden Society, nos. 18-19 (London: B. Quaritch, 1904-1906). Further details are often given in the histories and studies of towns listed in the bibliography supplied by Susan Reynolds, *An Introduction to the History of English Medieval Towns* (Oxford: Clarendon Press, 1977), pp. 202-23.
56. For the customs of Kent, see *SR,* 1:223-25, where they are described in terms of Kentish maxims.
57. Cirencester, a monastic town, had its own court until 1309, when the abbot outraged his tenants by forcing them to attend his manorial court. They eventually sought a remedy before the chancellor, but the abbot was able to purchase his privileges, and the town did not regain self-government until the nineteenth century. See H.P.R. Finberg, ed., *Gloucestershire Studies* (Leicester: Leicester Univ. Press, 1957), pp. 74-81.

(*juratores, custodes, gubernatores*) selected from among the more substantial citizens. They were granted the power to collect amercements of the green wax (from the exchequer) by Edward III, thus depriving the Sheriff of York of this privilege — one, incidentally, that sheriffs often abused in spite of King Edward's reforming statute of 1368 (42 Ed. III 9), which was widely disregarded, as a parliamentary complaint of 1393 (*RP,* 3.222) reveals. Such abuses are reflected in the Wakefield *Last Judgment* (line 281). The keepers of Beverley were also responsible for the assize of bread and ale, the amercements from which were delivered to the bailiff of the Archbishop of York, and they themselves heard cases of fraud. The town had a merchant guild and other craft guilds, but here the merchant guild was not the government of the town, as it was at Southampton, where the alderman of the guild was called the "mayor" in the fourteenth century. Among the ancient customs of the town was one in which if a burgess begat offspring upon a concubine, no such offspring could become a citizen of Beverley, even though the father later married the concubine.[58] Beverley Minster, noted for its magnificent Percy tomb (c. 1335-1340), celebrated the feast of "The King of Fools" until it was abolished by Bishop Thomas Arundel in 1388,[59] and the town sponsored plays.[60]

A small town might develop within the confines of an agricultural manor. Thus a settlement of cutlers, smiths, brewers, drapers, and carpenters grew up during the fourteenth century at Thaxted (Essex) near the manor house and the church. These tenants owed biennial attendance at the manorial court and elected a bailiff, but did not acquire a charter until the sixteenth century.[61] Generally, most boroughs included tenements and adjacent agricultural lands which could be

---

58. For Beverley's government and customs, see Arthur F. Leach, ed., *Beverley Town Documents,* Selden Society, (London: B. Quaritch, 1900).
59. Margaret Aston, *Thomas Arundel: A Study of Church Life in the Reign of Richard II* (Oxford: Clarendon Press, 1967), p. 293.
60. For the relevant documents, see Alan H. Nelson, *The Medieval English Stage: Corpus Christi Pageants and Plays* (Chicago: Univ. of Chicago Press, 1974), pp. 88-89.
61. K.C. Newton, *Thaxted in the Fourteenth Century* (Chelmsford: Essex County Council, 1960), pp. 20-23.

held independently of the tenements themselves. Some boroughs were dominated by prominent noblemen. Thus the lord of Leicester was the Earl of Derby (or later the Duke of Lancaster), although the town itself was governed by a mayor and twenty-four "jurats," or wealthy members of the merchants' guild. In 1375 John of Gaunt leased the bailiwick to this government for £80 a year for a period of ten years, the sum being a substitute for the profits from the fair court (which sat for a week at Michaelmas), the piepowder (i.e., "dusty-foot") or merchants' court, and the portmanmoot (presided over by the mayor and the twenty-four), granting at the same time relief from toll and tallage. But the duke kept his rents of mills and ovens, rents collected by the porter of the castle, and his right to the escheat of free tenements. The lease expired in 1385 and was not renewed until 1402. The town had its own elected coroner and chamberlain. There were a number of social guilds (neither craft guilds nor parish guilds), the oldest of which was the guild of Corpus Christi. Members of such guilds attended the funerals of deceased brethren, provided chaplains, held ceremonial dinners, and supported impoverished members. They also sought to supervise the moral behavior of their members, some of whom might be women. Here as elsewhere guilds proliferated after the great plague.[62] Guilds of various kinds, like that of St. Mary at Boston, supported plays, and some parish guilds supported dancing.[63] A guild like that of the Holy Trinity at Louth might also maintain in connection with its chantry a chaplain to instruct boys in manners and "polite letters."[64]

Although Winchester was not a royal manor, the king held the soil of the city, which paid an annual rent of 100 marks to the exchequer in the fourteenth century. It boasted the first mayor in England, legendary in 1184 and actual in 1200. He had twenty-four jurats or "peers" who made up his council, and he presided over a city court

---

62. For these and other details see Mary Bateson, ed., *Records of the Borough of Leicester,* 2 vols. (London: C.J. Clay and Sons, 1899-1923).

63. Dorothy Mary Owen, *Church and Society in Medieval Lincolnshire* (Lincoln: History of Lincolnshire Committee, 1971), pp. 130-31.

64. Ibid., p. 101.

that recorded property transfers, and that dealt with breach of contract or warranty, debt, and trespass. He also held a merchants' court mostly concerned with debts involving foreigners (or noncitizens from elsewhere). When the bishop held his fair at St. Giles, he received the keys to the city from the mayor for sixteen days, since all trade had to be carried out at the fair. The city's two bailiffs, selected from among four nominated by the jurats, were royal officers who acted as property custodians upon the death of a tenant, kept records of property transfers, collected rents and amercements, made presentments at royal courts, and supervised standards of workmanship. The city had a chamberlain, two coroners, whose records were checked against those of the bailiffs, and a cofferer, who kept records but not treasure. There were six wards, each with a chief tithingman (without the judicial powers of London aldermen) who supervised the bedels. Weaving was the chief trade, the products being blankets and burel cloth, so that the chief import was wool.[65]

Other towns might house prosperous merchants engaged in overseas trade. Southampton, for example, was granted freedom from the jurisdiction of the sheriff by Henry III, long before the larger and more prosperous cloth-exporting town of Bristol achieved "county status" in 1373. Southampton did not acquire freedom from tolls, passage, and pontage throughout the realm until the time of Edward III, although that freedom had been bestowed on Bristol by Henry II.[66] The city was dominated by the merchants' guild, which met at prime on the Sunday after Saint John's Day (June 24) and on the Sunday after Saint Hilary (Jan. 13). Such meetings lasted all day and might, indeed, extend for several days. The guild forbade quarrels among its members, punished swearing (without, incidentally, any taint of Lollardy), attended the sick, participated in funerals, and relieved the poor among its members. Members, either by heredity or purchase (not unlike the citizens of London in this respect, although some franchised citizens

---

65. The details here are from J.S. Furley, *City Government in Winchester*, passim.
66. The details concerning city government in the following discussion are from the excellent study by Colin Platt, *Medieval Southampton* (London: Routledge and Kegan Paul, 1973).

were here not members), shared purchased merchandise, and enjoyed freedom from local tolls and customs. The alderman of the guild held courts, supervised officers, kept the peace, summoned meetings, and kept records. His seneschal (steward) oversaw the maintenance of guild and town property, and he was assisted by a council of twelve and four "discreets" or echevins, who were respected older citizens. Two of the twelve were elected bailiffs; there were four jurats of the markets who maintained the quality of fish, meat, poultry, and bread; and twelve guardians kept the peace in five wards. Brokers supervised sales, and there were some sergeants and a clerk. Although local patriotism was intense, heirs of wealthy merchants often abandoned the town to become wealthy freeholders or "franklins."

Like many other towns, Southampton welcomed the Franciscans, providing stone buildings for them (contrary to the rule of the order).[67] A visiting provincial had them destroyed, but his timber and plaster houses were replaced by a stone church and other structures in the late thirteenth century. The church, like many other churches elsewhere, was used for business deals, and the Franciscans were widely respected in the town, for which they provided water systems, as they also did in Bridgenorth, Bristol, Chichester, Coventry, Lichfield, Lincoln, London, Richmond, Carmaethan, Newcastle, Oxford, Scarborough, and Exeter. Friars' churches became popular burial sites, to the disgust of writers like Jean de Meun and, later, Erasmus, and the burgesses often remembered the friars in their wills. It is quite probable, however, that the friars stimulated the growth of lay spirituality, and that their influence included the popularization of devotional literature and penitential treatises, and the conversion of popular lyrics and carols into more obviously devotional songs, however innocent of anything except a certain amount of figurative language the originals may have been. Their sermons, with

---

67. Other orders were promment in other towns. Thus, for example, at Clare, Suffolk, the Augustinian friars were prominent, enjoying the patronage of Elizabeth de Burgh and Lionel, Duke of Clarence. See Gladys H. Thornton, *A History of Clare, Suffolk* (Cambridge: W. Heffer and Sons, 1928), pp. 84-88. In London the Dominicans and Carmelites enjoyed close association with the royal government and the Augustinians were promoted by the Bohun family.

the literary adornments characteristic of Franciscan preaching, evidently captured the attention and sympathy of their local benefactors and their wives, and it is likely that they sponsored pageantry of one kind or another on high feast days.

The wealth of the friars, which sometimes contrasted sharply with their professed ideals, especially where Franciscans were concerned, and their rivalry with parish priests in preaching, hearing confessions, and burying the dead, promoted controversy not only among the learned but among lesser folk as well. The friars were sometimes accused of seducing women,[68] and it is quite possible that some popular lyrics are counteraccusations in kind inspired by the friars themselves. A historian of the manor of Winton in Sussex wrote, "It is curious that in the fifty years during which clergy are mentioned (1356-1408) only one name of a rector occurs, but it can hardly have been the same person throughout."[69] The name in question was "Sir John," which was indeed a common epithet for a rector. The songs "A Betrayed Maiden's Lament," "Our Sir John," and "Jolly Jankyn," where "Jankyn" is a contemptuous diminutive of "Sir John,"[70] may have been inspired by friars, although it is true that others besides friars, like Chaucer's Parson, for example, or Bishop Brinton, complained about lecherous priests; and the peace rolls afford many specific examples. Antifraternal songs are not always obvious at first glance. Thus the equation of fox with friar was a common enough bit of iconographic humor. In the lyric "The False Fox"[71] the predator "assoils" the geese before seizing his chosen victim, thus revealing his identity.[72] At times, as in the Vernon Lyrics, praise and blame of the friars may appear in the same

---

68. The accusation was actually based on 2 Tim. 3:6, originally used against the friars by William of St. Amour. See D.W. Robertson, Jr., *Chaucer's London* (New York: Wiley, 1968), pp. 192-96.
69. William Hudson, "On a Series of Rolls of the Manor of Winton," Sussex Archaeological Society Collections, no. 54 (1911), p. 181.
70. Rossell Hope Robbins, ed., *Secular Lyrics of the Fourteenth and Fifteenth Centuries* (Oxford: Clarendon Press, 1952), nos. 25, 26, and 27.
71. Ibid., no. 49.
72. This absolution for understandable reasons has disappeared from the American version of the song as rendered by Burl Ives.

collection.[73] It is true also that oppressive ecclesiastics like the Summoner at the Trial of Mary in the *Ludus Coventriae*[74] are often ridiculed in popular writings.

Southern coastal towns suffered especially from the wars. In 1360 Southampton, like Winchester and Plymouth, was exempted from war taxes on account of poverty. And in 1376 the town asked the king to take it into his own hands (a considerable sacrifice) and to prepare its defenses. After the coastal raids of 1377, the great architect Henry Yevele was asked to build a new keep for the castle, the construction of which was carried out during the anxious years 1382-1388. The same kind of danger affected towns elsewhere. On 30 November 1377 a writ was addressed to Leicester, as well as to other towns, to prepare a balinger for use in defense "at the cost of only the most honorable and richest men of the towns aforesaid."[75] The wine trade, important especially to merchants who exported cloth to Gascony, was often threatened. Thus in 1377 the king commanded that the vintage fleet be accompanied by the royal fleet, and orders were issued in 1384, 1385, 1386, and 1388 for the wine fleet to proceed in convoys.[76]

In times of peace, however, life, especially for the wives of well-to-do merchants, must have been rather pleasant, anticipating the situation discovered among wives of English merchants by Van Meteren during his visit to England in the sixteenth century. There are at least hints of this sort of thing in the song "On the Follies of Fashion,"[77] in Chaucer's description of the wives of his fraternal craftsmen in the General Prologue to his *Tales,* and in the Prologue to

---

73. Brown, *Religious Lyrics of the Fourteenth Century,* no. 103, ll. 49-60, and no. 117, ll. 49-56.

74. For a discussion, see Rosemary Woolf, *The English Mystery Plays* (Berkeley: Univ. of California Press, 1972), pp. 174-75. Other plays contain somewhat less obvious but telling examples.

75. Bateson, *Records of the Borough of Leicester,* 2:161-62.

76. Margery K. James, *Studies in the Medieval Wine Trade,* ed. E.M. Veale (Oxford: Oxford Univ. Press, 1971), p. 131. On the relationship between trade and war, see especially Kenneth Fowler, "War and Change in Late Medieval France and England," in Fowler, ed., *The Hundred Years War* (London: Macmillan, 1971), esp. pp. 4-8.

77. Brown, *English Lyrics of the Thirteenth Century,* no. 74.

the Wife of Bath's Tale, all, of course, disapproving. The Wife likes to dress in her best clothes and go to vigils, processions, and sermons, to go on pilgrimages, and to attend marriages. She also likes to see "pleyes of myracles," which must have appealed to persons of all degrees. Finally, like Van Meteren's wives, she liked to spend a great deal of time with her "gossips," although in Chaucer's time she might well have qualified as a "scold" because of the calumny she heaped on her old husbands. Guilds and fraternities held processions on the days of their patron saints, or on Corpus Christi, and members of town governments and guildsmen paraded through the streets with carols and minstrelsy on festive occasions dressed in colorful costumes. In London, Saint John's Eve (Midsummer) was just such an occasion, and in view of the antiquity of the custom and its widespread and enduring practice[78] — probably in celebration of the transformation of the Old Law into the New, for witches, elves, and fairies held sway until midnight — we can assume that leafy boughs and flowers were draped over houses and shops in towns and villages throughout England, that bonfires were lit in the streets about which the inhabitants sang and danced, and that officials paraded through the streets with minstrelsy all singing and dancing processional carols. The night's revels might be dangerous for girls, as the song "A Midsummer Day's Dance" reveals,[79] for not all of them enjoyed the supervising wisdom of Shakespeare's Theseus. Meetings of merchant guilds and fraternities were probably also graced with song or the reading of poetical narratives like *Havelok the Dane,* which offered an appealing combination of slapstick

---

78. See Richard Axton, *European Drama of the Early Middle Ages* (Pittsburgh: Univ. of Pittsburgh Press, 1975), pp. 147-50, 183-84; Adam de la Halle, *Le Jeu de la Feuillé;* Dunbar's *Twa Mariit Wemen and the Wedo.* Shakespeare's *Midsummer Night's Dream* deftly reflects the tradition. There is some information about the custom in Robert Chambers, ed., *Book of Days* (London: W. and R. Chambers, 1888), 1:814-17. For the London observance see R.R. Sharpe, ed., *Calendar of Letter Books Preserved among the Archives of the Corporation of the City of London* (London: J.E. Francis, 1899 et seq.), *Letter Book H,* p. 232; and J. Stow, *A Survey of London,* ed. C.L. Kingsford (Oxford: Clarendon Press, 1908), 1:101-3.

79. Robbins, *Secular Lyrics,* no. 28.

humor and outrageously stated but ultimately genuine civic patriotism to the fishermen of Grimsby, or later the more obviously comic *Tournament at Tottenham,* probably composed for a civic celebration of some kind. It seems quite likely that much literature of this kind has been lost, and, further, that some of the other surviving "vernacular romances" (a contradiction in terms where English narratives are concerned), the humor of which has been often overlooked, were used for town festivities.

Monastic towns, like monastic manors, enjoyed less freedom of self-government than other towns. Thus at Bury St. Edmunds (a cloth center), except in those areas subject to the manor of Clare or tenements held by the Hastings family, the sacrist was lord of the town and the obedientiaries held the town property and rented it to the tenants. The manor of Bury, consisting of some 212 acres of arable land in addition to heath, wood, and pasture, was controlled by the cellarer, who had the View of Frankpledge, market rights, the right to forestall, the right to dig clay, fishing rights, the profits of mills, and miscellaneous rents. The sacrist appointed the town bailiffs, held the View there (which was extended in 1383-1384 to all residents), presided over the assizes of weights and measures and bread and ale, acted as archdeacon in the ecclesiastical court, collected tolls, and had the right of tronage.[80] It seems obvious that the sacrist and the cellarer were busy men, deeply involved in worldly affairs. But the monastery was also active in providing plays and pageantry for the entertainment and instruction of the citizens and their rural neighbors.[81] At Chester both the Abbey of St. Wearmouth and the nuns of St. Mary's held franchises in the town, so that part of it was under monastic jurisdiction, a fact that gave rise to some friction.[82] The town itself had two courts, the "Prentice" court, which was the sheriff's court, and the Portmoot, or mayor's court, which entertained

---

80. See M.D. Lobel, *The Borough of Bury St. Edmunds* (Oxford: Clarendon Press, 1935), pp. 1-53.
81. See Gail McMurray Gibson, "Bury St. Edmunds, Lydgate, and the *N-Town Cycle*," *Speculum* 56 (1981): 56-90.
82. Douglas Jones, *The Church in Chester 1300-1540*, Chetham Society, 3rd ser., 7 (Manchester: Butler and Tanner, 1957) 39-42.

pleas of land, cases of forestalling, purpresture and encroachment, and trespass, which was, in fact, considered in both courts.[83]

Town court rolls usually present us with more or less routine business, including land transactions; violations of the assize of ale (mostly by women, who often appear year after year for this offense, apparently paying fines as a sort of license), or bread (mostly by men); cases of debt or covenant; cases of negligence, like leaving dung in the streets; or the punishment of scolds (technically by means of the cucking-stool, but more frequently by the more profitable means of amercements). They nevertheless sometimes afford us interesting glimpses of the people and their behavior. According to the *Court Rolls of the Borough of Colchester,* in that city (as in London) a man might be fined for carrying a knife,[84] victimizing Flemings by summoning them and punishing them (2:171), or eavesdropping, a widely recognized trespass (3:162). A woman might receive a very heavy fine for adultery (13s. 4d.; 3:110), a fact that should dispel the notion that such fines were imposed only on manorial bondwomen. Receiving or maintaining harlots could bring either a man or a woman before the court (2:24; 3:49,104). Harlots in Colchester were supposed to stay in Berislane, just as they were supposed to stay in Cock Lane outside the wall in London, and could be fined for seeking business elsewhere (3:177, 186). Women consistently outnumbered men brought before the court for forestalling (2:4, 13, 39, 76, 105, 130, 142).

The rolls sometimes reveal interesting characters, among whom at Colchester was one John Stanstede, appearing on the rolls first as a chaplain and later on one occasion as a rector. In 1372 the rector of St. Michaels of La Mylande, Colchester, was alleged to have wagered John Stanstede, chaplain, that if he could throw him he would give the spectators a gallon of wine and John two quarters of grain at Michaelmas. John threw him, but the rector refused the grain and denied the covenant. The rector failed to appear and was in mercy (3:11). Two

---

83. See A. Hopkins, *Select Rolls of the Chester City Courts,* Chetham Society, 3rd ser., 2 (1950): xviii-xxiii. The introduction to this volume contains useful comparative notes.

84. I.H. Jeayes, ed. and trans., *Court Rolls of the Borough of Colchester* (Colchester: Town Council of the Borough of Colchester 1921-1941), 2:226.

years later it was agreed at Colchester market that if Master Nicholas, a doctor, could solve a question put to him by William Dentone, John Stanstede would pay a cordwainer a pair of boots worth 2s. But when Master Nicholas solved the question, Stanstede refused to pay the cordwainer (3:59). These last cases illustrate the validity of verbal covenants before witnesses in local courts, not to mention a taste for playful humor among townsmen. To get a hearing before the royal justices concerning contract or covenant without a written record, it was necessary to allege a breach of the peace, *vi et armis,* an expression often followed by the formula "to wit, with swords and bows and arrows," although no such weapons might be involved. An entry in the court roll for 1377 mentions a death's-head mask, a tunic with tails, and other apparatus for playing "miracles" (3:140). We can assume, therefore, that this form of entertainment was available at Colchester as elsewhere.

A few more cases from the *Records of the Borough of Nottingham* will illustrate the kind of justice administered as well as something of the mores of the people. In 1360 one John Shakespere alleged that a servant of John de Spondon "vi et armis insultum fecit, et ipsum vulneravit, verberavit, maletractavit, et sanguinavit et alia enormia ei intulit ... contra pacem," committing 100s. damages. The court awarded him 40d.[85] In 1364 Thomas Hutton complained that on a day he was sitting in a tavern when Richard de Cobeley, shearman, "vi et armis ipsum Thomam insultum fecit, et ipsum verberavit, et quemdam ciphum plenum cervisiae in facie ejus jactavit ... contra pacem," committing 20s. damages. For this enormity the court awarded him a ha'penny (pp. 183-85).

In Nottingham a chaplain might be hired to educate boys. Thus in 1395 a chaplain complained to the court that one William Tole had neglected to pay him 3s. 4d. for teaching his boy for five terms (p. 263). Other chaplains might engage in less commendable activities. Thus in 1389 John de Bilby complained that Roger de Mampton, chaplain, broke into his close and entered his chamber, where John found him under the curtains of a bed. When John asked what he did there, Roger

---

85. W.H. Stevenson, ed., *Records of the Borough of Nottingham* (London: B. Quaritch, 1882), 1: 177.

replied that he did not come in any evil way. He promised not to enter John's premises again nor to be found with John's wife. Nevertheless, on a certain night, Roger broke John's wall and was with John's wife a long time "ubi secreta sua fuerunt." And so he did continually for a year to John's loss of two pairs of sheets, tablecloths, towels, a brass pot worth 13s. 4d., and the profit of four quarters of malt lost through Roger's coming and going to the damage of £100. Roger replied that he was simply making his rounds with holy water, a defense that may have produced laughter but won him small sympathy from the court (pp. 241-43). The peace rolls, incidentally, record many similar offenses on the part of chaplains.[86] The case reminds us a little of "A Midsummer Day's Dance," mentioned above, where the seducer is a holy-water clerk.

It is impossible to include "lords of manors" in a single social category, for they might include the king, the queen, greater and lesser noblemen or noble ladies, bishops, cathedral canons, abbots, priors, monastic obedientiaries, clerks, lawyers, merchants, tradesmen, parsons, self-perpetuating groups of trustees, colleges, town governments, or, in fact, almost any person or group of persons with sufficient wealth. The word *manor* is, moreover, a rather vague term, since a group of tenements in a town held by a single lord might be called a manor, and manors that were partly urban and partly rural were not unusual. Even in the countryside a manor might be chiefly residential, in some instances a place for monks to take their vacations from the routine of monastic life, and some agricultural manors were highly specialized. The modern historical vocabulary is here as elsewhere somewhat simplistic, especially where discussions of "the manorial system" are involved.

---

86. See for example, Elizabeth G. Kimball, ed., *Rolls of the Gloucestershire Sessions of the Peace 1361-98,* Transactions of the Bristol and Gloucestershire Archaeological Society (Kendal: T. Wilson, 1942), 62: 115-16, 122-23, 124-25, 130, 154; Elizabeth Chapin Furber, ed., *Essex Sessions of the Peace 1351, 1377-1379,* Essex Archaeological Society Occasional Publications (Colchester: Essex Archaelogical Society, 1953), 3:169; Bertha Haven Putnam, ed., *Proceedings before the Justices of the Peace in the Fourteenth and Fifteenth Centuries,* Ames Foundation (London: Spottiswood, Ballantyne and Co., 1938), pp. 112, 112-13, 139-40. Rectors, parsons, and vicars were sometimes similarly inclined. See ibid., pp. 113, 119, 120, 220, 369. Even an archdeacon might succumb. See Furber, *Essex Sessions,* p. 98.

We do have some descriptions of manor houses and their appurtenances. An especially fine one was the home of the distinguished warrior Sir Nigel de Loring, who had been knighted at Sluys, became a Garter Knight in 1344, and served as chamberlain to Prince Edward. In his later years he retired to Chalgrave manor, although as a man of substantial wealth, he held other manors elsewhere.[87] The house at Chalgrave contained first a great hall, where Sir Nigel, his wife, his two daughters, the chaplain, his steward (when he was not on his rounds), and visitors took their meals on a dais, while the household servants and perhaps the local reeve at harvest time ate in the hall below. Conventionally, there would have been a gallery built on the wall above the dais for minstrels or reading clerks, who might furnish entertainment or instruction at dinner, and somewhere in the hall was a large fireplace. In all probability the walls were decorated with Sir Nigel's arms and armor and perhaps some tapestries or decorative hangings. At the western end, where the dais was setup, there were the usual pantry, buttery, wine cellar, larder, a chamber for wood, three upper chambers, one with a latrine, and a basement below, perhaps containing a kitchen. An outer court enclosed a garden for vegetables and herbs. Adjacent to the hall at the eastern end was a chapel with an enclosed rose garden on the outside. There was a guesthouse with a garden and a gatehouse at the entry. Other buildings included a dairy house, a bakery, a malt house, a kiln house, an alehouse, a well house, a cart house, a stable, and several barns, including a large barn with seven bays, a haybarn, a strawbarn, a peas barn, and a granary. There were, in addition, two sheepcotes, a pigsty, a boarsty, a cowhouse, an oxhouse, a dovecote, and facilities for poultry, including geese. Within the grounds there were two orchards, one with two fishponds and one with three, as well as a nursery and a vivarium. A nearby field contained another pond. Altogether, Sir Nigel and his

---

87. Marian K. Dale, ed., *Court Rolls of Chalgrave Manor, 1278-1313*, Bedfordshire Historical Record Society (Streatley: The Society, 1950), 28:xviii. At his death Sir Nigel left bequests to the friars, to nunneries, and to churches in thirteen parishes where he held manors. For his manors in Devon and Cornwall, see *Calendar of Inquisitions Post Mortem*, vol. 16, 7-15 R II (1974), nos. 128-29, pp. 96-97; no. 326, p.116.

family must have lived in considerable comfort. We can assume a Bible and service books for the chapel, and probably prayer books, meditations, and devotional works, including a manual of penance, some of which were used when the family and their guests assembled in the chapel for evening prayers.

Many manor houses were, of course, far less elaborate than this one, which resembles the larger "inns" or residences in London except that it had more extensive grounds. Many lords among the nobility, like Thomas IV Lord Berkeley (1368-1417), were much given to the chase, hunting hares, deer, foxes, and badgers,[88] and some abbots maintained hunting dogs for the entertainment of their noble friends and benefactors, lesser monks being restrained from such pursuits. A bishop might have similar facilities.[89] Whether noblemen generally had literary interests has been the subject of some discussion. It was not necessary for a nobleman to be very literate to enjoy narratives, whether pious, historical, or jocular, read to him by a clerk or minstrel, or plays presented in a nearby town. It is quite likely also that active military men enjoyed songs and stories on festive occasions or at tournaments. Some of them had collections of books. Thus Guy de Beauchamp, Earl of Warwick, gave Bordesley Abbey some forty books, including some books of the Bible, meditations, saints' lives, romances and histories, a book of physic, one on surgery, a primer for children, an encyclopedia, and a miscellaneous anthology, all in French.[90] Clanchy has pointed out that by 1300 "an educated layman" was "probably familiar with three literary languages (Latin, French, and English)."[91] We do not know how many noblemen were "educated," but the proliferation of government documents of all kinds and the necessity for written records acted as a profound stimulus to learning. Chaucer, who was addressing a noble and clerical

---

88. See John Smyth, *The Lives of the Berkeleys,* Bristol and Gloucestershire Archaeological Society (Gloucester: J. Bellows, 1883-85), 2:12.
89. For a "chace of deer" held by the Bishop of Chichester, see Peckam, "Thirteen Customals," p. 124.
90. Clanchy, *From Memory to Written Record,* p. 60.
91. Ibid., p. 86.

audience, employs frequent references (not all of which are obvious at first glance) to the Bible, the Latin classics, and to medieval works in both Latin and French. We must assume that he did so because his audience appreciated them.

Noblemen were naturally interested in historical writings, especially in writings, whether actually historical or fabulous, that concerned their ancestors. Indeed, those with long military careers might well acquire works that contained material about themselves. We sometimes forget that the *Chronicles* of Froissart were at one time "popular" reading for boys throughout England and that men with military experience or aspirations were likely to have been even more interested in them earlier. The subject of history appealed to abbots as well. Thus we learn that one abbot sought to borrow a book that "temporibus Godefridi de Bolon' aliorumque nobilium conquestum continet terre sancte."[92] One rather notorious abbot, Thomas of Pipe, of the Cistercian abbey of Stoneleigh, became noted as a local historian, so that Dugdale was led to observe that "his memory will be of good esteem to all that are lovers of history."[93] His notoriety arises from the fact that during his administration the abbey — which, King Edward said, had been founded by his ancestors to provide chantries and other works of piety for his ancestors, himself, and his heirs — had neglected its chantries and had ceased both to give alms to the poor and to shelter pilgrims. He sent a commission to investigate in December of 1363. It was found that the abbot had alienated without any consideration or rent a messuage, a carucate of land, and ten marks in rents to his concubine, Isabella, and to their eldest son John, "de voluptuose affeccione quam habuit predicte Isabelle et filio eorumdem." He had also alienated a grange to some servants so that its income was used for the exclusive support of himself, Isabella, and her children, said to be "greater in number than his monks." Thomas had also disseized a tenant wrongfully through a false deed and then, to avoid discovery, reenfeoffed the holding to him in fee simple "to the

---

92. W.A. Pantin, "The Letters of John Mason," in *Essays in Medieval History Presented to Bertie Wilkinson*, ed. T.A. Sandquist and M.R. Powicke (Toronto: Univ. of Toronto Press, 1969), pp. 216-17.

93. Sir William Dugdale, *Monasticon Anglicanum* (London: J. Bohn, 1846), 5:445.

disherison of the aforesaid abbey." The king seized the abbey until a new abbot was elected in 1365. Oddly, Pipe was abbot once more in 1381, but retired in 1382.[94]

Erring abbots like Thomas of Pipe or the unfortunate abbot of Missenden in Buckinghamshire who was drawn and hanged for forging and clipping the royal coinage — a treasonous offense[95] — were rare, although others might be simply inefficient. More influential abbeys did a great deal of entertaining, becoming in effect social centers for noblemen, merchants, or lawyers, who exchanged gossip concerning current affairs (a source of rumors) and enjoyed the food served to them. We may safely assume that at dinner some instructive and edifying material (like selections from *Piers Plowman*, for example) was often read before the company. Larger abbeys, friaries, and cathedrals often maintained extensive libraries, which sometimes contained works that might be called "popular" in a restricted sense, like Holcot's commentary on *Wisdom*, the *De regimine principum* of Aegidius Romanus, or even romances.

Generally, medieval people in all walks of life were alert to wit and humor, and, at the same time, thirsty for practical moral instruction, appreciating both the "solaas" and the "sentence" that might be found in a great variety of works ranging from sermons (not always without humor), historical works, romances, songs and poems on the evils of the time, instructive works on law,[96] medicine, or natural history, to mere fabliaux. No one thought that there was anything very odd about speaking the truth with a smile. Their assemblies, whether associated with meetings ofparliament,[97] court sessions in counties, hundreds,

---

94. See G.O. Sayles, ed., *Select Cases in the Court of King's Bench*, Selden Society (London: B. Quaritch, 1971) 7: 133-35; Hilton, *Stoneleigh Leger Book*, xviii-xxi.

95. Sayles, *Select Cases*, 7:118.

96. For an example of humor in a law book, see the hypothetical case of a tenant who took a fish from his lord's pond in Maitland and Baildon, *The Court Baron*, pp. 54-55.

97. The mayor's accounts at Leicester for 1357-1358 include, among his expenses in London, 4d. paid to the King's fool. See Bateson, *Records of the Borough of Leicester*, 2:108. There is every reason to assume that diversions involving song and story were arranged by parliamentary representatives during their sojourns in London.

or manors and towns, festivals at churches, friaries, houses of canons, or monasteries, or fairs, markets, processions and town festivals, offered them opportunities to hear and enjoy what we might call "popular" literature. Lords could sometimes enjoy it in their manor houses, and, as the works of Chaucer attest, there were opportunities for literary entertainment at the royal court, and it seems quite likely that similar opportunities were available at the courts of prominent noblemen. However, I think that we should remember that there was then nothing like the large homogeneous audience available for writers today, when tastes are largely Epicurean in nature and when reactions to song and story are predominantly emotional. As has often been observed, medieval people were practical rather than sentimental, an attitude made more or less natural by the fact that life was then more difficult, a great deal shorter, and not very rich in opportunities for leisure, which was not regarded then as something to be cultivated in any event but as an invitation to irrational behavior. It will repay us when considering medieval popular literature (or any other kind of literature) to consider the question of the audience to whom it was addressed and, where possible, the kind of occasion for which it might have been used.

Chaucer and the Economic and Social Consequences of the Plague

D. W. Robertson, Jr.

In: *Social Unrest in the Late Middle Ages. Papers of Fifteenth Annual Conference of the Center for Medieval and Early Renaissance Studies,* ed. Francis X. Newman (Binghamton, NY: SUNY Binghamton Press, 1986), pp. 49-74.

I.

I hope you will pardon me if in this lecture I devote more attention to background than to the work of Chaucer, which I should much prefer to discuss. Again, you may notice a certain skepticism on my part concerning the topic announced in the title. The series of plagues that struck England during Chaucer's lifetime undoubtedly contributed to social change and to social unrest, but the effects of disease are difficult to isolate from those of other kinds of hardship, and it is also true that they might have been very different in a differently structured society with other means of response and other attitudes. Moreover, a change in ways of doing things in one area of human activity is likely to have repercussions in other areas and to produce situations that are in themselves, regardless of their origins, productive of further changes and developments. It may help to remind ourselves of what some of the "other kinds of hardship" were, and we are fortunately able to do so from a fourteenth-century point of view. In the jubilee address Edward III prepared to be read in Parliament, for he was too ill to attend himself, in the fiftieth year of his reign (1377), the king, who was about to announce a comprehensive pardon for various offenses and debts, spoke of "the great charges and losses which the said people [his subjects] have had and suffered in times past, as well as by the wars, and otherwise by the pestilence of the people, murrain of beasts, and the fruits of the land commonly failed by evil years in times past, whereof our Sovereign Lord the King hath great compassion ...."[1] It is noteworthy that the king mentioned "the wars" first, before going on to mention what might be called in modern legal parlance "acts of God," although it is true that a great many people, including King Edward, regarded all of the things he mentioned as being the providential consequences of sin.[2] Warfare was something for which Edward as king exercised primary responsibility, and after the resumption of the war with France in 1368 England did not fare very well. In addition to human losses in the field through military action or disease, war entailed onerous taxation, purveyance on a large scale, sometimes extortionate, the activation of commissioners of array who were not always honest, and widespread subjection to the misbehavior of troops either moving toward ports of departure or awaiting departure in the areas of ports. Again, returned soldiers often became robbers instead of settling down to honest labor. In fact, it was one of the first duties of the justices of the peace when they were established to seize and arrest such all persons who could be found.[3] In some coastal regions and in the Scottish

---

1. *Statutes of the Realm* (London, 1810–1828), 1. 396-97, (hereafter *SR).* May McKisack, *The Fourteenth Century* (Oxford, 1959), p. 396, calls the pardon a "colossal bribe," but this may be a little extreme. Edward's concern for his people, which he frequently expressed, should not be regarded simply as a device for gaining revenue.

2. On Edward's reaction to pestilence, see J. F. D. Shrewsbury, *A History of Bubonic Plague in Medieval England* (Oxford, 1975), p. 68. Cf. on war John Barnie, *War in Medieval English Society* (Ithaca, 1974), p. 28. And generally, see the "Verses on the Earthquake of 1382," in Carleton Brown, ed., *Religious Lyrics of the Fourteenth Century* (Oxford, 1924), no. 113, pp. 186-88.

3. *SR*, 1. 364-65. Returned military leaders with distinguished careers were also difficult to control. For example, Sir Matthew Gurney fought in France and Spain after 1340, and with the companies after the treaty of Bretigny. He was at Auray in 1364. In 1388, at age eighty, he acted as constable for Edmund of York, who went to Spain to aid Gaunt. He and his lawyer, John Janet, engaged in very dubious activities at home. Sir Matthew was indicted for trespass in 1380, but obtained a writ *supersedeas*. In 1381 he was pardoned for

border area many persons suffered from the ravages of enemy raiders, and commercial shipping was frequently impeded. During the following reign under Richard, England's fortunes in warfare steadily declined. Partly as a result of taxation that seemed ineffectual, partly as a result of coastal raids, and partly as a result of other factors, for some of which the government was responsible, a revolt broke out in 1381. By 1386 the country was faced by an enormous hostile invasion fleet and by simultaneous threats from the north and the south. The court had been disrupted into factions, the king was threatened with deposition, and a civil uprising led to the drastic actions of the Merciless Parliament. When it was not waged effectively war could lead to attacks on English ports and severe disruptions in trade, necessary to the welfare of all social ranks. [4]

During the last years of his reign Edward did not exercise very firm control of his government either in wars[5] or in matters of routine administration, although he did not mention this fact in the preamble to his jubilee pardon. But corruption or highhanded action could and did give rise to unrest. The king had been warned about these matters early in his reign, first by Archbishop Mepham, who observed that the illegal and extortionate behavior of household purveyors might lead

---

contempts, trespasses, and extortions. In 1385 he was in trouble for mayhem, but obtained another *supersedeas*. Nevertheless, he served as JP in 1381–1385, as well as being named in commissions of oyer and terminer, and, in addition, was constable for the court of chivalry. He was sued by a London weaver in 1388, who alleged that he and John Janet had imprisoned him until he promised to pay Sir Matthew, who alleged that he was his serf, £1000 for manumission. Sir Matthew was named on peace commissions in 1388–1392 and became a member of the royal council under Henry IV. He died finally at the age of 97. See Isobel D. Thornley and T. F. T. Plucknett, *Year Books of Richard II: 11 R II* (Ames Foundation, 1937), pp. xiii-xvi and 170-74. Another example is afforded by Richard de Aske of Aughton, who, although he received various pardons for felonies because of his service in France, frequently served on commissions, including oyer and terminer and sewers. See Bertha Haven Putnam, *Yorkshire Sessions of the Peace,* Yorkshire Archaeological Society, Record Series, vol. 100 (1939), pp. xxxix-xl.

4. For the effects on Southampton, for example, see Colin Platt, *Medieval Southampton* (London and Boston, 1973), pp. 125-28.

5. Cf. George Holmes, *The Good Parliament* (Oxford, 1975), p. 90.

to rebellion,[6] and then by Archbishop Stratford who threatened to excommunicate royal officers who at Edward's behest had imprisoned a number of persons without due process in violation of the Great Charter.[7] However, Edward issued a series of statutes to control purveyors for royal or baronial households, the most comprehensive of which in 1362 would have solved the problem if it had been faithfully enforced.[8] The failure of his early efforts to buy allies abroad also taught him the dangers of excessive taxation. It must be said in his favor that he sought to control the actions of sheriffs and bailiffs. A statute of 1340 (14 Ed III 1.7)[9] demanded that sheriffs be appointed for only one year, and that each have only one bailiff errant or "outrider"; for "outriders," it was said, had "notoriously destroyed the people." When Chaucer called his monk, probably an external cellarer, an "outrider" he was using pejorative language suggestive of extortion.[10] In 1354 (28 Ed III 7)[11] it was stipulated that no sheriff could succeed himself. And

---

6. See J. Moisant, ed., *Speculo regis Edwardi III* (Recensio A) (Paris, 1891), p.96.
7. The events surrounding this action are described in detail by G. L. Harriss, *King, Parliament, and Public Finance to 1369* (Oxford, 1975), chapters twelve and thirteen.
8. 4 Ed III 3, 4, *SR*, 1. 262; 5 Ed III 2, p. 266; 10 Ed III 2.1, p. 276; 14 Ed III 1.19, p. 288; 18 Ed III 2.7, p. 301; 25 Ed III 5.1, p. 319; 28 Ed III 12, p. 347; 34 Ed III 2,3, p. 365; 36 Ed III 1.2,3,4, p. 371.
9. *SR*, 1. 283.
10. Traditionally the manorial bailiff of a monastery was a cellarer. At St. Peter, Westminster, there were two cellarers, one "external" who oversaw the manors, and the other "internal." When the external cellarer spent several days in the monastery he took over the duties of the internal cellarer, who remained in the cloister. See Edward Maunde Thompson, ed., *Customary of the Benedictine Monasteries of Saint Augustine, Canterbury and Saint Peter, Westminster,* 2 vols., Henry Bradshaw Society vol. 28 (1904), 2:69. At St. Albans Abbey the cellarer acted as a kind of itinerant justice at the biennial Halimotes. See A. E. Levett, "The Court and Court Rolls of St. Albans Abbey," *TRHS*, 4th ser. 8 (1924): 60. The Benedictine Rule specifies that the cellarer should be "wise, mature in conduct, temperate, not an excessive eater, not proud, excitable, offensive, dilatory, or wasteful, but God-fearing, and like a father to the whole community." He should, moreover, be above all humble. See *The Rule of St. Benedict in Latin and English with Notes,* ed. Timothy Fry, O.S.B. (Collegeville, Minn., 1981), pp. 227, 229. Chaucer's monk hardly rides resplendent in these virtues.
11. *SR*, 1. 346. This statute was not consistently enforced.

in 1368 (42 Ed III 9)[12] it was decreed that estreats (or extracts from exchequer rolls sent to the sheriff so that he could collect fines and amercements) be clearly marked to identify their purposes and that they be sealed and totted in the presence of the debtor upon payment so that they could not be used twice for the same fine. Finally in 1372[13] sheriffs were forbidden to act as members of Parliament, along with lawyers doing business for the king. In addition to extortionate sheriffs and bailiffs the men of the shires had to contend with unscrupulous and greedy escheators.[14] A statute of 1360 (34 Ed III 12)[15] stipulated that escheators who seized land for alleged treason in deceased ancestors should warn their victims first with writs of *scire facias* so that they might present an answer on a given day, that the inquests held by escheators should be made before "good people of good fame," in the counties, and that inquests be indentured between the escheators and the juries so that the presentations of escheators could be verified. Further, tenants whose lands were seized because they had alienated without royal license, or were said to be heirs within age, could be heard at King's Bench if they objected. The abuses indicated are clear enough.

Perhaps more important were the remedies Edward decreed for abuses in the administration of justice, especially his great Ordinance for the Justices of 1346,[16] designed to prevent maintenance and procurement. If it had been enforced a great many miseries might have been avoided. The king, calling attention to the abuses just mentioned, said that he was "greatly moved of conscience in this matter," so that as much "for the pleasure of God and the ease and quietness of our subjects, as to save our conscience, and to save and keep our said oath, we have ordained the things following." I shall summarize them briefly:

---

12. Ibid., 1. 389.
13. Ibid., 1. 394.
14. On the duties of escheators, see *SR*, 1. 238-41.
15. Ibid., 1. 367-68.
16. Ibid., 1. 303-6. The oath covering the points of the Ordinance is given at length.

1. All justices should treat rich and poor alike with no regard to persons (a scriptural principle, incidentally[17]) and should disregard "any letters or commandment" either from the king or anyone else that might impede equal right, and should report any such letters to the king and Council.

2. Justices should take no fees or robes from anyone except the king, and no gifts beyond food and drink of small value.

3. They should give no counsel to anyone, great or small, in matters involving the king (or actions *contra pacem*, felonies, or cases involving lands held by tenants in chief).

4. The barons of the exchequer should treat rich and poor alike and avoid delays.

5. Justices of assize and jail delivery should take an oath to observe the ordinance.

6. No one in the royal household should maintain the cause of another, and each should keep the ordinance.

7. All great men should eliminate from their households fees and robes for "bearers and maintainers," who were to be brought before the king and his council.

8. The justices of assize were instructed to "inquire of sheriffs, escheators, bailiffs of franchises, and of their under ministers, and also of maintainers, common embracers, and jurors in the country" concerning the "gifts, rewards, and other profits which the said ministers do take of the people to execute their office, and that which pertaineth to their office, and of making array of panels [one of the chief duties of the sheriff], putting in the same suspect jurors, and of evil fame; and of the fact that maintainers, embracers, and jurors do take rewards against the parties,[18] whereby losses do come daily to the people...."

9. Such persons were to be punished "as law and reason requires" both at the suit of the king and the suit of the parties, and the chancellor and the treasurer should be alerted to hear complaints.

---

17. I cite only New Testament examples: Acts 10:34; Rom. 2:11; Eph. 6:9; James 2:9; 1 Pet. 1:17; Jude 16.

18. Cf. Ps. 14:5, a verse that plays an important part in *Piers Plowman*. See D. W. Robertson, Jr., and B. F. Huppé, *Piers Plowman and Scriptural Tradition* (Princeton, 1951), pp. 53-57, 60, 161, 210.

This Ordinance was repeated as a statute in 1384 (8 R II 3),[19] with the stipulation that those justices found guilty lose their offices, but it was repealed in the following year as being "too severe." An effort to revive it in 1386 when Chaucer was attending Parliament failed.

Edward reinforced his Ordinance in 1357 in a statute against champerty (31 Ed III 4.10).[20] In effect this pointed out that sergeants of the law and even court clerks act as maintainers, conniving with third persons to bring false suit against landholders to gain their lands, thus acquiring such lands at little or no cost to themselves. And in 1360 (34 Ed III 7-8)[21] a statute made it possible for even the poor, who could not pay a fine, to obtain a writ of attaint against a juror alleged to have taken anything to reach his verdict. In the same year the king established the justices of the peace in the counties[22] to "determine at the king's suit all manner of felonies and trespasses," stipulating that the justices assigned "be named by the court and not by the party," thus seeking to eliminate in part the evil of allowing those who brought suit to name their own justices whose actions they might control. These justices became responsible for enforcing the Statute of Laborers, to which I shall return in a moment, in 1368. Finally, Edward issued a series of statutes seeking to control the easy granting of pardons for felonies.[23]

Unfortunately, this considerable body of legislation in so far as it was designed to control corruption and maintenance was largely disregarded. If anything, maintenance of one kind or another increased, and the situation did not improve during the reign of Richard II, who seemed considerably less concerned about corruption than his predecessor, especially when he could use it to further his own ends.

---

19. *SR*, 2. 37. For a discussion of parliamentary efforts to stem judicial corruption after the Revolt, see J. R. Madicott, *Law and Lordship: Royal Justices as Retainers in Thirteenth and Fourteenth Century England,* Past and Present Society, Supplement 4 (1978), pp. 64ff.
20. *SR*, 1. 360. For a definition, see *SR*, 1. 145.
21. Ibid., 1. 366.
22. Ibid., 1. 364-65. These justices replaced the Keepers of the Peace.
23. 2 Ed III 2, *SR*, 1. 257-58; 10 Ed III 1.3, p. 275; 14 Ed III 1.15, p. 286; 27 Ed III 1.2, p. 330. However, felonies continued to be pardoned for a fee.

Sheriffs were sometimes almost forced to use extortion to collect the farm of the counties, impoverished by war or pestilence, or by the granting of hundreds to private parties; and officials of all kinds, both lay and ecclesiastic, enriched themselves through their offices. Extortion among coroners,[24] bailiffs of hundreds, and archdeacons,[25] became commonplace. As organizations, both lay and ecclesiastic, became more efficient and centralized, they tended at the same time to become more corrupt. Centralization also produced what has been called "bastard feudalism," although I do not think that "feudalism," much less "bastard feudalism," is a very useful term.[26] In this

24. R. F. Hunnisett, *Bedfordshire Coroner's Rolls,* Bedfordshire Historical Record Society, vol. 41 (1961), p. vi, observes, "All coroners practiced moderate extortion; bribes became an invariable prelude to the performance of their duties, and some coroners were much more oppressive." For an instance of a coroner who extorted 6s 8d from a man for viewing a corpse, see Bertha Haven Putnam, *Proceedings of the Justices of the Peace in the Fourteenth and Fifteenth Centuries* (Ames Foundation, 1938), p. 446. A Yorkshire coroner was fined for stealing 6s 8d from a corpse. See Putnam, *Yorkshire Sessions,* p. 108.

25. E.g., see the last will of William Donne, archdeacon of Leicester, as cited by A. H. Thompson, *The English Clergy and Their Organization in Later Middle Ages* (Oxford, 1947), pp. 60-61, who asked God's forgiveness for exactions and extortions, in which, he said, he merely followed the example of his brethren. On the specific activities of archdeacons, see Jean Scammell, "The Rural Chapter in England from the Eleventh to the Fourteenth Century," *EHR* 86 (1971): 1-21. The fact (pp. 17-18) that both the innocent and the guilty would pay to avoid citation pardy explains the opportunity for extortion. Archdeacons sometimes also extorted money for wills. See Margaret Aston, *Thomas Arundel* (Oxford, 1967), pp. 93-94. The following pages contain evidence of extortion by archdeacons' officials. Summoners or apparitors were notorious. See Brian L. Woodcock, *Medieval Ecclesiastical Courts in the Diocese of Canterbury* (Oxford, 1952), pp. 49, 111. Rural Deans, with whom archdeacons were associated, were also tempted in the same way. For a specific example, see Elizabeth Gurnsey Kimball, *Rolls of the Gloucestershire Sessions of the Peace, 1361-1398,* Transactions of the Bristol and Gloucestershire Archaeological Society, vol. 62 (1942), p. 128.

26. The term "feudal system" was first used in England in the seventeenth century. *Feudalism* is an artificial construct originating in the minds of historians, who have "defined" it in various ways and who frequently employ it very loosely. Its "origins," "history," and "decline" depend entirely on the definition being used. That is, it can be said to have "ended" in the later thirteenth century, in the Renaissance, at the time of the French Revolution, or, in England, with the passage of the Agricultural Holding Act of 1923. Similarly, its

connection some historians like to dwell on the evil consequences of the statute *quia emptores* issued by Edward I in 1290,[27] which in effect put an end to subinfeudation in fee simple, even though its purpose was to maintain ties between lord and tenant. The popularity of final concords, which gave free tenants of all kinds some of the convenience associated with transactions in borough courts, for transfers of land, rents, leases, and other holdings that were recorded as "feet of fines" and kept as central records, contributed further to centralization. It was quite natural that legal manipulation of one kind or another should have been used to supplement force.[28]

In the first Parliament of Richard II, memorable for John of Gaunt's spirited defense of his integrity, further statutes, for which the boy king was of course not responsible, were issued against maintenance. After a preliminary general decree on the subject, widespread discontent among serfs was attributed to maintainers who had "taken hire and profit of the said villeins and landtenants" to provide them with "certain exemplifications made out of the Book of Domesday" to prove that they did not owe their "services and customs" (1 R II 6).[29] As a result of their activities tenants were said to have formed confederacies

---

"origins" can be located in different times and places. Like many other "isms" it is a convenient label that often carries emotional overtones, although its concrete referents are vague. European societies called "feudal" were always complex with wide local variations and were always undergoing fairly rapid changes, a fact that the term tends to obscure.

27. SR, 1. 106. A. W. B. Simpson, *An Introduction to the History of the Land Law* (Oxford, 1961), p. 51, calls the statute "a striking illustration of the lack of importance which by this time was attached to the personal relationship of lord and tenant; lords were more interested in protecting their incidents than in selecting their tenants." The statute effectively discouraged grants in fee farm. But it did not prevent the granting of lucrative sinecures to faithful retainers.

28. We may compare the career of Lord John Fitzwalter of Essex with that of Sir Matthew Gurney (above, n. 3). For Lord John Fitzwalter, see Elizabeth Chapin Furber, *Essex Sessions of the Peace 1351, 1377-79*, Essex Archaeological Society Occasional Publications, vol. 3 (1953), pp. 61-62. Lord John's lands were seized by the king, whereas Sir Matthew, who had a good lawyer, continued in royal favor.

29. SR, 2. 2-3. Cf. *Rotuli parliamentorum* (Record Commission, 1783) 3. 21 (hereafter *RP*). For an example of such a person from Wiltshire, see Putnam, *Proceedings before the Justices of the Peace*, pp. 385-86.

to resist their lords, setting "an evil example to others to begin such riots." It is clear that what is known rather inaccurately[30] as "The Peasants' Revolt" was already getting under way in agricultural communities, and that it was being stimulated by unscrupulous persons with some literate competence for their own profit. The commons expressed a justified fear of "greater mischiefs, which God forbid, throughout the realm." Judicial inquiries were instituted to imprison the rebels and "their counsellors, procurers, maintainers, and abettors." This was followed by a statute (c. 7) against "persons of small revenue of land" who made confederacies with liveries of hats or other liveries and agreed to maintain one another in quarrels "reasonable or unreasonable." Another decree forbade enfeoffments of disputed land or other tenures to great men for maintenance. Other reform measures included one against clerks of the exchequer who connived to issue second writs for debts already paid (c. 5), and (c. 11) against the reinstatement of sheriffs within three years.[31] The commons had complained that sheriffs arrested people for homicide in their tourns without due process and held them in prison for high ransoms.[32] For their part some sheriffs complained that they could not collect the farm of the counties. The sheriff of Exeter and Hertford said that he had lost £100 a year, and that since the last pestilence the loss had been even greater.[33] Temporary remedies were supplied in the form of allowances granted to some sheriffs in succeeding years, but a solution to the problem did not appear until the first year of Henry IV,

---

30. Cf. R. B. Dobson, *The Peasants' Revolt of 1381* (London, 1970), pp. 13-15; M. M. Postan, *The Medieval Economy and Society* (Berkeley and Los Angeles, 1972), pp. 153-54. The latter points out that the facts do not fit the theory that the revolt was "a typical instance of the working class revolt against repression." I might add that the latter view is a typical example of the tendency among historians to view the past in the light of current "isms" and their attendant prejudices.
31. An effort to revive this legislation, which had been neglected, failed in 1384, *RP*, 3. 201.
32. Ibid., 3. 21.
33. Ibid., 3. 19-20. This complaint was repeated in the following year and brought a temporary remedy.

who realized that sheriffs could not pay the long-established farms "without doing extortion" (1 H IV 11).[34]

In their convocation the clergy in this first year of Richard's reign drew up complaints against the extravagances of the royal household, a traditional difficulty that was to become worse in the future, against the illegal seizure of clergymen by the officers of the Marshalsea, and against buyers and purveyors who, in spite of the warnings of Archbishop Mepham and King Edward's subsequent legislation, continued to seize goods. They were also burdened, they said, by the visits of sheriffs and their families to monasteries and priories, which caused heavy expense.[35] Again, they complained that laymen were forcibly oppressing ecclesiastical courts and preventing their functioning. For their part the commons asked that no "dean, official, archdeacon, or other curates" take money for the correction of sin but instead administer spiritual penances, that cures of souls are let to farm like lands and tenements in lay fee "for the increase from year to year," and complained further that curates take exorbitant fees for wills.[36] The contribution of corruption in ecclesiastical courts together with the effects of impoverishment of the clergy in many parishes and

---

34. *SR.* 2. 114. But this statute did not prevent extortion among sheriffs.
35. Dorothy Bruce Weske, *Convocation of Clergy* (London, 1937), pp. 72-72. Cf. *RP,* 3. 26, where escheators are also mentioned. Cf. "The Song Against Sheriffs" quoted by Helen M. Cam, *The Hundred and the Hundred Rolls* (London, 1930), p. 106. For an example of lay interference with an ecclesiastical court, see Elizabeth Gurnsey Kimball, *Some Sessions of the Peace in Lincolnshire,* 2 vols., Lincoln Record Society, vol. 56 (1962), 2:8. In this instance, the perpetrator, one John Racy, was later (p. 179) indicted for being a common thief who had stolen a horse.
36. *RP,* 3. 25; cf. *SR,* 1. 43. See n. 25, above. In 1392 John Lawrence, registrar of the bishop of Winchester, was indicted in Hampshire for having taken 13s 4d "by extortion" for probate of a will, 40s from another for the same service, and 10s and a silver seal worth 10s from two other executors. See G. O. Sayles, *Select Cases in the Court of King's Bench,* Selden Society, vol. 7 (1971), pp. 82-83. Even a bishop might be extortionate. Thus Henry of Wakefield, bishop of Worcester, and his suffragan were indicted for extorting money for consecrating chapels and altars. See Elizabeth Gurnsey Kimball, *Some Warwickshire and Coventry Sessions of the Peace, 1377-1397,* Dugdale Society, vol. 16 (1939), pp. 105-6.

the abandonment of many chapels as a result of pestilence have often been neglected as causes of social unrest. It is quite obvious that King Edward, who had for some years left governmental responsibilities to others, died at a time when his realm was in considerable disarray, harrassed by enemies abroad, and demoralized in its domestic functions by greed among both laymen and ecclesiastics. What the author of *Piers Plowman* called "Lady Meed," or what Chaucer in the *Pardoner's Tale* called *cupiditas,* seemed to be the true queen of the commonwealth.

This impression is strengthened if we glance briefly at parliamentary activity during the years immediately preceding the outbreak of large-scale revolt. In the second year of Richard's reign there was a complaint about extortionate summoners, a kind of anticipation of Chaucer's *Friar's Tale*. They were said to make summons out of malice, extorting money from the poor, or summoning them to distant places, making them pay fines they called "the bishop's alms."[37] There was also a complaint that agricultural workers had gone to vills, boroughs, and towns to become artificers, mariners, or clerks, so that husbandry was difficult to maintain.[38] This difficulty, which may be attributed in part to the effects of pestilence, and in part to the growth of industries,[39] was one that persisted throughout the century, as the rolls of the justices of the peace reveal. A statute was passed against mariners, who after having been arrested and retained for the king's service, fled with their wages, sometimes having bribed sergeants

37. *RP,* 3. 43. Cf. n. 25, above.

38. Ibid., 3. 46.

39. Cf. on the effects of the cutlery trade at Thaxted, Nora Ritchie, "Labour Conditions in Essex in the Reign of Richard II," in *Essays in Economic History,* ed. E. M. Carus-Wilson, vol. 2 (London, 1962), p. 93. On the manor of Thaxted the working of demesne lands by tenants except for a few acres of mowing ended in 1362, and the elaborate peasant hierarchy became a legal fiction. See K. C. Newton, *Thaxted,* Essex Record Office Publications, vol. 33 (Chelmsford, 1960), pp. 25-26, and on the cutlery trade there, pp. 20-23. The cloth trade was especially attractive to agricultural workers in some areas. See A. R. Bridbury, *England and the Salt Trade in the Later Middle Ages* (Oxford, 1955), pp. 36-37. Although the general effect of the cloth industry has been denied, it clearly did offer opportunities for agricultural workers where it flourished, as did other trades elsewhere.

at arms or masters of ships.[40] Another sought to punish those who spread false news and "horrible false lies" about prelates, dukes, earls, barons, and great men of the realm;[41] many such tales were spread about in the revolt soon to come, and it is quite probable that the process had already begun. Finally, it was agreed that no sheriff could be a justice of the peace.[42]

In the following year the commons of Norfolk, Suffolk, Kent, Surrey, Hampshire, Dorset, Devonshire, and Cornwall complained "that they and their houses are robbed and destroyed and wasted by armed men, archers and others passing in the service of the king and remaining a long time."[43] The commons of Northumberland were troubled by "mischiefs and damages" not only from the pestilence but from the Scots, so that they asked for wardens and garrisons to protect them.[44] The men of Staffordshire, Shropshire, Warwickshire, Hereford, and York asked relief from "devastation, rape, and mayhem" committed by bands of men from Chester, where a large area was a secular sanctuary protecting violent men.[45] Meanwhile, royal officers were still impeding justice. A petition complained that escheators suddenly disinherit and oust men from their lands and tenements who are delayed in their pursuit of justice either by force, by protection, or by other delays.[46] There was a strong complaint about benefices granted to aliens, sometimes "utter enemies of the king," who neglected to keep churches in repair, neglected divine service, and diminished reverence for the Church.[47] In response justices of the peace were given power to hear and determine concerning homicide, extortion, riding armed or in routs, lying in wait to commit mayhem or murder, and wearing livery of hats and other liveries for maintenance. The justices themselves

---

40. *SR*, 2. 9.
41. Ibid.
42. *RP*, 3. 64.
43. Ibid., 3. 80.
44. Ibid., 3. 80-81.
45. Ibid., 3. 81.
46. Ibid., repeated in the following year, *RP*, 3. 94.
47. *SR*, 2. 14.

were to be elected by the most sufficient knights and squires from each county, or by those then in Parliament, and to be paid in proportion to their rank. They were to meet four times a year or more often if necessary, and each justice was to take an oath "to do full right to all, to the poor as well as to the rich," and to avoid delays for benefits, promises, or "any articifice or stratagem whatsoever."[48] All this was perhaps a little late. In the following year there was a petition for better protection of the coasts, for the balingers of Normandy and other enemies were making great damages on the coasts, both in the north and in the south.[49]

It is obvious that there was considerable unrest throughout the realm before the revolt of 1381. The poll tax of 1380, as Sir Goronwy Edwards has recently explained, was a reasonable effort to avoid the inequities of the traditional tax of a fifteenth and a tenth, which was based on quotas established for each township and borough in 1344. During the intervening years some townships and boroughs had prospered while others had become impoverished. A tax to be collected in two installments based on an average of three groats per person, with the weak paying less and the strong more, seemed equitable and bearable.[50] However, when the initial proceeds collected in January seemed inadequate, the government ordered an inspection in March to check on the first collection, and this was sometimes regarded as a new tax without parliamentary consent. In any event, it precipitated riotous revolt,[51] by no means confined to peasants. The famous address to Parliament on the causes of the revolt by Sir Richard Waldgrave becomes much more understandable, I believe, in the light of the situation we have just been considering. He attributed the outbreak to "the government of the realm" which, he said, would be "lost and destroyed forever" if suitable remedies were not applied. Specifically, he called attention to the "outrageous numbers of familiars" in

48. *RP,* 3. 83-85.
49. Ibid., 3. 94.
50. Sir Goronwy Edwards, *The Second Century of the English Parliament* (Oxford, 1979), pp. 17-31.
51. E. Powell, *The Rising in East Anglia* (Cambridge, 1896), p. 4.

the royal household, in the chancery, king's bench, common bench, and exchequer. The implication of this statement was that there was widespread extravagance and corruption in the administration of justice, the chief function of the medieval king. He went on to elaborate by saying that there were "outrageous numbers" of embracers and maintainers "who are like kings in the country, so that right and loyalty are hardly made to anyone." Returning to the household, he said that the commons are "pillaged and destroyed" by purveyors for the household of the king and of others. They are distressed by "subsidies and tallages," and oppressed by "the ministers of the king and the lords of the realm," and especially by maintainers. Moreover, great treasures are levied for defense, but the commons, far from being defended, are "burned, robbed, and pillaged" by land and sea by enemies. These outrages and others, he concluded, had caused the lesser commons to revolt.[52]

Unfortunately, this address did not result in widespread reforms. In 1382 the commons said that there was not a bailiff in the counties who did not summon many good men for extortion.[53] There were complaints about rioters from Chester in 1382, 1384, 1390, and 1393.[54] A demand that justices of both benches treat rich and poor alike, and that the justices of the peace apprehend vagrants, thieves, and robbers was made in 1383, and a statute was issued against riding armed.[55] As one reads the parliamentary petitions of Richard's reign it becomes evident that Richard did little to enforce the reforming legislation of his predecessor, or even that of the early years of his own reign. In 1385 his chancellor failed to implement a series of reforms endorsed in Parliament, and in 1397 Richard accused a member of Parliament of treason for criticizing the extravagances of his household. Sir Richard Waldgrave's concern for the future was realized in 1386, when the king was threatened with deposition, and in the acts of the Merciless

---

52. *RP*, 3. 100-101.
53. Ibid., 3. 140. We can understand why the devil in the *Friar's Tale* should appear as a bailiff.
54. Ibid., 3. 201, 280, 308.
55. Ibid., 3. 138; *SR*, 2. 35.

Parliament. The domestic grievances of which Waldgrave spoke, especially that concerning "the outrageous numbers of familiars" in the government, were grievous to the lords as well as to the commons, and it is not surprising that Richard, who became fearful of his own people, was ultimately deposed.

II

Sir Richard said nothing about "the pestilence of the people, murrain of beasts, and the fruits of the land commonly failed in evil years." I shall not dwell on the subjects of murrains or bad years, but both probably stimulated corruption among officials. Mercifully, there were no direct taxes between 1361 and 1370, during years of peace, but this respite was spoiled not only by pestilence in 1360 and 1361, but by murrain, drought, and by a devastating storm in Cornwall. As Barbara Hanawalt has shown,[56] there was a correlation between crime and high wheat prices during the years before the great pestilence, and there is no reason to suppose that this correlation did not continue.[57] The early sixties, when prices were high, certainly witnessed a rise in crime generally.[58] Again, in 1389 there were devastating floods that moved the king to forbid exports of grain and to forgive the customs on imported grain in 1391. But these moves brought prices so low in 1394 that the poor could not pay their rents.[59] Similar dislocations resulted from pestilence. However, I shall not pursue here the chronology of fourteenth-century pestilences, nor discuss the controversial question of the various diseases involved or the mortality rates from each. Nor shall I describe in detail their effects on agricultural communities that have been described so well by Father Raftis and his students especially.

56. Barbara Hanawalt, *Crime in East Anglia in the Fourteenth Century: Norfolk Gaol Delivery Rolls, 1302-16,* Norfolk Record Society, vol. 44 (1976), pp. 14-15.
57. On high prices in 1361–1365 see A. R. Bridbury, "The Black Death," *EcHR,* 2nd ser. 26 (1973): 584.
58. John Bellamy, *Crime and Public Order in the Later Middle Ages* (London and Toronto, 1973), p. 6. For a local example, see J. A. Raftis, *Warboys* (Toronto, 1974), pp. 220-21.
59. L. F. Salzman, *English Trade in the Middle Ages* (Oxford, 1931), p. 284.

The response of the government to the great pestilence was to issue the Ordinance of Laborers,[60] soon to be followed by the Statute (25 Ed III 2,3).[61] The Ordinance began by calling attention to the fact that after the pestilence servants took advantage of the scarcity of labor and demanded "excessive wages," or even decided to beg in idleness. It was decreed that anyone under the age of 60, free or bond, without employment could be made to serve at the rate usual in 1346 and 1347, or in the five or six "common years" previously, on pain of imprisonment.[62] Agricultural workers who left service were to be imprisoned, as well as those who hired them. Employers who transgressed were to pay double to those aggrieved. Lords of towns or manors were to be "pursued" for triple the amount they offered. Artificers were to accept only their customary prices, and victuallers were to charge moderately. No one was to give anything to an able beggar. In the subsequent statute it was stipulated that agricultural workers were to be hired by the year, and wages for various services were specified. Such workmen wishing to be hired were to bring their implements to town and be hired publicly where everyone could see and hear. Wages of various trades were specified and prison terms set for offenders. To make these provisions more attractive it was stipulated that amercements were to be used in relief of the fifteenths and the tenths, the surplus, if any, being turned over to the nearest poor town. Measurements of cloths were specified and lax ulnagers were to be punished. There were regulations concerning victuals, a clause against forestalling (a common practice in towns, expecially among women), and one against the installation of mills, weirs, or kiddles in rivers where they might impede traffic. Sheriffs were forbidden, once more, to take fees from those entering or leaving prison, and justices were required to sit four times a year. The statute was supplemented in 1360–1361 (34 Ed III 9),[63] specifying terms of imprisonment and stipulating that carpenters and masons were to work by the day rather than by the week. Fugitive laborers were to be outlawed and might be branded on the

60. *SR,* 1. 307-8.
61. Ibid., 1. 311-16.
62. For a case involving this provision, see Sayles, *Select Cases,* vol. 7, pp. 60-61.
63. *SR,* 1. 366.

forehead with an *F* for falsity. Mayors and bailiffs of towns who refused to deliver fugitives might be fined £10. As we have seen, there was a complaint in Parliament in 1378 that agricultural laborers fled to towns so that husbandry was difficult. Efforts to enforce these statutes, especially after 1368 when the justices of the peace were given jurisdiction, were often assiduous, and these labors may have done much to stimulate the revolt of 1381.[64] However, the problem being addressed was by no means solved, as the petitions and statutes of Richard's reign reveal.

There was, for example, a series of complaints about improperly measured cloths, to one of which I shall return in a moment.[65] Although the great revolt itself was brought under control, it evidently stimulated a great deal of criminal activity) and a statute was passed in 1383 (7 R II 6)[66] against robbery, theft, and manslaughter by men riding in routs. Two years later another was issued against villeins who fled to cities and there brought suit against their lords for freedom (9 R II 2).[67] There was an outbreak of pestilence in 1383 that may have intensified the demand for higher agricultural wages, for it was decreed in 1388 (12 R II 3)[68] that servants and apprentices of artificers might be conscripted to help at harvest time. This was followed by a series of new labor statutes (12 R II 4-7)[69] concerning manorial servants. The preamble is instructive:

> "Because that servants and laborers will not, nor by a long season would, serve and labor without outrageous and excessive hire, and much more than hath been given to such laborers and servants in any time past, so that for scarcity of the said laborers and servants, the husbands and landtenants may not pay their rents, nor scarcely live upon their lands ... it is accorded and assented that the bailiff for husbandry shall take by the year 13s 4d, and his clothing once a year at the most."

64. Cf. Bridbury, "The Black Death," p. 585.
65. E.g., *RP*, 3. 159.
66. *SR*, 2. 33; cf. c. 15, p. 35.
67. Ibid., 2. 38.
68. Ibid., 2. 56.
69. Ibid., 2. 57-58.

The master hine was to have 10s, the shepherd 10s, the oxherd 6s 8d, the swineherd 6s, a woman laborer 6s, a deye 6s, a driver of the plow 7s at the most, and every other laborer or servant according to his degree. Similar stipulations were made concerning servants of artisans in towns. As Nora Ritchie has shown, workers were often demanding double or treble the amounts stipulated.[70] It was further decreed (c.5) that those who labor at husbandry under the age of twelve should "abide at the same labor, without being put to any mystery or handicraft." Moreover (c. 60), that "no servant of husbandry, or laborer, nor servant of artificer, nor of victualler, shall from henceforth bear any buckler, sword, nor dagger" except in the company of their masters or when going on message for them. They should instead have bows and arrows and "leave all playing at tennis or football, and other games called coits, dice, or casting the stone, or kailes [skittles] and other such importune games."[71] No servant was to leave his hundred, rape, or wapentake at the end of his term, except in some areas where it was customary, and none was to go on pilgrimage without a letter patent indicating the dates of departure and return. The justices of the peace (c. 10)[72] were ordered to inquire whether "mayors, bailiffs, stewards, constables, and jailers have done execution of the said

---

70. Ritchie, "Labour Conditions in Essex," pp. 91-111; cf. McKisack, *The Fourteenth Century*, pp. 339-40.

71. "Importune" or troublesome games had already come to the attention of local courts. For example, in 1373 six men at Colchester were accused of being common dice players, and one for being "a common player of chess." All were said to stay awake at night and to frequent taverns. And in 1375 three men were fined 6d each for playing unlawful games, and agreed to pay 6s 8d each if they were caught again. See I. H. Jeayes, *Court Rolls of the Borough of Colchester*, vol. 3 (Colchester, 1941), pp. 17, 81. The tenants of the Durham vill of Hetheworths were forbidden to play at dice on pain of 20s. Football ("soccer"), which led (as it apparently still does) to "gravis contencio et contumelia" was forbidden in 1381. See W. H. Longstreet and John Booth, *Halmota Prioratus Dunelmensis*, Surtees Society, vol. 82 (1889), pp. 166, 171. At Castle Combe such games were still being punished in the Renaissance. See J. Poulet Scrope, *Castle Combe* (London, 1852), pp. 330, 332, 335. The dice playing of Chaucer's Franklin's young son is reprehensible aside from the fact that it involves loss of money, which seems to disturb the Franklin. Ironically, many noblemen were fond of it.

72. *SR*, 2. 58-59.

ordinance," and offenders were to be fined 100s. Moreover, the justices were now to receive their wages from the sheriff, no steward was to be assigned to commissions of the peace (a provision almost immediately repealed[73]), and no association was to be made after the first appointment. The provision regarding town officials was evidently ineffective, for in 1391 the commons complained (15 R II 11)[74] that many villeins who fled to franchised towns could neither be approached nor apprehended, much less judged by their lords. Town governments were generally sensitive about their jurisdictions.[75] Complaints about liveries were expanded in 1388, for the commons wished to abolish not only liveries of temporal and spiritual lords, but also liveries of guilds and fraternities, which evidently gave them the appearance of being covins, or conspiracies.[76] In 1389–1390 the justices of the peace were cautioned to use discretion concerning wages because of fluctuations in the price of grain (13 R II 1.8).[77] And a statute was issued against inferior westcountry cloths (13 R II 1.11),[78] which were tacked and folded for sale, concealing the fact that the cloth inside might be

---

73. Ibid., 2. 62-63.
74. *RP*, 3. 296.
75. This fact is amusingly illustrated by the treatment of approvers (or convicted felons who obtained temporary respite by identifying and offering to prove themselves upon unidentified accomplices) who came from outside the liberty of Fordwick, the old port of Canterbury. Such an approver should enter the liberty with his equipment (probably a battle-ax with a leather blade and a leather jerkin). The custom of the borough as recorded by Mary Bateson, *Borough Customs*, Selden Society, vol. 1 (1904), p. 33, ran as follows. "He shall be led to the running water called the Stour, and he shall stand in that water up to his navel, with his equipment, in the manner of an approver, ready, as aforesaid, to prove his appeal. And the said freeman thus appealed shall come in a rowboat of three benches in the same river opposite the said approver, and the freeman shall wear a garment called a *skerp* (leather jacket), and shall have a weapon called an oar three yards in length, and his boat shall be made fast by a rope to the quay, and in the said water he shall fight with the said approver until the duel between them is finished." One can imagine the joy of the citizens if and when this custom was implemented.
76. *RP*, 3. 266.
77. *SR*, 2. 63. Cf. *RP*, 3. 272.
78. *SR*, 2. 64.

bruised, unevenly dyed, of inconsistent width, or made from various grades of wool. When merchants sold these cloths abroad they were "many times in danger to be slain, and sometimes imprisoned, and put to fine and ransom." This may lead us to wonder about the Wife of Bath, who was a west-country clothier.

The general situation revealed in the parliamentary records is confirmed when we consult manorial or town records. For example, the court records for John of Gaunt's Ingoldmells manor reveal eleven instances of tenants leaving the manor for excessive wages elsewhere between 1386 and 1389.[79] In an effort to maintain their incomes many manorial lords leased their demesnes, often to a single tenant, who could afford to pay the higher wages being demanded, and there was a widespread tendency to commute labor services for rents. Especially after the pestilence of 1360 many traditional peasant families disappeared, and their holdings, often consolidated into larger units, were taken over by rent-paying tenants without family ties to the land and interested chiefly in profits. Naturally, they were often employers of hired labor. At the same time workers in towns were demanding and receiving higher pay, and merchants and tradesmen were not only asking higher prices but selling defective goods, ranging from putrid meat or old fish to poorly tanned leather, candles without wicks, or the defective cloths just mentioned.[80] It is significant, I believe, that the word commonly used for excessive wages or prices was *extortion*. That is, workers and merchants from the point of view of contemporaries were doing exactly the same kind of thing that corrupt archdeacons, summoners, sheriffs, bailiffs, coroners, lawyers, or royal purveyors were doing. They were, at the same time, showing little interest in "the common profit" either of their own manors, towns, or shires, or of the realm as a whole. It must have seemed that the old ideals of fidelity and truth were rapidly vanishing from the face of the earth.

---

79. W. O. Massingberd, *Court Rolls of the Manor of Ingoldmells* (London, 1902), pp. 180-81, 185, 186.
80. W. H. Stevenson, *Records of the Borough of Nottingham*, vol. 1 (London, 1882), pp. 269-73, 315, 317-19. Cf. Ritchie, "Labour Conditions," pp. 95-96.

III.

Indeed, this is the theme of Chaucer's "Lak of Stedfastnesse," a balade addressed to King Richard, perhaps on his assumption of power in May, 1389.[81] It begins with a complaint that although a man's word was once an obligation, word and deed now bear little resemblance, for the world is now turned upside-down for meed and willfulness. A man is considered able if he can wrong or oppress his neighbor; covetousness has blinded discretion and "all is lost for lack of steadfastness." Chaucer urges the king to "hate extortion," to show his sword of castigation, to fear God, do law, love truth and worthiness, and to wed his people to steadfastness. Under the circumstances this was a large order. But the ideals are traditional, reflecting the kind of moral doctrines that Chaucer might well have found in John of Salisbury. The later fourteenth century was in many ways out of tune with them. It has been called an "age of ambition"[82] characterized by a widespread desire for self-aggrandizement and by a spirit of enterprise. The enterprise was not by any means always illegal, but even when it was not it seemed inconsistent with long-cherished ideals. A very brief glance at the General Prologue to the *Canterbury Tales* will show, I believe, that Chaucer used that work as a humorously exaggerated attack on the lack of "steadfastness" in the hierarchy of the realm. However, I

---

81. Geoffrey Chaucer, *The Works of Geoffrey Chaucer,* ed. F. N. Robinson, 2nd ed. (Cambridge, Mass., 1957), p. 537.
82. See especially F. R. H. Du Boulay, *An Age of Ambition: English Society in the Late Middle Ages* (London, 1970). May McKisack, *The Parliamentary Representation of the English Boroughs During the Late Middle Ages* (Oxford, 1932), p. 43, said that "in spite of the Black Death" and "the drain of the French war" the later fourteenth century was a time of "increasing municipal prosperity." More recent studies are more likely to emphasize prosperity in both agriculture and trade as a *result* of the Black Death, which is said to have reduced overpopulation. See most recently John Hatcher, *Plague, Population and the English Economy* (Economic History Society, 1977), pp. 31-34, who calls attention to the fact (p. 34) that the prosperity of the lesser folk outraged moralists like the chronicler Knighton, who in 1388 wrote of "the elation of the inferior people in dress and accoutrements ... so that one person cannot be distinguished from another either in splendor of dress or belongings, neither poor from rich nor servant from master."

think that we should consider the characters not as being "realistic," or even as "personalities," but instead as presentations of the ideals or the weaknesses of the groups presented.

Leaving aside for a moment the "idealized" characters, including the Knight with his modest entourage and his less worthy son, we encounter first the Prioress of the fashionable Benedictine nunnery of St. Leonard at Stratford at Bow.[83] Her studied but actually rather inept courtly manners, in part derived from the worldly advice of the Old Whore in the *Roman de la rose*, her false sentimental sensitivity that offers a poor substitute for true charity, her extravagant care for her little dogs, and her very expensive rosary with its dubious motto combine to form a picture of worldliness entirely inconsistent with traditional notions of what a nun should be.[84] Steadfastness is even less evident in the Monk, who holds not only his rule but monastic ideals generally in contempt, caring nothing for either work or study. In other words, he is from a monastic point of view "lawless." He loves "venery," probably of both kinds, is an "outrider" or bailiff errant, whose "dainty" horses are ostentatiously caparisoned as he is himself with expensively furred sleeves. He is well-fed, a lover of roast swan, the most expensive poultry available. Clearly, his wealth is not consistent with the usual monastic ideals. The Friar has no interest whatsoever in spiritual penances, but only in money, which he accepts as a substitute for true repentance. He is himself lecherous, a great singer who frequents taverns where he is familiar with barmaids. He likes especially the company of franklins, or wealthy landholders not of noble rank, of wealthy victuallers, or of any persons who can furnish him profit. In fact, he can even get a farthing from a poor widow. At "love-days" offering opportunities for maintenance he dresses like a master or a pope. The contemplative orders are obviously subject to the same kinds of weaknesses we have seen among other groups.

---

83. On the nunnery, see H. P. F. King, "The Priory of Stratford at Bow," *Victoria County History: Middlesex* 1 (1969): 151-59. In 1380-1381 there were only fourteen nuns, one of whom was called "Argentyn."

84. See most recently Chauncey Wood, "Chaucer's Portrait of the Prioress," in *Signs and Symbols in Chaucer's Poetry*, ed. John P. Hermann and John J. Burke, Jr. (University, Alabama, 1981), pp. 81-100.

Chaucer turns next to the Merchant, a dealer in wool,[85] who although in debt always talks about his profits. He makes money in the exchange in violation of a statute of 1351 (25 Ed III 5.12)[86] and practices illegal usury, or what Chaucer calls "chevysaunce," against which there was a parliamentary petition in 1390.[87] The Sergeant of the Law, who often served as a justice in assize, had many "fees and robes," which means that he was a "maintainer," and was a great purchaser of land in fee simple, probably through champerty. He knew all the cases and judgments since the time of King William, or before the time of legal memory,[88] an impossible achievement the implication of which is that he could readily cite fictitious precedents for his own purposes. With him was his friend the Franklin, who had been a sheriff and justice of the peace, offices he found to be extremely profitable and through which he became a wealthy vavasour or subtenant so that he could serve daylong feasts of costly fowl and fish with fine wines and rare sauces to the great men of the shire during sessions. Chaucer has these legal gentlemen, both of whom attended Parliament, ride along together, clearly suggesting cooperation in maintenance.

The so-called "guildsmen," actually members of a parish fraternity, ostentatiously dressed in liveries with expensive knives (illegal in the City of London), girdles, and pouches, seem to their wives (who would like to be treated like ladies) worthy to become aldermen. For they have gained through their "wisdom" sufficient property and income.

85. The Merchant is concerned about the safety of shipping "Bitwixe Middleburghe and Orwelle." After the French advance in Flanders in 1383 wool was sent to Middleburg, which became a compulsory staple in 1384. But in January 1387 convoys had to be employed between the two ports. The staple was restored to Calais in 1389. See T. H. Lloyd, *The English Wool Trade in the Middle Ages* (Cambridge, 1977), pp. 230-31. The Merchant's concern thus identifies his trade for Chaucer's audience and at the same time affords us an approximate date for the composition of the Prologue, or at least for this part of it.

86. *SR*, 1. 322.

87. *RP*, 3. 280-81. The commons petitioned that since both lay and spiritual lords practice "the abhominable vice of usury" and call it "chevance" the old statutes concerning usury should be confirmed. *Chevance* is clearly a variant of the term Chaucer uses.

88. On the limit of legal memory, see C. R. Cheney, *Handbook of Dates for Students of English History* (London, 1961), p. 65.

But no carpenter, weaver, dyer, or tapicer became a London alderman. These are small artificers who have clearly profited from high prices. To keep their appetites satisfied they have brought with them their own cook, who, appropriately, prepares dubious white sauce.

There is also a Shipman who steals wine from sleeping merchants on his return from Bordeaux, makes his enemies walk the plank, and knows all the creeks in Brittany and Spain, where he can readily engage in smuggling. A Physician was there who could impress his patients with references to famous authorities much in the same way that the Sergeant of Law could cite cases and judgments. He connives with his friend the apothecary to their mutual profit. He is generally penurious, but extravagant in his dress to make a good impression. Pestilences are especially profitable to him, and he is very fond of gold.

One of the most striking of Chaucer's figures is the Wife of Bath who probably owes her prominence to the fact that the cloth industry was flourishing in rural areas away from the control of the guilds and attracting many agricultural workers. She has become such a prominent member of her community that she proudly insists on being first at the offering in church, where she is expensively decked out in coverchiefs. Her hose are of the most expensive woolens, scarlet in grain (closely sheared wool dyed in kermes). She has been profitably married to five husbands, has accumulated enough wealth to make expensive pilgrimages, although she "wanders from the way" a great deal, and is expert in the "old dance" of love. We can be justly suspicious of the quality of her west-country cloths.[89] But the pilgrims are led out of town by a drunken Miller playing a bagpipe, a foul-mouthed character who practices both theft and extortion, especially oppressive to the poor who depend on his services for the preparation of their bread and gruel. The rear of the procession is occupied by the Reeve, a kind of competitor in extortion among the rural workers. He has risen to his office from his position as a manorial carpenter. His accounts are never in arrears, but he keeps his superior, the bailiff, and his fellow-servants on the manor in fear of him through his knowledge of their

---

89. Cf. my article "'And for My Land Thus Hastow Mordred Me?': Land Tenure, the Cloth Industry, and the Wife of Bath," *ChaucR* 14 (1980): 403-20.

little conspiracies, which he fails to report as he should to the manorial court. Meanwhile, he steals from his lord but subtly pleases him by giving or lending him his own goods.[90] He carries a rusty blade at his side in violation of the Statute of 1388. There is a Manciple of a temple who can profit greatly from his purchases of victuals in spite of the legal astuteness of his masters. The last two pilgrims, except for the host, are again ecclesiastics: a corrupt Summoner who would allow a man to have his concubine for a quart of wine, and an extortionate Pardoner, who with false relics earned more money in a day than the local parson gained in two months. And the Host himself, a worthy burgess, and exactly the kind of man the Friar likes to keep company with, turns out in the course of the journey to be amusingly deaf to the implications of the tales he hears.

It is not surprising, actually, that the majority of the characters on the road to Canterbury are singularly lacking in what Chaucer called "steadfastness." They not only deviate from the standards of behavior accepted as norms for their groups, but are frequently lawless, either explicitly or by implication. They illustrate very well the kinds of things concerning which the men of the shire courts, boroughs, and clerical convocations were deeply troubled, and which they hoped those they sent to Parliament would seek to remedy. Since Chaucer was a courtier, associated with the chamber, whose duties brought him into close contact with the exchequer and the courts, and whose friends at court were lords of manors, while some of his acquaintances were members of Parliament or sheriffs like Sir Arnold Savage, or bishops and other ecclesiastics, this fact is hardly surprising. The ideal characters in his General Prologue, who are steadfast in their offices,

---

90. For an example of a tyrannical reeve, see P. D. A. Harvey, *Manorial Records of Cuxham*, Oxfordshire Record Society, vol. 50 (1976), p. 669. Here the whole homage was in mercy for concealing the transgressions of the reeve for four years (clearly through fear). He had let his animals into the lord's pasture, stolen a small ash tree, and abetted a miller who stole grain from the lord's granary. For some light on Chaucer's lines

> Wel koude he kepe a gerner and a bynne;
> Ther was noon auditour koude on him wynne,

see Eleanor Searle, *Lordship and Community: Battle Abbey and its Banlieu* (Toronto, 1974), pp. 316-18.

are reminders of goals to be desired. The lack of success of English chivalry either in maintaining England's traditional holdings and allies abroad or in protecting the realm from foreign incursions, which became an acute problem in 1386, was often attributed to the lack of virtue among chivalric leaders, especially with regard to sexual conduct.[91] Chaucer's Knight, however, is worthy, wise, and humble; he loves chivalry, truth, honor, generosity, and courtesy, and has fought gloriously against the heathen. His son the Squire has been fighting Christians in areas reminiscent of Bishop Despencer's disgraceful crusade, not "in his lord's war," but in hopes to stand in the grace of his lady. The contrast between the humble Knight and the fashionably dressed Squire with his devotion to the seductive arts, reminiscent of John of Salisbury's Terentian braggart soldiers, is an obvious comment on chivalric decay. The Knight, unlike many of his degree who rode with ostentatious retinues,[92] is attended only by his son and one servant, his forester, who rides armed in the company of his lord but carries the bow and arrows appropriate to his station. The Clerk, who holds neither ecclesiastic nor secular office, studies hard and prays for those who have supported him at school. He speaks without verbosity of moral virtue. The Parson works tirelessly in his parish, which he does not desert for an easy position in London. He is content with a meager sufficiency, refrains from excommunicating the poor who cannot pay their tithes, and generally sets a good example in his own conduct for the ideals and virtues he preaches. Finally, his brother the Plowman follows the precepts of charity, works willingly to help his poor neighbors without pay, and faithfully pays his tithes.

As I indicated at the outset it would be difficult to ascribe the social changes that disturbed Chaucer to the effects of pestilence alone. His first long poem, *The Book of the Duchess,* celebrates the virtues of Blanche of Lancaster, who died of pestilence. He undoubtedly knew that the change in King Edward came after his queen died of pestilence. Pestilence plays a large part in only one of the Canterbury Tales,

---

91. I have discussed this point at length in an article now in preparation, "The Probable Date and Purpose of Chaucer's *Troilus.*"

92. See K. B. McFarlane, *The Nobility of Later Medieval England* (Oxford, 1973), pp. 105-12.

the *Pardoner's Tale,* and there it leads to an irrational abandonment of brotherly obligations in a deadly quest for gold. Chaucer was undoubtedly aware that its effect on the realm as a whole, which had long been susceptible to this weakness, might be very similar.

In conclusion, I should like to say that modern cynicism and sentimentality, reinforced by romantic or post-romantic political sensibilities, have often led to a denigration of Chaucer's ideal characters and to an elevation of his rogues. But the picture of Chaucer that results would have made him a mere trifler in his own time, unworthy of the respect as a "philosopher" he achieved among his contemporaries and the more discerning of his admirers in the fifteenth and sixteenth centuries. I do not think we shall understand him very well unless we can become better acquainted with the issues and attitudes of his own time, as well as with the intellectual and literary traditions he inherited.

The Probable Date and Purpose of Chaucer's *Knight's Tale*

by D. W. Robertson, Jr.

Studies in Philology 84:4 (Autumn 1987), pp. 418-439.

In recent years many rather diverse opinions have been expressed about the character of the Knight as Chaucer describes him in the General Prologue and about the significance of the tale attributed to him. To establish some rather basic probabilities about these matters it seems to me useful to consider historical events during the reign of Richard II, especially where relations with France are concerned, for the light they shed on what I believe to be the rather limited span of time when both the description of the Knight and the tale he tells would have appealed to many persons of power and influence at the English court and especially to those known to have been Chaucer's associates. The following discussion is largely confined to the General Prologue, although I hope to discuss the tale in future articles. For convenience it is divided into two parts, the first of which presents a sketch of historical events. The second contains an analysis of the description of the Knight.

I

The following "brief chronicle" is designed to provide a reference background for determining the approximate date of Chaucer's description of the Knight, the assumption being that Chaucer often reflects the immediate interests of his patrons at court. Since his most powerful supporter, either directly or indirectly through his own powerful friends at court, was John of Gaunt, who also was very active in negotiations with the French, I have devoted a great deal of attention to him and to his son Henry of Hereford. Meanwhile, certain actions of King Richard serve to illustrate the fact that he never sought to emulate the chivalric achievements of either Edward III or his own father. Some of the persons mentioned may not be familiar to most Chaucerians, but there is hardly room in a short article for detailed introductions to all of them, although a digression concerning one very influential international figure is included. If the result is somewhat difficult to follow, I can only ask the reader's patience. In 1381, on March 6, King Richard, probably at the request of a powerful lord, for he was then a mere boy, authorized a gift to his squire, Geoffrey Chaucer, of twenty-two pounds for his diplomatic journey to treat of peace in his own time and in the time of King Edward. As Froissart describes the negotiations at Montreuil-sur-Mer in 1377 the English were led by Guichard d'Angle (Earl of Huntingdon in July of that year), who had successively been Marshal to Prince Edward in Aquitaine, joint Marshal of the English armies in Spain in 1367, and tutor to young Richard. With him was Chaucer's friend Sir Richard Stury and Chaucer. Their purpose was to arrange a marriage between young Richard and Marie, daughter of Charles V, which would secure a peace.[1] The negotiations were complex and involved other English participants, including William de Montagu, Earl of Salisbury, with whose nephew, Sir John Montagu, Chaucer must have been well acquainted at court. He too was a poet, although he wrote in French, as Chaucer must have done in his youth. The war had not been progressing favorably for the English in spite of John of Gaunt's devastating march through France in 1373. Charles V was an effective strategist, and many in England hoped for peace, relief from taxation, and the burden of destructive coastal raids. But the negotiations failed. Charles V died in August, 1380, and in January of the following year Richard married Anne of Bohemia, daughter of the Emperor Charles IV. Hopes for an Anglo-French marriage disappeared for many years.

1. See Martin M. Crow and Clair C. Olson, eds., *Chaucer Life-Records* (Oxford: Clarendon Press, 1966), 49-50. Later factual material concerning Chaucer's career is also derived from this work but since it can be easily checked by consulting the very useful chronological table on 550-96, I have not included further footnotes to it.

The years 1385–88 need not concern us here, for they witnessed a developed French plan for an attack on England by sea, for which the French prepared a very large fleet, and a simultaneous advance by land through Scotland, the departure of Gaunt on his Spanish crusade, the revolt of the Appellants, and the Merciless Parliament. Chaucer's description of his Knight contains no references to English victories in Europe but confines itself to enterprises against paganism, which would hardly have had much relevance at a time when the war with France was of immediate and pressing concern.

On May 3, 1389, Richard declared himself of age and immediately undertook negotiations for a three year truce with France at Leulingham, the success of which brought widespread relief in both France and England. Gaunt, whose Spanish venture had been a diplomatic success for the realm and a financial success personally, returned home, having granted Chaucer's son Thomas an annuity for his service in Spain. Chaucer himself was named Clerk of the Works, the most distinguished office of his career. In the next year Marshal Boucicault of France, an outstanding exemplar of late medieval chivalry, arranged a tournament celebrating the truce at St. Ingelvert, for it was clear that the French had been suffering domestic difficulties and miseries from the war just as the English had. And it was also apparent that Christians would do better to fight the heathen on the borders of Christendom than to attack each other. After the tournament a large contingent of English knights, including Chaucer's friends Sir John Clanvowe and Sir Richard Nevill, joined Louis of Bourbon's crusade in Barbary, and Gaunt's son Henry of Hereford (the future Henry IV), having been spectacularly successful at the tournament, set out for Prussia. In July Chaucer's duties were extended to include St. George's Chapel, Windsor, the traditional meeting-place of the Knights of the Garter, then in need of extensive repair. This duty would have assumed a knowledge of and respect for the traditions of English chivalry. In May a return tournament for that at St. Ingelvert had been held at Smithfield, and there was another in October with lists and pageantry supervised by Chaucer.

In 1391 Sir John Clanvowe participated in a peace conference which secured a renewal of the truce with France. He, together with his close companion Sir William Nevill and Sir William Beauchamp, had supported Chaucer before the Chancellor, Bishop Sudbury, in 1380 against the claims of Cecily of Champagne. In October Clanvowe and Nevill died near Constantinople, although the nature of their mission is not clear. Clanvowe had long enjoyed an annuity from John of Gaunt, with whom he fought in France in 1373–74 and in 1378, as well as larger grants from both King Edward and King Richard, including a life annuity of one hundred marks granted in 1381 for his service as a chamber knight. Chaucer lost a friend, a fellow poet, and a distinguished knight.[2]

In February, 1392, the commons in Parliament expressed a desire for renewed negotiations with the French, recommending Gaunt as "the most sufficient person of the realm" to carry them out. Accompanied by the Earl of Rutland ("Aumale"), son of Edmund Langley, Duke of York, and Walter Skirlaw, Bishop of Durham, Gaunt met Charles VI at Amiens, where, although the two sides could not agree on terms for a permanent peace, a new truce was declared. In the following year Gaunt was again asked to treat of peace, an enterprise in which he was accompanied by the Duke of Gloucester (Thomas of Woodstock) who in this year joined Philippe de Mézières' Order of the Passion, perhaps having been encouraged by Chaucer's friend Sir Lewis Clifford, who had supported Philippe since shortly after 1385 and who in this year became a member of Richard's Council, and by Gaunt's friend Sir Thomas Percy. The conference was addressed in moving terms by Leo of Armenia, who had for some years been acting as mediator between England and France, hoping to unite them against the Turks, who had ravaged his kingdom. He was well received by both Gaunt and Gloucester, and in general the conference seems to have been strongly influenced by Philippe de Mézières, who had been urging a reconciliation between the Eastern and Western churches and a European crusade to counter the growing menace of the Turks. Thessalonika had fallen to them in 1387, Bulgaria was being gradually subdued, and at the battle of Kossovo in 1389 the Christian empire of Serbia was destroyed.

2. Clanvowe's career is summarized by V. J. Scattergood in *The Works of Sir John Clanvowe* (Totowa, New Jersey: Rowman and Littlefield, 1975), 25–27, which supplies further details.

The Turkish sultan (as he came to be styled), Bayezid I, whose father had been assassinated at Kossovo, having heard of the Anglo-French negotiations and fearing a Christian attack, sought to assemble larger forces to meet it. But the peace conference was interrupted by an uprising in Cheshire, Lancashire, Shropshire, Staffordshire, Warwickshire, and Leicestershire, led in part by Sir Thomas Talbot, a veteran of the French wars, who evidently thought that peace with France would amount only to a betrayal of England's traditional role on the Continent. The Earl of Arundel failed to oppose the rebels, although he was in a position to do so, a fact that led to open enmity between him and Gaunt and to his subsequent behavior toward Richard at Queen Anne's funeral, which was, to say the least, discourteous.[3] The conference reconvened in May, but was cut short by the illness of Charles. Henry of Hereford set out on a pilgrimage to Jerusalem, to which we shall return later, accompanied by one of Philippe's "evangelists," Oton de Granson, a distinguished knight and a poet much admired by Chaucer, who called him "flour of hem that make in Fraunce."

Before we resume the chronicle of events in England, a short digression concerning Philippe de Mézières may be useful.[4] He was born

---

3. See May McKisack, *The Fourteenth Century* (Oxford: Clarendon Press, 1959), 468-70. The present "brief chronicle" is derived from this and a number of other standard works. For relationships between England and France, however, I have drawn heavily on J. J. N. Palmer's *England, France and Christendom* (Chapel Hill: Univ. of North Carolina Press, 1972), rearranging the materials in chronological order. This is an extremely useful and stimulating book containing some important new insights based on wide research, but to have noted my indebtedness to it in every instance would have encumbered my text with notes. The task of seeking to arrange materials in chronological order from modern historical works is extremely difficult and involves a maze of cross-references when documentation is attempted. Further, I admit a certain sympathy for the implications of an observation made by the late Walter Ullman, *Principles of Government and Politics in the Middle Ages* (New York: Barnes & Noble, 1961), 33, "The atomization of our activities into religious, political, moral, cultural, economic and other spheres was a feature with which the Middle Ages were not familiar."

4. The fullest account of Philippe's life, although now in need of some correction in detail, is Neculai Jorga, *Philippe de Mézières (1327-1405) et la croisade au XIVe siècle* (Paris: Ecole Pratique des Hautes Etudes, 1896). There are briefer accounts in G. W. Coopland's edition and translation of Philippe's *Letter to King Richard II* (New York, 1976); in *Philippe de Mézières: Figurative Representation*

the younger son of a nobleman of Picardy around 1327, embarked on a military career at about eighteen, and served Luchino Visconti and Andrew of Hungary. He was knighted during a campaign against the Turks at Smyrna in 1346. The following year found him at Jerusalem, where in the Church of the Holy Sepulchre he had a vision enabling him to form his plan for a new chivalric Order of the Passion of Jesus Christ. At the close of the year he visited Cyprus but failed to interest King Hugh in a projected crusade. He did, however, win the support of Hugh's son, Prince Peter, and the two sought without much success to win the aid of European kings, princes, and noblemen in a new crusade. When Peter succeeded his father to the throne of Cyprus and to the title of King of Jerusalem in 1359 he exhibited a strong desire to restore the Latin kingdom. In 1360 he was joined by the Apostolic Legate to the East, Pierre Thomas, who was named Latin Patriarch of Constantinople in 1364.

The three travelled widely throughout Europe, seeking support for their crusade. In 1363 King Peter, with a great pagan king and a pagan lord in his retinue, visited England, landing at Dover where he was met by a party of noblemen, including Sir Richard Stury. King Edward greeted his visitors with appropriate festivities, including a great tournament on St. Martin's Day (Nov. 11), but when he was asked to join a crusade, Edward is said to have replied, "Certes, fair cousin, I have a good will to go on this voyage, but I am too old, and I shall leave it to my sons."[5] It was to be many years before one of his sons would respond. Peter and his associates were not spectacularly successful, but they did manage to organize an expedition which surprised and took Alexandria in 1365. After some unreserved pillaging and wanton

---

of the Presentation of the Virgin in the Temple, ed. and trans. Robert S. Haller, with an introduction by M. Catherine Rupp, O.S.M. (Lincoln, Neb., 1971); and, most recently in *Philippe de Mézières's Campaign for the Feast of Mary's Presentation,* ed. William F. Coleman (Toronto: Pontifical Institute of Mediaeval Studies, 1981). All of these works have their shortcomings, but a knowledge of Philippe's career is necessary to an understanding of his influence at the French and English courts in the later fourteenth century, even though the accuracy of some details may be questionable.

5. For Peter's visit to England, see C. L. Kingsford, "The Feast of the Five Kings," *Archaeologia,* 67 (1915-16): 119-26.

destruction the Europeans, unwilling to face advancing Egyptian forces, departed with much booty, to the disgust of Philippe, King Peter, and the Legate. Pierre died in 1366, and in 1369 King Peter was assassinated by some of his own noblemen, leaving Philippe, who was in Venice at the time, to carry on the campaign for a European crusade.

Before the coronation of Peter II of Cyprus in early 1372 Philippe was commissioned to represent Cyprus to Pope Gregory XI. At Avignon he delivered a discourse celebrating both the coronation of the new pope and that of King Peter in a joint ceremony. For over a year he remained at Avignon advocating the celebration of Feast of the Presentation of the Virgin in all western countries, finally winning approval for the Feast and for his Office.[6] He then returned to France where he became a close associate of Charles V, a member of his Council, and a tutor to his son, the future Charles VI. In the last capacity he compiled a list of books suitable for young Charles, recommending first the Bible but stipulating that for a proper understanding it should be read in Latin, and other books indicating common cultural interests at the French and English courts. For example, the list contained the *Consolation* of Boethius, reflected unmistakably in *The Knight's Tale,* Augustine's *City of God,* and *The Policraticus* of John of Salisbury.[7] After the death of Charles V when his son was still a minor and French affairs were directed by the royal princes, Philippe took up residence in the Convent of the Celestines in Paris, to which he had donated a chapel to the Virgin. There he engaged in extensive correspondence with notable persons. In 1388 Charles VI reached his maturity, an event that led to widespread hopes for a peace between England and France, the enthusiasm for which is well illustrated by the tournaments following the truce at Leulingham referred to above. Philippe regarded himself as a mediator and adviser to both kings in the conflict between

---

6. The liturgical play was printed by Karl Young, *The Drama of the Medieval Church* (Oxford: Clarendon Press, 1933), 2: 227-42. Cf. the editions of Haller (which contains Young's text) and Coleman.

7. For the full list see Philippe's *Le songe du vieil pelerin,* ed. G. W. Coopland (Cambridge: Cambridge University Press, 1969), 2: 18-20, 220-24. I cite it here only to suggest a common cultural milieu at the French and English courts, although there were some differences.

France and England, promoting his Order of the Passion with renewed vigor, so that, as Palmer has pointed out, between 1390 and 1395 over eighty French and English lords either joined the Order or pledged their support for it.

To return to the English scene, resuming the "chronicle," in January 1394, Parliament, which recommended that the Duke of York be substituted for Gloucester as a peace negotiator, was diverted by a quarrel between Lancaster and Arundel, whom Gaunt had accused of aiding Talbot and the rebels. Arundel made outrageous counter-accusations but was forced to apologize and to promise future good behavior. On February 28 Richard granted Chaucer an annuity of twenty pounds, having made him a gift of ten pounds early in the preceding year. An annuity of some sort was customarily granted to Clerks of the Works after their duties had been terminated and their accounts had been settled. Having made Gaunt and his heirs Lords of Aquitaine for the purpose of facilitating peace negotiations, Richard resumed talks, but these produced only another truce for four years. In this year three great ladies died — Queen Anne (7 June), Mary Bohun, wife of Henry of Hereford, and Constance of Castile. Naturally, there were speculations concerning important new marriages, especially where the king was concerned.

Meanwhile, in Aquitaine the counts of Armagnac and Foix revolted, renouncing any allegiance to Gaunt, for they wished to be subjects of the English Crown directly. For his part Gaunt had been preparing a crusade in Hungary in the company of Philip the Bold and Louis of Orleans. Pope Boniface IX ordered the crusade proclaimed, and secured the cooperation of the Venetians, who could supply transport. Late in 1394, having assembled an army of some fifteen hundred men, largely from among the rebels in Cheshire and elsewhere, Gaunt set out across France for Aquitaine, hoping to settle the revolt, the ramifications of which were extremely complex,[8] and to gather forces there and then proceed to Venice. Meanwhile, Richard set out for Ireland to counter the incursions of Art McMurrough and his followers

---

8. The Gascon revolt was a very complex matter, ultimately destructive of any real peace settlement between England and France. See Palmer, *England, France and Christendom,* chap. 9.

on English-held lands. He took with him Gloucester, Rutland, Nottingham (Thomas Mowbray), Huntington (John Holand), and March (Edmund Mortimer), as well as other lords.

At Parliament in 1395 (January) Bishop Thomas Arundel (the brother of the Earl) who was Chancellor praised the king's conduct in Ireland, where he had been winning the apparent allegiance of Irish leaders by granting them knighthood and wages from the Crown. This policy was expensive, and not as events were to prove effective, but at the request of Gloucester, who had been sent home to appeal for more funds, Richard was granted a tax. In March the king sent an embassy to Barcelona to ask for the hand of Yolande of Aragon, who was engaged to Louis II of Anjou. He in turn hoped for Aragonese support for his claim to be King of Naples. But Richard probably wished to further weaken French influence in both Spain and Italy. Charles VI objected strongly to the marriage, finally proposing that Richard marry his daughter Isabel, then six years old. Although its authenticity has been disputed, a letter purporting to have been sent by Charles to Richard on April 11 urged a new peace conference, a joint effort to unite the Eastern and Western churches, and "for the propitiation of the sins of our ancestors" a crusade to save the outposts of Christendom and to liberate the Holy Land. Together they would spread the faith "throughout all the parts of the East, demonstrating the gallantry and chivalry of England and France and of our other Christian brothers."[9]

Whether the proposal came in just this form and on the date indicated is not altogether relevant, for something very like it must have been advanced. In fact, it has been urged with some cogency that the Wilton Diptych was commissioned by Richard to demonstrate his dedication to a joint crusade with Charles.[10] He returned to England to discuss the marriage proposals with his Council. In May Peter the Hermit arrived with further letters from Charles and probably with the famous *Epistle* of Philippe de Mézières. The enthusiasm of all those

---

9. The letter, together with a defense of its authenticity, is printed *ibid.*, 180.
10. *Ibid.*, 242–44. On stylistic grounds some art historians have made the work either French or dated it in the early fifteenth century. My own suspicion, based on facial features in the painting, is that the artist, wherever he worked, was French. But this is merely a suspicion.

interested in the Order of the Passion can readily be imagined. In any event, the Council responded favorably to the French proposals and preparations were made for a peace conference. When it convened Richard's initial demands were extravagant, probably by design, and the ambassadors returned early in September without success. Later in the same month to quiet the rebellious lords in Aquitaine Richard sent them ambassadors to publish charters and grants that they would be subject directly to the English Crown, but this did not solve the problem. Meanwhile, a delay in the arrival of the Hungarian ambassadors at Venice made the plan for a joint campaign against the Turks impossible in 1395. The leaders, including Gaunt, returned home, leaving a depleted force with relatively inexperienced commanders in Venice to await better weather conditions for their departure in the next year. In this year Sir Richard Stury met Jean Froissart who returned to England for the first time since the death of Queen Philippa to present Richard with a copy of his poems. It may be significant, as we shall see, that the king entrusted the poems to a courtier from Cheshire, Sir Richard Cradok. Later in the year Stury died, depriving Chaucer of an old friend and companion.

Early in January 1396 Gaunt married Katherine Swynford, a union legitimized by Pope Boniface in September. Richard declared their children legitimate, for otherwise they could not inherit. On the first of February Henry of Hereford granted Chaucer wool for a scarlet robe, an action taken by some to mean that the poet was his retainer during 1395–96; in any event, the grant demonstrates that Chaucer still enjoyed the patronage of the House of Lancaster. Peace and marriage negotiations with the French continued, and on March 9 a truce for twenty-eight years and the royal marriage were agreed upon. In spite of the wedding, finally celebrated on November 4, the year was not unclouded. The crusading armies, having departed from Venice, marched across the Danube and besieged Nicopolis, thinking that Bayezid was preoccupied with his siege of Constantinople. But Bayezid, known as Yilderim or "Lightning" for the speed of his movements, quickly marched to relieve the city. His advance troops were easily disposed of, but when the main body arrived in September, the Christians unwisely charged into an ambush and were soundly defeated. Among the few survivors was the eldest son of Gaunt and Katherine Swynford, John Beaufort, who became Earl of Somerset in 1397. The defeat brought about a cancellation of the proposed Anglo-French crusade in 1397. The eastern and western Churches had not been united, no serious effort was made to curb the expansion of what was to become the Ottoman Empire, and the dreams of Philippe de Mézières and his followers ended in disappointment. There was no permanent peace between England and France, domestic discord broke out in both countries, in England marked especially by the September Parliament of 1397, which set the stage, so to speak, for the deposition of Richard and the triumph of Henry of Hereford. At Richard's court men from Cheshire were becoming increasingly influential, and the king may well have been acquiring a taste, or pretended taste, for alliterative verse,[11] which Chaucer's Knight parodies (A 2599–2615) and his Parson openly abjures with obvious contempt (I 42).

II

Chaucer's description of the Knight in the General Prologue offers almost unmistakable indications of that brief time in which what he says would have been of immediate interest at the English court. Some of the poet's closest friends had been concerned about domestic reform, which then meant moral reform, for many years, and would have been impressed by Philippe de Mézières' contention that Christian society was being undermined at home by *luxuria* (i.e., self-indulgence arising from idleness, especially Venereal self-indulgence), avarice, and vainglory. The plagues of mid-century and later, the corruption of institutions, both lay and ecclesiastical, domestic discord, and the devastations of warfare were widely (and perhaps from a medieval point of view sensibly) regarded as just punishments for the heedless pursuit

---

11. An argument that he did so is advanced by Michael J. Bennett, *Community, Class and Careerism: Cheshire and Lancashire Society in the Age of Sir Gawain and the Green Knight* (Cambridge: Cambridge University Press, 1983), 231–35.

of self-satisfaction at the expense of "the common profit."[12] The surge in popularity of *The Consolation of Philosophy* during the second half of the fourteenth century, with its emphasis on self-discipline, restraint, and personal responsibility under the aegis of a pre-eminently reasonable Providence (often misconstrued, Boethius explains, as the operation of chance perceived as Fortune), evident not only in Chaucer's translation but in the increasing frequency with which its themes appear in English church wall paintings, is a further manifestation of the same basic concern.

The need for reform was sufficiently obvious to produce a popular movement, sometimes radical as it is in the spread of Lollardy, and sometimes more sophisticated as it is in the pages of *Piers Plowman*, or in the penitential fervor inspired among townsmen by the friars.[13] The prospect of peace and a joint crusade against paganism which could unify the eastern and western Churches, unite rival factions at home, and marshal the forces of Europe against a new and menacing threat from the East, which proved ultimately to be menacing indeed, seemed for a time to be a practical and sensible solution. Modern historians and some Chaucerians have adopted a very cynical attitude toward crusades, but, as M. H. Keen has demonstrated,[14] and as the

---

12. Cf. D. W. Robertson, Jr., "Chaucer and the Economic and Social Consequences of the Plague," in F. X. Newman, ed., *Social Unrest in the Late Middle Ages* (Binghamton, NY: Medieval and Renaissance Texts and Studies, 39: 1986), 49-74. Most literate persons believed that a wise and just Providence controlled human affairs, a lesson strongly reinforced by the *Consolation* of Boethius. It was thus "sensible" from their point of view to attribute their difficulties to their own weaknesses.

13. On the friars and penitential literature, see D. W. Robertson, Jr., "Who were 'the People'?" in Thomas J. Heffernan, ed., *The Popular Literature of Medieval England* in Tennessee Studies in Literature, 28 (1985), esp. 15-16.

14. "Chaucer's Knight, the English Aristocracy and the Crusade," in V. J. Scattergood and J. W. Sherborne, eds., *English Court Culture in the Later Middle Ages* (London: Duckworth, 1983), 45-61. This article reaches very similar conclusions to those supported here. I have drawn freely on the factual material it contains, but reorganized it so that its relevance to Chaucer's immediate associates can be made clear. Again, in order to avoid tedious documentation I have not indicated in detail all of Keen's material I have used, but instead urge my readers to consult his excellent study, which deserves wide attention among Chaucerians. I do not agree with his occasional references

first section of this article has made abundantly clear, crusades were regarded with respect, and often with enthusiasm, by many European leaders, both lay and ecclesiastic, during the later years of the fourteenth century. The idea that a crusade might unite warring lords in a common cause was not a new one, and everyone knew that vainglory, lechery, and avarice might impair crusading success. The discipline of Philippe's Order seemed to promise better results. Chaucer's friend Sir Lewis Clifford, who had long been engaged in peace negotiations with the French, who had earlier been prominent among courtiers interested in reform gathered around Joan of Kent, and who had shown an early interest in the Order of the Passion, must have been especially pleased by the prospect of peace with France and an Anglo-French crusade.

Chaucer begins his description of the Knight by resorting to some generalizations. The qualities of a good knight as they were understood are well illustrated in the example of Sir John Chandos, described by Froissart in terms strikingly like those used by Chaucer. He was, Froissart says, "a gentle knight, courteous and amiable, generous, bold, wise, and loyal in every circumstance."[15] To these qualities we might well add piety, for Sir John wore an image of the Blessed Virgin, long regarded as an inspiration to chivalry, and especially to crusading activity, on his surcoat. Chaucer's friend Clanvowe, who had been present at the skirmish where Chandos lost his life, must have had many fine stories to tell about him.

At the outset Chaucer calls his Knight a "worthy" man, or a man fully competent in his profession, an idea echoed twice more in the next six lines. The idea of worth probably implied fortitude, or strength of spirit. For as Honoré Bonet (or Bouvet) says in his *Tree of Battles*, "strength of soul is the chief foundation [of true strength in

---

to "courtly love," but this is a minor matter in an article full of carefully researched factual information. See also the somewhat neglected study by A. S. Cook, *The Historical Background of Chaucer's Knight* (New York: Haskell House, 1956), especially chap. 2.

15. Quoted by John Barnie, *War in English Medieval Society* (Ithaca, New York: Cornell University Press, 1974), 89-90.

battle]: for according to Holy Scripture the man who is not loved by God will never be strong in battle, and it is virtue of soul to be of good counsel, and to know how to command well those who fight the battle.... God, who is above all in strength and power, will give the victory to him who is His friend, though he be feeble in body, rather than to him who is very strong in battle without love to God."[16]

The Knight's worthiness rested on the fact that he loved the virtues of chivalry, truth, honor, generosity, and courtesy. Chivalry, whose ideals are described in a number of readily available sources,[17] was not simply an abstract code, although adherence to "the laws of war" was important, a love of military panoply, the lecherous pursuit of impressionable women, and, to echo certain modern historians, a crazed love of warfare for its own sake were not. As applied to individuals it was a virtue to be loved,[18] but in a collective sense the "chivalry" of a country, consisting of those belonging to the order of knighthood, made up what we should call the "national defense" of a realm. Bonet observes concerning knights, "the first and principal thing is that they should keep the oath to the lord to whom they belong, and to whom they have sworn and promised to do all that he shall command for the defense of his land, according to what is laid down by the laws."[19] Chaucer mentions "truth" immediately. As R. E. Kaske has recently explained, "truth" includes "the knight's obligations to God and Christian morality, to the chivalric code, to the king and his immediate liege-lord, and to mankind at large," an idea fully apparent in the ecclesiastical rite for the ordaining of a knight.[20]

---

16. Trans. G. W. Coopland (Liverpool: Liverpool University Press, 1949), 119-20.
17. A number of them are discussed in a general way in M. H. Keen's recent *Chivalry* (New Haven: Yale University Press, 1984), chap. 1, and references are made to others in the course of the book. This study seems to me to be a much needed corrective to certain rather widely accepted ideas. Keen's earlier study, *The Laws of War in the Later Middle Ages* (London: Routledge & K. Paul, 1973) is also extremely useful.
18. Cf. D. W. Robertson, Jr., *Chaucer's London* (New York: Wiley, 1968), 138-39, where Peter de la Mare's speech at the October Parliament of 1377 is quoted.
19. Trans. Coopland, 131.
20. "Sir Gawain and the Green Knight," in George Mallory Masters, ed., *Medieval and Renaissance Studies* (Chapel Hill: Univ. of North Carolina Press, 1984), 24.

Generosity and courtesy were much admired among the noble. The first was an enemy of greed personally and a key to the maintenance of a body of faithful followers. The noble were traditionally urged to practise largesse but to avoid prodigality at the same time. Courtesy, when it springs from a good-natured or amiable regard for one's fellows, is a kind of generosity of spirit characteristic of those who are neither afraid, nor because of any fearfulness malicious, so that they may be effective and useful courtiers offering sound and disinterested counsel. New knights were expressly warned against malice in the ceremony of ordination. The opening of Chaucer's portrait describes his Knight as a worthy man indeed in easily recognizable terms but does not indicate a date beyond the fact that it is fairly commonplace for the later fourteenth century, although Chaucer manages his material succinctly and without much elaboration, leaving its connotations to his audience.

In spite of the fact that the specific campaigns mentioned in the following lines are early, their nature does suggest a date, specifically a time when the influence of Philippe de Mézières was strong in both France and England. The first military action mentioned is the conquest of Alexandria, the first victory celebrated by Peter of Cyprus and Philippe. Who at the English court would have known something about it? Sir Lewis Clifford, who had expressed an early interest in the Order of the Passion would undoubtedly have cherished its memory. Humphrey de Bohun, who died in 1373, fought there. Among Chaucer's friends, Sir John Clanvowe fought under Humphrey, received an annuity from him, and would undoubtedly have been able to talk about it in a well-informed way. Henry of Hereford was Humphrey's son-in-law and should probably be styled Earl of Hereford as early as 1384. He undoubtedly revered the memory of his father-in-law and his deeds. The Scropes also had memories of Alexandria, for Stephen le Scrope was knighted there. In 1393 Sir William Scrope replaced Sir Thomas Percy as vice-chamberlain, an office that would have brought him into

---

For the ritual of ordination, see R. P. Miller, *Chaucer: Sources and Backgrounds* (New York: Oxford University Press, 1977), 169-72. Miller's chap. 4 contains brief excerpts from other works bearing on the subject of chivalry.

fairly close contact with Chaucer. Because of his participation in the Scrope-Grosvenor trial, Chaucer would have known a great deal about the two Scrope families and their military careers. The significance of the conquest of Alexandria was probably well known, but there was only a fairly short time during which it would have been appropriate to give it pride of place among the experiences of an ideal chivalric leader in England to the neglect of English victories on the Continent.

The Knight had often "the borde bigonne / Aboven alle nacions in Pruce," participating in *Reisen* in Lithuania and Russia, "No Cristen man so ofte of his degree."[21] The Teutonic Knights operated over a long period of time so that no date is implied. But again this statement refers to crusading efforts, not to the victories of Edward III or his son Prince Edward across the channel, or in Aquitaine. French as well as English knights fought in Prussia, as we have seen, among the latter Henry of Hereford. He was diverted from a second venture in 1392, but proceeded to Jerusalem, moving through Prague, Vienna, Venice, and Rhodes to the Church of the Holy Sepulchre. He and his followers returned through Cyprus, Venice, Milan, Pavia, and Paris, where he consulted with French lords about conditions in the East. At Pavia Henry did homage at the tombs of St. Augustine and (as he was locally regarded) St. Boethius. Both tombs rested in a single church, a kind of memorial of which, the little Church of St. Augustine Pappey (Pavia) belonging to the Augustinian canons of Holy Trinity, stood at the end of St. Mary Axe Lane near Aldgate. The Bohun family had long been supporters of the London Augustinians, and Duke Humphrey declared in his will that he had venerated St. Augustine above all other saints. It was natural that Henry should have respected his views. Henry may also have sought to emulate his paternal grandfather, Henry of Grosmont, Duke of Lancaster, who had fought not only in Lithuania, but in Rhodes, Cyprus, and at Algeciras, winning for himself the reputation

---

21. On the "Table" in Prussia, see Keen, *Chivalry*, 172-74. Doubts that Chaucer's "borde" is a reference to it seem to me unwarranted. The portrait is characterized by a certain good-natured exaggeration, also apparent in the Tale. For the plausible theory that Chaucer's *Ruce* refers to Rossenia rather than to Russia, see William Urban, "When Was Chaucer's Knight in 'Ruce'?" *Chau R* 18 (1984), 347

of being one of the great figures in English chivalric tradition.[22] He was a generous founder of monasteries, churches, and hospitals, an abstemious man, acclaimed for his justice at home, especially for his willingness to hear pleas of paupers and widows. He is remembered today for his penitential treatise, the *Seintz medicines*, which has been praised as the best work of French prose produced in England in the fourteenth century.[23] As for Henry of Hereford, he was well educated, good-natured, interested in books and music, and noted for his chivalric prowess.[24] It is not surprising that A. S. Cook concluded that the portrait of the Knight was intended as a compliment to him, as it may in part have been, but the Knight Chaucer depicts is obviously a composite figure.[25]

Among persons about the court who had fought with the Teutonic Knights was Sir William Scrope, who joined them early in his career,[26] being only one among several of the Scrope family in its two branches to do so. Among the more distinguished figures about the court after 1393 was Sir Richard Waldegrave, whose memorable and prophetic speech before Parliament in 1381 must have attracted wide attention.[27] He was repeatedly a member of Parliament between 1376

---

22. On Henry's career, see John Capgrave, *De illustribus Henricis,* ed. F. C. Hingeston (London: Rolls Series, 1858), 161-64; the article in the DNB; and Barnie, *War in English Medieval Society,* 59-61. For the obligation of noblemen to emulate their noble ancestors, see Keen, *Chivalry,* 160. That this obligation was taken very seriously is vividly illustrated in John of Gaunt's defense of himself against charges of treason at the October Parliament of 1377, where he said, among other things, that "none of his ancestors on either side were ever traitors but good and loyal men. And it would be a strange thing indeed were he to stray from their path." See McKisack, *Fourteenth Century,* 401.

23. M. Dominica Legge, *Anglo-Norman Literature and its Background* (Oxford: Clarendon Press, 1963), 216-20.

24. For Henry of Hereford's interest in music, see Nicholas Orme, "The Education of the Courtier," in *English Court Culture,* 83. A very prejudiced account of Henry's early career appears in K. B. McFarlane, *Lancastrian Kings and Lollard Knights* (Oxford: Clarendon Press, 1972), chaps. 1, 2.

25. See the reference in note 14, above.

26. See G. Poulet Scrope, *Castle Combe* (London, 1852), 122-29.

27. For a summary of the speech, see Robertson, "The Probable Date and Purpose of Chaucer's *Troilus,*" in *Medievalia et Humanistica,* N.S. 13 (1985), 147.

and 1390, and in 1393 a royal knight and member of the Council. Early in his career he had fought in Prussia as well as in the Near East. Sir John de Montagu crusaded in Prussia in 1391–92, as did Gaunt's son John Beaufort and probably also Sir Thomas Percy. Thomas of Woodstock, Duke of Gloucester, sought to go there in 1391 in company with his son-in-law, Thomas of Stafford, but was turned back to the coast of Scotland by a devastating storm. But his crusading zeal did not diminish. As we have seen, he joined the Order of the Passion in 1393 and he entertained Philippe's ambassador Peter the Hermit in 1395 and Leo of Armenia in 1396. He was a devout and learned man who had a fine collection of religious and secular books, including a copy of the *Roman de la rose* purchased from Stury's estate.[28] During the negotiations for Richard's marriage, in which Gaunt played a prominent part, he seems to have felt that the concessions to the French were too generous, especially where Brittany was concerned, and he was undoubtedly depressed by the defeat at Nicopolis. Richard disposed of him in 1397.

Chaucer goes on to say that his Knight had fought at Algeciras, where Henry of Grosmont had also fought, as had the father of the Earl of Salisbury. This is followed by a series of campaigns in the Near East, including that at Leas ("Lyeys") and that at Attalia ("Satalye"), which are specifically mentioned among the accomplishments of Peter of Cyprus in Philippe's *Le songe du vieil pelerin*.[29] Humphrey de Bohun, Sir William Scrope of Masham, and Sir Richard Waldegrave had all been at Attalia. The Knight had been in Morocco, had fought in fifteen mortal battles around the Mediterranean, and thrice in lists at Tlemcen ("Tramyssene"), not for wealth or reputation but for "oure feith," on each occasion slaying his adversary. The final campaign

---

28. Thomas was also interested in music. There is a good account of his career in Anthony Goodman, *The Loyal Conspiracy* (London: Routledge & K. Paul, 1971), 74-85. Gloucester has generally had a bad reputation among modern historians, but it might be possible to respect him for the honesty and integrity of his views and to show some sympathy for the fact that he had not been rewarded quite so well as the other royal uncles.

29. Ed. Coopland, 1:295; 2: 91, 227, 419. Professor Paul Olson informs me that the battles were also mentioned in Philippe's *Ordo* which circulated widely among the English nobility.

mentioned, with the lord of Balat ("Palatye"), who was an ally of Peter of Cyprus, against another heathen in Turkey, has given rise to some adverse comment among Chaucerians; but John of Salisbury, who was not only a stringent moralist but the source of some of the basic ideals of chivalry as the English saw them, assures us that a Christian may fight in the service of a pagan so long as he keeps his faith.[30] Moreover, as we have seen, Peter of Cyprus visited England with two noble pagans in his retinue without causing any scandal. If, indeed, there is any scandal involved, it arises from the fact that Chaucer was not able to mention campaigns in Turkey under Christian leadership.

In the account of the Knight's career the clear allusions to campaigns under Peter of Cyprus, the reference to Turkey in the final campaign, as though this formed a kind of climax, and, finally, the omission of all references to Anglo-French conflicts all indicate that the portrait must have been devised at a time when hopes for a real peace with France were high and a joint crusade seemed a reasonable prospect. Before the peace conference of 1393, that is, the portrait of the Knight would have seemed irrelevant, and it became irrelevant once more after the defeat at Nicopolis in September 1396. I do not think that we should picture Chaucer regaling his audience with ideas that had little meaning for them. There is some reason for believing that the accompanying tale, which concludes with a peace established between two great powers with a royal marriage should place both the description of the Knight and his Tale after the death of Queen Anne in the summer of 1394.

Marriage had long been used as a figure for the restoration of both inner and outer order, and it forms a very important part of what the Knight has to recite. This does not mean that Athens should be identified with England and Thebes with France, or the other way around. Theseus, the legendary hero who established Athenian greatness, after

---

30. *Policraticus*, 6: 9, first sentence, "Nec refert fideli quis militet an infideli, dum tantum militet fide incolumi." Murray F. Markland's English abridgement renders this, "It makes no difference whether a soldier serves one of the faithful or an infidel, so long as he serves without impairing or violating his own faith." See, *John of Salisbury: Policraticus, The Statesman's Book* (New York: F. Ungar Pub. Co., 1979), 83.

a kind of "crusade" against the Amazons, who had destroyed marriage in their realm, settles their difficulties by marrying their Queen and establishing better customs for her subjects. On his return he attacks the city of fraternal strife, Thebes, freeing it from tyranny. Meanwhile, the role of the concupiscible and irascible passions in promoting "fraternal strife" in the "lineage of Thebes" is well illustrated in the figures of Palamon and Arcite. The irascible passions are self-destructive conventionally, and the solution to the concupiscible passions is not the lifelong service of Venus, which Palamon promises that goddess, but marriage, and this one simultaneously orders relations between Athens and Thebes. The whole tale is managed with good-humor, for Palamon and Arcite both comically abuse principles from *The Consolation of Philosophy,* while wise Theseus, in spite of certain recent misunderstandings, manages them correctly. This little comic epic[31] with its colorful decor of Classic legend, would have formed, and indeed now does form, a fitting opening for Chaucer's subsequent tales, which in various ways elaborate the themes it conveys. I realize that these are very brief remarks, not a systematic analysis of the Tale.

We do not know when a proposed marriage between Richard and the little French princess began to be discussed in French and English court circles, only that it was formally proposed during the Spring of 1395, and that Richard agreed to it on his return from Ireland, and that this agreement must have been celebrated with considerable festivity and rejoicing. There are, of course, obvious objections to so late a date for *The Knight's Tale* that have nothing to do with history. In the first place, if we assume that the General Prologue to the *Tales* was all written at the same time, we shall have to date it between 1384 and 1389 when the Merchant's concern for peaceful waters between "Middleburgh and Orwelle" (A 276-77) made sense.[32] But these years would hardly have been appropriate for the description of the Knight

---

31. On the *Tale* as an epic and for further information about Chaucer's friends associated with peace negotiations, see Paul A. Olson, "Chaucer's Epic Statement and the Political Milieu of the Late Fourteenth Century," *Mediaevalia,* 5 (1979): 61-78.

32. See T. H. Lloyd, *The English Wool Trade in the Middle Ages* (Cambridge: Cambridge University Press, 1977), 230-31.

as we have it, for England was being hard pressed by the French, and there were no hopes whatsoever for a joint crusade against paganism. It is true that the Duke of Lancaster departed on a crusade, but its real aims were to thwart the French by neutralizing their allies in Spain, and indeed the crusaders were forced to confront French opposition. On the other hand, in the period between late 1394, when Gaunt departed for a joint crusade against paganism with his French allies, Chaucer had every reason to think that a peace with France was imminent and that he could look forward to tranquil years under the patronage of the Lancastrians and their friends at court, who would form a ready audience for a long series of tales.

I wish to suggest that when he wrote the description of the Knight and his retinue he inserted it into the General Prologue, giving it a prominent place at the beginning where it would mark a new era in English history, and, at the same time, wrote a new conclusion specifying the Knight as the first speaker, planning a long series of tales elaborating in various ways the themes of *The Knight's Tale,* and setting aside the original *Man of Law's Tale (The Melibeus?)* for the time being. The introduction to the Man of Law by the Host sounds very much like an introduction to the first tale. Moreover, the original tale "in prose" (B' 95) was replaced by the verse tale now ascribed to him. It is quite possible also that he revised his description of the Man of Law in the General Prologue to make it humorously satiric. Chaucer and his son Thomas had some connection with the Stonor family, and his original Man of Law may have been much more respectable and his tale less a reflection of his shortcomings.

The Canterbury Tales as they survive were evidently put together by scribes who arranged them as best they could, in spite of clear evidence of a lack of auctorial revision, sometimes constructing "spurious" links for them. Thus the opening of *The Shipman's Tale* (B^2 10-19) looks very much as though the tale may have been intended originally for the Wife of Bath. There are lines in *The Merchant's Tale* that seem to imply a monastic speaker (E 1281, 1322). And in one instance, "The Words of the Host to the Parson" (I 15-21), Chaucer appears to have altered his ambitious plans completely, settling for one tale from each pilgrim on the road to Canterbury, without, however, altering the General Prologue so as to conform to this arrangement (I 15-21), a fact that strongly suggests that the tale should be ascribed a date even later than that of *The Knight's Tale*. The Parson is supposed to speak immediately after the Manciple, in spite of the fact that the Manciple spoke in the morning and the Parson did not begin until four o'clock (I 5). Meanwhile, the pilgrims have apparently not yet reached Canterbury. The *Canon's Yeoman's Tale,* finally, exhibits a rather subdued Chaucerian language, leading some to think it spurious, and sounds as though it might have been delivered to a group of canons regular rather than to the court (G 991-1011). It may be significant that it requires no additions to the General Prologue.

Perhaps it is not difficult to explain this situation. The royal marriage produced only a long truce, and this at the expense of disaffecting the Duke of Gloucester and others at home. In fact, fraternal discord broke out in both France and England once more. In England the September parliament of 1397, held in a temporary structure while Westminster Hall was being repaired, was menaced by the king's Cheshire archers, and at its conclusion demanded oaths with a statutory provision that anyone who sought to procure counsel to "repeal, abate, reverse, or annul" the statutes and judgments of the parliament be treated as a traitor. Richard was clearly becoming alienated from his own people and fearful of them. "Time-honored Lancaster," as Shakespeare called him, was growing old, and his son Henry, now Duke of Hereford, was soon to be exiled. Chaucer was losing his patrons at court while Richard may have been acquiring a taste, or pretended taste, for alliterative verse. The portrait of the Knight and the import of his tale, except for the basic moral points, became little more than reminders of causes lost and great enterprises forsaken. It is not surprising that Chaucer, who was losing friends who could bring his work before noble audiences should have curtailed and eventually abandoned his "literary" ambitions. In the later nineties Richard relied less and less on the Chamber knights for advice and used instead a hand-picked Council of his own.

A further objection to a late date for *The Knight's Tale* arises from the generally held opinion that the Knight's remarks about love (A 1785-86) are echoed in the first two lines of *The Boke of Cupid* by Sir

John Clanvowe,[33] who died in 1391. But the echo may well lie in the other direction, for Chaucer may have been paying a graceful tribute to an old friend, and, at the same time, enhancing the prestige of his Knight, who, not as an individual but as an exemplar of English chivalry might be thought of as among those assembled to hear Sir John recite his Valentine's Day poem before the Queen and her ladies at Woodstock some years earlier. Clanvowe had long been active in peace negotiations, had fought against the heathen with Louis of Bourbon in Barbary, and there were now hopes that the policies and ideals he stood for might soon bear fruit. There were probably some in Chaucer's audience who had been at Woodstock on that memorable day and would recognize both the tribute and its significance.

After listing his Knight's campaigns Chaucer returns to further generalizations. The Knight, he says, had a sovereign excellence: he was not only worthy, as the preceding lines amply demonstrate, but he was also wise. This means that like Chandos or Henry of Grosmont his impulses were well controlled by his reason. Froissart describes John of Gaunt as being "sage et imaginatif."[34] Wisdom was a virtue especially desirable in persons of high estate who were responsible for the welfare of those under them, for it implied not only prudent behavior under trying circumstances but in a tradition that stretches from Cicero to St. Augustine and beyond "a knowledge of things human and divine." Finally, the Knight is gifted with the highest of the Christian virtues, humility. In other words, he is never vainglorious. Humility's highest exemplar was, with her "grete humilitee," Mary, "whom God ches to moder for humblesse." As if to reflect this convention Chaucer says that his Knight was "meeke as a mayde," never speaking "villeynye" to anyone in malice, being in sum "a verray parfit gentil knight." The word "gentil" means "noble," and true nobility, as Boethius, Dante, and Chaucer's Parson all tell us, and as Chaucer himself

---

33. Scattergood, *The Works of Sir John Clanvowe,* 35 and 12-13.
34. Sydney Armitage-Smith, *John of Gaunt* (repr. New York: Barnes & Noble, 1964), 409. In his Tale the Knight says that Theseus "with his wysdom and his chivalrie" conquered "al the regne of Femenye," a place identified as being once called "Scithia," roughly the area across the Danube that was the goal of the Christian crusaders.

assures us in his "Balade" on the subject, rests not on lineage but on virtue. Appropriately he is modestly dressed, in spite of the Ellesmere illustrator,[35] and, unlike many fourteenth-century knights of prominence, rides with a very humble retinue consisting of his less worthy son, a squire of Venus, and his yeoman forester.[36] There is little reason to doubt that Chaucer wished to convey a set of genuinely revered ideals, emphasizing the need for Christian harmony in a joint effort against pagan encroachments from the north of Europe to the Byzantine Empire, and beyond that to Jerusalem itself in the portrait of his Knight. And there is a strong possibility that the Knight's comic epic tale was composed either to encourage or to celebrate Richard's marriage to his French bride as a solution to the "fraternal strife" that plagued relationships between Christian England and Christian France. In view of the career, tastes, and family connections of Henry of Hereford it is not surprising that he granted Chaucer wool for a scarlet robe in early 1396, nor that upon his eventual succession to the throne Chaucer should have addressed a laudatory poem to him endorsing all of his claims to that throne, to which Henry promptly responded. Again, it is not surprising that at the opening of *The First Part of King Henry the Fourth* Shakespeare should have depicted the king planning to lead his Englishmen in an effort

> To chase those pagans in those holy fields
> Over whose acres walked those blessed feet
> Which fourteen hundred years ago were nail'd
> For our advantage to the bitter cross.

Henry's crusading ambitions were remembered, even though that heritage of Thebes, fraternal strife, against which Chaucer had warned, came to occupy his whole attention.

Princeton University

---

35. Cf. Martin Stevens, "The Ellesmere Miniatures as Illustrations of Chaucer's *Canterbury Tales*," *Studies in Iconography*, 7-8 (1981-1982):
36. On the chivalric ideal of restraint in display, not often observed, see Keen, *Chivalry*, 153. Chaucer is here perhaps being admonitory. His friend Clanvowe severely condemned worldliness in his treatise *The Two Ways* and probably shared his views on the subject with his friends and associates.

The Physician's Comic Tale

by D. W. Robertson, Jr.

Chaucer Review 23:2 (Fall 1988), pp. 129-139.

It may seem strange to call the Physician's story of the death of Virginia "comic," and I confess at the outset that most critics have concentrated on its pathos so that what I am about to say may seem odd or even reprehensible. However, it has long seemed to me that Chaucer's less admirable characters tell tales that are inadvertent comments on themselves thus producing a humorous effect, even when the events described are rather serious, or would be serious if they were realistic rather than fabulous. Chaucer, not to mention a long series of earlier medieval authors, including Jean de Meun, had learned well from Ovid that fables permitted a witty or comic attitude toward imaginary events, that fabulous narratives could be manipulated in various ways for special purposes, and that even irrational violence vividly described along with its lamentable consequences might be amusing, provided, that is, that it appeared in a fabulous narrative. In the *Canterbury Tales*, again as in Jean de Meun, such humorous effects are enhanced when speakers distort or misrepresent sources that were fairly well known, whether those sources are Classical, Scriptural, or Medieval.

For this reason, and not for the purpose of determining "parallel passages," I believe that it may be profitable to consider the possible sources of the story of Appius and Virginia and the story of Jephtha and his daughter from the Book of Judges to see what the Physician does with them. And here I think that it is very important to distinguish between what Chaucer makes his Physician say and what he might have said himself. The story of the misdeeds of Appius Claudius was first told by Livy, or at least first in any available form. There are strong reasons for doubting that Chaucer's audience was familiar with

Livy. And in any event the Physician's narrative is clearly derived from Jean de Meun's continuation of the *Roman de la rose*, one of Chaucer's favorite books and one that did circulate widely among members of the fourteenth-century aristocracy. Chaucer's use of it both overt and allusive suggests strongly that his audience, or most of it, could recognize his allusions to it and could also appreciate the humor of deliberate distortions of what Jean had to say on the part of his narrators. The pathos of Virginia's death, emphasized by the Physician, has no real precedent in either Livy, where it results in outrage at the behavior of a tyrant, or Jean de Meun, whose Raison was interested in showing that charity is more important than justice.

There is little reason to suppose that Chaucer knew either the Latin text of Livy, the early French translation, or the later French translation by Bersuire at the time the tale was written. Although Nicholas Trevet had composed a commentary or gloss on parts of Livy's *History*, Livy's elegant Latin was very difficult for medieval readers, and his vocabulary was often obscure to them.[1] The early French translation did not circulate widely and was unknown even to Bersuire, and Bersuire's own translation did not begin to circulate until near the close of the fourteenth century and became popular only in the following century.[2] However, it will repay us to consider Livy's narrative, if only very briefly, to show that neither Jean de Meun nor the Physician paid much serious attention to it.

In the first five books of his *History* Livy's purpose was to describe the foundations of the Roman republic, a theme that would have

---

1. See the detailed account of Bersuire's translation by J. Monfrin in *Histoire Littéraire de la France,* 39 (Paris, 1962), 358-400. Bersuire made use of Trevet's gloss.
2. For the earlier translation of the first ten books see Monfrin, 365-66. This formed the basis for an Italian translation, and there was a copy in the library of Charles V of France, which may have been what Philippe de Mézières had in mind when he recommended Livy to young Prince Charles, the future Charles VI. See *Le Songe du Vieil Pelerin,* ed. G. W. Coopland (Cambridge, Engl., 1969), 2:222. Paul Olson informs me that there are French summaries of Livy's account of Appius in the translation of and gloss on Valerius Maximus by Simon of Hesdin and in the commentary on the translation of the *De civitate Dei* by Raoul de Presles, but I do not know whether these works were widely available in England in the 1380s.

elicited small sympathetic understanding among people who thought that social hierarchies were necessary after the Fall to maintain peaceful societies, a view perhaps most vividly expounded in John of Salisbury's *Policraticus*. The story of Appius Claudius in Livy's Book III was specifically concerned with the overthrow of the decemvirs and the restoration of the tribunate. The overthrow of tyranny is a stirring theme, and Livy develops it with considerable skill. Among the decemvirs, who at the time of our story had illegally maintained their powers, Appius was the leader and chief spokesman. His crime against Verginius and his daughter, which consisted of a device by means of which he persuaded one Marcus Claudius to plead before him that she was not actually the daughter of Verginius but his own servant so that Appius could enjoy her charms, followed hard upon the murder of the popular leader Siccius that Appius had arranged. The Roman people were outraged, there was an uprising in the army, and the decemvirs were overthrown.

A few details from this account, very little of which was preserved by Jean de Meun, may be helpful. Neither Jean de Meun nor the Physician says anything at all about Icilius, to whom Verginia had been betrothed, nor about the part he, together with Verginia's uncle Numitorius, played in preventing the immediate transfer of Verginia to Marcus Claudius when she was first brought before Appius to answer the charge of Marcus Claudius while Verginius was still with an army in the field. When they sought a delay until Verginius return, Appius granted it with apparent good grace, but he secretly issued orders to prevent the return of Verginius to Rome on the following day when the trial was to be resumed. But this effort failed, so that Verginius and his daughter were both before Appius when he rendered his final verdict in favor of his conspirator and pimp, Marcus Claudius. Appius now had reason to believe that he had finally gained access to Verginia after having failed in previous efforts to seduce her.

But when the decision had been rendered, Verginius asked for an opportunity to consult with Verginia and her nurse alone, ostensibly to determine whether there might be some truth in the claim of Marcus Claudius. A short distance away, but in view of the crowd, he seized a knife from a butcher and plunged it into his daughter's heart, saying that he could free her only in this way, and then shouted defiance at Appius. The tyrant demanded his arrest, but brandishing his knife and aided by a sympathetic crowd, Verginius escaped to a city gate, while Icilius, aided by Numitorius, displayed the body of Verginia to the spectators. When Appius, enraged, then ordered the arrest of Icilius, the popular leaders Valerius and Horatius, who had been seeking the restoration of the tribunate, intervened, so that Icilius escaped. He and Verginius returned to their armies, won their support, and came back in force to Rome. Subsequently Appius and the fellow decemvir who had most assisted him, Spurius Oppius, were placed in prison, where they killed themselves. Marcus Claudius was spared at the request of Verginius and exiled. The tribunate and Roman liberty as it was then understood were thus restored.[3]

Neither Jean de Meun nor the Physician displays the slightest interest in the restoration of Roman liberties, and the latter makes Verginius a dubious rather than a heroic character. Jean substitutes decapitation for the knife through the heart, performed, he assures us, out of love. The Physician follows him in this and adds no details from Livy that Jean omits. Both have Virginius (as I shall spell his name when referring to Jean or the Physician) place the severed head of Virginia before Appius. Jean de Meun may have wished to remind his audience of another lecherous tyrant, Tereus, and of the fate of little Itys as Ovid describes it (Met. 6: 619-74);[4] indeed, many in Chaucer's audience, although not the Physician himself, may have thought of it also, and of the vengeance of Procne and Philomela for the brutal rape of Philomela. The Physician has Virginius appear before Appius alone (which Livy's Verginius never did) and then go home to Virginia so as to permit a touching scene between the two, her reference to Jephtha, her complaint, based on that of Jephtha's daughter but differing from it in one very significant detail, and her statement

3. This moving narrative, here much abridged, is enlivened by impassioned speeches and vivid descriptions of the actions of the participants. Livy's Latin is still difficult except for trained classicists, but the narrative is conveniently available in *The Early History of Rome,* trans. Aubrey de Sélincourt, 2d. ed., Penguin Classics (Harmondsworth, 1971), 231ff.

4. On the association of lust and dismemberment, see John P. Hermann, "Dismemberment, Dissemination, Discourse: Sign and Symbol in the Shipman's Tale," *ChauR* 19 (1985): 302-37.

that she prefers death to shame. There are no references to Jephtha in Jean de Meun.

Of course, Livy, Jean de Meun, and the Physician were all concerned with justice in a general sense. However, Jean's Raison develops what is essentially a theological argument (in spite of assertions on the part of some that she shows no knowledge of theology), and Chaucer, who in all likelihood accepted her argument, probably had in mind a specific English legal abuse that would allow the Physician to further comment on himself.

But before we consider the legal abuse some explanation of Raison's "theology" may be in order. Perhaps *theology* in a technical sense is not quite the right word to use; something like "traditional Christian teaching" might be better, although theologians, like other Christians, were quite aware of it.[5] Raison explains to her stubborn pupil, the lover, who is overwhelmed by an idolatrous and purely selfish lust (some times amusingly called "courtly love") that because men did not behave charitably judges had to be established in order to bring criminals to justice. The lover asks to know something of justice and of the relationship between justice and love, not the kind of love he suffers, but the kind of love she advocates. She explains that love, by which she explicitly means charity, is more necessary than justice, for if men loved properly justice would not be necessary. For then there would be no need for kings, princes, bailiffs, or provosts and no need to protect men from the malice of their fellows. But unfortunately love of this kind does not reign, and many justices are corrupt, so that a judge often hangs a thief when he himself deserves to be hanged. Raison then recounts the story of Appius, which also illustrates the ill consequences of lecherous fixations like that experienced by the lover, and concludes by saying that justices often commit many wrongs.[6] As Professor Fleming observes, the story offers a "splendid

---

5. For a perceptive discussion of Raison's exemplum concerning Appius, see John V. Fleming, *Reason and the Lover* (Princeton, 1984), 131ff. The general principle adduced by Raison is discussed in D. W. Robertson, Jr., "Chaucer and Christian Tradition," in David Lyle Jeffrey, ed., *Chaucer and Scriptural Tradition* (Ottawa, 1984), 12.

6. See the *Roman*, ed. Ernest Langlois, lines 5434-5659, or Charles Dahlberg's translation (Princeton, 1971), 111-14.

exemplification of the impossibility of positive justice in the absence of interior justice."[7] Or, to put this in another way, those with judicial powers should take Chaucer's advice in Truth to heart: "Daunte thyself, that dauntest others dede."

In Livy and in Jean de Meun the focus of attention is on Appius. In the Physician's version through the inept comments of the Physician and the apparently inept introduction of the story of Jephtha our attention is shifted to Virginia, although the clear lesson of the corruption of justice through unreasonable love, which may take various forms, remains intact, if only by implication. This implication is anything strengthened by the reference to Jephtha.

In Jean de Meun's version Virginius decapitates his daughter immediately, but the Physician allows him to go home, where he explains to Virginia, who is unaware of the legal process involving her, has never been betrothed to anyone, and has never suffered the seductive advances of Appius, that she must face either death or shame. He calls her a "gem of chastity," explains the action of Appius, and asks her to accept death patiently. She asks him for mercy, embracing him and weeping. He asserts that death is the only remedy, and she, pointing out that Jephtha gave his daughter an opportunity to complain, her only crime being that she ran to greet her father upon his return home, asks to complain herself. She swoons, and upon recovering says (C 248-50)

> Blissed be God that I shal dye a mayde!
> Yif me my deeth, er that I have a shame;
> Dooth with youre child youre wyl, a Goddes name![8]

The reference to the complaint of Jephtha's daughter calls attention to the difference between the complaints of the two victims.[9] For the

---

7. *Reason and the Lover,* 131.
8. References to the *Canterbury Tales,* which include the fragment and lineation, are to *The Works of Geoffrey Chaucer,* ed. F. N. Robinson, 2d. ed. (Boston, 1957). In one instance I have altered the position of a comma in a line.
9. The contrast between Jephtha's daughter and Virginia is discussed by Emerson Brown, Jr., "What is Chaucer Doing with the Physician and his Tale?" *PQ* 60 (1981): 140.

daughter of Jephtha, still obliged by the literal Old Law commandment to "wexe and multiplye,"[10] asks for and is granted two months in the mountains with her companions to bewail her virginity (Judges 11:37-39), whereas poor Virginia, who has only a brief time at her disposal, thanks God for her virginity. This may well represent an effort on the part of the Physician to enhance the pathos of the scene, but, at the same time, it is an indication of a time under the New Law rather than under the Old. Meanwhile, the Physician makes her a pathetic character indeed. Her clearly manifested love for her father, her tears, her rather naïve pleas for a soft stroke of the sword, and her obvious innocence enhance this effect.

But the device he uses has, because of Chaucer's own stratagem as he lurks behind his character, a double effect; for it calls attention to that love which is more necessary than justice, an idea suggested at least in Virginia's concern for her virginity. The story of Jephtha could be taken both literally and figuratively, and indeed, it could be so regarded by the same person without any feeling that the two modes are inconsistent. Literally, it was often said that Jephtha should not have kept his rash oath to the Lord, for rash oaths that lead to sinful conduct are not to be kept, a principle often emphasized in the pastoral theology of the later Middle Ages. Thus he can be regarded quite legitimately as a dubious character, much in the same way that the Physician's Virginius, as distinct from his predecessors in Livy and Jean de Meun, can be regarded as a dubious character. On the other hand, the *Glossa ordinaria,* which often appeared in the margins of Scriptural texts, like the marginal glosses, for example, printed in the Geneva Bible, but more extensive, includes a traditional figurative interpretation making Jephtha a foreshadowing of Christ and his daughter a foreshadowing of Christ's human nature sacrificed willingly on the Cross.[11] Thus the figurative interpretation was a well known commonplace, and it would have been difficult to prevent reasonably literate persons from thinking of it. Moreover, the idea is reinforced by the Host's bit of profanity in his comment on the story? "by nayles and

---

10. See D. W. Robertson, Jr., *A Preface to Chaucer* (Princeton, 1962), 222-23.
11. *PL* 113:530C.

by blood!" (C 288). The oaths of our fair "burgeys" (A 754) are frequently unintentionally apt,[12] however much they may have debased his character in the minds of fourteenth-century audiences, and however stupid his comments may be.

The confusion of Harry's comments on the story he has heard is not difficult to discern. For after the oath just mentioned he condemns Appius as a "fals cherl and a fals justise," and proceeds to wish a shameful death to "thise juges and hire advocatz." But he immediately proceeds to demonstrate how he is moved by the death of Virginia, concluding (C 297) that "Hire beautee was hire deth," thus ameliorating the crime of Appius, who, presumably like Mars in Chaucer's *Complaint* (Section IV),[13] could not really help himself. All this undoubtedly amused those in Chaucer's audience who recalled the discourse of Raison in Jean de Meun. And, if anything, their amusement must have been heightened when Harry proceeds to call the Physician "myn owene maister deere" (C 301) and to compliment him further, as he thinks, by calling him (C 309-10) "a propre man, / And lyk prelat, by Seint Ronyan!" He now wishes to hear a "myrie tale," saying that his "herte is lost for pitee of this mayde," who was not, of course, responsible for her fatal "beautee," and turning to the Pardoner for "som myrthe or japes."

Before considering the "myrthe or japes" supplied inadvertently by the Physician himself, under the firm guidance of Chaucer, I should like to explain the legal abuse I believe to be reflected in the *Tale*. This is a form of "maintenance" known as "champarty."[14] Typically, a "maintainer" receives gifts or bargains from a party in a plea of land and unjustly "maintains" that party in whatever pleas he may advance so that he can recover the land. Hence the "fees and robes" of Chaucer's Sergeant (A 317), which were illegal. The robes

---

12. See Hermann, "Dismemberment," 325-26.
13. As Emerson Brown, Jr., points out, "What is Chaucer Doing?" 137, if Virginia's beauty is responsible for her death "then the moral of the tale has evaporated."
14. For references to fourteenth-century statutes on the subject, see Chauncey Wood, *The Elements of Chaucer's Troilus* (Durham, 1984), 178, n. 13.

indicate the number of his wealthy clients, and the fees he obtained from those clients enabled him to purchase a great deal of land in fee simple (that is, free of entailments, reversions, or remainders, and hence freely alienable, although not free from rents or services or both). A statute on "champarty" of 1357 adds the provision that "none of our officers great or small, sergeants or any clerks whatever, do make or carry out such maintenance, defences, or aids of parties upon such against justice, nor do obtain land so in plea,"[15] suggesting that champarty, although usually initiated by persons seeking to corrupt legal officials in order to gain land unlawfully (for example, by obtaining false charters or by altering feet of fines), might be instigated by legal officials who could bribe or threaten persons to institute false claims and later to transfer the land to them. As the Physician explains, Appius, having threatened Claudius with death if he reveals his scheme, "yaf hym yiftes preciouse and deere." His object was not land but power over Virginia, but the procedure is parallel with that in English land cases. His failure also illustrates the fact that (A 1947-50)

> wysdom ne richesse,
> Beautee ne sleighte, strengthe ne hardynesse,
> Ne may with Venus holde champartie,
> For as hir list the world than may she gye.

That is, although worldly wisdom, riches, beauty, and so on may induce Venus (the official) to inflame the proposed victim with her torch, that goddess does what she pleases. This is, of course, merely another way of saying that the reactions of women to a lover's advances are unpredictable, no matter how alluring or clever those advances may seem to the lover. Virginia was not at all moved by Appius and in fact preferred death to his embraces.

Maintenance and champarty are forms of conspiracy as the Physician indicates (C 149). But as he is described in the *General Prologue* he is not only a fraud, using what the more enlightened regarded

---

15. *Statutes of the Realm* (London, 1810-28), 1:145.

as purely superstitious astrological images,[16] but also a conspirator (A 425-27),

> Ful redy hadde he his apothecaries
> To sende hym drogges and his letuaries,
> For ech of hem made oother for to wynne.

He is, in a sense, a judge, but the fraudulent judgments he makes with his images are designed not to help his patients but to produce mutual profits for himself and his apothecaries, with whom he engages in a kind of champarty. Moreover, his citations of many learned authorities are undoubtedly like the cases, judgments, and statutes cited by the Sergeant (A 323-27) imaginary, a matter of seemingly wise words designed to impress his patients. He eats carefully and moderately but has no regard for the Bible, in direct disregard of the injunction of Matt. 4:4, "Man shall not live by bread alone, but by every word that proceedeth out of the mouth of God," as Chauncey Wood has explained.[17] But he dresses extravagantly to give himself an air of authority, a fact that probably inspired the Host to say that he was "lyk a prelat." Otherwise he is miserly, carefully hoarding "that he wan in pestilence," for he loved gold especially. The Sergeant conspired for land and fees, Appius for the satisfaction of his lust, and the Physician for gold. None of them cared anything for justice or for reasonable love.

But the Physician is not a "typical" physician, merely an exemplar of the falseness of some physicians, and these did exist.[18] For example,

---

16. Although it is true that some medical writers were still recommending them in Chaucer's lifetime, Robert Holcot in his popular commentary on the Book of Wisdom said that they were of no more value than the materials of which they were made. See D. W. Robertson, Jr., *Chaucer's London* (New York, 1968), 207-08. In his *Astrolabe*, moreover, Chaucer says that he does not believe in judicial astrology (II., 5, Robinson, *Works,* 551). St. Augustine had condemned it severely, and his arguments were still being echoed in the fourteenth century by Nicole Oresme and by Chaucer's friend Deschamps. Astrology is more popular today than it was in the fourteenth century.
17. "Artistic Intention and Chaucer's Uses of Scriptural Allusion," *Chaucer and Scriptural Tradition,* 44.
18. For some London physicians of Chaucer's time, see *Chaucer's London,* 205-08.

in 1382 a London doctor who undertook to cure a man by using a parchment charm, comparable with the Physician's more ostentatious "images" in efficacy, was made to ride backwards through the streets of the city "on a horse without a saddle, the said parchment and a whetstone for his lies being hung about his neck, an urinal also being hung before him, and another urinal at his back."[19] The purpose of this display was ridicule, for in any tightly knit community ridicule is a potent weapon of correction. Chaucer was quite aware of this principle and often makes use of it, however easily it may be overlooked by serious-minded modern readers, both in Ovid and in Chaucer. It is quite likely, I believe, that his fourteenth-century audience laughed, both at the portrait in the *Prologue* and at the stupidities of the Physician in the tale and those of the Host in the endlink. Meanwhile, it is possible that a fairly recent memory of the London doctor's ride may have inspired Chaucer to write what he did about his own Doctour of Physik, although it is true that false physicians were not unknown at any time.

The Physician introduces and concludes his tale with singular ineptitude, calling attention first to the perfection bestowed on Virginia by Nature and adding an extravagant description of her virtues (C 5-70), all of which helps to provoke the reaction of the Host later and helps to obscure the real implications of the fable. He goes on to discuss the behavior of mistresses ("Nannies") who govern the daughters of lords, irrelevant entirely to Virginia, as he soon admits, concluding (C 91-92),

> Of alle tresons, sovereyn pestilence
> Is whan a wight bitrayseth innocence.

It is true that Appius seeks to betray the innocence of Virginia, but it is also true that the Physician betrays the innocence of those who come to him "in pestilence," and this, he implies, is worse than the pestilence itself. Of course, the Physician, who is stupid, is unaware of this self-betraying implication, but certainly neither Chaucer nor the more alert members of his audience were unaware of it, and it is

---

19. *Chaucer's London*, 106. For the whetstone, see 47.

quite likely that the audience laughed. The Physician has just compared himself inadvertently with a treacherous mistress. Mistresses of this kind are, then, not quite so irrelevant as they may at first seem to be, even to the Physician.

He continues with another apparent irrelevancy, urging fathers not to be negligent in cherishing their daughters, since "Under a shepherde softe and necligent / The wolf hath many a sheep and lamb torent" (C 101–02), a principle he promises to illustrate in the story that follows. The story illustrates no such thing, for whatever we may say of Virginius, we cannot accuse him of being "soft and negligent." Virginia is remarkably obedient to her father. But is there a way in which the story does illustrate that principle? Are there "shepherds" who have allowed a wolf to betray innocent sheep and lambs? There are indeed, and they are the ecclesiastical and civic authorities who have allowed the sheep and lambs under their jurisdiction to be betrayed by the Physician. If they will not hold this wolf up to public ridicule, Chaucer will. Chaucer hastens to add, in order to avoid any misunderstanding (C 117), "The doctour maketh this descripcioun," wherein the "doctour" is not, as some would have it, St. Augustine on the subject of envy, not Jean de Meun, and not Chaucer, but the Physician, who is responsible for the entire opening "descripcioun," and for the inadvertent comments on himself that it contains.

On the other hand, the Physician is a fictional or "fabulous" character, like the characters in his tale. He is not a "personality" and not a "realistic" figure, merely a striking exemplar of medical fraud. The subtlety and wit with which Chaucer causes him to betray himself are Chaucer's own, and I believe that we do Chaucer a disservice if we fail to enjoy that subtlety and wit. But the tale is not over. The Physician goes on to describe the plot of Appius, to tell his story with its embellishment concerning Jephtha, which illustrates the fact that his "studie was but litel on the Bible" (A 438), and to formulate what he considers to be a proper moral. The general effect by implication is that false physicians like himself resemble conspiratorial "maintainers." In his famous speech before Parliament in 1381 on the causes of the Great Revolt, Sir Richard Waldegrave had said that maintainers

---

20. *Rotuli parliamentorum* (Record Commission, 1783), 3:100–01.

were living like kings in the country, destroying right and loyalty.[20] In the same way, Chaucer implied that false physicians by corrupting justice for the sake of gold and exhibiting no charity toward their patients were undermining confidence in the medical profession, especially in times of pestilence, an outbreak of which occurred in 1383. But the Physician is unaware of this implication. He says that his story shows "how synne hath his merite," in spite of the fact that his chief character Virginia was no sinner, and concludes, "forsaketh synne, er synne yow forsake," without realizing that he is a kind of Appius himself, and that in the fate of Appius he has described the fate he himself deserves. If our Host had been a little more astute he might well have wished a "shameful deeth" for "thise [doctours] and hire [apothecaries]," although this might have been a little immoderate (compare C 290–91). Chaucer, being more moderate, merely laughs at his fictional doctor and at the befuddlement of his equally fictional Host. His real interest, here, I believe, as always, was the welfare of his fellow Englishmen.

Princeton University

Wisdom and "The Manciple's Tale": A Chaucerian Comic Interlude

D. W. Robertson, Jr.

Essays in Honor of Edward B. King. Ed. Robert G. Benson & Eric W. Naylor (Sewanee, TN: The University of the South, 1991), pp. 223-237.

The Manciple's Tale has aroused very diverse reactions among Chaucerians, some of whom have not regarded it with deep respect. Considered in isolation as a "literary" work pure and simple it has few fervent admirers. But if we place it in its immediate cultural and historical context, it may yet be rescued and appreciated, at least in imagination, as it might have been appreciated at the time of its first public delivery. We shall find, I believe, that here as elsewhere Chaucer is being witty and amusing but at the same time serious beneath his witty exterior. His wit is often neglected.

This endeavor will require a rather lengthy discussion. I shall begin with an examination of the Tale's source in Ovid's *Metamorphoses,* in so far as possible with reference to its context there, but with some reference to Medieval reactions to it, a procedure necessary to determine what the Manciple, who is not Chaucer, has done with it. Since Ovid was concerned in the context of the story with the wisdom of "telling truth" and the often unfortunate consequences of doing so, some reference to conventional fourteenth-century ideas about this subject will prove useful. Against this background the Manciple's own opinions concerning wisdom and truth can be evaluated. Finally, certain historical considerations suggest a likely date for the Tale's delivery and the nature of the audience being addressed.

I The Wisdom of Ovid

Most members of Chaucer's audience were probably familiar with Ovid, whose work was often taught in schools. In particular, *The Metamorphoses* offered not only useful moral instruction, at least by Medieval standards, but also a great deal of information about the pagan gods, used since Carolingian times in Medieval Latin verse for figurative purposes and increasingly to adorn the works of poets in the vernaculars as their audiences became more literate and appreciative of subtleties that demanded some thought and were also amusing when they were understood.[1] Ovid's wit was widely appreciated down through the early eighteenth century, although more recently it has tended to disappear in favor of more feeling and sentiment.

In fact, in more modern times Ovid has been read in a variety of ways, depending on assumptions about his work. For this reason it is only fair to state some of the assumptions upon which the present discussion is based. The gods themselves are often ambivalent, appearing in both "celestial" and "terrestrial" roles, so that they may represent either virtues or vices. However, in *The Metamorphoses* deities who usually represent virtues sometimes relapse, so to speak, as a result of either habitual weaknesses or conflicts with other deities who may avenge themselves upon them. When this happens the result is not merely ludicrous, however devastating it may be; it demonstrates in a vivid and forceful way the manner in which a virtue may be corrupted. For the gods are personages of high estate and superior powers, so that irrational or irresponsible behavior is especially noteworthy in them, just as such behavior is noteworthy in humans of high estate who have an obligation to set an example for those who are dependent upon them.

Again, the stories Ovid tells should not be read as isolated units. First, it is important where possible to consider the character of the speaker when that speaker is not Ovid himself, just as in reading Chaucer we should pay attention to the character and status of the

---

1. On the medieval taste for the enigmatic, see D. W. Robertson, Jr., *A Preface to Chaucer* (Princeton: Princeton Univ. Press, 1962), 52–64.

person speaking. Moreover, a book of *The Metamorphoses* usually elaborates a theme, sometimes with a transition to a new theme in the final story of the book. Thus Book 2 describes the ill consequences of telling truth, sometimes as a result of rash promises or oaths, and sometimes because of the risk of offending others who would like to have the truth concealed. The world of the deities seems to be not very different from the world of men, and indeed Medieval commentators were probably right in thinking that Ovid was actually talking about people under the guise of mythology. Life in the Empire was not characterized by much respect for that *pietas* celebrated by Vergil, just as life in late Medieval England was not characterized by the kind of Christian *pietas* admired by Chaucer and the prominent Chamber Knights who befriended him and insured his patronage. Vanity, greed, and the uncontrolled appetites of the flesh are perennial enemies of family and community life, whether in pagan or Christian contexts. They also stifle truth.

The story of Apollo and Coronis appears in the second book of *The Metamorphoses* which opens with a description of the splendid Palace of the Sun, some of whose features found their way into the decorative motifs of Gothic cathedrals and churches. A statement Ovid makes about it is echoed in Abbot Suger's description of the decor of his new church at St. Denis, *materiam superbat opus,* "the workmanship was more beautiful than the material."[2] Its portals were decorated with the signs of the Zodiac, six on one side and six on the other, like the portals of Amiens or Notre Dame de Paris. Beyond the portals of the cathedrals were an immutable Truth and an immutable Wisdom. but within Ovid's portals amid representations of the cycles of Time and the Horae — Spring, Summer, Autumn, and Winter — equally spaced, sat Phoebus on his throne with his radiant crown almost too splendid for his son, Phaethon, who was approaching, to look upon. Meanwhile, Phoebus looked out with those unclouded eyes *quibus adspicit omnia,* "with which he beheld all things." Phaethon made his ill-fated request to drive the winged horses of the Chariot of the Sun for a day

---

2. See Erwin Panofsky, *Abbot Suger* (Princeton: Princeton Univ. Press, 1946), 61–62.

in fulfillment of an oath Phoebus had made to grant any request made by a true son. The father acknowledged that he had made a rash promise, sought in vain to explain the extreme dangers the boy would face, and wished that he would choose a wiser gift.

But Phaethon persisted and Apollo very unwisely heeded his own rash promise with disastrous results. For the boy's headlong journey upset the Signs, disturbed the stars, and burned the earth. Cities and nations burned, the Ethiopians turned black, and Libya became a desert. Even the rivers burned, and the Nile hid its head, which had not been discovered, Ovid says, at the time he was writing. The Earth cracked, and even the Lower World was terrorized. Earth prayed for relief to Jove, who released a thunderbolt, destroying the Chariot of the Sun and killing the foolish Phaethon. In grief Phoebus abandoned his journey for a day; the unfortunate Clymene found the remnants of her son Phaethon and mourned with her daughters, the Heliades, who became poplars; and Cycnus, grieving for his relative, Phaethon, became a swan. The foolishness of Phoebus disrupted the cycles of Time and the Earth almost returned to Chaos.

But the ill consequences of his folly persisted. For, having seen that the walls of Heaven were still firm, Jupiter carne down to Earth, especially concerned about Arcadia, whose rivers and flora he restored. And there, justifying Chaucer's epithet "the likerous" (*Form. Age,* 56), encountered a nymph with bow and arrows resting on the ground. Thinking that Juno would not discover what he was about to do, or that the falsehood to her would be worth it even if she did, he garbed himself as Diana. When the poor nymph, deceived, embraced him, calling him a goddess greater than Jove, he ravished her. When Diana later discovered that the poor girl was pregnant, she dismissed her from her service. After the birth of her son, Arcas, the nymph was turned into a bear. When Arcas was fifteen he encountered his mother, who recognized him and sought to approach him. Terrified by the bear, the boy raised his spear, but Jove intervened, turning both mother and son into neighboring constellations. The act increased the wrath of Juno, who was as usual aware of what her husband had done. She persuaded Tethys and ancient Ocean to deny those polar constellations any refuge. As she returned upwards in her chariot drawn by peacocks whose feathers were adorned with the eyes of Argus, the raven (*corvus*) who had been white was turned black. *Lingua,* Ovid tells us, *fuit damno,* "his tongue was his undoing."

Thus the poet introduces the story of Phoebus and Coronis. In Thessaly Phoebus discovered an extremely beautiful maiden, Coronis of Larissa, whom he favored *dum vel casta fuit vel inobservata,* "so long as she was chaste or unobserved," by her divine lover. He, we infer, no longer saw all things after he saw her, but remained for a time blinded by her beauty, just as he was later to be blinded by the beauty of Leucothoe (*Met.* 4.). As the speaker, one of the daughters of Mingas who refused to join the Theban Bacchanalia, observes (196–197). "Thou, who shouldst behold all things, dost gaze on Leucothoe, and on one maiden dost fix those eyes which belong to the whole world." The relevance of this unseemly blindness to the story of Coronis, incidentally, is clearly apparent to the Manciple, as his crow reveals in his remarks to his master. But, to return to Ovid, Apollo's raven observed Coronis bedded with a youth and set out on a journey to find his master and tell him about it. On the way he encountered the gossiping crow (*cornix*) who asked the news. When she had heard it she reminded the raven of her own fate, for when she reported to Minerva how Aglauros had revealed her secret the great goddess deposed her. She had once been a beautiful maiden but had been transformed into a bird by Diana to save her from the unwelcome advances of Neptune. Then she became Minerva's bird until she talked too much and was replaced by the owl. But the raven, bent upon speaking truth, disregarded the warning of the crow and told Phoebus how he had seen Coronis bedded with the Thessalian youth.

When Phoebus heard the story, he wrenched his head aside, losing the laurel crown he had dedicated to Daphne (*Met.* 1.559: "My hair, my lyre, my quiver shall always be entwined with thee, O laurel.") Taking up his weapons, he transfixed the bosom of Coronis. As he withdrew the arrow, Coronis said, "Twas right, O Phoebus, that I should suffer thus from you, but first I should have borne my child. But now two of us shall die as one." Phoebus repented his cruelty nevertheless, embraced the corpse, and hated both himself and his white raven, which he blackened and cast out. As Coronis lay on her funeral pyre, he rescued the babe Aesculapius, who was to inherit his powers of healing, from her womb.

The above summary is much abbreviated, but it touches on the main points. It is clear that Phoebus was blinded by the beauty of Coronis, which led him to violate his promise to Daphne and to be untrue to her memory. His desire for Coronis was frustrated by the truth told him by the raven, which led to an outburst of wrath. His music was destroyed, his harmony replaced by discord. Traditionally, wisdom was thought to control the concupiscible and irascible passions, but Phoebus, who had shown a lack of it in allowing Phaethon to drive his chariot, abandoned it once more when he allowed himself to be overcome by the superficial attractiveness of Coronis, and once more in his fit of jealous rage, directed first at Coronis and then at himself for the wrong reasons, and finally at the raven who had usurped his function as a revealer of truth.

During the Middle Ages music was regarded as fundamental to all of the disciplines. Human music specifically was thought to entail a harmony between the spirit and the flesh, maintained when the flesh obeyed the spirit under the guidance of wisdom. That the music of Apollo was thought of in a somewhat analogous way in Antiquity is well illustrated in the story of Midas, so amusingly mishandled by Chaucer's Wife of Bath. For Midas succumbed to the seductive pipes of Pan and judged Pan's music to be superior to that produced by Apollo's lyre. In the story of Coronis Phoebus shows himself to be sometimes worthy of those long hairy ears he bestowed on Midas. As for the raven, we may notice with some amusement that when the gods sought to escape from the wrath of Typhoeus, Apollo disguised himself as a raven (*Met.* 5.329), almost a kind of confession that the raven had once usurped his function and that he had, at one time, in effect, blackened himself. Meanwhile, Book 2 continues with accounts of other persons punished for speaking truth, one involving Apollo who, when he was a young shepherd playing his pipes and thinking of love at Elis, failed to discern truth.

II Wisdom and Truth

Before turning to the Manciple's treatment of Ovid, perhaps we should consider certain ideas concerning Wisdom and Truth current at the time Chaucer was writing. Christians were obliged to speak truth, regardless of the consequences, which at times might be severe, as they are in Ovid's second book. The most important authority on the subject was St. Augustine's *De mendacio,* which supplied what became the standard definition of a lie (1. 3.3.): to have one thing in the heart (or mind) while indicating another either verbally or otherwise. This, in fact, is the origin of later injunctions like those of Sidney or Shakespeare to the effect that a man should "look into his heart and write" or that we should "speak what we feel, not what we ought to say." That this ideal was current in the fourteenth century is well illustrated in two poems in the Vernon series which I shall summarize briefly. Parenthetically, St. Augustine did not regard poetic fables that are false on the surface as being lies when they conveyed useful truths.[3]

The first of these poems ironically condemns the attitude taken by the Manciple, taking its title from the refrain, "Who says the Sooth. He shall be shent."[4] The poet begins by saying that anyone who wishes to live at ease or to attain any respect should seek to please the "wicked world"; he must flatter and pretend in order to avoid difficulty. In short, he should lie (9-10):

> Herte & mouth loke thei ben tweyne;
> Thei mowe not ben of on assent.

A man should restrain his tongue, for "hos seith the sothe, he shal be schent." Thus the truth is hidden, and everyone abandons the text for the gloss and colors his words.[5] Every lord has his flatterers who lie

---

3. See *A Preface to Chaucer,* 59-60, 337-338.
4. For the text see Carleton Brown, *Religious Lyrics of the XIVth Century* (Oxford: Clarendon Press, 1924), no. 103, 152-154. For convenience I have substituted *th* for Brown's Middle English symbol.
5. For example, by using euphemisms or "polite" terms for reprehensible things to make them seem harmless. The word *glose* in Middle English, which had both Classical and Germanic origins with different connotations could mean either to supply an explanation or to "gloss over." Hence the humor in the observation of the Summoner's Friar, "Glosynge is a glorious

to him and blind him for fear of losing their offices. Thus we lack a physician to heal our maladies. Unless they are revealed we cannot heal them. And anyone who speaks the truth about them will be disgraced. If a friar tells us about our actual misdeeds he will get small thanks, risking disgrace at council and parliament. The world, the poet laments, has never been so untrue since the birth of Christ. But those who conceal the truth will rue that concealment on the Day of Judgment. Even children, who should be innocent, are brought up to heed the ways of deception. Indeed, the world is so corrupt that people cannot see their own faults; the father cannot trust the son, nor any man another. Falsehood is called "subtlety," so that, in fact, "Ho seith the sothe, he schal be schent."

In view of the widespread corruption in all ranks of society that seemed to grow steadily worse as the fourteenth century progressed, this sort of complaint is understandable.[6] The author of the second of our poems, "Truth is Best,"[7] makes use of the common epithet *Truth* or in Latin *Veritas* for Christ. He begins by asserting that the man who thinks about it will despise the falsehoods of this wretched world, for when the final Judgment comes, we shall find that "treuthe is best." He assures us that truth should be loved by kings, knights, and merchants, for if they do not love it they shall not enter Heaven. Truth [Christ] will do no mercy when He judges us, and we shall see that we have contradicted Him too long. Lords and those who "meddle with the law" should not destroy truth for the sake of greed. We should all rule ourselves with truth, rising from sin and sloth, and of "Chivalrye bere the flour."[8] Truth endures most in war and is strongest in the long run.

---

thyng, certayn." When he pretends to "glose" in one way, this flatterer is "glosyng" in another.

6. For some indications derived from a variety of primary sources, see Robertson, "Chaucer and the Economic and Social Consequences of the Plague," in Francis X, Newman, ed., *Social Unrest in the Late Middle Ages* (Medieval and Renaissance Texts and Studies, 39, Binghamton, NY, 1986), 49-74. For Chaucer's own view, see his "Lak of Stedfastnesse."

7. Brown, no. 108, 168-70.

8. Truth was the first obligation of a knight. Thus Chaucer's Knight loved Truth first among the chivalric virtues. This fact and some of its implications are discussed in Robertson, "The Probable Date and Purpose of Chaucer's *Knight's Tale*," *SP*, 84 (1987), 429-30.

For God's love we should succor and maintain Him. Once Truth was lord here and with Him all virtues. Spain, Brittany, and other lands will bear witness that we once endowed them properly and gave them lords to live in peace. They then loved Truth. Falsehood may rule for a time through the "maintenance" of Covetousness.[9] But his ground (i.e., the basis for his claim) will beguile him in in spite of his wisdom. When Truth prospers we shall hunt Falsehood as a cat does a mouse.

The "wisdom" of Falsehood is the wisdom of both the Host and the Manciple. Although the two poems above were clearly addressed to men of high estate, as was Chaucer's much better poem, "Truth," Chaucer discerned the same sort of falsehood among persons of lower rank. Thus for example his Reeve, a manorial servant, has made of himself a petty tyrant because he knows all of the "falsehoods" of the tenants of the manor that he should report to the manorial court but keeps concealed in return for their silence about his own deceits, and even has the bailiff, a servant of the lord, under his thumb, so to speak, in the same way.[10]

III The Wisdom of the Manciple

But exactly what has the Manciple done with Ovid's story, which is not actually about the crow, although he serves as a further illustration of the dangers of telling truth, but about Phoebus?[11] The question, I

---

9. This is a legal term used for legal officials who "maintained" the causes of lords, whether true or false in return for fees and robes like those granted to Chaucer's Sergeant. It could also be used for lords who "maintained" the causes of their tenants, or for "covins" of individuals of whatever rank who swore to "maintain" their companions in right or wrong. Here may be included, for example, bands of marauders, although even guilds and fraternities came under suspicion in the Cambridge Parliament of 1388.

10. Cf. the discussion of the Reeve in Robertson, *Essays in Medieval Culture* (Princeton: Princeton Univ. Press, 1980), 295-96.

11. Quotations from *ManT* and line numbers are from Donald C. Baker, *The Manciple's Tale*, in *A Variorum Edition of the Works of Geoffrey Chaucer*, 2, 11 (Norman, Oklahoma: Univ. of Oklahoma Press, 1984). Quotations from and references to the works of Chaucer elsewhere refer to the second edition by F. N. Robinson (Boston: Houghton Mifflin, 1957).

should emphasize, is not what Chaucer has done with Ovid but what he has made the Manciple do with him in order to further something Chaucer wished to say. The Manciple does not use the name "Coronis" but refers instead to the "wife" of Phoebus, and he does not mention Aesculapius. It has often been pointed out that he called Ovid's raven a crow, but this fact is not very significant, for he omitted the meeting between the raven and the crow, which could not have happened in his version because he put the crow in a cage. Moreover, *chough, crow, raven,* and *rook* are still used loosely in modern English. Further, they are all now classed as *corvidae,* so that the raven seems to have prevailed, but in English *corvidae* are "members of the crow family." Miller renders Apollo's disguise as a raven (*Met.* 5.329), *Delius in corvo,* "Apollo hid in crow's shape." However, like the Wife of Bath,[12] the Manciple distorts Ovid in other ways.

He begins by introducing Apollo, belittling him at once by calling him "the mooste lusty bachiler / In al this world" (107-108). It is true that Phoebus had a number of diversions with nymphs, almost always ill-fortuned, but these were diversions, not his most important characteristics.[13] Belittling him further, the Manciple says that he slew the Python as he was "slepyng agayn the sonne," hardly an accurate description of the slaying of that monster, an event memorialized in the Pythian games. Parenthetically, Cupid, proud of his own skill as an archer and irritated by this singular triumph with mere arrows, shot his own arrow at Apollo, provoking him to the fruitless pursuit of Daphne, a bit of unsuccessful "bachelerye." But the Manciple persists, this time producing a laughable self-contradiction, saying (125-129):

> This Phebus that was flour of bachelerye
> As wel in fredom as in chivalrye,
> For his desport, in signe eek of victorie

---

12. Cf. Robertson, "The Wife of Bath and Midas," *SAC,* 6 (1984), 1-20.
13. He was the god of truth and wisdom, although he was occasionally "diverted" from his proper course of action. The Latin verb *diverto* meant basically "to turn out of the way." Basic Latin meanings were still strong during the Middle Ages. Thus when a traveller stopped at an inn for the night, this was a "diversion" although his experience there might not be very "diverting" in the modern sense.

> Of Phyton, so as telleth us the storie,
> Was wont to beren in his hand a bowe.

He has just said that he was very handsome and filled with "gentillesse," "honour," and "parfit worthinesse," hardly consistent with his sleeping Python story. But even worse, "bachelerye" and "chivalrye" were by traditional standards inconsistent,[14] while "gentilesse," as readers of Chaucer's poem on the subject are aware, implies nobility of character. Moreover, John of Salisbury, who supplied many of the basic ideals for English chivalry insisted that knights addicted to lechery and splendid equipage are merely a temptation to enemy attack (*Policraticus*, 6.18). By this time the Manciple was already invoking laughter from Chaucer's audience, and we should laugh too. Meanwhile, his Phebus is beginning to resemble the "lusty bachiler" of the *Wife of Bath's Tale*.

Rationalizing and embroidering Ovid's account somewhat, the Manciple tells us that Phebus had a caged crow, white as a swan, and had taught it to speak and sing, so that no nightingale could sing "so wonder myrily and weel." Ovid's bird is not caged, and nothing is said about his musical abilities. Phebus, the Manciple says, also had a "wyf," who is not a wife in Ovid; in fact, what a person so devoted to "bachelerye" would want with one is a little difficult to see. In any event, like old John in *The Miller's Tale*, he loved her "moore than his lyf," and "kept hire fayne," but not like the crow "narwe in cage." But as the Manciple explains, echoing Theophrastus in Jerome's epistle

---

14. On the connotations of "bachelerye," see "The Wife of Bath and Midas," page 3 and note 6, where the quotation probably reflects John of Salisbury's condemnation of braggart soldiers devoted to luxuries. A young squire or knight bachelor might be valiant, but if he devoted himself too wholeheartedly to "diversions" and became a *miles amoris* like the Manciple's Phebus or Chaucer's Squire, he lost his worth. For the *miles amoris* see *A Preface to Chaucer*, pages 408-410. For OF *bachelerie* in this sense, see the illustrative quotation from the *Roman de la rose* in the Larousse *Dictionnaire d' Ancien Français* (1947) under that heading, where it is associated with song and dance. Phebus and the Wife's knight are *lusty* bachelors. Cf. Boethius, *De Cons.*, 3. m. 5. I am aware of the fact that the Middle English Dictionary defines "bachelerye" as a chivalric quality, but also very much aware that dictionaries, with few exceptions, offer only preliminary definitions, subject to revision by more detailed study of relevant texts.

against Jovinian,[15] all in vain, for a good wife needs no keeping and a bad one cannot be controlled, a principle he illustrates with the familiar examples of the caged bird, the cat, and the she-wolf, concluding humorously that these examples apply only to men, not to women, which of course makes them literally irrelevant and his conclusion an obvious example of *antiphrasis*, as one marginal gloss indicates.[16] On the other hand, if we take the remarkable "bachelerye" seriously, there are three uncaged birds that have returned to their natures in this story. But I shall return to this point later. Meanwhile, the Manciple continues, the wife had a lover, in Ovid simply "a youth of Thessaly," but now "a man of litel reputacioun," so that when Phebus was absent she sent for this unworthy "lemman" of hers. He then apologizes for the word *lemman*, not actually very shocking, and justifying it by citing Plato before going on, perhaps forgetful of the moral to his own tale to speak truth for a change. The Manciple is amusingly dense.

But to understand this we must first understand what Chaucer himself meant by citing Plato to justify his own use of profane language (I (A) 739-742):

> Crist spak hymself ful brode in hooly writ,
> And wel ye wot no vilenye is it,
> Eek Plato seith, whoso that kan him rede,
> The wordes moote ben cosyn to the dede.

For Christ's "broad" language, see, for example, the Sermon on the Mount (Mat. 5.28-32). Similarly, the Manciple justifies the use of the word *lemman* and introduces the observations to follow by saying (207-208):

> The wise Plato seith, as ye may rede.
> The word moot nede acorde with the dede.

The impression that this refers to some metaphysical principle seems to me to be mistaken, for it is a logical principle. It may be found, for example, in the Latin translation of Aristotle's *Posterior Analytics* attributed to Boethius where we are told (1.7) that the

---

15. The echo is indicated in a marginal gloss and supported in Baker's note, p. 101.
16. Baker, p. 108. For the figure, see Isidore of Seville, *Etymologiae*, 1, 28, 24.

demonstrative principles used in one discipline cannot be used in another discipline unless the two disciplines are based on the same axioms or unless one is a corollary of the other.[17]

Whether Boethius was in fact responsible for the Latin translation of Aristotle's treatise is not important; it is important that Lady Philosophy in the context of a carefully reasoned argument asserts that she has not violated the logical principle involved and attributes it to Plato (3. pr. 12. Robinson, p. 357):

> But natheles, yif I have styred resouns that be nat taken from withouten the compas of the thing of which we treten, but resouns that been bestowed withinne that compas, ther nys nat why that thou shoudest merveillen, sith thou hast lernyd by the sentence of Plato that nedes the wordis moot be cosynes to the thinges of which thei speken.

Chaucer knew this principle not only from this passage but also from Raison's defense of downright language in the *Roman de la Rose*.[18] Logical absurdities were regarded as being laughable in the Middle Ages, and when Medieval writers of reasonable literacy mingled religious themes with themes expressing venereal desires in lyrics or in the speeches of characters in narratives it is probable that they were not advocating a "religion of love" but were being jocular, making fun of the speakers, although there have been various kinds of modern efforts to form a doctrine of an idolatrous desire for self-satisfaction "reconciled" with charity. Be that as it may, Ovid's Apollo had no chivalric obligations, was not a knight, and could not be accused of "bachelerye" in its chivalric sense. Hence the Manciple is using words that are not "cosynes to the things of whiche thei speken," unless, that is, he is using them in a figurative sense to apply to an actual situation, as Chaucer often does. Apparently he is not, but Chaucer apparently was in this tale, as we shall see.

Further disregarding the lesson of his tale as he sees it, the Manciple goes on to tell us that there is no difference between a wife of

---

17. See *Essays in Medieval Culture*, page 142.
18. Cf. the discussion by John V. Fleming, *Reason and the Lover* (Princeton: Princeton Univ. Press, 1984), 97-115.

high degree who is physically unfaithful and a poor wench who is unfaithful in the same way, for "Men layn that oon as lowe as lyth that oother." In fact, it was conventionally held that those in high estate have a greater obligation to be virtuous than do the lowly, since their misdeeds affect more people. Even the Manciple knows this, for he reinforces his argument by proceeding to inform us that there is no difference between a tyrant, called a "captain," and a mere outlaw, but (231–234) because

> the outlawe hath but smal meynee,
> And may nat doon so gret an harm as he,
> Ne bryng a contree to so gret meschief,
> Men clepen hym an outlawe or a theef.

By these standards our learned speaker was quite justified in his observations about the Cook in the prologue to his tale. But they also serve to further demean the characters of Phebus and his "wyf." For the behavior of Phebus is indeed tyrannical, although it does not involve robbery.

But the Manciple distorts Ovid's narrative in such a way as to show that words must for the most part be suppressed, whether they are "cosyn to the dede" or not. In fact, they should be mostly suppressed. His "white crowe" in his "cage" witnessed the adultery of the "wyf" of Phebus but remained quiet until Phebus came home. Then the crow sang "Cokkow! Cokkow! Cokkow!" understandably provoking his master's curiosity. Perhaps the Wife of Bath should have been there to tell him that "the cow is wood" (III (D) 252). Lacking any such reassurance, he was forced to hear the assertion "bleryd is thyn eye," and a circumstantial account of what the crow saw in very plain terms — "in thy bed thy wif I sey hym swyve." Poor Phebus was heartbroken. He killed his "wyf" at once and in sorrow "brak his mynstralcye," which, surprisingly, included no lyre but instead "harp and lute, and gyterne and sawtrye." He then broke his arrows and his bow.

Lacking the confession of Coronis, Phebus proceeds to call the poor crow a traitor and his wife "sad and eek so trewe," without guilt. After some bitter comments on the evil of reckless wrath, he concludes that he will kill himself. Instead, however, proceeding to indulge in reckless wrath once more, he deprives the crow of his speech and song, pulls out his white plumage, condemns him and all crows after him to be black, and throws him out to "crye agayn tempest and rayn," as crows since, presumably, do naturally. The Manciple adduces a moral from this (309-13):

> Lordyngs, by this ensample I yow preye.
> Beth war, and taketh kepe what I seye:
> Ne telleth nevere no man in youre lyf
> Howe that another man hath dight his wyf;
> He wol yow haten mortally certain.

The same lesson was also appended to the story by Thomas Walsingham, probably a few years after the Manciple spoke.[19] Not content with this, however, our Manciple proceeds to deliver a little "sermon" taught him by his "Dame," the wisdom of the world, to the effect that a man should restrain his tongue, for no man is "shent" for speaking little and dissimulating, whether his news is true or false. The worldly will punish those who reveal truth or falsehood by in turn revealing the falsehood of those who speak against them. Remembering our lyrics, or even the real lesson of Ovid's second book, there is not much to be said for either the Manciple or his noble Phebus. Indeed, there is every reason to think that Chaucer's audience laughed at them. But perhaps they were laughing at someone else too.

IV The Wisdom of Gaston Febus

The idea that Chaucer (as distinct from the Manciple) was actually making fun of Gaston Febus, Count of Foix, has recently been argued cogently in a very thoroughly researched article by William Askins,

---

19. *Archana Deorum*, ed. Robert van Kluyve (Durham, NC: Duke Univ. Press, 1968), 2. 3. 37-38. page 53: "Fabula Phebi respicit sponsos ignaros qui maxime odiunt eos qui eis adulteria conjugum suarum nuntiant vel ennarant." The editor, page x, suggests a date for this work later than 1396. However, it is possible that Walsingham was here as elsewhere drawing on another source.

"The Historical Setting of the Manciple's Tale."[20] That is, he was using the amusing distortions of his Manciple figuratively to refer to an actual situation, thus making his own words, through the agency of his fictional Manciple, "cosyns to the thinges of which thei speken." The resemblances Askins indicates between the Count and the Manciple's Phebus are striking, as is also his account of the relations between the Count and the English. He had made himself a considerable nuisance both to Prince Edward (the Black Prince) and to John of Gaunt. Gaston vainly styled himself "Febus" as though he were a kind of reincarnation of Ovid's Phoebus and wore a blond wig to emphasize the resemblance, although this hair was hardly dedicated to Daphne. He was a famous hunter, a well-known cultivator of music, known for the splendor of his court, his exploits in warfare, but also for his "bachelerye," for he was the father of numerous bastards. Although he did not murder his wife, he did cast her off, installing four mistresses in his castle to replace her. And like the Manciple's Phebus he was subject to fits of uncontrolled wrath. He murdered his legitimate son, Gaston, having accused him of conspiring with his exiled mother to murder him. Then he tortured and murdered young Gaston's entire retinue, known for its splendor, in an effort to extract confessions from them as to his son's guilt. Again, he murdered a relative who was a guest at his castle when the unfortunate man tried to explain his allegiance to the English. Indeed, he was famous for his cruelty. It is true that some of the French, who liked courtly splendor, admired Gaston, and even John of Gaunt sometimes spoke of him in favorable terms, although his motives for doing so were probably diplomatic, for the castle at Foix commanded one of the most strategic and easily defended passes across the Pyrenees.

Ovid's Phoebus was not a knight and under no chivalric obligations, but Gaston was a knight, not to mention the fact that he bore the additional obligations of a count. The assertion of the Manciple to the effect that men rather than women are likely to "do what comes naturally," like the lover in Macabru's famous "L'autrier jost' una subissa,"

---

20. *SAC*, 7 (1985), 87-105. I do not agree with everything the article says, including its equation of "bachelery" and chivalry.

for example, makes no sense in the Manciple's story but does make sense with reference to Gaston. And at times Gaston did behave like an outlaw and a thief. Finally, the instruments of his highly prized minstrels probably resembled those discarded by Phebus. The splendid lyre of Phoebus wreathed in laurel would hardly have been appropriate for them. These hints, I believe, were sufficient to provoke Chaucer's audience to laughter at Gaston Febus.

It may be possible to suggest a tentative date and occasion for Chaucer's presentation of the Tale, and I shall seek to do so even though I am aware of the fact that many Chaucerians dislike thinking of Chaucer's tales as being "occasional." To do this a little excursion into history will be necessary, and again I am aware of the fact that many Chaucerians regard history irrelevant to Chaucer's literary productions.[21] But Chaucer was a royal squire associated with the Chamber, a number of whose knights were sympathetic to Lancastrian causes, a not unreasonable situation in view of the fact that the duke of Lancaster was the most powerful man in the realm beneath the king. Again, fairly regular entertainments were arranged for the Household and its guests, among whom were undoubtedly prominent lords, especially during sessions of Parliament. The likelihood that Chaucer's friends among the Chamber Knights arranged for him to recite his tales before the Household as a part of these entertainments seems to me to be very great.[22] Naturally, the tales were concerned with matters of current interest, frequently with issues of interest in Parliament. Chaucer's eloquence and his capacity for "speaking truth" probably were in part responsible for his ambassadorial appointments. He undoubtedly had also a reputation for "speaking truth" amusingly under the guise of poetic fiction.

---

21. For an interesting and provocative discussion of this attitude, see Paul A. Olson, *"The Canterbury Tales" and the Good Society* (Princeton: Princeton University Press, 1986), 3-18. The remainder of the book demonstrated the usefulness of historical knowledge in the interpretation of Chaucer's Tales.

22. For the suggestion that Chaucer participated in entertainments for the Household, or, more specifically, for the "upstairs" of the Household or "Chamber," see Chris Given-Wilson, *The Royal Household and the King's Affinity* (New Haven and London: Yale Univ. Press, 1986), 60-61.

With reference to the date, it is unlikely that a time after 1391, when Gaston died, would have been appropriate. He was no longer a problem, although his successor was, and there would have been little reason to make fun of him. After John of Gaunt's venture in Spain, which had distracted the French from their planned invasion of England, he tarried for a time in Aquitaine seeking to establish harmony in that troubled realm. He also granted Chaucer's son Thomas an annuity for his service in the campaign. He was called home by King Richard who needed more harmony at home among the great men of the realm. After landing at Plymouth in November, 1389, he met the king on the road to a meeting of the Council at Reading. Richard welcomed him warmly, and the Duke gave the king and the members of his retinue the kiss of peace. The factions among the members of the Council quieted in Gaunt's presence. When he went to Westminster the Duke was welcomed by the citizens and by the Abbot, and at London he was again welcomed at St. Paul's. Parliament met in January, 1390. On February 16 the Palatinate of Lancaster, which he had held as a tenant for life, was regranted to him in tail male. Finally, on March 2, with the full approval of Lords and Commons, Gaunt was made Duke of Aquitaine for life.

These events must have pleased Chaucer. The new Duke of Aquitaine did not visit his duchy at once, but sent Sir William Scrope to be his seneschal there. Parliament wished Gaunt to lead new peace negotiations with the French. A three-year truce was agreed upon at Leulinghen. To celebrate it Marshal Boucicault of France held a great tournament at St. Ingelvert, where Gaunt's son, the earl of Derby distinguished himself. Chaucer, who had been named Clerk of the Works in 1389, supervised the lists and pageantry for a return tournament at Smithfield in May. In July his duties were extended to include there furbishing of the Garter Chapel at Windsor Castle, said to be badly in need of repair. His friend Sir Peter Courtenay was named Keeper of the Castle in this year. As Given-Wilson points out, the St. George's Day festival was held at Windsor every year between March 15-31 and April 22-28. It was regularly attended by the king and his Household ordinarily travelled with him. With the renewed confidence resulting from the truce it is likely that the king and many of the magnates thought that the Garter Chapel should be more resplendent.

As Knighton informs us, Gaunt, whose relations with some of his fellow magnates had sometimes been strained,[23] held a great hunting festival at Leicester around the feast of Petrus ad Vincula (Aug. 1). His guests included the king and queen, who arrived on a Sunday (either July 31 or Aug. 7) probably accompanied by his Household. Other guests were the archbishop of York (Thomas Arundel), the duke of York (Edmund Langley), the duke of Gloucester (Thomas of Woodstock), the earl of Arundel (Richard fitz Alan), the earl of Huntingdon (John Holand), and many other bishops, lords, and ladies. The king and his retinue departed on Thursday to spend the night with Lord Beaumont at Beaumanoir.[24] This festival would have afforded an excellent occasion for the delivery of Chaucer's little comic interlude about the Manciple, for it would have amused and delighted the audience when they became aware of its relevance to a current situation. Of course, that interlude might have served equally well during the Parliamentary session when Gaunt was the center of so much attention.

Finally, as for uncaged birds, if they are birds who escape and return to their baser natures, both Phebus and his "wife" are such birds, not to mention the Manciple himself. But so also was poor Gaston, a vain and self-willed man, who abandoned his wife and luxuriated in the satisfaction of his senses, in those days an indication of "effeminacy" rather than of knightly virtue. Certainly, Gaunt wanted his guests to "speak truth," to be loyal to their sworn obligations, and to "bear the flower of chivalry." Whether Chaucer's Tale is a literary

---

23. Gaunt had been forced to defend himself against false charges of treason in the October Parliament of 1377. The royal favorite Robert de Vere had twice plotted to have him condemned falsely for treason, but he was no longer at court after the triumph of the Appellants.

24. Henry Knighton's chronicle was edited by J. R. Lumby in two volumes (Rolls Series, 1889-1895). For the hunting festival, see 2. 313-314. For Richard's retinue on his travels and an earlier visit to Beaumanoir, see Given-Wilson, pages 34-37. For a discussion of hunting parties and their use by magnates for considerations of policy, see Nigel Saul, *Scenes from Provincial Life: Knightly Families in Sussex, 1280-1400* (Oxford: Clarendon Press, 1986), 187-192.

success is a question I leave to the critics. But even they may grant that in view of the implications it sought to convey it is very carefully crafted.

Addendum

The Gascons met on Sept. 14, 1390, and refused to recognize Scrope as seneschal of Aquitaine. Although they praised the duke of Lancaster, they asserted that they wished to be subject to the king directly. Gaston Febus feared that his territories would be diminished by the new arrangement. Gaunt was probably aware that this reaction would be forthcoming. See J. J. N. Palmer, *England, France and Christendom,* (Chapel Hill, NC: UNC Press, 1972), 153-55. Although Richard later sought to remedy the objections of the Gascons and Gaunt ceased to style himself "Duke of Aquitaine," the essential problem remained unresolved as Palmer explains.

www.ingramcontent.com/pod-product-compliance
Lightning Source LLC
Chambersburg PA
CBHW031247230426
43670CB00005B/77